A *Backwoods Home* Anthology:

The Third Year

Published by
Backwoods Home Magazine
P. O. Box 712
Gold Beach, OR 97444

ISBN: 978-0-9846222-5-2

Editor: *Dave Duffy*

Art Director: *Don Childers*

Contributors:

Aku Kagazchi, Martin Harris, Jr., C.O. Callahan, Don Fallick, W. David Wright, Jj, Christopher Maxwell, Martin P. Waterman, Joel Davidson, Steven Gregersen, Chuck Hill, Carla Emery, Jan Cook, Jo Mason, Jennifer Brown, John Silveira, Vern Modeland, Mary Jo Frolick, Anne Westbrook Dominick, Marjorie Burris, Michael G. Hart, Michael Gohl, Neil Shelton, Jennifer Stein Barker, Bill Palmroth, Eric Large, Rodney L. Merrill, Richard Blunt, Pamela Kleibrink Thompson, Linda Rainey, Dan and Becky Ames, Melinda C. Long, Ilene Duffy, Rebecca and Leif Hietala, Joe Bratt, Rosemary LeVernier, Kelly Klober, Carl Watner, Tom Lane, Tim Haugen, Skip & Cathleen Thomsen, Ralph LaPlant, Rev. L. Dale Richesin, Gary Williams, Carl Carter, Don and Sharane Wilson, Robert L. Williams, Doug Stevenson, Kris Hartley, Leon Springer, Phil Wilcox, Anita Evangelista, Jojo Gunn, Mary Ann Hubbell, Lucy Shober, Scotty "Beezer" Matthews, Michelle Richards, Rudy Behrens, Russ Davis, Lance Bisaccia, David W. Christopher, Darlene Campbell, Windy Dankoff, R. Lee Rose, Jean M. Long, Vernon Hopkins, Barbara Elig, Natalie Lund, Dynah Geissal, Johnny M. Ernst, Theresa Neville, Reynolds Griffith, Jim Sullivan, Linda Parker, Susan P. Weiss, Michael Simmons, Lois A. Adams.

Contents —

Issue Number 16

Issue Number 17

Issue Number 18

Introduction

Well folks, here we are again bringing out our second volume of *Backwoods Home Magazine* back issues. We think you'll find this one as useful as the first one. It has an index at the rear to help you locate articles, and we've included a number of "*BHM* Writer's Profiles" to give you a glimpse of some of the people who have been bringing you the best self sufficiency information on the planet.

If you find this book useful, you may want to order the first book using the forms at the back of this one. And you may just want to subscribe to the magazine itself, also using the forms at the back of this book. Of course if you don't want to tear out the pages at the back (and many of our readers hate to disfigure their books and issues) just write up your order on a sheet of paper and send it in to us: *Backwoods Home Magazine*, 1257 Siskiyou Blvd., #213, Ashland, OR 97520.

John Silveira, left, Backwoods Home Magazine's senior editor, and Dave Duffy, BHM's publisher.

Backwoods

Home magazine

... a practical journal of self reliance!

January/February 1992
No. 13
$3.50 U.S.
$4.50 Canada

1908
& JANUARY

		1	2	3	4
5	6	7	8	9	10	11
12	13	14	15	16	17	18
19	20	21	22	23	24	25
26	27	28	29	30	31	

BACK~WOODS
HOME

WHY THE NEW YEAR
BEGINS IN WINTER...

SEARS

CATALOGUE

SOLAR POWER

HYDROPONICS

BREWING BEER

DRYING FOOD

LEARNING TO SHOOT

DON

WOMAN IN THE WOODS

Note from the publisher

New Backwoods' address

Backwoods Home Magazine has a new address in a new state. It is 1257 Siskiyou Blvd., #213, Ashland, OR 97520. For the two years of our existence we have had one foot in Oregon and the other in California, being an Oregon corporation but taking our mail at our California address. We've simply decided to move the whole operation to Oregon. Any mail sent to the old California address will automatically be forwarded to us in Oregon.

From Seattle to Salt Lake City

The final two Preparedness Expos — one in Seattle, Washington and the other in Salt Lake City, Utah — were very successful for us. It's apparent we're getting better known. Both cities are among the most beautiful and pleasant I've ever been in.

It can be a little tough getting into and out of the shows. After an 800-mile drive in my pickup, I arrived a day late for the three-day Salt Lake City show. When the show was over, I drove the first 200 miles out of Utah through snow, and by the time I got to Las Vegas the snow had changed to 50-mile-per-hour Santa Ana winds. I slept pretty soundly at the Sahara Hotel.

Remembering a Las Vegas knockout

Being in Las Vegas was a bit strange. It was my first time there in 20 years, and it brought back memories of my rather stormy past there.

I had been a news reporter for the *Las Vegas SUN* back then. Vince Anselmo, the managing editor, treated me like his son. He gave this 27-year-old kid choice assignments, such as investigating the Velvet Touch Massage Parlor as an undercover reporter, interviewing astronauts who had returned from the moon, and chatting with the likes of Muhammad Ali and Diana Ross as they passed through the town. I had a season pass to the Las Vegas Outlaws, a semi-pro hockey team, and I could watch the professional fights at Caesar's Palace anytime I wanted — with the beer on the house. It was a dream job.

Then a fellow reporter talked me into taking part in a union movement against *SUN* management in an effort to organize the city's news reporters. Somehow I got to be prominent in the union very quickly. I think it had something to do with my big mouth. Whatever, it was quite a happening, with most of the meetings taking place at my apartment in North Las Vegas.

Pretty soon the union movement, with me at its head, was locked in a serious duel with one of the most powerful men in Nevada — Hank Greenspun, publisher of the *SUN*. I remember a meeting with Greenspun in his big plush *Las Vegas SUN* office. All reporters were in attendance, and Greenspun used the occasion to humiliate A.D. Hopkins, a reporter he thought was the key element in the newsroom revolt. I remember interrupting Greenspun in midsentence and calmly telling him that his tactics of intimidation were out of place at the meeting. He glared at me like he was going to get out of his big fat chair and kill me, but I was supremely confident and found I could stare him down as easily as he had humiliated Hopkins.

A few days later, Vince Anselmo called me into his office and fired me. He also fired two editors — both union organizers like me. He called it a "layoff to cut operating costs." Before I left his office, Vince told me, "You might as well leave town Dave."

I thought he was kidding until I tried to get another job. Even though the *SUN's* main rival, the *Las Vegas Review Journal,* had offered to hire me away from the *SUN* only a couple of months prior, suddenly there was no job for me there. I couldn't even get a job at a local weekly paper at half my *SUN* salary. One newspaper editor told me, "Word is out on you Duffy; you're a union organizer."

At the *SUN* the reporters who so eagerly gathered at my apartment for union meetings now avoided me. I guess many of them were family people and were afraid for their jobs, but it was then and remains now the most disappointing experience of my life. It was almost embarrassing to go into the *SUN* offices because no one knew what to say. My old friend Vince took a week off.

Coincidentally, the engine of my Volkswagen blew up at the same time. Gene Vier, one of the fired editors, loaned me his second car, a beat-up wreck of a Volkswagen bug with a starter that didn't work. I'll never forget the feeling I had as I pushed that old Volkswagen by the driver's side door, then hopped in to jump-start the engine so I could get out of town.

I subsequently won a suit (filed on my behalf by the American Civil Liberties Union) against the *SUN*, but that was anti-climatic. *The SUN* was found guilty of "union busting" and had to pay my lost wages, which amounted to only two weeks worth because I landed a job in California right off — after lying about why I had left the *SUN*.

The man who drove through Las Vegas this time was 20 years wiser of course. I had no hard feelings toward Greenspun or Anselmo, both of whom have died. In fact, if Greenspun were still alive, I'd thank him for an important lesson about power and how to recognize when you have it and when you don't. Then I'd kick him in the knees. (Only kidding!)

Las Vegas is much bigger than when I left. The Strip has at least a dozen new hotel casinos, each filled with the same cold-faced pit bosses and scurrying keno girls I had left behind. I hadn't really missed them. In fact I hadn't really missed Las Vegas. I passed up a chance to gamble and left town in the morning, but on the way I stopped by the *SUN* to say hi. Only old Jim Barrows was still there. He had been at the *SUN* 10 years before I had arrived, and he was still there 20 years after I left. Goodbye Las Vegas. Thank you, Mr. Greenspun.△

Dave Duffy

My View

There's no stopping term limits!

Term limits for our elected officials is one of the best ideas to come along in 200 years. In fact, the effect it will have is in line with what our founding fathers had in mind for our leaders — serve awhile, then go back to your regular jobs.

To date, voters in three states — California, Colorado, and Oklahoma — have approved term limit initiatives and as many as 17 more will have them on the ballot in 1992.

What would have been the strongest term limit initiative yet, however, was defeated in November by Washington state voters after opponents — notably the entrenched political Establishment — mounted a last minute scare campaign that claimed the measure was a plot by neighboring California to gain control of Washington's natural resources. As absurd as the plot scenario was, it was carefully calculated to have just enough "day of judgment" credulity to confuse voters and cause the measure's defeat.

Chalk one up for a shrewd political Establishment that has become a master trickster in the art of perpetuating itself in power. But such trickery can work only once. "You can fool all of the people some of the time," Abraham Lincoln said, "but you can't fool all of the people all of the time."

Term limits are on the way in this country because it is such a good idea that it transcends the interests and imagined fears of individual states, and it will outlast all the tricks in the politicians' slick black hats.

Here's a few reasons why term limits are a good idea:

The Real World: The bulk of politicians today are professionals who don't know what it is like to make a living or run a business because they have barely had to compete in the real world. Because they don't understand how hard it is to earn a buck, they have never learned the wisdom of spending it prudently. Once elected, they act like children who have been given control of hundreds of millions of dollars — they spend it on everything in sight, divvying up the tax payers' hard-earned millions to every special interest group that comes begging. They are simply not equipped to understand the bottom line, which is essential to govern in a capitalist Democracy like ours.

Political mavericks: Our founding fathers never intended to establish a professional class of politicians. They saw enough of that in the European governments they fled. Instead they envisioned citizens serving a few terms in Congress to help the country, then going back to their farms and stores. George Washington set the precedent for the Executive Branch by declining to run for a third term, and Congress later made that precedent law. The two-term limit has worked well for the Executive

Dave Duffy

Branch, guaranteeing fresh blood and fresh ideas every eight years at the highest level.

Congress, on the other hand, has suffered from increasingly petrified ideas due to the inability to get long-time Congressmen with their well-oiled election machines out of office. The political maverick who has ideas and solutions, who understands the real world, and who is not beholden to the special interest groups that grease the skids of entrenched power seldom runs for office because he or she knows it's a hopeless effort. Term limits would help neutralize the political power machines and special interest groups, and encourage the political maverick to seek election.

Overblown Government: The big benefit of term limits is that it will give us a chance to stop Government from growing and encourage it to shrink. Long-term politicians have a vested interest in trying to increase their power because it is the nature of man — at least of political man — to control others. The professional politician has been given an efficient vehicle by which he can increase his personal power, and only lately have the majority of Americans reawakened to the realization that we, as a people, cannot stand to be overgoverned.

Government, both at the state and federal level, has never been bigger. It invades nearly every facet of our lives, with thousands of bureaucrats enforcing thousands of regulations and petty laws at every level of society. Every time a special interest group sneezes, the entrenched political Establishment passes a new law and hires more bureaucrats to enforce it.

Enough! We can't help but vote the bastards out.

Seldom has national need run headlong into such obvious solution. Term limit initiatives are grass roots politics at its best. The American populace is fed up and we are rising up to change our leadership in a most sweeping way. Political tricks be damned! Δ

A hydroponic greenhouse

By Aku Kagazchi

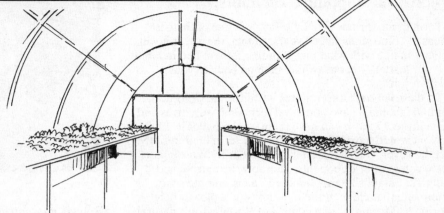

For three years my husband and I have been cultivating tomatoes hydroponically using the Nutrient Film Technique (NFT) method. We are still amazed at their growth rate—9-foot tall tomato plants are common. Just as in time-lapse photography, the plants seem to shoot up and unfold right before our eyes.

Our greenhouse resembles a concrete skating rink, 70 ft. wide by 100 ft. long, under a polythene dome. To bed the plants, we spread rows of 2-foot wide black polyethylene strips ("film") along the length of the greenhouse. The seedlings, which are grown in "Jiffy pellets", are placed one foot apart on the polythene strips. Then the sides of the polythene are brought up and stapled together forming troughs. The Jiffy pellets remain inside the troughs and only the stems of the seedlings protrude above the stapled edge. The water containing the nutrients is in a holding tank. It is continuously circulated through the troughs by means of a small pump.

Almost anything can be grown hydroponically—from strawberries to animal feed, flowers to trees, wheat to root vegetables. It is simply a matter of supplying the right nutrient to suit the particular needs of the plant variety. At the end of each row of tomatoes I planted some flowers with astonishing results. Marigold bushes were like miniature trees, and Gladioli were over a yard tall with large, perfectly formed blooms.

We started the venture with some trepidation: we were afraid the huge tomatoes forming on the vines would taste like water-filled balloons. However, we were agreeably surprised. Everyone who ate the produce said they were the best tomatoes they had ever eaten.

Of course hydroponic gardening has its own set of problems. In the case of tomatoes, such lush growth means excess foliage which has to be continuously removed so as not to strain or weaken the plants. Also, nine foot tall plants do need support. Suspended from overhead wires are 3000 strings around which the plants are wound as they grow.

Hygiene is the prime concern of the hydroponic grower. Since the growing medium, water, is constantly circulating through the greenhouse, diseases can spread very quickly. The grower often has to treat his greenhouse more like a laboratory than a farm.

Our biggest difficulty has been marketing the produce, and until consumers' prejudices regarding hydroponic vegetables are overcome, this problem will deter greenhouse operators. Friends who keep coming back for more of our delicious, firm and juicy tomatoes still jokingly refer to them as "artificial!" The notion that these vegetables grow in chemicals is what puts off consumers. But if they stop to think of it, what does a plant grown in organic fertilizers do? Surely it does not absorb the manure! In soil, the organic components are decomposed into inorganic elements such as nitrogen, potassium, calcium, iron etc. They are then taken up by the plant. In hydroponics, these elements are supplied directly in the nutrient solution, and the process of mineral uptake by the plants is exactly the same as in soil.

Before switching to hydroponics, we had grown tomatoes in a conventional greenhouse. Even with tender loving care we had never picked more than 6 lbs. of fruit per plant. Now we are picking an average of 14 lbs. In soil, vines would start to weaken at a height of about 4 feet. Now we cut the tops of the plants at 9 feet simply because the greenhouse doesn't go any higher! Plants are spaced much closer in NFT, thus making maximum use of valuable heated space. In our 7000 sq. ft. greenhouse we have 3000 plants.

Easier to control growth

With hydroponics the grower has much better control. It is possible to determine the exact amount of nutrient the plants receive at each stage of their growth—and plants' nutritional needs certainly do vary at different stages. One can also subtract as well as add fertilizers, something almost impossible in soil culture. If we find that any chemical or salt has reached unacceptable levels, we merely flush the system with pure water and wash out all toxic matter.

Plants react quickly to low or high levels of fertilizers, and a nutritional imbalance can easily be spotted just by observing the foliage. At the first sign of a disorder, we refer to tables of toxicities and deficiencies available in most good books on hydroponics. Because of the method of direct feeding, imbalances can be corrected quickly and easily.

Heating bills are greatly reduced. The temperature of the greenhouse can be lowered without harming the plants by simply raising the temperature of the water with an ordinary immersion heater.

What I like best about hydroponic gardening is the ease of the clean-up between crops. When a growing season is over, we simply roll up the polythene strips, plants and all, and throw them into large skips. Ask any conventional greenhouse operator about steam sterilizing or changing the soil in his greenhouse and he will change the subject! We just have a smooth concrete floor with no place

for bugs or slugs, fungi or bacteria, weeds and their seeds to lurk and attack the next batch of seedlings. When we hose down the floor, I say to myself: "It's no wonder the word **soil** also means **dirty**!"

In our experience, the advantages of hydroponics greatly outweigh the problems. Perhaps the greatest advantage of hydroponics is its versatility. From the hot desert, where every drop of water must be put to full use, to the ice caps, where soil is virtually non-existent, from farmland to concrete roof-tops, fresh vegetables and beautiful flowers can be grown. One never has to worry whether the soil is sandy or clay, rich or poor, salty or volcanic.

I don't intend to disparage the Good Earth—that would be tantamount to blasphemy. But secretly, I'm glad we haven't got any in our greenhouse! Δ

Puppy Love

*When I was a baby
I loved my Mommy.
When I was a boy
I loved my puppy.
When I was a teenager
I loved Mary Lou Perella.
When I was in my twenties
I loved all good looking women.
When I was in my thirties
I loved whoever I could.
When I was in my forties
I loved my wife.
When I was in my fifties
I loved my children.
When I was in my sixties
I loved my grandchildren.
Now that I'm old
I wish I had a puppy.*

Tom Chance
Ventura, CA

A Backwoods Home Anthology
The Fifth Year

* Odd-jobbin' can be a country goldmine
* How to keep those excess eggs
* Make better pizza at home than you can buy
* How we bought our country home
* Cooking with dried fruit
* Garden huckleberries
* Short season gardening
* The 10 most useful herbs
* Simplified concrete and masonry work
* Raising sheep
* Free supplies for your homestead
* Learning in the pickle patch
* Good-bye old friend
* Choosing and using a wood cookstove

* Three great bread recipes
* Build a fieldstone chimney
* Sun oven cookery
* Firewood: how and what to buy
* Choosing superior bedding plants
* A bit about ducks
* How to build the fence you need
* Improving poor garden soil
* Learn the basics of wall framing
* Determined woman builds distinctive vertical log studio
* Make better pizza than you can buy
* Good-bye old friend
* Turkeys — fun and profitable and not as dumb as you think
* Raising fish in the farm pond
* You have to learn to shovel crap before you learn to be the boss

---

There's nothing like metal roofing

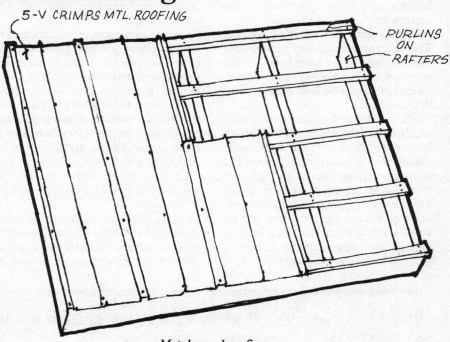

5-V CRIMPS MTL. ROOFING

PURLINS ON RAFTERS

Metal-panel roofing

By Martin J. Harris, Jr.

Americans don't, in general, have much of a sense of history. That's too bad, for it gets us in trouble not only on the world stage but also in minor domestic matters; such as, for example, the roof you put on your house.

It's my opinion, very simply, that metal roofing is the best option available; but, to most people, metal roofing is the rather unattractive, rusty corrugated stuff flapping in a half-loosened condition atop some old warehouse. It comes as some surprise to most folks that metal roofing was the material of choice for 12th century cathedrals in Europe, for 18th century public buildings in the American colonies, and for 19th century homeowners across the United States. In some parts of the Northeast -- Northern New England in particular, metal roofing has never lost favor; but in most of the land it has. That's why the stereotype has been so hard for the industry to overcome, even though major strides in technology, cost control, and permanence have been made in recent years.

The range of options in roofing runs something like this:

Shingles

The bulk of domestic roofing is executed in shingles, mostly triple-tab asphalt, but sometimes wood in either individual pieces or pre-fabricated runs. Shingles are typically installed atop a solid roof deck or closely spaced nailers and can't be safely used on a roof slope below about 3 on 12 (that is, the roof angle has a vertical rise of 3 inches for every horizontal foot of span) without special precautions. Asphalt shingles are manufactured in a wide variety of colors and a narrow range of surface textures; they usually cost between $8 and $12 per bundle (3 bundles to a square, or 100 square feet, the basic unit in which roofing is commonly discussed for estimating or installation purposes). Roofers usually charge between $75 and $100 a square for simple shingle jobs, which puts this material at the low end of the range for in-place costs. Shingles are attractive to the do-it-yourself market, since installation requires no special tools or skills.

Slate

Particularly in the Northeastern US, slate used to be the material of choice for the housing market. It came into prominence after the Civil War, replacing wood shingles, and remained popular (and reasonably priced) until after WWII. Since then its popularity has declined as its cost has increased; roofers now charge about $400 per square for the plain blue-grey colors, upwards of $700 for the rare red material. Slates are really stone shingles; they require the same underlying pitch, but the real cost of slate is increased by its weight, which calls for more structural strength in the underlying deck than shingles. It's also extraordinarily fragile, particularly in the thinner pieces now in common use. Simply walking on the roof will risk slate fracture, as will ice damage at roof valleys or eaves. Slate is not attractive to the do-it-yourself market, which is surprising because the special tools and skills needed are neither expensive nor complex. I'd guess it's just unfamiliarity based on a justified cost reputation which has lost slate much of its domestic market.

Specialty shingles

These include such items as metal units stamped and colored to imitate wood, slate, terra-cotta tiles, and so on. They represent a fairly new attempt to create a market niche, and have been most successful in the Western US. In cost they run between the low-end shingles and the high-end tiles; in weight they demand no special structural consideration; and in water-tightness they perform about as well as other shingle systems. They require simple metal-handling tools and skills for installation; they also demand—and this is a critical departure from the more traditional roofing systems—precision attention to deck dimensions. A roofer can't fudge spacings much with interlocking stamped metal units to compensate for a roof deck which isn't quite square or isn't quite the same width from bottom to top. There are ways of dealing with a roof width or height which doesn't work out to even units of these materials, but it's better practice to dimension the roof deck in the design phase so that fractional units aren't needed. This category used to include cement-asbestos shingles (now off the market); it also includes tiles (Spanish and otherwise); it might even include such rarities as thatch, now being used in a very small number of historic-authenticity situations and not likely to be of much interest to most homeowners.

Hot-mop systems

These bitumen-based roofs, built with melted asphalt or coal-tar pitch, go back hundreds of years and enjoyed good repute for low-slope or no-slope

applications until the '70's. By then, a mixture of asphalt and asbestos had pretty well pushed the more expensive coal-tar pitch off the market, but then virtually destroyed the entire industry when failures swept the country. Since then, the industry has clawed a renewed foothold with new modified bitumen systems, and has achieved some success in the commercial sector; but we tend to forget that bitumen-based flat roofs were modestly popular for housing of the "modernistic" style before WWII. Will these systems again achieve residential acceptance? I doubt it.

Membrane systems

When bitumen-based designs fell from grace in the 70's, the industry came up with a true innovation: large sheets of neoprene or similar materials which could be draped over a low- or no-slope deck, chemically welded to adjoining sheets at seams, and similarly detailed at flashings. In the domestic market, membrane systems have not been popular except for walk-out decks and porches above enclosed spaces, applications for which they afford truly reliable and relatively low-cost solutions. It's still not easy for do-it-yourselfers to obtain

membrane materials, as the manufacturers prefer to distribute only through franchised roofing professionals; but that situation is slowly loosening.

Roll roofing

This is a 70 year old technology based on three foot wide strips of asphalt-impregnated felts lapped on modestly-pitched roof decks. Edges and exposed nailheads are then daubed with roofing cement. Over the decades it has penetrated the cost-conscious commercial market but has never been deemed respectable enough for any but the cheapest housing.

Panel roofing

This is the category which includes pre-cut metal sheets, but here I'll include only the non-metallic panels, which are typically two or three feet wide, eight to 12 feet long, are corrugated for strength and drainage, and are edge-lapped and nailed through the high part of the corrugation onto the sloped roof deck. They're not recommended for slopes below 3:12. They don't need a solid deck, but can use a lower cost system of light spaced nailers over rafters. Cement-asbestos panels used to be popular in the non-residential market in this country, and are still the roofing of choice in rural areas throughout Eastern Europe. A composite material (trade name Onduline) has recently been introduced here, and has made some inroads into the agricultural market. It is easily handled by do-it-yourselfers, and can even be adapted to out-of-square roof decks.

Metal roofing

Here most people think of the pre-cut corrugated panels, but these are newcomers to an ancient industry which used long strips of metal folded over each other or sometimes soldered at the edges. Corrugated pre-cut panels came in during the '20's and a particularly popular variety, the five-vee crimp, was on every supply house's shelf until a decade or so ago.

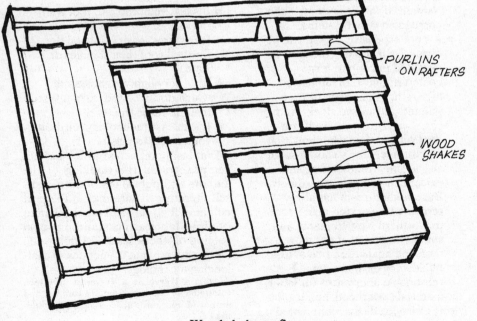

PURLINS ON RAFTERS

WOOD SHAKES

Wood-shake roofing

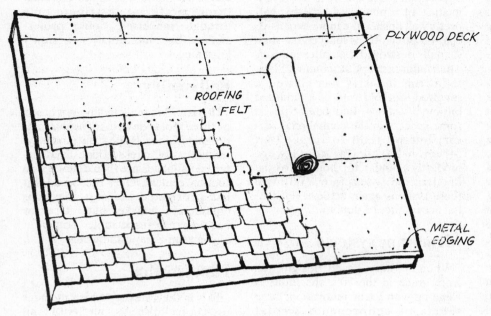

Asphalt shingles

The pre-cuts required only a tin-snips for cutting and a hammer for nailing, and have always been popular with do-it-yourselfers for ease of application and low cost (currently, the materials in galvanized steel cost about $40 per square). The pre-cut panels, with exposed fasteners and a more or less corrugated appearance, never appealed to the upscale market, never really competed with the traditional standing-seam or soldered-seam designs which go back to Williamsburg, Independence Hall, and the Capitol Building. It's the modern variants of these traditional designs; specifically the standing-seam, which have enjoyed such recent success in all sectors of the construction market, even the residential.

Only the do-it-yourself sector of the residential market has proven fairly impervious to both traditional standing-seam metal roofing and the new pre-shaped panels which are factory-fabricated to snap together on the roof. I'm not sure why that should be the case; after all, field-fabricated standing-seam is a technology which requires only simple tools and is easily mastered, while factory-fabricated requires only accurate roof measurements to ensure delivery of an easily installed product.

The rest of the domestic construction market has begun to re-discover standing-seam and I'd guess it's because of the following reasons:

- It's a good looking product. It always has been, as evidenced by its continued use in historic, reproduction, and high-end housing; but somewhere along the line, all metal roofing was "tainted" by association with the corrugated panel systems.
- It's not expensive. Yes, it can be expensive if you elect to have it executed in copper, terne-coated stainless, or similar metals, rather than plain or even painted galvanized stock. And yes, it can be expensive if you deal with roofers who think that all customers for standing-seam are wealthy trend-setters and price their services accordingly. But standing-seam has always remained a working-man's roof in Northern New England, and should be priced at not more than half again the price of asphalt shingles, based on reasonable allowances for labor, materials, overhead, and profit.
- It's long lived. Even unpainted galvanized will go a score of years before beginning to rust if protected from the run-off from dissimilar metals (TV antenna drip, for example). Painted, it can last centuries and has done just that here in New England.
- It's good at all slopes. Obviously, steeper is better, but a double-lock standing seam is industry rated down to 1 inch on 12. Don't even think about shingles at 1:12. Some factory-fabricated systems are rated down to 1/4:12, which is virtually flat.
- It doesn't necessarily need a solid deck. Lighter gauge material (28 gauge, usually) is used over a solid deck; but if, say, 24 gauge is used, a less expensive spaced nailer system is OK.
- It's non-combustible.
- It's less damaged by ice build-up at eaves and valleys than shingles. It's also less vulnerable to water penetration behind ice dams on the roof.
- It's based on a concealed-fastener system. Unlike nail-on panel systems, there are no exposed fasteners to cause leaks or wear around the fastener area.
- It's less vulnerable to wind damage than shingles.
- It's less vulnerable to foot traffic than slate.
- It requires fewer joints on the finished roof than shingles or slate.
- It's a very lightweight system which doesn't need extra investment in roof structure.
- It's an easy technology for do-it-yourselfers to master.

That last point is one which has not yet penetrated the thinking of the authors and publishers of do-it-yourself literature. Therefore, in the next column I'll go through the mechanics of field-fabricating standing-seam roofing on the job site. I think you'll agree with me that it's not a very challenging technology.

(Martin Harris is a Vermont architect, cofounder of the New England Builder, and author of numerous articles on home building.) Δ

The Third Year

New homes from old homes

By C.O. Callahan

Around the country people are fighting increasing mortgage costs by building their own homes. Not by hiring contractors, but by remodeling abandoned schoolhouses, stores, and barns, or constructing new homes from salvaged materials.

It's amazing how many abandoned buildings fill the countryside. In Wisconsin, Mr. & Mrs. Archie Barnie have a $15,000 home. Before, it was an abandoned school building, but today it is an expensive home that cost little to make.

How do you find abandoned buildings? Write to the Department of Education in the state of your choice and ask for the addresses of school administrations. Choose one from the area you're interested in and ask them for the locations of vacant buildings.

Old barns, homes, and ruined bars or cafes are usually owned by the state. These (and school houses) are usually auctioned, with prices ranging from $300 to $3,500. More expensive buildings have electricity, wells, and furnaces either ready to use or requiring a little repair. Your local auditing office can provide details concerning these auctions and can be found in the local courthouse.

Sometimes you'll find buildings not owned by the state, belonging instead to individual farmers/ranchers. The Hall of Records or City Hall can help you contact the owner of a land plot.

Another couple, this time in Washington State, found a better deal by collecting free railroad ties. The result—a rustic, 2,200 square foot, three bedroom home completed over five summer vacations. They built the outer shell by laying the ties like logs and filling gaps with mortar. Then they moved in and completed the job.

Granted, they spent a few thousand dollars fixing up the shell, but they could move in without paying a cent.

Building your home bit by bit over five years beats paying on a 20 year mortgage anytime.

The yellow pages can help. Look under the section called "Railroads". A listing of the company offices in your area should put you in touch with the right people.

Darrel Huff and his family of San Francisco used this same idea to transform two acres worth $5,000 into a comfortable house and property now worth over $45,000.

Their home is a post and beam California design with large windows and a stone fireplace the Huffs built by hand. Their first attempt was constructed with materials salvaged from a deserted home and sold to finance the second. They found the deserted structures by hunting or checking with the state.

Salvaging parts from abandoned homes, especially those partially ruined, is always possible. Landowners eager to get such 'trash' off their land would rather have you take it than put out the expense of hiring a demolitions crew.

More importantly, this $45,000 palace was built with an income no greater than $6,500 a year.

Building and/or remodeling your home may seem scary, but neither the Huffs nor the Washington couple had any experience when building their homes. Darrel did build a bookcase, but found houses easier because they had more tolerance as opposed to the exact measurements required for building cabinets.

But not everybody knows basic carpentry, and you'll want to know more about electricity before working with wires. Following are a few easy-to-find books written for do-it-yourselfers. Your library is loaded with more.

Time-Life Books Complete Fix-It Yourself Manual — 448 pages, Prentice Hall Press, Gulf + Western Building, One Gulf + Western Plaza, New York, NY. 10023, ISBN 0-13-921651-0. This is the best book I have ever seen on repairs, and I recommend it before you build/repair anything.

77 Furniture Projects You Can Build. -- 406 pages, TAB Books Inc., Blue Ridge Summit, PA. 17214. ISBN 0-8306-1122-0

From Ramshackle to Resale — 291 pages, TAB Books (see above address). Hardback: ISBN 0-8306-1362-5, paperback: ISBN 0-8306-3162-2 Δ

A fishing trip with a friend

(Daddy) said: "All children must look after their own upbringing." Parents can only give good advice or put them on the right paths, but the final forming of a person's character lies in their own hands.

Anne Frank
1929-1945

The Toolbox — hammers & drills

By Don Fallick

Breat drills: An old-fashioned tool that really works, the two-speed breast drill can replace a hand drill, boring brace, power drill and drill press. It's two or three piece chuck accepts virtually any kind of bit. Use low gear for boring bits, hole saws, for penetrating metals and hardwoods, and for driving screws. High speed works well for twist drills and spade bits, which require lighter pressure. some breast drills can be converted into hand drills by removing the stock and replacing it with the removable auxiliary handle.

Breast drills can be found in used tool stores, pawn shops, thrift stores, at estate sales and auctions. Antique dealers may have one or two, but they may not be functional, and will almost certainly be overpriced. A breast drill should cost somewhere between $15 and $25, depending on condition, features, and local demand. It's best to take some drill bits along to test the drill under actual working conditions. Avoid any drill with loose bearings, a bent shaft, or with a chuck that's hard to work or that slips under load. Bring along a wrench to check lock screws and nuts. Frozen screws will sometimes respond to a product called 'Liquid Wrench' but don't count on it. Finally, check for the feel of the drill. If it doesn't feel comfortable, don't buy it!

Claw Hammers: A hammer's a hammer right? Wrong! Claw hammers come in many different styles, depending on the weight of the head, the style of the face and claw, and the length and composition of the handle. 'Framing hammers' have a longer handle, frequently are made of metal or fiberglass, with a leather or rubber-coated grip. They usually have a heavy, straight "rip" claw, for sticking into the wood and pulling large nails, and may

have either a smooth or roughly "knurled" striking face. Many framers prefer the knurled face because it grabs the nail head, preventing bent nails. Framing hammers come in many weights, but most framers prefer a 20 or 24 oz. rather than the 16 oz standard

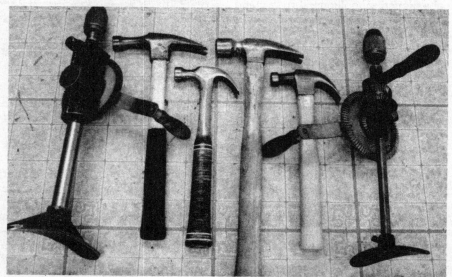

Left to right: breast drill with dial select gear shift, non-adjustable shoulder stock, and mising auxiliary handle; 24-oz. framing hammer with fiberglass handle and rubber grip; 13-oz. finish hammer with one-piece steel handle and leather grip; 24-oz. extra long handled framing hammer; standard 16-oz. general purpose hammer; typical breast drill with adjustable shoulder stock which can be replaced with an auxiliary handle. Crank can be quickly removed to change gears.

weight. The heavier weight drives the nail with fewer blows, reducing the chance of bending it. Finish hammers have lighter heads, for accuracy, and smooth faces which don't leave rough marks on the wood. Their curved claws pull small nails without marring the wood.

Many lighter weight, inexpensive hammers have very classy looking wooden handles. These are fine if kept in a climate-controlled workshop, but will dry out and loosen in hot weather and swell and weaken in wet weather. Hammers with weak necks or loose heads are dangerous in addition to causing bent nails. Sometimes the head is not hung properly. The face of

a properly hung hammer will rest flat on a surface when the knuckles of the hand are about an inch from that surface. If your wooden-handled hammer keeps bending nails, check the head for tightness and proper hang.

Believe it or not, many folks don't know how to use a hammer! They swing from the elbow instead of the wrist. This works but causes sore elbows. It's better to use the hand and wrist, slackening the grip with the fingers as the hammer comes back, then tightening the grip on the forward stroke. Do it properly, with little elbow motion and lots of power and you can hammer all day without joint pain.

Pros use several tricks to nail splintery wood without splitting it. Of course it helps to nail no closer than 1-3/8 inches from the end of the board, and drill pilot holes in extremely hard wood like oak or maple. Nearly everyone knows how to blunt the end of the nail so it'll chew its way through the wood. But even many professional carpenters don't realize that the nails themselves are designed with a diamond-shaped cross section at the point. Just positioning the nails so that the long edge crosses the grain of the wood will prevent most splits. Δ

Reliving "The American West" at the Hart Canyon Rendezvous

By W. David Wright

Low clouds cast a thin veil between the sculptured canyon walls as Highway 58 climbed the southern slope of California's Sierra Nevada mountain range. A cool wind pushed me up the steep grade toward my destination—the Hart Canyon Rendezvous—located in an oak and pine studded canyon high above the sprawling San Joaquin Valley. Bakersfield's fertile agriculture lay beneath me, and I could see a patchwork of grape vineyards and freshly plowed fields reflecting in the early morning sun.

The swift running creek beside the road bubbled loudly, carrying the runoff of early spring snows, now replaced by a golden carpet of mustard flowers. After several minutes of twisting dirt road, my quest for living history became reality. I parked and walked a short distance to the crest of the hill. Ascending the rise, near a cluster of huge boulders, I looked down a storybook scene straight out of the past—a historic timewarp splashed across the rolling canyon floor.

A small city of Indian tepees and white, canvas tents were sprinkled among ancient oak trees—a scene totally out of context with my modern world.

Opaque plumes of smoldering campfires contrasted the sun-splashed sky, while red-tail hawks circled overhead in winged vigilance. The crack of muzzle-loading rifles echoed through the hills, as hundreds of "mountain men" and their families milled about the camp in colorful, period attire, creating a collage of Rocky Mountain history.

150 Years Ago

This picturesque scene is the Annual Hart Canyon Rendezvous sponsored by the Breckenridge Buckskinners, a club dedicated to preserving this period of American history. The Hart

Recounting history around the campfire at Hart Canyon Rendezvous. (photo by W. David Wright)

Canyon Rendezvous is one of the many primitive rendezvous held throughout the year in different parts of the country attracting historians, artisans, craftsmen, and people interested in the history of the American West. The primitives adhere to strict rules pertaining to attire, lodging, artifacts, and weaponry, and no modern accoutrements or luxuries are allowed within the rendezvous site. From buckskins and feathers to moccasins and foxskin hats, the rendezvous spoke vividly of the pre-1840s Rocky Mountain fur trade. Reincarnations or mountain men with names like Bridger, Smith, Walker, and Colter walked the earth once again. I had come to the end of my contemporary world, and as I proceeded into the camp, I stepped 150 years back into the past.

Rendezvous were meeting where "free-trappers"—independent hunters who worked for themselves—sold their beaver, otter, and mink skins to fur brokers and re-outfitted after a long, isolated season of trapping in the mountains. The first rendezvous was held in July 1825 at Henry's Fork on the Green River near what is now the Utah-Wyoming border.

During this period, wagon trains of supplies were brought from St. Louis to predetermined sites throughout the Rocky Mountains where trappers, traders, and Indians engaged in contests, bartering, and debauchery that lasted from a few days to several weeks.

Rendezvous were held every summer until 1840 when fashion trends in the U.S. and Europe changed. This change ended the demand for beaver hats and other furs, bringing an end to the widespread fur trade and the mountain man's way of life. The rendezvous was to become the best known social and business institution associated with the mountain man during this period of Western history.

Living History

Although the original rendezvous are gone, they are not forgotten. This colorful period of American history still lives today throughout the United States and Canada, and is being preserved by organizations like the Breckenridge Buckskinners that are dedicated to keeping alive the customs and traditions of the American mountain man.

Attending to detail, everything used at a primitive rendezvous must be pre-1840s. From hand-made buckskin clothing to wooden water casks, the camps are authentic recreations of original rendezvous held throughout the Rocky Mountains between 1825 and 1840.

Although people from all walks of life attend rendezvous like the Hart Canyon to relive the days where survival was the key to life in the wilderness, the common denominator at these meetings is the love of history.

"It's getting back to the old times" Jeremiah, a modern mountain man from San Pedro, California, said. Jeremiah is a retired stock broker who vicariously relives history through rendezvous like the Hart Canyon.

"I was always interested in that time of history, the Lewis and Clark days, that's what set it off for me" he says, as he and his wife Kenokua sit in full mountain dress in front of their authentic Indian tepee. She dresses as an Indian squaw, and he wears the buckskins of a free-trapper. He fingers the necklace of grizzly bear claws around his neck while he explains his motives for being here. "I went through the cowboy era, but that didn't do it for me. I had to go back as far as possible. I think I was born 150 years too late. This all seems natural to me," he says.

Jeremiah designs and sews the clothing they wear, and their hand-crafted buckskins and authentic Indian artifacts displayed in camp are fine examples of skill and detailed craftsmanship. Jeremiah and Kenokua put on demonstrations and exhibitions for school groups, and use their interests as a tool for education and preservation of mountain man history.

I accepted their invitation, and stepped inside their spacious lodge where lush, fur robes were spread on the ground for sleeping and a small wood-burning stove created a cozy atmosphere that spoke of the past. "We even sleep on the floor at home," Kenokua says pouring me a cup of coffee laced with brandy from a hand-made jug. "We never get cold in here." I could certainly see why as I sipped my coffee and began to unwind from my tedious journey into the mountains.

Inside, my attention was drawn to the brightly-painted Indian warshields and breastplates adorning the walls. Puffs of smoke curled from the stove toward the opening in the top of the

Blackpowder shooter. (photo by W. David Wright)

tent. The coziness of their lodge overwhelmed me, and I had an urge to lie down on the fur- lined bed, but am content to sit and sip my coffee in the snug atmosphere.

Jeremiah and Kenokua are typical of those involved in recreating the rendezvous period, and throughout the camp names like "Lodgepole", "Long Trader", and "Bloody Hand", are given instead of real names.

Later I spoke to a buckskinner named "Leprechaun" who told me why. Sitting in front of his tent fashioning arrow and spear points from raw obsidian, he explained that most of the mountain men wanted to get out of a bad marriage. They took to the mountains, and if the word got out that they were up there, the law went looking for them.

Leprechaun is one of many craftsmen making authentic reproductions of old tools and weapons throughout the camp. By traditional percussion and pressure-flake methods used by Indians, he fashions arrowheads and spear points used in hunting and warfare. Leprechaun says he attends three to four rendezvous a year, selling his crafts to supplement his travels. "I started doing this in 1985; now I'm getting good at it," he says presenting me a perfectly rendered arrowhead. "This would be used to hunt small game."

Watching his meticulous labor, I see Leprechaun as an ancient craftsman preparing for the hunt, and I appreciate the time and skill required by Indians who made artifacts like these. Life was not easy then.

Black-powder firearms are a large part of all rendezvous, and many original and reproductions of pre-1840s rifles and handguns are seen throughout the camp. Contests are held every day showcasing the mountain man's weaponry and skill.

Held throughout the U.S.

Shooting rendezvous, held periodically throughout the United States and Canada, focus on different types of black-powder weapons used during this period of history. One of the largest annual rendezvous is sponsored by the National Muzzle-Loading Rifle Association (NMLRA) and attracts thousands of shooters who participate in regional contests.

"It's a nationwide organization that sanctions what they call 'nationals' in regions of the United States," Doyle Reed explains leaning on his long, smooth-bore muzzle loader. Reed is an 11-year veteran of rendezvous and says his love of history draws him to take part in these events. He dresses as a Scottish mountain man and wears a raked tam- o'-shanter with a ribbon hanging down the back representing his Scotch heritage. He says these rendezvous attract many people with similar interests. "The one in the Rockies is called the Western Nationals. Last summer, up in the Big Horns of Wyoming, the final count was about 4,000 people, and it's even more primitive than this." he says.

Like others at the Hart Canyon Rendezvous, Reed's interests are spent in creating the correct look. "The love of history, the research, everything you wear, everything you make is researched. You spend a lot of time in museums, you buy a lot of books. You find out what cut of moccasin is authentic for what period and how people dressed," he explained.

Authenticity by learning the old skills is what the primitives strive for. "We cook over fires; we don't use matches, we use flint-and-steel. We don't use flashlights, we use lanterns and candles. It's a whole new set of skills," Reed says.

Children take part too

Adults are not the only ones having fun reliving history at the rendezvous. Around Reed's campsite, his children dress in early 1800s fashion — with girls in long dresses, and boys in buckskins with wooden muskets on their shoulders, that march together in a game of follow-the-leader.

Next to Reed's camp, Jim Ernest tends his campfire while a pot of hot coffee steams. His tepee is painted with bright, plains Indian designs — moons and lightening bolts; colorful, red ribbons stream from the lodgepoles. "Come on in," he says. "Want a cup of coffee?" His invitation is sincere, and immediately I feel accepted as I sit down by his fire.

Ernest is a member of the Breckenridge Buckskinners and acts as advisor to the Hard Canyon Rendezvous, and says these family-oriented meetings are tranquil, but adds, "Fun is the bottom line!" Although debauchery and recklessness were part of the original Rocky Mountain Rendezvous, he pointed out that there are no problems at the Hart Canyon.

"We have never had a fist-fight or anything like that in the years I've been with the club. At night you can let your hair down and do some hell-raising, but we have never had a fight. "Most everybody up here are friends; it's like a big family. We are here as a group, reliving history...if you weren't into it, you wouldn't be here," he says.

Women and children dress the part also at the Hart Canyon, and are important in this period of time, Ernest said. "We have a lot of the ladies involved in the club and we couldn't get along without them." At the first rendezvous, white women were not present, but Indian squaws were. "So, you will see a lot of the ladies here depicting Indian squaws, because that's what was at the first rendezvous; the kids are our future buckskinners," he says.

Canvas tent trading posts line the main street where blacksmith's hammers ring out on huge anvils, and silversmiths and leather craftsmen sell period trade-goods, clothing, and hardware. From hand-made Indian flutes and flint-lock muskets, to beads for decorating buckskin clothing, various items representing the fur trade period are sold at bargain prices.

Walking through the tent city, I am enveloped in different cultures and styles of pre-1840s history. From the Santa Fe/Mexican style to Scottish tam-o'-shanters and fur hats, these free-trappers dress as if they had just stepped out of a history book.

Across from the blacksmith's tent, I talked with a man from New Mexico who dresses in the Santa Fe style. His wide sombrero, jingling spurs, and silver hand-worked conches adorning his leather pants depict the South-

The Third Year

western United States in the pre-1840s.

Dave Berge is a blacksmith from Glorieta, New Mexico, and says he travels to different rendezvous around the country selling his wares. He got interested in these meetings through his love of hunting. "I always liked hunting, and I finally started shooting a black-powder rifle which led me into these rendezvous," he says.

Berge started making and selling knives at rendezvous, and eventually started making other artifacts. Now, selling saddles, spurs, silver buckles, and conches, along with antique firearms, he explains about the money he earns: "Some days you're eating peanut butter, and some days you're eating steak. I've been doing this about 11 years. I do reproductions of the old things that pertain to the history of the pre-1840s."

Buckskinners with different interests attend the Hart Canyon Rendezvous. Behind the Santa Fe Trading Post, I met a man who belongs to an elite organization involved in the preservation of history.

"Lodgepole" Doyle is a member of the American Mountain Men (AMM)—a group of dedicated individuals who adhere to a rigid code in pursuing their ideals. Doyle is a road surveyor and uses rendezvous as a diversion from his contemporary life. "This is my escape," he says about his reason for being here. "I can come to these and get away. I love history, and can be someone else for a few days," he says. "I love dressing in the traditional style of yesterday. My wife and I come up here and have a good time with all these people. This is special, where else could you do something like this?"

The AMM is an international organization with 800 active members in California, Utah, Texas, Colorado, Arizona, New Mexico, Washington and Oregon along with chapters in the Eastern United States and Europe. "We have our rendezvous at one of the original rendezvous sites. We're going to Bent's Fork in Wyoming this year," Lodgepole says. The AMM is exclusively a man's organization, but women are welcome at some events. "Women are welcome to our national and state rendezvous, but when we get out and get on the ground, and go 100% primitive, they aren't," Doyle said sternly.

Behind a colorful tepee, Lodgepole introduces me to a man roasting a piece of beef over an open camp fire--juice drips into the flames causing a crackling sound as he explains about the organization. "The American Mountain Men is a historical group, it's not a shooting club, it's a brotherhood of man," Don Fraley, California Brigade, "Bourgeois" (commander) of the AMM says.

The aroma of barbecuing meat tickled my nose as he told me more about the group: "It's the basic foundations of man that would help one another survive the elements and whatever happened," he stated. "We have taken this group, 15-years ago, and started a survival group to pay back society, so to speak. We are teaching the basic skills of survival."

Fraley said the AMM's foundation is based on teaching survival by using, "the old ways, the Indian ways, the edible plants, trapping the animals to eat and make clothes out of. We are not saying go out and kill all the animals, don't get me wrong, we are conservationists like everyone else." He said they teach live-and-let-live, your word is your bond. A refreshing thought in our contemporary, fast-paced society. It's better for a person to cope with this environment and know that he can survive, rather than stealing from his neighbor.

To preserve the mountain man's history, the AMM is working to establish a museum featuring history, records and artifacts of this period. In keeping with the historical aspect of the rendezvous and the ideals of the AMM, Fraley said, "All of us have libraries, or are working on a library, all of us have to keep a journal."

A condensed history of the Rocky Mountain Fur Trade was thrust upon me by the many historians in camp, but one man who makes his living recounting this period is teacher and author, Raymond Glazner of Simi Valley, California. Glazner is a large, bearded man dressed in period attire--a colorful vest, split-tail coat, and a wide-brimmed hat shielding the bright sun.

Sitting at a rough hewn table in front of his tent, he leafs through a book looking for a historical point of information for an inquisitive buckskinner. "I go to rendezvous in California and back east also," he says. "This is one of my businesses, the other is "Images of the Past" which is a school/historical presentation. I also do consulting for the movie industry and museums on historical accuracy."

Glazner represents organizations involved in the preservation and presentation of the history of the United States, and is the National Field Representative of the NMLRA, and National Association of Buckskinners. He works from a huge tent-store housing a library and period literature, and speaks about history with a passion while he shows me the many authentic artifacts and reproductions inside. Tables lined with hand-made medals and buttons, toys of the period, and history books sit along the sides of the tent. As I browse thorough the contents of his store he explains the origin of his spacious tent. This style is called a marque; a style that goes back to the middle ages. They are very comfortable and big, with the store up front and the living quarters in the back," he says.

"Clacketey-clack." I hear a strange sound near Glazner's store. A woman sits intently spinning yarn, her long gingham dress flutters in the afternoon breeze. Her nimble hands twist red fibers onto an antique, foot-powered spinning wheel. "This wheel was used in Europe and brought over to the colonies in the 1600s, it's called a castle wheel," Jackie Taylor of Anaheim, California says. "This type was used by peasants sitting in castle stair-wells, which gave it the name." She spins baskets of colorful, raw wool that surround her wheel, and explains why she also likes the old ways. "I dye my wool with natural bark and bug dyes. It's richer," she explains. "The wool is from my sister's sheep. She doesn't spin or weave or knit, so I'm spinning her wool and will make her a sweater out of her sheep."

Taylor spins and weaves her own yarn on looms and spinning wheels she collects, and adds, "I have my great, great grandmother's wheel." She's

Walter McCudry, captain of American Mountain Men at the Hart Canyon Rendezvous. (photo by W. David Wright)

been interested in antiques since childhood, and started collecting antique firearms at age 13. Like most others at the rendezvous she declares, "I've always been interested in American history, that's why I'm here."

At the Hart Canyon Rendezvous, the pre-1840s live in spirited animation, keeping alive the traditions and customs of the mountain men and pathfinders who opened up the western wilderness for future generations. Hospitality, friendship and comradarie inundate the Hart Canyon Rendezvous promoting a feeling of well being and satisfaction throughout the camp.

With the dedication, interest, and exuberance exhibited by these "buckskinners" as they create a living history, I learned much about traditions and the quality of life in our environment by keeping the old ways alive.

When the sun began to set behind the surrounding mountains, I departed my living history lesson. I felt a mixture of sadness and joy having experienced a glimpse of the past. Sad that I was leaving, but comforted to know history is being preserved in our fast-moving world.

In retrospect, to those who wish to follow this path of adventure and return to the old ways, the following enticing notice was posted in the St. Louis newspapers in the early 1800s advertising for trappers to venture into the Rockies to seek their fortune:

For the Rocky Mountains.

The subscribers wish to engage One Hundred MEN, to ascend the Missouri to the

Rocky Mountains,

There to be employed as Hunters. As a compensation for each man fit for such business,

$200 Per Annum,

will be given for his services, as aforesaid. - For particulars, apply to J.V. Garnier, or W. Ashley, at St. Louis. The expedition will set out from this place, on or before the first day of March next.
Ashley & Henry.
jan. 18.

So, if you decide to follow your dreams, and seek fortune and fame in the wilderness, it would be advised to take stock in the mountain man's credo: "Watch your back trail, keep your eyes on the skyline!" Δ

The Third Year

Some tips on drying foods at home

By Jj Fallick

Drying is one of the oldest methods of food preservation still in use today. It is safe and can be quite economical. The nutritive value and palatability of dehydrated foods can range from the aptly-named "leather-breeches"—a dried greenbean recipe from great grandma's cookbook—to gourmet fruit leathers. It all depends on proper preparation.

Dehydrators

Your dehydrator can be a homemade solar model like we use, a commercial or homemade electric dryer or something as simple as racks laid in the sun, hung over the woodstove or even placed in a closed car sitting in the sun. I've used all these methods over the years, with varying success. Yes, they all work...but they all have drawbacks as well.

We all know how a closed car can really heat up. If you have an extra vehicle sitting around, even just a hulk with closed windows, it can make a good food dryer. I accidentally coated the seat of my husbands logging truck with strawberry "goo" when my Sunshine Preserves tipped over! I never did get all the sticky sweetness out of the truck and Don spent the rest of the summer fighting off the bees when he went logging. Not the way to improve your marriage, I'd say!

Suspending trays over the wood stove or laying them across the sawhorses outdoors has never produced much trouble for me. These methods are dependent on heat from the stove or HOT sunny days. Here in Washington State we often don't get many good drying days, but I used open air drying in western Colorado and southern California. DO cover your racks with cheesecloth or some such gauzy fabric to keep the bugs off and bring the racks into the garage or house overnight if they aren't done.

There are so many electric dehydrators on the market that I won't go into detail about them. I will caution you to TURN ON any electric dehydrator before you buy it. Many have fans to circulate the heat-- a good feature -- but if you plan to operate the unit in the kitchen you don't want a noisy one. Ours made such a racket that it drove me nuts even when I put it on the back porch!

Our homemade solar dryer came with the house. There are several similar ones in the area so I suspect they were built from plans that someone had. It is quiet, efficient and does a good job, now that I have plugged all the heat leaks. OF course, it doesn't work when the sky is overcast or it's raining and sometimes I have to end up with my food finishing off over the wood stove or by the propane oven's pilot light.

Herbs

Herbs are the easiest food to dry. I don't bother with the solar dehydrator for them, even here in the North. Laying herbs on racks in the sun for a day or two, at most, dries them well. As with all produce, pick at their peak of flavor, gently rinse off the dust and

Table 1. Drying vegetables

VEGGIE	PREPARATION	PRE-TREATMENT	TO DRY
carrots	select tender, non-woody roots, trim tops and root end; slice 1/8 inch thick or dice	steam-blanch 8-10 min.	spread in thin layer, dry until tough and leathery
corn	use "good eating" variety, at tender stage, cut from cob after blanching	steam on cob 10-15 min. (until "milk" is set)	spread 1/2 inch deep, stir often, 6-10 hours to dry, done when hard and brittle
peas	young, tender peas; shell	steam 8-10 min. or dip in boiling water 3-4 min.	spread on trays, 6-10 hours to dry, done when hard, shriveled and shatter when hit with hammer
summer squash	wash, slice 1/4 inch thick	steam 6 min.	spread in a thin layer, dry when brittle, EXCELLENT in soup
green beans	young, tender, wash	steam 8-10 min. or boiling water bath 3-4 min.	spread in thin layer, done when hard and brittle

Table 2. Drying fruit

FRUIT	PREPARATION	PRE-TREATMENT	TO DRY
apples	wash, peel, core, dice or slice up to 1/4 inch thick, coat with ascorbic acid (2 1/2 tsp. to 1 c. cold water)	soak 10-15 min. saline solution	arrange in thin layer, dry when leathery, no moisture when squeezed
apricots	wash, halve, pit, do NOT peel, coat with ascorbic acid (1 tsp. to 1 c. cold water)	soak 10-15 min. saline solution	lay on tray pit side up; done when leathery, no moisture when squeezed
nectarines	treat like apricots	treat like apricots	lay on tray pit side up; turn over when visible juice disappears. Done when leathery and somewhat pliable
peaches	use freestone, dry when ripe enough to eat but not fully ripe; peel, slice, pit; ascorbic acid like apricots	treat like apricots	arrange on tray in single layer. turn when visible juice disappears. Done when leathery and somewhat pliable
plums (prunes)	dry small ones, whole, large ones, halve and pit	blanch whole in boiling water 30 sec., halves, steam, blanch 15 min.	single layer, dry when pliable and leathery

dry them. No pre- or post- treatment is necessary.

Vegetables

The next easiest foods to dry are vegetables. Onions and peppers (sweet or hot) can be dried with little preparation. Onions are peeled and either sliced or diced and peppers are washed and diced. Spread either in a single layer on the dryer rack. At 140 degrees, these foods require 6 to 10 hours to dry. When done, onions are brittle and peppers tough. If you want onion powder, crush the dry slices or dices before storing. I use both of these veggies in spaghetti sauce, soup and stew. For "quick" sauces I presoak the dices in boiling water for up to an hour and add water and reconstituted pieces to the sauce.

Other vegetables require blanching—as for freezing—before the dehydration process begins. To blanch, immerse small quantities of the food in rapidly boiling water or steam briefly. This stops the enzyme action and makes your finished product more nutritious, tasty and better textured. Table 1 contains processing times and procedures for five commonly dried vegetables. This information is excerpted from Exten-

sion Bulletin 0700, Washington State University, Pullman, WA. Vegetables also require a pasteurization process after drying if they have been sun or solar dried, if they are cut into small pieces or if there is ANY possibility of insect contamination. This will save you the grief of losing an entire jar of dried food later. To pasteurize, heat the veggies in a 150 degree oven for 30 minutes or at 175 degrees for 10 minutes. Cool thoroughly before packing into clean, dry, insect and moisture-proof containers. I use canning jars and recycled lids; this is an excellent use for recycled mayo jars too.

Fruit

Some fruits can be dried with little preparation. Others require some treatment to prevent darkening which changes the taste and can make the food unsightly. While it is possible to sulphur fruits at home, I don't know anyone who does it. Most home processors use a saline solution (2-4 T. salt to 1 gal water) or ascorbic acid solution to treat fruit. Pure ascorbic acid, (available in pharmacies) is more effective than the commercial preparations which contain other in-

gredients and are used for freezing fruits.

Berries, cherries and grapes can be dried with no pre-treatment. They should be firm, free of stems and whole (except for cherries, which may be pitted) and laid in a single layer on the trays. When they are done, berries will be dry and have no moisture when crushed. Cherries dry much like grape "raisins". Table 2 contains processing options for a variety of other fruits.

Fruits must be "conditioned" and pasteurized. To condition, hold fruit in a sturdy, non-porous, non-aluminum container at room temperature in a well ventilated, protected area for a week. Stir the fruit daily. Then pasteurize in a 150 degree oven for 30 minutes or at 175 degrees for 15 minutes. Cool and store like dry vegetables.

Fruit leather

Fruit leather is an especially fun project. I use up the fruits that are a little too ripe to dry well whole or sliced, as fruit leather. You can make leather from virtually any fruit or combination you like. Wash and cut larger fruits into a saucepan until you have 2 - 2 1/2 cups of fruit pieces. Heat over low flame until soft, then puree in a blender or run through a sieve. Add 1-2 T. of your favorite sweetener (to taste) and 1 tsp. lemon juice to light colored fruits. Line your drying rack or a cookie sheet with sides with plastic wrap. Tape the wrap to the sides of the pan. Pour in the puree and distribute it evenly by gently tipping the sheet. Dry. Properly dried leathers will still feel sticky, but will peel easily from the plastic wrap. To store, roll up the cooled leather, plastic wrap and all, and store in a freezer bag, glass jar or other tightly sealed container. The leather is best if used within 3 months stored at room temperature but will keep up to six months under refrigeration, I'm told. I don't know...I never could hide it well enough.

Why dehydrate?

Modern food processing methods have made drying the least common form of food preservation. Living in the backwoods, however, makes drying foods more desirable. Dehydrated food is easy to process and easy and cheap to store. Proper preparation and storage of dried food can significantly affect the vitamin content of the foods. Recent research published in the Master Food Preserver Handbook (Washington State University Extension Service) shows us what can happen to the vitamin content of a fresh garden pea. When we eat the pea raw, fresh from the garden, we get 100% of the vitamin C. But cooking it, even fresh from the garden, reduces the vitamin C content to only 44% of the fresh vegetable. Comparatively, freezing, thawing and cooking leaves 39%, canning and reheating, 36%, freeze- drying and re-hydrating, 35% and dehydration and cooking leaves only 25% of the original vitamin C content. This is not a putdown of stored food. We cannot always eat fresh from the garden, and even "fresh" foods from the supermarket lose nutrition in the weeks of storage and shipping that bring them to northern tables. Processing your food fresh from the garden and using up-to-date methods maximizes nutrient retention. Blanching and pasteurizing minimize overall nutrient loss in dried foods. When you cook your vegetables in minimal amounts of water and include that water in your diet as liquid in soup, stew, gravy or sauce, you catch vitamins we used to throw away. Store your dry products at a low temperature in a dry place, sealed tightly in non-porous containers to maximize vitamin retention.

I use dried fruits and vegetables often in the winter to supplement my canned and cellared products. Since I can't have a home freezer, my stores of dried peppers, spinach, zucchini and onions show up often in winter soups and stews. In fact, my kids prefer when I use dry spinach and zucchini in soup. They don't cook up like their fresh or frozen counterparts and are therefore easier to fish out of the bowl!Δ

A Backwoods Home Anthology
The Tenth Year

The Third Year

USING GUNS AS TOOLS

Learning to shoot safely, effectively

By Christopher Maxwell

At one time practically every house in America contained firearms. Shooting lessons were part of every boy's education. The United States was never the "Nation of Riflemen" of myth, but in the past almost every American had at least some practical training and exposure to firearms.

Most Americans alive now grew up in cities or suburbs and the only knowledge about firearms most Americans receive is mis-information and lies from movies, TV, and "news" publications. The entertainment media's obsession with violence and the narrow urban perspective of the news media create a message that firearms are only useful for mayhem, and they are so dangerous that the mere presence of a firearm is threatening.

This creates two extreme types of attitudes among the people who are exposed to this mis-information: Rambo-fascination and Pollyanna-horror. Neither of these attitudes is reasonable or useful.

If one has the training to use them safely and effectively, firearms can help you put food on your table, protect your livestock from predators, protect your crops from rodents, and if all else fails, protect your home from violence. As any other tool, firearms can be dangerous if used carelessly or with malicious intent.

Learning to use firearms safely and effectively is not as easy as it once was. Political factors prevent safety information from being taught in most schools or by most police departments. It seems curious to me that some people who claim to be concerned about the potential for firearms accidents and misuse act to prevent the distribution of information which might prevent these problems.

The National Rifle Association's primary activity is training in firearms safety and use, not lobbying as you may have been led to believe. The NRA has certified instructors all over the U.S. A letter to them at 1600 Rhode Island Avenue N.W., Washington D.C. 20036 will get you a list of instructors in your area.

I recommend contacting a qualified instructor rather than trying to learn from one of your friends if possible. There are too many people out there who think reading a few copies of *Shooting and Blasting Magazine* makes them an expert. Even military training has very little application in civilian life these days. A responsible gun owner who shoots well may still not be able to teach.

I can't teach you shooting in a magazine article but the following tips should be helpful if you can't find a qualified instructor. They will at least help you spot a fake before you waste too much time and learn bad habits, and might serve to fill in the blanks in what you can learn from a friend.

Safety

If your instructor doesn't start with safety, get another instructor. Every accident with firearms I have ever heard of was caused by violating one or more of the basic rules listed here.

Do not allow a firearm to point at anybody or anything unless you are willing to shoot whatever you are pointing at.

Keep your finger out of the trigger guard until you intend to fire.

Make sure any shot you fire will be stopped by a solid backstop.

Keep firearms out of reach of children or irresponsible adults.

Thousands of accidents might be prevented if those journalists who are so concerned about firearms accidents would spend ten percent of the time they devote to relentless propaganda against firearms ownership to publicizing these rules.

Shotguns

For some basic information about shotguns, see *Backwoods Home Magazine* issue #11.

Shotguns are pointed rather than being aimed. This means you have to hold the shotgun so that it points where you look. Look along the top of the barrel, or along the rib between the barrels of a double, with your cheek against the stock. Tuck the butt firmly into your shoulder, so the recoil will push instead of hitting you. Once in this position you do not turn your head or swing the gun, you turn your entire body from the waist up like a turret.

When firing at a moving target, get in front and don't stop your swing to fire. The target continues to move while you squeeze the trigger, so you have to continue to move ahead of it.

Rifles

Issue #12 of *Backwoods Home Magazine* contains some general information about .22 rifles. Issue #14 will have some information about centerfire rifles.

A rifle is a precision instrument. To be useful, a rifle must be aimed precisely. A good rifle in skilled hands is capable of astonishing accuracy. In unskilled hands, a rifle is a very expensive and poorly balanced club.

The essentials of rifle marksmanship are: a steady hold, sight alignment, and trigger squeeze.

You must hold the rifle with minimal movement, ideally none, while aiming and firing. To do this from a standing position is very difficult and requires both strength and control. You will do better to begin learning with a .22 rifle from a benchrest or a prone firing position where you can rest the forend of the rifle on a log or sandbag. Practice holding your rifle in a standing position for a few minutes every day to build up the specific muscles needed.

Sight alignment presents a problem as you cannot focus at three distances at the same time. The solution is to look through, not at, the rear sight as you focus on the front sight. When you have fixed the location of the target, shift your focus back to the front blade or bead. The target will lose sharpness, and if colored protectively it may blur right out but you have to just remember where it was and keep your focus on the front sight. By looking through the rear and focusing on the front you will automatically center the front sight in the rear.

A telescope sight solves the focus problem by superimposing the crosshair onto the target so both are in sharp focus.

The idea of squeezing the trigger is to move the trigger without moving the entire rifle. Put the pad of the tip of your finger on the trigger, and squeeze with your entire hand. Practice, practice, practice.

Handguns

Handguns are generally aimed and fired the same as rifles but are much more difficult due to shorter sight radius, and less contact points to help with a steady hold while squeezing.

Notes for women

Firearms are one of the areas where women's fear and loathing of machinery causes unnecessary handicaps for them. Many women will be reluctant to consider use of firearms but there are more women than ever living by themselves. Even married couples usually work away from home so the odds are low that you can count on a man being around to handle emergencies. When the weasel gets into the henhouse, or the coyotes are dragging your newborn lamb away, or the escaped convicts come to visit, you may well have to deal with the situation yourself.

I don't recommend learning to shoot from your husband or boyfriend. For one thing, if he grew up in the city or suburbs he may not know any more about firearms than you do, and what he thinks he knows may be wrong. Even if your husband or boyfriend is a qualified instructor, there is still the potential problem of role playing between couples and the way women are trained to act helpless to make Mr. Macho Man feel important, and to get men to do things for them.

I have taught many women to handle firearms capably, but some of them can't seem to hit the target when their husband or boyfriend is present. This doesn't seem necessary. I don't believe most men are so insecure that they will feel threatened by any capability you may develop. If your is, maybe it's time to quit humoring him.

Another problem women face is that most firearms are made to fit average size men. This is OK if you are 5'9" and have large hands and long fingers, but if you are an average size woman you may need to have an inch or more removed from the stock of any weapon you will be using. Many popular firearms are available in Youth Models which are shorter and lighter and often made for less powerful ammunition.

If used skillfully and with responsibility, firearms can help your life in the country to be safer, easier and more productive. Without training and practice, firearms can be a menace and a dangerous source of overconfidence. Do it right or don't do it at all. Δ

A BHM Writer's Profile

Christopher Maxwell grew up in northern Arkansas. He has been a farmer, soldier, factory worker, janitor, salesman, gun dealer, writer and locksmith. He finally sold his locksmith shop and left Chicago because "business was too good." He is now working as an associate editor at BHM.

He has written numerous articles about home security, firearms, self-defense, politics, and the jury system, which have been published in many magazines and newsletters. He has been writing for BHM since issue #11.

Christopher is currently improving, expanding, and connecting his gun articles from BHM with additional material to produce the Backwoods Home Beginner's Guide to Firearms, which will be published by BHM.

Pals

WILD ANIMALS

A road kill could kill you too!

By Martin P. Waterman

Road kills fall into that category of accidents that we rarely think about, that is, until we are involved in that type of accident. This is unfortunate because many of these accidents can be avoided with just a little understanding of human and animal nature. This is important because there is usually more damage caused than just the loss of life to the animal.

Road kills have become a major problem in some areas. There are now over 40,000 road kills each year in the state of Pennsylvania involving deer. This does not include those animals that are often injured and return to the woods only to die.

There are many misunderstandings concerning road kills. Some people think that small animals such as squirrels, rabbits and raccoons pose no threat to the driver or the vehicle. In a sense, this is true. Unfortunately, human nature often kicks at the wrong time as the thought of crushing some poor helpless critter under your wheels distorts your actions. The natural reaction is to swerve to avoid the animal and this type of reaction can lead to loss of control, and injury or even death to the occupants of the vehicle. Another natural reaction is to hit the brakes. This is complicated further when there is traffic, poor visibility or poor weather. You may be able to stop in time to save the cute animal but the tractor trailer behind you may not have the same maneuverability.

Larger animals such as deer, moose and bears create the biggest problems because they cause the most damage to vehicles and loss of human life.

I hit a deer three years ago. It was a large doe. The circumstances seemed very strange at the time but after talking with a forest ranger at the Department of Natural Resources, who are the proper authorities here in Canada, I learned there is often a pattern and therefore the accident could have possibly been predicted and avoided. I was driving home from a long trip. It was three in the morning. There was a slight fog in the woods and the air was crisp and cool, typical of a late autumn day. I had just entered the city limits of a metropolitan area of 50,000 and had slowed to about 40 miles per hour. I came around the corner and saw three deer on the shoulder of the road, their eyes glowing red as if they were some type of alien beings. Two of the deer bolted into the woods while the third bolted onto the road and ran directly toward the front of my vehicle. All of this happened so suddenly that even though I had hit the brakes and had slowed the car dramatically the combined impact of the deer running onto the car and the car into the deer resulted in a crashing thump.

Instantly, there was a big puff of smoke which I later figured out was the vapor from the air conditioning compressor as it was broken. The deer was quickly spun around and fortunately was killed instantly. During the impact, I had hit the steering wheel and was shaken but not injured. Fortunately, I was driving a big car. In many instances when large game are hit with small vehicles the cars knock out their legs and the animals end up rolling up the hood and going through the windshield. In addition to the loss of animal life, this type of accident has also caused many human deaths. After hitting the deer, I immediately got out of the car and felt sick that such a large and beautiful animal had been killed. The impact had done close to $4,000 damage to my car and it was almost a write-off. Since I was within the city limits, I immediately went to a phone and called the police who then called the Department of Natural Resources to remove the dead animal from the highway. While I was being interviewed by the police for the accident report, I found out much information about road kills from the officer. Some of the information shocked me and has prompted to do more research into this area. He told me that they have about three such deer accidents a week and that there were also some very bad accidents with moose. Apparently, a few days before my accident a couple of senior citizens had come upon a large bull moose standing in the middle of the road. They had seen the moose, reacted in time, and come to a screeching halt just feet before impact. They were thanking the Lord and counting their blessings when the moose suddenly became livid. The moose started to butt the side of their car with its large rack of antlers. The moose was so powerful that it proceeded to roll the car over twice while pushing it off the road and into the ditch. The couple was shaken up but fortunately they were not injured. The car, however, was a total write-off.

Last week I learned from a friend about another unfortunate moose accident. Apparently, close friends of his were driving at night and came upon a moose. They were driving a small Toyota and were not able to stop or swerve in time to avoid hitting the large animal. The moose was so large that the Toyota was almost able to proceed under the moose's belly. "Almost" is the key word here. The top of the car hit the moose's abdomen and chest knocking out the front windshield and slicing the moose open. The moose was killed but not before the majority of its warm entrails had fallen on the laps of the driver and the occupant in the passenger seat.

This has been a record year for moose accidents here in the Northeast and because of this there are many stories I could tell. I have told these so that readers hopefully will take some of the precautions described in this article to help prevent unnecessary road kills.

I recently interviewed some forest rangers and found that there are several characteristics in common with all road kills. First of all, deer, moose, and even bears tend to be nocturnal. It is in the darkness of night that they often do most of their feeding and are therefore most active. As much as 95% of all road kills with large animals are at night. Therefore, when driving at night, it helps to be aware that your chances of hitting a large animal are almost 20 times greater than hitting one in the day.

The season that one is most likely to hit a deer is in the spring or early summer. Most people think the greatest hazard is in the fall. It was in the fall that I hit the deer. On the contrary, you are more likely to hit a deer or moose in the spring or early summer. The reason that this is more likely is that this is the time of the year when mosquitoes, black flies and other insects hatch while the woods are still damp from the winter. In a bad year this drives deer and moose into clearings or onto highways to get away from the insects which cause them great discomfort and irritation. This spring there has been an increase in road kills in Maine and it looks as if there could possibly be a record set for moose kills in some areas. Road kills also happen in the fall because this is the time when many animals such as deer are busy mating. As one ranger explained to me, "The bucks tend to get a little stupid and the does tend to move around quite a bit."

Deer are also attracted to lights such as headlights. This fact is well known among "deer jackers", who use lights to illegally lure and hunt deer. The deer are easy prey as they have been known to come within a few feet of the hunters' lights.

Another problem is that the deer population in many areas is at record levels. Historically, deer are not native in the Northeast. When the settlers came, deer were rarely found north of Pennsylvania. However, with the settlement of man and the disappearing grazing land being used for agriculture, they had to change their traditional habitat. In New England, there were historically caribou rather than deer. Caribou were hunted to near extinction but fortunately, they are now being reintroduced. Another reason for the abnormally high deer populations is the decline of their natural predators such as wolves, cougars, bears and coyotes which are now non-existent in many areas where there are deer. These natural predators of deer were eliminated be-

cause of their threat to livestock and poultry farming. In some states and counties there are now more deer than there are people and many of these areas historically had no deer.

Yet another problem is that deer are becoming less and less frightened by man. In fact, deer have become a big problem in some urban areas where they often feed on gardens and do not have the fear of being hunted or shot near cities where it is illegal to do so.

What else can we do to avoid these unfortunate road kills? First of all, we can extend hunting seasons. This may sound cruel to many individuals but deer are actually starving to death during many winters. It is better to have a large healthy herd than to have a weak herd that is going through the long painful effects of starvation that result from deer trying to survive off meager resources during the winter. A quick death is more humane than putting unfortunate deer through this starvation that results in a slow agonizing death. I once debated with an individual who wanted deer hunting banned. I explained that this would be a cruel idea and would lead to disastrous effects on the deer population. This could include increases in tuberculosis, Lyme disease, starvation, increased accidents and the damage to other animal habitat due to competition for food. My message did not get through until I asked him if he would support the same thinking for the rat population in New York City. Had they not the same rights as deer under his argument? Why should they be killed and not deer? Having run circles logically around this individual's increasingly weak arguments, I could see why he did what most ill-informed would-be do-gooders do best. He adopted a quick strategy of retrenchment and rudely walked away disturbed and confused.

It is unlikely that legislators are going to do much to increase deer hunting in the near future. The nature of our governments is to only act after there has been loss of life and after the problem is out of control. Often, they are still reluctant to act even then because of special interest groups who control large blocks of votes through disinformation campaigns. Members of these

groups, who often live in a self-created rationalized fantasy world where Bambi is symbolic of all that is good and all hunters are evil, irresponsible beer-swilling rednecks hell bent on destroying the world for their love of blood sports. It is this type of unscrupulous lobbying that can often prevent beneficial legislation from being passed.

Therefore, the major way to prevent road kill is avoidance. Be aware that animals are active at night and during mating season. Know that they are often attracted to the road because of road salt. Be alert when driving at night and do not hit the high beams when you see animals as this will not cause them to flee. In fact, they will usually freeze on the spot or run toward the headlights.

If you do much driving in wooded areas, you should pick up a set of Save-A-Life Deer Alerts. They are thumb-sized warning devices that are mounted on your vehicle that emit an ultrasonic sound. You cannot hear the sound but deer can hear it up to 400 yards away. They usually cost less than ten dollars and are available at many hunting shops and truck stops.

If you should accidentally hit an animal, do not touch it. Call the local or state police immediately. If the animal is still alive, mention this to the police and they will dispatch someone from the Department of Natural Resources or other appropriate agency to humanely kill the animal. Do not attempt to move the animal yourself unless it is in the middle of the road and poses a danger to other vehicles. If you do not call the police and fill out an accident report, you will probably have problems collecting from your insurance company. Depending on the jurisdiction dead animals are usually picked up by the highway department. In this area some of the road kills are given to a game farm where they are used to feed the wolves, coyotes, bears, and other wildlife in the area.

In our modern society road kills have become an unfortunate fact of life. Realizing the problem can help save animals which could include yourself. Δ

How an inverter fits into your solar electric system

By Joel Davidson

Early on in PV history, the use of inverters was downplayed and most people used direct current. PV systems were costly and small-sized. Inverters consume power, and when PV was two to three times its present cost, that power was too expensive to waste.

PV pioneers were willing to put up with DC systems. They either hunted up DC appliances, modified existing AC appliances, made gadgets from scratch or did without. It was a time of DC lights, fans and radios salvaged from cars and trucks. Much time was spent scrounging through catalogs and shops looking for military surplus DC motors and other goodies. Some very creative solutions resulted and a few DC PV businesses flourished for a time.

Even today the DC tradition has been passed on as part of the credo of energy conservation. A guideline for designing small PV systems is, if you can power something directly with DC, do it.

One idea that has grown less popular through changes in technology is record turntable modification. Since better belt-driven turntables use DC motors, it seemed logical to bypass the input transformer and go straight to the motor with 12 volts or whatever the DC requirement was.

For the non-technical: If you trace the power cord from the plug into some devices, the input transformer is the first thing you may find. The purpose of these coils with a magnet is to take the 120-volt AC utility power coming into the transformer primary coil and return reduced voltage from the secondary coil. That reduced voltage is then rectified to DC for use in the low-voltage DC circuitry of the solid-state electronics found in most everything nowadays. For the PV pioneer, much time was spent discussing which devices could be used

Inverters change a battery's direct current to alternating current so you can use the electricity with everyday household appliances.

directly in the DC mode. A voltmeter put across the secondary windings of the input transformer would often tell the story.

Reading the voltage and making modifications meant opening up the device. Electrical hazard warnings and threats of voided warranties notwithstanding, it was strange to open up a case which says "No Serviceable Parts Inside" or "To Be Opened Only By A Qualified Service Technician" and find 12 volts DC just waiting to be powered by PV.

Amateur radio operators and computer tinkerers were already familiar with these exploratory operations. They knew that most solid-state electronics were low voltage, usually 12 volts or less. Thus, ham radios and computers were among the first high-tech equipment to be PV-powered.

In the early 1980s two trends evolved. Tracking the growth of the recreational vehicle industry, all kinds of DC appliances began to appear. RVers

like gadgets, and the manufacturers were accommodating. In one automotive catalog, five models of DC vacuum cleaners were listed. I tried them all. To my disappointment, they were hardly more than toys (though some cost more than small home uprights). They worked, but were designed for small tasks, not cleaning a house in the country where dirt is always getting tracked in.

There are other examples of DC devices that couldn't quite do the job. There were blenders that couldn't crush ice, soldering irons that couldn't solder large wire, drills that broke after a few hours, bug zappers that missed the big ones. Needless to say, there was room for improvement, and things have improved. Nowadays, we can find better DC appliances—though at a premium price.

Fortunately, another trend was occurring. People were beginning to experiment with inverters. Users were willing to sacrifice the AC appliances they had stored away and to experiment with early square-wave inverters. Some people used old-style motor inverters and got satisfactory service but low efficiency. Some even bought expensive sine-wave inverters costing as much as their entire PV system.

The more technical PV users at that time were building their own. From early designs and testing came a new generation of inverters which was to change the nature of PV use and make the old DC bias obsolete.

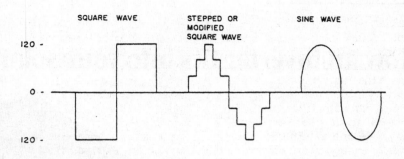

The wave forms of various inverters from the most primitive simple square wave to pure sine wave. For most applications, the stepped wave will work well and reduce inverter costs.

What is an inverter?

An inverter is a device that changes direct current to alternating current. (Converters, sometimes called rectifiers, change AC to DC). For our purposes, we are speaking of 12-, 24-, or 48-volt DC power inverted to 120 or 240 volts AC. (See Figure 1)

Don't let other approximate AC voltages confuse you. You will hear 110 volts or 115 volts or even 117 volts. The range is 110 to 120. However, actual readings may be greater or less. There are two conventions, 110 and 120. Old timers use 110, but the catalogs typically spec electrical equipment at 120 and 240 for utility voltage. Unless your equipment specifically requires something other than utility power, 220, 230, and 240 volts are also interchangeable. The simple test is if you can plug it into grid power, call it what you will — it's 120 or 240 volts AC.

Europe has different voltages, generally 230 volts 50 Hertz (named in honor of an early experimenter in electricity). The difference is the frequency at which the current alternates (thus, alternating current or AC). In the U.S. we use AC at 60 cycles per seconds or 60 Hz.

While the purist may want to operate his PV-powered home entirely on DC, there are some limitations. Besides limited availability of appliances, larger wire is required to carry the same power load. For example, a 200-watt load at 12 volts needs wire large enough to carry 16.6 amperes, whereas the same load at 120 volts is only 1.66 amperes.

Too often in PV discussions we hear a lot about inverter efficiency losses

and very little about the cost of large wire used for comparable DC loads. We won't mention wire loss inefficiencies because of undersized conductors. That kind of penny-pinching is, in fact, just throwing good money away. Sometimes those losses and costs can be as much as the difference in the cost of using an inverter. Factored into cost somehow should be the time spent making do with DC, but that is not often the case.

Inverters come in all sizes, shapes and price ranges offering a vast array of options. Some inverters produce the simple square wave suitable for most loads. While there is reason for concern about the quality of square-wave AC, it will do the job. Surprisingly, most computers will operate on square wave. Some computers have power conditioning equipment built into their power supplies which allows for almost any quality of electricity. This is done because grid power is so variable. I powered my Apple II Plus and two disk drives and Epson printer with a very simple 550- watt square-wave inverter satisfactorily.

Recently, my office was moved to the front of the building which is serviced by the utility company, while my PV system remained connected to the old office. One morning I turned on my computer and a surge or spike zapped the computer power supply resulting in costly repairs. When I got the computer back from the shop, I ran a 120-volt AC line from my old PV system to the front office, specifically dedicated for my computer. Needless to say, I am relieved to be back on smooth and reliable PV power again. (When I'm

on the road, I also avoid unregulated grid power from ruining my computer. A second battery in my car and a 300-watt inverter are my portable office power supply and Uninterruptable Power System. If I have to stay on location a few days, a portable PV array provides all the power my "office on the road" needs.)

More costly inverters put out a modified, or stepped, square wave which more closely matches grid power. Some test equipment needs the exact type of power produced by the utility company (60-cycle reference sine wave) to operate. In that case, a costly sine-wave inverter is necessary. The early sine-wave inverters were actually square-wave devices with ferro-resistant transformers to smooth out the flip-flop square wave. Thus, efficiency was sacrificed in the transformer to produce pure sine-wave inversion.

Now there is a new generation of inverters: relatively lower cost, very high-efficiency digital sine-wave inverters. They can power anything — just like grid power — and they are changing the way PV will be used.

So far we have been discussing solid-state, or electronic inverters. An old standby is the rotary or motor inverter. This device is a motor which drives an alternator. The DC power runs the motor. A common shaft ties the motor and alternator together, and the output of the alternator is sine-wave AC.

If rotary inverters put out a nice sine wave, why aren't they used more often in PV systems? The simple fact is that they are not very efficient. At less than 65% efficiency, and as low as 30%

efficiency with loads 20% of the rated output, rotary inverters are not particularly suited to PV. This is primarily due to the amount of energy required to move the motor and alternator. PV electricity is too precious to waste on spinning parts. But for the occasional, short-duration sine-wave load, a rotary inverter may be just the thing.

Also, the rotary, inverter output voltage varies in direct proportion to the DC input voltage. This means that as the battery discharges, the output voltage falls with it. Even though the output is a sine wave, you can see the voltages varying from as low as 90 volts to upward of 140 volts AC.

One nice thing about rotary inverters is that they can really take a beating. They handle motor-starting well. I know of cases where rotary inverters were used until they began to heat and smoke. After cooling off a while, they were called back into service and performed without any problem. You can't beat that for durability.

On the other hand, a good solid-state inverter should have enough protective circuitry to do the same. Of course, it shouldn't have smoke coming out of it, but if it can't take motor surges and occasional overloading, then it is under- designed.

I mention under-design because inevitably an inverter is called on to handle loads beyond its rated capacity. People have a tendency to pinch pennies when buying an inverter, opting for the smallest size they can get away with. Then they push it to the maximum. Inverter manufactures know this. For that reason, wise inverter builders factor in extra capacity to insure long life. But don't rely on the "fudge factor." Keep the use of your inverter within its factory ratings.

Solid-state inverters may also have an automatic demand on/off. This means that you can turn the inverter on and leave it on, using relatively, little power, until a load comes on. When it senses a load, the needed power is applied. Without a load, it waits. In the on and no-load state your inverter should use little power. If your inverter does not have a low no-load mode, be sure to turn it off when not in use. Do not waste your PV power.

What can you power with an inverter? Basically anything that operates from the grid can be operated with the modern solid-state inverter. Resistive loads like coffee makers, toasters, and hair dryers will operate with no problem, as well as incandescent lights. Fluorescents may not work well if your inverter does not interface properly with the fluorescent ballasts.

Some induction or brushless AC motors have very high starting surge requirements. Well pumps, garbage disposals, dishwashers, refrigerators, air conditioners, and washing machines all have high starting surges. These surge requirements can be as much as five times the normal operating power requirement. Thus, the 300-watt motor load of a refrigerator may not even start if your inverter is rated less than 1500 watts.

Some motors do not work well with some inverters. Why is this? Is it the fault of the motor or the inverter? The answer is both. Motors are made as cheaply as possible nowadays. Most manufacturers leave out what is commonly called the motor-run capacitor. The job of this capacitor is to smooth out the interaction between the load (motor) and the power source. Grid power with its pure sine wave does not create as much bad feedback (inductive reactance) with such loads, but some inverters do.

If you find that motors are not running up to normal speed with your inverter, try putting a 3- or 4-microfarad 400-volt electrolytic capacitor across the motor windings. Such a capacitor may be purchased for under $10 at most motor stores. Be sure to note polarity when installing the capacitor. If you don't know what you are doing, ask questions. Also, be sure to put the capacitor on the motor side of the switch so that it does not load your inverter when the motor is off. If you use an inverter designed for reactive loads, this should not be a problem.

Selecting an inverter

There are a few basic guidelines to use in selecting an inverter for your PV system. First, you need to know your power requirements. We always come back to this. The power requirements identify the loads and how long they will be used. Your power requirements list will give you an idea on what will be operating on AC and what AC loads will be operating at the same time. The inverter must be able to handle the combined AC loads which will be operated simultaneously. In fact, the inverter must be able to handle the surge of these loads, too.

Note the type of loads to be powered by the inverter. Are they motor loads with high starting surges? Is complex electronic equipment to be powered? How about kitchen loads? Will you be running the garbage disposal and dishwasher at the same time? If so, don't forget to include the well pump as you will be using water, too. And finally, don't forget the refrigerator. It can come on while all these other loads are running.

Total your automatic loads and surges. Then add up demand loads, such as dishwasher and washing machine, and your convenience loads, such as blenders and toasters, separately and in possible combinations of simultaneous operation. After you have done that, you may find that you will have to monitor your combined loads to keep the size and cost of your inverter to within reason.

There are a couple of other reasons to look at your power requirements when considering an inverter. When you size your system and allocate your budget, the inverter should be considered in your first purchase. Although inverters come in a variety of sizes, it is false economy to buy a small inverter you will soon outgrow. Buy the inverter that will suit your future needs now.

There's a good reason for up-sizing. When starting out, you may have lots of construction or remodeling work to do. A bigger inverter will help you through this period with ease. It sure is nice to have a quiet inverter instead of a noisy generator when you are doing carpentry. And besides, what if your generator breaks down? Then you are faced with a repair job before you can do the construction work.

The Third Year

Once you are settled in, the over-capacity of a larger inverter bought for construction purposes still has merit. Operating inverters at or near capacity may give high efficiency, but also may lead to shortened inverter life. Some over-capacity is good insurance.

On the other hand, a small inverter may be all you can afford, especially if you are installing PV in stages. Be sure to plan each additional part of your wiring though, or you will have imbalanced circuits. If you use a couple of smaller inverters for your loads, you have insurance in the form of redundancy. If one inverter should fail, you'll still have the other one. However, if the bigger one fails, will the smaller one adequately operate important loads?

This brings us to cascading inverters. While no inverters can be paralleled on the same circuit without one burning up the other, some inverters can be tandemed for increased capacity.

Heart Interface was the first company to address the needs of the inverter market and was the most popular inverter for remote home use. Thir first inverters reached peak efficiency at a very low load level, one or two lights. Their surge capabilities were good, and they ran motors efficiently. Among their deficiencies were reliability, changing internal adjustment and slow warranty repair. Many of these questions were met by Heart Interface. In 1985, Heart Interface began marketing inverters which could be tandemed for bigger loads.They did this to improve efficiency and to eliminate the costly 5000-watt inverter. Unless your loads are always big, a 5000-watt inverter is not such a good idea. It just doesn't make sense to use a 5000-watt inverter to power a 100-watt load. On the other hand, if you need an inverter to handle a 5000-watt, you must use one. Cascading or tandem inverters get around this mix. By stacking up to four 2500-watt inverters, you can handle big loads. The stack will be called on only if needed.

Should you ever have a problem with one of your cascading inverters, you will still have the others. Not a bad idea. For planning purposes, cascading inverters make sense, too. Let's say you are just getting started, and want to power your home with PV. Your eventual full complement of loads will be large. However, in the beginning you may be operating on a limited budget or requiring a limited amount of power. By using the first of a cascading inverter, you can squeeze by. Later you can add on as needed.

A word of warning: Never put two AC inputs on the same circuit or something will burn. That means never feed your generator or grid power into a circuit being powered by an inverter at the same time. Wire your home so that this can never happen. Never feed generator or inverter power into the utility grid without the power company's permission. In the first place, it is illegal. More importantly, it endangers power line workers.

Buying an inverter

When you buy an inverter, get one that can be repaired. And hope that the company that manufactured it and the person who sold it to you will stay in business. Buying close-out inverters is unwise. Where will you get technical support when you need it?

It is always a good idea to ask your seller if you can call for technical information after the inverter is in place. If you have hired someone to install your system, get a service contract that includes replacement. This may cost extra but it may be worth it because should the inverter fail you won't be without power.

All inverters must be tested when installed. Some may have to be adjusted for the specific installation. Be sure to ask "What if...?" If you don't like the answer, shop elsewhere. A reputable inverter sales outlet should satisfy your every need.

Probably the most popular inverter today is the Trace. The Trace Engineering Co. is a spin-off of Heart, and the company solved many of the problems in the Heart units. They boast a two-year warranty and so far there have been few warranty repairs. All units are delivered by UPS, meaning cheaper warranty repair and delivery price. These units have no adjustments to fail. The inverter is self-monitoring and modifies its internal workings and correspnding parts specifications as the temperature changes. These inverters have very high surge capabilities and will run large loads for the short periods of time that are needed in a remote site home. The basic 2000-watt 12 volt model or the 2500- watt 24 volt model will run the right 1/3 HP deep well pump and the right washing machine at the same time. Turn on voltage, turn off voltage, and charging ampere are all user selectable. The best part of all is that they are much cheaper than any of the competition.

Disadvantages

With all this talk about the wonders of inverters and their benefits, what are the disadvantages? We will not even consider poor quality, low-efficiency inverters. Of the good inverters, there will inevitably be problems, usually in the first few month, as they "burn-in" or get adjusted to regular use. Other problems occur because of bad installation, undersized DC input wires, rough handling, and overloading.

A disadvantage already mentioned is your reliance on the inverter to power all your loads. Should your inverter fail, even if fully warranted and all the repairs or replacement are cost-free, you will be without all or some of your load-carrying capacity. If everything electrical is AC, then you are out of luck – and power. Let's hope you at least planned in DC emergency lights and water to carry you through any waiting periods for parts and repairs.

A less important disadvantage of inverters is efficiency. This has become a secondary consideration since the advent of 90% plus efficiency field effect transistor (FET) inverter technology. But it still should be considered. If your system is small and your budget limited, perhaps an inverter is not for you. A 10% loss can be costly if you are operating on a shoestring.

Conversely, an inverter makes wiring a lot cheaper. You can use readily available low-cost standard wiring and hardware. Switches and breakers and all the other goodies used in AC homes are relatively inexpensive. The savings on the wiring along with the convenience and savings in using standard appliances makes shoestring DC almost a thing of the past.

The PV/grid connection

It is possible to install a medium to large-sized residential PV array and remain hooked up to the utility power grid. The advantage of this type of installation is that the battery storage system is eliminated. When the sun is not producing enough power to run the home's electrical appliances, or the peak load is greater than production, the grid-connect PV home gets its power from the utility company. When PV production exceeds consumption, the home is credited or actually paid for the power it produces and puts into the utility grid.

Although there are a few thousand grid-connect wind power homes, there are far fewer grid-connect PV homes. The two main reasons for this are economics and a lack of marketing. It has been difficult to present an economic argument for PV/grid homes because of their cost compared to buying a monthly electric bill. But like so many things that are not "cost-effective," PV/grid homes could have been marketed to the affluent for other than economic reasons. Unfortunately, they were not. On the other hand, Windworks, maker of the Gemini Synchronous Inverter, did an excellent job building a reliable grid-connect inverter for wind systems and did a good job selling it. In fact, they looked so good that a Wisconsin utility company bought the company.

In addition, Windworks was able to get parity pricing for their customers. They did all the system engineering with the approval of the utilities, and, in exchange, customers usually got one meter installed, which ran backwards when the system produced power. Nowadays we generally see two meters on these systems—one for buying power and one for selling. Parity pricing for alternative power systems is pretty much a thing of the past.

So the development of grid-interconnect windchargers proceeded smoothly with intertie equipment costing about as much as a battery

bank. Parity pricing and the elimination of battery maintenance were important selling points.

A few Gemini inverters were also used on PV systems. Today we see wind and hydro grid-interconnect systems using a variety of inverters similar to the Gemini.

Synchronous inverters are line-commutated, line-feeding inverters which change DC power to AC at standard line voltages and frequency. In operation, all the available DC power is converted to AC. If more power is available from the DC source than is required by the home, the excess flows into the AC grid where it is used by others. If less power is produced than is being used, the difference is provided by the AC grid.

The inverters have circuitry capable of handling unregulated DC power input. For PV arrays, where the maximum power output is not a function of a single variable, automatic tracking circuitry seeks the highest output by incrementally varying the loading of the array while monitoring the power output. Therefore, the array's highest wattage regardless of a standardized voltage is what the electric meter sees.

Do not confuse power tracking with physically tracking the sun. Power tracking is electronic peak power-seeking circuitry built into the power-conditioning equipment. In some DC PV water pumping systems, peak

power tracking is used to match array output to optimum motor operation.

The installation of synchronous inverters is generally beyond the scope of the average homeowner. An electrician is needed to do the job. In addition, utility company engineers will want to be involved to insure that the system is safe and producing power equal in quality to grid power.

The belief has been that when PV prices drop, more grid-interconnect

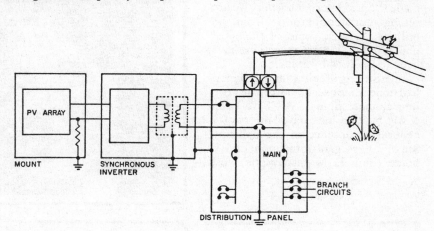

The synchronous inverter interconnects the solar array to the home and the utility company. At the main distribution panel, power can flow in two directions. During the day when an excess of PV power is being produced, it is sold to the utility. At night or when loads exceed PV production, power is bought by the utility.

systems would be installed. However, when PV modules were selling at half price (as they effectively were when the tax credits were available), there was no rush to install these systems.

Another factor that has limited the installation of PV grid interconnect systems is that utility companies considering grid interconnect of power fields have the advantage of economy of scale. Why would someone interested in PV and able to afford grid interconnect system do so if their utility company was going to do the same thing on a larger scale at a lower price per watt? Logically, by paying your monthly electric bill, you could buy utility solar electricity and support a much grander step toward a PV society.

As it turns out, few utilities are willing to put in PV power fields. Those utilities that have, publicize their efforts out of proportion and give the impression the they are "going solar" for their customers. Thus, rate payers are discouraged from the PV/grid connection because they mistakenly think their utility company has done it for them.

But even with short-term economics against them, some true pioneers have put in PV/grid-interconnect systems. Not only did they have to convince themselves of the merit of PV, they also had to convince their utility company. Now that a few people have made the grid interconnection, we are seeing more cooperation from the utilities. In fact, some of the most publicized grid interconnections have been those done by utilities.

Steve Strong, architect and designer, had done some excellent work on grid-interconnect homes. All have been costly, but they have paved the way for general acceptance of the concept. Steve's first grid-interconnect PV home (built in Massachusetts) cost about the same as non-PV homes in the same neighborhood. His work has been featured on the PBS series "The All New This Old House." Perhaps one of the most important impacts of his "Impact 2000" PV-powered home has been on Boston Edison, the utility that commissioned the job, for they are now able to see that PV can work in their locale. It is also providing valuable design guidelines for other architects willing to follow in Steve's steps.

Δ

(This article was reprinted with permission from Joel Davidson's book, "The New Solar Electric Home," which is available for $20.95 from aatec publications, P.O. Box 7119, Ann Arbor, MI 48107.)

A BHM Writer's Profile

Martin P. Waterman is a rural based writer whose work has appeared in numerous publications in Canada and the United States. He also writes a syndicated gardening column and is often a lecturer at horticultural symposiums.

Mr. Waterman is also involved in agricultural research and is a recognised fruit breeder striving to develop new hardier varieties for colder climates.

A BHM Writer's Profile

Vernon Hopkins gets a kiss from his great great granddaughter, Devyn, on his 80th birthday. Vernon is a retired trapper of 40 years, and he has witched wells for the past 30 years with a success rate of about 95%.

We profiled his extraordinary life in Issue No. 2 and he subsequently became a writer for the *Backwoods Home Magazine*. Vernon brings his extensive knowledge as a nuturalist and observer of the natural world to *BHM*.

Getting electricity from the sun

Opportunity is knocking for the country parson

By Steven Gregersen

Thousands of churches spread throughout small towns and sparsely populated counties are looking for someone to fill the pulpit on Sunday morning. The shortage in these areas is acute, not because there aren't enough preachers, but because there just aren't enough preachers who want to live and serve in smaller country churches. If you have the desire to preach God's word and serve others, to live in a relaxed atmosphere away from the hustle (and hassle) of the big city, to share in the joys and sorrows of caring people, then perhaps you should consider becoming a "country parson."

Opportunities are open for both men and women. Paid positions can be held as senior minister, youth minister, music minister, education minister, and sometimes other staff positions. Specialized knowledge or training is expected for each office according to the job title.

Be forewarned, if money is your primary reason for becoming a pastor in the church you'll be better off to find another occupation. On the other hand, serving as preacher doesn't require a vow of poverty either. What it does require is dedication. Dedication to God and his church.

Full or part time?

The duties expected from the preacher are often as varied as the educational requirements. Pastoring a country church may require as little as ten to twenty hours per week (preparing a sermon and preaching on Sunday mornings plus, performing wedding and funeral services), or it could consume sixty or seventy hours of work each week in a thriving full time ministry. The duties expected of you often

vary according to how much the congregation can afford to pay.

For preaching on Sunday morning and a few other duties such as calling on those in the hospital, and officiating at weddings and funerals you could expect to make from $75.00 to $150.00 per week. To hold this type of position you might or might not live in the community you are preaching in. Of course you will need another source of income unless you have the ability to subsist on earnings below the poverty level. Most of those who serve at this rate are Bible college students, local church elders who live and work nearby, or retired preachers desiring to supplement their income doing what they truly enjoy.

A common arrangement in some denominations is to have the same minister serve at several different churches in the same area. (This isn't far removed from the "circuit riding" preacher of frontier times.) The churches, seldom more than three, are normally located within a thirty mile area. They have the sermon at different times to allow the preacher to preach at one, then drive to the next one, preach and travel to the next church and preach again. This allows the preacher to devote his time and energy to ministry without the distractions and conflicts brought by secular employment. When the husband and wife are both ordained ministers they often work together in this type of arrangement. Each one will be assigned

their own churches to serve thereby covering a fair size piece of real estate.

In some cases a preacher will have one "major" church where he spends most of his time but will also offer interim or supply preaching to another congregation within reasonable driving distance. In this case the primary church is where he will devote most of his time and talent.

Many rural churches are large enough to employ a full time minister. Generally the pay scale will be comparable to what a public schoolteacher would make in the community where the church is located. Quite often housing is provided.

The minister and the IRS

The minister is in a different category with the IRS than most other people. Even though he is "hired" by the church and paid wages and benefits, he is seen as self-employed by the IRS. This has its good and bad points. The minister is entitled to many different tax breaks because of this tax status. Many benefits are not seen as income for tax purposes and many of the job connected tasks of the minister are tax deductible.

One problem occurs in the area of social security. Due to the self-employed status of the minister, he is liable for the full percentage of social security instead of half as regular employees are.

It isn't possible to cover tax benefits and liabilities in this article but the advantages are considerable. They often make up for the comparatively lower income many ministers make. The best option is to talk to an accountant **who is familiar with IRS rules for ministers.**

Job responsibilities

It's only fair to ask what preachers are expected to do, so, I'll tell you. Responsibilities include (but aren't limited to): preaching; counseling; calling (nursing homes, hospital, the home bound, and evangelistic); baptismal, wedding and funeral services; writing church newsletters, bulletins, and articles for the local newspaper religious page. The parson is also likely to be expected to attend meetings with elders, deacons, and other church committees. He will be expected to go to conferences, conventions, and workshops to keep current on new methods and ideas pertaining to his work and he must study for his own personal growth and education. Last but certainly not least, he's on call 24 hours daily, seven days a week. (Remember what I said about dedication?) Of course not every item on this list will be done every week but it does point out that the preacher must be versatile.

Educational requirements

The educational requirements are as varied as the churches you will serve. Some do not require any formal education at all. Others insist on eight years of formal education at a Bible college and seminary. Usually the smaller (and the non-denominational) churches have lower formal educational requirements but, don't make the mistake of thinking they have lower standards. A great deal of knowledge is still required to fill the role of pastor. These churches are just not as stringent about **formal** education credentials. In some cases the denomination headquarters sets the standards for ministers. The best place to get information concerning requirements in your denomination is to speak to your current pastor. Most are quite willing to help and will know what is required.

Education is available at Bible colleges and seminaries throughout the United States. Many offer two year associate degree programs in addition to their four and five year (and more) programs. There are also correspondence courses available for those who cannot attend a regular college or seminary. While college diplomas do open doors of opportunity, they aren't essential. Many fine preachers and

Daily life of the country parson

By Steven Gregersen

For the last two years I've been serving the Southside Christian Church, in Clay Center, KS. This is called a weekend ministry because I'm only here on the weekends to preach the Sunday sermon and, on occasion, teach the adult Sunday school class.

I'm currently a student at Manhattan Christian College, Manhattan, KS. I am not ordained yet but I am licensed by the state of Kansas to perform weddings. No license is necessary to conduct funerals in Kansas. I spend approximately fifteen hours per week in sermon preparation and another four hours traveling to and from church and attending services.

I became aware of the need for preachers in rural churches when, as chairman of the board of my home church, I was involved in the search for a minister when our minister resigned to move to a larger church.

My goal after graduation is to continue in a country or small town church. (Clay Center, where I currently preach, has a population of 5,000.) I enjoy the people and atmosphere of small town life and have absolutely no desire to live in a metropolitan area.

Other examples of small town ministries I'm familiar with include a preacher who was educated through correspondence school and now preaches full time in a town of 1200. A Bible college professor who preaches in a town of 45 (more people than that attend church there). Another close friend preaches full time in a small "bedroom" community of 700 located approximately 30 miles from Witchita, KS. He has small town life along with the services found in one of Kansas' larger cities.

I'm aware of one woman who preaches full time in a small mountain community in northern Montana and I have another close friend who serves in a suburb of Seattle, Washington. If you feel called to preach and desire to live where small town values and lifestyle abound...the opportunity is there. Δ

ministers had no formal college education—just years of experience. (And to be honest, many church elders aren't overly impressed by college educated preachers.)

Finding a church to serve

There are different methods for locating a church where a minister is needed. Probably the best method is to call or write to Bible colleges in the geographical area where you would like to live. Churches also advertise in publications aimed toward their denomination. The Christian Standard, 8121 Hamilton Ave., Cincinnati, Ohio 45231, is popular with independent Christian churches and usually has listings of churches that need a minister. Again, your pastor

might be the best source to ask for advice in this area.

Is this for me?

Being a "country parson" isn't for everyone but it might be for you. Just as in careers as a nurse, doctor, or counselor, it requires a love for people and desire to help. Opportunities abound in the rural areas throughout the United States at churches that are not attractive to preachers who want the prestige and/or benefits offered by large, urban churches. So, if you have the desire to preach God's word and serve his children in the slower paced places where neighbors still spend time on the front porch swing on balmy, summer evenings, maybe you have what it takes to be a "country parson." Δ

Clean up with house cleaning

By Steven Gregersen

How would you like to make more money per hour than your employer? It's not only possible, it's routine. At least it's routine if your work is house cleaning.

For the last five years my wife has been cleaning up (in more ways than one). She's been cleaning other people's houses and offices and making a pretty fair return on her labor.

Like most families today we found ourselves in a perpetual budget balancing act. When our children were small it was babysitting that brought in the extra bucks. But, babysitting has its bad points and after your own children become "potty wise" the thought of changing another dirty diaper becomes even less appealing. Sure she could have gotten a part time job somewhere but who wants to work for minimum wage? When a job cleaning the local doctor's office became available she called to check it out. That job led to another, and then another, until, she was turning down work.

Then, as now, she has found house cleaning to be a pretty solid way to set her own schedule, enjoy the benefits of a home business, and provide a steady source of income.

As the owner of her business, she controls the number of hours worked by the amount she takes on and controls her schedule by the type of work she accepts.

Housecleaning is an occupation that's likely to expand in the years to come. As more women enter the work force there will be a greater demand for someone to do the housework that neither spouse may then have time to do. Let's face it, after fighting rush hour traffic and listening to employers, customers, and children complain, who has the energy to do housework? Paying someone to clean the house is an investment necessary to ward off insanity. And many clients will pay more per hour than they make themselves.

If you can work without supervision and don't mind a job that's physically tiring but financially and spiritually rewarding (the people who hire you, unlike husbands and children, value the job you do and will show their appreciation) then you might want to consider cleaning up at house cleaning. After all, isn't it time you began getting paid for work you've probably been doing (until now) for free?

How much can you make?

There are two methods used to set the rates you charge. Both have good and bad aspects.

The first is to charge a straight hourly fee. This means you agree to work for a set number of hours at a per-hour rate.

This is more flexible for both you and your employer. It allows time for the unusual jobs that may be outside of your normal schedule. If your client wants you to leave the normal duties and spruce up a spare room for instance, it's no big deal. There's no temptation to rush through the house (and risk breaking things) when you work by the hour. One thing to watch

for, however, is the temptation to "drag your feet" instead of doing your very best.

Some people will not contract for your services unless it is by the hour. They've probably been "burnt" by previous house cleaners who charged a per-room fee and did sloppy work.

The second option is to price your work on a per-room basis. Fees are set for a bathroom, kitchen, bedroom, etc. and the amount of work done in each room is standardized. If for instance, in the bedroom, you agree to vacuum the floor, change the bedding, and dust, be sure your client understands that taking down the curtains for cleaning or window washing is not included in the base price. The expectations of both the client and you should be clearly understood or there will be trouble later.

This method of pricing is appropriate if you expect to hire others to work for you. It does provide incentive to work faster (and make more money) but, be careful, it's also easy to become careless and break things because of the emphasis on speed.

Ultimately the quality of your work will not vary with either pricing method. If you are a conscientious worker you will do a good job, if you're dishonest or sloppy your work will reflect it.

Set your prices to be competitive with local market conditions. Get some estimates for your own house from your competition and set your own rates near theirs. In the city we now live in hourly rates are in the $7.00 per hour range.

The type of work you do is up to you. You may limit yourself to house cleaning only or you may include laundry or other work as you desire. The business is yours to do with as you please. It is best to let prospective clients know of limits you've set before you make a commitment.

Hours/finding work

You can set your hours by the type of work you accept. If you decide to work in the evenings your best prospects will be businesses that are closed in the evening or night. My wife's first client was our local doctor. She cleaned his office and examining rooms two evenings per week. If you clean homes instead of businesses you will probably work during the day while the residents are at their job.

One of the main advantages of the house cleaning business is the flexibility you will have in setting your own hours.

If you are new to an area take out a classified advertisement in the local paper. My wife began like this in our present location. She made contact with two customers by this method.

She also answered two advertisements from people who needed a house cleaner. One of these people told her friends and three more clients were obtained this way. (This takes the turn of a soap opera now when two of her clients were married. She now remains working for them and the others.) She has limited herself to these five, working thirty-five hours per week total. This allows her to work extra hours occasionally if someone has something special scheduled and needs extra house cleaning done in preparation for the event.

Expenses/Uncle Sam

Like any business you must allow for expenses when you set your prices.

Equipement can be elaborate or you may want to use your household appliances. In many cases you can use the equipment and supplies owned by the homeowner you're working for. If you expand and hire employees you'll eventually need industrial grade apparatus. In the beginning it's better to rent what you don't have for those heavy duty jobs. Don't forget to include such expenses in your pricing structure.

Advertising is a business expense you may need to allow for. Usually once is enough unless you expand your business and begin hiring employees.

If you live in an area where litigation is a popular form of problem solving, you should consider buying liability insurance. My wife is rather selective in who she cleans for and we've decided not to buy insurance. You must make your own decision about this matter.

If you plan on taking a vacation be sure to add this expense to your pricing structure. You'll need to make enough during the year to finance your time off and you will need to plan for someone to do your work while you're gone. Most private homes will just do without you but most businesses will expect someone to clean while you're on vacation.

As a self-employed person you will be responsible for the full percentage of social security taxes and the normal overload of state and federal income taxes. Depending on your income you may need to pay an estimated quarterly tax payment to the IRS. The best advice I can give you is to find an accountant and follow directions.

There have been two articles in *Backwoods Home Magazine* that should be read. See "Taxes—a good reason for you to start your own small business" in Issue Number 7, and "A crash course in small business record keeping" in Issue Number 8.

House cleaning is an occupation that will allow you to set your own hours and pay. It can be tailored to meet the special needs of the single mother who needs a flexible schedule, the student who wants part-time work, the person who wants a business they can start with a small cash outlay and expand as needed, or anyone else who desires flexibility and independence in their occupation. ∆

Fathers

My sister said,

> *He lay in bed,*
> *His children around him,*

> *Except for his son,*

> *And to find solace*
> *In his dying,*
> *He called back through time,*
> *And spoke to his father.*

I wonder,

> *When I am dying,*
> *If he will be there for me.*

John Earl Silveira
Ojai, CA

Playing with a country cat

How to homebrew beer

By Chuck Hill

With the improvement of mail order technology (UPS deliveries and so on) it has become easier and easier to find do-it-yourself products available to those of us who live off the beaten track. Products for making quality homemade beer — and instructions and advice — are now as near as your telephone. Whether you enjoy European-style beers, English ales, or dark Irish stouts there are kits and special ingredients available to get you from package to mug in just a short time.

Equipment and supplies

Before we get into the method of home brewing, let's take a look at the equipment and supplies you'll need to get started:

To assemble and boil the ingredients for the beer (collectively referred to as "wort") you'll need a canning kettle of at least 20 quart capacity. This can be an inexpensive enamel model or a fancy heavy-duty stainless steel restaurant stock pot. Both are widely available.

To ferment the beer after boiling, you'll need a food-grade plastic bucket (primary fermenter) of 6+ gallon capacity. Larger batches require a larger bucket and boiling kettle but most recipes tend to make a 5 gallon batch and the equipment and ingredients are designed with this in mind.

Other equipment you'll need includes a stainless steel or plastic stirring spoon (these can be sterilized, whereas wooden ones cannot), a siphon tube and hose, hydrometer (for testing specific gravity), thermometer, airlock, bottle capper and caps, and beer bottles.

Ingredients for making beer include malt extract, corn sugar, yeast and extra additives if desired.

Most of the above equipment and supplies are included in kits sold pre-packaged or sold individually through mail-order companies specializing in home brewings.

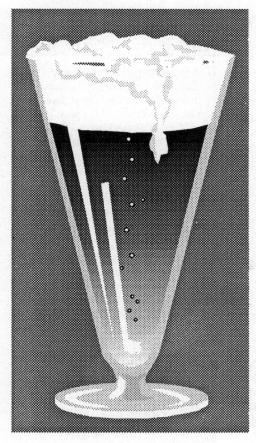

The method

Simply put, home brewing is converting malt sugar dissolved in water to alcohol by way of a yeast fermentation. The carbonation in home brew comes from a small secondary fermentation thak takes place in each bottle after bottling (a little extra sugar is added to accomplish this). The more sugar and/or malt in the starting wort, the higher the alcohol in the finished beer will be, 5% to 6% is a good mark to shoot for.

Step by step, the beer making process goes like this:

- 1. Your primary fermenter (plastic bucket) and stirring spoon should be steriled with a solution of sodium bisulfite or chlorine bleach, and then rinsed with water.

- 2. Add hopped malt extract and 2 lbs. of corn sugar to 2 1/2 gallons of water in your kettle and bring to a boil. Boil for 15 minutes to an hour. This boiling sterilizes the wort and thoroughly combines the ingredients. Also during the boil, more advanced brewers add flavoring ingredients like additional hops and grains. Check specific recipes for more information.

- 3. You must cool the wort before adding the yeast or the hot wort will kill it. Mix your 2 gallons of concentrated wort with cool water to make 5 1/2 gallons in the plastic fermenter and allow to cool until it reaches 68 to 72 degrees F. Sterilize your hydrometer and jar and test the specific gravity of the COOLED wort. (Hot wort will crack your hydrometer or at least give you a totally inaccurate reading.) The reading should be between 1.030 and 1.040.

- 4. Remove a half cup of wort and stir in your beer yeast. When it foams up in about half an hour, add it to the bucket and stir in.

● 5. Cover the bucket and fit the airlock in its hole. The airlock should be filled halfway with water. In about 24 hours you'll notice bubbles perking through the airlock. This is the action of the yeast converting sugar and water to alcohol with a by-product of carbon dioxide gas.

● 6. After 7 to 10 days of fermenting at room temperature (68 to 72 degrees F.), check the fermenting wort (now beer) with your sterilized hydrometer again. The reading should be about 1.000 to 1.005. If it is much higher than 1.005, you should wait another few days for the beer to complete its fermentation.

● 7. To bottle the beer, you must first sterilize and rinse your beer bottles and caps. Then siphon beer out of the fermenter into a vessel where you can mix the priming sugar (to create the bubbles) with the beer. Old time home brewers added a teaspoon of corn sugar to each bottle, but newer beer kits have streamlined the bottling process by providing a bottling tank to mix the sugar with the beer all at once. Fill the bottles with the sugar added before or added to each bottle then cap. If you added a teaspoonful to each bottle before filling, then invert a couple of times to mix.

● 8. Store the bottles in a moderately warm place (65 to 75 degrees F.) for two weeks so the secondary fermentation can add a sparkle to your beer. An additional four to twelve weeks of bottle age are needed for the beer to mature and lose the cidery, "green beer" flavor. Chill, serve and enjoy.

The don'ts

The above instructions are usually enough to get most anyone through their first brew without difficulty. However, you will encounter problems if you:

● 1. Don't sterilize equipment — beer is a living thing and there are bacteria and other spoilage organisms that can get into it and make it taste awful if you don't sterilize them away beforehand.

● 2. Don't try to make too strong a beer — high alcohol content will kill the yeast before it converts all the malt sugar. You'll end up with a sweet, low alcohol beer.

● 3. Don't have a warm place for the beer to ferment — the beer yeast needs at least 65 degrees to work quickly and efficiently. Low temperature (lager) fermentations are usually just the last part of the fermentation after the major work is done. Consult specific recipes and advanced brewing books for more info. In the meantime, keep your brewing area at least in the 68 to 72 degrees F. range.

Better beers, different beers

The brewing process outlined above is called "extract brewing" because you are using malt extracts that have had their sugars converted for you. "Mashing" (often referred to as "all grain brewing") requires that you convert the sugar from malted barley to maltose (fermentable sugar) yourself. Mashing is a subject best covered by curling up with a copy of *The Complete Joy of Home Brewing,* by Charlie Papazian. New equipment has made it easier to do at home, but it is definitely more time consuming.

With the broad range of malt extract powders and syrups available as well as adjunct grains and a wide variety of hops, you can easily create dozens of different beer styles without having to mash a single grain. Several popular beer styles are defined below and two complete recipes are included at the end.

American beer

If you're trying to brew Lite beer at home, you might as well go into town and buy ten cases to last a while. It will be cheaper, better, and easier. Homemade beer offers several advantages but making sodapop beer isn't one of them. If you MUST try to make your own version of Bud Light then use just a little real malt, rice syrup and corn sugar for the fermentables and just a touch of Saaz or Tettnang hops. After bottling, age at a cool temperature for 3 months. (Read the ingredients on a can of Bud sometime.)

Pilsner

This is the beer that American beers were patterned after until Prohibition forced a change in the drinking habits of American men and women. Use all light malt (no corn sugar, except for priming), a little crystal malt grain and lots of Saaz, Tettnang or Hallertauer hops added both at the beginning and the end of the boiling time.

English Ale

Several styles of English ale are popular. Try adding some crystal malt and Fuggle hops to the boil of a regular extract beer. Gypsum water hardener also helps the character of these beers. Many special malts and recpies are available in this area.

Scottish Ale

Amber malt, more hops and addition of crystal malt, malted barley and other grains give this style of beer more complexity and heavier body than regular English ale. Once again, you can find lots of recipes that will fine tune the specifics.

Stout and Porter

Stout is the rich, extra dark brew of Guinness and other breweries. Porter is a sweeter version that is not quite as dark. The dark and bitter character is achieved through the use of dark malt and lots of hops with chocolate malt grains and black patent malt grains added to the boil. It is very easy to make this style **too** dark and bitter, so be careful. I have found that a too-bitter batch responds well to extra aging time to mellow out (up to one year).

Sample recipes

Light American #1

A light American pilsner style that will please drinkers of lighter American beers yet with a hoppier character and more body. Recipe for 5 gallons

> *1 - 4lb. can Alexander's Malt Extract*
> *1 lb. Dry Rice Extract or 20 oz. Rice Syrup*
> *1 cup honey (optional)*
> *1 oz. Hallertauer Pellet Hops (bittering)*
> *1 oz. Hallertauer Leaf Hops (finishing)*
> *1 Pkg. Lager Yeast*
> *3/4 cup Corn Sugar for priming (bottling)*

Original Gravity—1.030 to 1.035
Terminal Gravity—1.004 to 1.010

Special Instructions: Add Rice Extract to 2 gallons of boiling water. Add honey if desired for more alcohol, malt and bittering hops and proceed as step 2 above omitting the 2 lbs. brewing sugar. Strain out leaf hops through cheesecloth afterwards or use hop bag.

Octoberfest

This style of amber German beer is the best known of the "Fest" beers. Smooth and malty, a great treat anytime. Recipe for 5 gallons

> *1 can Coopers Lager (yeast included)*
> *1 can Alexander's Amber Kicker*
> *3 lbs. Amber Dry Malt*
> *1/2 lb. Light German Crystal Malt—cracked*
> *1/4 lb. Chocolate Malt—cracked*
> *2 oz. Tettnang Pellet Hops (bittering)*
> *1 oz. Tettnang Leaf Hops (finishing)*
> *3/4 cup Corn Sugar for priming (bottling)*

Original Gravity—1.038 to 1.044
Terminal Gravity—1.014 to 1.018

Special Instructions: Add Crystal and Chocolate grains to 1/2 gallon water and bring to a boil. Remove from heat and let steep for 20 minutes. Strain out grains and add more water to make 2 to 2 1/2 gallons. Bring to a boil and add liquid and dry malts plus bittering hops. Proceed from step 2 above except do not add 2 lbs. brewing sugar.

For more information

The best source for information about a particular brewing problem is the shop where you get your supplies. If you're looking for inspiration, ongoing knowledge or a source of recipes, try *The Complete Joy of Home Brewing* by Charlie Papazian, or *The Big Book of Brewing* by Dave Line. Both are widely available from supply outlets.

Where to shop

There are many home brew suppliers who come and go, but the best of them have been in business for a long time and continue to provide good service, fair prices, helpful advice, and a full range of products. Check the Yellow Pages in your local directory for brew suppliers in your community and talk to the fellow brewers you chance to meet.

(Chuck Hill is the author of numerous articles about wine and beer, and is the author of The Northwest Winery Guide and Food and Wine Northwest Style. He lives in Seattle, Washington.) Δ

> *The distance from*
> *The top of my mattress*
> *To the ceiling:*
> *About the same as*
> *The distance from*
> *The bottom of a grave*
> *To ground level.*
> *God, I hate*
> *Lying awake at night.*
>
> John Earl Silveira
> Ojai, CA

Walking in the creek

... Final part in our 3-part chicken series
Butchering, cleaning, and cooking chickens

By Carla Emery

Chicken to eat comes from two basic sources: the broilers or cockerels you raise to butchering age and then put in the freezer, and the hens whose egg production is declining or stopped, that you cull out of your flock. The cockerels are your young, tender birds. At 8 to 12 weeks of age, they'll weigh from 1-1/2 to 3 pounds, depending on the breed. They can be cooked as a broiler, or a fryer. The 12 to 14 week- old bird will be around 4 pounds in weight and an ideal fryer from 14 weeks to 6 months of age, and from 4 pounds and up, the bird will make a fine roaster. A bird 6 to 9 months old is a judgment call. Older than that they are stew birds for sure. Culled laying hens have lived long enough to get tough, and so they are your classic "stew hens." A young chicken has soft cartilage at the end of the breastbone and pin-feathers. An older, stewing-type chicken has a rigid breastbone and long hairs on its skin.

Once you know what you're doing and have your system worked out, two people can kill, pick, and cut up about a half dozen chickens an hour-- or even more.

Dark meat, light meat: The color of muscle meat is a result of the exercise that muscle has experienced. Homegrown chickens tend to have relatively darker meat because they lead more active lives. A bird that flies will even have dark breast meat.

To catch a chicken: Enter the chicken's sleeping quarters well after dark, equipped with twine or a burlap bag. Carry a flashlight. Quietly grasp the bird you want by its two skinny legs (make sure the two legs are from the same chicken), and tie twine firmly around them. Or put the chicken in the bag and tie the bag with twine. Or haul it out with a firm grip around those two ankles and leave it for the night in an empty rabbit hutch, where you'll be able to easily reach in and grab it in the morning. Actually, holding a

bird by its legs can be a bit of a struggle because they're not crazy about being upside down and will flap their wings and try to get righted. Avoid that wing flapping. Better yet carry it the polite and friendly way, which is to hold the wings down and carry it under your arm with one hand on a leg or two, just in case.

To catch a chicken in the daytime, if you can't corner it, make a chicken hook out of a length of wire. Unwinding a clothes hanger gives you a good length. Or use a 4-foot piece of heavy wire. Make it single rod except for a miniature shepherd's crook at the chicken-catching end-- narrower than a chicken's foot, wider than its skinny lower leg, which is the part you hook it by. Or loop around the other end to make a better handle. Then you set out to pursue your quarry with the wire in hand. Pour a heap of grain on the ground. The chickens will all gather, heads down, backsides to the outside of their little crowd. When you get within reach with the wire of the one you want, suddenly stretch it out and hook the chicken's leg in the crook. Pull the chicken toward you and transfer the leg from the crook to your hand and get the other leg too. That works, but it's so much easier to catch a chicken while it is sleeping that I always do that. And if you can isolate the chicken the night before you butcher it, by leaving it in the gunny sack or, better yet in a wire-bottomed rabbit cage or something similar, you won't have to contend with such a full crop when cleaning it.

To kill a chicken: (However you kill it, it's best to plan a container arrangement to catch the blood.) To chop its head off (see killing cone below for probably the best way), grasp it firmly by the ankles and both wing tips with the left hand (if you're right handed), and place its body on the chopping block so that the neck is stretched out across the block. A chopping block is a large flat-topped and flat- bottomed log, with the grain running perpendicular to the ground. A heavy-headed ax is preferable to a hatchet for the job. Wear old clothes, and have a container ready, bucket or some such, and don't let go of the chicken's legs and wingtips after the head is severed. Then get the chicken neck down into that bucket as soon as possible to save on the mess. If you just drop it and run--because the chicken's body will flop around and scatter blood over amazing areas.

Getting the chicken to lie still with its neck stretched out across the top of the block while you aim the blade may require a bit of maneuvering. The chicken may retract its head just when you're all set. Have a sharpened ax or hatchet ready in your right hand for that moment when the bird is in the right position and then, quick before it moves, with one hard blow, bring the blade down and sever head from neck. Hit the chicken's neck clear across so you don't have it just half cut off with the first blow. (I've had to try twice to finish the job more times than I'd care to admit.) Cut it off as near the head and as far from the body as you can in order to save the neck for cooking, and to avoid cutting the crop which is located at the base of the neck. I know that method so well because that's how I did it as a little girl and as a young woman, too.

Since I first wrote the above paragraph, I've gotten some interesting advice from readers on how to make that chicken hold still while you're trying to chop its head off. One writer told me that she "hypnotizes" the chicken by putting the chicken's head under its wing, then swinging it around, and only then chopping its head off. Betty Lawrence of White Shan, Washington, wrote me that she hammers two nails about one inch apart on the surface of her chopping block. She leaves part of the nails sticking up. She lays the chicken's neck between the nails and pulls back gently until the head is next to the nails. If you use this system, you'll have to be careful not to hit those nails (hitting nails is very bad for ax blades), as well as not to hit the crop.

Wring-the chicken's neck: Some people prefer this method. It may be done by grasping the chicken firmly by the upper part of the neck or head.

Then get the body swinging rapidly, as you would twirl a heavy object on the end of a string. You go Swing, once, Swing, twice, Swing, thrice, and then SNAP, like you're doing crack the whip with the chicken's body. Then the body separates from the head you're holding. It WILL.

Death by shooting: A BB-gun won't do it. .22 will.

By hanging: Mrs. George Huckabey, Athens, TN, doesn't like chickens flopping around on the ground. "Find a low hanging tree branch, loop a twine string around it firmly. Place loop around the legs of the chicken. It will be hanging head down. Now grasp the head firmly and with a sharp knife, cut the chicken's head off just at the top of the neck." This way the chicken doesn't go flopping around leaving a trail of blood on your property and you can control the bleeding mess by having a container ready to put the bird in and making sure it gets in there and stays in there.

By severance: This popular professional method is to pierce the brain with a knife run through the roof of the mouth, then sever the blood vessels which are in the neck back of the earlobe. With this method, the bird doesn't flop about either, but it takes some know-how and experience to get it right.

Killing cone: This is the latest and best method of all, I think. You can buy a commercially produced killing cone mail order from a poultry supplier or from a local farm supply store or make your own. To make a homemade killing cone, cut off the bottom of a one-gallon plastic bottle. Cut about two inches from the top and handle. Nail the bottle to a wall or tree--or hang it by a rope or hook upside down. To use the killing cone, grab your bird by the ankles and put it, head downward, into the killing cone. Make sure the head and neck extend through the smaller end that you cut. Now proceed either "by hanging" method or "by severance" method or by grasping the head with one hand and pulling just firmly enough to create a small amount of tension on the neck, then cut into the neck on the left underside, just back of head and beak--which will sever the jugular. When

you do it the latter way it leaves the head on, just cuts the throat. Have something ready to catch the blood and this is the most manageable and least messy way. Commercially manufactured killing cones are not expensive and come in three sizes: one for broilers, pheasants and fryers, one for roosters, ducks, and guineas, and the largest for turkeys. (Rocky Top General Store, P.O. Box 1006, Harriman, TN 37748.)

However you get the unfortunate task accomplished, be sure and let the bird bleed out thoroughly, since this will improve its eating and keeping quality. When I was a little girl, chopping chicken heads off for grandma, I used to say a prayer for the chicken before I raised my ax. I would pray that if God had a place in Heaven for the souls of chickens, He should please take this one. In the animal graveyard beside our garden, where beloved departed cats, dogs, and mice lay planted, brother Dick and I also buried not a few chicken heads with full honors. There was a certain fascination to staging a really good funeral.

By then the feast would be ready, and Mama would call us to dinner. Oh, Mother's fresh fried chicken! With mashed potatoes and lots of gravy made with milk! Dick and I would eat and eat, the pile of bird bones beside each plate steadily heaping upward. The wishbones were saved and dried on top of the topside cupboard of Mother's wood cook stove for a week or two, until they'd become properly brittle. Then Dick and I each took hold of a side, got our wish in mind (you couldn't say out loud what it was or the magic wouldn't work), and pulled at the count of three. The one who ended up with the longest piece of wishbone could get his wish--or so we claimed.

Picking and cleaning the chicken

To pick the bird: First decide if you want to dry pick it, or scold before plucking out the feathers. Dry picking is more difficult than picking after scalding, because the feathers are harder to pull out. I think it's crazy to dry pick when you could scald. So skip to the next paragraph. (But I am sort of compulsive, gathering and putting down knowledge, so here are the directions for dry picking anyway.) To dry pick, start immediately after killing--even before the bird stops bleeding--before the flesh has a chance to become cold, which would set the feathers in tightly. Pick up the breast and up the side. Then do the wings, back, and finally the pinfeathers which can be removed with a tweezers or with a knife blade (you catch the pinfeather between the blade and your thumb and pull).

To scald: Have a metal bucket, or a big pan of water like a canner or roaster, on to boil before you go out to kill the bird. While the chicken is flopping and bleeding, adjust its temperature to about 130-180 degrees. Better to start out with your water too hot than too cool. Too hot will loosen the feathers plus cook the skin a little. Too cool won't accomplish anything. And your water will be cooling all the time, especially as you do a series of birds in it. If it gets too cool, stop and re-supply with hot enough water. (Rebecca Coufel wrote me that she and her husband do 70 or 80 chickens at a time by pre-wetting the dead birds with a hose or bucket of cold water, before scalding. She believes the hot water gets under their feathers better for the presoaking.) Spread out newspapers to do the picking on. You can roll them up afterwards with the feathers inside to keep them from flying all over your yard.

Now, grasping your bird by the ankles (the unfeathered legs and feet don't need to be scalded), immerse it in the hot water. If you are using a flatter-styled pan, like a roasting kettle, you soak the breast of the bird in the hot water, then turn it over and hold the backside in. Try to manage in such a way that every feathered part of it has nearly equal time in the hot water. Make sure you get the legs that you're holding in far enough to scald the feathered "knees". Make sure the wing and tail feathers get a good scalding, because they are the toughest to pull out. Over scalding any part of the bird will cause the outer surface of the skin to rub off--which doesn't hurt the meat any. Less than 30 seconds should do it. Hotter water does the job quicker, with cooler water you'd have to keep the bird in there longer. And how long you need to scald also depends a good bit on the size of the bird. Little birds like pigeons and quail need less scalding time. Bigger birds need more. A big turkey requires the most of all.

Older birds will take a higher temperature and a longer time than younger birds. You can scald several birds, one after the other, in the same water, so long as it doesn't cool below about 130 degrees. If your water gets too cool, add hotter water to bring it up. If the first dip doesn't loosen the feathers enough, you can give the bird another pass in the water. You have to have the bird in there long enough and with enough motion to get the hot water penetrated clear to the skin. Then take the bird out, let it drain just long enough so you can get your hands on the biggest feathers and start yanking.

It helps to have one person scalding and another picking. Begin picking immediately after pulling the fully soaked bird out of the hot water, starting with the wing and tail feathers.

Then do the body feathers, and finally the pinfeathers. Purists insist that feathers must be pulled in the direction in which they are growing. That's certainly true of the biggest ones. I pull short ones any way I can get them.

Singeing: After the pinfeathers have been removed, you will still have down and very fine long hairs, especially on an older bird. These are burned off with the singeing. Do it someplace where you won't set anything else on

A Backwoods Home Anthology
The Sixteenth Year

fire. Hold your bird by the ankles over a flame. Constantly change the bird's position over the flame, holding the bird with one hand and the cone with the other, until all parts having these hairs have been exposed enough to singe them completely away. It won't take long to singe all the chicken. If you don't have a gas stove, you can use a candle, propane torch, small alcohol burner, or a rolled cone of newspaper, or other paper (not with color)--rolled tight at one end (to be the handle), and wide enough at the other to flame readily. A burning paper bag won't blacken the bird as much as a newspaper. Don't touch the paper to the bird in this process, since that would dirty it with ashes. With practice you can do several chickens with one paper cone. Have all the chickens you plan to singe right there at hand when you light the paper. That's the way my mother and I used to singe them. Newspaper cone is probably the worst way--probably gives them a lead content or some such and it certainly risks setting something else on fire.

Cleaning the chicken: Now your chicken is ready to be cleaned or "drawn." That means you'll remove the head, feet, and innards. First, put the bird into very cold water in order to quickly cool the entire body. Get ready a bowl of clean cold water to rinse pieces in (or rinse them under the faucet), a very sharp knife, and an empty container to hold the cut-up pieces. Have a wooden cutting board to cut up the chicken on. Don't cut the chicken on newspaper because the ink could get on the meat. Have something to hold the disposables, like a wastepaper lined box, or a bucket. You can dispose of innards by burning, composting, or feeding to the pigs. Your chickens would be delighted to recycle the chicken butchering scraps--if you have no fear of parasite or disease transmission.

Head, feet, and oil sac: You need a small, but very sharp knife to do the next steps. If the head is still attached, cut it off and discard. If the head was chopped off and the chicken flopped on the ground and got dirt on the stump, cut the dirty part off and discard. Carefully feel for the knee joint right at the top of where scaly leg

meets feathered knee. Bend the knee and cut across each joint until the foot is off. Some authors tell you to cut off the small oil sac at the end of the chicken's back on the "north end going south." That isn't necessary. It's presence doesn't affect the taste. It is necessary with certain other birds such as goose, and duck and game birds.

Outing the innards: Place the chicken on its back with its hind end closest to you. Carefully cut across the abdomen from thigh to thigh (or from below the breastbone to just above the anus--it doesn't matter which), making sure you do not cut into any of the intestines in the cavity. Reach inside carefully between the intestines and the breastbone until you reach heart level. Loosen the membranes between the innards and the body wall and gently pull out the entrails in one pass. The gizzard, heart and liver will come out with it. Be especially careful of the gallbladder, a greenish sac embedded in the undersurface of the right lobe of the liver. If it should break, the bile which it contains would make bitter and undesirable any part of the chicken that it touched. You'll probably have to remove the light pink lungs nestled between the ribs.

To finish extricating the innards: Cut carefully around the outside of the excretory vent, allowing plenty of room so as not to cut into it or the attached intestine, so that it can now be discarded along with the intestines. The kidneys in the back cavity adhere closely and should now be at least partly removed. Just scoop out what you can with your fingers of

the soft, brown kidney tissue. It's impossible to get all the kidney out. Don't worry about what's left. It will be cooked along with the rest of the bird. Now, finish up the front end of the chicken: cut the skin the length of the back or the bird's neck. The crop tears very easily. The crop is a thin-skinned round pouch off the birds esophagus that serves as a first stomach. You must gently pull it apart from the skin next to it. Then carefully pull crop, esophagus and windpipe out of the bird and discard them.

The giblets: "Giblets" means heart, liver and gizzard-- usually the neck, also. To get the liver, cut off the part of it that contains the gallbladder-- allow plenty of leeway (better safe than sorry), and discard the gallbladder along with its attached liver section. Rinse the remaining liver and put it into your giblets bowl. Cut the gizzard open along its narrow edge. Continue the cut to three-quarters of

A BHM Writer's Profile

Vern Modeland's writing career began as a media journalist and news service stringer in Iowa. He went on to writing and media relations in the aviation, health care and travel industries and for the U.S. Food and Drug Administration.

Vern grew up in a rural community near free running streams, woods, and wildlife that have made a lasting impression. For the past 25 years, his home has been in the Missouri Ozarks on acreage that overlooks Table Rock Lake. From there, he writes environmental and life-style articles and contemporary fiction. He is also a freelance editor.

the way around. Inside the gizzard there will be food and grit. Empty that out onto your newspaper. Carefully peel off and discard the yellowish inner lining of the gizzard. If you can get that lining separated from the gizzard proper at some point along your cut edge, the rest of the lining hopefully will strip out easily connected to it. If it tears and doesn't all come out the first time, you'll have to work it loose at some other point, then pull again. When the lining is all pulled off, discard it. Rinse and save the gizzard, cut the heart away from its attached arteries, rinse, and put in your giblet bowl. Cut the neck off at the base and add it to your loose pieces in the bowl.

Outing the innards: poultry shears method: An alternative system popular with owners who must butcher many small birds (like gamebirds), duck owners and efficiency lovers in general, is to cut off the oil-gland on the bird's tail. Then carefully cut around the vent until the anus and attached intestine is separated from the rest of the bird, and then use the poultry shears to cut all the way up the back on one side of the backbone. The bird is then opened out from that cut and the innards will basically just drop out. Sort out and deal with heart, liver, gizzard, and neck as above. (Poultry shears are wonderful. You can also use them to simply halve and quarter the bird and be done with the cutting up process, too!)

Dealing with the waste products: At this point you have feathers and innards. You can make use of the small feathers, or you can bury the whole works in your compost bin. Make sure no creature can dig it up again.

June Scherer, Eastman, Wisconsin, wrote me that she washes and scrubs the chicken's skin with dish soap at this point. She told me, "It's surprising how dirty they are, and the soap leaves no taste. Just rinse good".

Chicken Foot Soup: Scald feet with boiling water until the skin and claw cases will peel off, then place cleaned feet in cold, salted water and cook slowly with stew-type veggies and seasonings to taste.

Using Giblets: If your bird is a roaster, you can use the giblets (except for the liver) in the dressing or gravy.

(Cook and dice them, then mix in.) If your bird is to be a fryer, fry the giblets right along with the rest of the pieces. If it's a stew bird, use the giblets (except the liver) right with the rest. Another way to use giblets is to grind them up for taco and pizza meat. When chicken is canned, the hearts and gizzards are canned separately and the livers are not canned at all.

About bird livers and pate: The liver gets left out of most recipes because its flavor is just too distinctive to blend successfully. From extra livers you can make the gourmet delicacy called pate. The livers of about 5 or 6 average- sized chickens will give you 1/2 pound of chicken livers. If you just do a couple every Saturday for Sunday dinner, you could add the fresh livers to your supply in the freezer until you have enough to make pate. You can make pate out of any bird livers; recipes are by weight of liver and variety of bird doesn't matter. If you have a food processor or blender, that helps to get the pate perfectly smooth. After the pate is made it's stored in a small crock or bowl in the refrigerator. Old-timers kept the vulnerable pate from contact with air by smoothing the top and pouring clarified butter over it until completely covered. Nowadays you can do that or you can cover it with plastic wrap pressed close over the top of the mixture. Make pate in small amounts because it doesn't freeze successfully and needs to be eaten up within a few days to a week at most. Pate is good with mustard or tart jelly like red currant or crabapple, or with chutney. It's good served cold with sliced apples, crackers, toast fingers, melba toast or to make fancy sandwiches.

Plain pate: Cook 1/2 pound livers slowly in 2 tablespoons butter with 2 chopped onions until the onion is soft and the pink in the liver has disappeared. Remove the liver, mash with a fork, and force it through a sieve, or blend until smooth. To the sieved liver, add 1/4 cup sour cream. Salt and pepper to taste.

Gourmet seasoned pate: Saute 1 large onion, chopped, and 2 minced cloves of garlic in 1/3 cup butter until vegetables are limp. Add 1 pound chicken livers and saute until pink has

thoroughly disappeared. Add tarragon (1 tablespoon if fresh or 1 teaspoon if dried), 1 teaspoon salt, 1/2 teaspoon freshly cracked black pepper, 1 teaspoon dried thyme, 1/4 teaspoon cayenne pepper, 1/4 teaspoon cloves, and 1/4 teaspoon allspice. Process mixture until smooth. Add 3 tablespoons dry sherry, and blend again until smooth. Pour into bowl, cover, and refrigerate overnight before serving.

Using unfinished eggs: When butchering cull hens, eventually you're going to encounter one with clusters of eggs of all sizes, from almost like grains of sand to soybean size to almost regular egg size. They look like little egg yolks, and that's what they are, for the addition of an egg white and a shell are the last two steps on a hen's ovarian conveyer belt. The sight will give you awful pangs of guilt, as you will have obviously goofed in your culling and butchered a hard-working egg layer. But such mistakes do sometimes happen. So forgive yourself. At least you can avoid tasting the unborn eggs. Carefully remove them, rinse, and save. Use fairly soon. They are good food. You can cook them in the chicken broth for soup, scrambled them together with regular eggs, or stir into any rice-vegetable mixture that you want to turn into a fried rice.

About stuffing: The bird may be stuffed both through the opening you made to remove the crop and in the abdominal cavity. Stuff sufficiently to fill it, but loosely, since stuffing expands when cooking. When the body is full of stuffing, sew up the skin or close with a combination of skewers and thread. If the sides are very slack, skewers alone could do the job. The loose skin of the neck is drawn over the stuffing in that neck cavity and sewn or skewered. A bird for roasting may be frozen with the stuffing in it for up to 2 months. Make the stuffing ahead and pre-chill so it is thoroughly cold before stuffing and freezing the bird.

About trussing: A roasting bird is "trussed" by drawing the thighs and wings close against the body and fastening them securely with skewers or tying with string. Trussing keeps those appendages from drying up while the thicker parts of the bird are still baking.

To roast a bird: Roast 2 2-1/2 lb. chickens at 400 degrees for 1 to 1-1/2 hours and they will brown well. Roast 2-1/2 to 4 lbs. chickens at 400 degrees for 1-1/2 to 2-1/2 hours. (If cooked at a lower temperature they will require a longer time to cook and won't be as brown.) Roast 4-8 lb. chickens at 325 degrees for 3 to 5 hours. If your bird is stuffed with a dressing, allow 15-20 minutes additional cooking time.

To freeze a roaster: Trim away and discard excess fat. Cool bird in refrigerator or soak in ice water until it is well cooled. This may take 6-8 hours. Then drain thoroughly, like 20 minutes, since the dryer it is when it goes into the freezer, the better it will keep. Wrap the giblets in freezer paper, put the giblets into the bird's empty cavity, then slip the bird containing giblets into a plastic bag. Lower the bird in bag into a can of lukewarm water. Be careful not to let any water get inside the bag. The water will press the plastic against the bird and expel all air. Twist the part of the bag remaining out of the water tight. Then loop the tag end of plastic double and fasten with a wire twist or a strong rubber band.

Marketing your dressed poultry: There are exemptions for small producers in the Poultry Products Inspection Act. There are some state variations in regulations. For information, before dressing and selling poultry directly off your farm, check with your state department of agriculture.

Halved and quartered birds

To prepare a halved bird (broiler): Traditionally, you start with a bird in the 1 to 1-1/2 pound range. Split the bird into two halves, down one side of the backbone and along the breastbone. If you want, you can also cut along the other side of the backbone and remove it completely. **To freeze the broiler,** place two pieces of freezer paper between the halves to make it easy to separate them, then wrap well in a plastic bag or freezer paper, label with date of freezing and "broiler."

Quartered bird: You just cut each half in half again so that you end up with two breast-wing pieces and two thigh- drumstick pieces.

Old time frying pieces

To separate legs and wings: For fryers, I would cut off both legs and wings before opening the abdomen to remove the entrails. But a person can cut them off afterwards, too. You may leave the drumstick connected to the thigh and serve the resulting larger pieces as one, or you can feel for the joint by wiggling it with one hand and feeling with the other until you locate it and then cut them apart. To get the thigh off of the body, you have the chicken lying on its back, pull the thigh away from the body, cut through the skin that is thus exposed, between the thigh and the abdomen. Now bend the thigh sharply away from the body cavity until the ball of the thighbone pops from the hip socket. Cut between ball and socket and finish separating the thigh from the body. Do the other leg the same way.

Wing joint cut: For a big piece, press the top bone of one wing against the body. Feel for the shoulder ball-and-socket joint. Cut through the joint, pull wing outward from body, and cut it from body. By this technique a portion of breast meat will come away with the wing. (It makes the wing piece more significant than it is otherwise.) If you prefer just wing and no breast meat with it: pull one wing upward to expose the joint connecting the outer wing to the body and cut through that joint. Do the other wing the same way.

Cutting up the body: Insert knife blade into the cavity of the bird. Cut parallel to the backbone, slicing through the ribs at approximately the halfway point. Do the same thing on

A BHM Writer's Profile

Russ Davis has spent more than 50 years camping, hiking, canoeing and hunting. A family therapist and clinical hypnotherapist, he is also an Iowa Law Enforcement Academy ceritified instructor and is active in teaching and training police officers. His widely varied teaching ranges from Boy Scout Camp wilderness cookery to graduate level courses for counselors.

He has authored a number of books, including two outdoor cook books and several technical books for law enforcement. He also writes for police, gun, and outdoors magazines.

the other side. Pull apart the breast and back. You'll see the meat-covered shoulder blades that unite them. Slice down through these bones to separate the breast section completely from the back. Cut across the backbone where the chicken's rib cage ends to divide the back into two equal pieces. To finish, place the breast skin side up and cut down the length of the breastbone to divide it into two equal pieces. If this were a very large bird, like a turkey or goose, you could make extra cuts to get more breast pieces.

To freeze cut-up chicken: Chicken in pieces is more compact than a roaster, and so takes up less freezer space. The freezer life of a chicken is about 6 or 7 months. If you freeze cooked chicken, it will stay prime only 2 or 3 months.

To can chicken (and other poultry, small game or rabbits): Use cut-up pieces. Remove as much bone as possible so it will pack more compactly. You can include the neck, but do something else with the gizzard, heart, and liver. Instead of canning the wings, which are bone and don't have much meat, use them for old-hen recipes, soups, or dog biscuits. Boil chicken pieces one hour to pre-cook. Pack jars loosely. Leave 1-inch headspace. Put on lid and process in pressure canner at 10 pounds, 75 minutes for pints, 90 minutes for quarts. To **can giblets**, pack hearts and gizzards in pint jars. Add broth to cover giblets, leaving one-inch headspace. Process in a pressure canner at 10 pounds 75 minutes (for pints).

Good recipes for old hens

You can use these recipes for other small, tough old creatures (like rabbit) simply by substituting "creature" for "chicken."

Chicken and noodles: This recipe is delicious and warms up well. Put your stewing hen in a deep pan. Add all giblets except liver. Cover with water and add 1/2 teaspoon salt for each pound of chicken. Add 1 carrot, 1 small onion, 1 clove, and 3 peppercorns. Bring to a boil, reduce heat, and simmer until the meat will easily come off the bones and is very tender. That will require at least several hours or

more, depending on how tough your old bird is. Cool it down enough to work with. Take the chicken off the bones and discard bones, skin, and cartilage. Return the meat to the broth. Mash the vegetables in the broth. When you're almost ready to serve this, heat it to boiling. Pour in noodles and cook, frequently stirring to make sure nothing is sticking, until the noodles are done. Serve. I always make this with homemade egg noodles.

Chicken stew: Prepare the chicken as for Chicken and Noodles but, instead of adding noodles, add potatoes, more carrots and onions, and peas (or any other vegetables you have and enjoy in stew). Cook until tender.

Chicken potpie: Make Chicken Stew or use leftover chicken stew to make this. Brown 7 tablespoons flour in a frying pan with 4 tablespoons butter. Gradually add enough chicken broth to make a good gravy (about 2-1/2 cups). Butter a baking dish. Put the vegetables and meat from your chicken stew in the dish. (Hold back any excess broth to use in another recipe.) Pour the gravy over it. Make a dumpling dough by your favorite recipe. Drop the dumpling dough by marbles or teaspoonsful (depending on how you like to make it) on top of the meat and gravy. Bake at 350 degrees until the dumplings are done.

Chicken and dressing: Cook the chicken and giblets (except liver) until you can easily separate the seat from the bones. Let cool, remove bones and

cartilage, and then grind the chicken skin and giblets. The chicken meat is nicest sliced thin. Make a bread dressing base from bread (homemade) plus egg, seasonings, and chicken broth and milk. In an oven pan put a layer of dressing, then a layer of chicken, a layer of dressing again, and so on. Bake, covered for 40 minutes at 350 degrees.

Ivy's chicken loaf: Ivy Isaacson is a beautiful person, a real old-timer. Her husband, Dick, has experience driving oxen and knows how to make an ox yoke, starting with the right size tree. Here is Ivy's recipe: First, boil your old hen by the chicken noodle recipe (minus the salt), until it is so tender you can pick out the bones and discard them. Keep the chicken meat and broth. Mix 1 small loaf bread torn into pieces with 4 cups corn bread and add enough of the chicken broth to moisten the breads thoroughly. Now add 1/2 to 1 cup chopped celery, 1/2 to 1 cup chopped onion, salt, pepper, and sage to taste. Place mixture in a buttered 12 x 15-inch pan. Cover with the chicken meat. Mix 1/4 cup melted butter with 3/4 cup flour. Add 2 cups milk. Cook same as any white sauce until thickened. Cool, add 6 eggs, beaten. Pour over chicken. Sprinkle with buttered bread crumbs. Bake at 350 degrees for 1 hour. This will give you 15 to 20 servings. Good to take to a potluck!

Gertrude Johnson's chicken spread Cut stewing chicken of 2 or more pounds into pieces, place in casserole

A BHM Writer's Profile

Dynah Geissal lives and farms in Western Montana. When not down on the farm tending the livestock she can be found trekking the mountains, canoeing the rivers, skiing the backcountry, or running the roads of Montana. She lives with her husband Bob Koss and has three grown children: John, Greg, and Gypsy.

that has a tight-fitting lid. Dot with 4 tablespoons butter. Add 1 onion, peeled and quartered, 2 carrots, halved, 2 ribs celery, halved, 2 pepper-corns, and lay 3 lemon slices on top. Cover casserole tightly and bake for 3 hours at 325 degrees or until chicken is very tender. You might want to just serve the chicken for supper right at this point in the recipe! Otherwise, remove chicken and cool. Discard the vegetables, spices, bones, and skin. Run meat through a meat grinder 2 or 3 times, or whirl it in a food processor until smooth. Put chicken in a mixing bowl and blend in 4 to 8 tablespoons of softened butter. Stir in l/2 teaspoon Worcestershire sauce, salt and pepper to taste. Press your chicken spread into small jars. Pour a 1/4 inch layer of clarified butter over the spread in each jar. Cover tightly and refrigerate until ready to make sandwiches.

<u>Dog biscuits:</u> You can use any of the excess broth from any other old hen recipe to make this, or you could cook the chicken specially to get broth, use the meat in another recipe, and use the broth for dog biscuits. (Actually you can make this recipe with other types of meat broth, too.) This recipe will yield 60 medium-sized dog biscuits which your pet will consider a great treat. Mix together 3-1/2 cups un-bleached flour, 2 cups whole wheat flour, 1 cup rye flour, 2 cups cracked wheat, 1 cup cornmeal, and 1/2 cup skim milk powder. On the side, dis-solve 1 tablespoon (or 1 pkg.) yeast in 3-1/2 cups lukewarm chicken broth. The richer this broth is, the better your dog will like the biscuits. Let yeast-broth mixture set 10 minutes. Then stir in flour mixture. Roll resulting dough out 1/4 inch thick. Cut dog biscuit shapes from dough. Brush biscuits with egg wash. Bake on greased cookie sheets at 300 degrees for 45 minutes. Then turn oven off and leave biscuits in there overnight to finish hardening.

(This is the third and final article in a series of articles on chickens by Carla Emery. The series is excerpted from her book, "The Old Fashioned Recipe Book," available from her for $28.50 (Canadian residents add $3.50 for postage and handling) from P.O. Box 209, Kendrick, ID 83537.) Δ

**The winter road to the
Backwoods Home Magazine office**

A BHM Writer's Profile

Carla Emery is the author of <u>The Old Fashioned Recipe Book: An Encyclopedia of Country Living</u>, an 800,000-word basic reference in the field of self-sufficiency. Her book is a practical manual on how to grow, harvest, preserve, and prepare every kind of food — plant or animal — and a few more topics. It's also a chatty letter and pooling of information with a few hundred thousand of her closest friends.

Originally self-published, mimeographed, and sent out punched for three-ring binders in "installments," <u>The Old Fashioned Recipe Book</u> made the <u>Guiness Book of World Records</u> as the largest mimeographed book ever, and the most copies sold of any self-published, self-marketed book.

Carla is a mother of seven, goes way back when with the back-to-the-land movement, and is currently working on the next 500,000 words to be added to her classic.

Creating with Saltdough

By Jan Cook

Saltdough modelling became popular in Germany in the early 1900s when the Christmas tree became the focal point of holiday decoration. Peasants used to make their decorations from bread dough. Then, to protect them from being eaten by mice and vermin, they began loading them with salt. This was the beginning of salt dough.

This is something you can do with or without your kids on a rainy day with items you probably already have in your kitchen.

There are no specialty tools involved. All you'll need are things you can probably find in your kitchen junk drawer (comb, toothpicks, small scissors, etc. for texturing). Don't work in a room that's too warm (no more than 75 degrees) otherwise the dough becomes too soft to work with.

The mixture

> 2 c. white flour (don't use self-rising)
> 1 c. salt (use regular table salt)
> 1/2 c. water (approximate)

Kneading

Mix ingredients together either by hand or with a mixer (one with a dough hook is ideal). Then knead until smooth. **Not** kneading the dough thoroughly will cause it to be crumbly and it may crack easily.

Storing

Keep the dough covered, preferably in an airtight container, when not working with it. Don't refrigerate, but keep it covered in a cool place and it will stay fresh for a few days and can even be combined with a fresh batch. However, it's best to work with smaller amounts.

Modeling

The absolute easiest project for a beginner to start out with is the cookie-cutter-cutouts. Roll dough to 1/4 inch thick on a bread board or other flat surface. Use cookie cutters of varying shapes to cut out your dough or trace a pattern of your own with a paring or exacto knife. Smooth edges with a little water and your finger or a modeling tool

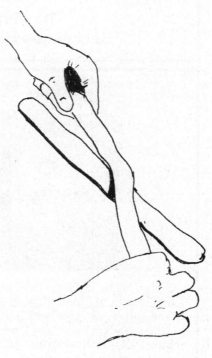

Another easy and pretty project is a twisted wreath. Separate the dough into two equal pieces and roll them evenly into ropes between 12 and 16 inches long. On a cutting board, carefully twist them together, slice the ends straight and press them together, forming a circle. The wreath can then be trimmed with dried flowers, or dough flowers and leaves (using the same technique as for frosting flowers if you're a cake decorator).

Drying

For this project we'll stick to air drying (but I'll tell you about oven drying just in case you're adventuresome and impatient) because there is less chance of cracking. A place in the sun is the best place to air dry your models. This saves gas and energy especially for thick models but depending on the thickness, could take several days or weeks. **Remember, drying too quickly will cause cracks**, so if you choose to use your gas oven to speed the process, keep the door half way open at the very lowest temperature setting for the first hour. Have it open only 1/4 of the way or less for the next hour (I prop it open with a metal measuring cup). The door may be closed for the third and subsequent hours. Natural gas has a high degree of moisture, which allows the top to dry slowly while the moisture in the center evaporates more quickly causing less problems for a beginner. Models dried in an electric oven will take twice as long. For example: It will take about 1 hour per 1/4 inch of thickness in an electric oven and approximately 1/2 hour for the same thickness in a gas oven.

Browning

If you like the brown, baked bread look, **dried** models can be baked to browness. Heat oven to 400, bake until the desired color is obtained. But watch carefully, models crack more easily at this stage. If your work shows signs of cracking, turn oven off, open the door and rest your model on the door (Cooling too quickly causes problems too.)

Repairing

Grind dried saltdough crumbs to a powder, add enough water to moisten and use like glue to cement broken pieces together.

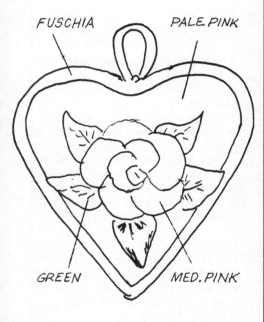

FUSCHIA PALE PINK

GREEN MED. PINK

Coloring

You can use food coloring, one drop at a time to color dough before it's dried, then knead until doughball is evenly colored. For a marbleized effect, stop kneading when it looks marbled. For dough that has been dried, watercolors, poster paints or acrylics work just fine. Spray with a light coat of varnish when paint is completely dry to preserve colors and dough. Δ

A Backwoods Home Anthology
The Fifth Year

- Odd-jobbin' can be a country goldmine
- How to keep those excess eggs
- Make better pizza at home than you can buy
- How we bought our country home
- Cooking with dried fruit
- Garden huckleberries
- Short season gardening
- The 10 most useful herbs
- Simplified concrete and masonry work
- Raising sheep
- Free supplies for your homestead
- Learning in the pickle patch
- Good-bye old friend
- Three great bread recipes
- Firewood: how and what to buy
- A bit about ducks
- Choosing superior bedding plants
- How to build the fence you need
- Improving poor garden soil
- Learn the basics of wall framing
- Build a fieldstone chimney
- Sun oven cookery
- Determined woman builds distinctive vertical log studio
- Turkeys — fun and profitable and not as dumb as you think
- Raising fish in the farm pond
- You have to learn to shovel crap before you learn to be the boss
- How to build a low-cost log lifter
- Choosing and using a wood cookstove

Just for kids — logic puzzles

By Jo Mason

Mystery of the yellow room

Madame Dewberry has just said good-bye to the guests who stayed in her upstairs rooms. Each room is named for a color: red, gold, pink, green, blue, and yellow. The maid discovered that the guest who stayed in the yellow room forgot his or her squash racket. Using the clues below, can you tell who the racket belongs to?

- 1. Professor Prune was one of the guests.
- 2. Dr. Date stayed in the red room.
- 3. The person in the yellow room was right across the hall from Countess Kiwi.
- 4. Col. Cranberry stayed right next door to Dr. Date.
- 5. Lady Lemon's room was between the green room and Miss Mango's room.

red room	gold room	pink room
Hall		
green room	blue room	yellow room

Solution:
red/Dr. Date
gold/Col. Cranberry
pink/Countess Kiwi
green/Prof. Prune
blue/Lady Lemon
YELLOW/MISS MANGO

What color is your house?

Richard, John, and Mike are neighbors. One boy is 10 years old, one is 11 years old, and one is 12. One lives in a red house, one lives in a green house, and one lives in a white house. Using the clues below, solve the problem: **How old is Mike and what color is his house?**

Clues:
- 1. Richard likes to play ball with the eleven and twelve year old.
- 2. The boy who lives in the white house is ten years old.
- 3. John is older than Mike.
- 4. John lives in a red house.
- 5. Mike has a baby sister.

Bonus
One clue is **not** needed to solve the problem. Which is it?

Solution:
Since Richard is not eleven or twelve, he's ten, and so he lives in the white house. Since Richard is ten, John must be twelve, and Mike eleven. Since John lives in a red house, and Richard lives in a white house, Mike lives in the green one. Clue #5 was not needed.

Princess Belinda

The royal family eats dinner at a large round table. Each person always sits in a certain spot. Using the clues below, can your tell which is Princess Belinda's place?

- 1. King Xavier's place is #1.
- 2. Prince Manfred sits at place #8.
- 3. The Duke of Dorkshire sits next to Queen Zora.
- 4. Princess Georgette's spot is directly across the table from the king.
- 5. Queen Zora sits just to the king's left.
- 6. The Duchess of Dorkshire sits between the Duke and Princess Georgette.

7. Prince Yancy's place is between his sisters, Georgette and Belinda.
Solution:

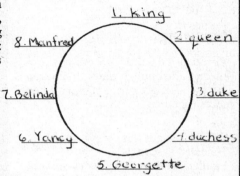

Wayne's birthday party

Wayne's friends, Buddy, Arnold, and Kenneth, attended his birthday party. One boy gave him a basketball, one gave him a toy truck, and one a jigsaw puzzle. One boy's gift was wrapped in green paper. Another's was in a shiny box. One boy didn't have time to wrap the gift. Using the clues below, solve the problem: **Which gift was not wrapped and who gave it?**

Clues:
- 1. The boy who gave the toy truck likes parties.
- 2. The boy who gave the jigsaw puzzle rode to the party with Buddy and Kenneth.
- 3. Kenneth put his gift in a shiny box.
- 4. The jigsaw puzzle was wrapped in green paper.
- 5. Buddy gave Wayne a toy truck.

Bonus
One clue is **not** needed to solve the problem. Which is it?

Solution:
Arnold must be the one who gave the jigsaw puzzle, wrapped in green paper. Since Kenneth's gift was in a shiny box—that means buddy's gift, the toy truck, was not wrapped. Clue #1 was not needed. Δ

Why does the year begin in January?

By John Silveira

"What's the topic of your article for this issue?" Dave asked.

I cringed.

Dave Duffy is the publisher of this magazine and he asks me questions like this because the credits page now lists me as Senior Editor and the senior editor should know what he's going to write about. But I didn't have a clue.

"Which issue is this?" I asked.

"January/February."

I pulled my desk calendar closer and flipped through the pages.

New Year's Day...Martin Luther King Day...Presidents's Day. My Mom's birthday is in February; I never remember to send her cards and she never forgives me. I was born on her birthday.

I flipped a few more pages and I was into March. I looked up and Dave was staring at me.

"I'll think of something," I said.

"When?"

"Later," I added.

"Remind me to ask Mac something when he gets here," he said.

Mac is Dave's poker playing friend who drops in from time to time.

"Mac's in town?"

He nodded.

"What do you want to ask him?"

"There was a conversation down at the coffee shop this morning: When does the 21st century begin—January 1, 2000 or January 1, 2001?"

"That's easy—January 1, 2000."

"Some say it starts January 1, 2001."

"That doesn't make sense. The century changes as soon as the first two digits of the year change."

"Actually, the whole thing's a big waste of time to think about," he said and got up to leave.

"Then why ask Mac about it?"

"So I'll stop thinking about it," he said and left.

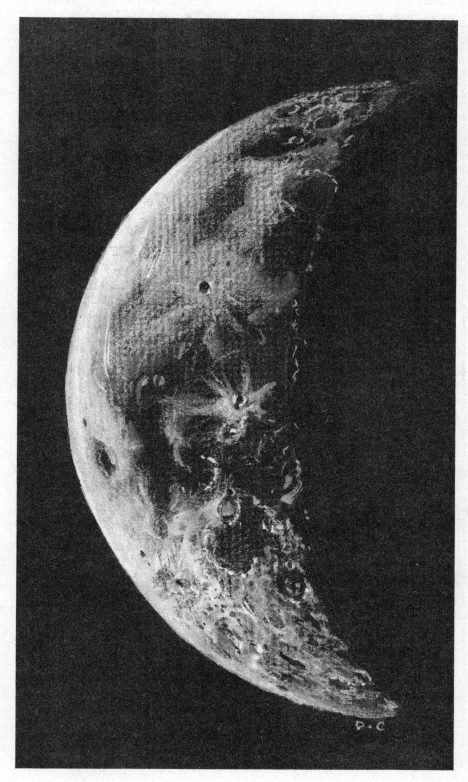

The Third Year

He was out most of the afternoon and I worked alone editing a few submissions, rejecting others.

The subject of my article was as elusive as ever. Now and then I'd push away from my desk and read the newspaper. Once in awhile, I'd pull the desk calendar closer and fan through it. I wondered what Mac would say about the beginning of the 21st century.

The more I flipped through the calendar, the more I realized how peculiarly a calendar is put together. The months have different numbers of days. New Year's Day is on January 1st and there didn't seem to be any good reason for it to be on that day.

Then there's leap year. I wasn't sure what it was for. I looked to see if 1992 is a leap year. It is. I remembered something about years being leap years if they were divisible by four so 1991 wasn't one. I checked the 1991 calendar and confirmed it.

The more I went through the calendar, the more peculiar it looked. September, October, November, December. Sept-, Oct-, Nov-, and Dec- stand for seven, eight, nine, and ten. Yet, they're the ninth, tenth, eleventh, and twelfth months.

I heard the door open in the other room and I yelled, "Dave, you know what I'd like to find out? Where the calendar came from and why it's set up the way it is? It doesn't make sense."

A moment later, I looked up and there was Dave's friend, O.E. Mac-Dougal, standing in the doorway to the office. He held an empty coffee cup in his hand. "Where's the coffee?" he asked.

"I thought you were Dave," I said. "The pot's up on the counter near the sink."

He left the room.

I pushed the calendar back and decided to at least look busy while I had company.

He came back with a full cup in his hand.

The Roman calendar

"We actually came by our calendar by way of the Romans," he said. "Is this the cover for the new issue?" he asked

as he looked over Don Childers' artwork.

"Yeah," I said.

He nodded approvingly.

"You say we got our calendar from the Romans? Are you sure?"

He looked up from the artwork and nodded, then sat in the chair Duffy usually sits in and picked up my newspaper.

I asked him: "Ever notice that September through December are the ninth through twelfth months of the year when their names seem to imply they're the seventh through tenth months?"

He looked around the newspaper. "At one time they were."

I looked at him expecting more.

10-month calendar

"According to Roman legend, Rome was founded by Romulus and he was credited with having devised the first Roman calendar. That calendar started with March and ran 10 months until December. There were six 30-day months and four 31-day months."

"Wait, wait," I said scribbling with pencil and paper. "That's only 304 days."

He nodded.

"What about the other 61 days?"

"Who cared? They were only winter."

"Are you kidding?"

"No. For some reason the Romans didn't recognize winter at first. Romulus' successor is said to have divided this uncounted time between two more months and created January and February and tacked them onto the end of the year."

"You mean the beginning of the year."

Janus for January

"The year used to begin with March. The New Year was later moved to January."

"That doesn't make sense."

"Actually, beginning the year on the first day of spring probably makes more sense than anything else. Think about it."

"Then why'd they move it?"

"They had an Etruscan king for awhile who moved the New Year to the festival for god of door and gates—Janus, a god with two faces, one looking forward and one backward, and for whom January was named. But it didn't stay there for long. It got moved back to March. It would be centuries before January 1st was again accepted as the New Year."

Unlucky even numbers

I made some notes. He read. Then I said, "Can I ask you something else?"

He lowered the newspaper.

"Do you know why they make all the months different lengths?"

"The Romans considered even numbers unlucky so later on they made their calendars with all the months having an odd number of days—except for February."

"Why was February made even?"

"With an odd number of days and an even number of months you need at least one even month to have the year add up to an odd number of days. They chose February because it had lousy weather and they thought it was the month given over to the infernal gods."

"I was born in February," I said.

He smiled.

"So this is the calendar we now use?" I asked.

"No," he said. "The Roman republican calendar was a mess."

355-day year

"It was?"

"It was only 355 days long. Every once in a while they inserted another month to try to keep it in step with the seasons, but even then the average year was 366.25 days long, a day longer than an actual solar year. It was always slipping out of step with the seasons and finally it slipped out completely."

"A 355 day year? That doesn't make sense," I said.

"Sure it does. Calendars originated with natural events like the phases of the moon or the cycle of the seasons. The phases of the moon are the easiest to plot as well as the most striking. In 12 lunar months there are between 354 and 355 days—close to a solar year. It

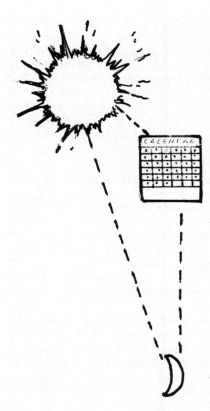

became an easy way to mark time. But because neither the return of the new moon nor the solar year are an exact number days, there's a drift in the calendar unless it's adjusted periodically to bring it back to the solar year.

"But, clergymen and politicians being what they are, there's always resistance to change, even if it's to change a calendar that's wildly out of step with the seasons it was meant to measure and forecast.

Julius Caesar reforms the calendar

"In fact, when the calendar was adjusted, it was often by Roman politicians who manipulated it to political ends—like to increase their time in office. Over the centuries, the calendar of the Roman Republic got so far out of sync with the seasons that Julius Caesar invited an astronomer from Alexandria—Sosigenes—to advise him on how to reform it.

Sosigenes prompted Caesar to abandon the old lunar calendar, so Caesar replaced it with a solar calendar. The year 45 BC became a year with 445 days in order to bring it back into step with the seasons, and a leap year was devised to account for that extra fraction of a day in a solar year. This became the primary calendar used in the West for the next 1600 years."

Renaming the months to honor the Caesars

Julius Caesar, I thought. "I remember once learning in school that July and August were named for Julius and Augustus Caesar."

"They were.," Mac said. "July was originally called Quintilis, where quint- is for five, but was renamed in honor of Julius Caesar."

"By who?"

"Julius."

"Himself?"

He nodded.

"And August?"

"In honor of Augustus. The month used to be called Sextilis where sext- is for six."

"Let me guess—renamed by Augustus himself."

He nodded.

I shook my head. "Talk about vanity."

"In fact," Mac added, "Sextilis only had 30 days, but Augustus—feeling his month should have at least as many days as his uncle's—took one from February which had recently been given 29—and 30 in a Leap Year."

"I get the feeling there have been quite a few other calendars."

"There have. In fact, some cultures have operated with more than one calendar, and the Egyptians used three.

"That sounds crazy."

The Jews and Babylonians

"It's not. Sometimes, the second calendar merely had religious significance. Like with the Jews today."

"That's why the Jews use their own calendar nowadays?" I asked.

"They don't use their own. They use the Babylonian calendar."

I looked at him for signs of a joke.

"At one time, the Jews had their own calendar," he said. "We have very little knowledge of what it was like. Scholars have deduced it was a lunar calendar with 12 months and it was adjusted periodically, to keep in step with the solar year—but we don't know how the adjustments were made. We know the months had Jewish names, though we don't know what all the names were, and we know that what they called *the beginning of the months* was Passover, though we don't know if they recognized a New Year.

"What we do know is that they adopted the Babylonian calendar after the Babylonians conquered Jerusalem early in the 6th century BC and, except for the intervals of the Macedonian and the Roman conquests, they've used it as their religious calendar ever since. Along with the Babylonian calendar they adopted the Babylonian New Year and the Babylonian names for the months, and they still use them—though I'll bet most Jews don't know that."

"Where did the Babylonians get their calendar from."

Kidenas and the lunar calendar

He put the newspaper down and stroked his chin. "As far as we know, it was developed by a Babylonian astronomer, named Kidenas, who headed the astronomical school at Sippar. All the original creators of calendars, in every civilization, were astronomers. No matter who took credit for them—popes, kings, Romulus, or revolutionaries—the astronomers did the work.

"Among other things, this Kidenas discovered the precession of the equinoxes and he introduced a lunar calendar based on the phases of the moon instead of the sun and the seasons. The calendar was 12 months long, but as this makes a year of just over 354 days, seven extra months were inserted over a 19 year cycle to keep the calendar in step with the seasons.

"Did anyone else use lunar calendars?"

"I think most did, and because lunar calendars were so much more readily adopted than solar calendars, religious festivals are very often lunar festivals, so it was hard for a lot of cultures to change to a solar calendar."

"What's the precession of the equinoxes?"

"The precession of the equinoxes comes about because the ecliptic—the sun's apparent path through the sky—appears to cross the equator at a different point each year. That point moves about one degree west every 75 years."

"One degree? And this precession has to be figured into the calendars, too?"

He nodded.

"And some guy figured that out back then, without the benefit of telescopes and without knowing for sure that the world was round?"

He nodded again. "If you want to hear how good he was, his calculation of the length of the lunar month differs by less than one second from that calculated by modern scientists with all their telescopes and computers."

"Whew."

"One of the quirks in the Babylonian calendar, and subsequently the Jewish calendar, is that the intercalary adjustment used to keep the calendar close to the solar year makes the Jewish year vary from as little as 353 days to as many as 383 days long."

"What does intercalary mean?"

"An intercalary period is a period of time inserted in a calendar to adjust its length."

I wrote it down. "How do Jews number their years? For example, we're going into 1992. What year is it on their calendar?"

"The numbering of the Jewish years is supposed to count the number of years since Creation."

"Yeah, but what year is it now on the Jewish calendar?"

He looked at me for the longest time. "I don't know. Look it up."

I don't get many "I don't knows" out of Mac.

(Editor's note: at the time this is being written, it is 5752.)

The Greek influence

"The Jews are not the only ancient people to adopt someone else's calendar. India now uses the Gregorian calendar because it was introduced by the British. But before that, when Alexander the Great of Greece went out to conquer the world, he dragged along his calendar and got as far as India, where the Hindus adopted much of it. Alexander also brought with him the signs of the Zodiac and astrology, and although they substituted Sanskrit names for the signs of the Zodiac, the Hindus retained the Greek symbols and their meanings.

"They also adopted a seven-day week and named the days for the seven known planets—which included the sun and the moon—just as the Greeks had done."

I didn't know what to ask next. As I went over my notes, Mac went back to reading the newspaper.

The Venerable Bede

I cleared my throat. "Ah . . . getting back to our calendar . . . then we now use the Calendar of Julius Caesar."

He looked over the paper again. "No, there were still problems with it. The Julian calendar—that's what Caesar's calendar came to be called—was reckoned to be exactly 365.25 days long and the Romans inserted a leap year every four years to keep it accurate. But, by the 8th century AD, The Venerable Bede, an Anglo-Saxon monk, calculated the true solar year to be 11 minutes and 14 seconds shorter than the year of the Julian calendar. This added up to about a day every 128 years.

But another 800 years went by before anyone did anything about it. By 1545, when Paul III was Pope, the actual first day of the vernal equinox was 10 days earlier than the calendar said. It wasn't something that could just be ignored anymore and the Church decided something had to be done to correct the drift. But bureaucratic inactivity ensured 27 more years would pass before Gregory XIII decreed that the Jesuit astronomer, Christopher Clavius, and a physician, Luigi Lilio, would determine how to adjust it.

The leap year

"One day in 128 years amounts to a little over three days in 400 years. Clavius figured that if three leap years were dropped every four centuries, the calendar would be closer to being in step with the solar year. He and Lilio proposed that, once the calendar was adjusted to correct centuries of slippage, every fourth year thereafter would be a leap year, unless it was a year that ended a century. But the centesimal year would be a leap year, too, if it was divisible by 400. That way, three leap years would be skipped every 400 years. So, the year 1600 was a leap year, but the years 1700, 1800, and 1900 were not. And the year 2000 will be one."

"Why was February chosen to have the leap year day?"

"It was a carry-over from the days when it was the last month of the year."

"Oh?"

He scratched his head. "Starting in 222 BC, March was the beginning of the calendar year as that was when the consuls took office. In 153 BC, this was changed to January 1st. The beginning of the year moved back to January because of it."

AD, BC, & Easter

"You keep saying AD and BC; do you know who came up with that?" I asked.

He rolled his eyes back and looked at the ceiling for a moment. He got out of his seat and reached for the bookcase. Dave has a one volume encyclopedia on the bottom shelf. He looked something up, then put the book on the shelf and sat down again.

"Dionysius Exiguus, a Christian canonist devised the Christian Era calendar around 525 AD by reckoning the birth of Christ to be around 1 BC. In the end, he was probably off by several years, but the AD-BC convention stuck."

"Did the Church do this because farmers were having trouble knowing when to plant or something?"

"Farmers had nothing to do with it. It was a concern over Easter."

"Easter?"

He nodded. "Despite the opinions of numerous six-year-olds, Christmas is not the most important day of the Christian year. Easter is. And when it falls determines most other Christian feasts.

"Easter is tied to Passover. The Crucifixion occurred just before Passover, and Passover occurred on the 14th day of the Jewish religious month of Nisan. Because of that, some Christian Churches took that day as Easter no matter what day of the week it fell on. But most of Christiandom chose to observe Easter by tying it to the moon and the first day of spring. It was calculated as the first Sunday following the first full moon that falls on or follows the vernal equinox." He looked at me critically. "You got that?"

I read my notes carefully and nodded.

"And if the full moon falls on a Sunday, Easter is on the following Sunday."

I wrote it down.

"Consequently, it was very important to know when spring began. Using the Julian calendar, Easter was difficult to predict because the Julian calendar erroneously calculated the first day of spring.

Gregorian calendar and January 1

"With the Gregorian calendar—that's what the modified Julian calendar we now use is called—Easter is more readily predicted and always falls between March 22nd and April 25th each year."

"I've always wondered why it jumps around so much," I said.

"The Gregorian calendar also finally established the modern convention of making January 1st the New Year. In Great Britain, December 25th was regarded as New Year's Day until the 14th century. Then March 25th was assigned as the first day of the new year. Everyone who adopted the Gregorian calendar assumed the convention of New Year's Day as being January 1st."

"So everyone adopted the calendar then," I said.

"No. Because of rivalries within the Christian Church—between the Eastern and Western Catholic Churches and between Protestantism and Catholicism—the Gregorian calendar, despite its obvious advantages, was not immediately adopted.

"Countries most influenced by the Vatican, like Spain, France, Portugal, and the little states that made up the Italian Peninsula, adopted it in 1582. Most other Catholic countries followed within a few years.

U.S. adopted present calendar in 1752

"Protestant countries—particularly those influenced by the British—took almost two centuries. By the time the British adopted it, their calendars were 11 days out of whack. But they and their colonies, which included what was to become the United States, finally adopted it in 1752 and the day following September 2nd of that year was officially proclaimed to be September 14th.

"Legislation providing for the change was carefully worded to prevent legal problems..."

"Like what?"

"...like the calculation of interest. Lenders didn't get 11 extra days of interest on legal technicalities. They tried to ensure that anything that was time dependent was calculated by the number of days, not the calendar. By the way, you can put this in your Gee Whiz File: The word 'calendar' is from the Latin word "kalendarium," which meant a moneylender's account book—something that probably makes sense to anyone with time payments."

I nodded. It made sense to me.

George Washington's birthday adjusted to suit new calendar

"Birthdays were recalculated as well. George Washington was born on February 11, 1732, but after 1752 his birth date was adjusted by eleven days to February 22nd to keep it on the same day of the solar year. Yet, despite the careful planning and the explanations to ensure the calendar's change would be painless, there were protests by people who thought that 11 days had been legislated out of their lives, and they wanted them back."

"Takes all kinds," I said.

"Gradually, one country after another adopted the Gregorian calendar but some didn't until this century. The Soviet Union didn't adopt it until 1918 and Greece, not until 1923."

Egypt's 3 calendars

"Can we go back to something you said earlier?"

"Sure."

"You said the Egyptians had three calendars."

"Yeah. Like almost everyone else, their first calendar was a lunar calendar and religious days became associated with it. So they kept it.

"The second was a solar calendar. It was actually an agricultural calendar. To keep it in step with the seasons, the new year was proclaimed to start when the star we now call Sirius first rose above the horizon in the spring. This was important because it always occurred just a few weeks before the Nile began to flood.

"You've gotta realize, the entire Egyptian civilization revolved around the Nile and its cycle of rising and falling, and the Egyptians became very good at predicting when it would happen without ever understanding what caused it. The Nile comes to them through a virtually rainless desert so they came to believe that the rising of Sirius caused the Nile to flood."

"Why does it happen?" I asked.

"Seasonal rains on the upper reaches of the Nile, well beyond the Nile the Egyptians knew."

"Oh."

"Their most generally used calendar was a civil calendar, introduced around 2500 BC. It was a 365-day calendar that was an attempt to create a lunisolar calendar. But, as it was based on a 365-day year, it started to fall out of sync with the solar year from the day it was introduced. But it continued to be used by government and administration."

New World sophistication

"Let me ask something: With this hubbub about Columbus now, did the

The Third Year

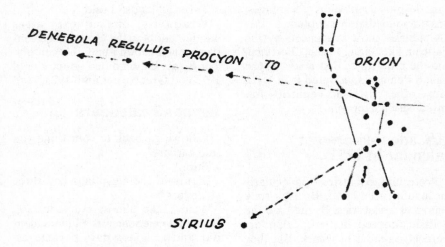

DENEBOLA REGULUS PROCYON TO ORION

SIRIUS

The appearance of Sirius in the spring marked the new year in ancient Egypt.

Indians in the New World have any calendars?"

"Boy, did they. It's difficult for people to appreciate the level of development of the civilizations in pre-Columbian America. The indigenous people in Meso-America may have been behind the Europeans in things like animal husbandry, metallurgy, and navigation, but they were ahead in agriculture, astronomy, and even calendars. Their level of mathematical sophistication rivaled that of the Arabs, and surpassed the Europeans—until the Renaissance."

"I didn't know that."

Aztec human sacrifice

He nodded, as if saying that's okay. "The Mayan used two calendars. They were more accurate than the Julian calendar Columbus used. The Aztecs had two calendars that were derived from these. One was a ritual calendar of 13 20-day months and the other was a civil calendar of 18 20-day months with 5 intercalary days called nemontemi which were considered unlucky. The beginning of the Ritual and Civil calendars coincided every 52 years and was celebrated with, 'the new fire ceremony.'"

"What was that?"

"All the sacred and domestic fires were allowed to burn out and a new fire was started by priests on the chest of a sacrificial victim. From this all the fires were started again.

"Yucko."

"They do it differently, now."

"That's nice."

Some had no calendar

"Mac, It seems like everyone has a calendar."

"Not everyone did."

"Who didn't?"

"Few, if any, of the North American Indians had them, regardless of whether or not they had time-marking methods and even though they recognized the passage of the seasons. Days and phases of the moon were frequently used to measure time but calendars just weren't part of their cultures.

"This is not to say one wouldn't have happened. It's natural to develop a calendar. Civilization depends on agriculture, agriculture depends on the land, the land depends on the seasons, and, because of this, it is crucial, in every civilization, to keep track of the seasons with a calendar.

"Not only that, the stars were seen to move through the sky in an orderly progression that was repeated year after year. Spring flowed into summer and summer into fall, and winter followed that. It was like the cycle of birth, growth, maturity, and death. Many an ancient—many a modern—

felt if these things could be plotted, a man's fate could be predicted."

"We don't appreciate it now because the seasons don't mean the same things to modern man. Lettuce magically appears in the supermarket 365 days a year—and once more in leap years. The stars have nothing to do with it.

"All we use the seasons for now is to predict when the World Series will start and when we're going into summer reruns.

"Still, the invention of the calendar and the ability to accurately forecast the seasons ranks as one of the landmark inventions of mankind. It even appears that the invention of the lunisolar calendar and writing occurred at about the same time, and it's difficult to say just how one influenced the other."

Measuring the day

"So, there are lunar calendars and solar calendars, but everything else is about the same."

"What do you mean?" he asked.

"Well, the calendar can vary from culture to culture, but the day can't."

I knew from the look on his face I was wrong.

"Determining when a day begins has always depended on the culture you came from," he said. "We reckon a day from one midnight to the next. More primitive people, myself included, measure from sunrise to sunrise. Throughout most of Western history, it was measured from noon to noon. The Jews, who adopted most of their time reckoning from the Babylonians, measure the day from sunset to sunset. Hindus and Egyptians, on the other hand, measured the day from dawn to dawn, and the Romans, like us, measured it from midnight to midnight.

"Until a little over a hundred years ago, each town in this country reckoned its own noon by 'high noon,' and all the clocks in a particular town set their clocks that way. But if you set your clock in one town and went due west to another, your clock was suddenly several minutes fast.

Railroads standardized time

"This was okay when travel was leisurely and no one punched a clock but with the advent of the railroad, schedules were impossible to make and keep. So the railroad disregarded what individual towns did and created arbitrary time zones and set their schedules accordingly. The result was that the trains ran on time and the towns along the way followed suit. Ultimately Congress made the time standards created by the railroad law, and then took credit for standardizing the time. But it was actually the railroads that did it."

I write slowly. Mac pauses. Mac is patient.

"And from days we get weeks," I said and opened another can of worms.

Measuring a week

"Weeks varied from culture to culture. In many cultures the length of a week was originally determined by the interval between market days, so it varied from one people to another—from four days in West Africa to 10 days in ancient Egypt.

In Rome the week was nine days. But once again it is because the Babylonians had a seven-day week that we have the seven-day week, and the reason the Babylonians had a seven-day week was apparently because seven most nearly divided the lunar month, and each of the four lunar phases is about seven days long."

Varying length of seasons

"But everyone has four seasons," I said, glad to be able to interject at least one thing I knew to be true without Mac telling me differently.

"Even the number of seasons varied from culture to culture," he said and I winced. "In some there were only two—rainy and dry. The Egyptians had three seasons, corresponding to the levels of the Nile. The first was for when the Nile flooded, the second was when it flowed in its bed, and the third was the dry season. Cultures in the higher latitudes tended to have four seasons. Some American Indian tribes had five.

"We like to think we time the seasons scientifically with the summer and winter solstices and the spring and autumnal equinoxes. However, on our civilized social calendars summer ends with Labor Day, not with the autumnal equinox."

I looked at the stack of notes I'd acquired while talking to him, and said, "All this just to have a calendar to hang on the wall," and Mac immediately made me wish I hadn't.

"Not all calendars hang on the wall to advertise tires or girlie magazines."

"What do you mean?"

"The passage of the year can be marked by a number on a page. But it can also be marked by the movement of the stars. At the equator, the rising stars seem to rise vertically from the horizon. The closer you get to the poles, the shallower the angle they rise at, until at the poles they seem not to rise or set at all but just travel in great circles—with the exception of stars near the horizon which may seem to appear and disappear because of the wobble of the earth on its axis.

Stonehenge

"Structures were built to mark points along the horizon where particular stars appeared at the same time every year. The seasons could be marked this way. Stonehenge was one of these, and after many fanciful theories about its purpose, it was finally realized that it is a giant calendar—built about 4000 years ago—to allow primitive men to mark the passage of the year. It marked the solstices and equinoxes, and it also marked the lunar months and even predicted eclipses."

"Are you kidding?"

"No. There are some good books on it. You should read one.

"In fact, evidence of more than 600 such structures have been found in Britain alone, and others have been found on the European continent. Stonehenge just happens to be one of

The ruins of Stonehenge is but one of 600 such monumental calendars found across England.

Here's what we believe Stonehenge looked like when complete.

The Third Year

the better preserved and certainly the most spectacular of the bunch."

Varying length of day

My hand ached from writing and my penmanship was turning into a scrawl. I made one more attempt to make a statement Mac wouldn't refute or amend. "Well at least the length of the day is the same in all cultures."

He sighed and I knew I'd blown it again.

"The lengths of the days and nights not only depend on the season, they depend on how far from the equator you are. As you get closer to the North Pole during the northern summer the day gets longer until, at the Pole itself, the sun doesn't appear to set for weeks on end. In the winter, everything is reversed. Meanwhile, at the equator itself, the sun appears to rise and set at the same time everyday, no matter what the season."

Varying length of an hour

"Do hours ever vary?" I asked knowing somehow they were going to.

"Not anymore."

"You mean they once did?"

"Days and nights were split into 12 hours each in ancient Egypt. But these were not hours in the way we think of them. They were simply 12 equal segments. So because the days are longer in summer than in the winter, the daylight hours in the summer were longer than those in winter. In fact, a daylight hour could vary from 75 minutes to 45 minutes, depending on the season."

"Isn't anything sacred?" I asked.

He didn't answer.

"At least everyone uses a year that's a year long, nowadays," I said.

He shook his head and I winced.

"The Muslim calendar is a true lunar calendar. They recognize a year of alternating 30 and 29-day months with the last month occasionally being 30 instead of 29 days to keep it in sync with the phases of the moon. But there is no attempt to keep it in step with the solar year. So, a Muslim year is 354 to 355 days long and the months regress

in relation to the seasons, repeating roughly every 32 years."

"Anything else?" I asked hoping there wasn't. My writing hand was starting to cramp up.

The Chinese calendar

He knew my enthusiasm was flagging. "Well, the Chinese had a very accurate calendar. They calculated the length of the solar year to be 365 and a quarter days and the lunar month to be 29 and a half days at least as early as the 14th century BC and had developed their own intercalary methods. In fact, historians feel that Chinese understanding of astronomy exceeded that in the West until the 13th century AD."

I sighed.

"But we don't have to go into that," he said.

"Just one more thing," I said. "Has anyone ever attempted to improve the calendar since this Clavius guy?"

The French Revolution

"There have been attempts to reform the calendar since the Gregorian calendar was adopted. After the French Revolution, the French actually adopted and used a calendar which they purged of any religious significance. It had 12 months of 30 days each, and the months all had new names. The seven-day week was abandoned and the months were split into three 10-day decades. They even decimalized the day by splitting it into ten units but this became the first part of the new time reckoning that was abandoned. And New Year's Day on this calendar fell on the first day of autumn."

"Twelve months of 30 days each make only a 360 day year," I said.

"That's right. The remaining five days—six in leap years—were designated as feast and vacation days.

"They adopted their new calendar in 1793—after backdating it to 1792—and abandoned it on January 1, 1806."

"Why?"

"No one else adopted it. They were out of sync with the rest of the world. Though the world adopted France's

system of measurement—the metric system, the best system of measurement ever devised—it didn't want their calendar.

"Are there likely to be any new calendar overhauls?"

Present-day adjustments

He thought about it. "There will always be adjustments. Every once in awhile you'll hear a news item that astronomers have adjusted the solar year and you'll wonder what it means just before you forget it forever. It usually means that due to the precession of the equinoxes or the slowing of the earth's rotation due to tidal forces, the length of the solar year is adjusted.

"It's not something that's going to affect the setting on your alarm clock. In fact, it has no bearing on your day-to-day life at all.

"But there have been other reform movements afoot. Some reflect changes instituted in the French Republican calendar and the Aztec calendar with months of equal length. One would have 13 28-day months and one odd day—two in leap years—that would not be part of any month or week. A calendar like that would ensure that a date always fell on the same day of the week so, if you were born on a Tuesday, your birthday would always fall on a Tuesday forevermore."

"Will we adopt a new calendar?"

"No."

"Never?"

"Never's too big a word. Let's just say not in our lifetimes or any time reasonable in the future."

"Why not?"

"Why should we? For a prettier calendar? The calendar's a little awkward but only a little. Changing it would be expensive and there's no guarantee other countries would go along with it—that's why the French calendar failed—and all we'd have to show for it would be a pretty calendar."

"So you don't think calendar reform is real important?"

"No, and I put the people who think it is in the same class as people who compulsively think everything has to be neat and iron their underwear."

He went back to reading.

"One more thing?"

He looked at me over his newspaper.

The 21st Century

"When does the 21st century officially start?"

"January 1, 2001."

"There are a lot of people who disagree with you . . . Not me," I added.

"The years haven't always been thought of as beginning on January 1st and ending December 31st, but by today's reckoning they do. So the first year of the Christian Era ended on December 31 of the year 1 AD. The second year ended on December 31st of the year 2 AD. The hundredth year ended on December 31 of 100 AD. It takes 100 years to make a century so, the second century AD started on the first day of 101 AD. Centuries have begun on the odd year ever since."

"But a lot of people think it should start as soon as the year reads 2000."

"Those people probably iron their underwear."

He was reading when he asked me, "Ever wonder why we called this the 20th century and not the 19th when all but one of the years begins with a 19?"

I squirmed in my seat. I didn't have the slightest idea.

Dave walked in. "You're here," he said to Mac as he walked by. "Are you staying to have supper with me and Lenie?"

He dropped an armload of the day's mail onto his desk. Without waiting for Mac to answer, he turned to me. "I think you're right, John, the 21st century begins on January 1, 2000.

I winced again.

He turned back to Mac. "The nights are a little chilly," he said, "but we're having a barbecue in the backyard tonight. You're welcome to stay."

Mac nodded.

"Actually, that's not quite right about the 21st century," I said. "It starts January 1, 2001."

He hesitated. "How do you figure?" I looked at Mac, expecting him to jump in but he kept reading the newspaper.

"Well," I said, "the first year of the Christian Era ended on December 31 of the year 1 AD. The second year ended on December 31st of the year 2

AD. The hundredth year ended on December 31 of 100 AD. It takes 100 years to make a century so, the second century AD started on the first day of 101 AD. Centuries have begun on the odd year ever since."

"Is that right?" Dave asked Mac.

Mac looked up from his paper for just a second. "Sounds right to me."

"What are you writing about for this issue?" Dave asked.

"Calendars," I said.

"Calendars? Calendars. Hey, I like that. It fits in with the New Year. Are you going to have a thing on leap years, and stuff like that?"

"Yes."

"Good. Why don't you put in something about when the 21st century begins."

"Okay, Dave." Δ

Warnings,
To the young,
Go unheeded.
I say,
LiveYour life.
They reply,
I am,
And will not realize,
Until too late,
So said I

John Earl Silveira
Ojai, CA

A Backwoods Home Anthology
The Eleventh Year

* Wild greens: when weeds become vegetables
* A portable bench for your better half
* Keeping poison ivy under control
* Cooking for a crowd
* Rural building: Construction q's and a's
* Radiant floor heating
* Jackie's tips for hardcore homesteading
* Solar building design
* Make a sure-fire live trap
* Good homemade jerky
* A passive solar-heated tower house
* Preparation for successful painting
* An easy-to-make pot rack
* Make your own insulated waterer
* Home canning safety tips
* Masonry stoves — what's old is new
* Lye soap making in the modern home
* Integrated PV/roofing
* Basic livestock vetting
* Tale of a country family
* Dealing with ticks
* Electricity from the wind: Assessing wind energy potential

The Third Year

Some ideas for remodeling and living from Catamount Ridge Farm

By Vern Modeland

In front of a crackling fire on one of the lead-gray, ice coated days that make up the bottom of winter in the Missouri Ozarks, Walker Powell likes to talk about spring.

Spring can come early along the Missouri-Arkansas state line, sometimes as early as February with the right combination of warm southerly winds and sunny days. Walker Powell has seen 74 Springs come to the hills and hollows where he's always lived the kind of life to which many of us still only aspire. Walker was born just a half-mile from where he lives today. He grew up learning self-reliance and a healthy life style based on the resources of the land and the wildlife it supported. He played, hunted and fished around the limestone ledges that caught and channeled clear water from springs and run-off, and sometimes shared the locations of cool, damp caves.

Those caves included one Walker's father uncovered in 1921 while hunting rabbits. Opened to visitors, to help pay off the mortgage, it has been an Ozarks tourist attraction for 70 years.

Life for Walker Powell has always moved in harmony with what the land along the White River attracted and nurtured. But adapting so completely to the natural, quiet lifestyle seems more surprising for Johanna Powell. She grew up in Tulsa, Oklahoma, worked at jobs that involved lots of traveling, and lived 20 years on the wind-scoured western Kansas high plains where earth and weather are not very cordial. Then, in 1971, Johanna took a seasonal job at Silver Dollar City, a tourist attraction near Branson, Mo. She met Walker there, demonstrating one of a dozen homestead crafts that form a backdrop for the theme park's paraphrase of turn-of-the-century country living.

In 1974, the couple hired a carpenter-helper and started remodeling Walker's 672-square-foot, one-bedroom bachelor's house.

Walker and Johanna Powell of Catamount Ridge Farms

"It's a we-done-it-ourselves project," Johanna says with pride. It's a house hidden by forest and shrubs at the end of a lane that doesn't fight how the land drains but flows with it. The lane hugs a side of the ridge named for bobcats that, although far fewer in number today than in Walker's youth, still visit there in the night.

The design and building project doubled the size of the 24- by 28-foot one-story frame house Powell built in 1969. To the east, a new living room, bath and bedroom space were added, preserving the back stoop and its four steps up as entryway to the kitchen. A beamed ceiling slopes upward from the native stone fireplace wall. The slope directs warmed air toward the upper level of the house through the former back door opening.

The new living room's windows afford a view of wooded valley and capture winter sunshine. Built-in seating conserves space. Other furnishings mix home-made, antique and antique-with-innovation. Cast iron bases cast off from spent wood stoves support a TV and, with glass cut to fit, make sturdy tables.

Five-inch-thick native stone covers cement blocks behind the fireplace. A door in the wall hides a firewood bin. Access from outside allows replenishing the wood supply without having to haul it through the house.

Walker Powell harvests his firewood from the 280 acres that remains his today out of the 2,280 acre homestead.

"I cut diseased or dead trees, weak trees, or where they grow too close together. And I only cut what I need. I don't stack wood for all winter. Termites get too much that way. I cut what I need when I need it. I like to burn

Johanna and Walker Powell pause on stone steps in front of their "did-it-ourselves" home in the Ozarks. Living room addition is on the right, and screened summer room above them. Outside entrance of guest quarters is beyond the carport.

some green. Green wood holds a fire longer, gives better coals," he says with native conviction.

There's a second wood-burning stove in what was Powell's living room and now is the dining area. A forced air, dual- fuel central heating system also was added in an addition on the north side of the original house.

The furnace burns wood and propane. It will accept logs up to five feet long, is self-igniting and has a thermostat to monitor each heat source.

"Takes about three or four logs about three times a day on real cold days," Powell observes. That keeps the well-insulated house at about 72 degrees F. daytime and 65 F. at night during the coldest of Ozarks winters, he says.

Five-hundred gallons of propane is more than a year's supply to back up both heating and cooking needs. The propane tank gets topped off whenever the price seems the most attractive, Powell points out.

Directly above the furnace is a 12-foot-square greenhouse. Its unusual shady-side location is based on taking advantage of the furnace as a secondary heat source. The greenhouse's deck-like floor allows furnace heat to supplement solar energy collected through white corrugated fiberglass roofing. Even on cloudy days, Walker Powell says his greenhouse's temperature can easily reach 120 degrees. Excess heat is regulated by the low-tech method of opening one or more of the screened windows cut into the sides of the addition.

The greenhouse's prime use is for seedlings and tender plants. Johanna also cultivates a few decorative tropical plants, herbs, and a massive aloe. Later in the year, fruits and herbs will dry there.

When warm weather comes, the Powells spend more and more time in the 18-foot by 30-foot screened room added to the sunniest side of their house. A sliding glass door connects the summer room with the rest of the house through the dining area. There also is an 8-foot covered deck beyond the screened in space.

"We practically live out here, even sleep here when it gets really hot," Johanna says in describing the screened room. Both bedrooms are on the north side of the house.

Thirteen feet high to its ridge beam, the screened room has a green translucent fiberglass roof. Ceiling fans and bamboo shades hold back the hottest sun and supplement the house site's natural affinity for cooling breezes.

Recalling her summers spent in Kansas, Johanna Powell originally insisted they splurge for central air conditioning. A three ton unit was installed. When it was turned on only a handful of times in four years, it came out and was sold to a newcomer building down the road, who ordered all trees bulldozed off his construction site, Walker Powell recalls with one of his gentle smiles.

Powell figures his total annual heating and cooling expense now as "near zero."

The summer room and its deck shelter parking space large enough for two cars. There had been a basement garage. It was remodeled to become a small apartment for Johanna's daughter. Today, is a private place for houseguests.

The cement block foundation also houses a laundry room and space for cool storage of food and canned goods. A bermed storm shelter down hill from the house contributes additional underground storage space.

The Powells continued another country tradition when remodeling by finding space for a summer kitchen, for canning time which generally also is the time of year when Ozarks daytime temperatures hang monotonously up toward the top end of the thermometer. The summer kitchen uses space that was a front porch. Closed in with fiberglass and wood panels, it was fitted with a counter top electric oven and an antique propane stove.

Output of a 500-foot-deep well is conserved and supplemented by a 1,400 gallon above-ground cistern. It was placed to collect and store run-off from the east half of the low- pitched roof. Cistern water is the primary supply for the Powell's livestock, for watering plants, and for outside cleanup chores. In the basement storeroom, there also are dozens of water-filled, gallon-size plastic milk cartons on the floor and on shelves. Each is labeled as to the date filled and is replenished regularly. The oldest water goes to house plants and for scrubbing floors.

The Third Year

Two 750 gallon stock watering tanks were originally placed to catch the rain run-off. When the galvanized tanks got rusty and began to leak, they were replaced by a single container made of cement blocks. (For construction hints see "Build your own ferro-cement water storage tank" in Issue No. 5). The stock tanks were recycled by moving them to a sunny spot nearby where one was filled with dirt and became a raised garden for tomatoes and asparagus.

"Raised gardens are easier to weed. I don't have to bend over," Powell says with a twinkle in his eye.

The second stock tank is now a composting container.

A few goldfish in the cistern combat the growth of algae and mosquito larvae. The Powells also keep chickens, including some ornamental breeds. "For their eggs and the pleasure of their company," Johanna says.

Three cats are responsible for rodent patrol.

Three Airedales have the run of two fenced acres around the house at night. The dogs spend their days in shaded pens close to the house where each dog has its own sturdy shelter and private fenced run appropriate to the 100-pound size of the breed. Airedales are a family tradition as watch dogs, according to Walker Powell.

"Good hunters too," he adds. "My dad used to hunt wild hogs and bear with them."

A handful of guinea fowl wander free and are praised for their ability to keep the cricket, grasshopper and tick populations at a minimum.

Jeannette and Elmer, a pair of donkeys, add their braying to the clatter of the guineas as they watch the comings and goings on Catamount Ridge from a pasture close by. Pets, the donkeys are retired from the theme park, Silver Dollar City, to spend the rest of their days contributing fertilizer for compost and plant beds.

"We have a no-mow yard. It's a no-rake yard, too. The leaves don't seem to stick," Johanna Powell says in explaining her choice of a ground cover of periwinkle and ivy that now climbs both sides of limestone steps that lead toward the front door.

Native and hybrid fruit trees also grow close to the house. A few were transplanted to grow among the native ornamentals that include dogwood, service berry and other spring-colorful Ozarks under-forest varieties. Fruit trees that generally do well in the Ozarks include apple, pear, persimmon, wild cherry and mulberry varieties.

Five courses of water-sealed cement blocks will hold 1400 gallons of rain runoff, conserving water use on Catamount Ridge Farm.

Other productive landscape plantings are wild strawberry, gold and black raspberry, dewberry, high bush huckleberry and domestic grapes. The annual harvest is frozen by Johanna or enjoyed as pies and cobblers, jams and jellies.

Deer, turkey and squirrels that Walker Powell hunts are the couple's primary source of meat.

"Healthier, and has more taste," Powell says of wild game. "We haven't bought three pounds of beef in 20 years."

Recycling and composting leave little unusable trash and garbage. What cannot be recycled goes directly to the county commercial landfill, or to a recycler.

The Powells look unkindly on littering, a growing problem in the tourist-laden Ozarks. People who elect to throw cans, bottles and other trash from the windows of their cars or recreational vehicles in the vicinity of Catamount Ridge Farm can be in for a delayed surprise. Johanna Powell tells of being behind a car when the occupants dumped a sack of trash along the state road near her home.

"I got the license number before I stopped and gathered up their trash. Then I got their address from the license number. Littering is a crime, you know. I packaged that trash and mailed it to them in Kansas City along with a note that said it came from their friends in the beautiful Ozarks."

Over a cup of mullen tea sweetened with honey, the Powells also easily share their thoughts on what it takes to be happy living on a place like Catamount Ridge Farm.

"Some can make it, some can't. You have to love nature, peace and quiet, and not having neighbors," Walker says.

"People still want to know if I'm scared to death living here," Johanna adds. Her answer: "It's safer than a city." Δ

My Backwoods Philosophy

By Mary Jo Frolick

You don't have to be young with hate for the establishment in your heart to seek a home in the backwoods. You can be any age and want to take command of your life. Maybe you just want to live a simpler way. All it takes is a plan, fair health, a will to work, and guts enough to break away from the commercialized crowd. I am 64 years old. My son, Gary, is 35, his wife is 30. They have 3 small children and another on the way. I do my work with Gary's part-time help. The things I don't know how to do, we learn. We are making progress in shaping 40 acres into two homesteads.

Few women would choose to live as I do. More men are inclined to like the wilds but they are usually too busy making a living to live. Perhaps I have found the Philosopher's Stone that turns the copper pennies of necessity into golden coins of just enough for contentment. I find the simpler my life, the cheaper I can live. I realized somewhere during my years that money, by itself, is a useless empty thing. It cannot buy the important intangibles such as love and contentment. To live without money seems to be morally good because we have been taught from childhood to adulthood that money is the root of all evil. This is not a realistic viewpoint either. You need to pay Caesar his taxes and there are other things that require cash. Dollars are the medium of exchange but I see no reason to stack them up.

Most of my life I have wanted to live in deep woods on the bank of a river. It was a western book written by Zane Grey called *Rogue River Feud* that planted the idea inside my mind many, many years ago. I was country-raised but spent my young adult years living in the city hemmed in and feeling smothered. From age 30 I have lived the country life again, but I put my

dreams on hold and tried to help my husband achieve his.

Suddenly in January 1989, I was a widow. My girlhood dreams came back. Could I, at the age when most people are ready to quit, fulfill my dreams? Most of my family thought I had come unhinged when I began to make my dreams into plans and put my plans on paper. I think it takes both visualizing and drawing plans on paper to firm up dreams and make them into substance. While my mother and other family members bad-mouthed the plan, Gary and his family thought I had a good idea and wanted to move with me. East Texas was getting a mite crowded for them too.

We decided to look in western Arkansas. The county we chose is located in the Ouachita (Wash-a-taw) Mountains with lots of public land in national forests. It is sparsely populated. I find fewer people and less crime. The mountains are small but are high enough to block some of the inclement winter weather.

We went into a real estate office and told them our requirements: 40 acres of wooded land with a small river along one edge. We wanted solitude and privacy with deeded access. If it had a habitable dwelling, I would consider it a bonus. They brought us here. I came, I saw, and I bought. It was exactly what I asked for. My 40 acres are wooded and to my south across the river are several thousand acres in Ouachita National Forest.

The cabin was a derelict, two-room, cement block shanty located a half mile from hard-topped highway. There was some question about whether it was liveable. A rich man had built it in 1974 for a fishing camp and let it go to ruin when he got tired of playing. It could have been the flood of 1982 or perhaps it was after the cabin was robbed that he gave up. The house had been vacant a long time and its tin roof had many generous leaks.

October 1989 I moved in. The electricity and telephone were hooked

up the next week. There was no pump in the well so I dipped my flushing and bathing water from the river by bucket and borrowed my drinking water by the gallon from a neighbor on the hill. I had a propane tank, cook stove, and a small heater installed in November. Hurrah! No more cooking on a campfire outside.

We had a month of cold weather in December. Some of it was below zero. There was not enough heat to warm the house. Ice was floating in my flushing buckets. I layered my clothes. Did I ever!! I think I must have had on my whole wardrobe! I replaced the plumbing and well pump in January. Aahhh---luxury! A pot that flushes by handle and a hot shower. I think the hot water heater was the only thing I didn't replace. Gary put up my old wood heater in January too. I was warm and snug the rest of the winter.

Gary and family live up the road a piece in an elderly mobile home.

Spring opened with a deluge of rain. Of course, I flooded. Ten inches of rain in my watershed and I have water in the house if the rain falls for a couple of days. I bought the place with my eyes wide open. The high water mark on my bathroom door is 33". Flooding usually occurs every 8 to 10 years but it can happen anytime. Eight inches of muddy water was exploring my house in April 1990. Water backs in here, lap by lap. It has to climb a 12' bank first, then travel 100 yards and rise another 4" to get inside the house. It does little or no damage to my block house with it's cement floor. One flood and I realized that for my house to grow, it would have to get taller. So Gary and I built 4 rooms and a bath upstairs. We didn't know how but we had a good how-to book. We even built a stairway. We started in September 1990 and are still building-- finishing actually. I hope to complete it by the first of the new year. A "plain-jane" house to live in—no prestigious place for me.

I read long ago that prestige makes a poor bedfellow. Since I don't sleep around, I never met this scalawag. I do, however, have a speaking acquaintance with the Jones family—as in "keeping up with". I have paid little attention to their lifestyle, but if their

The Third Year

"proud-of's" give them the boost of importance they need for feeling good, I'm happy for them.

I suppose I'm not an ordinary person. It doesn't matter if I'm popular with my neighbors or thought of as a recluse. I please myself with what I do. I pick and choose my friends and companions. I am a person who is unafraid of opinion and selective enough to prefer one-on-one conversation. I dislike people in bunches.

I have a social security income so money is not a problem, but making it stretch—to do all the things I want—is. Am I living in poverty? Perhaps. I don't feel deprived. I feel blessed. I have learned to make, grow, build, repair, or substitute for most of my necessities whether they are needed or only desired. I live in comfort. My needs are small and my wants are few. These are my 10 needs:

- 1. To own a bit of land
- 2. Have an ample supply of pure water
- 3. Food to fill my stomach
- 4. A tight roof over my head
- 5. Firewood to warm me
- 6. A soft bed to rest on
- 7. Woven threads to clothe me
- 8. Work of **my** choosing to do
- 9. Folks to neighbor with
- 10. And a few friends on my bookshelf

I need all these things to have a well-rounded life, especially work that I like to do. It sounds as if I live primitively but I'm not missing many modern conveniences.

So I own a few acres on the bank of a river and I work when I want to, rest when I get tired, do almost as I please. I don't have much "back-pocket" money but I am rich in the things that count. I have plans for an orchard. I have already planted some fruit trees. I have a "raised bed" flower and vegetable garden in the works. A chicken house and pen for 12 hens is planned. I need chickens to take care of the insects and for eggs. However, I might have to teach them how to swim in the wet years or turn them into ducks. I keep adding things as I can afford them, which is 1 or 2 major items a year. Not much money is invested, just a great amount of thought, muscle, and sweat. Δ

Animal lifesavers — CPR & comfrey

By Anne Westbrook Dominick

Over the years I learned a lot about the fragility of life but it took whimsical, willful goats to teach me how to save it. Two methods, one a commonly recognized lifesaver and the other a diagnosed carcinogenic, have rescued two of my goats (one dead, one declared dying).

CPR: Everyone should learn cardiopulmonary resuscitation (CPR). It works on livestock—or pets for that matter—as well as humans. A foundry where I was a molder taught me, but where employees don't do it, state agencies and local communities offer free lessons. CPR takes only a few minutes to learn. Using it just once more than pays back for all that time lost.

I first used it—within a couple months of learning how—to revive the heart and return breathing to a dead goat. First though, I had done what I knew I shouldn't: staked out one of the goats to clean up a weedy spot. She strangled.

I heard an unusual cry from her and ran to the spot to see her in the last throes of suffocation. By the time I had cut through the still tightening snarl of rope to release her, she gave all evidence of death—not breathing, no heart beat. I rolled her onto her back and gave her the heart thrust and was about to start the respiration part but she gasped, shuddered, and definitely took one inhale. Then she quit. Panicking, but hopeful, I gave her another sound, sudden drive to the heart. This time she really took a hold of life and sucked in air while her heart heaved her sides. In about 30 seconds she opened her eyes. In 10 minutes she was standing. In a couple hours I think she forgot she had died.

CPR is easy to learn, easy to remember, and easy to do. It also really does save lives.

Comfrey: Now, on the the other life saving trick a goat ingrained into me: the use of comfrey in a way I hadn't come across in any herbal book. Comfrey has been found to cause liver cancer in rats. Whether or not it has the same effect on goats and/or humans is uncertain, but comfrey herb tea has been outlawed in Canada. It is a scientifically recognized external healer of skin lesions. Still goats love its flavor and when mine get loose they rush straight up the hill north of the barn to devour it. I keep some there, near the barn, because it saved a mighty sick goat a couple years ago.

That summer we came close to losing her to mountain laurel poisoning. She hadn't eaten or been able to drink water for 72 hours and she had quit vomiting—something a goat starts doing a few hours after eating laurel and continues for 12 to 24 hours before eating again. This one had not only gone beyond vomiting, she had also lost her rumen (cud) with all its necessary digestive ingredients.

After taking her to the veterinarian (who told us we had little hope of saving her and to take her home to die where it would be cheaper to bury her), we tried coaxing her into nibbling at caprine favorites: clover, maple leaves, cabbage seedlings, day lilies, anything. None inspired anything beyond one obedient, weak nibble. Finally we tried a comfrey leaf. She tasted it tentatively, and finished it as eagerly as she could in her condition. She ended up eating six large leaves. The comfrey was good enough to start her ruminating a bit later so we didn't have to steal the cud from another wily goat to get her started.

I don't feed my goats comfrey regularly. It isn't even an occasional treat, but it is always there for medicinal reasons. I can't even imagine a barn without comfrey nearby anymore. Δ

March/April 1992
No. 14
$3.50 U.S.
$4.50 Canada

Backwoods Home magazine

... a practical journal of self reliance!

EARNING A LIVING
IN THE BACKWOODS...

METAL ROOFING

RV's AND SOLAR

WOOD COOKSTOVES

FIRE ANT INVASION

HOME REMEDIES

CENTERFIRE RIFLES

DON CHILDERS

My View

Recession and AIDS

The threat of a deepening Recession and the threat of a growing AIDS epidemic loom over America like two mindless bullies. Who will be layed off next? What friend, relative, or neighbor will become infected with the AIDS virus next?

Where do we turn for help. The Government? In my lifetime I've never known the Government to successfully grapple with a major problem. In fact the Government caused this Recession by mismanaging the economy. They raised taxes on the middle-class and further strangled business with mindless regulations and increased taxation. By the time Government finishes playing politics with the recession and AIDS, the country will be in Depression.

How about the AIDS activists? AIDS activists who hand out condoms to teen-agers as they leave school are not doing those students any favors. While giving those teen-agers condoms, I wonder if they tell them that condoms fail to do their job about 20% of the time, thus leaving them wide open to an AIDS infection? They might as well be handing out a five-chambered revolver with only one bullet in it and tell them to spin the cylinder, point the gun to their head, and shoot.

Solutions from the past

Here is an older solution that should work pretty well for both the Recession and AIDS. Go back to the way our grandparents lived and become relatively self sufficient in our family lives and relatively chaste in our personal lives.

Olga Robertson, 60, grew up on a farm in Manitoba, Canada. She said you could hardly tell the Great Depression was going on. "We read about in the newspapers," she said. "But we weren't touched by it; we were completely self sufficient. We had our animals and our food storage. The only ones who lost their farms were the ones who got too deep in debt. My father didn't believe in getting too deep in debt."

There's a lesson there for us in this Recession. Put yourself in a position so you are not dependent on a big corporation or on the Government. The company will kick you out the door when times get tough, and Government will do nothing because they have never known how to do anything right when hard times come along because the Government is usually the one who brought on the hard times in the first place with unwise spending, unbalanced budgets, and their catering to special interests groups rather than to the people at large.

Set yourself up to be a self sufficient person, not dependent on Government or big business for money. Start your own cottage business and become part of the real back-

Dave Duffy

bone of America. Don't just move to the country; also stay out of debt and work hard at your business. You'll do more good for the country than any 1,000 bureaucrats could do with their massive spending plan remedies.

It's easy for Americans to blame the country's economic woes on the Japanese, and the self-serving politicians and big business tycoons do just that every chance they get. But the Japanese are not to blame. We are. The problem with America is that too many Americans have lost the work ethic that our grandparents had. America, once the land of the free, has become the land of the free-loader. America, once the land of the brave, has become the land of the crybaby, and all the crybabies want the Government "to do something."

Forget the Government. It's time for **us** to get our work ethic back, and the only way to do that is by working hard, as individuals, for our own individual goals. If enough Americans do that, we'll kick the Recession out the kitchen door.

Now what about that other bully—AIDS. Scary isn't he. So why not avoid him the way our grandparents avoided other sexually transmitted diseases. Just say no to sex before marriage. Do I hear laughter from the more liberal readers who believe "teen-agers" are going to have sex anyway, so why not given them a condom so they'll be safe.

There is no law that says teen-agers have to go out and prove their manhood or womanhood by having sex at the earliest opportunity. It is a phenomenom of the last 30 years or so. Our grandparents—many of them— did not have sex until they were married. Is that such an old fashioned idea that it should be laughed at?

We dig up ancient herbs to cure our bodies. We delve back into time and find things like acupuncture and transcendental meditation to help relieve our pains and stress. Why not go back 40 or 50 years and dig up some old fashioned morality and common sense to help us through this AIDS epidemic.

Dave Duffy

Note from the publisher

Two-year-book

Backwoods Home Magazine: The Best of the First Two Years, our 480-page anthology of the best of our first two years worth of articles, has become an instant success. Our first printing of the book was 5,000 copies, and we sold 1124 of them before it came off the press. Not bad for an American- made product.

The book is one-inch thick and is a quality softback volume. We did not scrimp on print materials. It would look nice on your coffee table, or on a friend's. I recommend it as a nice gift for someone you like.

Hottest on the newsstand

Our distributor, American Distribution Services (ADS), tells me we are their hottest magazine on the newsstand. Yet the most frequent telephone call I get is: "I can never find you in the bookstore! Are you still in business? What stores are you in?" If you are in that boat, ask your bookstore to call ADS at 708-498-5014 and order Backwoods Home Magazine for their shelves.

But in spite of my personal frustrations at not getting BHM more widely distributed, ADS tells me we'll be printing 80,000 copies by the end of 1992.

Making a living

Notice that in this issue we have a lot of articles on "how to make a living" in the backwoods. It is one of the themes that is rarely touched upon by country magazines, yet it is the most important aspect of country living. If you can't make a living, you can't live in the country. Period. In all future issues, we will pay special attention to "how to make a living" articles. If you readers have something to share with other readers along these lines, please let me hear from you.

Shows

We'll have booths at several upcoming shows, beginning with the Environmental Exposition February 21-23 at the Ohio Expositions Center in Columbus, Ohio. We'll be at booths 211 and 213.

On March 6-8 we'll be at the Los Angeles Convention Center for the Ecological Exposition. And on June 19-21 we expect to be at the Midwest Renewable Energy Fair at the Portage County Fairgrounds in Amherst, Wisconsin.

Banned by Mother

I regret to report that Backwoods Home Magazine has once again been banned from advertising in The Mother Earth News. After Mother went "belly up" for about a year,

Ilene Duffy at work with sidekick Jacob

then was purchased by British businessman, John Colman, I assumed Mother would see the light and once again publish a magazine worth reading. She did for a couple of issues, but then began following in the steps of the old, recently departed Mother that had just folded.

Mother Earth News is a microcosm of what is wrong with America. When Mother was young, and under the guidance of John Shuttleworth, she realized that quality was what mattered. Now that she is old, and like America out of the hands of the founders who steered her straight and true, she seems to feel that gimmicks and fast-talking salesmen are all that she needs. You are wrong Mother, and you are wrong America.

I don't care if I ever advertise in Mother again. She has so lost her readership that my ads get few results. American Survival Guide and Good Old Days magazines do much better for us. But it bothers me that such a great instituion has strayed so far from a good path.

A family business

Mother Earth News should try operating like us. No big bottom line to worry about. No big advertisers to please. No big shots to wine and dine. Just us and the readers getting together for a friendly exchange of information.

This particular issue was a real family affair. Annie got a used computer and mouse for Christmas, so typed in a poem—by Linda Hutton—on page 69. Since producing "The Best of the First Two Years" book put us behind on everything else, Lenie typically has been holding baby Jacob on her lap as she typed articles or entered new subscribers into the database.

As I write, we're on deadline for this issue. It's a little past midnight. Silveira has fallen asleep on the floor. He couldn't do that in a regular office in some big company. They'd tell him to go home. I'll just trip over him in the morning when I get up to turn on my computer again.

"Want some coffee John?" I'll say.

Wow! — field-fabricated standing-seam metal roofing!

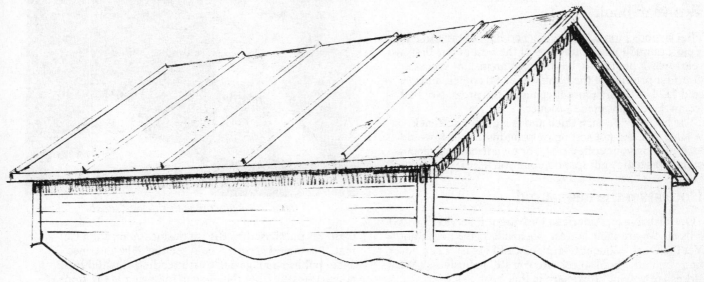

By Martin J. Harris, Jr.

Americans of the do-it-yourself persuasion display a curious kind of self-censorship in the trades they are (and are not) willing to practice. Do-it-yourself house-framing is common; do-it-yourself masonry construction is not. Do-it-yourself roofing using asphalt shingles is common; do-it-yourself metal roofing is not.

This article will pick up where my last one ("There's nothing like metal roofing" in Issue No. 13) left off and show you how easy it is to execute high-quality metal roofing, and thereby, perhaps put a dent (no pun intended) into the self-censorship which exists in that particular trade area.

In terms of function—keeping the weather out—all kinds of metal roofing, both field-fabricated and factory-manufactured, are high quality. When applied in accordance with manufacturer's instructions or generally accepted trade standards, they'll perform well. In fact, they're less subject to accidents of natural or human origin than, for example, shingle roofing systems.

Standing-seam design

Nevertheless, I want to focus here on metal roofing of the field-fabricated variety. Just about anyone will take the dare to install a nail-on metal-roof, but few will tackle the traditional standing-seam design. That's a shame, for it's a great system with fine qualities of function, appearance, and even history to its credit.

Good results in standing-seam roofing start with a nice, smooth wooden roof deck. No ridges at the plywood edges, no raised nailheads, no dirt on the deck: they'll quickly telegraph their presence through the relatively thin sheet metal. If the deck isn't a perfect rectangle, not to worry—standing-seam can accommodate to such problems as stamped metal panels usually can't. For our purposes building a single-lock roof system, a deck slope of 3:12 is the minimum acceptable; pitches down to 1:12, if necessary, can be accommodated with a double-lock system which is somewhat more complicated to install.

Felt and edge-strip

Atop the deck goes a layer of 15-lb. roofing felt. You can staple it down if you plan on finishing the roof quickly, but roofing nails and washers are better if even a few days of weather exposure are possible. Run the felts horizontally and lap them about 3 inches or so at the seams.

On the deck edges eaves and gable rakes, but not the ridge goes a continuous band of metal edge-strip. You can buy these pre-shaped or you can make your own. Any design is OK as long as it offers a projection of about an inch over which the roofing-panel edges can be bent, and the other leg can be nailed to the deck, or the roof facia. The edge-strip should be 28-gauge galvanized stock (26 or 24, being heavier, are of course better, but 28 gauge has been used with fine results for many decades), same as the roofing itself. All nails should, of course, be galvanized, too.

Comes in coil form

The roofing stock itself comes in coil form, usually rolls 26 inches wide and 100 feet long. (Other sizes are available, if you prefer a narrower or wider seam spacing on the finish roof.) For our purposes, let's use the 26-inch width. For a single-lock standing-seam, we'll need to bend one edge up

This photo shows felts and eave edge strips in place, as roof panel installation proceeds. Roof pitch at 6:12 is steeper than it appears.

the first set of nailing tabs. You make these up, also of 28-gauge stock, to dimensions of about 2x4 inches. Make a lot of these tabs, because you'll need one for every two feet of panel seam. Fold them at the half-point so that they make a right angle. Then, starting at the center seam line, nail down each tab with a single roofing nail, so that 2 inches of tab lies flat on the deck and two inches stands up vertically. With the first run of tabs in place, we're ready to install the first panel.

Installing the panels

Cut the panel length so that it's about three inches longer than the roof deck dimension; if you know the deck is perfectly rectangular, you can cut the panel more precisely to allow 3/4 inch overlap at the eave and a full inch

at right angles for a height of, say, one inch. We'll bend the other edge up 1.5 inches, so that when it goes on the roof it stands next to the one-inch leg of the adjacent panel and the half-inch overlap can be bent over and crimped tight to form a watertight seam. Taller seam heights are OK, if you wish, as long as the bend-over flange is about a half-inch taller than the receiving flange on the adjacent panel.

These flange allowances will take up 2.5 inches of the overall 26 inch panel width, so when we go to lay out the roof

pattern on the deck, we'll use a seam spacing of 23.5 inches. The final product will look best if you start at the center of the roof and work to the two gables, where the last panels need not be standard width anyway, since they will be cut about 3/4 inch too wide and that overlap bent tight around the edge-strip.

Nailing tabs

Having chalked the seam pattern on the roofing felts, we're ready to install

Here the standing seam is being closed by bending over the longer flange with a hard rubber mallet.

overlap at the ridge. Place the panel on the deck, hard up against the tabs already nailed down, and hold it there (a helper is useful here) while you bring up and place the second panel so that the tabs are sandwiched between the two standing flanges. Bend the taller flange over the shorter one, including all the tabs in the bend as you go; cut off any tab length which projects, and go back over your bend a second time, crimping it good and tight and making a good sharp standing seam. At this point the tabs are holding the two panels firmly onto the deck along the seam between them, and you'll no

Roofer installs a nailing tab adjacent to the last sheet set. Note how the sheet overlaps the ridge with enough material to construct the ridge joint.

The Third Year

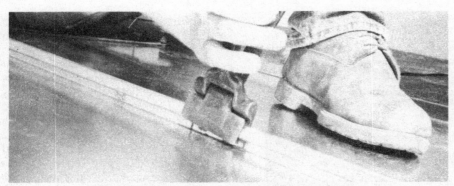

Once bent, the seam is crimped tight with a pair of crimpers.

Helper flanges a sheet on a work table at ground level.

longer need that extra set of hands. You're now ready to install the next set of tabs, along the loose edge of the installed panel.

With the tabs in place, bring the next panel up onto the deck, slide it up against the tabs, and fold the overlapping flange over as you did the first one. Keep repeating the process until you get to the last seam before the gable edge of the roof. On that seam you install the tabs as before, but when you cut the last panel, make it only 3/4 inch wider than the remaining exposed roof deck and flange it only on the inboard side. Once up on the roof and the standing seam crimped tight, the outboard overlap is bent over the edge- strip and also crimped tight.

Finishing the edges

At this point, each panel has two unfinished edges; eave and ridge. Finish the eave edge by folding the overhanging 3/4 inch back under the

edge-strip and crimp it tight—you'll find it makes a better bend if you nip off the corners at 45 degrees. Finish the ridge edge by bending it so it stands straight up in the air. Cut it to a 1-inch height, so that when the matching panel from the opposite side of the roof is placed against it, cut off at 2 inches, and bent over, the 1-inch flange of the first panel is completely enclosed in the standing seam thus created. If you live in an area with heavy doses of wind-driven rain, you may wish to caulk that joint with silicone before you crimp it tight.

The description so far explains fabrication of a simple pitched roof without valleys, dormers, or other complications. It illustrates the basic principle involved: all edges are manufactured by folding adjacent sheets over each other, and incorporating hold-down tabs in the folded seam. Since the nails holding the tabs to the deck are in all cases concealed, it can be described as a concealed-fastener system (as opposed to nail-on systems, where various gasketing and caulking materials are used to make the exposed fasteners waterproof).

The same principle prevails where complications occur. Examples:

Once flanged, up the ladder it goes. Note edge-strip at eave and rake.

The Third Year

For long slopes

If your roof slope is too long for you to handle a single sheet covering from ridge to eave, you could consider multiple sheets, each with the same sort of folded overlap at top and bottom horizontal edges. If your sheet length is, say, 8 feet, you may find it convenient to have the flanges pre-bent in a sheet-metal shop using a mechanical

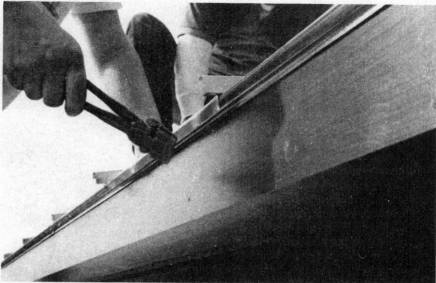

Using crimpers, the roofer bends the eave overlap around the edge strip.

The 3/4-inch overlap at the eave is about to be bent around the edge-strip. Note the roofer taking 45-degree cuts at the corners.

break, thus saving a lot of time and producing much more precise bends.

For valleys

If your roof design incorporates a valley, flash it with half-coil width material (13 inches) with each edge flanged back an inch. Then each roofing sheet which ends at the flashing has a 3/4 inch flange to fold under the valley flange: hammered flat, the joint thus created sheds snow, ice, and rain perfectly. For extra insurance, you may wish to use silicone caulk. Valley flanges can be secured to the roof deck

with tabs installed so they engage the valley flange but not the roofing panel flange.

For walls

If your plan incorporates a side-wall flashing situation (a chimney or dormer, for example) simply allow enough panel width so that you can fold about 6 inches up (rather than the usual 3/4 inch down) as a base flash. The counter flash, then, secured into the brickwork of the chimney or the sideall of the dormer, overlaps the base flashing in traditional fashion. If you like you can create a folded joint for more security against leakage.

For pipe projections

If you need to deal with projecting waste line vents or similar items requiring cuts in the middle of a panel, you won't be able to use a typical folded-seam design. Your best bet is a purchase-item flashing pre-cut to the appropriate pipe diameter, which you then seal to the panel surface by means of soldering or silicone caulk. For the latter you may not be able to avoid a few exposed fasteners, as the caulk alone won't make a mechanically strong joint.

What about maintenance: Should you paint a galvanized standing-seam

The roof was too long to be done with full-length panels. Here a panel folded at the top horizontal edge awaits the next sheet.

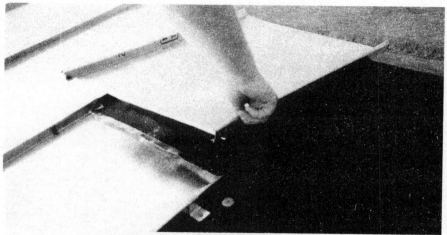

Here's the next sheet. Note the fold in its bottom edge to engage the sheet already in place.

Whether you paint or not, sit back and enjoy your roof. You've just joined an architectural tradition and a construction trade with roots at least eight centuries deep.

Footnote: for craftsmen who like to work "by the book" no better guide exists than the "Architectural Sheet Metal Manual" published by SMAC-NA, the Sheet Metal and Air Conditioning Contractors National Association. At about $80 or so, it's a bit pricey, but well worth it for serious would-be tin-knockers. The illustrations of complicated seaming folds are amazingly clear and well worth the price. Send your check to P.O. Box 221230, Chantilly, VA 22022 after

roof? Only if you don't like the silvery color, which will change to dull grey after a year or so. Rust won't be a problem unless you're located near salt water or unless you've got some dissimilar metals up on the roof (a TV antenna, for example) causing electrolytic action at the drip line. In that situation you'll lose the protective zinc coating of the 28 gauge coil stock rather quickly. If you choose to paint, you'll have to remove the manufacturing oil before the paint will adhere; the alternative is to allow natural weathering a season or so to remove the oil for you. Use any paint labelled for application to metallic surfaces.

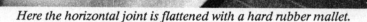

Here the horizontal joint is flattened with a hard rubber mallet.

verifying the exact cost.

(Martin Harris is a Vermont architect, cofounder of the New England Builder, and author of numerous articles on home building. Photos in this article are of the McClintic Family Roofers, Charlotte, VT.) Δ

Among other things, this view clearly shows an expanse of finished roof surface.

Marvels in small packages

By Marjorie Burris

This spring when you are startled by a small, brightly colored, long-billed bird zipping in and out of your line of vision, stop, locate the bird, and enjoy watching its antics for awhile. You are privileged to be seeing a hummingbird, the smallest of all birds. The hummingbird is a marvelous creation with strength and capabilities far beyond what would appear to be possible in a speck of life that weighs less than four ounces.

Found only in the Americas

Although there are about 750 species and sub-species of hummingbirds, most of the birds live in the Andes Mountains regions of Columbia and Ecuador. Only about 15 species of the feisty little birds nest north of Mexico, and only one specie—the Ruby-throated Hummingbird—nests east of the Great Plains in the eastern part of the United States. The Rufous (meaning reddish) Hummingbird flies farther north than any other hummer and nests in Alaska. All hummers migrate south of the U.S. for the winter and most winter as far south as Central and South America.

Fly at 55 mph

After migrating to the southern states, the Ruby-throats fly across the Gulf of Mexico some 500 to 600 miles non-stop to their winter home! Since a Ruby-throat has been clocked at 55 miles an hour, this figures out to be a trip of at least ten to twelve hours without rest or food with an average wing motion of 55 strokes a **second**. This means the bird flaps its wings 3,300 times a minute, 198,000 times an hour, and almost two million times in a single flight over the Gulf. One

wonders that the wings stay attached with such rapid, continuous use.

Heart rate 8 times a human's

All the motions of a hummingbird are quick and lively. A hummer's heart beats 615 times a minute (the human heart ideally beats 72 times a minute) and food is soon used up. Because a hummer expends so much energy, the birds must eat almost constantly during daylight hours. The birds drink nectar from flowers, thrusting their long bills deep into a blossom and transferring pollen from flower to flower in the process. They also sip tree sap, and with their long tongues, flick out aphids, small insects and spiders from under tree bark and from inside blossoms. A mother hummingbird will feed her babies at least once every 15 minutes during the day with the partially digested nectar and insects she has collected by pushing her long bill deep into the nestlings' throats. A hungry little hummingbird, especially one with babies to feed, can do as much good as several bees and more good than three cans of bug dust—without the toxic effect of chemicals.

They even fly backwards

All species of hummers have many things in common: unlike any other bird, hummers can fly backwards, or straight up or straight down. They can also hover, and are able to drink

flower nectar without actually landing on the blossom.

They are pugnacious and will defend their nest fiercely, driving away predators many times larger than themselves. No hummer is larger than about five and one-half inches long, and most are three to three and one-half inches long. Their feathers are usually iridescent, and most males in all species have jewel-like throat feathers called gorgets.

All make tiny cup-like nests of lichens, bits of leaves or soft grasses which they bind together and to a bush or tree branch with spiders web. All hummers lay two little, completely-white eggs no bigger than a white pea bean which take about 15 days to hatch. Though their calls are different, all hummers make some kind of shrill, squeaky notes and a whirring sound with their wings, hence the common name "hummingbird".

A bird's feet tells how it lives. For example, a bird with a webbed foot lives on or near water and uses the foot like a paddle for swimming and diving; a bird with long, sharp claws uses its feet to catch and hold its food. The hummingbird, like the swift, has weak feet and legs and cannot run or hop, but uses its strong wings while gathering food. Hummers do not fall off their perch while asleep because each toe is connected with a cord inside the leg. When the leg is bent, the cords stretch tight and pull the toes around the branch binding the bird onto the branch.

Identification of a hummer is easy in the eastern half of the United States: there is only one specie and it is the beautiful Ruby-throated hummingbird which comes to mind when thinking of hummingbirds. The Ruby-throat has a metallic green back, forked tail and the male has a fiery vermillion-red throat which gives it its name. The female, however, has a white throat and is virtually indistinguishable from several other species of birds found in the western part of the U.S.

One of the easier to distinguish hummingbirds of the west is Anna's Hummingbird which summers mostly in California. This bird looks very much like the Ruby-throat, except the red of its throat extends up to and covers the crown of its head.

The Rufous Hummingbird, another recognizable western specie, is mostly red-brown with an iridescent orange-red throat and sides of the head. It summers as far north as Alaska as well as across most of the western U.S. It is the most fierce fighter of all the hummingbirds.

A third easily recognized western specie is the Black-chinned Hummingbird. It has a blackish metallic-green back with a black throat bordered with iridescent purple. It has a slightly forked tail and lives in dry scrub, woodlands near streams, wooded canyons and mountain meadows all through the west.

Because so many species of hummingbirds have such minute differences in their markings, I would refer you to Roger Tory Peterson's book, *A Field Guide to Western Birds* for more technical and detailed explanations for identification of other hummers.

It is easy to attract hummingbirds with a feeder filled with sugar water made of one cup sugar dissolved in two cups of water. There are many inexpensive ready-made feeders on the market, but a small glass bottle partly painted with red nail polish and hung about five feet off the ground will make an irresistible feeder. There are two drawbacks to sugar-water feeders however: bees will come in abundance as well as hummers, and, once started, a feeder should not be discontinued for the rest of the season. The birds quickly become dependent upon the feeder and will starve if the feeder is not filled every day. This can get to be a very expensive, if entertaining, project.

A better way to attract the helpful little birds is to plant vines and flowers they like. They especially like red, orange, or red-orange tubular flowers. In the west the Hummingbird trumpet (Zauschneria californica) is a natural for the birds. It has beautiful, long red tubular flowers. It grows easily in seemingly inhospitable habitats, including desert lowland and high barren ridges, on cliffs and rocky streambeds — all places the hummingbirds like as well.

Other tubular flowers such as the honeysuckles, are attractive to hummingbirds as well as some purple and blue colored flowers including vinca and chicory. Most good nurseries have a long list of plants desirable to hummingbirds, and will help you select those which grow well in your area.

How to feed a baby hummer

At some time or another you might find a baby hummer stranded out of its nest and unable to care for itself. The best thing to do is put the baby back into the nest and stand well away from the nest so the mother will come back if she is able. Discreetly watch the nest for a couple of hours, and if the mother returns, fine. If she doesn't return, you may want to become a surrogate parent to the tiny creature.

If the nest is where you can reach it easily, leave the baby in the nest and only take it out for feeding. If the nest is hard to reach, break off the branch with the nest attached and put it in a place where the baby will be safe and warm. The nest is the most secure surrounding for the baby and should be used until the baby is able to be on its own.

To handle a baby hummer, or any hand size bird for that matter, grasp the bird firmly without squeezing with the bird's back in the palm of the hand. Let the head extend between the first finger and the middle finger, then close the thumb and the fingers comfortably around the bird. Turn your palm up so that the bird is laying on its back. Turned over on its back, the bird stops struggling and seems to relax and lose its fear.

To feed a baby hummingbird, make a syrup of one part sugar to two parts water. Force the liquid down the bird's mouth with a long medicine dropper. After about ten days give the little bird its first protein by mixing a very small amount of pablum or finely sifted dog food into the sugar-water. You should feed a baby bird often during the day; remember its mother would feed it about every 15 minutes. And you should especially feed it at night before it goes to sleep. However, young birds should be handled as little as possible, and they should not be fed too much at a time. Being a parent to a hummingbird is an awesome task, probably only equaled to being a parent to a newborn preemie human baby.

For the past 12 years my forest-ranger neighbor has put out sugar-water hummingbird feeders. A meticulous diary keeper, he has recorded every year the dates when the hummers appeared and when they left. Recently he went through his records and was astounded to find that the birds have appeared every year within a 48 hour period the middle of March, and they have left within three days of the same time the last of October.

Since we are very close to the same latitude as San Juan Capistrano in California, we have wondered if there is any connection between the migration habits of our hummingbirds and the famed Swallows of the California Mission which appear every year about March 19 and leave around October 23.

If you decide to become an observer of the tiny, but marvelous, hummingbird, you might find it interesting to keep records and see if the birds are as punctual in your area as they are in our mountains.

Yes, wonderful things do come in small packages.

For more reading:
Peterson, R.T., Field Guide to Western Birds
Lincoln, F.C., Migration of Birds
Pettit, T.S., Birds in Your Backyard
Mason, C.R., Picture Primer of Attracting Birds (a good book for children) Δ

Greechie, the hummingbird!

By Marjorie Burris

According to the papers filed at the county courthouse in Prescott, Husband and I own Homestead Entry Number 77, Yavapai County, Arizona. I really should go and have the papers changed. But somehow I'm just not up to standing on one foot, then the other, while some clerk with one eyebrow raised two inches above the other looks at me and says, "You wanna change the ownership of the Homestead to a hummingbird? We don't have the forms for that."

I first met the daring little bird last spring while I was bent over dropping pea seeds into the garden. I was wearing my new pioneer-days style red calico sunbonnet, made for me by my artsy-craftsy sister, when all of a sudden — THUMP — something hit the brim of my hat. Startled, I jerked up just in time to see a tiny bird flying away from me. Then, the bird stopped, reversed gears, and flew **backwards**. It hovered right in front of my face, and looked me straight in the eyes! Bright green feathers covered her back. Her throat and underside were white, and she had a long, needle-like bill. Her wings were beating so fast they were just a blur. From the tip of her beak to the tip of her tail she was less than four inches long.

"Hello!" I said, surprised. "And who are you?"

"Greech, greech," she squeaked in a loud voice and circled my head. So — I named her "Greechie".

But then she flew up a few feet above my head and made a kamikaze-style dive right into the crown of my hat! Before I could duck, she flew at me again, and again, and again, beating her wings so fiercely that I thought she would hurt herself and tear my hat. Finally, I dropped my peas and ran to the house with Greechie dive-bombing my hat all the way.

"Help!" I shouted to Husband in the house. He pushed open the screen door and slammed it after me, just barely missing Greechie as she went into formation for another attack.

"That's FUNNY!" Husband laughed. "Beat up by a hummingbird!"

I didn't think it was so funny. I decided I'd better read up on hummingbirds. I found out that hummingbirds are the only birds that can fly backwards, that their wings beat 55 times a **second** when they fly, and that they are particularly attracted to

things colored red.

So I tried an experiment. If I wore my old ragged sombrero, Greechie would fly circles around my head and call her funny little greeting. But if I wore my sunbonnet, she immediately began to attack me. That little bird weighing less than a MacDonalds quarter-pounder hamburger made me put my red hat away for the rest of the summer.

One day I noticed Greechie flying back and forth to a dark spot on a low juniper branch hanging over the front gate to the garden. I got the step-ladder and carefully climbed up to where I could see. Stuck on the branch was a little nest about the size and shape of a one-fourth cup measure. Inside the nest was a tiny white egg which looked just like a small white soup bean. I did not touch the nest, but quickly took

down the ladder and left. For a month we walked all the way around the garden to the back gate so we wouldn't disturb Greechie in her house keeping duties. She eventually hatched and raised a teensy baby, a miniature copy of herself.

When the weather got warm Greechie began taking a bath in the drinking fountain. Just outside our back door we have a spring-fed fountain which bubbles all the time. The water shoots up about five inches above the top of the fountain with such force that we get our faces wet every time we take a drink. We call the fountain "Old Faceful".

Greechie would hover on one side of Old Faceful picking up speed, then dash through the water. On the other side she would turn and fly back through the cascade like a dare-devil flying through Niagara Falls. I was afraid the strong force of the water would wash her down the drain, so I set a lawn sprinkler with a gentle spray beside the fountain. She ignored the sprinkler and continued to take her daily bath in Old Faceful.

Our family traditionally celebrates the fourth of July with a picnic and we always have watermelon for dessert. Greechie hovered nearby while we ate our sandwiches, but when we cut the watermelon, she went wild! She zoomed down and stuck her bill in the juice of the cut melon. And once, when Husband tried to take a bite of melon, she actually stuck her bill in the piece he was lifting to his mouth!

We tried to shoo her away. She refused to leave. Fearing we would get a bite of hummingbird, we left a piece of melon on the picnic table and retreated to the screened-in front porch. Eating watermelon on the porch wasn't much fun though. We couldn't have our annual seed spitting contest.

Now I ask you, "Who **really** owns the old homestead?" Δ

> "A free people ought to be armed."
>
> George Washington

Now that you have your little slice of heaven, how do you go about paying for it?

By Michael G. Hart

To those of us who own our little slice of heaven, or are planning to, there is no greater benefit than the freedom to enjoy our hard-won backwoods home by making our living there as well.

When I was young, I owned a company called General Enterprises. I rounded up a bunch of friends and passed out fliers that said that we would do just about anything as long as it was legal. In a few weeks, we were on the front page of The San Jose Mercury News and were getting hundreds of phone calls. We washed cars, painted houses, walked dogs, held garage sales, baby-sat, mowed lawns and cleaned-up some really disgusting garages. In short, we were willing to do things that other people didn't want to do. We had no real cash investment in our business and our labor was free. The idea here is that there are opportunities all around you, the question is: Is there enough money to be made to justify your time?

What does it take?

Since that first business, I have owned a dozen different ventures. Some were successes, but I also learned a lot of hard lessons in ways how **not** to make a million dollars. I have found that you need three things to be an entrepreneur:

the idea
the resources to make that idea real
the determination to make it happen

The idea

The first prerequisite for a home business, the idea, can be easy. I have found that good ideas are a dime a dozen. I have drawers full of products and services that I see the need for, but lack the other two ingredients to make real. A quick look around you will provide you a host of possibilities: even looking in the back of this magazine will give you ideas others have to offer. The only word of caution I would add is to make certain that the idea is one that is either currently in demand, or one that you are certain will be in demand once you begin. This may sound obvious, but I know of many people who had a great idea for something that they needed or wanted and just assumed that everyone else would too. I have to admit that a number of my ideas remain in the drawer because they are things for which I would be the sole customer!

Resources

The second ingredient for your own business is the resources necessary to make your idea a reality. This requires a careful look at what you have to offer. You need to compare the requirements of your idea with your circumstances. Becoming a computer programmer requires lengthy and expensive training: becoming a car washer, less so. You need to review your talents and resources to see what you are able to provide. Talent is an important resource; there is no point in becoming an artist just because you have a garage full of canvas and a barrel full of paint. If you lack the prerequisite talent to make salable art, try opening an art supply store instead!

Determination

The final element for becoming an entrepreneur is the determination to accomplish your objective. Whether that objective is to make money, see an idea become reality, or start a family business you must have the determination to see it through. I work at my home perched high on a mountain, out of sight and out of mind of the rest of the world. Sometimes it would be so easy to let the answering machine take the calls and slip down the hill to the Redwood grove where I can forget about the idea that I am championing. Sometimes, I admit, temptation wins...

If you choose the path of an entrepreneur, you alone are responsible to make the phone ring. If you fail to send out letters, don't look crestfallen when the mailman arrives with nothing more than a batch of Victoria's Secret catalogs. You need to plan every day. You are the boss. You are the only one who can make certain that the sun will never set on a day when you haven't made a buck.

Sound like more than you want to handle? Get a real job. Just because I am an advocate for the life of an entrepreneur doesn't mean that I advocate it for everyone. People are different. I would make a lousy employee. I tried it once and found that I was always trying to reinvent the process or the product. Some people need another person to set their schedule. Others need the absolute assurance that barring corporate takeover they will get a paycheck each week. But for the entrepreneur, there are risks to be taken. The future is an empty book waiting for them to provide the story.

Don't waste capital

I have given lectures on starting businesses and am often asked by students how it is possible for someone just starting out to afford starting a business. Many people have the mistaken image that business people look like a character in "L.A. Law," wearing tailored Italian suits and those awful power ties. I have seen more start-up businesses waste precious capital on walnut walls instead of setting money aside for the inevitable bad months ahead. A business can start with nothing. In fact, the best businesses often do. *Backwoods Home Magazine* is an example.

Where I grew up, Bill Hewlett and David Packard started a huge corporation out of a small garage. Steves Wozniak and Jobs launched Apple Computers out of a two-car garage down the street from where I went to high school. All of their resources were poured into the idea, not trappings of a business front. Ken Hakuta, known as "Dr. Fad" for his phenomenally successful "Wacky Wall Walker," started his enterprise on an ironing board and eschewed expensive business cards in favor of putting all he owned into his product. There will come a time when your business can afford to pay for some luxuries, but for right now, focus on what it will take to bring your idea to market as inexpensively as possible.

Tools of the trade

If you are going to sell products, I highly recommend getting an account with United Parcel Service (UPS). They can find even the most remote home and are the backbone of any product-oriented business. If your product is something that you plan to make yourself, raw materials can come in to you via their big brown trucks, and your finished product can go out with them as well. In my area they charge about $5 per week to stop by my house each day to see if I have anything going out. If your product will be something made elsewhere, UPS is still a must. You will also need boxes, tape, labels, and a scale (a bathroom scale will do) for shipping. You should plan on putting together some promotional literature on what you have to sell. If you plan to take orders over the phone, you will need either an answering machine, or an answering service. Some of these ser-

vices can provide 24-hour 800-number service for about fifty dollars per month. To the rest of the world, you can look like any New York-based catalog company, but there you are, out by the creek, waiting for the orders to roll in.

Manufacturing

You will find that no matter how unusual your idea is, someone, somewhere makes something similar. The trick is to see if the company making that product would be willing to make your product as well for less than it would cost you to set-up your own assembly line. More often than not, I have found that an established manufacturer is willing to produce my product for a fraction of what it would cost to make it myself. Often, they are even willing to make a limited run of your product, so that you might test the waters for a higher per-item cost. Don't expect to make any money on your first sales; just do it to find out if there is a demand at the price that you need.

When I started making "Mai-Tie" Hawaiian neckties, I was spending over $4 per tie, and I had a very difficult time getting any sort of volume to market. I found a tie manufacturer that was willing (though he thought my idea of cotton Hawaiian ties was crazy) to make my ties using his staff and high-volume equipment for just $2 per tie. The ties arrived at my home and I repackaged them and sent them out to my wholesale customers for $8 each. In addition, I sold directly to individual customers for $20 per tie! What I found was that the real money is in selling the product, not making it. For the manufacturer, all of his costs are already sunk, and he has a huge payroll to meet. Sometimes the line is slow or idle and sending someone else's product through it is just so much extra profit.

Intellectual properties

Many of my students asked what kind of protection I used when approaching other businesses with my ideas. I encourage them to not be too

worried about the other guy running off with your idea. The sad truth is that there are very few new things under the sun. If your idea is truly novel, then most people will take a wait-and-see approach to see if it succeeds. "It's easy to spot the pioneers; they're the ones with the arrows sticking out of their backs" goes the manufacturer's motto! If anyone does decide to copy

you, it will be after the product has proven itself in the marketplace. At this point your own manufacturer (who is succeeding with you) will be the least of your worries.

It is prudent to keep good records of your relationship with your manufacturer and those that you approach before the idea hits the streets. There are lots of books on intellectual property rights. Your specific situation is unique, and you may need more protection than I have suggested. I also strongly recommend that you trademark your name and copyright any text that is uniquely valuable for your idea. I once failed to get a trademark for $200 when I had the chance, assuring myself that I could get one once the product proved successful. Ten thousand dollars in attorney fees later, I finally eliminated the last competitor who decided to use the name that I had popularized.

In my opinion, the patent is over-rated and usually is little more than expensive ornamentation. If you wait until you get your invention fully patented before you try to bring it to market, it can be like selling eight-track tape players to Compact Disk owners. Too many inventors mistakenly believe that their better mousetrap is so valuable that anyone would want to steal it from them and that they will only be safe under a patent. An idea is not like wine; it does not get better with aging. Move it before the moment passes. I believe that if anyone started selling better mousetraps, all the inventors of the world would beat a path to their door, with their own versions of course!

Knowledge-based business

If you have a reliable power source, and at least one direct phone line, you are ready to sell your knowledge to the world at large. The question is what knowledge do you have for which others would pay? If you have a unique hobby or specialty that others could use, there may be an option. If you have just bailed out of a particular profession or industry, there may be a future for you mining your past.

If you have some sort of knowledge or skill that a company was willing to pay you for before, there is the possibility that you can find gainful employment as a consultant. A consultant is a valuable asset to a company in hard financial times; you don't ask for health care, benefits, a parking space or a "golden parachute." They ask you to do a job that you are able to do, and you are paid for the job. When a lay-off strikes a company and people hit the streets, more often than not, many of those ex-employees are brought back in as consultants to fill vital roles that cannot be filled by the remaining workers. Often these returning workers find themselves earning far more as a consultant than they ever did as an employee. The biggest bonus comes when you are struggling with a big project on a weekend just as you did as an employee, but now you are getting paid for it!

To get started in consulting you need a few vital tools, these include a business card that is neat and accurately describes your specialty, a sizable rolodex (or your old company's directory), a facsimile machine, and a good telephone. Stationery is a must if you are going to correspond with your customers through the mail, or deliver any sort of written reports. Get a comfortable desk with a good light and leave room for your reference library and a filing cabinet.

The ubiquitous fax

I know it sounds trite, but the fax is really the way business communicates; without one, you simply are left out. A relative in the timber industry receives faxes from perspective buyers, cuts their name off the top, puts their order on his own stationery, and faxes it to his suppliers for bids. The incoming bids have their prices added to his outgoing fax and the customer's order comes back the same way. His business is one of huge orders and narrow margins; it would be impossible without the fax. I was forced by customers to buy a fax and now will never go back. There is something about waking up in the morning and shuffling to my office in my bathrobe to find that my east coast and European customers have been thinking of me while I slept. Nothing like having a huge order sitting on your desk before you've even had a chance to shave...

Our friend, the computer?

Why not a computer? Sorry folks, the big computer productivity hype was just that, so much hype. Most studies of the American workplace have found scant gains to those companies that bought in on the computer revolution. Even those gains are eroded when you consider the incredible capital expense that went into buying the hardware, software, and training. Their only new use seems to be mid-level managers using Lotus 1-2-3 to keep track of their stock portfolio and to count-down how many days till retirement. What I am saying is that there is no prerequisite for having a computer just because you are going into business for yourself. This is not to say that they are not useful to specific businesses; for many tasks they are invaluable! First evaluate what your business needs to do to function, and then decide if any of those tasks really need to be automated.

For most people, their real assets are between their ears, and a computer can be just an expensive typewriter. I say this as a software designer and developer. For many people, the immense amount of time you will spend setting-up a computer, learning a few rudimentary programs, and at least a half-dozen video games, would be better spent on the phone. Just like the fancy office and power suits, their time will come. For now, put the two grand you would have dropped on a computer into a fax and some phone time to drum up some business!

Service business

By far the most approachable business for most of us is the service sector business. If you are skilled in one of the trades, you already know how to make a living! For the backwoods handyman who is truly a jack-of-all-trades, perhaps there is a small industry in taking care of your neighbors needs for a small fee. Where I live I could use such a person just about every day.

You can charge by either the hour or the job. As you get proficient at what you do, you'll discover the secret that makes lawyers rich...after you do something once, the next time is far easier and takes far less time. You will find that billing by the hour as you learn is a smart way to start. As you get proficient with your job you will see how much customers seem comfortable paying. Use that as your fixed price and work like mad to beat your old time! My attorney once charged me 10 hours at $250 per hour to "draw up a contract." He had thoughtfully typed my name at the top of one he had already stored on his computer. It was how long it had taken him the first time...

If you do have a skill, like being able to repair small engines, replace broken windows, fix locks, install solar panels, or design rural water systems, you could have a viable business. Find out what other people in such a business charge in your area, and try to offer more service for less money.

If there is no one offering the service in your area, you have either a potential monopoly or an idea that is impractical for your area. Try to find a neighboring area that has someone who does what you want to do, find out what they charge and double it! Just kidding. No need to gouge your neighbors. In fact, when you talk to a customer about say, sweeping their chimney, don't just think of it as a $100 job. They will need to have their chimney swept every year. Let's say that you moved up to your backwoods home and are planning to live there for at least 30 years; that neighbor is worth $3,000 to you. Not to mention the word-of-mouth sales that you could get from a satisfied customer.

There is a whole religion of customer satisfaction with Tom Peters as the crusading leader. If you chose to go into a service business, or any business for that matter, I strongly suggest that you read at least one of his books.

Now, what if you are living someplace where there just aren't enough neighbors to support your proposed 24-hour cuckoo clock repair service? This is where our friends UPS and the U.S. Postal Service come into play. Anything that you can fix has someone who may want to have it fixed by you. Frequently, if the item you are most skilled at working on is odd or rare, there will be other people across the country or around the world with the same interest. Try advertising your skills in magazines, newspapers, and computer bulletin boards and see if you can have them send the work to you. You then have the freedom to set your own hours, doing what you want to do, in the place where you would most like to be. I'm certain that many readers are nodding over this article as they sit in their workshop filled with cuckoo clocks that they make a living fixing. Again, think about your resources and see what it is that you can do that would make your time valuable to others.

Marketing $ $ $

For any of these businesses there is the obvious prerequisite that you have customers of some sort. The question is how do you get to them? You need to reach your customers in as inexpensive and direct a way as possible. It is too expensive to use the "shotgun" of television to spread your message to thousands of viewers, when your small market is best reached with the "rifle" of a few well placed classified ads. If you are going to sell hardwood walking sticks by mail, then by all means advertise in walking magazines. If you are going to offer a service that covers a broad area, "let your fingers do the walking." If perchance you want to repair a rare and specialized item, be sure to advertise where owners of those items will look. If you intend to consult, not only should you attend professional conferences, but you should advertise in the appropriate literature as well. I strongly recommend "Ogilvy on Advertising" if you want to explore the mind of the true advertising expert.

To fill your mailbox with incoming checks, one should fill it first with outgoing direct mail. Depending on what your product, service or field is, there is probably a list of names out there for you. By renting a list from a list broker (look under Mailing Lists in the Yellow Pages) you get a very narrowly defined set of mailing labels for people that you think will be prospective customers. For example, you could ask for a list of only homeowners in your county that own swimming pools and have incomes over $50,000 per year. For your business with the cuckoo clocks, you may be able to rent the list of people who belong to a club for clock fanciers, subscribers to clock magazines, or the list of people who have purchased items from your competition! It's all out there. All you need is the right product or service coupled with a good price wrapped up with the right message.

For one of my businesses, I decided to go the direct mail route. My wife and I spent weeks stuffing thousands of letters with our marketing letter, return envelope, order form, and catalog sheets. The problem was we bought the mailing labels from the lowest bidder who maintained a lousy list. After all of that work, a full 25% of the letters came back marked "Undeliverable." We spent months haggling with the company that sold us the list. The best we got was a refund for the cost of the list. I had been told that the industry standard for responses was 2-5%; we were greatly disappointed to find that a fraction of a percent of our total mailing responded with an order. In later mailings I went to reputable brokers, got really refined lists that had been recently updated, and got much better responses. If you want more information about selling by mail, I recommend the comprehensive "Direct Marketing" by E.L. Nash.

Other sorts of marketing include display advertising in newspapers and magazines and their much less expensive cousin—classified advertising. When you run such an ad, your product or service will be visible to a large number of potential customers. The key is picking the right publication. You can ask the advertising department of just about any magazine or newspaper for their demographics and pricing. Compare their readership carefully to what you perceive to be your target market. If you find a suitable publication, try to negotiate a reasonable price for your first ad. You may find that they are willing to come down on price if you are willing to be flexible about which issue you go in and where your ad is placed. Always give your potential customer an easy way to order or respond. Look at similar ads in the publication that come back month after month; their style clearly is suited to the tastes of the readership.

Of all the marketing techniques, none even approaches the value of meeting your prospective customer face-to-face. I once flew to England (strictly on business) to meet with a potential customer; his opening order paid for the entire trip! This was a customer who was impossible to deal with over the phone and who ignored my direct mail. Going there to meet with the buyer directly and to share my enthusiasm with him made it all possible. There is no better salesman for your product than you. No one can have as much enthusiasm, or has at much at stake as you do. If you ever wanted to travel, owning your own business is the best way to do it; not only is it a way to expand your market, but much of it is tax-deductible!

Tradeshows are another good way to meet with potential customers. The only drawback is that they are usually held in cities like New York City or Las Vegas, exactly what we have moved away from! A tradeshow has thousands of booths filled with vendors like you dwarfed by county-sized booths of the few large companies that dominate your industry. Into this arena come thousands of buyers from all over the country or region. They usually spend almost all of their money on those products from the big vendors, but everyone is looking for a bit of something different. This is where you come in. If you were clever and called prospective customers weeks ahead and made appointments, you may get a brief chance to sell your product face-to-face with that buyer from Macy's.

If you don't know anything about the tradeshows in your prospective industry, ask the buyer of a store you want to market what tradeshows he or she attends. Contact the tradeshow and ask for literature on displaying your goods at the show. A tradeshow can be very expensive, but it is one of the best ways to get your product in front of the largest market possible all at once. If you want to find out what stores are out there and who does their buying, I suggest that you obtain a copy of the Buyer Guide for that particular industry. Buyers Guides are available through the company of the same name in New York City.

Taking a risk

There is a popular misconception about the risks taken by the entrepreneur. There is an image of the daring businessman with the devil-may-care grin tossing a briefcase filled with money on the roulette table of life and letting it ride. Inspirational perhaps, but the assumption that there is

a gambler behind that grin is far from the truth. A friend of mine recently bought a 120,000-square-foot greenhouse in the outback of Colorado to raise purple bell peppers. To the rest of us this may sound like a wild and risky gamble. But my friend, a true entrepreneur, was taking no risks. He had spent 10 years studying hydroponics, markets for produce, and regions for growing. He knows down to the dollar what he could afford and what the greenhouse was worth. When he found out that the greenhouse was available, and the price, he leaped on a plane and in fact did throw a briefcase full of money to the astonished sellers. It may have looked like a risky maneuver to anyone else, but for him it was all but a sure thing.

There are genuine risks associated with any venture, but the entrepreneur minimizes those risks with knowledge. Behind the devil-my-care grin are the same concerns that I felt when I made a bid at 12 to mow a big lawn for a flat five bucks. I hadn't done my homework on that one and spent the rest of the day getting my education the hard way. Before you take the plunge, read about the field, talk to friends, go to another town and talk to people that are doing exactly what you want to do. If you have to go on a bunch of long walks with your beloved and hash out all of your fears and concerns, do it! But once you have decided that it is a good idea and that you have a reasonable chance at success, set aside your fears and put on the trademark devil-may-care grin of the true entrepreneur! Δ

A BHM Writer's Profile

Ilene Duffy is the business manager for *Backwoods Home Magazine*, but she also has written articles and book and video reviews. As the main proofreader for each issue, she is responsible for the remarkably low number of typographical errors that appear in *BHM*. A former bilingual kindergarten and first grade teacher for nine years in California, she originated *BHM's* very popular "Just for Kids" pages.

Ilene gave up teaching to become *BHM's* business manager shortly after she married the magazine's publisher, Dave Duffy. She says the biggest benefit of working with the home-based magazine is being able stay at home with her two young sons and to raise her family in a quiet, country setting.

An overview of centerfire rifles

By Christopher Maxwell

A good rifle in skilled hands can be used to do things that cannot be done with any other instrument yet devised. The proper rifle, used well, can eliminate the cautious predator who attacks your livestock or the sneaky varmint who eats your garden from as far away as you can see them. A rifle will be more selective and less dangerous for these uses than traps or poison. You can put 100 pounds of venison in your freezer with a cartridge weighing less than an ounce.

A good rifle will help you do these things and more but you need to know what you are doing. Rifles are more

specialized than the versatile shotgun, and not as forgiving of imprecise shooting.

A rifle fires a single, spin stabilized projectile. Black powder rifles were often used with a plain round ball but modern rifles usually fire a long pointed bullet called a spitzer which has higher section density and less drag for better long range performance.

Rimfire rifles were covered separately in *Backwoods Home* Issue No. 12. In a rimfire the priming compound is distributed in a projecting rim around the base of the cartridge. The firing pin crushes this rim causing the priming compound to ignite and light the propellant powder.

More powerful cartridges require stronger cartridge cases. In these the priming compound is in a separate cap which is pressed into the center of the base of the cartridge. Thus, all high power firearms are centerfire.

Centerfire rifles are made for a variety of different cartridges depending on their intended use. The light rifle used to protect your sheep from coyote might fail to bring a deer down immediately, wasting both the shot and the deer. The rifle you would use for deer wouldn't leave enough of a rabbit to be worth the price of the shot.

I warn you, rifles can be addictive. Once you learn to shoot well and see what a good rifle is capable of, you may strain your ingenuity trying to think of reasons why you have to get another, or a few more, or a lot more.

The most common types of rifles in the U.S. are: bolt action, lever action, and semi-automatic. Pump action and single shot rifles are also made but are much less popular.

Bolt action

The bolt action is the most accurate, the strongest, and is made in the widest variety of calibers.

If you are in the woods where your shots will rarely exceed 100 yards, the difference in accuracy is not enough to matter. If you will be shooting on open plains or in the mountains where the ranges are longer, the bolt action is the rifle for you.

The strength of the bolt action does not mean other types are unsafe. What it does mean is that bolt actions can be made in more powerful calibers than other types. In the medium calibers a bolt action rifle can be much lighter than a semi-automatic and still have the extra margin of safety to handle the rare defective cartridge. A bolt action .30-06 can weigh less than 7 pounds where a semi-automatic may weigh almost 10 pounds.

If you have to carry your rifle a long distance to fire one shot, or you carry a rifle often but rarely fire it, you may want to accept some extra recoil to save weight. I don't recommend a lightweight high-power rifle for beginners because the recoil may prevent you from becoming proficient with your rifle.

The fact that the bolt action is available in the widest variety of calibers may be important if you find you need more than one rifle but ensuring that the safeties and other operations are the same on all your rifles may prevent fumbling, embarrassment, and accidents.

Lever action

The lever action is the traditional American rifle and is still very popular. The flat, compact design is very convenient and easy to carry and the low to medium powered cartridges are all many people need.

The most popular lever action rifles made today were designed in the 1890's. They fire the .30-30 Winchester cartridge, which is considerably less powerful than the .30-06 Springfield, the most popular cartridge for bolt action rifles.

The design of these rifles is inherently less tight and rigid than the better bolt action rifles, lessening the potential accuracy. The ammunition in these lever action rifles is located in a tubular magazine under the barrel, with the tip of one cartridge resting against the primer of the next. This design allows a large magazine capacity in a compact rifle, but requires the use of flat-tipped bullets to prevent detonation of the primers. Flat-tip bullets lose velocity quickly. This limits the useful range of these rifles to 100-150 yards.

Despite all this, if used for game under about 150 pounds in the woods or brush, these rifles will serve well. Simplicity, compactness, traditional appearance and adequate performance for many may keep these rifles going for another hundred years.

There are some more powerful lever action rifles. The unconventional Savage 99 and the traditional looking but modern designed Browning BLR are made in modern high-velocity cartridges such as the .243 and .308.

These rifles have stronger breech locking and don't have tube magazines so they are able to fire high pressure cartridges with spitzer bullets for better performance at longer range. They still don't have the intrinsic accuracy of a bolt action but they do provide substantially more power and range than a .30-30 in a compact rifle.

Revolver owners and wannabe cowboys keep the Marlin 1894 going strong. This lever action carbine is now made in modern calibers such as .357 Magnum—which will also fire .38 Special, .44 Magnum—which will also fire .44 Special, and .41 Magnum if you can find one.

The longer barrel greatly increases the velocity of the Magnum revolver ammunition and the easier aiming of the carbine make these popular brush deer rifles.

Semi-automatic

Semi-automatic or autoloading rifles have been available in the United States since about 1905, despite the propaganda campaign in the media which pretends they are new and somehow especially menacing.

A semi-auto fires one shot when you squeeze the trigger. Then some of the recoil energy or some gas pressure tapped from the barrel is used to open the action, eject the fired cartridge case, cock the firing mechanism, and reload the rifle. The trigger must then be released and squeezed again to fire and repeat the sequence.

Obviously, a semi-auto is no more deadly than a bolt action, lever action or a single shot rifle which fires a cartridge of comparable power. The ability to fire subsequent shots faster than you can aim is of very limited value. If you don't hit on your first shot when you have plenty of time and your prey doesn't know you are there, how will you hit on your second shot when you are in a hurry and your target is trying to break the land speed record?

Some who hunt in thick brush prefer autoloaders because a deflected shot may wound an animal instead of killing it instantly. A quick second shot may be needed to prevent the animal escaping to suffer a slow death.

Some believe autoloaders to be less reliable than other action types. While this may be true in theory, in practice I find autoloaders more reliable than other types because the "fumble factor" of trying to operate your rifle with your heart pounding and your fingers frozen is eliminated.

Autoloaders usually recoil less than other rifles of similar power. This is partly caused by the autoloader's greater weight and partly because the mechanism shows the recoil and spreads it over a longer time.

Civilian style semi-automatics from Browning and Remington are popular and work well. They are not quite as accurate and durable as bolt actions from the same manufacturers, but are very well made rifles.

Most of the modern military style autoloaders are much heavier and more awkward than other rifles of the same power. Many of them are very durable and accurate and have very light recoil. People who don't have to carry them far like them.

The venerable .30-06 M-1 Garand rifle of World War II fame and the M-14 in .308, a later development of the same action, fall about midway between the modern military semiautos and the civilian semiautos in weight, appearance, and handling.

They are heavier than the civilian designs but don't have the same appearance of the modern military designs. While they do look military, they don't look like machine guns. Their construction is wood with steel forgings rather than plastic and stamped sheet metal. They are accurate enough for anybody but benchrest competitors.

There are a number of lightweight semi-automatic rifles and carbines which have become popular with rural dwellers in recent years. Among these are the Ruger Mini-14 and Mini-30, the Chinese SKS carbine, and the U.S. M1 carbine.

The Mini-14 in .223 caliber is popular as a varmint and predator control rifle, while the Mini-30 and SKS in 7.62x39mm will serve as a hunting rifle for small deer at brush ranges without being too destructive for small game.

Remington makes a pump action high power rifle which is similar in appearance, and uses many of the same parts, as their semi-auto hunting rifle. If I was used to a pump action shotgun I would consider this rifle. Otherwise I don't see any advantage to it.

Self protection

Sadly, many have discovered that moving to the country does not guarantee leaving all of society's problems behind. Drug smuggling gangs, lunatic cults, and political and racist fanatics have established hideouts in the country, and most of America's overcrowded prisons are located in rural areas.

While you are much less likely to experience violent crime in the country than in the city or suburbs, if you do encounter trouble, help may be an hour or more away. Many consider self-protection a vital part of self-sufficiency, and buy these small light, low recoil carbines for this purpose.

Another urban problem which gets dumped in the country is unwanted dogs. There are some areas in the U.S. where feral dogs run in hunting packs and decimate wild game, kill livestock, and occasionally attack people. If you wander into such an area on foot, a Ruger or SKS might be comforting.

Cartridges

One look at the shelves in any gunstore or the pages of any ammunition catalog will convince you there are many more types of ammunition made than necessary. At one time everyone who invented a new gun also invented his own ammunition and every country had to have it's own special rifle cartridge which was not interchangeable with any other even though they were all very similar in power.

Generally speaking, the most popular rifle cartridges are popular for good reason so if you are considering two rifles or two cartridges which are similar in power you can safely choose the more popular. Popularity means volume production, lower prices, wider availability and more selection of brands, bullet weights and types.

For example, the .222 Remington and the .223 Remington are both accurate, flat shooting varmint cartridges but the .223 is also known as the 5.56mm NATO, the rifle cartridge of half the world's armies. This results in the .223 being much more widely available here as well as providing inexpensive surplus ammunition for training and practice.

Table 1 is a list of the most popular cartridges and their uses.

If you need a rifle for moose or grizzly bears you'll need something bigger. You'll have to ask somebody else about that as I have no experience. However, I would suggest you learn how to shoot with a .308 or .30-06 before you even consider a larger rifle.

Some obsolete foreign military rifle calibers are excellent, and remain in

Table 1. The most popular centerfire cartridges	
.223 Remington:	Varmint and predator
.243 Winchester:	Heavy varmint and predator or light deer, antelope
7.62x39mm:	Predators and brush rifle for small deer (under 150 lb)
.30-30 Winchester:	Deer in woods and brush
.270 Winchester:	Deer and larger game in open country or mountains
.308 Winchester:	Deer and large game
.30-06 Springfield:	Deer and large game

production because of the low-cost finely made surplus rifles which fire them. These include the .303 for the British Enfield, 8x57mm for the German, Czech, Belgian, and Yugoslav Mausers, 6x5.5mm for the Swedish Mauser and 7x57mm for the Spanish Mauser and Mauser rifles made in several European countries for South America. There are others which are also very good but aren't very popular.

These cartridges won't do anything the more popular American cartridges can't do and there is no good reason to choose them unless the rifle is such a bargain you can't pass it up.

Ammunition will be covered in much greater detail in *Backwoods Home* Issue No. 15.

Sights

Any rifle is only useful if you can hit what you shoot at. Whether you hit or miss will depend partly on your sights.

The most common and least satisfactory rifle sights are the open type. These will consist of either a blade, post or bead front with a notched blade rear. The notch may be square, "V" or "U" shaped.

Aperture or "peep" sights are available for most rifles and are much better. When you look through the hole in the rear sight and focus on the front sight, your eye will automatically center the front post in your field of vision. The open type always requires some concentration to center the front sight in the notch, which distracts from

focusing on the front sight and tracking the target.

Try an aperture sight before you put a telescope on your rifle. It has always seemed a shame to me to mount an awkward telescope on a graceful little woods carbine.

There are all sorts of telescopes available for rifles. On most rifles I like a 2 or 3 power long eye relief. If I was setting up a .223 for long range shooting at small targets I would probably go with a 6x. The only sort of rifle I might use with a variable power scope would be a .243 which I intended to use as both a long range varmint and predator rifle and a short range deer rifle.

Bear in mind that telescopes can and do break. Your rifle will still need iron sights.

That's enough for this issue. I'll be back next issue to tell you how to get the most from your working guns by selecting the right ammunition for your purposes. Δ

Getting ready to ride

Fire ants on the march in the U.S.

By Jo Mason

We hear a lot these days about the damage man is doing to the environment. But one of God's non-human creatures is wreaking havoc. It could come straight out of the pages of one of Stephen King's horror novels; it makes the killer bees look like a joke. Unfortunately, it's not fiction and it's not funny.

I'm talking about fire ants.

In a few short years they've spread across the South like one of the plagues of Egypt. A U.S. map showing the areas they've infested resembles a map of the confederacy during the Civil War. There are trillions of them, and lately, they scare the hell out of me.

They arrived from South America by ship, landing in Alabama in the '30's. By the '60's, they'd invaded much of the Deep South and portions of East Texas. Now they infest 250 million acres in 11 southern states. (There's also a small colony in Santa Barbara, California.) They like warm temperatures, and experts say they're expected to spread anywhere the average minimum temperature is greater than ten degrees. Future projections, then, have them in western Texas, southern Arizona, the better part of California, and up the Oregon and Washington coasts.

They are aptly named **Solenopsis invicta** — meaning invincible. Scientists have given up on eradicating them, the focus being, according to the Texas Department of Agriculture, on "control." And they haven't had much luck with that.

For some reason, they are attracted to electricity, and have cost southerners thousands — perhaps millions — in air conditioning repair bills. They crawl into relays and other parts, and then become electrocuted. The bodies pile up and cause malfunctions. They mess up traffic lights. A study by the Texas Transportation Institute at Texas A&M University, found they've infested traffic signal cabinets in six southern states. There has even been speculation that the proposed super collider in Waxahachie, Texas, may be jeopardized by these ants.

People go about their business as usual in town, the ants having little visible impact there. But in the rural areas their destruction becomes obvious. We live less than a mile from the city limits, yet can look out the window and see dozens of mounds in our neighbor's pasture. My husband has given up trying to grow anything but tomatoes, after they ruined his beets, okra, corn, and cucumbers. He also tried using organic materials — until the ants set up housekeeping in it. It's a painful activity working with fire ant infested mulch! They crawl under the bark and kill trees. They eat the insides out of vegetables — if they haven't already devoured the blossoms. And, oh yes, they kill earthworms.

They even sting like a bee

Once I saw an entomologist discussing them on TV. When he mentioned fire ant stings, I guffawed. **Ha! Some bug expert!** Didn't he know ants don't sting, they bite? Seconds later, I stopped laughing when a magnified shot appeared of a fire ant on a victim's arm. It grasped the victim's skin with its mandibles, then, sure enough, jackknifed its body and stung just like a bee. Unlike bees, these ants can live to sting again and again. They inject bacteria along with the venom, and this raises a small blister, which later itches. First you feel a slight irritation (the bite) then a burning sensation (the sting). To make matters worse, these creatures are highly aggressive, and tend to swarm over their victims. When you get stung, you're liable to get several stings. Enough stings can be fatal.

Life's not the same any more. From the first thaw as early as February, until the hard freezes begin in perhaps December, you have to be on the alert. Going barefoot is a thing of the past. You wear thick socks while mowing the lawn. You watch out for your kids and puppies. The new by-laws of survival? Don't stand in one spot too long. Be careful where you sit. And never, ever lie down on the grass. I nearly cried one day when I saw my teenaged daughter suntanning on top of the car.

Even the most environmentally aware rural residents have stopped trying "green" methods of fire ant proofing. (Using wood shavings and motor oil; boiling water; cream of wheat; and transferring ants from one mound to another.) After spending a small fortune on air conditioning repairs, we had to resort to poison. Even that doesn't get rid of them, it just keeps them off the A/C for awhile.

After discovering a dead mouse in a trap in our storage shed, I picked it up gingerly with a shovel, and placed it on a bench outside the back door, planning to let my husband dispose of it. I forgot to mention it to him and 36 hours later I went back to the bench. What was left of the mouse? A little pile of grey fur and a skeleton.

But these ants from hell don't wait for killed prey. They take matters into their own mandibles and attack anything living—especially the young, the slow, the vulnerable. They kill setting hens and baby chicks. They'll get into the eggs if there's a slight crack in them. They kill mother rabbits and baby rabbits. They attack calves, beginning with the eyes.

About the only thing safe are fish—if they're in the water. You don't dare leave your stringer on the bank. I saw a sorry sight last summer. A friend fishing on the Brazos River sat in a folding chair in about a half foot of water, his bait can tied to the armrest.

(Had he not taken these precautions, it's a toss-up as to what the ants would have had for breakfast first: Randy or the night crawlers.) Cold weather only slows them down. They burrow deeper into the earth waiting for their spring assault. A deer hunter isn't safe if he picks a tree where they're hibernating under the bark.

The things I've observed out here have made me wonder what's going on out in the woods. How many newborn fawns are meeting the same fate as the calves? How many wild rabbits, squirrels, quail nestlings? So I consulted our resident outdoors "expert"—my son. I said I hadn't seen any statistics about the damage fire ants are doing to wildlife, and I asked him what he thought. Was the situation as bad as I suspected?

"Sure, they're killing off everything," he said. "You can't find a bobcat, a 'possum, a coon. They're messing up the whole ecosystem."

Once I recovered from the shock that my kid knew the word **ecosystem**, I asked why you don't hear more about the problem. "Why doesn't somebody talk about it?" I asked. "Why doesn't somebody write about it?"

He shrugged. "Somebody ought to," he said.

One of my fondest memories as a child, was on summer nights when my parents would spread a blanket on the grass, and we'd all sit under the stars and sing "Deep In The Heart Of Texas" and play "20 Questions." That sort of activity isn't possible now. I have about 20 questions. Will life outdoors ever be the same? Will our wild creatures survive? Will anything stop these invincible ants? And, if the earth is warming, as most scientists believe, how long before you find fire ants in **your** back yard? Δ

A Backwoods Home Anthology
The Eighth Year

Charging RV batteries with the sun

Photovoltaic panels provide electricity for this trailer.

By Michael Gohl

There are three general types of photovoltaic systems for charging batteries in recreational vehicles (RVs) here in the Southwest Desert. Innovative people use the sun to keep batteries charged in a variety of ways ranging from the quick and simple to the sophisticated and complex.

A lot of people think that since solar panels are a state of the art device, it must be a difficult task to install them in some sort of a workable system. This is not necessarily the case. A lot of people here in the desert simply attach two wires on to the solar panel, one positive and one negative, and simply hook those leads to the positive and negative battery terminals. Point the panel toward the sun and bingo! Your battery is being charged.

This method works just fine for a lot of folks although there are a few disadvantages with this system. The first problem is securing the panel in such a manner that it won't be wind damaged, tripped over, or stolen. These panels are most often constructed with tempered glass that is capable of withstanding all sorts of inclement weather conditions. Extreme physical abuse tends to break the glass rendering the solar panel subject to the ill effects of moisture on electrical con-

nections. The second problem is the extra daily effort it takes to take the panel out of storage, attach the panel to the batteries and secure it properly. Also, when it is time to pack up and travel, the panel needs to be stored out of harm's way. This is a real problem considering the typical lack of extra space in an RV. Also inherent with this system is a safety issue: any time you attach wires directly to a battery, you risk reversing polarity, explosions from arcing battery connections, or fire hazards from wires shorting against metal objects and not being able to handle the current flow from the batteries. What initially seems to be a quick and easy hookup may turn out to be a disaster without constant attention to detail.

Another typical photovoltaic installation on RVs involves permanently attaching the panel on top of the vehicle. It is important to find a location away from TV antenna storage pods and air conditioners to avoid shadows during the day. They should be attached securely onto the roof rafters with screws and liberal amounts of silicon caulking. Most of the time, 12/2 stranded double insulated wires are run down through the refrigerator vent either directly to the batteries with an in-line fuse located near the batteries (with lower voltage self regulating panels) or via a voltage regula-

tor placed in a convenient location and then to the batteries or DC fuse box.

This installation is the more typical RV installation and proves to be a safe and trouble free method of taking advantage of most of the attributes of solar battery charging. It can provide ample power for DC lights, TV, and pumping water and, with occasional moderate use, heater fans, CBs, and ventilating fans. With this system, you don't need to be taking the panel out of storage, attaching wires to the battery and securing it down on a daily basis. However on the negative side with this method you need to park in the sun and are not able to track the sun throughout the day as easily as the first method.

With these systems, folks here in the Southwest can have all the conveniences of home as well as the quiet and solitude of the desert. They have ample electricity for all their DC electrical requirements and, with the addition of an invertor to change their DC to AC, they operate microwaves, video cassette players, and satellite dishes — without the noise and inconvenience of generators.

In the final, analysis photovoltaic and RVs are a perfect combination for anyone interested in enjoying the conveniences of electricity and the quiet solitude of Mother nature.

(Michael Gohl owns The Sun Works, P.O. Box 1545, Niland, CA 92257. Telephone: 206-794-5427) △

A photovoltaic panel and an RV spell independence.

Creating your own life at home without special tools

By Neil Shelton

You'll get a lot of well-meaning advice these days on how to launch your new life in the country and subsist on very little. Well, what I want to know is, what do you do when your truck blows up? I mean, I agree that simple life is most likely a better one, but what if you move out into the country and suddenly you're faced with a financially catastrophic situation? Suppose you've honed your budget to the point that you can get by on the tiniest of incomes, and then your appendix bursts? Do you try to barter your laying hens for surgery? Think fast now, remember, you're in excruciating pain.

Obviously, there are a few flaws in the subsistence plan. However, I'd like to suggest to you that with the means available in the latter part of the twentieth century, if you can make a living in the city (or maybe even if you can't) then you can do just as well, probably better, working for yourself, on your own schedule, out of your own home, even if you're living at the sort of end-of-the-road location that I enjoy. I'm not just talking about making money. It stands to reason that if the people you work for can turn a profit on what they pay you (and you wouldn't be around for long if they couldn't) then you can find a way to make **at least** as much as you're making now working for yourself. But to address a broader goal, living your own life in the environment you choose should be your first concern rather than what the dreary business of getting by day to day dictates.

Ten years ago, I was a rural real estate broker. This was an okay thing to be, but it took a lot of my time, and most of that time was wasted. I once figured that I spent an average of one full day with all the wailing and gnashing teeth that my dinner guests here at the farm are often treated to: about

how the expenses kept going on whether anyone bought anything or not, but suffice it to say that the overhead was considerable.

But what was I going to do? I'd already tossed out my college degree to get into real estate having discovered that I was allergic to my boss, and after

Neil Shelton with partner, Catherine Ault.

all, you can't run a real estate company by mail order.

Or can you?

In 1982, my partner, the lovely and talented Catherine Ault, and I started Woods & Waters Inc., our small corporation dedicated to selling and financing rural Ozark land in a manner as stress-free as possible for both ourselves and our clients, while being profitable enough for us to maintain lifestyles we could enjoy, spending most of our time in a peaceful, rural environment.

I'm not saying that **you** should start a land company like ours, (or if you do, I strongly recommend that you **not** call it Woods & Waters) but I am suggesting that if we can take a one-on-one high-intensity business like real estate and turn it into a mellow, yet profitable cottage industry, you can probably find a way to do the same with

whatever business or hobby appeals to you.

If this is truly your ambition, then I'm confident you can achieve it. We've put together some rules, based on our experience, that should help you in your escape from the system.

Rule number one: start small and evolve

Don't quit your job and sink your life savings into your new business. Cathy and I started with one small tract of parcels that didn't cover it's monthly expenses for an agonizingly long while. Since then, we've made a number of changes. We've seen some of our bright ideas bud and bloom while others proved to be the entrepreneurial equivalent of blossom-rot. It was a few years before I stopped working on commission and she stopped preparing income taxes. We thought that since most new businesses fail in the first six months, this was an obvious sign of poor planning in itself. If your new business can't support itself through a six-month slump, it's not time to quit your steady job.

Rule number two: reach beyond your local economy

Many of the things that make living in the country so attractive also make it a poor place to try to locate a conventional business. (You notice there aren't lots of fast food joints located on unpaved roads.) So unless your idea of living in the country means locating on the edge of a major city (here the author holds his nose and makes "peeeyeww" noises) then your first thought should be of finding a market for your goods or services that is as broad as possible. Due to the Persian Gulf War, we made more sales in the past year to Americans in Saudi Arabia than we did to residents of sleepy little Willow Springs (our home-town). We accomplished this through nothing more complicated nor expensive than classified advertisements in national magazines such as this one, and we overcame any disadvantages our location may have caused by telephone, fax, and overnight mail.

Rule number three: stay small by thinking through sub-contracting

You will be hard pressed to find employees who will show the enthusiasm for your business that you have, and this lack of enthusiasm often translates into poor customer service. The phone company may be able to afford to treat it's customers the way it does, but you can't. Still, your company can become as large as it needs to be by subcontracting the parts of the job that are either too labor intensive, or require too much investment in equipment, or both. For example, keeping all of those classified ads paid and up-to-date was quite a time consuming chore until we found that an advertising and public relations agency in our nearest city would do it all for us for **free**. They get a 15% slice of each ad from the magazines, and we get to spend a couple of more afternoons a month down by the creek.

Additionally, if we ever feel ourselves in a pinch for art or production help, their staff of professionals is available to us. When we need a road built or a trash dump eradicated, we have $150,000 worth of excavating equipment and the necessary operators at our beck and call because we've worked out a good long-term relationship with an excavation contractor. Let **him** worry about how much it costs to fix a broken road grader.

Rule number four: stay small by thinking big through technology

In any given month, we will write approximately seven times as many contracts as my old brokerage did during its most shining moments. Yet we don't have any salesmen (unless you count me) or employees. Besides the obvious savings in commissions and wages, we avoid the mind-numbing hassle of IRS W-2 forms, FICA withholding taxes and other bureaucratic abominations. Some of these savings we pass on to the customers, some of it we keep and a relatively tiny amount of it goes into what makes it all possible: computers and associated goodies. We sell small tracts of land for small monthly payments that would normally mean more bookkeeping than left-brain types like us could fathom. For the computer, it's just a warm-up exercise. We need to produce an up-to-date catalog of a quality that will impress our clients. With today's desk-top publishing software and equipment, I can do work that would have tied up a whole advertising department 15 years ago. Just be thankful Hitler didn't have a laser printer.

Rule number five: get your financing from those who stand to benefit from it

Banks are much more interested in making loans to the financial scandals of tomorrow than to small businesses run out of the home, and with the rates and terms they insist on, you're just as well off without them. A better deal for you is to finance your expenses on **your**

terms by negotiating with the people you pay for goods and services. Since most of Woods & Waters' income is monthly, we have traded our loyal repeat business for monthly terms on our printing, roadbuilding and advertising. (I stress the fact that we have made these deals with people who know that they can depend on us based on past experience.) When we buy land, we choose it carefully and only buy from sellers who will finance a portion of the price. Banks want the option of changing the rate of interest or the term at a later date. When you work out your own financing, you can set your own terms.

Rule number six: be unique in your approach to the customer

Spend a weekend thinking about what you do for a living (or what you'd like to do) and how it could be made more attractive to the customer. (Hint: cheaper, faster and easier are very, very popular.) Conventional merchants rent a storefront, buy a huge inventory and give up 40 to 60 hours of their lives each week to provide a convenient place of business for their customers, but if you can do business in your home, you virtually eliminate these major expenses, while **your** customers don't need to go any further than their phone or mail-box. Already you've got a decided advantage. Most anyone will readily choose to pay less for quicker, easier, goods or services **if** they are confident of your quality and integrity. So guarantee both and stand behind your guarantee.

Rule number seven: have fun

I didn't tack this on to the end just to give this piece a homey touch. It's essential. If we didn't enjoy what we were doing, we might as well be working in a factory. Cathy and I feel strongly that there is a sort of a mystic relationship here whereby our enjoyment of the work is the real driving force that makes it successful. Maybe this isn't mystic at all but just common sense. Δ

Cooking with woodstoves

By Jennifer Stein

As I stood by the stove stirring my big pot of potato soup today, I meditated on the usefulness of the appliance it was sitting on. Here in the backwoods, our wood cookstove cooks and bakes our meals, heats our water, and keeps our house toasty warm in all kinds of weather. We hang our coats up on the wall close to the stove so they'll be dry in the morning, and I keep an old stoneware pot full of herb tea on a trivet on the side away from the firebox. Work gloves hang over the edge of the woodbox to keep warm, and when I make pancakes, the syrup pitchers go on the warming shelf before I even start mixing up the batter.

Our wood cookstove is a modern airtight stove. Back in grandma's day, a wood cookstove was the center of the kitchen because she was cooking all day to feed her family, but that cookstove required a lot of attention and coaxing. Grandma was constantly feeding it pieces of fuel that had to be chopped small enough to keep a good roaring fire going in the tiny firebox. If she wanted to control the temperature of the oven, she had to carefully gauge the proportion of green wood to dry, and then know exactly when to add more wood, and how much, because the wood in the firebox would burn out before the bread or cake in the oven was baked. And there was no way you could heat the house with it because the heat all went up the chimney and the fire was out at night almost before you had the bed warmed up!

You can still buy an antique or a reproduction of grandma's old stove, if you want to, but if you're going to live with a wood cookstove, you'll probably want to keep the care and feeding of it to a minimum. There are several wood cookstoves on the market which are, or claim to be, airtight. I will describe and compare only the two brands

which I have lived with and cooked on extensively, but I'll point out features you should look for and compare carefully in purchasing a cookstove.

The Stanley

My first wood cookstove was a Waterford Stanley. When I went to buy it I asked the salesperson, who sold both Elmiras and Stanleys, which one he would buy if he had to live with it day in, day out. The Elmira was prettier and more costly, but he recommended the plain-jane Stanley for efficiency and durability. I cooked meals for up to fifteen people at my ski lodge, on that Stanley, and I was never unhappy with it in the eleven years I lived there. I found that with a little practice it was very simple to control the oven temperature for baking, and if I didn't sleep in too late in the morning, the fire which I'd carefully fed my highest quality wood the night before would

still be glowing in the firebox. The stove that looked so plain next to the shiny Elmira took on a patina of its own from use, and it looked just right next to my simple New England antiques.

The Pioneer Maid

Then I sold the ski lodge and moved here to Oregon, to my friend Lance's place. He already had his own wood cookstove, a Pioneer Maid he'd ordered by mail and had shipped to him from Ohio. It is a black box of a stove that sits massively in the middle of the house. Instead of a spin-draft in the ash-door and a fire built on grates, it has down-draft controllers on the side of the firebrick-lined box. Through the airtight lid on the stovetop, you can feed the fire with eight- or ten-inch diameter unsplit log lengths. The bed of coals and ash in the bottom of the box will glow all through the longest night and still be ready to flare up when you feed the fire after a lazy morning. The broad stovetop has room enough for a variety of temperatures which let you perform a wide range of cooking chores (such as fry, boil, simmer, and warm) at the same time. And the large oven has room for six loaves of bread in a baking!

The Pioneer Maid isn't perfect. The oven temperature isn't as easy to regulate as the Stanley. The flues are a little more difficult to clean, and they need cleaning more often. But its design is far superior, and it doesn't depend on maintenance to retain its airtight quality. It holds a fire longer than any other space heating or cookstove I have ever seen, and it uses far less wood for the heat it puts out.

How to kindle a fire

With any wood cookstove, the first thing you want to do is start the fire. Look at your stove or a diagram of it. Figure out where the drafts and dampers are. One damper controls whether the heated air goes around the oven, or directly up the chimney from the firebox. You always want the air to go up the mainline to the chimney until you have your fire kindled

The Third Year

and the wood burning hot and cleanly. Another damper may control the speed or amount of air going around the oven. Leave this open too! Finally, open your air-intake draft all the way. Just for kindling, you can leave your ashpan door or other air supply ajar. Your chimney should be able to handle all this air supply. If the chimney smokes, it's time to clean the chimney. If the stove smokes, clean the flues.

Light the fire, using several pieces of kindling and a chunk or two of good dry wood. When the wood is burning well, you can fill up the firebox. After everything has caught, close the ashpan door, but leave the air intake draft and oven dampers wide open. At this point, it's desirable to have a stovepipe thermometer so you can tell when your fire is burning hot and clean. Both Waterford and Vermont Castings (who don't make cooking stoves but make very good non-polluting heating stoves) say that a fire should be burning at 500 degrees before you choke it down, to minimize particulate emissions and creosote buildup. Cookstoves don't have catalytic converters so if you live in an area where pollution is an issue, it's important to be conscientious.

Now that you have your fire burning well, you can begin to regulate it. Here's where the airtight models really show their stuff. If you have an airtight model, you've got a load of wood in the firebox that will burn for hours. Once you get the oven temperature adjusted, you're ready to bake. Adjust the oven temperature by controlling the supply of air to the fire. If the temperature is climbing very rapidly, you'll want to start regulating the air supply about 100 degrees before you reach the desired temperature. Experience will tell you just how early and how much to adjust the air supply. It took a year for me to get really accurate with the Stanley, and only a couple of months to adjust to the Pioneer Maid. It can be helpful to use an oven thermometer to check and see if the built-in one is accurate. I had to adjust my baking temperature in the Stanley for good results, but the Pioneer Maid's built-in thermometer seems to be perfectly accurate.

Keeping warm all night

You're warm and well-fed, but the temperature is plummeting unseasonably, and you want to make sure the frost stays outside tonight! If you've got a Pioneer Maid, all you do is throw several of your big chunks on the fire, wait till the wood is burning well and heated through, then shut the spin-drafts almost all the way. You'll be toasty in the morning. If you've got a Stanley, well, it's a little more difficult. Wait till the fire has burned down to a good bed of coals. Then take about three large chunks of your best and hardest wood. (In the east, most any hardwood will do. Here in the northwest, tamarack or maple is best). Load them in, and let the fire catch and warm up the wood for just a few minutes. Then shut down the spin-draft all but a quarter turn, and close both the oven and chimney dampers all the way. There is enough air passage around the end of the oven damper to keep the fire going. When the stove is new, this technique will produce an eight-hour burn, but as the stove ages, it gets harder and harder until you give in and replace and gaskets and the adjustment screw in the spin-draft.

Now we're cooking!

What can you cook or bake in your wood cookstove? Just about anything! The only thing I don't try to do is broil. The variable heat on the stovetop provides better temperature control than any gas or electric stove I ever used. The further you move the pot away from the area over the firebox, the slower it cooks. As far as the oven goes, the all-around heat provides for even baking and wonderfully crusty baked goods. Some ovens bake more evenly than others, with airtight rating the best in my experience. With the Pioneer Maid, the only reason I take my baked goods out and turn them is to check on how well they are getting done, and judge how much more time they need. I often put a stainless steel bowl of hot water in the bottom of the oven to modify the dry heat produced by the wood fire.

What is your cookstove made of?

The material your cookstove is made of is very important. Sheet steel will only do for an old-fashioned style stove which makes no pretensions to being airtight. This is because airtight stoves produce creosote, a very corrosive liquid. In a cookstove, the creosote will run down the chimney and pool in the area under the oven, where it will sit and do its nasty work until it eventually dries out. The folks at Pioneer Place discovered that if they tested stoves under worst-case conditions, with lots of green wood and choked-down fires, they could rust out a 12-gauge sheet metal stove in just over a year. They decided to make their Pioneer Maid stoves out of 304 stainless, guaranteed never to rust or corrode. Waterford makes their Stanleys with an all cast-iron fire path. Cast-iron is not quite as good as stainless, but far better than sheet steel. If you figure you're only going to buy one wood cookstove to last the rest of your life, then checking the quality of the materials is very important.

Where to buy them

Stanleys are available at many Waterford dealers around the country. For the dealer nearest you, write: Waterford Irish Stoves, Inc., River Mill Complex, 85 Mechanic St., Lebanon, NH 03766.

Pioneer Maid cookstoves are only available by mail order. For more information, write: Suppertime Stoves Limited, Route 4, Aylmer, Ontario N5H 2R3, Canada.

Elmira cookstoves may be found at many dealers throughout the country. Δ

> *"Americans have the right and advantage of being armed-unlike the citizens of other countries whose governments are afraid to trust the people with arms."*
>
> James Madison

HEALTH

Carob — the chocolate alternative

By Bill Palmroth

Both sugar and chocolate have been in bad graces with health authorities for quite some time. Many health-conscious Americans have turned to honey or maple syrup as a substitute for sugar. Meanwhile, a strong case is being made for carob as an alternative to the evils of chocolate.

Ceratonia siliqua

Since biblical times, the carob tree has grown near the Mediterranean Sea. Its long, dry pods nourished the Israelites, Mohammed's conquering armies, and the Romans. According to the bible, John the Baptist survived on the pod's sweet pulp during his days in the wilderness. The carob, a dark evergreen, grows up to 50 feet in height in Arizona and Southern California.

Often called St. John's Bread, the carob looks like an apple tree and has small flowers. Its brown, leathery pods, 4 to 10 inches long, are ground into a nutritionally rich powder resembling cocoa. But that's as far as the resemblance goes. Carob is rich in protein, has 2-1/2 times the calcium of chocolate, is non-allergenic, and is virtually fat-free. Easily assimilated, carob contains a high amount of pectin, a valuable ingredient that offers natural protection against diarrhea.

Carob contains as much thiamine as asparagus, strawberries or dandelion greens, as much niacin as dates or lima beans, and more vitamin A than equal amounts of eggplant, beets, raisins, or onions. It also contains good quantities of important minerals such as potassium, phosphorus, iron, copper, and magnesium. The riboflavin content in carob is comparable to that found in brown rice.

Carob aids digestion with none of chocolate's drawbacks. Nutritionally, chocolate has disadvantages. It is 52% fat, and is highly allergenic. Naturally bitter, over 40% white sugar is added to make it sweet (a 3-1/2 oz. candy bar has 538 calories).

Chocolate is rich in calcium, but high in oxalic acid, which interferes with the absorption of calcium. It also contains caffeine and theobromine, alkaloids which stimulate the nervous system. Carob is 50% natural sugar and is used as a sweetener as well as a chocolate replacement.

Despite its nutritional drawbacks, many people continue to eat chocolate simply because it tastes good. Well, carob also tastes good and it is nutritionally good for you. Since it doesn't taste like chocolate, you should think of it as an alternative rather than a substitute.

Look for carob powder/chips and soya-carob flour in health food stores, food co-ops, or in supermarkets' natural food sections. If you like baking, try using carob-soya flour. And to satisfy your sweet tooth urge without the usual guilt trip, try one of the following delicious carob recipes:

Wholesome carob candy

1 c. honey or maple syrup
1 c. peanut butter, plain or chunky
1 c. carob powder
1 c. sesame seeds
1 c. sunflower seeds or chopped nuts
1/2 c. unsweetened coconut, shredded or flaked
1/2 c. dates/raisins/dried fruit

Heat honey and peanut butter together on the stove. Add carob powder. Remove from heat. Stir in the seeds, nuts, fruits, and coconut. Put in baking pan, cut in squares. Refrigerate until firm.

Soya-carob bread

2 Tbls. dry yeast
1 c. lukewarm water
3 c. warm water
1/2 c. vegetable oil
1/2 c. powdered milk
1/4 c. raw honey
10-12 c. soya-carob flour
1 Tbl. salt

Dissolve yeast in 1 c. lukewarm water and wait for bubbles. Meanwhile, mix honey, oil, and 3 c. warm water in mixing bowl. Add salt, powdered milk, then add proofed yeast and enough flour to make a kneadable dough. Knead on floured board until no longer sticky. Place in oiled bowl, let rise until doubled. Punch down, let rise again. Punch down, shape into 3 loaves. Let rise in well-oiled bread pans until dough reaches at least the tops of the pans. Bake in a pre-heated 375 degree oven until the loaves sound hollow on the bottom (about an hour). Δ

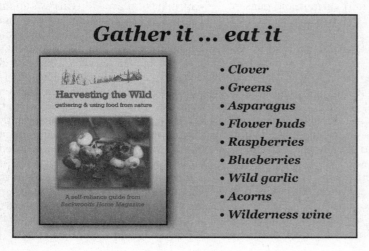

Gather it ... eat it

Harvesting the Wild
gathering & using food from nature

A self-reliance guide from
Backwoods Home Magazine

- *Clover*
- *Greens*
- *Asparagus*
- *Flower buds*
- *Raspberries*
- *Blueberries*
- *Wild garlic*
- *Acorns*
- *Wilderness wine*

Seed starting the easy way

*By Jj Fallick
(photos by Eric Large')*

Have you gotten tired of spending the price of a packet of seed for only six plants? Have you ever wanted to try a new variety but found only the "old standbys" when you went shopping for transplants? If so, maybe it's time for you to begin starting your own transplants from seeds. It doesn't require costly equipment—only a few scrounged materials, a bit of potting soil and a sunny window—or extensive training. After learning a few tricks of the trade, anyone can save a bunch and have the varieties they want by growing their own seedlings.

The first consideration is timing. Even the best greenhouseman can't rush a seedling! Garden experts often say seedlings require 6-8 weeks after germination to reach transplant size. It's true that overmature seedlings suffer more transplant shock. In my experience, backyard gardeners have less than optimum growing conditions and need to allow a little extra time for their plants to reach transplant size. How do you determine when to start your seedlings? Determine your best transplant date and count back the required number of weeks from Table 1. For help in determining the best transplant date for your garden, refer to my article "It's Not Too Late to Start Your Garden" (BHM #9) or check with your county Extension Agent.

Table 1.

Squash, melons, cucumbers	4 weeks
Lettuce	6 weeks
Tomatoes	12 weeks
Peppers, leeks, onions	14 weeks

To make sure that you have seeds to plant on the early planting dates you'll probably have to mail order or use last years seeds. For most vegetables either option is viable. If stored in a cool, dry place, most seeds will germinate adequately the second year. My local garden store, which is usually well supplied, doesn't get new stock until after I start tomato seedlings, though. I prefer to mail-order new seeds for my early spring planting, to take advantage of new varieties. Don't forget to allow time for your order to be packed and shipped. I put in my first order right after the new year and send additional orders as needed throughout the spring.

You will also need planting medium and containers. This is where you can easily eat up your savings. You don't need fancy supplies. Some folks even mix their own potting mix from sifted compost, soil and other materials. This can be tricky, so I watch for potting soil on sale cheap throughout the year and buy it to have a ready supply. Regular potting soil is what you want; some of the custom blends are not good for veggie seedlings and they all cost more. You don't need to buy planting flats or peat pots either. I used to buy Jiffy Pots, compressed peat pellets for my squash and melons but now I make plantable pots from newspaper for those crops that don't like transplanting.

For basic flats I use cutdown cardboard boxes lined with plastic. You can use milk cartons, old pans or any container that will hold soil. Don't cut holes in the bottom of the container; it's messy and can lead to uneven soil moisture. You'll avoid soggy roots by learning proper watering techniques and one of my tricks.

If you want just a few plants, milk cartons work just fine. Be sure to rinse them in cold water immediately upon emptying and then wash with soapy water. This will help prevent fungal and other infections. To make the most of your carton, cut the spout side off lengthwise (illustration 1).

If you are growing more than just a few seedlings, you can use any cardboard box, cut to 3" deep, and lined with plastic. I recycle old plastic bags and weathered plastic big enough to completely line the box and extend past the edges a couple of inches. Fill the lined box with potting soil about 2" deep, smoothed out and patted down.

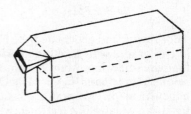

ILLUSTRATION 1.
MILK CARTON MINI FLAT

Water the flat now so that you don't disturb the seeds. I water the flats with a pitcher in a crosshatch pattern (illustration 2) until the soil is damp but not soggy. To test soil moisture, grab a handful and squeeze! If you squeeze out a few drops of water it's moist. More than a few and you overdid it; less and it's too dry.

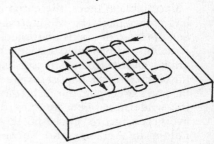

ILLUSTRATION 2.
WATERING PATTERN

Sprinkle or place seeds in rows about 2" apart. I usually don't worry about crowding tomatoes (I thin them when I transplant the first time) but take care not to get lettuces, onions and leeks too close together. The plants you transplant directly to the garden want lots of room to grow in the flat. Seeds that you can handle individually (like peppers) you might want to plant on a 2" grid (like the bean seeds I used for illustration in photo #1). While it is possible to put different veggies in the same flat, life is easier if you group them by species so they all germinate at the same time. Cover seeds with 1/4" potting soil and pat gently.

Photo 1. Bean seeds planted on a 2 inch grid.

Now comes the secret of keeping the soil moisture even! Encase the flat in a clear plastic bag or cover it with plastic wrap (photo #2). If your flat is too wide for a single piece of plastic, "drugstore fold" two pieces together to make a cover (illustration 3). You may need to trim the lining plastic and tape down the plastic cover to make your mini-greenhouse.

Your "babies" will need a warm place to begin their life. A few seeds, like lettuce, prefer germination temperatures a little on the cool side...but most

like a nice room temperature. Peppers like it especially warm, so much so that my northern window sills and coolish rooms aren't good enough. I start pepper seedlings on the coolest part of my woodstove's warming shelf, moving them to the window once they are up and growing.

After germination, the seedlings need light. I've tried "grow lights" and other kinds of artificial illumination and still prefer the original light source, the sun. Any south-facing window into which the sun shines can

make a good greenhouse window. If your window sill is narrow or you lack space to sit your flats, make a set of temporary hanging shelves. Attach two screws, hooks, eyes or even nails to the top of the window frame. Tie the middle of a length of clothesline rope to each fastener, then tie an overhand knot in each set of ropes about 10" below where you want each shelf to sit. Make sure to allow lots of room between shelves for the plants to get sunlight. It **will** take a bit of fiddling to get knots and shelves level. I "fine tune" the level after sliding my shelf (an old board or piece of drywall will do) between the ropes above the knots (photo 3). Place the flats on your shelves and you're all set.

Check your flats daily from the beginning but do **not** open the plastic or add water until you see lots of little green babies reaching for the sun. Then, remove the plastic and begin

ILLUSTRATION 3. "DRUGSTORE FOLD"

checking the flats twice a day. The sun shining in the window can get really hot, and the bigger they grow the more your seedlings will need to eat and drink. The soil can look dry but still have enough water in it for the plants. **Feel it.** You don't want them to be soggy, but you don't want them to wilt either. You will need to turn the flats regularly, also, since the sun only shines on one side. When the plants begin to reach seriously for the sun, turn the flat 180 degrees.

Commercial transplants are fed often with chemical fertilizers. Even if you don't want to use these products, your seedlings will need feeding to grow strong and sturdy, because potting soil is not fertile. Choose a product you like and use at the dilution recommended for houseplants. I use liquid fertilizer and replace a

Photo 2. Cover the flat with plastic.

The Third Year

Photo 3. Temporary hanging shelves.

regular watering with the diluted plant food at least twice during the growing period.

Once they have their first real leaves, your veggies may need transplanting to a roomier flat. As a rule of thumb, if they more than just touch each other and it will be more than two weeks until they go into the garden, **transplant**. Make a flat that is a little deeper (about 4"), lift your seedlings gently with a fork and plant 2" apart in the new flat. The best thing you can do for tomatoes and peppers is to bury the stem completely to the level of their seed leaves. These plants grow roots from their stems and this gives them a good boost.

Melons, squash and cucumbers need a little different handling. These plants are picky about transplanting. They don't like having their roots disturbed, so you can't just put them in a flat. For these veggies, use individual containers like the Jiffy Pots, pint milk cartons, or my favorite -- the recycled newspaper creations my kids love to make with the "potmaker" tool. Put your mini-pots in a plastic-lined flat, plant 1-3 seeds per pot and proceed as before. When you plant these veggies out in the garden don't unpot them. Plant pot and all. If you use a milk carton, carefully cut away the bottom of the carton before planting.

Don't forget to get your tender hothouse babies ready to go outdoors gradually. At least a week before transplanting day, gradually acclimatize the seedlings to the outdoors. Place them out in the morning in a protected location and bring them in at night, gradually increasing the length of time they are outdoors. When they are ready to stay out full time they are considered "hardened off" and ready for transplanting.

If you are at all like me, it will take you a few springs to get the hang of all this. Keep at it though, and eventually you will succeed. With any luck you won't end up killing off your seedlings like I did the first two years...first with an unplanned vacation (my mom took care of the plants for me; the houseplants survived but the seedlings didn't) and the next year with hospitalization. That year my husband, remembering the previous year's disaster, made sure they got **plenty** of water. They drowned. Δ

The summer road to the Backwoods Home Magazine office

A BHM Writer's Profile

Jo Mason lives with her husband Rodney and two grown children on twelve acres outside College Station, Texas.

In addition to her articles in *Backwoods Home Magazine*, Jo writes for *Capper's, Family Circle, Dell Logic Puzzles, Best Recipes*, and *Maine Organic Farmer and Gardener*.

The bonus of blackberries

By Bill Palmroth

Because of their juiciness, texture, and a distinct, slightly tart flavor, blackberries get high ratings from most berry lovers. Nevertheless, in spite of the abundance of blackberries, fewer people are picking and eating them than ever before.

While blackberries are found all over the world (except desert regions), they are native to the Northern temperate regions of the Old and New Worlds. Many native varieties grow wild in the U.S. and Canada.

Blackberries, of the genus Rubus (the rose family) comprise many varieties. There are upright types in the erect and semi-erect categories, as well as trailing types. Botanists believe that the original 20 or so species have hybridized and segregated into literally tens of thousands of varieties. All are brambles, usually compound-leafed, and their thorny branches, called canes, often arch toward the ground. A cane leafs out in its first year; in the second year, it flowers, fruits, and dies. Generally, the flowers are white, but they can be pink or red. Ripe blackberries range from black to reddish purple and dark purple.

American Indians made good use of wild blackberries. They collected them to eat fresh, add to other foods, and to dry for use during the long winter months. Great Plains Indians dried blackberries and mixed them with lean dried (jerky) buffalo meat, pounded into a fine mix, and then added buffalo fat to make pemmican, a concentrated energy food that took up little space and could be easily carried by an Indian brave, either walking or on his horse. An Indian brave could easily carry a supply of pemmican which would last for many days.

Blackberries were also a favorite of early American colonists and were commonly eaten throughout rural America until recent times. Most farms had an area where blackberries grew wild, and berry picking was a regular summer activity, and the berries were eaten fresh and also canned by farm families for use during the winter months.

All major seed and plant catalogs list several varieties of blackberries, including special thornless varieties that bear large, juicy berries in abundance. Domestic and commercial production, which began only in the latter part of the 19th century, is confined primarily to the U.S.

Approximately 10-20,000 acres are devoted to blackberry cultivation in the U.S. In the United Kingdom, blackberry cultivation takes up only about 1,000 acres, and there is even less emphasis on blackberry production in Europe. In the United Kingdom and Europe, blackberries are commonly used as a hedge plant and the berries are harvested as a premium.

All cultivated blackberries are derived from native North American wild varieties. Horticulturalists have produced many superior varieties such as the Thornless Evergreen, Marion, Boysen, Olallie, Youngberry, Cherokee, Comanche, Dewberry, Cheyenne, Humble, and Darrow. The most important commercial blackberry producing areas in the U.S. are Oregon, Texas, Oklahoma, and Arkansas. However, commercial blackberry production is increasing in other parts of the country.

Blackberries are among the easiest and most rewarding home fruits to grow. They're a wise choice for impatient gardeners because they begin to produce in their second year and they have the advantage of providing a permanent planting. As long as no serious disease problems develop, rows of blackberries can be maintained in the same place for 10 or more years. Blackberries, like raspberries, are relatively carefree and provide a bountiful crop for a minimum amount of effort. What's more, they take up very little space. One 25-foot row will supply enough berries to satisfy the appetite of a family of four.

Hardiness is a very important consideration in the selection of a variety for planting. Darrow and Ebony King are among the hardiest of the upright varieties and they will produce well in cold climates. The trailing types of blackberries, such as the Loganberry, are not as hardy as the upright ones. In the south, many of the trailing varieties won't survive because they are susceptible to endemic diseases.

Probably the best way to choose blackberry varieties for your own garden is to find out what other people in your area are growing successfully and to contact your local agricultural extension agent.

In selecting plant stock, make every effort to obtain certified, disease-free plants from a reputable nursery. Guaranteed, disease-free stock may cost more, but it is well worth the investment. Obtaining starts from a friend's garden or a nursery which doesn't guarantee disease-free stock is a gamble which could prove costly. You could end up not only losing your planting but also contaminating the soil and ruining it for future plantings.

Practically any type of soil is adequate for growing blackberries, although the subsoil should be deep and well-drained. Slightly sloping hillsides are excellent because they provide for cold-air drainage in winter.

Moisture is the key to good blackberry production. You won't have to water as often if you cover your blackberry bed with a mulch of straw or grass clippings. A deep mulch not only retains moisture and prevents erosion, but it also nearly eliminates the tedious task of weeding.

Space upright types (erect and semi-erect) 2 to 3 feet apart, with about 4 to 5 feet between the rows for cultivation and picking. Trailing blackberries should be planted anywhere from 6 to 12 feet apart, depending on how well they thrive in your area.

When planting your blackberries, be sure the roots don't dry out. Set them in the ground approximately 2 inches deeper than they grew in the nursery.

Give each plant a good soaking once it is in the ground.

To increase production and to simplify the care of blackberry plants, proper training and pruning is a must. The easiest way to keep upright blackberries in line is by installing a sturdy 4 to 5-foot high post at each end of the row. Place a crossbar at the top of each post and another at 3 feet, stringing heavy wires between the crossbars along either side of the row.

Trailing blackberries are vigorous growers and need to be tied to a trellis. Arrange posts at 15 to 20-foot intervals along the row and string a wire at 3 feet and another at 5 feet. Loop the canes over the top wire and fan them out along the lower one so they receive as much sunlight as possible.

As upright blackberry plants begin growing in the spring, top, or cut off, the upper ends. Cut them to between 18 and 24 inches in height.

With trailing varieties, let them grow freely and do no pruning during the first year. Then, in late winter, prune the canes back to about 10 feet in length. In areas where there is a long growing season, the canes of Dewberries are sometimes cut back to the ground after harvest. They seem to be less susceptible to pests and disease when treated this way.

Since blackberries are biennials—growing one year, bearing the next—each shoot must be grown two years before it produces and dies. Near the end of the first growing season, each cane sends out lateral branches which, during the next season, sprout several small fruiting branches. You should cut back these laterals to six buds each, early the following spring.

In all varieties of blackberries, as soon as the canes finish fruiting, cut them close to ground level. To prevent disease, destroy all pruned canes. By thinning out the patch you are making room for new canes to grow from the crown.

You will need to fertilize your blackberry beds in early spring. Apply a 10-10-10 fertilizer, 1 pound per 10 feet of row.

Weeds are always a problem for blackberry growers. They rob the bushes of nutrients and also serve as a breeding ground for diseases and insects. However, you can keep this problem under control by deep mulching. One effective and inexpensive method is to lay down thick sheets of newspaper, then cover them with grass clippings. Leave the soaker in place throughout the growing season so that you water your blackberries during dry weather. Give the plants 1 to 2 inches of water per week.

Pick your blackberries at least twice a week, keeping the pails in the shade. Remove overripe or diseased fruit from the plot. Once harvested, blackberries can be canned, frozen or dried and held over for later enjoyment.

From time to time, you may encounter problems with insects, particularly the Japanese beetle. Either remove them by hand or apply wettable Sevin according to the manufacturer's instructions.

By planting disease-resistant varieties and by following the cultivation practices mentioned herein, you can add delectable blackberries to your family's diet without paying a premium price.

Even if you don't wish to grow your own berries or go out and pick the wild varieties, that doesn't mean you have to miss out on enjoying the delightful taste of sweet blackberries. Fresh blackberries are becoming available in markets and blackberry juice concentrate is available in most health food stores. It is a great flavoring, it makes delicious beverages and, when sweetened with honey, makes an excellent gelatin.

Blackberries are loaded with nutrients. They contain Vitamin C and iron and, being a low calorie fruit, they are ideal for weight watchers. They are an excellent source of calcium, phosphorus, potassium, and niacin, and contain small amounts of protein. They also provide dietary fiber.

Blackberries are ideal for use in any recipe that calls for berries. They also make for a rather tasty addition to cold cereals. Pureed, they are excellent over ice creams and puddings. Fresh blackberries can also be used to garnish and decorate countless other dishes.

The biggest bonus of blackberries is that they are ready to serve in any form with little or no preparation.

Berry Good Syrup

> 4 cups blackberry juice
> 2 cups granulated sugar
> 1 to 2 cups light corn syrup (see note)
> 1 tablespoon lemon juice, optional

To extract juice, mash a small amount of fruit, using a food mill, juicer or food processor, then sieve to remove seeds if desired. (Some people prefer not to mash all the fruit, but leave some whole.)

Place juice, sugar and corn syrup in saucepan. Boil for 3 to 5 minutes. Place in boiling water bath and process for 10 minutes (from when water returns to a boil) to ensure a seal. The yield is about 3 1/2 pints and it makes a nice topping for desserts or pancakes.

Corn syrup is used in this recipe to thicken the juice. Simply adding more sugar without the syrup will tend to make jelly, rather than syrup, and if too much sugar is added, sugar crystals will form.

The amount of syrup can be varied depending on the amount of pectin naturally present in the berries. The riper the berries, the less natural pectin available, and the greater amount of corn syrup is needed to thicken the syrup. The longer cooking time is needed if there's not as much natural pectin, in order to thicken the syrup.

Blackberry Jelly

> 6 cups blackberry juice
> 1 1/2 cups liquid pectin
> 3 tablespoons lemon juice
> 12 cups brown or raw sugar

To obtain juice, wash berries, crush. Place in jelly bag; squeeze out juice. Mix berry juice, lemon juice and sugar in large saucepan. Bring to a boil as quickly as possible and add pectin at once, stirring constantly. Bring to full rolling boil and boil hard exactly 1/2 minute. Remove from heat; skim and pour into hot sterilized jars. Seal at once. Δ

Preparing yourself for springtime floods

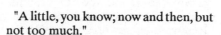

© *By Rodney L. Merrill, PhD, MPH*

When I was growing up in the New Hampshire backwoods, springtime always brought mixed emotions. After being cooped up in the cabin through a long, brutal northern New Hampshire winter, frantic, like I'd stayed underwater too long and run out of breath, the feeling of just bursting out the door on a warm spring day, half-dressed, defies description. But, because we lived along a river, springtime also meant preparing for a flood.

Every spring, when the snow melted, water came rushing down from the mountains, and the river rose up, heaving and tumbling great, groaning chunks of ice that became thirty- or forty-foot walls when they reared up. And just about every year those great walls of ice found a bottleneck in the river and dammed it up tighter than a drum. That's when we started hauling our possessions up the path to higher ground.

Living at "The Hideout" (as the cabin was called) taught me some valuable lessons about flooding. Until I saw my first spring along this otherwise placid river, I couldn't imagine why it was referred to as "The Wild Ammonoosuc." You'd certainly never believe "The Hideout" was in any danger. But it was.

So, if you plan to buy a backwoods home in an unfamiliar area, I suggest you find out if the place is subject to flooding. Who do you ask? Don't overlook the obvious. Step right up to the seller and ask. Backwoods folks tend to accept hardships as a fact of life and many won't even try to hide it from you.

But if the conversation goes along this vein:

"Place flood any?"

"Some."

"What do you mean, exactly, by some."

"A little, you know; now and then, but not too much."

. . . then you might want to use other sources to refine this estimate. Local insurance agents are a good source.

Be prepared

If your property is subject to flooding, prepare for it.

Keep the gas tank at least half full during flood season. There's no point in abandoning your home in a car that's going to run out of gas. Gas pumps are often out of commission during a flood.

Clearly mark a tall object in the flood's path (like a tree or flagpole) so you can easily see how fast the water is rising during a flood. This bit of information can be helpful. It might even save your family.

Keep an emergency box stocked with a first aid kit, an extra supply of any special medications needed by family members, blankets, canned foods, bottled water, a portable radio, flashlights, extra batteries. Ideally, there would be two of these boxes: one kept on high ground in a weather-proof and varmint-proof shelter, and another in the attic. A citizen's band walkie-talkie is a plus.

Have an easily accessible escape route to higher ground and practice using it. Although it may seem easy, you usually can't think as clearly in an emergency situation.

Work out a realistic plan for getting everyone and the upstairs box of emergency supplies up to the roof, just in case the house floods and you can't get out. It happens.

Check your homeowner's insurance policy carefully. Most standard homeowner's policies do **not** cover any flood loss. You may find yourself paying a 30-year mortgage on a house that no longer exists.

If you can't get satisfactory flood coverage through your homeowner's company, ask your agent if you are to purchase coverage through the National Flood Insurance Program. You might want to check into NFIP anyway because a chief feature of the program is its low cost.

Take pictures of your real and personal property and update them periodically. Augment these with itemized descriptions. Documentation and photographs will help you get the most from your insurance adjuster and help you validate tax deductions for any uninsured losses.

Put documentation and insurance policies in a safe place—either on higher ground or in a safe deposit box at your bank.

When it happens

If you made a marker as suggested earlier, keep your eye on it. Flood waters can rise suddenly.

Rinse the tubs, sinks, and any jugs with bleach to sanitize them, then fill them with cold water. If your water supply gets cut off or contaminated by flooding, you'll be glad you have those extra gallons of water. (See "Emergency Quick-Fix Tricks" in Dec/Jan 1989 issue for tips on emergency water treatment.)

If it looks like the house is going to flood **and you are certain there is enough time,** you can help minimize damage by closing the main gas valve and turning off the electricity at the main switch. If there is any doubt about time, forget utilities; get everyone to safety. **Caution:** If the house is damp, you must stand on a dry, nonconductive material (like a dry piece of wood) and wear rubber gloves and rubber-soled shoes to be sure you won't get shocked. This is nothing to take chances with—you can be electrocuted.

If the water rises faster than you expected and you are caught in the house, resist the urge to swim for safety. Flood waters can be deceptive and many people drown needlessly in floods because they abandon their homes with no place to go—except into a swift, ever-widening, ever-deepening river that is too strong for them to resist.

Instead, go to the second floor, if there is one. If there is no second floor, head for the roof. Hopefully, you will have planned and practiced how to get everyone and the box of supplies to the roof. If time permits, dress everyone in rain gear first. Staying dry is crucial to staying warm. You may be up there awhile. But, it is a good place to be. Most floods don't reach the rooftops. And, guess where rescue workers are trained to look for survivors?

If you can safely evacuate by car, be sure to take your emergency supply boxes with you. Don't leave the relative safety of your house unless the gas tank has plenty of gas to get you to safety. Don't drive over flooded roads—floodwater often rises faster than you expect and can sweep the car downstream; cross currents can pull the car off the road; water may be deeper than it seems; parts of the road may be washed out. For all the reasons just mentioned, a stalled car can become a death trap. If your car stalls, abandon it immediately and head for high ground.

After a flood

If your home has been damaged, make sure it is structurally sound before going back in. If your home is hooked up to natural gas or bottled gas, make sure there are no leaks before using flames or electrical equipment. If you have electricity, avoid using it until an electrician has checked it out for short circuits.

Before you start fixing or cleaning anything, take **lots** of pictures—inside and outside. Don't miss anything. If it takes a while for the insurance adjuster to get out and assess the damage, you will need the pictures to explain the rental fee for a sump pump, dry cleaning, and so on.

Remove mud as soon as possible to minimize damage to walls and floors. Be sure to clean out plumbing, air conditioning, and heating systems before mud has a chance to solidify.

Take all wooden items outside to dry. Remove all drawers and other movable parts so the air can circulate. Let them dry slowly in a covered or shaded area. Direct sunlight will warp and split water-soaked wood.

Pump out flooded basements. However, the Federal Emergency Management Agency, says draining out the water too quickly can cause serious structural damage. They advise waiting until **after** the floodwater around your property has subsided, then draining the water from your basement over a three day period—about 1/3 of the volume each day.

When your insurance agent inspects your property and assesses the damage, he or she will decide whether damaged items should be repaired or replaced. If the agent recommends repairing something and you want to replace it, insurance will probably cover a repair bid and you'll have to make up the difference minus whatever salvage price you can get for the damaged item.

Flood insurance

Until 1968, most folks couldn't get flood insurance. Private insurance companies considered flood insurance too risky and either refused to write coverage at all or charged such high premiums that rural homeowners were out of picture entirely.

In 1968, Congress created the National Flood Insurance Program. The government offered to underwrite an affordable flood insurance plan in return for local implementation of risk reduction programs.

I checked with Anna Townes, my friendly and helpful State Farm insurance agent here in Wauwatosa, Wisconsin, and she assures me the National Flood Insurance Program still exists. She says not many inquire about it; but she did write a policy just last week. Anna says any insurance agent can write an NFIP policy and rates are set by the government. Rates do vary a little from one place to another based on a risk assessment.

As someone who grew up along "The Wild Ammonoosuc" in the backwoods, I appreciate NFIP. It works efficiently through entrepreneurial agents. It encourages personal independence and small scale property ownership by putting the security of disaster insurance within the reach of ordinary folks. And that makes springtime a bit easier to enjoy. Speaking of which, I'm outta here!

For more information:

Federal Insurance Administration: 1-800-838-8820 or 202-646-2781

Office of Disaster Assistance Programs: 202-646-3615, or write either office at: **Federal Emergency Management Agency, Washington, DC 20472**

This agency also sells a 41-page booklet (*"In Time of Emergency"*) which gives practical advice about floods, hurricanes, winter storms, tornadoes, earthquakes, and fires. Send request for publication #459 and 50 cents to: **R. Woods, Consumer Information Center-T, P.O. Box 100, Pueblo CO 81002.**

(Rodney Merrill is an associate editor for "Backwoods Home Magazine." He currently lives in Wisconsin and writes for a variety of publications on health and environmental topics.) Δ

Dare to dream with Michael Andy Darr

By Pamela Kleibrink Thompson

A wood-burning potbelly stove heats the Silverton Artworks gallery but visitors warm up to Andy Darr's friendly open personality and his unique vision of abandoned mines and ghost towns of the Colorado Rockies. The walls of this century-old house are adorned with images of mining operations that capture the essence of the rugged mountain landscapes surrounding the small town of Silverton, Colorado. The home serves as workshop and gallery, both for his watercolors, photographs, and pen and ink renderings as well as his wife, Ruth Ann's handmade pottery, weaving, and baskets.

Ten years ago when Ruth Ann suggested "Honey, quit your job and we'll move to the mountains and become artists," he thought the idea was crazy, but decided to try it anyway. Today, this 28-year old Colorado artist enjoys a lifestyle that city folk and others often dream of, but rarely take the chance to discover.

Dressed in flannel shirt and jeans, Andy looks like an unpretentious, typical resident of any small town in the rockies. If you catch him playing golf, leading his son's Scout troop, or serving on the local Chamber of Commerce, he would strike you as he describes himself—"an ordinary guy who happens to paint pictures." But the spirit of the independent artist shines in his eyes when he gazes at his surroundings, the former mining camp of Silverton wedged between the impressive peaks of the San Juan Range. He has something in common with a former resident of Silverton, Bat Masterson, as a man who takes chances with his life.

Like other artists before him, Andy's parents had different expectations of what he could or should accomplish with his life. His childhood was very atypical. His mother, Ann Gedney, a

professional artist, influenced him to pursue the art industry but his father, the field supervisor for Federal Steel and Supply, a high steel erection company, wanted him to continue his education and seek regular employment. Andy admits that "the hardest thing to learn is giving up the crutch of a steady pay check and security of a real job." His mother, wife, and collec-

Andy Darr in front of his home studio in Silverton, CO. (photo by Joe Darr)

tors of his work encourage him to continue in his life's choice of being a self-supporting free-lance artist.

The Colorado artist has gained national recognition. Andy was recently commissioned by the Bureau of Land Management to create commemorative limited edition prints of America's scenic highways. When a BLM director showed one of Andy's San Juan Mining District posters to his colleagues, they decided that this artist should be hired to paint Colorado's

backcountry byways. Marvin Paioff of Colorado owns the original 22x30 painting of "The Empire Chief," the model for BLM's Alpine Loop poster. So far Andy has produced, published and sold 600 posters and 2000 prints of the Alpine Loop.

Andy just completed the painting for another poster commemorating the scenic byways of Colorado. The painting depicts Driggs Mansion at Thimble Rock. Eighteen hundred posters of the Unaweep/Tabaguache byway in western Colorado will be issued. (Price $22.75) 200 limited signed prints (price $145) and 35 artist's proofs (price $195) will also be available.

Ruth Ann and Andy decided to move to the picturesque mountain community of Silverton, Colorado the day they happened to drive into it. Although Ruth Ann was concerned at first about the remoteness of this community, Andy believes she now likes it even more than he does. From May to October, this small village of 700 people caters to tourists from around the world who ride the historic Durango-Silverton narrow gauge railroad through the majestic peaks of the San Juan mountains. Its population swells to 1200 during the summer months but never loses its charm for Andy and his family. "We love the beautiful surroundings, the close friends and community. There is no place better for scenery, people, and weather." The nearby majestic peaks serve as inspiration and subject matter to his art.

Andy was born and grew up in Alton, IL, a suburb of St. Louis, a small town of 48,000 people. With a touch of irony he recalls he dreamed of moving to a big city. Overrun by poverty and people on welfare, Alton offers little inspiration to its native son although he admits he misses the river. "The river is a magic place." He returns to this town of old glassworks and steel mills to visit his family. Intending to pursue a career as an architect, Andy studied architecture at the Southern Illinois University at Edwardsville. While still in high school he had designed homes with a general contractor. He also designed pizza restaurants. This experience would later help him to design and build the studio at Silverton with Ruth Ann.

Architectural influences are reflected in his paintings; buildings play a prominent role in his work. Andy's background in draftsmanship and precise pencil rendering gives his watercolors detail and precision. Influenced and inspired by the work of Ivan Bilibin, a Russian illustrator, Sam English, and Andrew Wyeth, Andy's work captures the heritage and legacy of Colorado's mining days. Like Wyeth, Andy's paintings depict uncrowded rural scenes that are reminders of earlier American life. Works of both artists include pictures of old buildings with bare windows and cracked ceilings, weathered paint and a sense of isolation. Both painters concentrate on scenes that portray the remains of past activity rather than the accomplishments of the present. While Wyeth painted Pennsylvania

and Maine, Andy paints his adopted Colorado.

His watercolors capture the essence and haunting beauty of the deserted mining operations. He believes collectors like the way they capture this sense of place. Perhaps that is why J. Michael Hudson brought home "Old Hundred Boarding House" to Oklahoma or Jean Baldauff recalls her Colorado visit in her Florida home when viewing "On the Way to Tomboy." Andy's paintings are in private collections from Albuquerque to Australia. With names like "Treasure Mountain Trio" (collection of Eugene Schrock of Colorado Springs), "Falling Giant" and "Spring Thaw," Andy's paintings evoke a sense of time as well.

A sense of detachment and yearning, of serenity and a bucolic peacefulness beckon the viewer to explore memories of a bygone era when miners tapped the snow-capped peaks of the San Juan in search of silver by the ton, gold, and other precious metals. The prices of the metals have closed most of the mines in the surrounding area, but Andy has captured the remnants of this once prosperous industry forever in his watercolors. Andy feels that the most compelling aspect of his work is "the spareness of the high altitude environs."

Andy works in a studio rather than on location. He paints from photographs he has taken of his chosen subject. Much like French impressionist Claude Monet who

The Old Hundred Boarding House

The Third Year

"Near the Black Prince."

painted the same building at different times of the day to explore the effect of light and changing atmospheric conditions, Andy photographs his subject 15 times during the year, in different weather conditions and seasons. First to admit it goes against his sense of ecology, Andy says he "puts a nail in the ground to mark the spot where his tripod goes." With his cache of photographs viewing the building from the same angle, but with different lighting and surrounding scenery, he selects the shot that he feels will help him to convey "the beauty and mystery of high mountain places."

"There is not a day that I don't think how lucky I am to be able to make a living as an active artist. I also love the ability to spend so much time with my family."

A work desk placed near the pot belly stove reminds the visitor that this artist is a businessman as well. He admits that he is "one of a few lucky artists who can think business and create too." He discusses the importance of merchandising and marketing his work. He cites Bev Doolittle as the most popular example of that rare combination of artist and businessperson.

Andy says the myth of the starving artist keeps many from following their dreams. But as he has proved, artists can thrive by pursuing their muses. The two most important qualities an artist needs to succeed is determination and self-belief. He advises aspiring artists to "maintain your own style and stay ever vigilant to your trade. Keep pushing your ability. Never stay just comfortable with what you do. Push, always push." He recognizes that it's difficult to make a living and raise a child on an artist's income but he and Ruth Ann are demonstrating that it isn't impossible. They cherish the freedom of their chosen profession which allows them time to enjoy their 10-year old son, Joseph Caitland.

Andy's future plans include painting larger canvases. He is working on a series of San Juan Mining District Posters to celebrate the history and culture of hard rock mining. "Eventually I would like to have a published hardback book featuring my works from start to present."

Colorado galleries representing Andy's work include the Toh-Atin in Durango, The Mining Gallery in Leadville, The Ouray Gallery in Ouray, Barton's of Steamboat in Steamboat Springs. Andy's artworks are obtainable by calling him direct at 303-387- 5823 or writing to him at Silverton Artworks, 1028 Empire Street, Silverton, CO 81433. Δ

Sirens in the Night

Night after night,
Ambulances, firetrucks, and
*   police cars*
Pass below my window.
I sit on my bed reading,
Listening with one ear
To a distant wail:
Someone else's nightmare
*   is coming true.*
I put my book down and wonder
*   how many years*
He listened to the sirens come
*   for others,*
And now they've come for him.
I am safe in my little room
But a chill crawls over my skin
Like snakes in a swamp
Though the night is hot and humid
And I think,
Someday, someone else will sit
*   in a room like this*
And listen
While past his bedroom window
The nightmare comes for me.

John Earl Silveira
Ojai, CA

A country ride

Make a crazy quilt

By Linda Rainey

Since the days of the pioneers, country women have been recycling. Crazy quilts were a way to make use of old clothes, while at the same time preserving memories. Crazy quilts were made from patches of material that held special meaning, such as a swatch from their wedding dress, a piece of a dead child's christening dress. You can preserve these memories in the same way.

Materials

- 1. Patches of any kind of material
- 2. 1 skein of 4 ply knitting and crochet yarn
- 3. An old blanket of commercial batting
- 4. An old sheet or material for backing

Instructions

1. Measure the size of your anticipated quilt.
2. Cut patches of material and sew them together.
3. Trim to match your measurements after you piece your quilt, leaving allowance for a 1" hem.

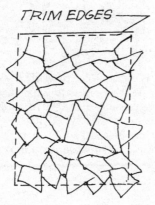

TRIM EDGES

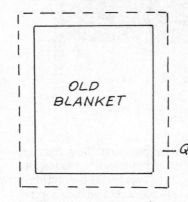

OLD BLANKET

QUILT TOP

QUILT TOP

4. To remember what each patch means, you can embroider or paint on each patch.
5. Next find an old blanket or use commercial batting to

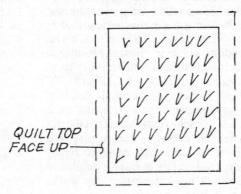

QUILT TOP FACE UP

use for a filler. Pioneer women used frayed old blankets because they never threw anything away.
6. Pin your quilt top, back down, to the old blanket.
7. Turn the quilt over and pin an old sheet or batting, the size of the old quilt, to the blanket.
8. To hold the quilt together you need to tie yarn at intervals over the quilt using a random pattern. To do this cut strands of yarn 6-8" long and thread through a darning needle. Draw the needle

through all three layers and back out again.
9. Remove the needle from the yarn, then tie the yarn together three times. Repeat

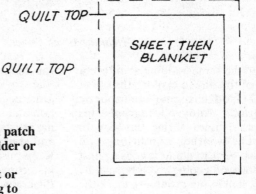

QUILT TOP

SHEET THEN BLANKET

this until the quilt is covered.
10. Trim the ends of the yarn to within a 1/2" of the blanket.
11. Now you are ready to hem your quilt. Turn the quilt over and fold and pin the edges around the quilt. Using the darning needle and yarn hem the edges using a whip stitch.

Now you have a warm quilt to keep you toasty on a cold winter night and an heirloom to pass to your children. Δ

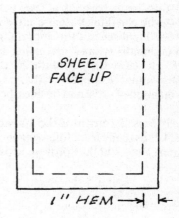

SHEET FACE UP

1" HEM

Heat your upstairs by cutting holes in the floor!

by Don Fallick

Many old, two-story houses have upstairs rooms that are impossible to heat in the winter time. In nearly every case, the problem is that the rooms were built with no way for the cold air in the room to get back to the furnace or stove downstairs. Since there's no place for the cold air to go, the warm air downstairs can't get into the upstairs rooms to warm them up. As a result, the downstairs bakes, while the upstairs freezes. If this describes your house, don't despair. There's a cheap and easy way to fix it that may also save you money on your total heating bill. The solution is to cut a hole in the floor of each upstairs room, through the ceiling downstairs, so the cold air has somewhere to go.

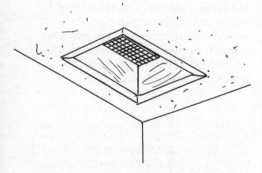

Location of your hole is very important. It should not adversely affect convection downstairs. But more important, it should not prove a safety hazard to people upstairs or compromise the structural integrity of the floor. If you place the hole between 2 joists, it is unlikely to weaken the floor. If you can place it under a large item of furniture, such as a bed or dresser, it is unlikely to prove a safety hazard, even without a grating over it. (But you will put a grating over it anyhow, right?) Examine the room with an eye to moving the furniture later. Will a change bring the hole into a new traffic pattern? When you have tentatively decided on a location for your hole, go downstairs and see where it's going to come out. Dust, dirt, and small objects sometimes fall through floor holes, or are pushed through by children. It's not a good idea to put holes directly over dining, cooking, or sitting areas. No one wants to catch dirt in their soup or a marble on their head.

Finding floor joists

To prevent cutting floor joists you must locate them positively. If the floor is wood, you may be able to tell where the joists are by looking at the nails. Tongue and groove flooring is usually laid with the nails hidden, so you can't tell where the joists are by looking. Rugs can be removed, but wall-to-wall carpets and glued-down linoleum make a harder problem. Sometimes you can tap with a hammer on the downstairs ceiling and listen for the "solid" sound that indicates the location of a joist. This does not work well with old-time wooden lath and plaster ceilings. An electronic "stud finder", available in discount stores for about $15, may prove helpful. The surest way I know to locate joists is in the ceiling downstairs, by turning off the electricity and removing a ceiling light fixture. The junction box may have knockouts removed, which will give you a hint about which side of the box is nailed to a joist. Even if it doesn't, you know that ONE of the sides is a joist. By carefully drilling a small hole in the plaster on each side of the box, you should be able to find the joist because the drill bit will penetrate the lath and plaster on the other 2 sides, but on the joist side it will stay in wood the full length of the bit. Use a fairly long bit, since lath and plaster in some old houses can be over an inch thick. Keep your holes within the area that will be covered by the light fixture when you replace it. Sticking masking tape to the plaster before you drill will keep the plaster from breaking out around the hole. Wear eye protection.

Locating the hole

When you know which way the joists run, measure from the joist whose location you know, in multiples of 16 inches, until you get close to the proposed location of your hole. In most houses, floor joists are placed 16 inches apart. But if the upstairs was an addition to an original one-story building, the joists may have been laid 24 inches center to center. Since 16 and 24 are both multiples of 8, they may coincide right next to your hole. Or the joists may be nowhere near where you want them to be. In any case, when you think you know where the joists are, pencil in lines where you think the edges of your hole should be. The hole should be a rectangle about 1/12 the size of the upstairs room. So an 8 ft. x 12 ft. room should have an 8 in. x 12 in. hole. If the room is much larger than this, it may need more than one hole for proper circulation. The hole must not cross a joist. When the hole is laid out on the ceiling, turn off any electric circuits that might be running through the ceiling, and drill a series of small holes, in a line at right angles to the joists. Start at the center of your pencilled rectangle, then an inch on either side of the center, then two inches, etc. Eventually you will either find a joist or reach one of your pencilled lines. If you find a joist, you can locate your hole precisely, with confidence. If you don't find a joist, your hole will be just fine where you've drawn it.

Cutting the hole

This is easiest to accomplish if you can locate the hole on the floor above. Cutting plaster ceilings from below will get you a face full of plaster dust, maybe an eyeful, too, even with eye protection. If you have a rotary power saw, start cutting through the flooring and subflooring, gradually deepening the cut, until you are just cutting all the way through, to avoid cutting wires that may be below the floor. You will have to finish the cuts at the corners with a hand saw or a chisel. Once you've got the flooring out, you'll be able to tell if there's any wiring in the way. Next, the lath and plaster ceiling can be cut out with a keyhole saw from above, or from below with a saber saw or reciprocating saw.

If you can't locate the hole on the upstairs floor, you'll have to cut from the bottom up. Again, make sure you're not going to cut into any live wires, then cut **carefully** using a non-electric saw such as a keyhole saw, so you'll feel any wires you may run into before you sever them. Saw carefully and don't allow the saw to drag against the plaster when you pull it out at the end of each stroke. To further prevent plaster at the edge from chipping out, hold a piece of scrap wood tightly against the ceiling along the kerf as you saw. Work over a drop cloth or spread newspapers on the floor to catch plaster dust, and wear eye protection.

Once you have the ceiling removed, you can locate the hole upstairs by drilling a small hole in each corner. If there's carpet on the floor upstairs, **don't drill**. A drill can pull the pile out of a carpet faster than you'd believe. Instead, locate the corners by nailing nails up through the floor, or nail down from the top approximately, then measure from the nails to the actual corners. Cut the carpet with a razor knife, about 1/4 inch outside of the actual hole, so you don't catch the carpet with the saw. Then saw out the hole.

Finishing the hole

It's a good idea to line the inside of the hole to prevent dirt and dust inside the ceiling from raining down on the lower floor. Use wood of the same width as the floor joists. If the floor joists are 2x8s, use 2x8 or 1x8 boards. Modern lumber is milled about 1/4 inch narrower than the old-time, "rough cut", or "full size" boards. If you

can't find the same size lumber, get the next larger size and rip it (cut it lengthwise) to fit exactly. Often your lumber dealer will do this for you for a small extra charge. If you have to do it yourself by hand, it's a lot easier using 1x stock.

Check the thickness of your floor grate and cut back the flooring to the proper depth, 3/4 inch beyond the edge of the hole, all the way around it. Set your rotary saw to the exact depth and make your cuts, then finish the corners with a sharp chisel then turn the chisel **bevel down** and mortise out the ledge.

Do not go any deeper than the top of the subflooring. Make each board the same length as the actual side of the hole it is covering, **plus** an amount equal to the thickness of the board. Place the board between the floor and ceiling, with all the "excess" length to one side of the hole, and nail in place with casing nails driven up through the ceiling and down through the subfloor. Then butt the end of the next board tightly against the "excess" length of the first and nail it in place. To aid in handling these pieces of wood, screw a couple of wood screws part way into the face of each board, and remove them after it is nailed in place. Finish the ceiling with corner moulding, available wherever wood products are sold. Paint or stain the moulding before you put it up, and miter the corners, or it won't look right.

Floor grates

Even if the hole is under a piece of furniture, it needs a floor grate on top. If nothing else, this will keep "dust bunnies" and large objects from falling through. Floor grates can sometimes be found in old houses that are being demolished, or they may be improvised from any number of things. Old treadle sewing machine parts work well. If you can't find anything cheap, try a scrap metal dealer. As a last resort, you can have grates made up by a furnace dealer or sheet metal shop, but expect to pay custom prices. If your grate is nearly the same thickness as the flooring, you can set it right on top of the subfloor. If it sticks up

slightly above the floor, trim around it with moulding of the appropriate thickness, to keep people from stumbling on the edges. Miter the corners of the moulding, and paint or stain it before you nail it down. Special metal trim for finishing the cut edges of carpets is available at most hardware or builders supply stores.

For grates that are too thick to set on top of the subfloor, form a ledge inside the hole at the appropriate depth by gluing and screwing 1x4 boards to the sides of the hole. If you know you are going to do this, it's a real good idea to use 2 inch thick boards for the sides of the hole, and use 16 D (16 penny) box nails to secure them to the floor and ceiling.

Heating bills

When your cold-air returns are complete, you will be amazed how much warmer your upstairs rooms will be. You may even discover that your total heating bill goes down. The energy that you used to expend over-heating the downstairs, in a vain attempt to warm up the upstairs just a little, now is not needed at all. Now the warm air downstairs rises and heats the upstairs as well, doing double duty, before returning to be reheated. Δ

Getting more cash from your crafts

By Dan and Becky Ames

The practice of self-reliant living often requires a person to do several different things in order to bring in needed cash. We've found that selling our crafts is an excellent way to generate income.

I make gifts and utility items from driftwood and hardshell gourds. Becky is the real artist in the family. She created "Thumbprint Originals", a line of handcrafted clay sculptures in miniature. The little animals, children, and scenes are always top sellers.

Participating in crafts shows seems to be the most popular and well known method of selling crafts, and we've done a lot of them. It has been our experience that three or four good craft shows a year uses most everything that we can produce and provides substantial income.

Visiting with the people is one of the fun benefits of craft show selling. We've met lots of interesting folks this way. We get to demonstrate our crafts and talk to them about their crafts and their desire to sell them.

There are four questions from would-be craft sellers that we hear most often at our booth at craft shows. The answers to those questions may help encourage you to start a craft selling venture of your own.

How can I tell if my craft will sell?

First, a caution! Don't rely on the "ooohs and aaahs" of your friends or relatives as a reliable indication of your crafts acceptability and saleability. These folks mean well. They wouldn't hurt your feelings for the world, so they won't be too critical or objective about your work. They may boost your ego, but they won't help your selling effort much.

There is only one way to find out if your crafts will sell. Submit them to the cold, impersonal eyes of prospective buyers in the marketplace! Participating in a craft show is the quickest way to test your crafts "saleability".

If your craft is recognizable as a true craft; if it has original form and function; each piece well designed and crafted; if it is reasonably priced, you should find a ready market and willing buyers.

How do I get started selling at craft shows?

First, find a non-juried show near your home. Non-juried means that your work doesn't have to be judged. Anyone who pays the entry fee can show and sell.

Next, get acquainted with a fellow crafter who has done shows before. Ask around. My guess is one of your friends, or a friend of a friend, can be found to help you get started.

As an exhibitor, you will usually be required to provide your own table, chairs and all the other trappings for your craft display. You should check and re-check to make sure you've taken everything you need for a good show. Do it **before** you leave home!

We suggest you make a list of all the things you need to take, and all the things you must do to get ready. After years of doing craft shows, we still make a list. It has saved our hides more than once!

There is a lot of packing and toting that goes along with doing a craft show. Don't worry. It won't be long until you've developed an easy system for moving your crafts and stuff from home to the show.

The type of show (indoors/outdoors), how many days you'll be there and how far you must travel are just a few of the things you will need to consider in deciding what you must take. You will constantly change your "take

and do" list, depending on the circumstances.

Take a **person** with you. If possible, find someone experienced at craft show selling to go along. Otherwise take a friend, relative, wife/husband or your mother-in-law, but take someone with you! Don't try to do it alone, at least not the first one. You are going to need some help.

You will also need: table, chairs, display stands, your stock of craft items, nail apron or cashbox, money for making change, pad and pen, receipt book, string or small rope, scotch tape, pocketknife or scissors. Whew! What else?

Consider making the day as comfortable and pleasant for yourself as possible by taking: thermos for coffee or cold drink, doughnuts, lunch, small box of tissues, aspirin (or other needed medication), a spare set of car keys, sun glasses, tarp or other shade, rain gear and plastic sheet to cover tables in case of rain.

Dress in layers so you can dress up or down as comfort and temperatures dictate. Take anything else you can think of that will help you have a really great day at the show.

How can I get the most sales for my effort?

The most important thing here is to stay involved. Once you get to the show and get your display set up, continue to stay involved in the selling activity. We are always amazed by people who put time, money and effort into going to a show and then totally remove themselves from the selling activity!

For example, don't sit in the corner and read a book. We see this at every show. People have a built-in aversion to interrupting. If you're sitting there with your nose stuck in a book, you're going to miss a lot of sales.

Please don't sleep! We attended a craft show last Saturday and saw this again! This old-timer had a really good display of grapevine wreaths and stick furniture. People were avoiding his booth like the plague. The crowd literally moved sideways around it.

When we got closer we saw why. The fellow was sitting in the shade in one of his beautifully handmade stick chairs — sound asleep! Great advertisement for the comfort of his chair, but no sales.

So, stay involved. There are many ways to create interest and excitement for your craft display. Here are a few tips for you.

Use activity. Do something. Demonstrate making your craft. Create something beautiful right before their eyes! Carve the wood. Polish the jewelry. Sculpt the clay. Activity, especially during slow times, will get a crowd coming your way.

During the day you should arrange and rearrange the items in your display. Replace sold items with fresh stock. This will keep the display looking full. This is staying busy and involved with your showing and selling activity.

Use an attractive display. Put some thought and effort into how you display your items. They should be arranged neatly, not just stacked about. Always use a large, sturdy table for small and medium sized items. Large items may be arranged on the floor (ground) around the table. Make it easy and fun to shop your booth.

Use attitude. Pleasant/friendly/positive, these are three big, important keys to your successful craft selling. Do it! Whether the sales have been good or not; whether the weather is lousy or not; whether you feel like it or not, do it. This will put cash in your jeans!

Use show and tell. I do, where it's appropriate. Remember the old time circus barker, "Step right up Ladeeeze and Gentlemen!"? Well, just refine that a bit and it still works. As people pass in front of your display, hold up one of your craft items and call attention to some interesting feature about it. I absolutely guarantee you'll have a

crowd. I have personally seen folks run toward my spiel and gathering crowd.

How can I sell crafts other than at craft shows?

When most folks think of selling crafts, the big four come to mind. Craft shows (fairs, festivals); a retail outlet of your own; consignment to retail outlets or wholesaling. The last three on this list are good possibilities, but can be time consuming and expensive.

Over the years, we have developed and tested many different, successful methods for selling crafts. We've been asked so many times, "how do you do this, or that". So, we've collected all this information and written it into a

Becky sets up for another show.

report that helps experienced as well as beginner craft sellers get more cash from their crafts.

While the report goes into detail with helps for the standard method of selling, it also lists many alternative ways to sell crafts. The information shows you how to either sell crafts directly or to get exposure in the marketplace which leads to sales. Here are a few.

Use your local library. This is an excellent way to get exposure for your crafts. Call or visit the Head Librarian. Get an appointment to show samples of your work. You may be allowed to create an attractive display for the lobby area. In our town, we're usually

allowed to leave it up a week or two. In three of four months do it again.

Ask for the library promotions calendar and plan your display around their special emphasis. This becomes the theme for your display. Example: Native American Week, use Indian designs on wall hangings, pottery, etc.

You may or may not be allowed to price your work for this display. Ask the librarian what their policy is. You may show a neatly lettered sign or your business card, so folks can contact you.

When you remove your display, be sure to thank the Librarian. Establish a good relationship with her and you will be invited again.

Bank lobby areas are excellent for getting exposure for your work. Sales will be generated by bank customers who pick up one of your prominently displayed business cards.

Contact the bank services representative, show your samples and discuss the type of display you have in mind. Be open to this person's ideas and incorporate them where possible. The bank will be happy to display your work as a "customer service". You've helped the bank with unusual decoration and a point of interest for its customers.

Contact your local County Extension Agent for information about Home Demonstration Units (HDU). You may be able to arrange to teach your crafts and may charge students a reasonable fee for instruction and materials. Classes usually meet at an HDU designated place one or two evenings a week for four or five weeks.

Be sure to plan your instruction carefully. Good communication skills are a must. The goal should be for each student to have mastered the principles of your craft and to have completed at least one item (project) by the end of the course.

Your local HDU chapter schedules many community activities and the director may suggest other ways you may participate. You may not always be able to actually sell your crafts at a particular event but, the exposure you'll get will be priceless!

Get acquainted with your Avon lady. These ladies have regular established customers and routes that are valuable to them. While they can't usually sell your crafts, they may be willing to take you along when they make their visits and introduce you to their customers.

Take along a few samples of your crafts for a brief presentation and take orders for future delivery. You'll want to deliver and collect on your own time. Don't bother the Avon lady with this. Be sure to offer her a 10% commission on every sale you make.

Remember to include your business card with each order you deliver and ask for referrals from your new customer, (their friends or relatives who might be interested in owning one of your crafts).

This method works well with any direct salesperson in your area, Mary Kay Cosmetics, Knapp Shoes, McNess Products, Stanley Home Products are all possibilities.

Life is for the living! Selling your crafts will be a great little adventure for you. You will meet some interesting people and make some lasting friendships. Some of the nicest people we have ever met are craftspersons. We hope you will give it a try. You'll be adding one more nice guy or gal to our ranks.

(Dan Ames publishes a report titled "How to Get More Cash From Your Crafts - Twentyfive Different Ways," available from him for $8 from P.O. Box 785, Ottawa, KS 66067.) Δ

A BHM Artist's Profile

Don Childers is the artist who paints each of *BHM's* scenic covers. He has spent many years working for the Defense Industry, painting mock-ups of military equipment still in the planning stage. The stealth bomber and fighter, the HARPOON and TOMAHAWK cruise missiles, and a variety of other once secret weapons are among the many mock-ups he painted at various stages of their development.

He is also an amateur astronomer who has built many of his own telescopes, an amateur inventor of a graphic arts tool to sharpen exacto knives, and has illustrated various historical books. Many of his paintings have been sold to private collectors, and many more hang on the walls of admirals and generals around the country. The Dijon Museum in France exhibits one of his paintings, and several hang in English pubs.

A BHM Writer's Profile

Jan Cook has been with *BHM* since the beginning, as a writer, an editor, and as the principal typist for entire issues. She is an associate editor for the magazine.

A technical writer for the Department of Defense for 15 years, Jan lives about 700 miles from the *BHM* office, but thanks to the reliability of Federal Express and the wonders of computer text-scanning technology, she still inputs most of our articles onto computer disk, then sends them to us.

Jan says she's a cut-to-the-chase kind of person with little tolerance for things that are supposed to work but don't. She believes in life's simpler things, like poems should rhyme and people should be as good as their word.

Growing Christmas trees —
a year-round part-time business

By Melinda C. Long

Now that Christmas is a long way off again, it's time to start thinking about how to use the season to help you make a living. For some of you, that may mean growing Christmas trees.

In the late 1970's my father, William Hardy, was looking for something to produce for sale on the poor, hilly soil of his farm, so he planted White Pine and Scotch to be sold as Christmas trees. He was surprised and delighted at the demand for them, and for the past three years, his ten acres of trees has shown a steadily increasing profit beginning at $2,000 a year.

Requirements for starting a tree farm

A good thing about growing Christmas trees is that they are not particular about where they grow. They will grow on sandy flats, under power lines, on top of old dumps and in hilly areas. Actually, poor soil suits Christmas tree farming very well. It doesn't produce quite as many weeds and that reduces the risk of seedlings being choked out.

To start a tree farm you need at least an acre. One acre can grow 600-700 trees. Seedlings can be bought from some state nurseries for 10 cents each. Making allowances for some trees that die or are deformed, the profit can be about $5,000 an acre by the time all the trees are harvested.

Your money won't come all in one year because the trees won't mature all at once. A White Pine can be ready for sale in six years, while a Scotch Pine takes longer to grow. And to maintain constant production you must not plant the whole farm the first year. For the first three years, plant only a third each year of the area you plan on tending overall. Then your supply won't be depleted the first year or two that the trees are ready for sale.

Selecting the right species of tree to grow on your farm will depend on your area. Selecting the right species is important. Plant the most valuable variety your soil will allow to get the highest return on your investment. Planting at least two different varieties offers the customer a choice.

Christmas trees enjoy trends of popularity. Cedars were popular during the 1860's. Douglas Firs and Fraser Firs are preferred today, along with Scotch and White Pine. If you are not sure what variety to choose, get in touch with the District Forester in your area or the Soil Conservation Office. These services, or the County Extension, can also give you the address of a state nursery where seedlings can be bought.

Finally, another essential requirement of the business is patience. It takes an average of seven years to grow a tree to salable age. If you have children, now would be a good time to plant. My father started planting trees when my brother and I were grown. He regrets not having started sooner. But it is not too late for his grandchildren. My twelve-year-old son, Vincent, is already involved and takes pride in instructing his little sister about the trees. There is hard work to the business, but not so much that an older child can't be a big help. Mostly, the work is repetitive. The money earned from Christmas trees can be put towards a child's future. It is a profitable family business that can last into the generations.

Planting

Two-year-old seedlings arrive from the nursery in early spring, and they are planted like most other tree seedlings. The hole must be deep enough so the roots have enough room to run straight down. Cover the stem an inch above the roots with soil. Carry the seedlings in a bucket of water to keep the roots from drying out.

Just like planting a garden, a stake will keep your sights and your rows straight. Don't set trees close to the woods. The shade makes the trees one-sided and difficult to sell. Set trees five feet apart in the row. Leave twelve feet between rows if using farm equipment, such as a tractor and a brush cutter to mow around the trees. Leave six or seven feet between rows if using narrower equipment.

Mowing

Young trees must be protected from being choked out by weeds. This follow-up care is especially crucial in the first year. And two and three-year-olds do better if mowed around more than once. After three years, mowing once a year can be enough.

For a large farm, a brush cutter is necessary. But for an acre, a gas-powered weedeater or heavy duty lawnmower will do to keep weeds down. As the trees mature, early fall is a good time to mow. Not only does it help the trees, but it also clears the way for cutting time.

Trimming

While growing Christmas trees can easily be a part-time job, it is definitely a year around business as each season has its purpose of activity. Early summer brings the important job of trimming. Trimming creates the pyramid shape that Christmas trees are known for. Cutting part of the spring growth causes new buds to appear for next year's growth, and the trees bush out during the summer.

With a tree pruner, start trimming a tree when it is at least three years old. To begin, select a top branch (there will be several) that is straight and healthy. This is the tree top. Trim it down 8 to 12 inches. It must be trimmed, otherwise it will create a bare gap leaving only a long straight spike. Now going all around the tree, clip at an angle the new growth (called candles) to the shape you want it to be. If a tree hasn't grown much that year, still clip the candle ends. After a tree is three years old, this trimming ritual is repeated every summer.

Cutting, replanting, and drawbacks

When a tree is cut, it is best to cut it even with the ground. This speeds up the root rotting process. After a tree is cut, the soil around the stump seems to be depleted, and a seedling won't grow well in the former tree's shade for at least a year. To give a seedling a two year head start, plant it between trees that are a couple of years away from sale. By the time the mature trees start to crowd the four-year-old, they will be gone.

Insects and disease are generally not much of a problem. Fire can be, and drought will stunt growth. But a real plague to the business is trees that are stolen. You'll always know too, because you have worked the trees long enough to know each and every one.

Marketing

After nearly a decade of diligence, you may feel a touch of attachment to your trees when cutting time comes. But it's also a proud feeling to know your trees are being enjoyed by others.

One way to market your trees is to invite customers into your field to choose-and-cut their own. This method of marketing is becoming extremely popular. Reminiscent of the days when all trees were cut from free stands, roaming over the fields in search of that special tree is a treat for many people.

My father opened his fields and was surprised by the number of repeat customers and new ones. It was word-of-mouth that brought them. My father has yet to advertise and each year he sells every tree ready for market. Some customers even come as early as October to tag their tree and insure a good choice.

He sells trees at retail price to visiting customers and wholesales the rest to a local grower because he can order fresh trees as he needs them. Before, the trees had to be ordered as early as August and shipped from large farms weeks in advance. Inquiring with local produce and grocery markets may find a wholesale outlet for your trees. And don't overlook non-profit organizations. By offering to help church, scout or civic organizations raise money, you are also helping yourself.

If you decide to take your trees directly to the customer, a lot near a busy street intersection will give your trees plenty of visibility. A place where people stop such as a busy gas station is also a good location. They stop at your site anyway, and with the holiday spirit drifting freely in the air, what's a few extra minutes to check out your beautiful trees.

Advertising can be worth the small marketing investment, especially if

you offer a variety. Dug trees and miniature trees are becoming increasingly popular. Have some burlap on hand for the orders of dug trees. Miniature trees have been popular in Europe for years. They are becoming popular in this country as well. They make fine tabletop trees. Additional Christmas greenery such as Holly and Mistletoe, if it is available, will also add to sales. Carrying your customers into the field by tractor or horse drawn wagon to choose-and-cut their own tree adds nostalgic charm. And kids love it.

Prices

In the end, trees are worth what you can get for them. When people see an opportunity they naturally flock to it.

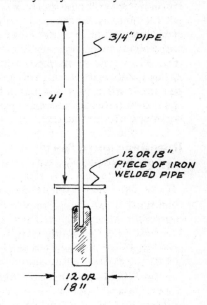

If you have access to a welder, a hand-crafted tree planter will speed the job of planting seedlings three times faster than a spade.

Locations around larger cities may be able to charge more, but keeping your prices low will keep the customers coming back for the Christmas break you can give them. Ten or even twenty dollars is a long way off from the $35-$50 trees that some places charge, and your trees will be just as beautiful.

(For additional information on growing Christmas trees, write to the National Christmas Tree Association, 611 E. Wells Street, Milwaukee, WI 53202-3891.) Δ

The all purpose power food — soybeans!

By Rebecca and Leif Hietala

You may have heard of soybeans and how widely touted they are for being the "ultimate food". In this world of diminishing food chain returns, a beef cow would have to eat ten pounds of soybeans to produce one pound of beef. Why shouldn't anybody be able to take advantage of a versatile kitchen staple?

Dried soybeans are about 35% protein, and when properly prepared, this protein is readily assimilated by your body's digestive processes. In the vegetable world, the soybean is about the closest thing to meat there is. They're almost as easy to grow as kudzu, and are a nitrogen-fixing legume. There are no waste products left over after processing soybeans.

Our collection of soybean recipes is large and diverse, ranging from main courses to fillers to desserts to drinks, so I won't go into any recipes here. There are many cookbooks on the market that can guide you in soybean cooking.

What a lot of them don't tell you though, is how to make some soybean derivatives like tofu, soymilk and okara. We'll see if we can't enlighten you regarding these useful foods.

For the respective steps you will need:

1 cup dried soybeans, soaked overnight (soaking will expand the volume to about 4 cups). Remove hulls that float to the top if you want.
7 cups of nearly boiling water.
Blender.
Saucepan, at least 5-qt capacity.
Strainer, ricer or colander
Dishtowel (non-terry) or other lint-free cloth
Two large bowls
5 cups cold water
3-4 tablespoons lemon juice or vinegar

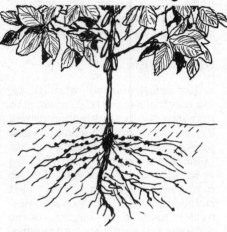

One 15-oz. can of beans (don't open)

Step One:

Soak one to one and a quarter cups soybeans overnight in six cups of clean water. Next day, rinse the soybeans once with hot tap water. Warm beans are a must for the next step.

Measure one cup soybeans and one and a half cups of the nearly boiling water into the blender, and blend for 30 seconds on the highest setting. Be careful how you turn your blender on, as hot spray from the sudden spinning can burn! Dump the results into a large saucepan. The water you blend with must be hot, as it is the heat used here that prevents your end products from having a beany taste.

Proceed as above until the soybeans are used up. If your math is good, you'll notice there's going to be a cup of hot water left over. Use it, again blending on high, to rinse the blender, and pour that into the saucepan too.

Bring the contents of the saucepan to a rolling boil. While the temperature is rising, stir frequently. The soy mash will tend to stick some to the bottom of the pot. Don't worry, that's normal. When the mixture comes to a boil, turn the heat down to maintain a low simmer, but continue stirring until the vigorous boil has settled. If the mash looks like it's about to boil over and won't stir back down, simply lift the pot off the burner for a few seconds.

When the mash is simmering calmly, cover loosely and set your timer for twenty minutes. No stirring should be required during this stage. While your mash is simmering, prepare for the next step.

Step Two:

Wet and wring the cloth in cold water, and use it to line the ricer or strainer. Place the strainer over one of the bowls to catch the soymilk you will be pouring through the strainer. Have the five cups of cold water measured out and ready.

Note: Becky prefers to do this step in the sink, since some splashing is sure to occur, and having everything happen a few inches lower makes the heavy pans easier to handle, and everything easier to see.

When the twenty minutes are up, slowly and carefully pour the contents of the saucepan through the strainer. Pause to let the strainer catch up with you if it doesn't drain quickly. While the mash is draining, take a minute to wash the saucepan. I've never seen it, but Becky says soymilk will make a crust that makes dried-on breakfast cereal look timid.

The mash has been draining into a bowl. Empty the bowl back into the saucepan, and put the bowl back under the strainer. Now use the five cups of cold water to pour through the mash. Work slowly here, and knead the cloth liner once in a while to make sure fresh water gets to all the contents, as we're trying to cool them off enough to handle bare-handed. Stirring gently with the handle of a wooden spoon will also help. Empty your bowl as often as necessary into the saucepan. When the last of the cold water has drained through, and the mash has been squeezed fairly dry, empty the catch bowl into the saucepan one last time, put the saucepan back on the stove, and once again bring it to a boil. The result is soymilk. Once you've reached this point, you can shut everything off and stop. Soymilk is a healthful (though low in calcium) milk substitute that takes well to flavoring. But if you really want to get the whole soybean experience, move on to step three.

Step Three:

Once the soymilk has again reached a boil, remove it from heat and add the lemon juice or vinegar, one tablespoon at a time, stirring very, very gently for a few seconds between each tablespoon. At some point, somewhat gradually or even quite suddenly, the soymilk will separate into curds and whey. When it does this, add another half tablespoon of juice or vinegar and stir that in too. Always be gentle at this stage. The curds are tofu. The whey is whey. Don't throw away either one.

By this time you should have removed the mash from the cloth that is lining the strainer. Make sure the liner is well rinsed, and re-line the strainer with it. Now pour the contents of the saucepan through it again. Be sure not to lose any of the whey! That stuff is useful! If you have to, stop and change bowls (thought I forgot about that second bowl didn't you). When the saucepan is empty, fold the liner over the tofu, and set the can of beans on top to supply a steady, gentle pressure.

Anywhere from five to twenty minutes is good for pressing the tofu. The longer it's pressed, the firmer it will be, so that is dictated by your preference.

Now that you've got all these soybean products, let's see what you can do with them.

Tofu

Tofu can be fried with flavorings, ground up and added to hamburger, added to mashed potatoes, grilled, smoked...anything you can do to meat or cream cheese you can do to tofu. It can even be freeze-dried. Tofu will not melt however.

One thing I recently discovered was frying it with some Worcestershire sauce and just the tiniest bit of oil (tofu has no oil of its own), and making a sandwich with it. Light and tasty! If you can't immediately use up the pound or so of tofu that you've just made, store it in a covered container,

under water, in the fridge. We've kept ours for up to two weeks.

Okara

The mash is called okara, and it can be used both wet and dry. In the wet state it will store for up to a week, refrigerated, or you can dry it in the oven or food dehydrator. Kept dry, okara will last, well, until you use it up! Okara can be treated just like cornmeal or flour for the purposes of baking, but don't forget that, just like the whole soybean, okara absorbs and holds lots of moisture. Therefore, it is not the best choice for light, delicate pastries. But for anything else you've got that you want to add some protein to, this is an easy way to go. Okara also has no gluten, so it will not make bread alone. Substitute one cup in every five of flour with okara to give your bread more protein, a moister texture and a longer shelf life.

Okara tends to dry in lumps. You can run these through a grinder or blender if you prefer a finer texture. Okara has little if any taste, and what taste it does have is so neutral that it won't clash with anything. You can use okara to stretch out your meatloaf, give a little protein kick to your favorite bread recipe, even grind it up fine and add to a milkshake. Okara works well in just about everything.

Soymilk

What can I say? Use it like milk. It has less of a flavor, and isn't as white, and has no calcium. If these don't deter you, then you ought to have about a gallon of a perfectly useful milk substitute if you followed our recipe, if you didn't make tofu. We have yet to discover a recipe or even an instant mix where soymilk can't be substituted directly for milk. You can even use it to stretch out your regular buttermilk. There's virtually no difference between soybuttermilk and the real thing. However, try to start with at least a half cup of original buttermilk and don't add more than a quart of soymilk to that, or the new stuff won't sour properly.

Whey

Whey is the clear yellowish liquid left over after you've made tofu from your soymilk. Pour it into a bottle and keep it in the refrigerator. Whey can be used as a mild detergent for both clothes and dishes, a mild shampoo, and can be used as a high-protein, lecithin-rich cooking water for vegetables and meats. Lecithin helps your body get rid of cholesterol, and adding a little more protein to your diet won't kill you.

If you find you're not satisfied with the suds unadulterated whey makes, add a tablespoon of Dawn dishwashing detergent to a cup of whey. This combination cuts grease as well as any other dishwashing soap from the store, doesn't leave that irritating film like uncut Dawn does, and is non-toxic if you don't get it all rinsed off. Plus, you can make one bottle of Dawn last a whole year this way.

Some special notes

Heed the boiling and hot water instructions religiously! Soybeans have in them a natural component called a trypsin inhibitor which prevents human digestive enzymes from breaking down the available protein, and it is all the heating involved that breaks the trypsin inhibitor down. If you don't boil your soybeans long enough, then they're pretty much going to go straight through you without doing you any good whatsoever. So where the recipe says boil it, boil it.

Soybeans and related products are cheaper ounce for ounce than the foodstuffs they can replace. Where we live, soybeans can be had for as little as eighty cents per dry pound, from which we can produce as much as three pounds of tofu, a little more than two gallons of whey, two gallons of soymilk (we never have enough soymilk!) and nearly a quart and a half of dried okara! All for eighty cents! When you figure in all the different uses for your soy products, you may start to wonder how you ever got along without them. Δ

Straw bale houses — an alternative

By Linda Rainey

"A straw house!," scoffed my husband. "It will just blow down." These are the words most people say when they are told of this alternative type of building. The scoffing of my husband prompted me to research straw houses.

Straw bale construction originated in the early 1900's, in the United States. The settlers of the Sandhills of Nebraska found grass covered sand dunes with no trees. The soil proved too sandy for sod construction so an alternative type of shelter had to be found. Hay was the most important crop of this area and a desperate farmer probably saw the possibilities of using bales of hay or straw as building blocks. There are still homes, barns and even airplane hangers still in use in Nebraska today.

The 1973 edition of Shelter had an article entitled Baled Hay. This article revived interest in this type of home construction in the western United States.

Several homes, where I live in New Mexico, were built as a result of this article. One home that I visited, looked like the typical southwestern style adobe with the flat roof, deep windows, and the attached porch. Plastering of the interior and exterior concealed the fact that the building blocks used were bales of straw instead of adobe. This small home, with outside dimensions of 20x32 feet, costs less than $7 a square foot to build. This also included electrical and some plumbing.

The windows are set to the outside, leaving an 18" window sill which is home to plants and knick knacks. This southeast facing home has a cement floor that forms a heat sink to absorb sunlight through the southeast windows. This plus the insulation of the straw bale walls and insulated curtains keep the warmth in on a cold winter's night. Only 1/2 cord of wood is needed a year to supplement for heat.

In the summer, the porch shades the house. The insulated drapes are kept

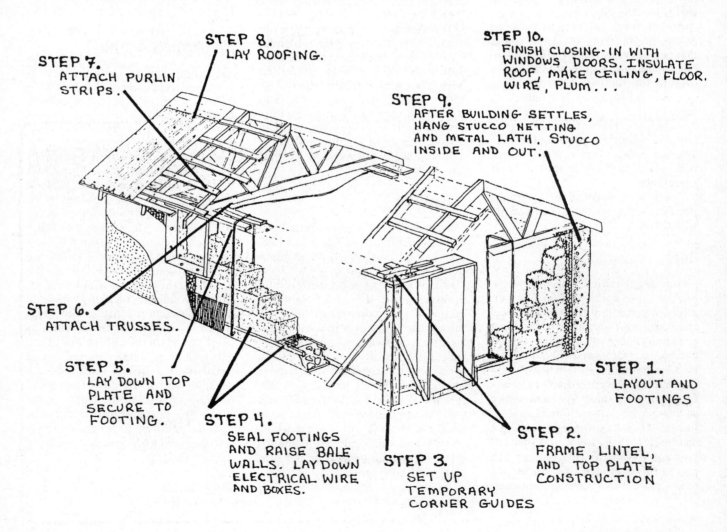

STEP 7.
ATTACH PURLIN STRIPS.

STEP 8.
LAY ROOFING.

STEP 10.
FINISH CLOSING-IN WITH WINDOWS, DOORS. INSULATE ROOF, MAKE CEILING, FLOOR. WIRE, PLUM . . .

STEP 9.
AFTER BUILDING SETTLES, HANG STUCCO NETTING AND METAL LATH. STUCCO INSIDE AND OUT.

STEP 6.
ATTACH TRUSSES.

STEP 5.
LAY DOWN TOP PLATE AND SECURE TO FOOTING.

STEP 4.
SEAL FOOTINGS AND RAISE BALE WALLS. LAY DOWN ELECTRICAL WIRE AND BOXES.

STEP 3.
SET UP TEMPORARY CORNER GUIDES

STEP 2.
FRAME, LINTEL, AND TOP PLATE CONSTRUCTION

STEP 1.
LAYOUT AND FOOTINGS

closed during the day to preserve the night coolness.

These facts encouraged me to participate in a straw bale workshop. This workshop used the hands on approach to learning. Construction was based on the step approach as illustrated here and also is found in *A Straw Bale Primer* written by S.O. Mac Donald and illustrated by Orien Mac Donald.

Step #1 We layed out the dimensions of the house and built footings to the width of the straw bales.

Step #2 Next we learned to build window and door frames and lintels. Afterwards we built the top plate that would be used to hold the walls to the footing and also to attach the trusses to the walls.

Step #3 This involved the actual construction of the baled walls. Prior to erecting the walls we covered the footings with felt to act as a vapor barrier. Construction of the walls was accomplished by staggering the bales, like laying bricks.

Step #4 With walls finished, we placed the top plate on the finished wall. The top plate was attached to the wall by a cable, that was hooked to loops in the footing. The cable was drawn over the wall and attached to a loop on the opposing side.

Step #5 We next attached prefabricated trusses to the top plate. We then attached the purlin strips to the trusses. This would serve as a base for the roof. As a final part of this step we placed sheets of painted galvanized steel on the roof.

Step #7 We next learned how to apply stucco netting and metal lath used to hold the stucco to the walls. We learned the proper way to make stucco for the outside and plaster for the inside.

Step #8 The final step of house construction was the finish work. The windows and doors were hung, the roof insulated, and a ceiling made. The wiring and plumbing was finished after laying the floor.

At the end of the course we reviewed what we had learned and many suggestions were made for improvement.

The advantages to this type of construction is that it is simple enabling the owner/builder to make changes without great cost. This kind of construction is energy efficient, economical and also uses a resource that is burned in some parts of the country as waste.

The main disadvantage is that it is not covered by most building codes. A study made by the Canada Mortgage and Housing Corporation should give sufficient support for this type of building.

These are resources that can give you more information on this unique type of building:

Bainbridge, D.A., 1986 High performance low cost buildings of straw. Agriculture, Ecosystems, Environment 16: 281-284.

Bainbridge, D.A., 1988 Straw bale construction. Dry Lands Research Institute, University of California, Riverside, CA. Working Paper #5 11p.

Canada Mortgage Housing Corporation, Housing Technology Incentives Program, Ottawa, Canada 1984. An innovative straw bale/mortar wall system. NHA 5799 84/08 3p.

Doolittle, B. 1973. A round house of straw bales. Mother Earth News. 19: 52-57.

Mac Donald, S.O. and Orien. 1991 A straw bale primer. Available for $10.00 by writing the author at Box 58, Gila, NM, 88038

Mc Elderry, W. and C. 1979 Happiness is a hay house. Mother Earth News 58: 40-43

Myhram, Matt, Out On Bale (UN) LTD 1037 E. Linden St., Tucson, AZ 85719 (602) 624-1673. Platered Bale Designs, workshops, and consulting.

Strang, G. 1985 Straw-bale studio. Fine Homebuilding 12/84- 1/85: 70-72

Welsch, R.L. 1973. Baled Hay Page 70 in L. Kahn, ed., Shelter. Shelter Publications, Bolinas, CA 176 p. △

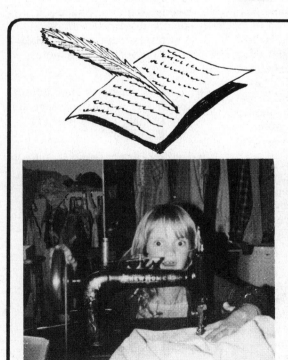
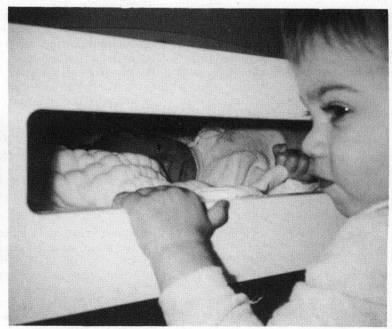

Future writers for Backwoods Home Magazine? Annie Duffy (left) uses a treadle sewing machine. Jacob Duffy (right) sneaks a peek at his newborn brother Robby.

The Third Year

Good food for hard times . . . or any time

By Jo Mason

The other day at the store, I stood in front of the shelf for five minutes, debating over which brand or size of salsa to buy. Finally, I couldn't bring myself to pay $2.58 for a jar, so I went home and made some. And it took less time than I'd spent trying to decide! (About three minutes)

The ability to "cook cheap" may not be something you'll use every day—or even every month. But like a nest egg tucked under the mattress, it's a nice thing to have when you need it. The bonus? Good nutrition and, generally speaking, foods in their more natural states are less expensive, naturally higher in complex carbohydrates and fiber, and lower in fat and sodium.

But are they really worth your time? Only you can decide that. As for me, I figure I made (saved) around $28 an hour on the salsa and I make a $59-an-hour pizza whose name tells it all. And it's better than any you can buy. The recipe is at the end of this article.

What do you need in the way of equipment? Basically, just your everyday, common pots, pans, and sense. (Like me, you may have a favorite appliance. The blender and crockpot are two of mine.) But I've found that some "labor saving" devices actually create work. A food processor, for instance, is a great help when you have a ton of cheese or cabbage to shred—but then it must be taken apart and cleaned. For small jobs, I simply use an old-fashioned grater.

As in any important endeavor, you need a blueprint for success—in other words, a **plan**. This means not only a grocery list, but a detailed, weekly menu. Remember that coined word from the women's magazines— **planned-overs**? It still makes sense not to just recycle leftovers, but to plan on them when you draw up your menu. Like any good manager, you take in-

ventory, order supplies, and keep the merchandise moving. You also try to eliminate waste. This planning session will take time, but it is vital. And in the long run, it'll save both time and money.

Revive the time-honored art of "making do" (substituting) and making items from scratch. Get in the habit of reading the list of ingredients on labels on your favorite sauces, salad dressing, etc. Not only will you save money and a trip to the store—you won't be adding all those preservatives. Here are some more tips:

- You can tell a good grocery store the same way you can spot a good road side diner—by the number of "rigs" parked out front! Avoid stores with empty parking lots.

- **Ranch dressing**: Combine 1/2 cup mayonnaise, 1/4 cup buttermilk, 1/4 cup milk, 1 packet Ramen beef-flavored seasoning (from the soup mix), juice from 1/2 lemon, 1 tablespoon onion powder, and 1/4 teaspoon garlic powder. Blend well and refrigerate.

- **Oven-fried potatoes**: Wash and scrub (unpeeled) potatoes. Make thick slices. Put 2 tablespoons vegetable oil on cookie sheet. Place slices on sheet and sprinkle with onion powder, salt, and paprika. Bake at 450 degrees for 30 minutes, turning once.

- To mimic the flavor (but not the cost or fat) of Italian sausage in your spaghetti, use a pinch of fennel seeds.

- **3-minute salsa**: Drain 1/2 cup of liquid from a 28 oz. can of tomatoes. (Save for another use.) Chop tomatoes while in can. Place chopped tomatoes in jar. Add 1/2 teaspoon garlic powder, 1 or more diced jalapenos, and 1/2 chopped onion. Stir, cover, and refrigerate.

- **Low cholesterol eggs**: Combine several egg whites with only 1 yolk, add a drop of yellow food coloring. (To save remaining yolks, place in small bowl, cover with water, then cover with plastic wrap.)

- Investigate your area for a "no frills" grocery store. Fewer employees, shorter store hours, and no advertising means lower prices.

- **Orange julicious:** In blender, combine 1 6-oz. can frozen orange juice concentrate (partly defrosted), 1/4 cup honey, 2 cups non-fat dry milk (liquid), 1 tablespoon vanilla extract, and 1 cup cracked ice. Whirl until frothy.

- For your next cookout, look for some meaty pork neck bones. These are often as good as spareribs—and are about half the price.

- Do you feel you need Omega-3 fatty acid in your diet? Don't buy expensive (and possibly dangerous) fish oil supplements. Use canned tuna instead. What's even cheaper? Canned mackerel.

- Take your recipes with a "grain of salt." You don't **have** to use as many chocolate chips, nuts, or mushrooms as is called for.

- **Quick seafood cocktail sauce:** Place 1 cup catsup in jar. Add the following according to taste: prepared horseradish, celery salt, cayenne pepper, and lemon juice.

- When preparing whole chickens—always freeze that little packet of giblets. When enough chicken livers accumulate, you'll have the fixins for a fantastic appetizer—chopped liver.

One last word—don't get "carried away" by economizing. Immediately throw out any suspicious canned goods—especially home processed items. **Do not taste.** Swollen and dented cans are not bargains. Botulism has no odor or taste, and is one of the most toxic substances in the world.

For the following recipe, I use bulk mozzarella cheese and pepperoni sausage, which is less expensive than buying them already grated or sliced.

Also, I use bits & pieces of mushrooms, which are cheaper than whole button mushrooms.

$59-an-hour pizza

1 loaf frozen bread dough
3 tablespoons extra-virgin olive oil
1 6-oz. can tomato paste
1 can water
1/2 teaspoon garlic powder
1 teaspoon sugar
1/4 teaspoon black pepper
1/2 teaspoon dried oregano
1/4 teaspoon fennel seeds
1/4 teaspoon basil
dash of salt
1 lb. grated mozzarella cheese
1/2 lb. hamburger, cooked and drained
4 oz. sliced pepperoni
1 8-oz. can mushrooms
1 small can pitted ripe olives
1/2 medium onion, chopped
1/2 medium bell pepper, chopped
1 small can anchovies (optional)

(Note: For a thicker crust, use only 1 loaf for one pizza. You can add more or less of the suggested amounts of the last seven ingredients, or omit any of those items.)

Grease loaf with vegetable oil before thawing. Grease 2 pizza pans. To prepare sauce: combine olive oil, tomato paste, water, sugar, salt, and spices in small saucepan. Stir and let simmer over low heat for 15 minutes.

Preheat oven to 400 degrees.

(All ingredients should be ready before doing this step because once the dough has been patted out, it should not be allowed to rise.) Cut loaf in half. Place 1 half in each pan. By stretching and patting, spread dough over each pan. Spread on sauce. Sprinkle on cheese and other ingredients. Bake 14-20 minutes (oven times will vary) until cheese is melted and crust lightly browned. Serve with Parmesan cheese and dried hot peppers. Makes two 12-inch pizzas. Δ

Backwoods Home Cooking

- **Breads**
- **Casseroles**
- **Cookies**
- **Desserts**
- **Jams & jellies**
- **Main dishes**
- **Salads**
- **Seafood**
- **Soups**
- **Vegetables**
- **Our favorites**

The Builder

She chooses her nesting spot
 carefully,
This young robin, opting for an
 open
Beam bathed in sunlight all day
 long.
Plenty of fresh air for her nestlings,
With a delicatessen nearby for her
Shopping. Her strutting mate
Approves, they sign the lease, and
Mere humans lose the use of their
Front door and porch to new
 tenants.

Linda Hutton
Hayden, Idaho

Parakeets for cash

By Joe Bratt

You are probably asking why parakeets? Most rural areas don't have pet shops, but many rural residents would like a pet bird. Parakeets are the best selling and most popular pet bird around. They are not difficult to raise if you have some experience with livestock.

You can expect to sell your birds for approximately $10 to $30 depending on the variety you raise. The most popular varieties are what is known as color birds, Lutino, Albino, Australian Banded Pieds, Yellow-Faces, and Spangles. Some other varieties are Crested, Clearwing, Greywing, and Harlequin (recessive pied).

Budgerigars (parakeets) in the wild are gregarious birds, they live in flocks and breed in flocks, when breeding, this is called the colony system and probably the easiest for a newcomer to the business. In order to breed your birds in a colony system you should follow some simple rules. Only start with mated pairs, do not introduce new birds to the aviary and make sure you have about 1/3 more nest boxes than you have pairs. You can pair your birds by placing males and females in a cage and watching to see if they pair up. Males have blue ceres and females have brown or ivory colored ceres (the fleshy part above the beak with the nostrils). When you see the birds feeding and preening each other and in general acting like lovesick teenagers, you have a pair. Once you have several pairs, release them all at the same time in the colony flight.

In order to raise these varieties you should know a little about the genetics of these birds. Yellow-faces, Australian banded Pied and Spangles are **Dominant** varieties. In other words, only one parent need show the markings to pass it on to their offspring. Clearwing, Greywing and Harlequin are **Recessive** varieties. In other words, both parents have to

carry the genes for the markings to show. Lutino and Albino are called **Sex-Linked** because the characteristic travels from father to daughter (i.e. if the cock bird is "ino" (albino or lutino) and is mated to a bird other than "ino", any chick that shows that characteristic has to be a hen). It is sex-linked. The male chicks are split for the sexlink characteristic and do not show the color involved. Generally if you breed Dominant to Dominant you will get all Dominant. If you breed Recessive to Recessive you will get Recessive. And if you breed Sex-Linked to Sex-Linked you will get all Sex-Linked.

One other hereditary factor to remember is that green is dominant to blue. If you have a green bird and breed it to a blue bird you will get visual green youngsters (I say visual green because all those youngsters will carry the blue factor). If you breed these youngsters together you will get both blue and green. It is best to breed blue to blue or green to green until you become familiar with the basic genetics.

It is important to care for your birds properly and give them the same thing you do for all other livestock. Good clean water and fresh food. Parakeets eat seed and greens and various forms of protein. The basic diet should consist of seed in the form of millet and canary. Other seeds such as oats and wheat can be added. The birds like carrots, broccoli, endive, corn, peas and most other greens you will grow. I give my birds an egg protein in powdered form (available at the feed store). A friend of mine feeds his birds leftover chicken, ham, fish or whatever else they had that night for supper. A good choice is chick start or other protein enriched feed.

You do not have to go overboard in your feeders. Use empty tuna cans or pineapple cans; an open dish, saucer, or jar lid will serve for a waterer.

Parakeets do not build nests like a robin but breed in hollow trees in the wild. If you give them a wood box approximately 6"x6"x8" they will be happy. You could use those pieces of firewood with hollows if you want to. The birds are not fussy and they will breed in just about anything that gives them privacy.

Once the birds have picked out their boxes the hens will start laying eggs about 10 days after mating, the usual clutch is about 4 to 8 eggs, sometimes less, sometimes more. The first egg should hatch in 18 days and then every other day until they are all hatched. The young are fed a "crop milk" by the parents, usually the hen, for the first couple of weeks and then by the cock bird. The young chicks will be eating on their own in about 5 to 7 weeks. At this point they are called barheads and are the most desirable of pets.

It is not difficult to build an aviary or flightcage. They usually range in size from 3' x 3' x 4' to 5' x 8' x 10'. You can use old screen windows or chicken wire but the most durable seems to be welded wire 1/2 x 3/4 inches, available at most feed or hardware stores.

Since parakeets are not domestic birds, your state may ask that you have a license. Here in Florida, it costs $25 per year if you have 10 or more birds. These birds are kept and raised in every state so ask your local Fish Game and Wildlife Commission or the local Agriculture Department about regulations.

I recommend that anyone interested in raising budgies do two things prior to starting.

• Join or visit a local bird club.
• Read some books on the subject.

There is not much that bothers these little birds if they are treated right. The most common problem is probably scaly mite. Although usually not fatal, the traditional method of treatment is to rub vaseline on the affected areas. Recently it is being treated with Ivermectin, a common wormer for horses and pigs. There are feather mites and red mites that can be eradicated with most any poultry powder containing pyrethrum. Psittacosis (ornithosis) is a flu-like disease, caused by a virus, communicable to humans. It is rare in budgerigars and treatable with antibiotics and other drugs. See your local veterinarian if you suspect any problems and isolate those birds showing signs of disease or lethargy.

There is a great satisfaction to be had raising these delightful little creatures and should be a nice addition to the ordinary home-raised livestock.

More reading on parakeets:

"The Budgerigar Journal" (magazine), Rt. 6 Box 151-E, Jackson MS 39208
"Budgerigars in Colour" by A. Rutgers
"Inbreeding Budgerigars" by Dr. M.D.S. Armour
"The World of Budgerigars" by Cyril H. Rogers
"The Budgerigar Book" By Ernest Howson
"The Cult of the Budgerigar" by W. Watmough
"Bird Diseases" by I. Amall and I. F. Keymer
"Budgerigar Handbook" by Ernest Hart. Δ

The Best of the First Two Years
Our first big anthology!
In these 12 issues you'll find:

❋ A little knowledge and sweat can build a home
      for under $10,000

❋ Tepee to cabin to dream house

❋ From the foundation up, house-building is forgiving

❋ A first time horse buyer's guide

❋ A greenhouse offers advantages for the organic gardener

❋ Canning meat

❋ Backwoods Home recipes

❋ In pursuit of independence

❋ Canning blueberries

❋ How we keep humming along on the homestead

❋ Pioneer women on the trail west

❋ Some tips on first aid readiness for remote areas

❋ Whip grafting—the key to producing fruit variety

❋ The basics of backyard beekeeping

❋ Co-planting in the vegetable garden

❋ How to make soap—from fat to finish

❋ The instant greenhouse

❋ The old time spring house

❋ Getting started in a firewood business

❋ For battling ants or growing earthworms,
      try coffee grounds

❋ Sawmills: a firm foundation to homesteading

Family works together at successful home-based business

By Rosemary LeVernier

Deep in the Selkirk Mountains of northern Idaho lives a family that works together to make a living. Bill Lanphar, his wife Sue, and their sons Brian, 14, and Luke, 13, operate Selkirk Mountain Collection, a home-based craft business featuring handmade wooden products.

"People like objects that function," said Sue from their home near the small town of Sandpoint, Idaho. "All of our articles are functional." The Lanphars make swan and dove-shaped candleabras, and wooden baskets in various shapes and sizes, each one cut from a single piece of oak.

"The graceful doves were first designed by a woodworker in Arkansas sometime during the 1940s," Sue said. "As for the beautiful swans, they were designed by Bill and a friend in the winter of '88."

Both the candleabras and baskets are collapsible, and when folded flat, become useful as a trivet and store away easily. "When opened, the folding hardwood baskets make an intriguing piece for displaying flower arrangements, fruit, bread or your own special treasures," said Sue.

From start to finish, the business is a family enterprise. It begins in the workshop located next to their home in the woods. Bill performs the tasks of planing, cutting, power sanding, and assembling each item. Brian and Luke trace the patterns onto the wood, and sand each assembled item by hand.

"I take over from there," Sue explained, donning a mask and rubber gloves as she dipped baskets into a tray of stain in the finish room. "I stain each piece, attach brass grommets, and pack the finished product into boxes until we go to a craft show, where we sell them. We're all salespersons too.

"We like wood," she said. "The beauty of the natural grain enhances each item with its own unique personality. And oak is great to work with." Woodworking gives her the satisfaction of handling a natural and esthetic raw material she would otherwise have little reason to associate with, she said.

"I'm proud of what we make. I'd love to put every piece in my home, but I don't have the room. I'm glad that

Sue Lanphar in the packing room. Though most of their products are sold at craft fairs, satisfied customers often call to order more. Sue includes complimentary candles with each candelabra.

each one will give someone else enjoyment, and that I played a part in it."

Selkirk Mountain Collection evolved slowly. Bill supported the family for many years by logging in the woods of northern Idaho. The time came when he decided he would rather work for himself.

Bill and Sue's first venture was marketing various manufactured products. "But we had no control over the quality of the merchandise we were selling," Sue recalled. "We wanted something more personal, something we could make with our own hands."

Four years ago, the Lanphars created their first handmade wooden items: bent-wood furniture made of natural alder collected in the forests of Idaho and Montana. It sold well, but because of its size and the inconvenience of hauling it to craft shows, they eventually turned to something smaller.

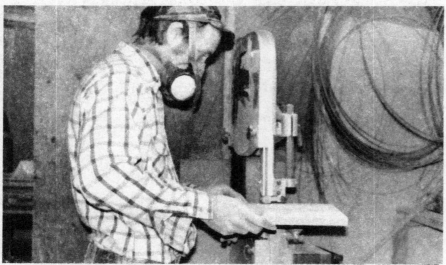

Bill Lanphar at work in his shop. Because of the huge amount of sawdust, he wears the mask to protect his respiratory system. Here he cuts a piece of oak at the band saw.

Sandscapes were their next product. Sandscapes consist of sand and colored water sandwiched between two sheets of glass in a wooden frame, and form fascinating patterns when turned upside down.

When competition stiffened as more crafters began selling sandscapes, the Lanphars knew it was time for a change. Their baskets and candleabras followed, which they have been producing since January of 1989.

"Usually our ideas for new items come from customers. We're catering to the public. We depend on people for our livelihood, so we make what they like," Sue said.

A large calendar hangs on the office wall inside the Lanphar home. The locations of craft shows they will at-

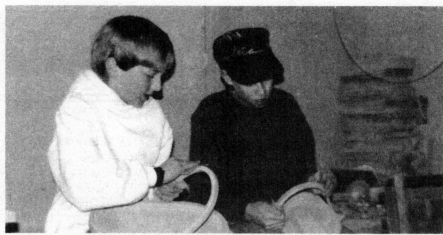

Luke (left) and Brian Lanphar at work in the shop. They are responsible for hand-sewing the assembled items.

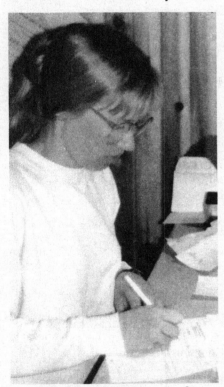

Sue Lanphar taking care of the business side of Selkirk Mountain Collection in her office at the family home.

tend dot its pages. The Lanphars sell at the higher level craft shows throughout the Pacific Northwest. Because the shows are juried, the Lanphars must submit photos of their work to a panel of judges who decide if they will be allowed to enter. Com-

petition is tough at these quality shows.

"It's important to take an active part in selling. You can't just sit and read a book, or your sales will walk right by," said Sue, emphasizing the role dynamic salesmanship plays in their business.

"Craft shows are fun," she said. "And tiring! During our busy season (summer and just before Christmas), we average three days a week away from home. The hardest part is Monday morning following the show. Everybody's drained." The Lanphars often see as many as 5,000-10,000 people at a single show. "After three days of watching thousands of people walk by and talking to a good many of them, we're worn out."

There are benefits to showing at craft fairs beyond marketing their products, Sue said. "We meet new people. We trade merchandise with other crafters. We exchange ideas too." On a practical note, she added, "You learn to read a map, how to get where you're going, and how to fix your car if it breaks down."

As if the family business isn't enough to keep her busy, Sue also takes on the role of teacher. She homeschools her boys. Two desks sit prominently in the living room, next to a shelf filled with books. Each weekday morning, Sue can be found working on lessons with Brian and Luke.

"The boys are old enough to do a lot of their schoolwork on their own. We

plan independent study for days when I'm staining. If they have question, Bill or I are around to help."

Brian and Luke are gaining a practical education beyond the academic. They have their own products, called Rhythm Sticks, which they make and sell. Rhythm Sticks are a wooden toy requiring coordination and concentration to operate. Both boys are experts at using them, and actions speak louder than words when it comes to making a sale.

"They have the capability of making a decent living at it one day if they choose to," Sue stated, proud of her boys and their business and woodworking skills.

During the summer, when a free moment at home occurs Sue makes a break for her large garden. There she tends to a variety of fruits and vegetables, all organic. Amid her hectic schedule, she somehow finds the time and energy to create homegrown, nutritious meals for her family.

"Working together and our determination to make a living are the things that make this business successful," Sue said. "It's a full-time occupation. We have about six weeks off during the slow season, after Christmas. During that time, we play," she laughed. "We sit back and relax."

And what better place to do it, than in the peaceful forest they call home? Δ

The Third Year

Home remedies

By Linda D. Rainey, R. N.

Mothers have passed down home remedies to their daughters for generations. Something got lost along the way with the break up of the extended family. Today's young mother depends almost exclusively on their physician or the emergency room. What happens when you can't get to a doctor?

Here are some home remedies that have been passed down. They are not scientifically but rather mother researched.

Household Item	Recipe	Healing Action
Garlic juice/vapor rub	Mix together into paste. Place on square of flannel. Place on chest.	Aids in relieving congestion
Garlic juice	Apply to affected area	Numbs ant bites
Garlic juice, lemon juice & sugar	Mix together in cup of warm water	For sore throat
Powdered mustard	Mix with water for a paste. Place on square of flannel then on chest	For congestion
Honey, lemon & rum	Mix together in cup of warm water	For cough & sore throat (never give honey to children under the age of one year)
Hot chile peppers	Eat raw	Relieves nasal congestion
Olive oil	Warm teaspoon of olive oil. Place a few drops in ear then cotton	Earache
Baking soda	1 teaspoon in glass of water	Indigestion
Essence of peppermint	A few drops in warm water	For Stomach/intestinal cramps
Horehound	Mix juice of herb with water	Cough/asthma
Oats	Fry with salt & apply to affected area	Pain reliever & removes spots & freckles from body
Onion	Roast in embers then eat with honey	Helps cough
Parsley	Boil; then eat	Good for urinary stone & takes away eye inflammation
Lemon	Squeeze fresh juice into palm and inhale	Nasal congestion

Ginger	Mix with water and boil	For suppressed menstruation, promotes sweating, relieves early symptoms of colds
Mud	Apply to affected area	Relieves pain & itching of stings
Bleach	Dilute with water & apply to affected area	Athlete's foot
Cucumber	Slice & apply to affected area	Soothes tired eyes
Salt pork	Apply to affected area	Draws infection from wound
Potato	Peel, slice & place on affected area	Soothes burned eyes
Corn starch	Use as powder to affected area	Soothes skin irritation & also can be used as a deodorant
Nutmeg	1 teaspoon in glass of warm milk	Helps to sleep
Soap/water	Apply to affected area	Antiseptic to cleanse wounds
Anise	Mix in water to make tea	For asthma, bronchitis, cough, congestion & heartburn
Salt water	1 teaspoon in quart of warm water; gargle	For mouth sores & sore throat
Aspirin	Crush & mix with water to make paste; place on affected area	Will help relieve dry itchy skin
Vegetable oil	Apply to affected area	Will help relieve dry itchy skin.
Egg whites	Apply to affected area	Helps soothe & cool burns
Ice	Apply to affected area	Use to reduce swelling of sprains & strains for first 24 hours
Tobacco	Remove from cigarette or use pipe tobacco. Mix with water & make paste - Apply to affected area	Soothes & relieves pains of bee stings
Aloe vera	Break or split fresh leaves & apply to affected area	Sunburn, scrapes, rashes & other skin irritations
Oatmeal or starch or baking soda	Mix with water & make paste or place in bath water	Helps relieve itching

The use of home remedies and medicinal plants are becoming more important to those seeking an alternative lifestyle.

The following reference books are excellent and your library will have more:

Ferrara, Peter l., *Natural Remedies*, Pinnacle Books, New York 1984

Moore, Michael, *Medicinal Plants of the Desert & Canyon West,* Museum of New Mexico Press, Santa Fe, 1989. Δ

The Third Year

Good farm management puts money in your pocket

By Kelly Klober

When a farmer is told that he or she doesn't need the latest in new technology it should be headline news, but just seeing it on the printed page of a recent farm magazine was quite a start: "Some Farmers May Not Need a Computer".

This doesn't forgive the small farmer that has been keeping his or her records on coffee shop napkins and scraps torn from feed sacks, but points up the fact that simple record keeping systems kept up to date still have great value on the smallholding. Most farmers seem to find record keeping even more distasteful than time spent on the business end of a manure fork, but few are the farm tasks that return more per hour invested than the time spent on bookwork and making management decisions based upon good books.

Too many small farmers use the "I'm just a little guy" excuse to justify a bookkeeping system that is little more than a shoebox full of pink and yellow receipts and a scribbled up checkbook. If tax time finds you rooting through the glove box in the pickup and under the cushions of your favorite chair for needed papers you have some very big holes in your record system.

Most farmers are well aware of the ups and downs of the various markets they sell on, but very few know their costs for a unit of production be it bushels of green beans or hundredweights of feeder cattle. And even the producer with a flock or herd so small as to know every animal on sight and by name can become a bit "barn blind" in evaluating production from them.

A herd of 12 cows that produces 11 calves at weaning has a very respectable 91% calving percentage, but that only scratches the surface of performance evaluation. Did the calving period extend beyond a 45 day period thus giving an uneven set of calves at weaning? Is a problem calving forgotten months later at weaning time? Would the added costs of a pre-conditioning program be justified in this herd? What market outlet will be best for these calves? Are any of the heifers good candidates for herd replacements?

These are questions that can't be answered just sitting on a gate watching them graze. And trying to rely on memory and serendipity just isn't good management. Memory is a very selective thing and we all are prone to forgetting most of the bad and recalling most of the good. A favorite cartoon of mine shows a cow in a squeeze chute with all four feet sticking straight up and in about every third position in the run up chute is another cow on her back. The caption has one cowboy saying to another, "she's a bit silly, but she has a heifer calf every year."

There is an old country bromide that the best looking sow in the herd and the best doing sow are never the same sow. The only way to tell them apart is through proof of their performance in black and white. To that end, each animal in the breeding herd needs to be clearly identified upon sight and in the farm records. You and your wife or husband may know that Fawn has a bigger star in her forehead than Pet, but the neighbor that does chores for you upon occasion, the vet, and the AI technician will be better able to tell the difference between cows ear tagged 36 and 37.

Identification options include ear tags, neck chains, ear notches, heat or freeze branding, tattooing, and paints and crayons for temporary marking. A small, round ear tag that fits within the shell of the ear works best for most livestock species. It is not a least-cost option and it can be pulled free, but it is less likely to than larger tags, is legible from a reasonable distance, and has good durability.

Good record keeping begins in the field and that means it has to be simple, quick, and durable. To this end nothing has yet to beat the shirt pocket notebook and no. 2 lead pencil. They can be used to record breeding dates, due dates, ration changes, and the general day-to-day data of running a farm. In the evening such notations can be transferred to more permanent records kept either at the barn or house.

An individual record sheet should be kept for each animal in the breeding herd. On it should be logged the animal's genetic background, breeding and due dates, birth performance, weaning information, sire, health treatments, and any other pertinent data. For males, it should track the performance of females mated to him, health history, and producer observations on offspring performance. Many producers improvise a simple 1 to 10 rating system for animals in the breeding herd based on birth weights and numbers and numbers and weights again at weaning to evaluate female performance. Two low ratings in succession and a female is considered for culling.

A simple idea is to begin a 3"x5" index card on each female as she begins her productive life and moves through the facilities on the small farm. In group pens they can be kept inside a jar with its lid nailed to a post top. The card can be clipped above a farrowing unit or lambing jug when the female is placed in it, follow her through lactation, and then back to the breeding pen. As needed, the cards can be collected and that data on them transferred to permanent records.

The jar method also works with pens of growing animals. There the producer can record ration changes, health treatments, weights, amounts of feed, and performance observations. When the group is marketed, the cards can be collected and the data transferred to permanent records. Good livestock records should tell a producer where his or her animals are in their growth or reproductive cycles and how well they are performing.

Wean 26 pigs from 4 females and you know you have a bit of a problem. With good records you should also have a bit of a handle on an answer. Were the litters small because there were first-litter gilts in the group? Were there older sows that might have produced a greater number of stillbirths? Were they all by the same boar and might he be the blame? Old time breeders like to say blood tells, but you have to be able to tell where it is in the herd and what it is doing there.

Crop farmers need to similarly designate the fields and pastures with which they work. Farmers have talked of the back forty for generations, but proper designation and then simple mapping are where good management begins. A simple map of the field showing where weedy patches are and what varieties have been a problem, where drainage problems exist, where sloping occurs, and other aspects of the field will aid in planning and making management decisions. Such maps will need yearly updating, but they are the only way to take a field in to the house and work with it when the snow flies.

Logged with the maps should be a listing of crop varieties planted previously, fertilizer and other soil and crop treatments, planting and harvest dates, dates when other management practices occurred, weather and rainfall records, soil testing records, and yield results. Much of the data on a growing crop can be recorded on a calendar and transferred to permanent records at the end of the growing season. Every year during the holidays, Dad would make the rounds of local businesses collecting several calendars to record such information upon and then, at the end of the crop year, he would roll them up tightly, and store them away for future reference with the little blue student notebooks he kept for note taking.

The further fields are apart, the more important it is to log such information about them individually, so, they can be managed accordingly. Fields on the opposite sides of even the smallest towns can experience vastly different rain patterns over the course of a growing season.

There is more to a good record system than tracking money into and out of an enterprise. In point of fact, separate records need to be kept on each separate enterprise on the smallholding. It is too easy to lose track of inputs when the only record for purchases is a canceled check. What was covered in that last $100.00 check to the elevator? It could have been pig starter and cedar chips, salt blocks and dog food or chicken scratch and steel fence posts. Such a lack of distinction may not bother the producer, but it will sure concern the IRS.

Serious numbers crunching to determine enterprise performance can only occur if both income and expenses are defined clearly in the records. This may be best achieved by the small farmer with a simple columnar record book. This system lists each expense and credit in a general column and then in a second for those in its specific category. Crop producers then should know seed, fertilizer, fuel, lubricant, hired labor, machinery, and other costs at a glance.

And while the income tax form for farm income allows lumping feed expenses together, the small farmer will benefit from knowing how much is regularly spent for feed grains, protein supplements, hay, complete feeds, minerals, and starter feeds. One figure that seems especially high can alert the producer to the need to work on paring this cost. With inputs logged in by date of purchase, type and amount, and cost the producer then has hard information for determining costs and feed per pound of gain, seasonal fluctuations in consumption and growth, and just how well management, genetics, and nutrition are working together.

Logging in credits by category, size or amount, and time of sale is vital in determining those all important cash flows for planning any expansion or other change. By noting categories of sales, feeder stock, butcher stock, breeding animals, cull stock, and to what outlets they were sold one can begin forming a marketing plan rather than wandering around asking, "What will you give me?"

We have come to a time when bankers look for a lot more than a firm handshake when it comes to making a loan. They need cost and return projections, an idea of the producer's track record, realistic projections for production levels, and a budget built upon substance and not wishes. That data exists already in a good record keeping system.

Previously, we pointed up the need to record things in the field as they occur. To be useful, farm records have to be kept current and to that end, many producers set aside a few minutes at the end of each day to bring them up to date. Producers need to get into the habit of keeping good records. A trick taught by one of my high school vo. ag. teachers was to do record keeping in ink; his thinking being that if a mistake is difficult to correct, you're more apt to do it right the first time.

Farm records should be kept for more reasons than to satisfy the tax man and please the banker. They should guide the operation of the enterprise dictating decisions on everything from what to cull to the potential for future expansion. There is an old saying that in the dark all cats are gray. On a farm without good records all sows, cows, ewes, and fields can begin to look the same too. Only good records can bring black or red out of all this gray.

Good records, an eye to the bottom line, livestock and crops grown for the clear purpose of producing a livable income for the farm family denote a smallholder on the land to stay and may become a necessity, in time, for income tax purposes and to participate in government farm programs. Hard data, the knowledge of a small farm's strengths and weaknesses, can come only from a clear-eyed look beneath the surface. And, unlike a car where to get such a look one has to open the hood, on the family farm, the family business, one has to open the books. Δ

The Third Year

Teach your kids the fun, safe way to split kindling

By Don Fallick

Bang! Bang! I raised my groggy head from the pillow. "What's going on?" Then I remembered: eight-year old Mandy had volunteered to light the fire this morning. "Hey! She doesn't know how to use an axe!" Thud/Clang! "Daddy!!! I hit my knee with the axe!" Two hours and several stitches later, after setting a new land speed record on the way to the hospital in town, I vowed to teach **all** my kids to split kindling safely—even the youngest. You just never know when they might need the knowledge.

Granny's way

I learned to make kindling from an old homestead granny who's been splitting her own for 60 years and still has all her fingers and toes. She uses an old, double-bit axe, but instead of holding the wood and swinging the axe at it, she sticks the axe in a stump and drives the wood down on it with a club. This wouldn't work well with hardwood or wet wood, but it works fine with bone-dry pine, fir, or cedar, which is what you want for kindling, anyway. I like to start with a piece of super dry wood, split into quarters with an axe or maul. Hold the wood vertically, so one end is resting lightly on the upward-pointing blade of the axe and strike down on the other end.

Make a club

You could use a hammer or a mallet, but you chance damaging the axe or cutting the mallet. It's easy to make a club out of a small piece of firewood that will last for years if kept out of the rain. Just thin the end of a 3-inch diameter stick with a hatchet, then shape a handle by whittling with a Scout knife. The whole club should be

about 18 inches long. Adjust the length and handle size to suit the strength and hand-size of the user. We keep several clubs of various sizes in the woodshed. Allow 2 or 3 inches for the club to taper down to the handle thickness. If you don't taper it, the handle will break when you strike the wood. Besides, it's easier to make that way.

Good kindling

The best kindling comes from old cedar telephone poles. Every year when I'm getting in the firewood I go by the electric company and ask if they have any useless old poles for sale for kindling. I've never had to pay for one yet. Sometimes, they even cut them to stove length for me. **Don't burn** the creosoted ends! It fouls the air, and it's a waste, as they can be split into excellent fence posts. The rest of the pole can be cut into billets of very fast-burning wood that splits easily into pieces

as thin as you want. If you try to split thin slices off a thick piece, the thin slice will "run out" to a long, tapered splinter, because the thin part flexes more than the thick part. The trick is to split each piece approximately in half. Old cedar poles split so well that you can easily get them down to matchstick size if you want.

Safety tricks

When the pieces get really thin, it's best to lay them horizontally on the axe bit and strike lightly with the club. If you have stuck the axe **firmly** in the stump, you can **pop** the pieces off by starting them with the club, then pulling the end of the wood to one side. Kids love watching the split run down the length of the wood, and hearing the **sproing!** as the piece flies off. That's the best thing about splitting kindling this way—your kids will beg to do it for you! Δ

Backwoods Home magazine

... a practical journal of self reliance!

May/June 1992
No. 15
$3.50 U.S.
$4.50 Canada

RELIGIOUS FREEDOM

RIGHT TO BEAR ARMS

RIGHT AGAINST UNREASONABLE SEARCHES

SOVIET NUCLEAR WEAPONS !
WHAT EFFECT ON OUR RIGHTS
IF THE TERRORISTS GET HOLD OF THEM?

FREE PRESS

FREE SPEECH

RIGHT TO SPEEDY TRIAL

AMATEUR RADIO

HOUSE FOUNDATIONS

USING GUNS AS TOOLS

SOLAR WATER HEATING

BURYING YOUR OWN DEAD

DON CHILDERS

PIE RECIPES

NATIONAL HEALTH INSURANCE

Note from the publisher

Eating ants in triumph

The other day I munched on CHEEZ-ITs while helping to unload eight tons of *The Best of the First Two Years of Backwoods Home Magazine*. When the task was done I left the CHEEZ-ITs on a shelf in an unused trailer in front of the house.

The next day, while feeling triumphant and admiring that huge pile that contained *BHM's* first book, I retrieved the box of CHEEZ-ITs from the trailer and munched on them in my usual fashion—grabbing big handfuls and stuffing them in my mouth.

They tasted slightly stale and bitter as I wolfed them down. (The Cookie Monster has nothing on me when it comes to devouring food.) So I grabbed another fistful and jammed them into my mouth. This time they tasted real bitter, so I spit some out on my hand. And there they were—hundreds of ants crawling all over my hand and the soggy, broken CHEEZ-ITs. I thought I was going to puke. Instead I screamed, "ANNIE!"

Annie's head popped out the house door. "Get me some water! QUICK!" I told her

Annie came running out of the house. "Daddy," she said in her astonished 9-year-old voice, "you have ants all over your undershirt and head."

I tore off my undershirt and went for the garden hose and hosed off my head. Annie started laughing. "Daddy they're on your back. "Quick, hose me off," I said, and she grabbed the hose and blasted me. "In the mouth," I said, and she blasted me in the mouth and I spit out more ants. Then she blasted me all over to get them off my pants. We were both laughing like crazy by the time Lenie came out to see what was happening.

It was all over in a matter of minutes. Both Annie and I needed a change of clothes. An inspection of the box of CHEEZ-ITs revealed thousands of small black ants swarming inside the box, and a thick trail of ants leading from the box across a counter and down the wall into a crack in the trailer floor. I estimate I ate about 300 ants, and hope they have all died inside of me and are not building a colony. Imagine the horror movie: ants crawling out of your nostrils in the middle of the night.

The best bargain for BHM's first 12 issues

Speaking of our first book, *The Best of the First Two Years of Backwoods Home Magazine*, it is your best buy for getting the first 12 issues of *Backwoods Home*. It contains 90% of the articles. It is not sold in any store, although that possibility still exists. The discount (50%) you must give the stores takes most of the profit away, so it's hardly worth selling the book.

Since our goal is to stay solvent, out of debt, and always in control of the business (rather than have a bank or ad-vertisers in control), we'll probably just sell it from here. At $16.95 a copy, plus $2 shipping, for a total of $18.95, it's a very good value. It's fat (1 1/8-inch thick), big (8.5 by 11 inches) beautiful, well-bound, and well worth the money. The order form is on page 98.

If you can't find Backwoods Home at your newsstand, call 708-498-5014

Backwoods Home Magazine is sold in approximately 6,000 stores in the United States, Canada, Australia, and New Zealand. Unfortunately, there are thousands of other stores that don't sell it. So, if you can't find it at your favorite newsstand and wish it was there, there is something you can do about it: call American Distribution Services (ADS), which handles the distribution of *BHM*, at **708-498-5014**, and ask them where you can find *Backwoods Home Magazine*. Not only will they will tell you, but they will alert the appropriate wholesaler to increase distribution to the stores in your area. And that will be a great help to the magazine.

Preparedness, energy shows coming up

Two great shows on the horizon and we'll have booths at both of them. The first is Preparedness Expo '92 May 29, 30, and 31 at the Cashman Field Center in Las Vegas, Nevada. Lots of self reliant types at this show. For details call: 801-561-8242.

The second is the 1992 Midwest Renewable Energy Fair June 19, 20, and 21 at the Portage County Fairgrounds in Amherst, Wisconsin. Solar and electric cars are big at this one. For details: 715-824-5166.

Last issue we announced we'd be at the Environmental Expo in Columbus, Ohio in February, but we didn't make it. Sorry! That's unusual for us not to keep a commitment. The magazine's move to Oregon and all the physical activity that it took simply overwhelmed us and forced us to cancel out. That's not likely to happen again.

Tell us if you change your address

If you change your address, don't forget to tell us. Magazines are mailed third class, and are not forwardable. So if we send a magazine to your old address and you are not there, the post office just throws the magazine away. To change your address, go down to your local post office and get a "change of address" card and fill it out and mail it to us. Δ   *Dave Duffy*

My View

New World Order — old world stench!

Here's the main front-page headline of the Los Angeles Times newspaper on a recent morning:

World Leaders Urge U.N. to Safeguard Rights Everywhere

Dave Duffy

The article beneath it described a summit gathering of world leaders at the United Nations at which most of the major powers called on the U.N. to expand its role and move to "protect human rights everywhere in the world."

French President Francois Mitterand even called for the establishment of a permanent U.N. military force that could be dispatched to enforce U.N. decisions. Besides Mitterand, the meeting included all the big U.N. guns: U.S. President George Bush, British Prime Minister John Major, Russian President Boris Yeltsin (assuming the former Soviet seat), and Chinese Primier Li Peng, who was the lone dissenting voice.

Even Japanese Prime Minister Kiichi Miyazawa was there saying he expected Japan will be given veto power at the U.N. by 1995 since it will be expected to foot the bill for these U.N. adventures. Japan's former World War II ally, Germany, was also there, predicting it too would soon enjoy veto power at the U.N.

Someone pinch me. Am I living a soap opera or a nightmare? It's hard to tell whether to laugh or cry. The "morally correct" bosses at the U.N., still feeling jubilant and righteous a year after their victory over Iraq in their first "world policing" action, now want to clean up the rest of the world in accordance with their views of who is morally correct and who is morally wrong.

Is this what President Bush had in mind when he kept referring to The New World Order during the Iraq War? Is this the beginning of World Government, or a transitional step to it? By gosh I think that's exactly what these leaders hope it is.

So why aren't the people in the streets protesting? Are we all asleep? Didn't East Bloc Communism with all its Big Governmenet totalitarianism just crumble under its own misguided weight? Didn't Democracy just triumph in country after country? Weren't we just celebrating the victory of individual freedom over state totalitarianism? Or was all that just a pleasant dream?

Are we now back to the nightmare of reality? Big Government with all its trampling on individual freedom is not dying afterall. It has merely regrouped and is, in fact, on the rise in the form of The New World Order, in the shape of what these world leaders at the U.N. hope is the beginning of World Government.

We, as free people, should be shaking in our boots. These are not boasting flunkies like Hussein; these are the most powerful politicians on the planet. And much of the mass media is treating their suggestions like they're pretty good ideas, like they may even be the inevitable evolution of government. These world leaders, with the help of an applauding media and our own lethargy, could well pull off World Government in the midst of what we thought was a world triumph of individual freedom.

And they are not even being very original how they do it. Moral excuses like "protecting human rights" have always been used to justify the increase of government power. It sounds good! Wo would object? Certainly not a mass media that believes strongly in Big Government.

But examine the history of the U.S.; ever since our founding fathers laid ink to that special parchment we call our Bill of Rights, Big Government "do-gooders" have been chipping away at our individual freedoms in the name of "protecting the human rights" of someone or other. Trouble is, every time someone's human rights got protected, our personal freedoms got diminished.

That's how the old Soviet Union grew to be so big. They wanted to protect the rights of workers. The Soviet Union didn't collapse because the Communists lost their zeal for their cause; they simply ran out of money.

The zealots in the West who still see Big Government as the way of the future have not lost their zeal for their cause either. Despite Communism's fall, they still think all of societies' problems can be solved by Big Government forcing solutions down the throats of all of us. This World Government idea is right up their alley. It's a big hammer that will be used to smash individual freedoms in the name of "protecting human rights" somewhere around the globe, or somewhere in our own country.

I thought the demise of Communism around the world would give us a reprieve from Big Government. But instead of a reprieve, the powerful politicians in the West see an opening for even bigger government — their style of "morally correct" Big World Government.

Talk about nightmares: Old World War II enemies and old Cold War enemies all together in one Big World Government. And Japan the banker! George Orwell should be here to see this. It's his story. Δ

Foundations . . . from pole to slab

By Martin S. Harris

Just because foundations for most houses and other small buildings are usually fairly massive constructions in stone, masonry, or concrete doesn't eliminate other choices. Particularly for the sweat-equity builder, other foundation systems — some ancient, some modern — may be far more logical and economical.

Here are three which make practical sense in many situations.

Pole foundations

This is a design system which has been around for 10,000 years. It was invented by Pleistocene-Age lakeside condo-dwellers and has been in use ever since. Only the technology has changed; today we're more likely to use pressure-treated squared timbers or round poles than raw tree trunks.

Poles can be installed by hand labor where mechanical excavating equipment and transit-mix concrete trucks can't go. They can be used to level off sloping sites, and with minimal environmental impact, to create dramatic building locations. They can raise bottomland dwelling levels above flood risk. And, they can save the builder a bundle in comparison with the cost of more conventional foundations.

Floating slabs

This is a design system which has been around, in contrast, for barely 100 years. For most of that time, it has not enjoyed the approval of the "official" concrete industry, although just recently the experts have taken some tentative steps to recognize what non-experts have been doing successfully without approval. It's based on the common-sense idea that a concrete slab doesn't require below-frost-level footings to be freeze-proof; if it "floats" on a thick bed of fast-draining coarse gravel, damaging frost-heaves won't occur even if freezing does.

PWF systems

PWF is the lumber industry acronym for "permanent wood foundation," a design with conventional wood framing and plywood sheathing in lieu of conventional deep-wall-and-slab concrete work. PWF has been around for roughly a score of years, and enjoys official recognition from the engineering establishment although some of us in the countryside remain a little skeptical. PWF advocates argue that it is less expensive than concrete, but some of that argument traces back to the same line of reasoning that calls PWF the "all-weather" foundation: in other words, builders save by being able to send out the carpenters when, presumably, the concrete trucks can't roll.

Let's take a more detailed look at each of these options, and let's start by outlining some sizes and costs for a conventional poured concrete foundation. The average new house size in the U.S. today is 1200 square feet, and most new housing is 1-story, requiring a 1200 SF foundation. Typically, here in rural new England, the full-depth poured concrete foundation-wall and floor slab will run about $7 per SF, or $8400 for the concrete work alone, professionally done. That number probably isn't much different in other rural areas around the countryside. Not included here are the costs of excavation, perimeter drainage, waterproofing, backfill, or restorative landscaping of the site.

Pole option

Against that benchmark, let's look at the pole option. One of the best ways to avoid high per-square-foot costs in construction is to avoid the use of ex-

This cross-sectional view of a pole foundation shows the poles (a) and their pre-cast concrete base pads (b) which may be necessary to distribute the load onto the sub-soil. Also shown are the bracing (c) and the deck (d). Note that the deck can readily be designed to be multi-level.

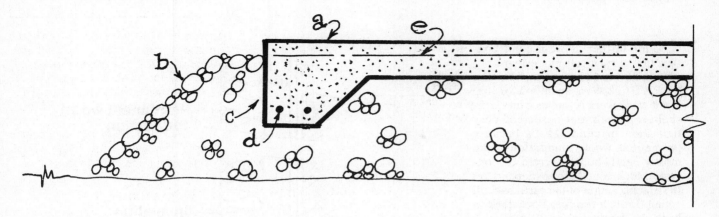

This cross-sectional view of a floating slab foundation shows the way the slab (a) "floats" atop a pad of coarse crushed stone (b) providing excellent drainage. The slab should be haunched at the perimeter (c) and reinforced with steel reinforcing rod (d) around the edge. It should also contain woven-wire fabric reinforcing (e) or a new substitute, glass-fiber reinforcing which is mixed into the liquid concrete before pouring the slab. Also not visible in this sketch is the polyethylene vapor barrier between the slab and the crushed-stone base, and the foam thermal insulation which would be desirable in colder climates.

pensive construction equipment: poles small enough to be manhandled (to be politically correct, I should say personhandled) into place will result in an economical building platform; poles large enough to require specialized excavating or driving equipment won't. In Vermont, years ago, one could enlist the local phone company's augur-and-derrick truck at nominal cost, but those days are now gone. However, unless your site is a breakneck slope, it doesn't matter: reasonably-sized poles (say, 8-inch diameter and 14-foot length) can be placed with hand labor. They can be used for the basis of a 12 x 12 framing grid, which makes for reasonable floor framing as well.

A 1200-SF building size could thus be accommodated in just about any overall grid configuration with 16 poles. They'll cost about $160 apiece, roughly $2600 for the lot. That's commercial pressure-treated lumber: cedar you cut from your own woodlot will be almost free.

Holes can be mechanically augured, even in somewhat rocky soil, in half a day for under $400 — more where drilling or blasting is needed. Drainage, waterproofing, backfilling, and site restoration are virtually eliminated as cost items.

On the other hand, pole systems create a couple of cost items not found in conventional foundations: the need to build a freeze-proof water-and-sewer enclosure from below the frost line up onto the house deck; and the need to enclose and insulate the underside of that deck. These items are not terribly expensive, and total cost, therefore, should run about a third of the concrete alternative.

The "floating slab"

The "floating slab" option, in contrast, rests on the ground rather than dug into it. It works best on reasonably level sites for modest-sized structures, although it has been used for industrial applications and even used in combination with deep-wall foundations.

For our typical 1200 SF house, we'd simply remove the topsoil, place an 18-inch-thick bed of coarse crushed stone, and pour a concrete slab on top of the stone. Utilities are trenched in during excavation with vertical risers to project above the finished slab surface; since they'll be completely inside the finished structure, no special insulation for the risers is needed. You'll probably want to place some insulating foam board at the perimeter of the slab.

I'd cost out the floating slab like this:

- topsoil stripping and sub-slab utility trenching: 1/2 day backhoe time, say $400.
- crushed stone, delivered and placed, with 10% allowance for edge-slope and waste: 74 cubic yards, say $1000.

- reinforced and haunched concrete slab, 4-inch thickness, vapor barrier under slab, steel-trowel finish, formed, placed, and finished: say $1.15 per SF or almost $1400.
- site restoration: 1/2 day backhoe time, say $400.

All this adds up to $3200. If you choose to have the concrete delivered on site for you to place and finish in edge-forms you've pre-built, you reduce the concrete cost to about $55 per cubic yard or $1100. Either way, you're looking at a floating slab cost well under half the cost of a conventional foundation.

With a floating slab, obviously, you won't have a basement, so it's interesting to look at the numbers the other way: for a rough $5000 above the cost of a floating slab, you can have 1200 SF of usable full height space. That works out to under $5 per SF, surely a bargain in anyone's calculations. This arithmetic recalls to mind the economic logic behind earth-set or earth-sheltered construction, where a major part of the final living space can be built at (no pun intended) bargain-basement prices. We've examined this subject in earlier columns, and will probably do so again.

No matter how low the cost of basement space, it's no bargain if you don't need it: the floating slab option, therefore, offers an economical solution similar to the pole option in creating a deck for further above-ground construction at relatively modest cost.

If you do want a basement, however, the PWF folks have an option for you. But it won't work if you have an earth-sheltered, walk-out-basement configuration in mind. That's because permanent wood foundations, like mostly lightly-built concrete or concrete block foundations, depend on the bracing action of the earth backfill acting through the first-floor deck to keep the foundation walls from tipping in. In a walk-out design, there's nothing to brace the side opposite the walk-out, and a properly engineered retaining wall design, not dependent on bracing in the wood deck, is essential.

PWF is based on the idea that a wood box, set deep into the ground on all four sides, can be self-bracing just like conventional deep-wall foundation design. The wood is protected against ground moisture by anti-decay treatment and by careful attention to site drainage: that includes waterproofing membrane outside the perimeter walls, a gravel base under the whole system, and perforated-pipe drainage carrying ground water away from the site. It's the sort of drainage design that should be, but frequently isn't, used on every conventional deep wall foundation.

Drainage costs, as outlined above, are part of the reason why it's difficult to evaluate the economy claims made for the PWF system. Those same costs, you'll note, were not included in my thumbnail estimate for conventional concrete, simply because they're so frequently excluded from the design. It's also tough to evaluate when PWF sponsors resort to such claims, as, for example, 40 SF of extra space per house because the foundation walls are thinner than in concrete.

On the other hand, some claims for PWF are quite valid. Given the notoriously low insulating value of concrete, it's clear that the insulated stud-wall system which is part of the PWF system performs far better in energy-conservation terms. It's also obvious that such walls are easier to run wires and pipes in, and easier to finish with sheetrock for living-space use.

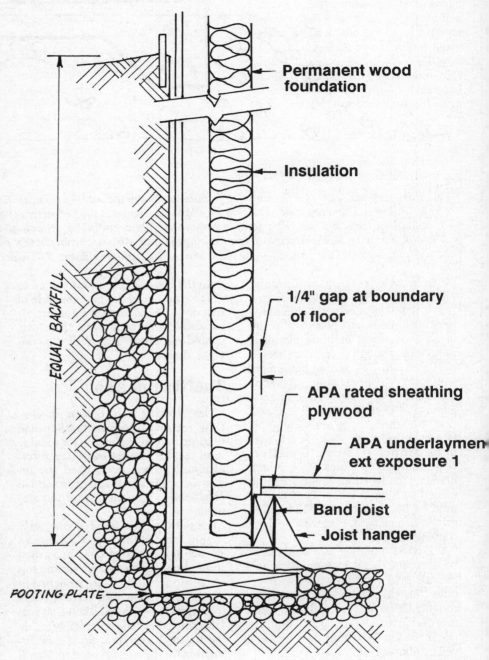

This cross-sectional view of a PWF foundation, courtesy of the American Plywood Association, shows how typical wood framing is used in a below-grade situation. The sketch does not show the perimeter perforated-pipe drainage all around the outside of the foundation to carry ground water away. Nor does it show the upper part of the basement, where the floor joists act as braces to keep the walls from tipping inward because of soil pressure.

Of these three options, PWF is the only one to offer usable full-height space as part of the foundation design. Whether it does that at less cost than the conventional, deep-wall concrete system is, in my view, questionable. I'd summarize this way: PWF is less suited to the heavy wet soils of the North Country than to the light dry soils of the High Plains and the Great Basin.

It's less a way to save a significant chunk of change on the foundation of a building than it is a way to use modern lumber technology in an unusual setting. For real savings, therefore, I'd focus on the pole or floating slab options, and if my design needed basement square footage I'd stick with more traditional concrete or masonry.

Weak links

No discussion of structures is complete without some mention of structural failure: what's the weak link for each of these options?

For conventional concrete or masonry, the traditional weakness has always been wall failure under backfill loading, particularly in wet heavy soils where frost goes deep. It shows up in cracks and leakage at first, then progresses into wall tipping and even collapse.

Basements of walk-out design are particularly vulnerable because of the absence of the effect of deck bracing. Proper use of steel reinforcing could have prevented the weakness, but after it's happened one can only do three things: demolish and re-build, pour a new wall outside the existing one to stabilize things, or excavate to install a fast-draining backfill and improved drainage piping. It would have been a lot cheaper to put steel into the concrete and to invest in proper drainage at the beginning.

Pole foundations usually fail for one of two reasons: soil overload or pole tipping. The nature of pole design is to concentrate a lot of load at the pole base, and all too frequently that load exceeds the bearing capacity of the soil, even with the little concrete pole-bases that are sometimes used by better-than-average builders. In rock and gravel soils there's almost never a problem, but for any other soil conditions I'd use any good pole construction manual as a guide to running the numbers and determining the needed size for the concrete pole base. Pole tipping is evidence of inadequate lateral bracing: it can be corrected easily and bracing added.

Floating slabs fail for two reason: the coarse stone sub-grade settled after the concrete was poured, or doesn't drain properly and therefore causes frost heaves. It's almost impossible to correct either defect after the fact. Don't confuse superficial shrinkage cracks in the concrete surface with serious structural failure. Almost all slabs display shrinkage cracks, which can be prevented only by tooling construction joints into the slab as it is being finished.

PWF failure is something I've never seen, but I'd imagine that it would work much like failure of a conventional system, and be just about as difficult to fix.

Of these options, someone will ask, which do I prefer? I'd have to nominate the pole system: not only because its almost always the most cost-effective and the most responsive to sweat-equity investment, but also because it offers the most design flexibility. And maybe there's another, more romantic reason: most of us are descendants of those Pleistocene lake-front condo-dwellers who invented this oldest of non-hole-in-the-ground systems.

(Martin Harris is a Vermont architect, cofounder of the "New England Builder," and author of numerous articles on home building.) Δ

Grow your food
Can your food

The Third Year

Soviet nuclear weapons.....

What effect on our freedoms if terrorists get hold of them!

By John Earl Silveira

I hate sitting in front of the computer, staring at a blank monitor, waiting for inspiration. But that's how Dave, the fellow who publishes this magazine, found me this morning when he walked into the office.

"Have you finished your article, yet?" he asked.

I stared at the screen without answering.

"Any calls?" he asked. I heard someone else come in behind him.

"Some subscriptions were called in," I said without turning to see who was with him. "I got the information. It's all on your desk."

"Want coffee, Mac?" Dave asked.

I turned and saw O.E. MacDougal, Dave's poker playing friend.

"There's a fresh pot," I said before Mac could answer.

"What's your article going to be on for this issue?" Dave called as he left the room.

I didn't answer.

Mac crossed the office, found a cup, and poured some coffee.

"You look tired," he said from across the room.

"Couldn't sleep," I said. "You don't look tired. No poker game last night?"

He shook his head and walked over to where I sat in front of the blank screen.

I turned back and faced the computer.

"How come you couldn't sleep?" he asked.

"I think I'm holding this issue up," I said.

He didn't say anything.

"The rest of the magazine is set to go to the printer. Dave just needs my article before he sends it."

"What do you have in mind?"

Some of the former Soviet Union's tactical nuclear weapons are small enough to fit into a suitcase, or even an attache case, and most any of them would fit into a small car.

"I'm thinking of doing something on next fall's Presidential election."

He didn't comment.

"What with the economy the way it is, I figure it's likely to be the most important issue of the year."

"You do?" he asked.

I didn't answer and I could hear Mac sip his coffee behind me.

"Don't you think so?" I asked.

"What angle do you plan to take?" he asked.

"I don't know."

I continued to stare at the screen. I could hear Dave doing something elsewhere in the house. Mac sipped his coffee again.

"What do you think is the most important issue of the year?" I asked.

"I think we may be at a crossroads in civilization," he replied.

"With the election?"

"With the bomb."

I looked at him out of the corner of my eye. "Is this a joke?"

"Not to me." He sipped his coffee again.

"What bomb?"

"I'm talking about the nuclear weapons in the former Soviet Union. It's in all the newspapers," he said.

"I've read about them. What's got you worried about them?"

"Well, now that the Soviet Union's breaking up, the Cold War's over and, while that may be good, we may be falling into something worse."

"What could be worse?"

He eyed me a little critically. "Fifteen republics that once formed the Soviet Union are going their separate ways and the vast war machine they once controlled may also be out of control and could alter civilization in totally unexpected ways."

I stared at him.

"Do you want me to go on?" he asked.

I grabbed a steno pad and a pencil and said, "Yeah."

50,000 warheads

"Well, you've first got to realize the Soviet Union had between 13,000 and 15,000 strategic nuclear warheads and another 30,000 to 40,000 tactical nuclear warheads, in their arsenal when they broke up. What's going to happen to them? Over the next seven years, the Russians are supposed to take all the strategic weapons, not currently in Russia, back behind the Russian borders. They're also supposed to draw back all the tactical weapons by July."

"This July?"

He nodded. "They claim they're even going to scrap some of them as they do this. But we're talking about some 50,000 nuclear warheads. What with the economic turmoil over there, several of the republics at the brink of civil war, and the emerging Moslem zealotry, I wonder if they can control them all."

"What's the difference between strategic weapons and tactical weapons?" I asked.

"Think of the strategic weapons as the ones they had pointed at us with their ICBMs, submarines, and long ranged bombers. They're the city busters that range from hundreds of kilotons to several megatons in yield. The tactical warheads are battlefield weapons. They're smaller in size and smaller in explosive power. Some are small enough to be fired from cannons and a lot of them would fit into a suitcase or even an attaché case, and most any of them would fit into a small car."

"Are you kidding. That small?"

He nodded. "Small enough to smuggle out of what was once the Soviet Union.

"The bright side is that all the Soviet's strategic weapons are concentrated in Russia, Ukraine, Kazakhstan, and Byelorussia, and the tactical weapons are just in Russia, Ukraine, and Byelorussia. Makes them a little easier to keep track of."

"What's the downside?"

"Not only is there social and economic turmoil over there, but several of the republics are having second thoughts about letting the Russians take them all home with them."

"Why?"

"A history of Russian domination. These other republics joined the Soviet Union because the Russians forced them to. Then, though they were all ostensibly equal partners, the Russians never really shared the power. For example, they made sure almost all of the important posts, in each and every republic, was filled by ethnic Russians. It would be as if in this country all the highest posts in each state were filled only by people from New York."

"They feel justifiably scared that the Russians are going to continue to dominate them after the split."

"Do we care who gets the bombs?" I asked.

"Sure we do."

He walked back to the pot and topped off his coffee. When he came back, he pulled up a chair.

Dave was standing in the doorway, a box full of doughnuts in his hand and a puzzled look on his face. I don't know how long he'd been there. He stepped in and put the doughnuts on my desk and got a chair for himself.

Cash crop of export bombs

Mac said, "First of all, the old Soviet economy is bankrupt and the military arsenal they once held represents one of the few 'hard cash' exports they can readily sell for Western currency."

"Do you think they'd sell them?" Dave asked.

"It's not likely that any will be sold officially. But it's possible. Of more concern are the hard times and poverty now endemic over there. An individual or group could make one or two of the 50,000 bombs 'get lost' during the accounting and try to use them to strike it rich."

"And they'd sell them to...?" Dave asked.

The bomb buyers

"Who do you think? Iraq, Iran, Libya, or directly to a terrorist group like the IRA, the Tamil rebels of Sri Lanka, the Basque Separatists, or even some drug baron who has a use for one.

"But the biggest problem, right now, is in the Middle East. Eleven percent of the population of the Soviet Union was Moslem, several of the republics, like Tadzhikistan and Azerbaijan, are predominantly Moslem, and they don't have a great deal of love for the Russians—or us."

"Okay," I said, writing.

"I'm not saying all these things are for certain, anymore than the end of civilization was a certainty during the Cold War. It's just a new danger we have to face."

"But what you're saying is that terrorists can get some bombs, set them off and end the world."

Using a nuclear bomb to change politics

"No, the threat isn't that they can end the world like World War III could. The threat is that nuclear terrorists could change the political climate of the world, forever, and they could change the politics of this country, too.

"Think of how we'd react, politically, if a terrorist group smuggled a small nuclear bomb into the United States.

"Is it possible for them to get one into this country and set it off?" Dave asked.

Smuggling a bomb into the U.S.

"Of course," he said. He looked over the doughnuts like he was about to make a lifetime investment in one. "And they aren't going to need a missile or a long ranged bomber like the Russians. All they need do is follow the examples set by any major drug dealer or the people who smuggle aliens in. Then, once here, driving a bomb to within a few blocks of the White House, the Capitol Building, or the Pentagon will be easy. Or they could place one in a car on a street next to the World Trade Center in New York City." He shrugged. "No problem at all."

"But **how** would they get a bomb in here?" Dave asked.

"We have long, undefended borders. Drug dealers cross them regularly with small planes and land on makeshift airstrips in the desert. Diplomatic pouches are never searched. In fact, it's illeagal. Or, hell, they could hide it in the hold of a cargo ship or a luxury yacht and set it off in one of our harbors." His hand poised over the box.

"We have a lot of individual rights in this country but we have traditionally had fewer during war, and the siege mentality that could afflict us if some of these weapons got loose could create a situation tantamount to a state of perpetual war."

"How do you think our rights would be affected?" Dave asked.

"If a bomb goes off in this country, warrantless searches are going to become a matter of course and no one will dare speak out against them.

"And Moslems in this country who are good citizens, will be persecuted simply because of their beliefs. Jews will suffer if there's a backlash blaming them for Moslem animosity.

"And what will become of dissenting opinions? Censorship is almost inevitable. I pity any individuals who speak out against the injustice of curtailing our constitutional rights.

"Secret trials will not be unheard of."

"I don't believe any of this," I said.

"What do you mean?" Mac asked me.

"These are just not things that can happen in America," I said.

America curtailed freedoms in the past

He smiled. "This is the greatest country that ever existed," he said, "but we're not without our faults. Look at the record. We allowed the lynching of blacks in this country—2,000 from 1910 to 1930. We acted as if they didn't have rights.

"We interred hundreds of thousands of Japanese during World War II because we suspected their allegiance and patriotism without a shred of justification. We imprisoned them in the desert. Yet, Japanese-Americans saw themselves as Americans first as Japanese second—just as you think of yourself as American first and Portuguese and whatever else you are second. But did you know that the Nisei units were far and away the most heroic, dedicated, and decorated combat units the United States ever fielded—in any war? Did you know that among white American soldiers, the desertion rate in combat during World War II was about 10-15%, but among Japanese-Americans it was zero. Yet, even as the war wore on and their dedication was apparent, we kept their families interred until the war was over, and they lost their homes, their businesses, and their feeling they could depend on their fellow Americans.

"Let's face it, we forced Indians, the natives on this continent, onto reservations as if they were foreigners.

"We staged military trials of suspected German spies and performed executions during WW II, right here in the States, without the public being apprised.

"These things have happened and though it may be hard to believe we would do anything like them again, politics and the social climate are funny things subject to drastic and dramatic changes.

Dictatorship in the U.S.?

"We could lose it all because of some crazy terrorist and a mushroom cloud. And we could lose it forever. We could trade away our rights for the feeling of security. It would be like George Orwell's *1984* where the government has become a dictatorship and justifies it with the excuse that a constant state of war exists."

His hand hovered another moment, then he took both a lemon filled and a chocolate covered chocolate.

"*1984*?" I asked.

"Read it," he said.

Dave said, "Then it sounds like, if we can help the Russians ensure that all their bombs are accounted for, we can solve the problem."

Mac said, "Maybe, although I'm not sure the Russians really want us getting close to their bombs. We're not exactly allies, yet.

The danger of unemployed nuclear scientists

But that brings about another aspect of the problem. Even if all the bombs can be accounted for, there are thousands of scientists and technicians who worked on the Soviet nuclear programs. They've suddenly been unemployed in their own homelands. They need jobs, they can build a bomb from scratch, and there are people who'll pay them to do it." He started to eat the lemon-filled doughnut.

Dave looked at me writing in my steno pad.

"Are you taking this down?" he asked me.

I nodded.

"Could you put aside the article you were working on and write something on this?"

I nodded again, and looked at Mac who didn't seem surprised that this was now my article.

"How many scientists are we talking about?" I asked.

"There was an estimated 100,000 scientists and technicians involved in the Soviet nuclear weapons programs, including 3,000 who had the highest levels of expertise. Now, quite a few of them are out of work and the ones who have jobs are getting paid in worthless rubles.

Similar to WWII aftermath

"In some respects, we're seeing a repeat of the situation that existed after World War II when the Americans and Soviets scrambled for German scientists and technicians in war torn Germany.

"Are you aware that the birth of military missiles, germ warfare, and the space programs, in both East and West, were midwifed by German scientists grabbed after the war?"

Neither Dave nor I answered.

"Well, today, it's Third World countries vying for the brains and knowledge of a defunct and impoverished Soviet Union, and they want 'the bomb.'

"There are oil-rich countries beckoning these scientists and technicians with offers that run into the hundreds of thousands of American dollars each. A friend told me over lunch just the other day that she'd heard of an ad appearing in a Moscow newspaper advertising jobs available in Moslem countries for unemployed Soviet scientists."

"What are the chances they'll go?"

These scientists once lived privileged lives in the old Soviet Union. They had the most interesting jobs and loved their work. Now, they have nothing. Thousands of scientists. Some of them are going to be tempted."

"But I read that this country is going to give the Soviets some $25 million to help employ them at home," Dave said.

"40% of the Soviet gross national product went into maintaining their military. Half of that was spent on nuclear weapons alone. $25 million isn't much. And how's the money going to be spent? Will it buy the kind of jobs with challenges that these people thrived on in the nuclear heydays? If they're not, what we're talking about is scientific welfare, and that alone may send some looking for more interesting jobs in Baghdad."

"Couldn't they be harnessed to develop computers or something?" I asked.

He drank a little more coffee. "Not just by throwing money at it. The widespread use of computers didn't happen overnight in the West. A consumer base had to be developed and market forces determined where they were needed. Right now the Russian economy is in shambles; it would make no sense to put these scientists to work on scientific projects for which there are no markets.

"Not only that, but the job skills and knowledge in nuclear and missile fields don't readily translate to computer jobs, anymore than piano tuning translates to diesel mechanics. Most of them would be years away from making any significant headway.

Scientific welfare

"We've just got to be careful we aren't creating a sort of scientific welfare. Scientists are not the welfare type. They want real, meaningful jobs and the stature that goes along with them. If we do it wrong, they'll work for someone who can give it to them."

"What about other aid?" Dave asked. "According to Yeltsin, the dangers of the West not giving aid to the new republics is that if things get worse over there, a dictator will arise and we'll be back into a cold war followed by a hot war."

"In other words," Mac said, "if we don't pay tribute, somebody is going to start World War III with us. I don't believe it. I think the whole thing is a ploy to save Yeltsin's political behind."

"Then we shouldn't give them aid?" I asked.

I saw just a tinge of exasperation on his face. "Don't put words in my mouth. We should help them, but do it right. Make capital investments. You know, create businesses and jobs—those things we have over here that we tax so we can have social justice and welfare.

"We should do what we did after World War II; we invested money in the Japanese and German economies. They thrived and both countries became free market democracies that give us a run for our money. Even Vietnam is turning around because Western and Asian businesses are investing there—not because someone's giving them handouts. Most of the so-called aid we give out has been a failure because it hasn't been capital investment. We're trying to become a welfare system to the world."

"So you're saying, 'give them jobs,'" Dave said.

"Yeah. One McDonalds franchise is worth a trainload of welfare."

"Back to the nuclear bombs, what's the worst case?" Dave asked.

A worst case scenario

"The worst case is that a nuclear bomb actually explodes in a Western city. Maybe we don't know who does it, or maybe it's some zealots who don't care if we strike back. The threat is that if they can set off one, they can set off another. That mentality would affect the very fabric of Western society and the way we live.

"Why do you think the Israelis bombed that nuclear power plant outside Baghdad back in 1981? It was because they feared it could be used to manufacture nuclear bombs. They have a keener appreciation of what a nuclear weapon would mean in the hands of someone like Hussein. Just the existence of a terrorist bomb in the Mideast will bring about the end of their state in a way the four Arab-Israeli wars could not.

He looked at the ceiling. "You know, a bomb doesn't even have to be detonated. Imagine if one were found in Washington, D.C., set to go off, but

left as a just warning, along with the claim that there were more.

"We're talking about the bomb in the hands of people who have thought nothing of blowing up airliners with hundreds of people aboard, planting car bombs at busy city intersections, and sending suicide squads to attack military installations and inflict losses that ran into hundreds of lives."

"You mean, like the Marine barracks in Lebanon," Dave said.

Mac nodded. "These were not tactics the Soviets used. We and the Soviets had an all-or-nothing mentality in dealing with each other. Muamar Khaddafi or Saddam Hussien have not only condoned and encouraged such terrorist acts, they may even have contracted for them. Setting off a bomb may not be too horrifying for them to comtemplate.

"So," Mac said, "though the danger of ending civilization faced us during the Cold War, it did not translate into a serious curtailment of civil rights and today we live in the freest society that has ever existed. But those freedoms will go away if we live in society with a siege mentality. In fact, terrorists may dictate what rights we have and which ones we don't."

"So what's the answer?" Dave asked.

"Bomb them first," Mac replied.

Dave looked horrified. I must have looked worse.

"I'm just kidding," he said. "No, the answer is to encourage the Soviets to keep track of all the weapons, to ensure employment for as many scientists as possible—even if it's nuclear weapons development and even letting some come to the West until an economic base can be established that employs them in other sectors, and to encourage Western business investments."

"No handouts," Dave said.

"No handouts," Mac said. "We're not dealing with Haiti." Δ

> *Our constitution is in actual operation; everything appears to promise that it will last; but in this world nothing is certain but death and taxes.*
>
> Benjamin Franklin, 1789

The Third Year

Walking that last mile with a loved one ...

... a guide to caring for your own dead

By Carl Watner

When a family member dies, most Americans instinctively grab for a telephone and call one of their local undertakers. But there was once a tradition, before the telephone and the advent of licensed morticians, where "home funerals were the practice everywhere, and each community had a group of women who came in to help with the 'laying out of the dead'."

Even today, in 41 states, a family or support group has the right to handle all death arrangements without the assistance of outside professionals. In the other nine states, if the family (and friends) can find a cooperative funeral director they may, if they wish, "take on at least some of the duties usually assigned to a funeral home." Let's consider the legal and moral considerations, and the practical procedures to be followed in the event you or a family member opt for a funeral without an undertaker.

Involving yourself in the mourning process

In Lisa Carlson's book, *Caring For Your Own Dead*, she writes that this can be one of "the most meaningful" ways "to say goodbye to someone you love." Like homeschooling, homebirth, and homecare (hospice) for the terminally ill, home funerals allow us to take control of critical areas of our lives. Not everyone may be emotionally prepared for this choice, but grief therapists have long recognized that the American way of death usually offers no satisfactory way of actively and physically involving the bereaved in the mourning process.

Participation of close friends and family in construction of a casket, transportation of the body, preparation of the grave, scattering of "ashes", or other related activities helps them accept the fact of death—both emotionally and intellectually. For most people who have done it, involvement in a home funeral is a special time, not frightening or aversive. In effect, it is "going the last mile" with the deceased, and customizing their last rites. By not turning over the funeral responsibilities to people who never knew the deceased as an individual human being, we not only offer our last respects, but engage in an emotional process which helps us cope with their death. To be around the body of one who has just died gives us the "unparalleled opportunity" as one death educator has put it, "to let go gently into the light," "to act out one's grief by confronting the reality of death."

Certainly the decision to care for your own dead should be taken seriously, discussed beforehand and accepted by all concerned relatives. Religious, cultural, and personal beliefs, as well as the individual wishes of the deceased and the needs of the surviving family and friends must all be taken into consideration. Not everyone will want nor be able to cope with a funeral without an undertaker.

Saving money not the prime goal

While it is quite possible to save money, the primary motivation for caring for your own dead should normally not be financial. (In fact, this author urges that it not be.)

It should be a moral, caring concern, regardless of what choice is made. Those who choose to employ an undertaker miss their loved ones just as much as those who choose to do it themselves. Both should have the right to arrange their affairs any way they wish, so long as it is peaceful. There is nothing in home funeral practice which violates this rule.

Since family and friends can duplicate the services of the funeral director (except embalming the body—and this need not be done in many instances) there is absolutely no reason why they should be prohibited from caring for their own dead.

Funeral home services and costs

What are the services performed and products ordinarily supplied by your local funeral home? First of all, they usually transport the body from the place of death to the funeral home. There the morticians prepare the body for placement in a casket, which they normally supply. The body then stays in the funeral home (for one or more days) for viewing or family visitation. Then the undertaker transports the casketed-body to its place of final disposition—normally a crematory or cemetery.

They may make certain cash advances: to the newspapers for obituary notices, to the florist for flowers, or to clergy for honoraria. They may also try to sell you a grave vault, liner, cremation urn, or grave memorial, depending upon their product line and your needs.

The funeral home personnel will handle all the necessary paperwork, including obtaining copies of the state death certificate, the transportation permit, and will probably assist in the completion of paperwork at the cemetery or crematory. They will probably also present you with a whopping bill, beginning at $300 or $400 for the most basic cremation and possibly running into many thousands of dollars if you select an expensive casket and let them take charge of everything.

Knowing your state law

In the final version of the Federal Trade Commission's "Consumer's Guide," published in 1982, funeral directors are required to give you a general price list which contains the cost of each individual item and service offered. The purpose of this regulation is to allow you to comparison shop between undertakers, and to better allow the family decide exactly which services and products it wishes to purchase. You should be able to obtain this list of prices over the phone or in person. It would probably be wise for a person thinking of an at-home funeral to familiarize him or herself with at least one such price list and their particular state law governing the disposition of the dead. The Department of Health and Vital Statistics in most states will be able to direct you to the appropriate statutes or furnish you with a copy of the law.

Embalming not mandatory

The FTC rules also require funeral providers to supply information about embalming. Embalming is an ancient practice reflected in Egyptian mummification.

Today, the process involves arterial embalming ("draining the blood and filling the veins and arteries with pre-

servatives") and cavity embalming, which removes body wastes from the abdominal and chest cavities, and then fills them with a formalin solution. After embalming, the body would be cosmetically restored by the funeral director, if so desired by the family.

The basic purpose of embalming is simply short-term preservation of the body for the purposes of viewing it until the day of final disposition and holding the body until distant relatives and friends can arrive for the funeral. There is little scientific evidence that standard embalming prevents long-term decomposition, or prevents the spread of disease.

An alternative would be refrigeration of the body, which is both legal and practical in many areas. Thus embalming is not mandatory, except in certain circumstances, and the family opting for an at-home-funeral would be wise to familiarize itself with the law. If they desire embalming, they should locate a professional mortician that will perform this service for them at a reasonable charge.

Things to remember to do

The family who has experienced the death of one of its loved ones, and desires to handle arrangements on its own, must be prepared to provide services and products normally supplied by an undertaker.

Before transporting the body of the deceased, **they should have a physician sign a death certificate and obtain the necessary transportation permit from their local health department.** This form will have to be presented to the cemetery or crematory, and eventually be returned to the local health department.

The family will have to **build or obtain a suitable box in which to place the corpse.** Some crematories and funeral homes sell what they describe as an **alternative container,** which may be used in lieu of an expensive casket. **Such a container is generally a heavy-duty cardboard box** of casket dimensions. Since it is combustible it is suitable for a crematory disposition. If such a container is used, **a piece of**

plywood should be placed under it, to make it rigid and assist in handling. "The board enables the deceased to be readily moved from a vehicle into a church, for example." If family members are going to construct a casket, they should consult with their cemetery or crematory to be sure that the one they build is not too large for the crematory oven or cemetery liner or vault.

Burial clothing/jewelry

Before placing the deceased in a container, the family will either have the body embalmed (depending upon their wishes and state law) or else bathed and dressed in appropriate burial clothing. They should not forget to remove jewelry from the body, if that is their desire. (If the body is to be cremated, and the deceased had a pacemaker, do not forget to have it removed since **the pacemaker's lithium batteries will explode when subjected to extreme heat.**) They should also be prepared for changes in the body. The blood will have settled to the lower points, leaving the upper portions of the body pale and waxy looking. "Some parts of the body may swell a little." There may be some discharges from the body cavities, so it is advisable to use absorbent materials like towels or sheets or newspapers under the deceased. Sometimes zippered body bags may be used to prevent leakage or seepage of body fluids.

The body having been casketed or placed in an alternative container, the family may wish to participate in religious, or memorial services or may simply take the body to the place of final disposition, and conduct its services at another location after this is done. The basic choices with regard to final disposition of the body are:

- 1 The body may be cremated at a crematory.
- 2 It may be buried in the earth.
- 3 The body may be entombed in an above-ground mausoleum.

If cremation is chosen, the box containing the body must be combustible. The cremation process may take one

DON CHILDERS

to three hours. When the combustion chamber has cooled down what remains is three to seven pounds of clean, white bone fragments, known as "cremains." The cremains are processed in a pulverizer and then placed in a temporary container of tin, plastic, or cardboard, all of which are mailable. Permanent, attractive cremation urns and vases may be made by the family or purchased from the crematory or funeral home. The cremains may be scattered over land or sea, buried in the earth, placed in a columbarium, or kept at home, as they pose absolutely no health hazard.

Burial or entombment

The other methods of final disposition, if the family chooses not to cremate, are earth burial or above ground entombment in a mausoleum. Ordinarily this would take place at a cemetery, where the family has purchased a grave site or mausoleum space.

Commercial or religious cemeteries all have their various rules and regulations, so it behooves the family to familiarize themselves with the requirements that affect them. Many cemeteries will not let family members dig or backfill the grave, although sometimes special requests are honored. Practically all charge a fee for opening and closing the grave.

Additionally, most cemeteries today require some sort of concrete burial box, known as a vault or liner, whose primary purpose is to prevent sinkage at the grave site. Wooden or metal caskets in direct contact with the earth will eventually rot or rust, and if heavy cemetery equipment is moved over the grave, sometimes serious settlement of the earth can occur.

A **vault** is a concrete container with a seal between its upper lid and box-like bottom, designed to keep underground water from entering. The **grave liner** is an unsealed box and lid, usually with holes in the bottom. Its only function is to prevent settlement of the earth over the casket. The cemetery would normally sell these concrete containers, or they may be obtainable from outside sources such as a funeral home or a manufacturer of septic tanks.

Rural areas

In rural areas home burials are usually possible if they conform to local zoning ordinances. The lay of the land and local soil conditions must be taken into consideration. Burial sites should be away from low lying areas and away from all water sources. There is no particular reason to use a concrete grave liner, unless the family wishes to do so.

Home burial plot

A family must realize that if it establishes its own burial plot, that someone else in the future may choose to disregard its dead. Cases abound of abandoned family cemeteries, disrupted by building expansion and development. But the satisfactions of

a home burial are great. No one sets visitation hours, and plantings or markers can be appropriate to the family or individual. Depending upon the place of burial, the family has a number of options in marking the grave. Memorial park cemeteries usually only permit bronze markers, which sit flush with the ground. Traditional cemeteries permit these markers as well as tombstones. Even cremains, which are sometimes buried in the ground, may be memorialized with bronze tablets or conventional type monuments if the family so chooses.

There is much good information and many suggestions in the literature about caring for your own dead. For example, I have not discussed organ or body donation as a family option. The books listed at the end of this article will shed light on other options.

Bureaucratic resistance

If you live in an area where at-home funerals are not common, then you

should be prepared to expect hesitancy and even resistance on the part of those normally involved in the process. Local bureaucrats, including hospital personnel, may be reluctant to permit you to proceed, but if you have studied the law and know what you are doing, their unwillingness and indecision should be easily overcome. Plenty of advance planning and forethought is necessary. Timing is important, as cemeteries and crematories have cut-off hours.

Death is certainly part of life, much as we are conditioned to reject this idea. Active involvement following the death of a loved one or friend is actually a labor of love. It is often the best type of grief therapy, for there lies the power, the terror, the pain, the finality of death and the truth. Because caring for our own dead makes us personally and fully involved, directly and naturally, we are free to grieve and move into reality. We are in reality, not protected from it.

Further reading

Patricia Anderson, *Affairs in Order: A Complete Resource Guide to Death and Dying*, New York: Macmillan Publishing, 1991.

Lisa Carlson, *Caring for Your Own Dead*, Upper Access Book Publishers, Box 457, Hinesburg, VT 05461. 343 pages, published in 1987. Softback edition $14.95 + $2.00 shipping. Must reading. Presents a detailed study of all aspects of home funerals, plus analyses on a state-by-state basis.

Funerals—Consumers' Last Rights by the Editors of *Consumer Reports*. Copyright 1977 by Consumers Union, Mount Vernon, NY 10550, and published by Pantheon Books.

Ernest Morgan, *Dealing Creatively with Death: A Manual of Death Education and Simple Burial*. Order from Celo Press, 1901 Hannah Branch Road, Burnsville, NC 28714. Another must- be-read book. Second only to the Carlson book.

(Carl Watner is editor of "The Voluntaryist" newsletter, Box 1275, Gramling, South Carolina 29348. Sample copy available on request. 6 issue subscription - $18.00.) ∆

Sample funeral home charges

The following prices are those given by a funeral home operating in an upstate South Carolina town of 3,000 people. Prices will naturally vary from business to business, and from locality to locality.

Basic professional charge (non-declinable; applicable to every funeral except direct cremations) (includes availability of staff and facilities on a 24-hour basis, 365 days a year; consultation with family and clergy; arrangement and direction of funeral services; preparing and filing of necessary permits and authorizations; care and arrangement of floral tributes; coordinating with those providing other portions of the funeral, such as cemetery or crematory; continuing assistance to the family with business concerns after the funeral)...$750.

Embalming (Includes dressing and arranging in casket)...$225.

Use of facilities for visitation...$150
Church services...$125.
Graveside services...$100.
Automotive equipment (local use of hearse)...$65.
Merchandise
caskets...$350 to $2879
liner (for a perpetual care cemetery)...$425.
vault...$550 to $8200.
Direct cremation (no services, visitation or public viewing)
professional services charge...$400.
cremation...$320.
container for cremation...$30.
Cremation (with services, visitation, public viewing, etc.)
professional services charge...$750.
see above prices for other service and merchandise costs
cremation...$320.
Grave opening charges in this town are generally $300 to $350. ∆

Understanding ammunition will make your working guns more versatile and useful

By Christopher Maxwell

Knowledge about the different types of ammunition which are available for your firearms will enable you to use them to maximum effect, and to use them for more different purposes than you might be aware of.

The ammunition catalogs list so many variations of each cartridge that they tend to overwhelm rather than educate the novice. Many manufacturers' claims about their products are also somewhat optimistic.

In this article I will try to give you some of the basic information about ammunition for the most common types of firearms. This will help you get the best effect and give you the basic groundwork to learn more if you care to.

Ammunition components

All firearms ammunition for cartridge firearms contain the following components.

- **Projectile:** This will be shot, in ounces for shotguns, or bullets weighed in grains for rifles and handguns. Shot comes in different sizes for different purposes, and bullets are available in different shapes and compositions.

- **Propellant:** In shotguns this will usually be stated in dram equivalent. No good reason, it's just the way they always did it. In rifles and handguns, no quantity will be stated. .22 ammo will be high velocity or standard, handgun ammunition is stand-

ard or +P. Rifle ammunition will almost always be full power.

- **Primer:** This lights the propellant and will not be optional unless you assemble your own ammunition.

- **Case:** The cartridge case or shell holds the whole assembly together. Again there are no real options offered.

So every time you buy ammunition you will need to know what type and weight of bullet or size and weight of shot you want. Plus you may want to select an appropriate power level for the job at hand in your shotgun or .22.

The popular .22 rimfire

The .22 rimfire is the most popular cartridge in the world. It is available in different lengths. Each length is available in different power levels and different weights and shapes of bullets.

The .22 short is the oldest self contained firearm cartridge still in production. This cartridge was developed by Smith & Wesson before the Civil War. Today the only guns made specifically for this cartridge are gallery rifles, Olympics grade target pistols, and some European pocket pistols.

But any gun made for the .22 long rifle cartridge will fire this cartridge and many like the low noise and low power of these tiny cartridges.

Low velocity and high velocity are offered; both use a bullet of about 29gr. The high velocity hits a little harder, but the low velocity may be more accurate in your gun. Hitting what you shoot at with a low velocity works better than missing with a high velocity.

Hollow points are available in the high velocity version, but I can't tell any difference in the effect. Any of these will do for game or pests the size of a squirrel or smaller. In truth, I see little use for this cartridge.

The .22 long cartridge is deservedly obsolete. This cartridge offers the same performance as the .22 short in a longer case. Don't ask me why.

.22 long rifle

The .22 long rifle is the cartridge most people mean when they say .22. The .22 long rifle is the lengthened case of the .22 long with a heavier bullet and more power. The difference in power and accuracy makes the .22lr one of the most useful cartridges in existence.

The standard (target) velocity .22lr fires a 40gr bullet at about 1150 feet per second from a rifle. This cartridge is accurate and powerful enough for small game hunting or pest and predator control up to about 5 pounds and about 100 yards in skilled hands.

The high velocity .22lr fires a 40gr bullet at about 1350fps. The hollow point version is more destructive on small game at close range but is also more effective on pests and predators up to about 10 pounds.

The standard velocity is more accurate than the high velocity in every rifle I have tried them in, but the high velocity functions better in semi-automatic rifles. That may be due to the higher energy of the high velocity or it may be because the better brands of high velocity ammunition are made with copper washed bullets which reduce friction and fouling. Copper coated bullets do shoot noticeably cleaner.

.22lr hyper-velocity

Recent years have seen the introduction of a new type of .22lr ammunition, hyper-velocity. CCI's Stinger is the oldest and best known of these but every major manufacturer makes a similar cartridge.

The idea is to take a bullet of about 30gr and load it to about 1500fps or more. Testing rarely confirms the manufacturers claims, and most of these cartridges suffer a loss of accuracy compared to other .22lr ammunition.

They do too much damage to shoot anything edible with, but are effective on predators up to 30 pounds or more if your rifle will shoot them accurately.

CB caps

Another useful load on the opposite end of the power range is CB caps. These are extra light loads in a .22 long case. They are powerful enough for light pest control duties and will take small game if used carefully. The reason they sell is because they are very quiet, and are safe enough for indoor practice. They can be fired comfortably without ear protection, and a few large metropolitan Sunday papers will serve for a backstop.

Your .22 rifle will have an ammunition preference

Your .22 will show a definite preference for one brand of ammunition in whatever you choose as your type of load.

The only way to find out what brand your rifle will prefer is to try every brand you can find from a steady rest and see which shoots the smallest groups. Don't pay any attention to which load hits closest to point of aim.

When you find which shoots the smallest groups you can adjust the sights to bring the point of impact in line with your point of aim.

You may want to experiment with a few brands of **match grade ammunition** in your .22 rifle. This ammunition costs 3 to 5 times the price of standard ammo, but if the rifle and shooter are good enough, this ammunition can be frighteningly accurate.

Shot cartridges

Another useful type of ammunition for .22 handguns is shot cartridges. If snakes are a problem in your area you will want to experiment with these.

CCI makes the best of the shot cartridges I have tried. The shot is contained in a plastic capsule and seems to be very effective on rats or mice to about 10 feet.

.22 Magnum

The .22 Magnum is the most powerful rimfire cartridge made at this time. It fires a 40gr bullet at about 2000fps from a rifle. Velocities fall off rapidly as the barrel gets shorter.

A .22 Mag fired from a 6" handgun barrel will rarely reach 1500fps. A friend once had a pair of deringers, one in .22lr and the other in .22 Mag.

We fired both through a chronograph to see what the difference was and found the .22lr at 900fps and the .22 Mag doing 950fps. He traded the .22 Mag deringer the next day.

In a rifle that shoots it well, the .22 Mag can be a very useful varmint and predator cartridge. It usually doesn't shoot as accurately as .22lr, it costs much more, and guns chambered for it will not fire any other cartridge.

Handguns for .22 Mag seeem a waste of time and money to me. The only thing you get from a .22 Mag compared to .22lr is more flash and blast.

Some revolvers are made which have two cylinders, one for .22 long rifle, and one for .22 Mag. Some of these can be very effective with the CCI .22 Magnum shot loads. The .22 Magnum shot loads are much more powerful than the .22lr shot loads. They also contain more weight and a larger size of shot.

Shotgun terminology can be confusing

Shotgun ammunition has been made much more confusing than necessary. Even the size of shotguns is arcane and confusing.

Gauge

Gauge in shotgun bores is the number of lead balls you can make to fit your bore from one pound of lead. You can make 12 balls to fit your 12 gauge shotgun from one pound of lead. I can't think of any reason why you might want to, but there it is.

At any rate, that's why 10 gauge is bigger than 12, which is bigger than 16, which is bigger than 20 gauge.

Of course there's an exeption. They do it on purpose. The .410 shotgun is the diameter of the bore in decimals of an inch—like rifles and handguns are measured.

Power

Then there is the method of stating power. On most boxes of shotgun shells you will see a dram equivalent stated. This is not an accurate weight of the powder contained in the shell. It is the weight of black gunpowder equal in power to the smokeless propellant in the shell. Black powder hasn't been used in shotgun shells for almost 100 years.

Now pick the magazine up from the corner you threw it in when you read the last paragraph.

Power levels in shotgun shells are also described as low base, high base, and magnum. This refers to the height of the brass base which was needed with the old paper shotshells. This brass base isn't really needed with the new plastic shells, and some manufacturers are starting to leave them off and make all plastic shells. Low base means less power.

Different lengths of shells in each guage are also available. In 12 gauge the 2 3/4" length is standard; 3" magnum is also made and there is a new 3 1/2" super magnum for masochists and those who want to try to shoot high flying waterfowl with the Federally required steel shot.

You can use shorter length shells in shotguns chambered for longer lengths, but **don't ever try to fire a longer shell in a gun chambered for a standard length.** It will fit, but when it tries to open the chamber will not be long enough.

Weight of shot

Another bit of information given is weight of shot. In a 12 gauge this will be somewhere between 7/8 and 1 1/2 ounce. After some experience, you will learn which weight of shot works better for each purpose you may want to use your gun for.

You want enough shot to make a dense, effective pattern at the range you will most likely shoot, but not enough to pulverize your target. The more your shot weighs, the more recoil you will feel. There is no sense beating yourself to death using goose loads on quail.

Size of shot

Size of shot will be the next choice. You should select your shot size according to the size of game you will be shooting.

I find #6 the most generally useful. It will work on anything from field mice to turkeys if you watch the range.

For best results when you know what you are after, smaller shot like 7 1/2 works best for small birds like quail and smaller rodents while 2 or 4 shot works best for ducks, turkeys, or larger animals like jackrabbits or weasels.

The larger shot size you use, the less pieces of shot per ounce. Shooting at a mouse with #2 shot at 30 yards will probably be a miss because your pattern won't be dense enough.

Smaller shot spreads more rapidly than large shot. This can be useful at times if your gun won't give you the pattern you want at the range you need. Often just changing shot size will do the trick. To get a bigger pattern at short range, use smaller shot. To get a smaller pattern at long range, use larger shot.

Buckshot

Buckshot is another option available for shotguns. There are 4 sizes of buckshot made in 12 ga shells at this time; #4 buck, #1 buck, #00 buck and #000 buck. Each are available in high base, 2 3/4" magnum and 3"magnum. Recoil ranges from excessive to brutal.

A standard load of #4 buck contains 27 pellets, each .24" in diameter. The 2 3/4" magnum contains 34 pellets and the 3"magnum contains 41 pellets. 27 seems like quite enough to me.

The #000 buck is loaded with 8 .36" pellets in regular, 9 in 2 3/4" magnum and 12 in 3" magnum.

Buckshot is still used for deer hunting in the southern woods. It is also useful for larger predators, feral dog packs, and two legged predators.

The standard high base loads are effective if you choose the right size for the range you may use them at. The #4 buck is good for a wide, dense pattern at closer ranges, but it loses its power and doesn't hit very hard past 20 yards.

#00 buck works better at longer ranges, but doesn't spread fast at short range.

Even the largest size of buckshot loses velocity quickly. The round ball shape is not ballistically efficient and even the buffered, copper plated

buckshot suffer some deformation during firing. Buffered, copper plated buckshot such as Federal Premium performs much better than unbuffered lead buckshot, but even at its best the effective range is under 50 yards.

Shotgun slugs

A slug is a single shotgun projectile used for deer hunting and in some places for protection from dangerous animals.

The traditional hollow base slug lacks range, accuracy, and stability. Few shotguns can shoot a 6" group at 50 yards with them. For close range deer hunting in the woods they can serve. With a .73 caliber 1 ounce projectile you don't have to hit your target between the eyes.

Several other slug designs are available which improve on the range and usefulness.

The Brenneke slug is heavier, solid, and more aerodynamic than the hollow base made by most U.S. manufacturers. This improves the accuracy and penetration.

I have read several accounts of Brenneke slugs being used for protection from grizzly bears. I wouldn't go looking for a grizzly bear with a shotgun, but if a grizzly came looking for me I would want my shotgun to be loaded with Brennekes.

I have shot a few 6" groups at 100 yards with Brenneke slugs but at that range they have probably lost at least 1/3 of their velocity. At point blank range they should stop anything in North America.

For those who have shotguns with interchangeable barrels or interchangeable choke tubes, the BRI sabot slug is an interesting option.

This slug is about .50 caliber and is fired in a plastic carrier which separates from the slug after leaving the bore. The hourglass shaped bullet performs well if spin-stableized by a rifled barrel or rifled choke tube, and retains velocity better than any other shotgun slug.

If you can put some good sights on your shotgun, these slugs make 100 yard shots on deer practical.

BRI slugs have been difficult to find until recently, but now Winchester Ammunition has bought BRI and the patents have expired so Federal is also producing a similar slug. Distribution will be much better.

These slugs are not hard enough for protection against dangerous large animals, but they are a significant improvement over traditional slugs and can double the range of your shotgun for deer hunting and livestock protection.

20 gauge

The 20 gauge is much less popular, so there are less choices available in 20 gauge ammunition.

Usually a 20 gauge shell will contain about 2/3 to 3/4 the amount of shot as an equivalent load in 12 gauge. You should not expect the same range fron a 20 gauge as from a 12. A smaller size of shot and a less tight choke is needed to produce good pattern density with less shot.

Only a single buckshot loading is made, and the slug loads for the 20 gauge do not have the range or power of the 12 gauge.

The 3" magnum 20 gauge is roughly equal in power to the 2 3/4" high base 12 gauge load, but is much more difficult to find than 12 gauge ammunition, and less sizes and types of shot are available.

Generally, you are better off buying a bigger gun and using less powerful ammunition when you don't need full power than buying a smaller gun and trying to streth its performance when you need more power or range. This is true for rifles and handguns as well; you can always shoot a small animal with a big gun, you can't always shoot a big animal with a small gun.

.410 shotgun

The .410 shotgun is often recommended for beginners. I do not think it is a good choice. The 2 1/2" .410 does not contain enough shot to produce an adequately dense pattern once the pattern size gets beyond about 15", and even the 3" .410 only contains about half the shot of a 12 gauge.

The .410 is pleasant to shoot, but unless you are very skillful you will wound and cripple more game than you kill. A slug load is made for the .410. I'm not sure why. The .410 slug doesn't have the power to kill large animals, or the accuracy to hit small ones.

Rifle ammunition

Since Dave doesn't want this article to take up the whole magazine, I'm not even going to try to tell you about all the types of rifle ammunition available.

Some calibers, like the .30-30, offer some fairly meaningless choices. Ammunition in .30-30 is offered with 125 grain, 150 grain, and 170 grain bullets. The only shape offered is a flat-nosed soft point, so even if the lighter weight bullets were loaded to higher velocities they would not offer any increase in effective range. The 170 grain is the only real choice. It is adequate for deer at woods ranges.

In cartridges for bolt action rifles things get more interesting. The .30-06 and .308 cartridges are offered in a wide variety of bullet types and weights which offer some real differences in performance and usefulness.

Bullet weights range from the 55 grain saboted .223 bullet of the Remington Accelerator for varmints to the 220 grain bullets which will bring down a moose.

The most generally useful bullet weights in this caliber are from 150 to 170 grains. These are the most accurate and will serve for anything from larger predators to mule deer.

The spitzer soft points perform well on most animals at most ranges, but if you may be shooting at ranges much beyond 200 yards you may want to try boattail soft points.

For game over 250 pounds you will want to switch to heavier bullets and get closer before you shoot.

Any time you switch loads you will need to check your zero, since different bullet weights and different velocities will change your point of impact.

Military & generic ammo

For low cost practice and training, surplus military ammunition and white boxed "generic" ammunition is available in these calibers. This ammunition will have hard full metal jacketed bullets and should not be used for hunting. Military ammunition is required to be made so that it will not expand on impact, and it will shoot clean through most animals without bringing them down.

As a cautionary note, this ammunition will also shoot right through cars, brick walls, refrigerators, and almost anything except a tank or a mountain, and it will bounce off most things it won't shoot through, **so be careful**.

Military surplus and generic ammunition works well enough on pests and predators, but shooting a large game animal with it can mean a slow painful death for the animal, and a slow painful tracking job for you.

In some states, hunting laws forbid the use of FMJ ammunition outside of target ranges during hunting season.

For pests and predators, ammunition manufacturers make several special loads in .308 and .30-06. Higher velocity rounds loaded with very fragile 110 grain bullets are devastating killers of small pests and predators at long ranges, but many rifles do not shoot these loads with the same accuracy as standard loads. The same is true of the Remington Accelerator. This cartridge fits a .223" 55 grain varmint bullet into a .30 caliber plastic sabot. The lightweight bullet can be driven to extremely high velocities in a .30 caliber rifle but usually the accuracy suffers.

Due to the recent changes in U.S. import laws, many countries have cleared out the WW2 weapons from their armories. This has caused a renewed interest in cartridges such as the 8mm Mauser (also known as 7.92mm, 7.9mm, 8x57mm).

U.S. manufacturers load this cartridge at considerably less than its potential power because of the many rifles of weaker design which were converted to fire this cartridge.

In a '98 Mauser in good condition this cartridge can be loaded to pressures over 50,000cup but U.S. manufacturers load it to 38,000 or less.

The most common load is a 170 grain spitzer at about 2350 fps. This is only a little more powerful than the .30-30, but will perform better at longer ranges since it is loaded with a pointed bullet. This is a very effective hunting load for animals up to about 200 pounds without the recoil of the full power loads.

Full power 8mm Mauser ammunition is available in several brands imported from Europe: Norma, Geco, and occasionally Hirtenberger. This imported ammunition is expensive, but you can use the domestic ammunition for most purposes and keep a box of the more powerful ammunition around for special purposes.

This ammunition launches a 198 grain bullet at 2550 fps and will take anything in North America but the largest bears. If you switch back and

forth between these loads, be sure to adjust your sights because they will not shoot to the same point of aim.

The performance of these two loads is so much different that it is almost like having two rifles. This type of flexibility is usually only available to those who assemble their own ammunition. It isn't a good enough reason to buy an 8mm Mauser, but it's a good reason to use it if you have one.

I want to stress that full power 8mm ammunition **MUST NOT BE FIRED FROM** '91, or '93 Mausers, '88 Commision rifles, or from converted Carcanos or '95 Steyr rifles. If you have an 8mm rifle, ask a gun dealer or gunsmith what it is. If it isn't a '98 Mauser, do not use the full power loads.

Military surplus ammunition in 8mm Mauser is also loaded to very high pressure, and most is loaded with corrosive primers. This is no reason not to

use it for practice and training; just scrub the bore out with hot soapy water after firing.

The warnings given about FMJ ammunition before are applicable here and in any other caliber also.

There are many other rifle cartridges made, and many of them are very useful and effective. If I did not cover your favorite, that does not mean I have anything against it.

The information given here covers the basics about the most common and useful rifle cartridges. The same general guidelines apply to other calibers and cartridges. With this background you will be able to understand what you may read in other sources and what the guy at the gun store tells you.

Store your ammunition in a cool dry place away from solvents and sources of heat and sparks. Δ

A Backwoods Home Anthology
The Thirteenth Year

* Emergency solar for $950
* The survival garden
* How do you live without electricity
* Long-term food storage
* Disaster preparation
* Storing fuel
* Tools and hardware for
    the backwoods home
* The return of home emergency shelters
* Raised bed gardening — neat
    and productive
* Dorper sheep
* What to do when there's no doctor
* The self-sufficient barnyard
* Happy chickens, healthy eggs
* Get to know your herbs
* Build a graceful footbridge

* A river rock shower
* Fencing for livestock and poultry
* Make a quilt of Levis
* Planting fruit, nut, and shade trees
* Bread: The staff of life
* Making baby food at home
* Build a portable woodstove for $30
* Horseshoe projects
* Harvesting the wild upland game birds
* Two livestock feeders and an
    insulated water bucket
* Dehydrating fruits and vegetables
* Can she bake an apple pie, Billy Boy?
* Avoiding heat illness
* Harvesting the wild asparagus
* Morels...A taste of springtime
* The fall garden

Amateur radio — a sensible communication alternative for people who are self-reliant

By Vern Modeland, WAØJOG

The kids have quieted down, the day's chores are completed, the fire curls lazily, the TV is boring and the night is yet young. What a great time for a little armchair adventuring!

You might meet up again with Uri who taught you how to pronounce Severd Sibirskaya Nizmennost, and sent you to your atlas to find out exactly where that is. Maybe you'll chat again with Will who is building a bootstrap business charter-flying his Cessna out of Dillingham, Alaska. Or you and Carlos might be able to continue that conversation you had going about the South American way to coax a better grape harvest out of a few vines like yours. Carlos lives in Chile's bountiful fruit basket. Most of the grapes consumed in the U.S. off-season come from there. You didn't know that until you ran into Carlos on the airwaves.

Every one of the above examples shows how hooking up so casually with such interesting people can be a rewarding bonus of the self-reliant lifestyle once you've discovered amateur radio. And once you're hooked, you'll find the rewards gained from obtaining an amateur radio license can be about as limitless as are the imaginations and innovations of the 534,503 Americans and several million world-wide who enjoy the hobby today.

But why would a busy homesteader go to the time and trouble of studying for a radio license and buying more electronic stuff? Because just like this magazine, amateur radio is a resource for people who value personal independence and self sufficiency. Amateur radio is a way to network-- wherever you live, wherever you

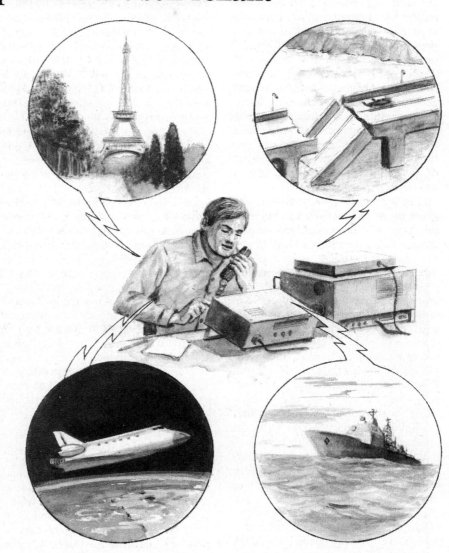

travel—and link up with people who might have experience, educational background or contacts from which you can learn and benefit.

Swapping info & ideas

A chance conversation by radio that begins with a routine exchange about the weather and comparison of radio equipment and what kind of antenna you are using, can easily move along to discovering that the she or he at the other end has years of experience raising milking goats, or knows a source of parts for your little old Farmall, or cans meats, or collects quilt patterns, or is educating kids at home.

Not every amateur radio conversation is guaranteed to solve a pressing homestead problem or initiate a regular schedule of contacts, but everyone can be interesting and rewarding in some way or another. A benefit for parents is the ability of amateur radio to contribute to and reinforce homework assignments about geography and the global community.

Visiting and trading ideas and information by amateur radio sometimes leads to invitations to stop by the home of the other ham — if you ever drive by Trail, Oregon, Flippin, Arkansas, Deming, New Mexico, or Stafford Springs, Connecticut. They're usually sincere invitations. A common interest in amateur radio has built many rewarding friendships that have lasted for decades.

Getting started is easy

In this age of de-regulation and government re-direction, getting into amateur radio has never been easier. Anyone can do it. Really. The hobby has no limits as to age, gender, physical ability, social status or the size of your discretionary income. It's off-grid compatible, too. Modern ham radio's tightly packaged transmitters and receivers — transceivers is the term — will coast along for hours of communicating on a small fraction of the energy in any healthy deep-cycle 12-volt battery. The newest ham radio sets also are small enough to ride along in the family pickup without cramping the space of your significant other or that dog in your life. Either of them might require some re-training, however, to get quiet when you're chatting with someone in another state or some other country.

Learning the technicalities, the legalities, and the etiquette of the airwaves needed to obtain a U.S. amateur radio operator and station license and then be welcomed back by those you encounter on the air, is generally convenient wherever you choose to live. Printed and computer-compatable self-help programs are available. Local study courses are in place in many adult education programs, in some public schools and at most local amateur radio clubs. Volunteers in your area administer license examinations for the government.

Learning Morse Code no longer a barrier

Learning the Morse Code was once a major barrier to getting started in amateur radio. Understanding Morse Code remains a requirement by International agreement for border-hopping radio communicators. But today, you can enter domestic ham radio through a code-less Technician license class that only requires you to pass two written tests with a total of 55 multiple-choice questions. (See related story page 33.)

For those for whom making sense out of the dit-dahs of Morse Code poses no great problem, a Novice amateur radio license gets you on the air after a five-word-per-minute code comprehension test and a 30-question written exam about basic electronic theory and FCC rules and regulations.

More advanced steps up the ladder of amateur radio proficiency include pushing that code speed on to 13 words per minute, or maybe 20, and passing tests about more complicated theory, operating and regulation topics. The rewards for the extra effort involved in obtaining the higher General, Advanced, or Extra Class license are access to larger portions of the radio spectrum in which to communicate to other states and around the world.

Talk to astronauts

Or beyond. Both United States and Russian manned space flights have at times included crew members whose hobby is amateur radio. Owen Garriott was the first. In 1983, he carried a 4-watt hand-held amateur radio transciever with him and an innovative antenna that fit against a window on the spacecraft Columbia. Other astronauts and Cosmonauts who have followed Garriott's lead have, when off-duty while floating along 200-some miles above the earth, traded greetings with thousands of hams. U.S. ham-astronauts have visited via amateur radio hookups direct with school classes, enhancing youthful understanding and appreciation for the sciences and geography.

Ham satellites

There also are sophisticated satellites in orbit that were conceived, built and funded privately by the amateur radio community. American ones carry the acronym of OSCAR. That stands for Orbiting Satellite Carrying Amateur Radio. These satellites are open for use to communicate freely by voice, code and computer. One new ham satellite even beams back home-brewed remote imaging of the earth and weather from space. The average desk-top computer will play back its pictures with TV-like clarity.

A great disaster tool

When disaster strikes, amateur radio frequently plays a pivotal role in restoring communications. Ham radio has a long history of being first to report earthquakes, major fires, storms and floods, and to fill in when local phone systems or power lines go kaput.

Practice for such emergencies often takes the form of public service communication activities by hams. That includes passing along greetings from special events and fairs, linking first aid stations for marathons and races, going to Scouting jamborees, and annual Field Day exercises. Each summer, Field Day sends dedicated hams packing off to remote locations where they set up temporary stations and antennas and operate continuously for 24 hours, competing among themselves to see how many other U.S. and international amateur radio stations with which the participants can trade call signs.

Being prepared for emergency service is a responsibility most hams feel goes with the privilege of having been granted a license to use a part of the increasingly crowded radio spectrum. U.S. law sets forth the basis and purpose of the Amateur Radio Service as recognizing and enhancing a voluntary non-commercial communication service, particularly with respect to providing emergency communications. The Act says that amateur radio "contributes to the advancement of the radio art," and "expands the reservoir of trained operators, technicians and electronic experts," and "recognizes the amateur's unique ability to enhance international good will."

Ham radio's answer to cellular phones

Having an amateur radio license also can link you with the web of ham radio repeaters that is casually accessed by miniature low power, very-high-frequency FM radios. The hand-held sets fit in a pocket, slip into a purse, or clip to your belt. They, and CB-sized FM mobile rigs, are amateur radio's answer to cellular telephones without the monthly usage bills. (Keep in mind, though, that the law prohibits using amateur radio for business-related communications.)

Repeater radio systems

Amateur-built or modified commercial radio equipment has been hauled to the top of mountains, tall buildings and lofty radio towers and installed there in order to automatically gather up weak signals and repeat them with gusto. This repeater radio system allows joggers and hikers and folks on the road to stay in touch and easily communicate and network with friends and family, or call for help, or get directions when lost. It's a sort of local wireless party line. Some of the systems allow telephone calls to be made through the radio so that you can check up on the rug rats or see if an extra stop by the grocery store might be in order before you head home from town.

Packet radio

An even newer technological twist allows amateur radio operators who are comfortable with computers to get in touch through radio-linked "bulletin boards," leaving messages for each other and catching up on the news. Electronic communication via what is called "packet" radio can be routed to another ham who might live far across the country. The message will burp its way automatically from one amateur radio packet repeater to

another until it arrives within reach of the addressee.

The cost?

So, what's the tab? No more than what a good camera or a new TV costs today can get you started in ham radio. The new transceivers start in price at around $1000. More elaborate sets sell for well above that figure. The extra cost is for added automatic and sophisticated features such as memory and scanning for favorite frequencies, automatic antenna tuning, and com-

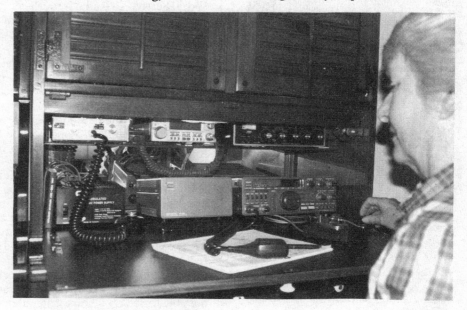

Beverly Modeland lisstens in on the ham radio from her home in Reeds Spring, Missouri. Modern amateur radio equipment is homestead-friendly.

puter interfacing for control and display of operating information.

However, there is an active market in used amateur radio equipment and sound investments are possible. There are many hybrid and pre-transistor amateur radio sets that seem to have been designed to outlast this century. They are priced at much less than the fancy new compact rigs. Older generally means bigger and will consume more power, but spare parts and radio tubes to keep older ham radio sets going are still available for the more popular makes and models. Some manufacturers continue to offer technical support for their out-of-production sets. Entrepreneurial ser-

vice centers for older radio equipment also exist.

Hand-held and small mobile or fixed FM radios, for use with the local repeater networks, can cost $400 or more for the latest version that packages frequency storing memory and scanning, and perhaps multi-band operation or auto-dialing of stored telephone numbers. The traffic in used FM amateur radio sets also is active at half that new-set price and below.

Prices for used amateur radio equipment generally depend on the set's condition, features and popularity more than on age alone.

Antenna requirements

Antenna installations are another consideration in the hobby of amateur radio. High frequency radio communication usually requires a tower or a pole 30 feet or more in height that is sturdy enough to support a sizeable beam antenna in all kinds of wind and weather. The beam antenna is normally hooked to a rotator to allow it to be pointed toward the state or the part of the world where your interest is focused remotely from the radio operating position. However a few dollars worth of Number 12 copper wire, shot into the treetops with a bow and arrow and held in place by nylon rope, might suffice. One of these random length wire antennas has served the author in reliable global communication for many years, from home, motel rooms during business trips, and hugging the perimeter of a third story efficiency apartment floor during two years in a restrictive Maryland apartment complex.

Very high frequency antennas for the FM repeaters and local radio contacts are generally much more compact and lighter in weight—but necessary, especially if yours is a homesite remote from the local repeater location. But again, in town, you might get by with a few inches of wire supported by a magnet attached to a favorable window's curtain rod.

There appear to be as many opinions and solutions for what is the right combination of radio equipment and antennas as there are hams. Once you've gotten the amateur radio urge and made connection for learning the ropes, doing some reading and asking lots of questions will begin to reveal

From Scud missiles to sea rescues, ham radio puts you into the action

By Vern Modeland

Most newer amateur radio high-frequency transceivers offer the enthusiast a wide selection of frequencies outside of the limits of the amateur radio bands. As a result, it's never been easier to dial in daily to the BBC World Service, to Radio Nederland, Radio Canada International, the Swiss Broadcasting Service, The Voice of Spain, Deutsche Welle, radio from Moscow, Paris, Rome, Quito and Peking, to get a second and third opinion on the news of the day.

You can "be there" when governments are in turmoil. You could have heard the alert and directions to put on gas masks when Scud missiles were on their way toward Israel. You can enjoy soccer tournament play-by-play "live and direct" from Australia.

Nearly every major nation of the world produces its own daily radio broadcasts in English. Some include lessons for understanding native languages on their menu of ethnic news, music, drama, interviews, and features on lifestyles and history.

In the spectrum space between international short wave broadcasting allocations, you can count the heart beats of a world alive with human activity and strife. You can listen real-time to rescues at sea, military movements, airliners dodging storms in far-flung skies, commercial fishermen comparing their luck in the Gulf of Mexico and diplomats calling home.

Plug in a couple of accessories, and some modern communications radio receivers will turn what sounds like discordant, scratchy music into facsimile pictures and weather maps, or will print out international press dispatches and weather data transmitted as radio teletype. One adapter makes it possible to see on a home computer screen the pictures that a half-dozen U.S., Russian, and Japanese satellites transmit.

Resource publications for tuning in the world include:

The World Radio-TV Handbook, Billboard Books Division, Watson-Guptill Publications, Inc., 1 Astor Plaza, 1515 Broadway, New York City, NY 10036.

Popular Communications Magazine. CQ Communications, Inc., 76 North Broadway, Hicksville, NY 11801.

Monitoring Times Magazine. P.O. Box 98, Brasstown, NC 28902

DX Listening Digest Review of International Broadcasting, Box 1684, Enid, OK 73702.

Journal of the North American Short Wave Association, 45 Wildflower Road, Levitown, PA 19057. Δ

ways to get started on even the most limited budget.

Bartering is one way. Often you'll discover an experienced ham who has equipment he or she is using infrequently or maybe not at all. The ham might be willing to trade for something you have, or something you can do, or

will offer to lend you an unused set in order to see an eager newcomer get started in this fascinating and rewarding hobby.

(Vern Modeland is a free-lance writer who lives on Deer Mountain in the Missouri Ozarks. For more than 25 years, his amateur radio call has been WA∅JOG.) Δ

New rules for ham radio license

By Marjorie Burris, N7RZN

In 1989 the Federal Communications Commission (FCC) reorganized its rules governing Amateur Radio and began to adopt many changes which recognize the advances made in radio and electronic technology. Not the least of these changes is the new code-free Technician license which first became available February 14, 1991.

By international treaty, knowing the Morse Code is a basic requirement for operating on any amateur band below 30 MHz, and prior to the February date, all classes of U.S. radio hams were required to pass a Morse Code test as well as a written exam on radio technology and FCC rules. Now, with digital communications (radio-teletype on personal computers and packet radio) image sending, and the many, many kinds of radios made for sending and receiving on the radio spectrum above 30 MHz, the Morse Code requirement for a Technician's license has become archaic. However, due to the international agreement, all classes of ham license above the technicians's class still are required to pass a Morse Code test because the higher class licenses permit use of the radio spectrum below 30 MHz.

There are five U.S. amateur license classes. Each class has its own regulations and requirements—the higher the class, the more stringent the requirements and the greater the privileges. Entry level into the world of ham radio is the Novice class. This license gives one the privilege of sending Morse Code (called continuous wave or CW in radio lingo) on several bands plus the use of telegraphy and radio-teletype (RTTY) and voice on a few bands. To earn a Novice license, you still must be able to send or receive Morse Code at the rate of five words per minute and pass a written test on elementary radio theory and regula-tions. The amount of power a novice can use is considerably less than that allowed for the higher class licenses.

The next class of license is the Technician class. Even before the Tech license became codeless, it was both the largest and the fastest growing category of amateur license. It is still possible to earn a Technician's license including CW, but the privileges for both the code and the codeless tech-

nician are the same—except if you don't pass a code test you can't use CW on the air, of course. The written test includes 30 questions from the Novice pool of questions plus 25 slightly more difficult questions from the Technician's pool. The Technician is licensed to use voice on many bands including the popular 6 meter, 2 meter and 70 centimeter bands. This gives the Technician access to the thousands of repeaters and telephone auto-patch machines all over the United States. With a good antenna, a Technician can "work the world."

The third class of license is the General class; Advanced and Amateur Extra make up the last two classes. These classes of license require higher speeds of Morse Code and quite a bit of radio theory. As of April 30th of this year there were only 54,887 Amateur Extras in the United States.

Morse Code still has its place in the radio world; not only is it fun to use, it can often get through static and adverse weather conditions when voice cannot, and it uses a much narrower band on the spectrum than voice. But it is no longer a hinderance to those of us who have minor hearing difficulties. The new FCC rules do make accommodations and some exceptions for a severely handicapped applicant who is unable to pass a 13 or 20 word per minute Morse Code examination, however. Information on examination accommodations on Morse Code exemption is available from the American Radio Relay League (ARRL). To request a copy, send a long SASE to: Handicapped Information packet, ARRL/VEC, 225 Main Street, Newington, CT 06111. Even though some handicapped individuals may be excused from the higher speed Morse Code tests, no one who aspires to a license class higher than technician is exempt from the initial five word per minute CW test.

Another change made by the FCC is the way U.S. amateur exams are administered. Previously, the FCC gave all tests. The tests were extremely difficult and were given at inconvenient locations and times. Then, in the early 1980's, government budget cutbacks greatly reduced the number of FCC exams and the FCC almost eliminated field tests completely. The Amateur Radio Relay League, recognizing an impending disaster, worked for legislation to permit voluntary assistance in the examination process. Now, all classes of tests are given by Volunteer Exam Coordinators (VEC's), an organization that has entered into an agreement with the FCC to coordinate efforts of volunteers in preparing and giving amateur radio exams. The fee for taking the ARRL/VEC test in 1991 is $5.25 per person and the tests are given frequently and regularly in all parts of the country. To help you locate a test session, the ARRL/VEC maintains a computer data base of all test sessions being conducted by ARRL teams so you can get the most up-to-date information about tests being given in your area. For information about tests contact Bart J. Jahnke, KB9NM, Manager ARRL/VEC, 225 Main Street, Newington, CT 06111, Telephone (203) 666-1545 or (203) 666-1541 or Fax (203) 666-7531.

The League also has prepared study books which include all questions from the FCC question pool and their answers. These excellent books make learning amateur radio easy and prepare you for all questions on the exams. The newest book is *Now You're Talking*, "the only book you'll need to get your first ham license". It is available from the American Radio Relay League, 225 Main Street, Newington, CT 06111. The cost is $19.00 plus $3.00 for U.S. Mail or $4.00 UPS.

There was one thing not changed by the adoption of the new rules, however. Amateur radio is strictly for amateur use. No business of any kind can be conducted over the radio with two exceptions: you can buy, sell, or trade, amateur radio equipment over the air if you are not in the radio equipment business, and, in an emergency, you can contact any business that will save property or lives, i.e., call a tow truck, an ambulance, paramedics, or the fire department.

There are radio classes available, but my husband and I chose to study on our own. We bought a study book and

made a concentrated two week study while we were snowbound in March. We passed the codeless Technician's test in early April, then had to wait for six long weeks before the FCC sent our licenses. Although ham radio can be an exciting hobby, we use our units strictly for necessary communications. It is indeed comforting to know that we can get outside help quickly in the case of an emergency.

We have excellent reception with our Ringo Ranger II Antenna and are told we are heard clearly by those we contact. We have two small hand held transceivers which broadcast only on the 2 meter band, but they do have punch button keys for dialing a telephone through an auto-patch repeater. For us, the new regulations have brought great peace of mind. N7RZN monitoring on 145.350. Δ

Government is not reason, it is not eloquence — it is force. Like fire, it is a dangerous servant and a fearful master.

George Washington

Information sources for ham radio

By Vern Modeland

Here are some places to write for information on how to find an amateur radio club near you, get the dates for licensing classes in your area, locate volunteer examiners, and obtain study materials:

The Federal Communications Commission, P.O. Box 1020, Gettysburg, PA 17326. The FCC will supply its Form 610 necessary in applying for and renewing an amateur radio station and/or operators license, and copies of Part 97 of the Commission's rules. Part 97 contains all the pertinent regulations that govern American amateur radio operation, operators and equipment.

The American Radio Relay League, Box BHM, 225 Main Street, Newington, CT, 06111. The ARRL is a non-profit organization and the largest organization of radio amateurs in the United States. It publishes QST, a monthly journal, and many aids for getting started, setting up and operating an amateur radio station.

CQ Communications, Inc., 76 North Broadway, Hicksville, NY 11801. Publishes *CQ Radio Amateurs Journal*, a monthly magazine of interest to amateur radio operators, and many other publications in support of radio as a hobby.

Wayne Greene Enterprises, WGE Center, Forest Road, Hancock, NH 03449. WGE publishes 73 *Amateur Radio Today*, a monthly magazine covering mostly technical and operating news. WGE also recently introduced *Radio Fun*, a tabloid-format monthly described as "a beginner's guide to amateur radio." WGE also sells information books for the beginner and technically-interested ham.

The W5YI Group, P.O. Box 565101, Dallas, TX 75356. The W5YI Group offers printed and computer-based study guides and audio tapes. It also coordinates more than 600 volunteer examiner teams involving some 10,000 examiners.

The National Amateur Radio Association, 16541 Redmond Way, Suite 232, Redmond, WA 98052. NARA publishes study aids for use in obtaining an amateur radio license and maintains a directory of volunteer examiners.

Worldradio, Inc., 2120 28th Street, Sacramento, CA 95818. Publishes Worldradio, a tabloid-format monthly newspaper covering events, operational and social activities and other news of interest to amateur radio operators. Δ

Marrying solar thermal and photovoltaics to create a top notch closed loop solar hot water system

By Tom Lane

An interesting aspect of the solar industry has always been that there is little crossover between solar contractors. Most of the contractors involved in solar thermal systems have hardly any experience in solar electrical systems, and conversely, solar electrical

Collectors mounted on the north roof facing south. This strategy keeps the collectors from being mounted on the front of the house. Note the photovoltaic panel attached to the side of the thermal panel.

contractors who are on top of "what works" in photovoltaics do not seem to have a clue about what is a good buy, or value, in a solar hot water system and what the pitfalls are in solar hot water system design.

In this article we'll marry both technologies and show you how to build a

dependable, top quality solar water heater.

Presently, I am heating water for six people: my wife, three boys, my mother-in-law, and myself using a 120-gallon closed loop solar tank, two 4x10 black chrome U.S. solar collectors, a SX-20 photovoltaic module which functions as the controller and power to run a 12-volt Hartell HEH Brushless DC pump.

For circulating the solar loop, the Hartell HEH Brushless DC pump connected to a small photovoltaic module, is my personal preference. Because of its inherent simplicity, immunity from scaling and freeze damage, and low cost per square foot of collector area, this component configuration has shown itself to be the

best solar water heater available today.

Some costs

Solar hot water systems can be an excellent investment; however, you owe it to yourself to make sure you are getting a good investment—not just a gimmick "token" solar system that heats a little water and makes you feel "environmentally correct."

Solar hot water heating for showers, dish washing and laundry will cost about $110 per person per year if LP gas costs $1.15 a gallon, or if electricity costs $.07 a kilowatt hour. At $.10 a KWH it costs $646 a year to heat water for four "average" people. A solar hot water system with a 120-gallon tank and 64 to 96 square feet of collector area will typically save about $500 to $600 out of the $646.

Never forget that all savings are in nontaxable income which would be equivalent to $600 to $750 that you earned and paid taxes on to the IRS. If you are heating hot water for two or more people and you are not hooked to natural gas pipelines, then you need to carefully evaluate solar hot water as an investment **and look for value**— total BTUs delivered into **storage**. All you need is a sunny spot where you are not shaded from 9 o'clock to 3 o'clock on December 21st (the lowest the sun drops in the northern hemisphere) facing within 25 degrees of due south.

Closed loop and open loop system

There are basically two types of solar hot water systems. Open loop systems, in which the same water for your showers etc. goes through the thermal collectors and a closed loop system, which typically uses a glycol antifreeze and a heat exchanger built into the tank. The main criteria for these systems is how hard the freezing weather is where you live.

Open loop systems should be used where you don't get any freezes. If your local area can grow mangoes, avocados, or citrus groves without danger of being damaged by a mild freeze, then you are in an area that can directly circulate water through the collectors. If not, use a closed loop system or one day you will have a visit from Mr. Murphy and your collector will freeze and burst. Since 95% of the U.S.'s population, including central Florida and most of southern California and Arizona are in areas where freezing conditions do occur, I will discuss my experience with closed loop systems to show solar hot water as an investment.

System sizing — storage

The most important consideration for the homeowner is to make sure to get enough storage (gallons in tank) and enough collector area (square feet of collector) to give you a real return on your investment in solar hot water. Plan on at least 20 gallons per person for the first four people and 15 gallons for each additional person. Solar hot water tanks are manufactured in 80, 100, and 120 gallon sizes so the choice in tank selection is one of three. When choosing a tank, you'll find that the 120 gallon size tank typically costs only $125 to $150 more than an 80 gallon tank and the money is well spent considering you are adding 50% more storage capacity for a small increase in dollars.

System sizing — collector area

You should have at least 40 square feet of collector area for the first two family members and add 12 square feet of collector area for each additional family member in the sunbelt, and add 14 square feet of collector area for each additional family member in northern climates. However never add more than 64 square feet to an 80 gallon tank or 96 square feet to

a 120 gallon tank. Keeping tank size at a ratio of 1.25 gallons or more to a 1 square foot of collector area will keep the solar system from grossly overheating in times of little demand and assures that the collector to storage ratio is efficiently matched. In Arizona and southern Florida keep the ratio at least 1.5 gallons to 1 square foot of collector area. Overheating a hot water tank dramatically decreases its lifespan.

The typical sizes available for flat plate collectors are 4' by 6.5' (26 sq. ft.), 4' by 8' (32 sq. ft.), 4' by 10' (40 sq. ft.) and 4' x 13' (52 sq. ft.) The bare minimum collector area size worth investing in is one 4' by 10' in a closed loop system. I strongly suggest two 4' by 8's with at least an 80 gallon tank for more than three people, or two 4' by 8's, two 4' by 10's, three 4' by 8's, or two 4' by 13's with a 120 gallon tank for larger families.

Use copper

Always use thermal collectors that have **all** copper tubes **and** absorber plates for collecting the solar energy, and have a tempered glass cover above the absorber plate. **Never** use plastics or fiberglass covers instead of tempered glass or any other material than all copper collector plates for absorbing the heat. Avoid using evacuated tube collectors for heating domestic hot water. It is like hunting rabbits with a cannon and can grossly overheat your tank.

A 120 gallon tank with two 4' by 8' or 4' by 10' collectors **is the best investment in dollars per BTU delivered into storage.** Avoid like the plague companies that sell solar systems with less than 40 square feet of collector area. Even in south Florida or Arizona less than 40 square feet of collection is simply not worth the investment. All solar water heaters depend on capturing sunlight to heat water and no matter how exotic the bottom end of a solar water heater might be it cannot create more solar energy than falls on the collector area in less that 40 square feet just is not enough square footage in an active open or closed loop system.

Avoid external thermosyphon systems

Also avoid external heat exchangers that rely on thermosyphoning of heat. Thermosyphon heat exchangers that work off natural convection will typically only heat the top half of the tank **no matter how you plumb the tank.** External heat exchangers only work well if you double pump the heat exchanger in counter flow. Or as is the case with the Copper Cricket, pumping the water side of the heat exchanger through the tank and back through the heat exchanger.

Another serious problem for external heat exchangers is scaling due to hard water. If you have hard water, especially calcium and magnesium, **do not** use an external heat exchanger unless you have a water conditioner or an antiscale filter to condition the hot water system in your house.

Rheem/Rudd and State closed loop tanks

Fortunately the two largest manufacturers of hot water tanks in the country, Rheem/Rudd, and State Industries, manufacture 82, 100, and 120 gallon solar tanks with closed loop heat exchangers that are bonded to the lower half of the solar tank's wall. This enables you to use a closed loop system and avoid the two biggest problems for solar hot water systems — 1) freezing and 2) scaling due to hard water. These tanks also keep the system incredibly simple since you need only one pump to pump the heat exchanger side of the system.

The Rheem or Rudd tanks use copper tubing bonded to the exterior wall of the tank. This enables you to use Prestone II car antifreeze (the best) in 2 gallons of antifreeze to 3 gallons distilled water mix ratio to run through the heat exchanger. If your coldest freeze on record is above 0 degrees F. use 1 gallon of antifreeze to 2 parts distilled water.

State Industries uses an integral single wall heat exchanger that is bonded to the lower half of the outer tank wall. The State Heat Exchange Tank works extremely well, however, you cannot use ethylene glycol (Prestone II) but must use its cousin, inhibited propylene glycol a nontoxic antifreeze used in all soft drinks and many other foods. The mixture ratio is the same and the excellent heat transfer properties are identical for either ethylene or propylene glycol.

Never use hydrocarbon oils, silicone oil or alcohol as heat transfer fluid because they have low specific heat characteristics and are poor choices for heat transfer fluids. We have either the State or Rheem closed & open loop solar tanks available. The cost is about $600 for a closed loop 80 gallon tank, and $700 for a closed loop 120 gallon tank.

Caution on materials

The entire collector loop, all fittings and pipe, must be copper or brass. All copper fittings must be soldered with 95/5 tin/antimony, or brazed. Never use 50/50 lead solder. The antifreeze/distilled water solution will not need to be changed for over five years if you do not mix metals in the loop to the collector and back and mix your antifreeze with distilled water only. **Never** use steel galvanized pipe, CPVC, or **any** plastic pipe or parts.

Solar electric pumping and control

The most efficient trouble free control and pumping system is to use the 12-volt Hartell HEH Brushless DC pump connected to a small solar electric module rated at a minimum of 1.2 amps to a maximum of 2 amps under full sun conditions (typically an 18 to 30 watt PV module). The solar electric module, pop-riveted to the side of the frame wall of the solar thermal collector, will slowly start pumping at the correct solar intensity at a variable speed.

Solar thermal and solar electric energy are completely different forms of energy from the sun, however, they are always in the same proportion based on the intensity of the sunlight. The choice of a solar electric or PV module rated 1.2 to 2 amps matched to the Hartell HEH Brushless DC

pump not only enables it to provide power to run the pump but also to act as a variable speed controller to start and stop the pump and vary the speed at the correct solar intensity. The Hartell Brushless Pump features a Panasonic D.C. motor without brushes to wear out, sealed dual ball bearings, and a graphite bearing impeller to ensure optimum reliability with an extremely long life.

A smaller PV module (less than 1.2 amps) will start too late and a module bigger than 2 amps would start too early and run too long. Use only single crystal or polycrystalline PV module—do **not** use an amorphous PV module. Just connect the positive and negative leads from the PV module to the positive and negative leads on the Hartell HEH Brushless pump with 16 gauge stranded PVC jacketed wire. This control strategy means no sensors to fail, no differntial thermostats, (which means it cannot malfunciton and run at the wrong time), no AC power outage problems from the utilities.

After the hurricane that hit Tallahassee, Florida in 1985 the city lost utility power for several days but the solar systems with solar electric powered pumps were still providing hot water to their homeowners. Do not let anyone try to sell you on the obsolete differential controls with sensors and an AC pump. Tell them to send their dinosaurs back to the city dump.

Piping the system in

All lines in the solar loop from the tank to the collectors and back should be in type L soft and/or hard 3/4" (inside diameter) copper pipe. Use hard type L copper around the tank and collectors and use soft type L coils on the long attic pipe runs. Insulate the lines with 3/4 inch thick elastomeric insulation (trade name Rubatex or Armaflex) available at air conditioning and heating parts distributors. Use 1" wall thickness on the pipes in northern climates.

Do not slit your insulation and tape. Slide it over the pipes. Do **not** use polyethylene rigid pipe insulation! The heat from the solar thermal panel

can melt it. All exterior insulation exposed to sunlight must be protected from UV light. One way to accomplish this is by encasing the pipe and insulation in PVC or ABS plastic pipe. But the best way is to spray it a couple of times with automotive undercoating spray and touch up as needed in the future.

Seven basic parts

Besides the pump, there are only seven simple parts in the system. 1) A pressure gauge (0-69 PSI) to simply let you know your system has not lost its charge of antifreeze and water. 2) A solar expansion tank (about the size of a basketball) that allows the solar solution to expand into it as the antifreeze fluid heats up. 3) A check valve above the pump to prevent reverse flow thermosyphoning at night. 4) A pressure relief valve rated at 75 PSI (not a pressure and temperature relief valve). 5) One boiler drain (hose bib) valve at the lowest point in the system for filling and draining. 6) A two way ball valve, to create a bypass around the check valve. This item, #6, enables you to fill and also drain from a single drain hose bib, and if you go on vacation you can let the system dump all the heat back to the roof each night by reverse thermosyphoning if the ball valve bypass is open. If you vacation for a week or more and do not have a means to keep your tank from overheating you will definitely shorten the tank's life. 7) A 100 PSI air vent at the highest point in the system to vent during charging.

Once the system is completely installed it will be time for charging. All you will need for system charging is two washing machine hoses, a drill pump for the end of a 3/8" or 1/2" power drill, and a bucket.

Charging the system

Add your antifreeze/distilled water mix, to the bucket as your drill pumps the water into the washing machine hose connected to the lower boiler drain. (If the collectors are extremely high, cover the collectors, remove the air vent, and slowly fill from the top with a funnel). Each collector will require about 1 gallon of mixture; the tank one gallon, and each 100 feet of pipe about 2 gallons.

Keep charging until your pressure gauge reads 20 PSI plus 1 pound of pressure for every 2 feet the solar collector is higher than your tank. One way to crank the pressure up is to connect the washing machine hose to a 100 feet garden hose that you fill with your mixture through a funnel. Connect that garden hose to a hose bib on the tank drain or an outside spigot and let your city or well water pressure crank your pressure up by forcing the extra mixture in by water pressure through a washing machine hose connected to the boiler drain at the bottom of the system.

Two weeks after the system has been running check your pressure. Add more mixture if necessary and then tighten down the air vent cap on top of the system.

The winning decision

An 80-gallon closed loop system with two 4' by 8' collectors and components will cost about $2000 for the equipment and save about $556 a year at $.10 a KWH or LP gas at $1.60 gallon. A 120 gallon tank with two 4' by 10' collectors and components will cost about $2300 and save about $720 a year at $.10 a KWH or LP gas at $1.60. Piping and insulation will cost about

$1.25 a foot. The tank and heat exchanger should last 20 years with no maintenance other than to change the antifreeze mixture every 5 to 10 years. However, the absorber plate in the thermal collectors may need to be replaced every 50 years, about twice in the 150 year life of a good flat plate collector. The Hartell pump should last 15 years with no maintenance.

It is ironic, a family of four that has LP gas or high electric rates will pay for a solar hot water system in utility bills over the next 4 to 8 years, whether they get one or not. You can invest, wisely, in a solar hot water system and have something to show for your money or send the money you would have saved on solar each month to the utility company and have nothing to show for your money but more NO_2, SO_2, and other air borne pollutants or more nuclear waste.

The winning decision is to stop paying each month to be hooked on utility power and start owning what you are already paying for and not getting. Your savings will more than offset the monthly payment on a five year loan and you'll actually own a solar system at the end of five years instead of feeding it to the utility.

Tips on installing closed loop systems

Flush the system out with water through the top of the collector

without the air vent for 10 minutes to get all the flux out of the system before charging.

Use a street 45 degree elbow and regular 45 elbow instead of a 90 degree elbow on long pipe runs to reduce pressure drop.

If you cannot find a solar contractor to help you install the system try to get an air conditioning contractor since the techniques for dealing with installing and charging a solar hot water heater are known concepts in that trade.

Do not use dielectric union or any type of plumbing unions. Use only couplings and fittings that can be soldered or brazed to prevent leaks. Keep threaded fittings to a minimum, and use liberal amounts of teflon tape or paste when making this connection.

One or two weeks after the system has been charged with anti-freeze and operating, close the air vent down tight. At this point all the air left over from charging the solar loop would have been expelled.

(Tom Lane owns Energy Conservation Services, 4110 SW 34th St., #15, Gainesville, FL 32608. Tel.: 904-373-3220. FAX: 904-338-0056. ECS has installed more than 2,000 solar hot water systems in north Florida.) Δ

"A free people ought to be armed."

George Washington

The wolves of Mission:Wolf

By Tim Haugen

Back in 1986, Tracy and Kent Webber did not envision that their search for land would eventually lead them down the path that they are following today. They just wanted a remote place where some lucky, captive-bred wolves that had come under their care could live out their lives in as natural a setting a possible. They found their home on 36.5 acres in southern Colorado's Wet Mountains, bordering on the San Isabel National Forest about 14 miles from the nearest neighbor.

But then they began hearing from others who had heard about their place, and who wondered if they had room for more wolves. The wolf population of the Wet Mountains grew. Visitors began to find their way down backcountry roads to see the wolves, and informal learning sessions about wolves evolved to satisfy visitor curiosity. Soon it became evident that not only did wolves need a home, but also the public needed to learn about the species. Thus, the Mission:Wolf refuge and learning center came to be.

Mission:Wolf is currently home to 11 pure wolves and 14 wolf-dog hybrids. Most were bred to become pets, but ended up at the refuge when their owners learned the hard way that wolves are not like domestic dogs. They do not adapt well to life as a pet, even when they are bred in captivity. Also, at least one of the current residents of the refuge arrived there from a fur farm.

Because these animals were born in captivity and have had a history of contact with people, they are not candidates for release in any wolf reintroduction program. While most are quite shy, they still do not avoid contact with humans to the degree that would be considered natural in a truly wild wolf. Consequently, it is likely that they would get into trouble with humans if they were released into the wild, with a dead wolf being the most probable end result.

The wolves at Mission:Wolf have been given the opportunity to live their lives in a habitat that is as large and natural as is feasible in captivity. They live in large open enclosures situated in a grove of trees on a hillside. They have been allowed to form packs so they can develop fairly natural wolf relationships. This is interrupted only in breeding season. Breeding is not allowed because that would only result in more wolves being forced to live their lives in captivity.

Still, there is a message that comes through very strongly from seeing these animals in their enclosures, and if the thought does not occur to the visitor spontaneously, then the people of Mission:Wolf are very inclined to bring it up. That is that wolves do not belong in cages, or in back yards, or in people's homes, or even at Mission:Wolf. They belong in wilderness. They belong in that portion of our land that remains wild. This is the primary message of the Mission:Wolf education program.

Whether viewed as an adorable pet or as the bloodthirsty nemesis of Little Red Riding Hood, the wolf is a very misunderstood animal. Perhaps the most obvious symptom of this misunderstanding is that the wolf has been eradicated throughout much of its historical range. While wolves once ranged from southern Mexico to northern Canada and Alaska, populations south of the Canadian border have been extirpated, except for populations in northern Minnesota and northwestern Montana. A small population of red wolves has been re-established in the southeast, and unconfirmed sightings of remnant populations have been reported elsewhere.

The people of Mission:Wolf would very much like to see viable populations of wolves re-established in those areas that can support them.

Whether wild or captive-bred, wolves instinctively seek to form rigid social hierarchies. A wolf will seek to establish and improve its place in the pecking order of the pack, whether the pack consists of other wolves or of people. This can have especially serious consequences when a wolf seeks to establish dominance over family members, especially children. One current resident of Mission:Wolf was sent there after dominating a child, with the result that the child required 70 stitches. That animal did what would be natural in the context of wolf interrelationships in a pack setting. In the family setting, what comes natural to a wolf can be disastrous.

Mission:Wolf can teach you a lot about wolves in one of two ways. First, self-sufficient visitors prepared to camp out in a remote mountain setting are welcome. By writing in advance of your arrival,(Mission:Wolf, POB 211, Silver Cliff, CO 81249) you can get directions and be assured that someone will be prepared to talk with you. Since they are a certified non-profit organization dependent entirely on contributions for their continued good work, a SASE and a couple dollars to help them cover the cost of responding to your inquiry would be much appreciated.

But if you do not anticipate meandering around Colorado's back-country roads at any time soon, then it may be possible to arrange a visit by Mission:Wolf to your area. Their traveling education program has given people all across the country the opportunity to meet a wolf.

Be warned, however. Once you learn about wolves and meet them face to face, the countryside will seem a little empty. You will long for the day when you can be serenaded by wolves wherever it is that you have chosen to build your backwoods home.

(Tim Haugen publishes "The Wild Ranch Review;" a quarterly newsletter offering in-depth profiles of community-based environmental groups.) Δ

> *"The great object is that every man be armed. Everyone who is able may have a gun."*
> Partick Henry

The Best of the First Two Years
Our first big anthology!
In these 12 issues you'll find:

❋ A little knowledge and sweat can build a home
for under $10,000

❋ Tepee to cabin to dream house

❋ From the foundation up, house-building is forgiving

❋ A first time horse buyer's guide

❋ A greenhouse offers advantages for the organic gardener

❋ Canning meat

❋ Backwoods Home recipes

❋ In pursuit of independence

❋ Canning blueberries

❋ How we keep humming along on the homestead

❋ Pioneer women on the trail west

❋ Some tips on first aid readiness for remote areas

❋ Whip grafting—the key to producing fruit variety

❋ The basics of backyard beekeeping

❋ Co-planting in the vegetable garden

❋ How to make soap—from fat to finish

❋ The instant greenhouse

❋ The old time spring house

❋ Getting started in a firewood business

❋ For battling ants or growing earthworms,
try coffee grounds

❋ Sawmills: a firm foundation to homesteading

The Third Year

Moving "back to the land" and making it work

By Skip Thomsen

Many of us dream about moving "back to the land"; going back to a simpler, more self-sufficient lifestyle. To many of us, a dream is all it ever is. Of those who actually take the big step and leave the city behind to try and make a go of it out in the woods, only a few manage to pull it off with any degree of success. Why?

Why is the simple life so difficult to attain? In spite of what we used to read in *Mother Earth News*, it takes a little more than desire, a half-dozen chickens, and an old Chevy pickup just to survive, let alone to put together a self-sufficient lifestyle.

The bills won't stop

Even if we move onto a paid-for piece of land with enough extra trees for the lumber to build our house, and space to raise all of our own food, the tax man will still want his annual donation. And what about when the kids get sick? Who will pay the doctor bill? Or buy gas for the pickup—not to mention tires, insurance, and repair parts? There will be things we have forgotten and events we haven't anticipated. In short, we have to have some income, no matter how self-sufficient our homestead is.

How do we cut the margin of error to minimums? The key to success is careful and realistic planning. The following paragraphs outline some of the things we need to consider before dropping everything and taking off.

You are the key

The most important element of this move to independence is, of course, you. Are you a self-motivated person who does well with no supervision? Are you skilled in most of the areas that you will need to make it on your own away from the city? Can you deal competently with mechanical things—the kinds of things that need to be fixed when nobody else is around to fix them?

Sharing with a partner?

If you are planning to share this experience with a partner, the first step is to establish the move as a joint venture. Do your skills complement each other's? Do both of you have sufficient skills and talents that one of you isn't going to have to carry an unfair share of the load most of the time? Lack of

Doing the wash in the country is not always the same as doing it in the city. Here Cathleen and Jake Thomsen share the chore.

togetherness can make or break a move to the country.

We moved to a 108-acre piece of forest beyond the power lines back in 1979. During the ten years we lived there, we watched about a dozen families and individuals, both young and old, leave the city for new lives.

Including ours, only two families made it. Of those who didn't, some lasted a few years, some a few months. Some ended in divorce, all ended up disillusioned.

Togetherness in thinking

There are several things that all of those who failed had in common. One was poor planning. Another, and a part of the poor planning, was undercapitalization; they ran out of money and had no form of income. But the biggest factor that the couples—with or without children—had in common was their lack of togetherness in their thinking.

It is imperative that all members of the family agree that they are seeking this new kind of lifestyle. We heard many versions of a basic disagreement. Often we heard them as part of our introductions to our new neighbors. "This is my idea of heaven but my wife thinks it's the pits." "I've wanted to do this all my life and George here is just wonderful for coming along for the ride. George already knows it won't work." Or the parents both loved it but the kids hated it. Or the parents and the little kids loved it and the teenager hated it. Or Mr. thought that kids should be raised on a farm and Mrs. thought that they would be culturally deprived, lonely, and forever dirty. The list is endless.

If you are absolutely certain that you are ready for a backwoods lifestyle and your spouse isn't convinced, don't bank on being able to change his or her mind "later." The time for both of you to be convinced is before you make the move.

Where will you go?

Let's say you and yours have it all together in the dreams and goals department. It's time for constructive planning. First of all, where will you go?

Considerations in choosing your new location may include weather requirements, availability of water, access to maintained roads, proximity to nearest town and schools, local building regulations, proximity to relatives, and even such things as the political climate of your chosen state or locale.

Whether you will be starting from scratch or doing any building at all, talk to the local building officials. Different areas have widely differing rules governing what can and cannot be done in the areas of construction. (For example, here in Oregon, the State's building codes are getting more unrealistic each year. Oregon puts absurd limitations on those of us who would like to build a home that doesn't look like a tract house in the suburbs.) Be specific in announcing your intentions so that you won't be disappointed when you try to get a building permit.

Give yourself a year to prepare and accumulate

You will do yourself a giant favor if you allow a year or so to get it all together before actually pulling up stakes and moving out. During that year, you can accumulate most of the stuff you will need in your new environs. It is so much easier to find good deals on tools and equipment while you still have access to city sources. (Classified ads, garage sales, and auc-

Country life can be rewarding for a youngster. Here, a young Jake enjoys a carefree rock by the barn.

tions are all excellent sources.) If you wait until you have moved onto your new place, you'll be busy with all your exciting new chores and when you discover you need something you hadn't thought of, you'll no longer have nearby supply sources available. It's also easier to make the purchases while you still have your regular income.

What will you need? Depends on what you will be doing when you get there. Will you be building your own house? Farming the land? Setting up a home business? Will you need snow removal equipment?

Some folks are disgusted at the thought of power tools, electric lights, and other traits of civilization. Others won't do without them. You will have to decide that for yourself. But if you think that you will be comfortable with kerosene lamps instead of electric lights, an axe instead of a chainsaw, and shovels instead of a tractor, be **very** objective in your thinking. Visualize yourself in your new lifestyle a few years down the road.

You might be very happy living a life that is as simple and basic as camping, for a while. Then in a few years when the novelty wears off, you may find it extremely difficult to make an adjustment back to a more contemporary lifestyle, unless you have set aside funds for just that eventuality.

Planning your move a year ahead of time has all sorts of benefits. During that year, you can not only accumulate most of the things you will need, but you can learn some of the skills that you will need in your new life as well. Are you going to be building your own house? There are a number of great books available that show how a house is built from the ground up. Thinking of making your own electricity? You should not only have all of the equipment together before your move, but you should know exactly how it's all going to work. The same goes for water resource management or the handling of animals and growing of your own food.

Cash reserves a must

An essential part of your planning year should be spent methodically salting away the cash reserves that will make all the difference in the world to your survival. This is serious business. More often than not, when we talked to would-be homesteaders who tossed it in and headed back to the city, it was because they were broke and had no source of income. How much you will need in the way of reserves will depend on whether you are moving into an existing, operating out-in-the-boonies homestead or starting from scratch on bare land.

Moving into an existing homestead might well not be a whole lot different than just moving anywhere else. Starting from scratch, on the other hand, means that you will be real busy for as long as it takes for you to build your shelter and get your homestead in some sort of livable condition. During that time, it would be real nice not to have to worry about having to generate income just to stay alive. It would be even worse to have to quit working on your half-built house because you ran out of money.

So how do you determine a reasonable sum of money to set aside? If you haven't already amassed most of your materials and equipment before your move, what will it cost to buy the rest? Assume that you will have no income for your first year. What will be your cost of living for the year? Don't skip anything here: land payments, property taxes, insurance (which you will probably be required to carry if you are making payments on your land), groceries, gas and car expenses, and of course, the materials you will be needing to build, remodel or finish your home and any other buildings in your plans.

After you carefully assemble your anticipated-expenses list, add it up and then double it. This may seem a little extreme, but it isn't. There will always be unanticipated expenses, so to rely simply on the list of expenses you're sure that you will have is unrealistic, at best.

What worked well for us was to get as many of the expenses out of the way during the planning year, while we still had an income and while we were in a better position to shop for the best prices. For example, we knew that we would need a tractor and snow-removal equipment. We spent a good deal of time chasing down ads for affordable (read: old) tractors, and finally found a gem at a good price. Then we built a six-foot wide, three-foot high snowplow blade that mounted easily on the tractor's loader arms. The tractor also came with a heavy-duty, three-point mounted grader blade, which proved indispensable for maintaining our half-mile of driveway. It felt really good to have that piece of equipment bought and paid for ahead of time.

Another contribution to your peace of mind might be to pay your land payments up a year in advance. Remember, if you are pretty well starting from scratch, you should not count on having any income for that first year or so.

An interim move

Purchasing most of your equipment, materials, and supplies during the year before you move to the woods presumes that you won't be moving across several states. If your move is far enough that transporting all that stuff would be impractical, there is another possible solution. How about an interim move to the town of reasonable size which is nearest your new homestead?

If you are of an entrepreneurial nature, here's another idea for you: in that town near your new destination, buy a fixer-upper house. During the year before your final move, refurbish the house to the point where the profit from its sale will furnish most of the capital you will need for your stash. A number of folks have made this system work very well.

Independence

Making the move to independence requires thoughtful planning. We acquired several neighbors over the years who had not bothered to consider that our winters often brought five feet of snow. Since we were the only ones on our ridge with a snowplow, we ended up plowing about eight miles of neighbors' roads for every mile of our own. In return for this favor, we were spared the bother of cutting our own firewood.

Country neighbors are generally wonderful folks who are happy to lend a helping hand. Your own thoughtful planning will make it possible for you to become a good country neighbor as well.

A source of income

Independence also requires that you eventually have a source of income. We've had neighbors who derived their income from all sorts of enterprises. Some worked at straight jobs in town (a thirty-two mile round trip), several were artisans who did their craft at home and participated in country fairs to sell their products. One young woman used her commercial sewing machine to manufacture various products for sporting goods dealers. Another neighbor hired out to do dozer work for neighboring farmers and ranchers, as well as neighbors. And we operated a desktop publishing business.

Backwoods Home Magazine is an excellent resource for home business ideas.

Two vehicles are handy

One more element of independence is transportation. Make sure that your vehicle is in good repair and is equal to the tasks you will demand of it. Will you need four-wheel-drive in the winter and during the spring thaw? Will you need a heavy-duty pickup? We heartily recommend two vehicles if at all possible.

Heavy-duty pickups and trucks or vans can be terribly expensive to operate. They gump indecent amounts of fuel, and have big, expensive tires that wear out fast if used for daily transportation. If you have an efficient, small car, you can save the truck for when you need its utility.

Another real bonus of having two vehicles is that when one becomes inoperable for any reason, you have the other as a backup. This becomes more important the farther you are from town.

Of course, if you won't be very far from town and plan on very few trips anyway, you could just get by with one vehicle—perhaps a light pickup. Again, you need to evaluate carefully your needs, and plan your equipment accordingly.

Although we sold our place on the mountain a few years ago and are now living in a small (200 souls) town, the ten years we spent being as independent as we knew how were indescribably rewarding in many areas of our lives. And we will do it again, as soon as we find the next perfect spot.∆

The Third Year

Looking for love in rural places

By Jo Mason

Those who live on a farm or ranch, in the backwoods, or in a small town, lead a special life. They enjoy the solitude...yet they want companionship too. But they face problems finding that certain someone. As one Texas farmer explains, "I can go into any big city and get a date. But when they find out it's 130 miles from my house to the nearest supermarket, they don't want anything to do with me."

After a stressful divorce, Michelle Burns (not her real name) tried the singles bar scene in Houston, but it and the men she met didn't jibe with her wholesome, rural upbringing. So she headed back to the small Texas town she calls home.

Burns says there are almost no social activities in the country. She explains, "For a woman, your name is **mud** if you hang out in a beer joint in a small town, especially when the small town has only one beer joint."

That's why this single mother of two teenagers was "ecstatic" when she heard about Singles in Agriculture (SIA), a national organization that provides opportunities for friendship between unmarried rural people. This determined lady vowed, "I knew immediately **we were going to have a Texas chapter** unless someone got in **my way.**"

Thanks to her effort, and those of a handful of other singles, the Texas chapter is now a reality. It's part of a 12-state, nationwide group composed of over 1200 members of all ages. It began in 1984, when a reader asked Farm Journal for help in meeting other single people with similar interests. They devoted a special section of the magazine to this, and 2700 readers responded. The section was eventually discontinued, but Iowan Marcella Spindler took over where they left off, and helped set up the organization. In the five years since then, there have been 200 marriages of people who met through the group.

Besides attending national conventions, the members enjoy state and regional activities. They get together for fish frys, campouts, barbecues, dances, and boat trips. Recent activities by the Texas chapter include a New Year's Eve weekend at a ranch resort (no heavy drinking allowed!), an old-fashioned box supper auction, and a barn dance. Future plans include a polka dance and Caribbean cruise. They also have frequent smaller get-togethers, such as fishing (bring your own rod and reel), and dominoes (bring your own folding chairs and table).

Perhaps the greatest benefit of SIA, is that they all speak the same language. When one member talks about canning, or making pickles, or how the crops are doing, everyone else knows what they mean. For instance, an item in one of the newsletters warns: "Please keep my gate closed so the cows don't get out."

At present, there are SIA chapters in the following states: Illinois, Ohio, Indiana, Colorado, Texas, Missouri, Iowa, Kansas, Nebraska, Oregon, Oklahoma, and Wisconsin. For information on joining or starting your own state club, write: Singles in Agriculture, 5297 Ill. Rt. 73 So., Pearl City, IL 61062. Δ

"The Perfect Shot" by Cindy Myers, Oxnard, CA (original drawing)

Here's a new way to remove a fish hook

PUSH

PULL

Pushing down and pulling at the same time should remove the fish hook.

By Ralph LaPlant

It seems that for anyone who fishes or spends a lot of time around anyone who does will sooner or later get "caught". Often an imbedded fish hook is easily removed as it may be only barely under the skin's surface, not grabbed by the barb. The barb is there for a purpose—not to let the fish get off the hook. Why should a person be any different?

If the hook is imbedded and not easily removed, I suggest that the victim be seen by a doctor. Under a controlled situation a doctor can cleanse the area, infiltrate the immediate area with an anesthetic, remove the hook, and dress the area of the wound. A tetanus shot can be given if need be.

If you are away from medical care and these luxuries are not available, you might have to try the removal yourself.

There is a method that has been taught for years. That is to push the hook through until the barb is visible, then cut off the barb, pulling the hook out back the way it entered. It works, but is somewhat painful.

There is another method that is less painful. It works slick, but should not be used with hooks that have multiple barbs and should not be used when the hook is imbedded in areas of the face, neck, or areas having connective tissues such as tendons close. I would suggest this method be used on arms and legs and other such areas.

All you need is string and if you're fishing, you should have plenty of that. Use strong string and wrap it around the hook, push down on the hook and pull the string. The hook should come out before you know it. It is important to pull in the long axis of the hook and to pull fast, actually snapping.

What happens is this—pushing down on the hook prevents it's barb from digging into the path it made going in while being removed. Pulling simply removes it.

A couple of cautions. The hook can fly and no one should be in its potential path as we've just removed it from one person and don't want another stuck. If you have no luck and it does not come out easily, treat it as any other imbedded object by packing it in dressings to prevent further movement and seek medical attention.

After removal and as with all minor wounds, cleanse the area and dress it. An antiseptic ointment might be a good idea also. By all means seek medical attention if signs of infection appear such as warmth, redness, and swelling of the immediate area. Everyone should have a current tetanus shot to prevent later complications.

Next time, catch fish, not people! Δ

The Backwoods Home Magazine office in the Siskiyou Mountains of Oregon

Miles per gallon vs. miles per hour

...or... things to consider when buying a car

By Skip & Cathleen Thomsen

Maybe an article on cars is not what you expect to find in your favorite homesteading magazine, but what the magazine is all about is self-sufficiency. A big part of self-sufficiency is not spending your hard-earned cash in the wrong places. Enter this article.

Ask fifty people what the term "economy car" means, and you'll get fifty different answers. An economy car, by definition, should be economical, right? "Economical" implies that it will cost less than one which is less economical.

Gas mileage alone is not the answer. If you are looking for an excuse to go out and spend a small fortune on a new mini-car, and you elect "better gas mileage" as the rationale, read on.

An example

Let's use Joe and Mary Smith as examples to illustrate the entire concept of "economy car."

Joe and Mary now drive an eight-year-old Maxicruiser with a small V-8 engine, automatic transmission, power steering, and air. It shows 87,000 miles on the odometer, and is in better-than-average condition. It gets about 14 mpg in town and 20 on the highway.

Joe just got a new job (he's a computer programmer) and his Maxi was the only big, old car in the company parking lot. Joe "needed" a new car. In their quest for reasons to replace the Maxicruiser, Joe and Mary settled on better economy.

After several trips to various new- and used-car dealers, they finally decided on a three-year-old Minicar. The new ride was equipped with a five-speed transmission, a nice radio and air. It showed 30,000 miles on the odometer. Its price was $6995, which they skillfully negotiated down to $5995.

For their Maxicruiser the dealer allowed them $1000 against the purchase price of the Minicar. They were given the usual choice between buying an extended warranty or signing the AS-IS clause; they opted for the $400 "warranty." After subtracting the value of their trade-in as their down payment, and paying outright for the license/tax/transfer fees, they signed a thirty-six month contract for a balance of a little over $5400, drove their new car home, and proudly parked it in the driveway. They now had a car just like everyone else's on the block.

Mary wasn't happy to find out that their insurance premium had doubled because of the new car. Their agent explained that they had carried no collision coverage on the old Maxicruiser; but since they were financing the new car, the lender insisted they carry collision coverage. And as expensive as the newer cars were to repair (even a 5 mph tap on the front bumper of their Minicar could do over $1300 damage), it just wasn't bright to drive without collision, even if it weren't required. Mary understood, but the extra $120 hurt just the same.

Since most of their driving was the commute to work — nearly all highway driving — the Minicar was getting about 33 mpg. Maybe they could make their payments out of what they saved on gas, as the salesman had promised them.

The arithmetic

Let's figure it out. The Smiths drove about 15,000 miles per year. The Maxicruiser averaged 17 mpg. 15,000 miles at 17 mpg comes to 882 gallons of fuel. At $1.10 a gallon, that's $970 annually. The Minicar uses 500 gallons annually at its average of 30 mpg. That comes to $550 for a year's supply of gas. So far, the Smiths show a savings of $420/year, or $35/month.

The added $120 for insurance coverage not needed for the old car cuts into their savings a bit: now they're down to $300/year, or $25/-month.

Oh, yes, car payments. $5400 for thirty-six months, financed at a low 11%, comes to "easy monthly payments" of only $179.36.

But they are saving $25 a month, right? Right. So for driving a car half the size, half the comfort, half the utility, and a fraction of the safety when compared to the sturdy old Maxicruiser, John and Mary pay only $154/month more to drive the Minicar. Keep track of this figure for a few moments; we'll get back to it.

Figuring only principal, interest and the down payment, they will have spent a total of $7457. After three years, they'll actually begin saving that $25 a month, because the Minicar will be paid off.

The difference in gas mileage from one car to another is almost never a good reason to change to a more expensive car.

But will they be able to live with their basic Minicar for longer than three years? Won't there be sufficient social pressure by then to justify another new car?

Three years later

Let's take a look at the two hypothetical cars after three years. Had they kept the Maxicruiser, it would now be showing 132,000 miles. If they had serviced the car properly during those miles, chances are good that they would have experienced no major problems. The Minicar would now be reading 75,000 miles. It, too, probably would not yet have needed any major repairs.

But let's suppose that at 100,000 miles, the Maxicruiser needed a $300 transmission overhaul, and let's figure that into the overall picture. Let's also figure in another expense: depreciation.

The Maxi was worth $1000 three years ago. If it still looks and drives well, it's still worth $500. The Mini was worth $6000 three years ago when John and Mary paid for it. At six years and 75,000 miles, it has a market value of about $2000.

The Maxi depreciated $500, the Mini, $4000. It cost the Smiths $3500 more in depreciation to drive the Minicar than it would have to keep the Maxicruiser.

After deducting $300 for the Maxicruiser's transmission repair, the Smiths spent only $3200 more to drive the miniature car. Added to the $7457 in direct expenses (principal, interest and down payment), the total comes to $10,657 for John and Mary to drive their "new" car for three years.

Let's go back now. $3200 over three years comes to about $89 per month. When we add that to the direct monthly increase of $154 (mileage, insurance, and car payments), we find that it cost the Smiths **$242 MORE per**

month for those three years of Minicar entertainment than it would have cost to continue driving the nice, big, comfortable, fully- equipped Maxicruiser

If the Smiths could **afford** to shell out nearly eleven thousand dollars over the course of three years, if they had decided that they would rather spend the money on replacing their present car than on a down payment on a house or a lengthy vacation in the tropics, then there was nothing wrong with their purchase.

If, on the other hand, they purchased their Minicar the way many people do — blind to actual costs — they deprived themselves of things more important than having a car that blended better in the office parking lot.

One more "if": If John and Mary had opted for a **new** car instead of one three years old, their expenses could have been thousands of dollars higher. The lesson here is to figure in ALL the expenses, not just gas mileage.

The difference in gas mileage from one car to another is almost never a good reason to change to a more expensive car. Certainly, if you are about to replace your present car anyway, and fuel economy is a factor, you would be wise to pay attention to the mileage figures of your prospective purchase. But buying a more expensive car simply because of its better mileage requires some careful arithmetic to make an intelligent choice.

Big bargains

In today's used-car market, bigger cars, particularly older ones, are almost always bargains compared to the little "fuel-efficient" models. The same applies to many models of pickups. The bigger vehicles generally go farther before needing major repairs. If you can buy a nice, big, comfortable cruiser for a thousand dollars less than a miniature car in comparable condition, you might **never** save enough on gas to pay the difference.

Let's use another example. We need a car, and we just happen to be in love with a mid-eighties full-size Olds. Our consciences tell us that we should buy a Honda to save money on gas. We

drive 15000 miles per year, mostly highway.

An '86 Olds with the overdrive transmission will get an easy 20 MPG. Let's give the Honda a break and say it will do 40 MPG. In 15000 miles, the Olds would use 750 gallons of gas; the Honda 375. At $1.10/gallon, it would cost $412 more per year to drive the Olds. If we planned to keep either car for three years, we would have to buy the Olds for about $1200 less than the Honda to come out even. Time to shop around.

Not everybody loves big cars. We do. If we had a specific amount of money available with which to buy a car, we would choose an older cruiser over a newer econo-car for the same amount of money.

Important concept: To make a rational decision, decide not only which car to buy, but whether to replace the old car in the first place.

Matter of fact, that is exactly what we do. Our family car has always been a loaded cruiser bought for peanuts because it showed seventy thousand miles on the odometer. It was always selected because of its as-new condition and the obvious (and often documented) care that it received.

We have never had to do a major repair to any of these cars, and we have driven several of them, without a hitch, to well over 150,000 miles.

Ultimate miles per gallon

Let's talk for a moment about **ultimate** miles per dollar. Did you know that there are lots of good, dependable cars available for less than one thousand dollars? Even less than five hundred dollars?

We have been joyfully driving cheap cars for years. Not because we can't afford to drive a car just like everyone else does, but because we enjoy squeezing all of those free miles out of a good piece of machinery.

Example: Back in 1984, we bought a beautiful 1971 Oldsmobile "98" sedan

The Third Year

with every conceivable option (and they all worked) from a used car lot for $450. The Olds showed 97,000, was exceptionally clean, and ran like new. By 1988, we had logged another 60,000 miles on the car. During that time, we installed a new set of discount-store tires and a water pump. Our total expenses to date, including the price of the car, amounted to $750.

Unfortunately, about this time, we loaned the car to a friend who thoroughly trashed the still-beautiful-but-thin brocade upholstery on the front seat, and soon after that, the windshield developed a crack. It was time to move on. We sold it to a clunker dealer for $300.

Four years and 60,000 miles use of this ultra-comfortable cruiser had cost us $450. That's a lot less than most owners of new, itsy-bitsy, disposable mini-cars spend on their first year's interest. Miles per dollar.

One of the best things about a $500 car is that it cannot possibly depreciate more than $500, no matter what you do to it.

Matter of fact, any car which looks decent and runs well will likely always be worth $500. Your only expense of operation will be any required repairs. Again, if you apply your expertise in selecting such a car, there will be no repairs other than the nickel-and-dime stuff that occasionally happens to any car.

In our younger days, we drove nothing but older, excellent cars which we bought for next to nothing. Often we drove one for a few years and sold it for more than we had paid for it.

We regularly receive comments regarding our big old car, and how can we afford to buy gas for it. (Our current big old car is a thirteen year-old Dodge.) It is a well-maintained, comfortable cruiser with all the toys, and it gets about 18 MPG. We paid $800 for it two years ago when it had 65,000 miles on it. We now live in a little coastal village and never leave here unless we absolutely have to, so we log less than 5000 miles a year on the car.

The last person to berate us for driving a gas-guzzler had just shelled out a little over $7000 for a new econo-mini-car which he claims gets 40 MPG. In the last two years, we have spent about $700 on gas for our cruiser. In the last two **weeks** the econo-car owner has spent three times that much on depreciation. When he reminds me that depreciation is non-polluting, unlike all that gas we burn, we wonder how much gas we would have to burn to equal the amount of pollution produced in the manufacture of his new disposable-transportation appliance.

Smaller bargains

Not all cheap cars have to be huge-mobiles. There are lots of fifteen year-old Toyotas, Mazdas, Datsuns and the like available in the under-$1000 price range, too. You do have to be more careful with the little ones, though. They are not as robust as the bigger cars, and when something does need to be fixed or replaced it will usually cost more. Old Toyota Coronas are a prime example of a durable Japanese car. It is not unusual for a reasonably well cared-for Corona to go well over 100,000 miles before needing any repairs at all.

The trick is to know what your budget limits are and stick with them. Find the best car you can for the money you have allotted. If you feel the need to get rid of your cruiser or that big, thirsty pickup and find a smaller rig, you might have to settle for moving back a few years to an older model if you want to do it without spending any additional money. The age of the vehicle is never as important as the condition.

If your goal is the absolute highest attainable ratio of miles per dollar, as opposed to miles per gallon, there is no substitute for a good, old, depreciation-proof, cheap car.

What counts is **miles per dollar,** not miles per gallon.

(Skip Thomsen and his wife Cathleen have recently retired from about 30 years in various facets of the automobile business and have written a book which is both an expose of the car selling/repairing industry and a guide on how to survive the occasional necessary encounter with it, financially intact and with minimum brain damage. This article is an excerpt from the book, "Games Dealers Play," which is now being published by Oregon Wordworks, 406 Pine Ave., Box DD, Manzanita, OR 97130.) △

War without End

*You have no idea about the conditions
over there, he said. The people over there
are not Free. Hell, I'll take you over there
sometime to Poland, Hungary, Czechoslovakia
and then you'll see how it is not to be
Free.
And he picked his nose forcefully and frowned.*

*Stop wasting your time, she said to him,
the Americans harbor a million illusions.
It's no use trying to make them understand
since they have never been Invaded.
Us, we were Invaded!
France was Occupied!
We were Prisoners!*

*He points to his wrist and stretches
his hand out flat and says,
You give the East
This
and they will take
That.
And he draws a line at his shoulder
as if he would cut off his arm.*

*She says, I'd rather have a Reagan.
We loved Nixon, you know.
Carter was a pansy.
The Hippies were wrong,
all the Liberals were dead
wrong.*

*You don't know how we starved! he cries.
You don't know how it is to be bombed!*

*They look at each other and nod
and nod and nod. The raspberry ice-cream
flattens out in the bowls.*

Kyle Jarrard
Suresnes, France

MONEY

Tips to help make your car go 150,000 miles!

By Rev. L. Dale Richesin

I am no mechanic or car expert. I am a minister and I drive a great deal. And I don't have much money, so I must get the greatest value from the money that I spend on my car. Here are a few easy tips that should enable you to drive over 150,000 miles on your car. I have had four cars in the past 20 years and all went over 100,000 miles, three went over 180,000 miles. These are very simple rules, but often easily ignored.

1. Buy a used car, 2-4 years old, with about 20,000 to 40,000 miles. The cost will be greatly reduced, and most of the initial bugs will have been worked out.

2. Avoid extras. No air-conditioning, no power windows or locks, no automatic transmission. If you must have any of these, you should realize that at about 65,000 to 85,000 miles you should expect another $300 to $700 in added repairs. And all extras subtract from mileage and performance.

3. Fill 'er up. Every time you get gas, fill the tank. Don't let your car settle overnight with less than 1/4 tank. An empty tank allows air and moisture to condense in your gas line and can corrode your gas line and rob your carburetor of efficiency and mileage. Of all of my tips, this is the most important!

4. Check the oil. At any given moment, over 54% of all cars are low on oil. Check it every time you get gas. And change the oil and filter every 3,000 miles. My best advice is **don't** do it yourself. Go to a quick oil change place. They can recycle the oil, which is good for the environment, and they can often spot problems that might be more expensive later.

5. Check the water. Over 34% of all cars are low on water at any given time. Change your complete water and anti-freeze system every two years or 40,000 miles. When you change it, make sure that your heater water is changed at the same time. Corrosion can affect your heater much easier because the heating elements are not as durable as the radiator. Remind your serviceman about this because sometimes they might forget.

6. Check your tires. Low pressure can cause uneven wear. At least once a year have your tire alignment checked. You might go to one of those places that offer a lifetime alignment. If you own the car for 150,000 miles, the expense will be worth it.

7. Brakes, mufflers, and shocks. There are several places that give lifetime or extended warranties for these items. Patronize them. After 150,000 miles you will have used 2-4 sets of brakes, shocks, and mufflers, and your repairman will have become a good friend.

8. Battery and alternator. These have much shorter warranties than other items. But you should expect to use several in the lifetime of your car. Anticipate the expense and don't let it surprise you.

9. Road trips. The best way to extend the life of your car is to take an occasional road trip. These trips are fun and enjoyable and you can also see the relatives or the beach or whatever. A drive of 200 plus miles several times a year will help to burn out some of the accumulated dirt and corrosion in your engine. Your car will run better. Tell yourself you could use the break in your routine.

10. Positive attitude. The only way that you can drive a car for 150,000 miles is with a positive attitude. Some people talk to their plants. You can also talk to your car. Keep a careful list of your major repairs and the mileage when those repairs were needed. Also note the symptoms that prompted those repairs. If you heard a funny noise that resulted in a new alternator at 48,000 miles, you might listen for that noise when your car reaches 96,000 miles. You might even do preventive maintenance and replace the item before it fails. Be-tween 40,000 and 90,000 miles you will need to expect to replace and/or repair several major systems. Don't be irritated. Expect it. Don't postpone those repairs. They will be much more expensive and inconvenient later. If you spend $25 for an oil change every 3,000 miles, you will postpone a $1,000 repair by many, many years.

(Rev. L. Dale Richesin is Pastor of the First Christian Church, Maywood, Illinois.) Δ

Greener Grass

He traveled
with his head
held high and both eyes
fastened
on the sky, disdaining
worldly passions
all and harking
to a higher call.
The straight
and narrow path
he trod, his feet
in tandem on the sod.
No jug of wine
approached
his lips. No buxom
lassie's comely hips
enticed him
from his chosen way
nor showed him where
base pleasures
lay. And he lived
good and kind
and just a man
whom everyman could trust.
So when his span on Earth
was done he reached
the heavenly
plane he'd won. There
from his lofty
cloud-strewn perch he wandered
his new height to search,
peered down to see
what might be seen on Earth
and oh! the grass
looked GREEN.

Cathleen Freshwater Thomsen
Manzanita,Oregon

National Health Care — will it work in the U.S.?

By Martin P. Waterman

It used to be that most Canadians felt that each was a beneficiary of one of the best National Health care systems in the world. However, with the recent economic changes many Canadians are concerned about the integrity and longevity of a system that has not lived up to expectations.

The current discussion over a National Health Care system has spurred heated debate with both supporters and opponents providing emotionally packed arguments. A National Health Care system, if passed into law, may be the most important piece of legislation in the decade. It will probably also be one of the most expensive with one expert claiming that a Canadian-style system for the United States would cost taxpayers an additional $350 billion a year.

Not a simple "yes" or "no"

National Health Care, unfortunately, is not a simple yes or no, black and white proposition. There are many sides to the debate and the issues can be so complex and affect so many people and special interest groups that you almost need a program to keep score. Knowing what interest group has the most to win or lose will help most people make an informed assessment of the benefits and pitfalls of National Health Care.

In preparation for this story, a study was made of articles and editorials appearing in national and regional newspapers on both sides of the border concerning attitudes and facts concerning the Canadian and any potential U.S. system. The volume of facts and figures was staggering.

A friend had expressed a special interest in knowing the truth about whether a national health care system would work in the U.S. He had quit his job to pursue the American Dream. He started his own business, and with the enterprise in the formative years, he was not yet drawing a salary. Naturally, the concern lingered about what to do if he or members of his family needed emergency health care.

It's a political vote-getter

Four years ago, listening to the then current crop of Democratic Presidential hopefuls and their passionate pleas for a national health care system, one got the impression that national health care had become a panacea for almost all that ails America. We are hearing those calls for national health care again.

Unfortunately, national health care is being used as a political football by many dream merchants who have found it to be the new flavour of the month they can sell to get elected or re-elected. However, another cure-all system, Medicare, which was introduced in the 1960's has seen expenditures go up 1,200% and has earned a reputation as being riddled with inefficiency and fraud.

National health care will continue to be a hot topic in the media and most should realize that there is much disinformation and many misleading facts being expounded by all sides. Arguments are not always being supported by evidence. One passionate article for the establishment of a health care system was written by a Doctor who tells of sending his patients to Canada for prenatal care.

However, he never once mentioned the high cost in extra taxes needed to pay for a system, and these costs were not paid by his satisfied patients. If his readers had to pay 10-20% more in Federal taxes, two and a half times more for gasoline, and higher costs for electricity, rent, utilities, and food (to cite but a few examples), they may not have thought that our system was such a bargain.

It was disheartening to read so many articles and editorials that only expound the good and not the bad. As in all debates, the radical left and the radical right arguments require special scrutiny.

The Canadian Health Care system that many proponents in the U.S. want to duplicate is the system as it once existed and not the nightmare that it has become for some. It seems that every week there is a news report on hospitals cutting or limiting services, people dying or being sent to U.S. hospitals because of a shortage of hospital beds, and user fees being imposed since the system is running out of money.

Canadian health system based on British system

Canada's system was based on the British system, which has over 800,000 people waiting for surgery. Some patients in Canada have had to wait over two years just to get a magnetic resonance scan for a brain tumor. There are many controversial cases such as patients who have died waiting for operations or have died because they have been bounced from one hospital to the next. The reason for this is usually a shortage of beds, equipment, or hospital administrators trying to control costs.

The U.S. safety valve

The Canadian system would be even worse except for one thing: the system uses the United States as a safety valve. We are shipping patients to U.S. hospitals. If the United States has a duplicate system that so many are pleading for, where would the safety valve be for the American system? Mexico?

For some, the question of whether or not to have a national health care system is a question of how much faith they have in the government being capable of effectively and efficiently delivering the benefits of the system. But, for many, resolution of the question rests in their belief that the U.S. Government has a moral or social responsibility for the health of its citizens.

But is the U.S. government capable of administering a system such as national health care? After all, there is not much faith in the ability of the public sector these days to administer Social Security and welfare, and faith in government is near an all time low.

How to pay for it?

What about the cost? Will the tax increases necessary to fund such a system hurt the competitiveness of America? In Canada, everyone, in theory, has access to a national health care system but there are extremely high taxes to pay for this program.

Under the recent Free Trade Agreement, hundreds of Canadian manufacturers have already headed to the United States as a matter of financial survival because the tax load has become so burdensome. As a result, hundreds of thousands of Canadian workers in the affected industries have lost high paying manufacturing jobs. Are Americans, who are already concerned about American jobs being shipped overseas, prepared to deal with this—to pay for "free" health care?

The Government in control?

Furthermore, there is no reason to think, once the government controls health care, that it will be conducted in the interest of the people as a whole. Congress is heavily influenced by the hordes of lobbyists who continually comb the hill for special interest groups that represent insurance companies, doctors, religious concerns, pharmaceutical companies, hospitals, and others who will want their own interests protected regardless of how it affects the average tax paying citizen.

And what do the people who pay those taxes want from a national health care system? Many already have adequate health care systems through their employers. Some take the attitude that they will never be critically ill.

An argument against it

One common argument against national health care is rooted in the new perception that some individuals are taking government systems for a ride while others pick up the tab. For instance, many believe that if you take care of your health, eat right and exercise, why should you pay thousands of dollars in extra taxes for your neighbour who drinks like a fish, smokes four packs of cigarettes a day, and who may in his lifetime cost a health system hundreds of thousands of dollars.

In Canada, there have been many instances of people taking up hospital beds just because they do not have enough to eat or a warm place to sleep.

A whole new bureaucracy

What about the cost of the administration of the system. There are the buildings, computers, clerks, investigators—in a sense a whole new massive federal bureaucracy with high paid boards that could be loaded with more political appointees and patronage appointments at the top.

Will it be fair?

Then there is the question of universality. Will the poor black family in Mississippi have the same access to a quality health care system as an affluent white family in Westchester County, New York? Can the system provide the same expensive medical equipment to both areas?

Will only powerful Congressmen and legislators be able to get the new hospitals and new equipment in their districts while districts with Congressmen who do not have the same seniority have their districts go without only to have the inequity switch once a seat changes?

In Canada, under our national health care system, many rural areas are not getting the same level of service that is available in urban areas.

Misuse & the baby boomers

What about the inefficiencies, overbilling, fraud, and waste that these national programs bring? Members of Congress have proven that they cannot even balance their own checkbooks, let alone the checkbooks of the nation. What about the baby boomer generation? As they age, the tax burden to the rest of the nation could be staggering.

One of the many reasons that the Canadian system is going broke is that since it is free, some people naturally take full advantage of the system. They go for repeated visits and often have a variety of unnecessary tests. If a doctor refuses, there are hundreds of others willing to offer abundant tests since this is how they get paid.

With the Canadian health care system, the focus has changed for many and the need for preventive maintenance has been replaced by the false security that the system will always by there to take care of them.

Differences between Canada and the United States

There are many differences between the Canadian and U.S. medical establishments that proponents for a U.S. system will never point out. In Canada, doctors do not have the same worries about malpractice suits since Canadian courts have consistently taken the position to limit such settlements. However, in the United States, doctors already feel compelled to order every test imaginable to lessen the possibility of any malpractice suits. With factors such as this to consider, the price tag of such a system may be many times higher than the costs as calculated using the Canadian model. And really, how many federal programs have ever come in below or as budgeted.

The taxes and the debt

Whatever the cost, the government can raise your taxes to pay for a national health care system. However, the new tax revenue will not go to pay for the system. It will probably go to pay the interest on the debt to pay for the system. Because of the enormous federal deficit, your tax money will be paying interest to the lenders, many of them foreign nations. This will no doubt put pressure to reignite inflation and high interest rates. If everyone's taxes go up, everyone will raise their prices to try to compensate for the adjustment.

Insurance companies

The powerful insurance industry is naturally against the government getting into the health care business. The insurance companies are doing very well and want to hold onto this important part of their business; resolving

the health care issue could be a choice of who you trust more—insurance companies or your government. To many, this is not a calming choice to be made. Still, private enterprise has almost always been able to deliver a service or product cheaper than a government agency can. It's difficult to find any exceptions.

The Singapore system

In the debate over national health care, many facts are being neglected. For instance, Singapore has a system that seems to work. Have you heard of this system? You probably never will. In Singapore, the government allows medical savings accounts to which the individuals or their employers can make contributions. These accounts are sheltered from taxes and have other benefits besides.

With these accounts people are allowed personal control of their health plans instead of the insurance companies, doctors, hospitals, or the government. The people can buy high deductible policies for catastrophic coverage and pay most of the expenses from their medical savings account. Any money not spent is theirs, which provides an incentive to control costs.

The Singapore system should be considered before committing to a national health care system but it would probably be fought tooth and nail by many special interest groups because it puts the power in the hands of the people and protects the integrity of the free enterprise system at the same time.

So what is the answer for my friend concerning national health care for the U.S.? If it means trading off the economic health of the nation I would find it hard to justify supporting it. The high price of private health care premiums are small compared to the cost of turning the U.S.A. into a high taxed country with a stagnant economy which could extinguish the dream for many of owning a house, starting a business, or going to college.

The idea of government taking care of you still appeals to many. Sociologists argue that this is why people in the former Communist Bloc countries are unable to change.

Perhaps the real question concerning a national health care system is how much more empowered should the government become? The question is a hard one to avoid. You are already being asked (depending on the Presidential hopeful) to endorse or reject such a system.

To quote a founding father of the United States of America: "A government that governs least, governs best." Based on past government programs in both countries, it appears that caution should be used when the people delegate their powers and rights to the government. Once relinquished to the state, rights are hard to get back.

Pro and con arguments are sure to become more prevalent and emotional in days to come. Do not believe anyone who says there will be no cost in instituting a national health care program. There is no such thing as free health care.

(Martin P. Waterman is a Canadian citizen living in New Brunswick, Canada.) Δ

Work at home at your convenience as a paramedical examiner

By Steven Gregersen

If you like being a health care professional but don't like working on

had something to do with nursing skills. Partly to satisfy my own curiosity and also because I thought her career might interest others, I arranged an interview so she could explain what a paramedical examiner is.

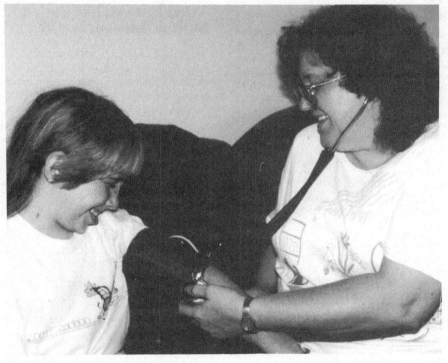

Paramedical Examiner Chris Tawney checks the blood pressure of Amy Gregersen, the author's daughter.

holidays and weekends, maybe you should consider a career as a paramedical examiner.

If you're an LPN, RN, or EMT, you might qualify as a paramedical examiner. The pay is good, the hours are flexible, and work is available throughout the United States.

I'd never heard of a "paramedical examiner" before I met Christine Tawney. I didn't know what Chris actually did but I knew she worked from her home, set her own schedule, and it

What does a paramedical examiner do?

Chris: "A paramedical examiner is sent out by an insurance company to assist people in properly filling out the health history forms that are needed before an insurance policy is issued.

"When the insurance company sells a new policy they contact the paramedical group they use. The paramedical group then provides me with the name of the applicant.

"Next, I set up an appointment to meet with the applicant in their home or office, my home, or somewhere else where there is a degree of privacy. I guide them through the application and help them understand what information is needed by the insurance company. I help define what is meant by some of the more ambiguous questions such as, excessive use of alcohol, shortness of breath, and/or dizziness.

"I also measure the client's height, weight, and blood pressure. In the case of some male applicants I take chest and stomach measurements.

"Since the advent of AIDS, many insurance companies require blood tests before issuing a policy. It's my job to draw the blood sample. Sometimes the insurance company will require that an EKG be taken and sent in for evaluation. I am expected to do that also.

"Usually examinations more in depth than this will require a visit to a doctor or hospital."

What skills are needed to qualify?

Chris: "It varies from state to state and even between different paramedical firms. Some states have licensing requirements for paramedical examiners. Some paramedical firms have a short training period done by the company.

"In most cases you will need a good medical background. In a basic exam the job includes completing an accurate health history of the client, taking a urine sample, and checking blood pressure.

"Perhaps one of the most important qualifications is to enjoy working with people."

What equipment is needed?

Chris: "You'll need a good notebook or briefcase to carry the necessary insurance forms. Accurate scales measuring up to 300 pounds are a necessity (bathroom scales are adequate **if they are accurate**), plus a cloth tape measure at least six feet long (eight feet is better).

This is the equipment Chris takes with her to perform an exam. It all fits in two satchels and the cooler.

"A small ice chest will give you more time to get to the lab with blood work during hot weather. A medical dictionary is helpful for spelling medical terms correctly.

"Kits for taking blood and urine samples are usually furnished by the insurance company."

How did you hear about this type of work?

Chris: "I answered a newspaper advertisement in the help wanted section. I had never heard of a paramedical examiner before then.

"Once I was established at one firm I started doing work for others. I now have several companies who call me when an examiner is needed.

"Without an ad, the best way to find which firms are used in your area is to call local life insurance agencies and ask them for the names and telephone numbers of the paramedical firms they do business with. Paramedical examination firms can be hard to locate because they don't normally advertise unless they need help."

Are you an employee or self-employed?

Chris: "It depends on the paramedical group. In most cases I am considered a self-employed contractor.

However, one firm has redefined my status to that of an employee this year."

How are you paid?

Chris: "I'm paid by the paramedical group after the exam is done.

"Each firm has their own pay rate that varies from $12 to $27 for a basic exam (health history, blood pressure, urine sample). The basic exam takes from thirty to forty-five minutes.

"When "blood work" is involved I'm paid more (blood work includes taking the blood sample and filling out the proper "chain of custody" forms to keep track of the sample on its way to the lab). If an EKG is required, the pay increases accordingly. (Equipment to do the EKG is rented from the paramedical group when needed.)

"I began part time while going to school to become an R.N. (I was already an L.P.N.). At first I did about 100 exams per year on a part time basis. When AIDS testing began that figure went to 600-800 per year. Now I do between 60 to 100 per month on a full-time basis.

"Most of the time the workload is fairly stable. If an insurance company is having a sales promotion or contest among the salesmen, there may be a surge in examinations for that company as they sell more policies. For the most part though there are no seasonal fluctuations as in some occupations.

"I take calls within 100 miles of home. I think this gives me an advantage over those who won't go out of town to do an exam. Some firms will reimburse mileage expenses and some won't.

"You should keep accurate records of all mileage and business expenses for tax purposes." (See *Backwoods Home Magazine*, "A crash course in small business record keeping," in Issue Number 8, and "Taxes—a good reason for you to start your own small business" in Issue Number 7.)

What is it you like the most about your work?

Chris: "I enjoy helping people. What I do is a convenience for the client. I often go the their home for the exam. Because people are usually more comfortable at home their blood pressure is often lower than if they were at a doctor's office. It also give me an opportunity to answer their questions. Many people don't know what normal blood pressure is or how it's measured. Often people ask questions about certain diseases such as diabetes or hypertension.

"My hours are flexible. There's no set schedule. Appointments are made according to the client's convenience and my own. If the work slows down I can take some time off.

"I enjoyed working as a nurse but I didn't like working weekends and holidays. Now I'm doing the work I love and I spend weekends and holidays at home. What more could anyone want?" Δ

The Milli Vanilli Poem

'

,

.

"   ,

."

,

?

John Earl Silveira
Ojai, CA

International ways with chicken

By Jennifer Stein

Now that you've all read Carla Emery's excellent article on raising chickens, (in issues #11, 12 and 13 of BHM) you'll want to know all you can about cooking with these versatile birds. Chicken dishes abound in international cuisine, and almost every region of the world has created its own style of cooking with eggs and chicken meat. Styles range from America's simply seasoned roast chicken to exotic African and oriental dishes where the chicken can hardly be found among the many other ingredients and strong spices. A tender fryer or a perfectly fresh egg lends itself well to being the centerpiece of the meal, while an old hen whose meat may be a little tough can be boiled to melting tenderness and stretched to feed a dozen or more in the stewpot.

Keep clean around chickens

One of the advantages of growing your own chickens is freshness. Another is health, both yours and your chickens'. While your homegrown birds are much less likely than factory chickens to carry salmonella, the possibility still exists. Hens can even pass salmonella to their eggs before the shell is formed. Be reassured, though, the solution is simple: keep cool, clean well, and cook thoroughly.

Keep all eggs and meat products refrigerated at all times up to preparation. Refrigerated means between 33 and 45 degrees. If you are thawing a chicken which has been in the freezer, the recommended way to do it is in the refrigerator. However, this can take a couple of days, and if you're in a hurry you can place the frozen bird in a basin of cold water to thaw. Change the water frequently, and never **never** leave meat out at room temperature to thaw.

Clean all surfaces and utensils that have come into contact with chicken meat thoroughly before using them to prepare any other foods, especially vegetables and salads which will not be fully cooked. Wash your hands after handling chicken.

The third step is to cook chicken meat or eggs thoroughly. With eggs, this means cooking to 140 degrees and holding at that temperature for 3 1/2 minutes, or cooking to 160 degrees. Sorry, this means no more sunny-side ups! Yolks should be at least semi-firm. For chicken meat, the recommended serving temperature of 185 degrees is enough to kill any bacteria.

If you take these simple precautions: keep cool, clean well, and cook thoroughly, you should find your homegrown chickens to be a healthful source of food for your family.

Following are three simple ways to cook eggs and chicken:

Tofu fooyong

1 cup bean sprouts
1/2 cup frozen peas
1 lb. medium tofu
1 clove garlic, minced
3 eggs
freshly ground pepper
1/2 teaspoon toasted sesame oil
3 green onions, sliced thin
2 Tablespoons tamari or
2 teaspoons Maggi seasoning
peanut oil for frying

Bring a medium saucepan of water to a boil. Place the bean sprouts in a strainer, and dip them in the boiling water for a few seconds, then lift them out and drain thoroughly. Pour some of the boiling water over the peas to thaw them out. Discard the used water, or save for soup stock.

Cut the tofu into 1/2" chunks. In a skillet, fry the chunks, turning occasionally, until they are golden. Remove them to a bowl, and add the garlic and eggs. Mash and beat everything together until it is blended, then add the bean sprouts, peas, pepper, sesame oil, green onions, and tamari or Maggi. Stir until the vegetables are evenly distributed. In the skillet, heat a few tablespoons of peanut oil over medium-high heat until a drop of water will sizzle in the pan. Pour the Fooyong mixture into the pan and cook until the mixture is golden on the bottom and begins to set up. Flip with a spatula and cook the other side until golden. Serve immediately. Serves 4.

Oven-baked oriental chicken

1/2 cup tamari
2 cloves garlic, minced
1 Tablespoon toasted sesame oil
3-4 lbs. cut-up fryer

Wash and cut up your chicken carefully. Break open the joints before you cut them, and cut the meat between the bones. Discard all fat, and remove the skin if you wish. Combine the tamari, garlic, and toasted sesame oil in a bowl, and add the fryer pieces. Marinate, covered, in the refrigerator for at least two hours, tossing occasionally to coat all the sides with the marinade.

Preheat the oven to 400 degrees. Place the fryer pieces in a roasting pan with space between them and bake them for at least 35 minutes, or until well done.

Hungarian chicken paprikas

a great dish to feed up to 12 from one old hen
Feeds 8 or 12
To feed 8:
2 stalks celery, sliced thin
2 large onions
4 cloves garlic, minced
2 Tablespoons olive oil
1 chicken, cut into pieces
1 teaspoon freshly ground black pepper
6 Tablespoons sweet paprika
1/2 cup water
2 bay leaves
6 cups water
1 cup dark beer
2 Tablespoons tamari or
1 teaspoon salt
2 1-lb. cans tomatoes
3 1/2 cups rice
2 Tablespoons lemon juice
parsley for garnish
yogurt or sour cream for garnish

In an 8 quart dutch oven or stockpot, braise the celery, onion, and garlic in the olive oil. Each time the vegetables begin to brown, add 2 tablespoons of water and cook till the water evaporates and the vegetables acquire a golden glaze.

Add the chicken pieces, black pepper, paprika, and 1/2 cup water. Cook uncovered, stirring frequently, until the water is evaporated and the ingredients are beginning to brown.

Then add the bay leaves, 6 cups water, beer, and tamari or salt. Bring to a boil, then turn the heat to medium-low and simmer gently until the chicken is tender, anywhere from 35 minutes to 2 hours depending on the age of the chicken and the size of the pieces.

Remove the chicken pieces to a cutting board, draining carefully to keep the juices in the pot. Cut the meat into bite sized pieces, discarding the bones, skin, and fat. Return the chicken meat to the pot and add the tomatoes, rice, and lemon juice. Bring back to the boil and turn the heat to medium-low, cooking slowly until the rice is tender and the sauce thick, about an hour.

Serve hot, with a garnish of yogurt or sour cream and a sprinkle of chopped fresh parsley. To really get in a Hungarian mood, serve this with braised red cabbage, pumpernickel bread, and dark beer!

For 12, use one and one-half times all ingredients except the chicken. You will find the dish is still plenty hearty. Δ

Pie recipes

By Jennifer Stein

Ah, the aroma of a baking pie! It's hard to resist, and when the pie comes out of the oven, those who didn't do the work of baking it have been known to give in to the temptation to steal a taste before the pie is even cool enough to cut. The cook guards his or her work jealously until it reaches that point of perfection, then serves it proudly as the centerpiece of a meal for everyone to admire.

Today's pies have a reputation for being fattening, sugary, and empty of nutrition, but it hasn't always been that way. In the middle ages, a pie was a main dish, the hearty pastry serving both as a container for the juicy meats and vegetable cooked within, and a bread to sop up the juices. Today's Cornish Pastry is the descendant of that pie, and Cornish workers tuck them in their lunchboxes to eat cold out of hand as the noonday meal.

Dessert pies don't have to be full of sugar and butter either. Ripe, luscious fruit needs only enough sweetener to bring out the flavor, and a binder to keep the juices in the pastry instead of running over the plate. Whole wheat crust goes well with either a main dish pie or a full-flavored dessert pie.

Whole wheat crust! Cooks have always been scared of it, but why not put a wholesome crust around your nutritious filling? When I first wanted to make one, everyone told me it was impossible to make a whole wheat crust that wouldn't be tough or fall apart when it was rolled out. Well, it is possible, but you have to forget everything you know about white-flour-and-shortening pie crusts. Whole wheat, if you treat it gently and handle it well, can produce a crisp, tender crust that will do justice to the savory main dish filling, or sweet and tangy fruit filling.

Whole wheat pie crust

Makes one crust:
1 cup flour
1/4 cup milk
2 Tablespoons canola or safflower oil

Measure the flour into a heavy bowl. Then, drizzle the oil slowly into the flour while tossing the flour with a fork. The oil should form little droplets in the flour, about the consistency of coarse cornmeal.

You may have to adjust the milk measure. Flour soaks up differing amounts of moisture depending on the humidity where you live. Start with 1/4 cup of milk. With a spoon, fold the milk **gently** into the flour mixture. The idea is not to break the little droplets of oil. If the dough has a tendency to break, add more milk to your recipe a teaspoon at a time. If you get the dough too soft to handle, it's a simple matter to sprinkle a teaspoon of flour over the dough to soak up the extra moisture.

When the dough holds together well, dust your hands lightly with flour. Take up the ball of dough and fold and work it gently into a ball. When it comes together well, set the ball back in the bowl and let it rest for a minute before rolling it out.

Flour the board lightly, then with your hands flatten the ball of dough into a disk and lay it on the floured board. Roll it out a little larger than your pie plate, using gentle strokes with the rolling pin. To transfer it to the pie plate, fold it in quarters or roll it round the rolling pin. Do not rim the crust until you have put the filling in and the top crust on (if used). To put the top crust on, moisten the edges of the bottom crust with milk. Place the top crust over the filling, and pinch the edges gently together all around the pie. Do not fold the crust over. Trim the edges even with the edge of the pie plate.

Savory vegetable pie

We had broccoli and carrots in the fridge, and a pot of sorrel on the window sill, so that's what we used. Design your own pie to use what's in your fridge and on your spice shelf (how about cabbage, mushrooms, onion, dill and thyme?) Makes one 9" pie.

> 1 Tablespoons olive oil
> 1 onion, chopped
> 2 cloves garlic, minced
> 1 medium potato
> 1 stalk celery
> 1 carrot, sliced thin
> 1 lb. can tomatoes, chopped with juice
> 1 stalk broccoli
> 1 1/2 teaspoon tarragon
> 4 sorrel leaves, chopped
> 1/2 cup frozen peas
> 1/4 cup dry sherry
> 2 Tablespoons tamari
> 1 dash Tabasco
> 1 Tablespoon cornstarch

Heat the olive oil in a heavy skillet and add the chopped onion and garlic. Braise and re-glaze as follows: saute the vegetables on medium-high until they begin to stick to the pan and turn golden brown on the bottom. Add a couple of tablespoons of water, stir, and repeat the process until a golden haze coats all the onions and garlic. Add the rest of the vegetables as you prepare them, along with just enough liquid (water or tomato juice from the can) to prevent sticking. Quarter the potato and slice it thin, then slice the celery and the carrot. Add the tomatoes from the can, the broccoli, tarragon, sorrel leaves, and peas. Turn the heat to low and allow the flavors to blend for a few minutes, while you mix the sherry, tamari, Tabasco and cornstarch in a cup. Dissolve the cornstarch well, then pour the mixture over the vegetables. Cook gently until the mixture thickens, then pour the vegetables into a pie shell and cover with a top crust. Cut vents in the crust and bake for about 40 minutes at 375 degrees, until the crust is golden brown. Allow to rest for 10 minutes before serving.

Rhubarb pie

Rhubarb used to be called "pie plant" for a good reason. If you don't have one in your yard, you should, and here's why: Makes one 9" pie.

> 1 cup honey
> 2 Tablespoons cornstarch
> 3 Tablespoons flour
> 7 cups (about 2 pounds) diced rhubarb
> 1/4 teaspoon cinnamon
> 1/4 teaspoon ground cloves
> 2 teaspoons grated orange rind

Mix the cornstarch, flour, cinnamon, cloves, and orange rind. Pour them over the rhubarb, and toss to coat. Drizzle in the honey, and stir until it coats everything. Pour the mixture into an unbaked pie shell and smooth the top as well as you can, then cover with a top crust. Cut vents in the top crust. Bake at 375 degrees for 45-50 minutes, until you can see the filling bubbling and thick through the vents and the crust is golden. Allow to cool on a rack before serving.

(Note to readers: this article on pies was written in response to a special request. Is there something you've always wanted a recipe for? Please send requests for vegetarian recipes to the editor, Backwoods Home Magazine, 1257 Siskiyou Blvd., #213, Ashland, OR 97520, and he will forward them to me.) Δ

Immortality

The oldest tombstones
In this cemetery
Are barely
A hundred years old
And already
The names are fading.

John Earl Silveira
Ojai, CA

Using your "stockman's eye" to care for your livestock

By Kelly Klober

To see them for what they are and to see them for what they need, the stock raiser needs a very special kind of sight.

Actually, it is a form of insight that comes from experience and study of the animals one works with every day. This skill, this insight, is termed the "stockman's eye". The stockman's eye enables the producer to focus all of his or her senses on the animals being raised to determine their level of comfort and well being and to take a truly honest reading of their condition and quality.

My grandfather had a lifetime of experience with draft animals and livestock and he began his day among his animal charges and he ended it there, too. He would walk among them looking, listening, and even smelling for anything out of place or upsetting to the creatures about him. It also made them more comfortable with the human presence and easier to handle and restrain when treatment was needed.

The 30 minutes just before full daylight and just before sunset are perhaps the best times of day to monitor the state of a herd or flock. They are good times to check for signs of estrus or imminent birth, observe for respiratory problems, and watch for any injuries or changes in condition from the day or night just passed.

Look and listen to your stock

The best advice to give a beginning stock raiser, one wishing to develop the stockman's eye, is to go out often and just look at and listen to the animals being tended. Begin focusing on them even before the pen or housing is reached and learn what is normal behavior. For example, when approached, a pen of healthy pigs will quickly rise up, move to the opposite side of the pen, and then work their way back toward the visitor out of curiosity.

As an animal rises up or lies down it presents an excellent opportunity for examination for potential health problems. The feet and legs are most clearly displayed and lameness and some of its causes may be more clearly noted. Do joints appear swollen? Is there injury to a hoof or hooves? Do hooves appear chipped or cracked? Is there tightness in a shoulder? Does the animal move away with a mincing or shortened gait? Is a foot being put down in an unnatural way? Is an animal lying down more than is the norm or otherwise favoring a limb?

Check respiratory activity

It is also a good time to note respiratory activity. Is the animal taking short, irregular breaths or breathing in a hard, rasping manner? This is sometimes termed "thumping". Does the animal pant or cough upon coming to its feet or after a short bit of exertion? It could mean simple, flu-like symptoms or maybe a developing pneumonia. In fact, it may be best to pause outside of a building or a short way from a pen and listen for sounds of irregular or hard breathing or congestion before moving up on the animals.

As well as the senses of sight and sound, the senses of touch and smell can be used to evaluate an animal's state of well being. For example, the fecal material produced by pigs stricken with the disease TGE (transmissible gastroenteritis) quite often has a most distinctive odor, quickly making it distinct from the diarrheal symptoms of other baby pig diseases. As for the sense of touch, there is no better means of evaluating the condition of a bottle calf than to pop a finger in its mouth. If the mouth feels cold and the animal displays little or no nursing activity and interest, it is a calf with some very real problems. Rubbing the hand down a lamb's back is the time honored approach to measure fleshing and body condition.

A symptom of many health problems, one with very real consequences of its own, is dehydration. A young animal moving much beyond 5% dehydration is in very real danger of going into shock. A good measure of the degree of dehydration is to

pinch up a fold of skin in the shoulder region and then watch how long it takes for it to return to its natural position. The slower it is to return to position, the less elastic it is, and the more dehydrated the animal is.

Focus at animals' level

For the senses to give the most exacting reading of the state of the animals they must be focused at the animal's level in the environment. How things are functioning at animal level is not easily determined with a simple walk-through. Are waterers and feeders operating properly? Are the animals truly comfortable? Are there rough surfaces, raised nails or bolt heads or draft sources at animal level?

The producer experiences most things at his or her head and shoulder level. A few years ago we had a few pigs develop a problem with navel ill and hard knots developing on their abdomens. It could have been genetic and pointing to a weakness in herd genetics. Tracking the problem, we traced the pigs all back to one farrowing hut with a 2x4 nailed to the floor at the mouth of the pig bunk. Climbing over that kept the navel area raw and set the stage for the navel ill to develop. We were able to clear that problem up in a couple of minutes with a crowbar.

Variations from normal behavior

The stockman's eye is attuned to the slightest variation from normal behavior. I've heard it said that the good hands catch them when they're not even sick, just thinking about it. An animal that removes itself from the group, goes off of feed (one of Dad's first tests of just how sick an animal was was to offer it a choice morsel of food), holds the head at an odd angle, appears unusually dirty or shows other haircoat irregularities or appears listless is sending out a message that it doesn't feel well or is undergoing some sort of stress or discomfort. Detecting some of these more subtle signs will take the full focus of the producer.

The earlier a health problem is detected the quicker it can be solved and at the least cost. Treatment options are often more varied with early detection also. Logging symptoms as they develop also helps with the diagnosis and can be a real help if the vet has to be called in to pinpoint the problem. And call him or her in quickly before you have a real wreck on your hands with little or nothing to save or salvage.

Appraising an animal begins, quite literally, from the ground up. The positioning of the animal's feet and legs, it's stance, can tell a great deal about the animal. A calf that looks like all four feet would fit in a teacup with back bowed high, and leaning against a gate or wall is trying to ease obvious internal discomfort. An unusually arched back, mincing steps or a walking-on-tiptoe appearance, and a reluctance to rise are all ways an animal expresses pain or its efforts to ease pain.

Signs of ailing

Signs to look for about the head of a potentially ailing animal include: a dull, sunken eye; discharge from the eyes or evidence of it by streaking down the face from the corners of the eyes; a clouded or discolored eye; sniffling or a nasal discharge; the head cocked sharply to one side; excessive head shaking; and knots and abscesses along the jaw line. Especially to be noted in hogs are signs of twisting, swelling or other misalignment of the snout as they are classic symptoms of the performance-robbing disease, atrophic rhinitis. An animal with a head that appears too large for its body or has long, coarse hair on the head has been stunted.

Equally as telling can be the haircoat itself. Flat, matted down, dull looking, discolored with fecal matter or hair on end is typical of animals undergoing some type of stress. A litter of baby pigs all piled together and with hair on end are badly chilled. Erect hair is the body's effort to hold whatever traces of warmth are possible.

Signs of trauma or infection can take the form of small abscesses or pockets of swelling under the skin. Old timers in the Midwest call such abscesses "walnuts". Typical injuries can range from cuts and puncture wounds to dislocations and sprains to broken limbs. The hands-on approach will be necessary to determine the extent and full involvement of any injury and points up the need for the animals to be comfortable with the human presence and accustomed to regular handling.

The estrus cycle

The estrus cycle also triggers a group of activities in farm animals that are readily identifiable. We once owned a Guernsey heifer that hit the road at nearly every one of her heat cycles and led us on many a merry chase. This increased walking activity at the time of estrus is quite common in cattle and to determine estrus in dairy cows to be artificially inseminated, a type of pedometer is often attached to a hind foot. When a reading indicates increased walking activity, one begins checking for other signs of estrus.

Typical indications of the onset of estrus include an enlarged and reddened vulva (the external female genital organ), a possible slight discharge from the vulva, roaming or other ill at ease behavior, sniffing of the genitalia, and attempts to mount or ride another female. The female doing the riding is the one most often in season. A hog in standing heat will respond with erect ears and by standing rigidly still when pressure is applied to the hindquarters just above the hams.

Similar behavior can be noted as the time for birth approaches. Things to watch for can include increased walking activity and the female removing herself from the herd or flock to a more isolated area; some type of nest building activity in some species; enlargement, reddening, and possible discharge from the vulva; moving in a circular pattern and sniffing at the ground; twisting toward and sniffing at the hindquarters; enlargement of the udder segments; and the presence of milk. Not all of these indications will be present at every birth however.

At each observed birth, the producer must determine when things are going well, when nature is on course, and when some human intervention is needed. A first delivery will probably be the most stressful and a bit prolonged, but any birth process in which labor has been unproductive and prolonged, blood is being discharged or an out of place limb is being presented, signals that intervention is needed. In most species, this point comes 2 to 4 hours into the labor. In the farrowing process baby pigs arrive at intervals of roughly every 20 minutes or less with the smallest pigs arriving at the beginning and end of the farrowing.

A female that does a lot of getting up and lying down, circles the birth area a great deal, strains excessively or otherwise demonstrates a great deal of stress needs attention. The young could be improperly positioned, the young animal could be excessively large or otherwise abnormal or the birth canal blocked. The passing of a weak or dead animal through the birth canal will take longer as all of the effort of the delivery must come from the female.

The greatest number of births go quickly and simply with no need for intervention. In fact the tendency is to get involved too quickly and when there is really no need. The literature is full of examples of a litter of pigs being farrowed over a period of several days and twin calves born many days apart. A female that cannot deliver and get her young off to a good start should be seriously considered for culling from the herd or flock. The best thing to learn in preparation for an expected birth is good old fashioned patience.

Even with the birth process passed, the producer needs to remain observant as the female moves to tend her new offspring. A slight clear or whitish discharge from the vulva can be expected following a birth, but should it turn dark, thick, blood-tinged or foul smelling, a problem is at hand. The female should be observed closely to be sure she returns to her feet safely and that she has milk and all young get to nurse. The first milk or colostrum imparts a great deal of natural immunity to the young and is a must for their survival. The udder should be monitored for signs of hardening, fever and/or loss of milk flow. All are signs of an infection or complex most often termed 'milk fever'.

Signs of health

A healthy farm animal will have a bright, alert manner; the eyes will be clear and bright; the haircoat bright and clean; will move freely and easily; have a good appetite; display a bit of curiosity about what is going on around it; maintain good body fill; regularly drink; have good bowel and urinary function; and appear comfortable and at ease in its environment. Changes in temperament, withdrawal from pen mates, a gaunt appearance, excessive urination, constipation, diarrhea, and soundness problems are all rather obvious, but the stockman's eye can and will pick up on much subtler signs of looming health problems and quite early.

Is that last shoat out of the bedding in the morning a sick pig or just a lazy one? Is that cow in the far corner of the pasture near to calving or just enjoying a choice bit of grazing? Is that old ewe losing condition to age and bad teeth to parasites? Sometimes the stockman's eye doesn't even detect any hard evidence, just a feeling that something isn't right, that the animal has a need for something more. A $5.00 investment in a rectal thermometer will do much to either assuage or verify that feeling that all is not right.

Fever is a part of the body's effort to throw off infection and is one indication that natural systems are still in working order. More to be feared actually are below normal temperature readings. The normal rectal temperatures of the more common farm animals are: 101.5F for cattle, 103F for sheep, 104F for goats, 102F for hogs, 102F for dogs, and 102.5F for rabbits.

Making those incisive early calls comes from day-to-day experience and contact with the animals on the smallholding. The producer knows the animals in his or her care as individuals, has chosen or bred them for the home farm which is like no other, and sees in them their weaknesses as well as their strengths. He or she will know which trimester of pregnancy a female is in, what rations are being fed to them, when they were last treated for parasites and with what, whether there is a family history of health problems, and will be breeding to correct existing weaknesses.

The eye and other senses were the first tools of the stockman's calling, the first calling of civilized man. For them there can never be a replacement. Δ

The Glen

Remember that hike when you flushed the quail?
We stumbled on that hidden trail.

It led us over a rocky-ridge, needling the brush,
Running through a glen where the breeze whispered hush.

There wasn't a soul anywhere in sight,
Sunlit by day—moonlit by night.

When we took a deep breath, the air was sweet,
Honeysuckle and morning-glory tangled our feet.

It appeared to us, the place we found
Was some forgotten sacred ground.

It seemed to be a thousand miles away
From any development of our day.

But all to soon, the things we cherish
Become discovered and then they perish.

Recently, I returned to that hidden place
Where I could embrace nature face to face.

Sadly I had my fill
Discovering the clear-cut hills.

There were no trees, no grouse,
Just broken down cars framing a trailer house.

Hal Meili, Cheney, WA

The Third Year

Make a colonial shoulder yoke

By Don Fallick

Our Colonial ancestors certainly knew what they were doing when they devised the carrying-yoke. As anyone who has ever had to haul water to animals by the bucket has discovered, there just has to be a better way! The water sloshes all over you, your hands die a thousand deaths, and it feels like your arms are about to be torn from their sockets. A carrying yoke ends all these problems and is **easy** to make.

Wood

Begin by selecting a piece of sound wood 6" x 8" or larger and at least 16" longer than the width of your shoulders. Exact dimensions aren't critical, and the wood can be of any handy species, but it must be free from large knots and splits. If you use a hunk of a round log, it should be at least 8" in diameter, to take advantage of the strong heart wood at the center of the log.

It's best to cut your rough piece a few inches longer than you anticipate needing. When the yoke's done it'll be simple enough to trim any excess off, and even if you don't use the extra inches, it's handy to have some place to hold on to the wood while you're working it.

If you're working down a log, strip all the bark off right at the beginning. It makes it easier to draw on the wood with a carpenter's pencil, felt-tip marker, or lumber crayon. Wood is **much** easier to shape when it's "green", but the dimensions will change as the wood shrinks so make your yoke a little oversize and wait til it has seasoned a month or two before doing the final fitting.

Lay-out

Begin by drawing the top view of the completed yoke on the top and bottom surfaces of the wood. If you are using a 6x8, the 8-inch dimension should be horizontal. Now turn the piece 90 degrees, and make a series of vertical saw cuts 1 inch apart, down to the lines for the **back** surface. See figure 1. Then turn the piece over and repeat the procedure for the **front** surface, including the **neck cut-out**. Finally, chop the scrap out from between the saw cuts with a mallet and chisel, as in figure 2. You now have the front and back contours roughed out.

Rest the yoke on its back and draw the top and bottom views on the front and rear surfaces. Saw down to the lines and rough out with mallet and chisel as before. The yoke should look something like figure 3. The next step is to hollow out the shoulder cavity.

Draw the cavity as wide as the shoulders of the person who will be using the yoke. Leave about 2 inches between the back of the cavity and the rear surface of the yoke. Part of the scrap can be removed by sawing and roughing out, but the actual hollowing has to be done with a gouge, or an in-shave, or with a very narrow straight chisel. I have even used a piece of bent steel pipe cut and sharpened on a 35 degree diagonal, then heated in the stove to cherry red and quenched in used crankcase oil. It doesn't hold an edge as well as an "official" chisel, but it sufficed for hollowing 3 yokes and cost nothing at all. See figure 5.

Smooth curves

At this point your yoke still has lots of excess wood on it. Round off all the corners with a draw knife or a rasp. The easiest way to do this is to clamp one end of the yoke in a shaving bench and shave the rest of the yoke down, then reverse the yoke and shave the other end. See the accompanying article on the construction and use of a shaving bench. If you don't have a shaving bench or a draw knife, a large vise and a coarse rasp or surface forming plane will work.

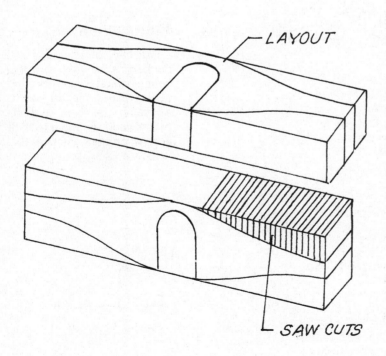

LAYOUT

SAW CUTS

Figure 1.

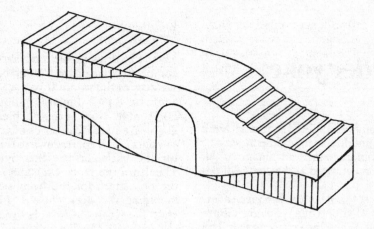

Figure 2. Knocking out scrap with mallet and chisel.

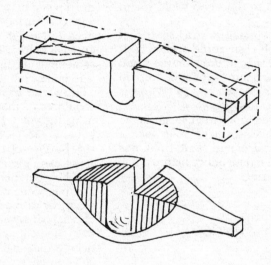

Figure 3. Rough-out yoke.

Thin the wood all over so all the curves are smooth and the wood around the shoulders is no thicker than 1 1/2 inches. The arms where the buckets hang should taper to 2" diameter. It is important to get the **curves** smooth, as jagged areas not only can catch on clothing, they actually weaken the finished yoke. Also, you're going to have to carry this thing, along with the weight of the water, so you want to get it as light as possible while preserving strength.

Be sure to thoroughly round, thin, and smooth around the neck hole. If the yoke will be worn over bulky winter clothing, make the neck hole extra large. I allow at least 6 inches for the neck. The surface can be rasped and sanded as smooth as you like, or you can just scrape off the splinters with a broken piece of glass. See figure 4.

Fitting

The secret to comfortable hauling with a yoke is in the fit. Each yoke must be custom-fitted to its user, or the whole weight of the load will bear on the shoulder bones, causing intense pain. Rest the yoke on the user's shoulders and mark where it hurts. Remove some wood there and try it on again. When you think it's right, try it with a couple of buckets of water.

When the shoulders fit perfectly, hang the buckets from the arms and see where the ropes need to go to place the bucket handles in comfortable reach of the hands. Mark the spots on the yoke arms and cut, saw, or chop a notch in the top of the arms there, to keep the ropes from sliding. It's handy to add another notch an inch to either side of each main notch, to aid in balancing loads of uneven weight. Carry the heaviest weight close to the body.

Ropes and hooks

You can, of course, just tie your buckets to the yoke with a couple of baling twines. This works OK, but it's unnatural to squat down with the yoke on your shoulders to pick up the twines and loop them over the yoke's arms when you want to lift the buckets. It feels a lot better to have the ropes

Figure 4. Ready to fit.

hanging from the yoke, with hooks on the ends of the ropes. In this way, you keep your hands hanging down below your waist all the time, making it much easier to balance with the yoke on your shoulder. S-hooks from the hardware store work fine, or you can make your own out of 20d nails, or a forked stick, for authenticity. Metal hooks are not as prone to breaking as forked sticks are. If you use a stick and it breaks, you'll probably end up with **both** buckets of water dumped on you!

Using the yoke

It may take you a while to get the hang of walking with 80 lbs. of water swinging at knee level. Adjust the ropes so you can hold the bucket handles comfortably, to steady them. It's best to let them swing naturally, **a little**, to avoid sloshing. With practice, you'll be able to carry two **full**, lidless buckets over fairly rough terrain without spilling a drop. It requires a

sort of a skating motion, to eliminate much of the up-and-down movement of normal walking. A side benefit of carrying water with a yoke is that it lowers your center of gravity, making it nearly impossible for you to fall, once you get used to the increased inertia. Δ

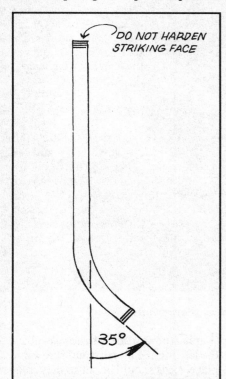

Figure 5. Making a bent pipe gouge. Heat pipe and bend to 35 degrees, then cut and grind face to make a bent gouge. Reheat face to cherry red and quench in oil to harden edge.

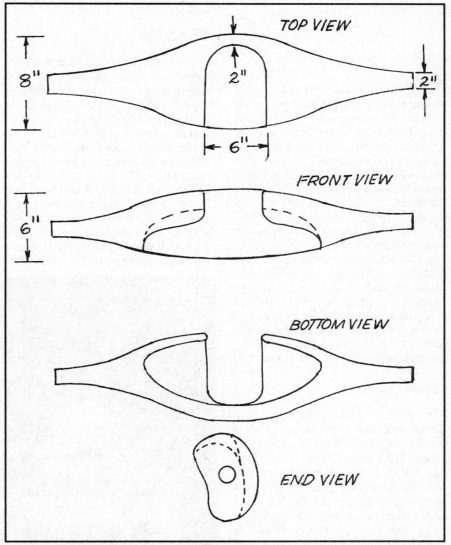

Figure 6.

*I would like to lie in bed,
And watch you put on your makeup in the morning,
And wonder what changes
You were trying to effect,
And try to figure out who it is
You are trying to become,
When you stand before your mirror,
Putting on your makeup in the morning.
And maybe I would know who you are now.*

John Earl Silveira
Ojai, CA

Build a shaving horse

By Don Fallick

Old time woodworkers used a home-made "shaving horse" or shaving bench, to clamp odd-shaped and round pieces of wood, allowing them to produce their own tool handles, chair legs, even carrying yokes, easily and with minimal tools. The bench provides a sturdy place for the worker to sit, and a solid clamp for the wood to be worked, with "geometry" designed to greatly amplify the woodworker's power.

A shaving horse can be made from virtually any kind of materials handy, even un-barked logs, and will give many years of service with minimal care. Best of all, exact dimensions and techniques are not required to make one, so the project is well within the abilities of even the novice carpenter.

The bench

A shaving horse is nothing but a large, massive "saw horse" with a device on one end for clamping the wood. See Figure 1. Traditional shaving horses in the Appalachians had three legs, since they were mostly used outdoors on uneven terrain, but other European traditions produced horses with four legs, so either design is authentic. Shaving horses I have seen were all about six feet long, to give the woodworker room to maneuver. Most had massive bench tops made out of split 8-inch diameter logs, or 6x8 timbers. The exact dimensions are not at all critical, but the top should be stiff enough not to flex at all, wide enough to be comfortable to straddle, and thick enough to provide adequate support for the legs, especially in the direction along the length of the horse. That's the direction you'll be pulling and leaning when you use the horse. See Figure 5.

The table

At one end of the horse is a sloping "table", to support the work, and provide a hinge point for the swinging "head", which actually clamps the work. The table should be about 2 1/2 feet long, and should be set at such an angle that it points just below your elbows when you are in working position. The table is supported by the bench itself at one end, and by a short block of wood at the end facing the worker. Attach the table to the block with wooden pegs or dowels, or at least with **deeply** countersunk screws, to avoid damage to the drawknife

Don Fallick works on his shaving horse.

blade if it should slip and contact the table. If you make the table about 2 inches thick, and as wide as the bench, it will have adequate strength to support the head. Both the table and the bench itself will have to be morticed to pass the neck of the dumbhead, and the table will also have to have a hole drilled through it horizontally to receive the hinge pin. A long, 3/8" bolt

makes an adequate pin. Leave it loose so the jaw opening can be adjusted.

Legs

Legs can either be flat lumber, morticed into the bench seat, like a conventional sawhorse, or can be round branches of trees, set into holes drilled in the seat. Round legs should be 2-3 inches in diameter for strength. One way to secure them is to slit the upper ends and wedge them like an axe handle. If you do this, **be sure** the width of the wedge is pointing across the grain of the seat, to avoid splitting the seat when the wedge is driven.

Or make flat legs from 2x4s or 2x6s. To accurately fit a flat leg, so there is no play in it, lay it on the edge of the seat and scribe along it with a pencil. Then saw the edges of the mortice about 1/32" **within** these lines. After

shaping the mortice with a chisel, drive the leg into the mortice and screw it in place. Legs should be set so they splay outward for stability, and be long enough to raise the seat to a comfortable height of 18-20 inches.

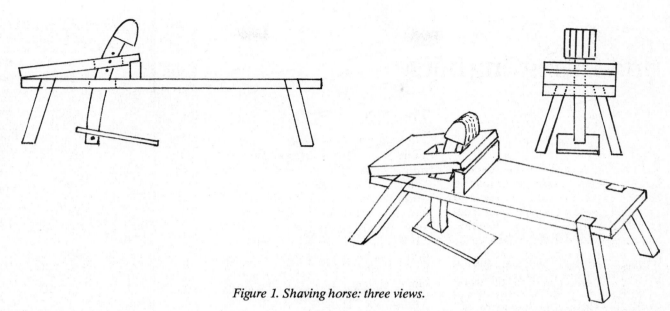

Figure 1. Shaving horse: three views.

The working parts

The clamp gains its power from the fact that it acts like a lever, multiplying the strength of the leg muscles. To maximize this clamping power, maximize the ratio of the lower section (treadle to hinge pin) to the **effective** upper section (hinge pin to **bottom** of jaw). The top part of the head, above the jaw, must be massive to keep the jaw from breaking off, but it does not affect this ratio. In other words, make the lower section of the shaft as long as your legs and the height of the bench will allow, and the upper section as short as the thickness of the work to be grasped will allow.

Because you will likely be working pieces of different thicknesses, you'll need to make the jaw opening adjustable. This is done by making several holes in the dumbhead's neck, so the hinge pin can be moved. You'll need to allow for this when planning the length of the dumbhead. Make the hinge holes along the **front** side of the shaft (the side towards the user), so the jaw will tend to fall open, instead of closed. This will greatly facilitate repositioning the work.

The dumbhead

The dumbhead can be made from a 30" length of a 6" diameter log, or a similar piece of a 6x8 or larger timber. Use wood that's hard to split if you've got some. It can be difficult to envision the finished dumbhead within a round log, so I recommend starting with an already squared piece of a timber, or laminating one from 2x8 "dimension" lumber. If you laminate a dumbhead from 2x8s, be sure to glue and securely bolt the laminations together. Counter-sink the bolt heads and nuts if possible to avoid striking them with the edge of your drawknife in use.

In carving the dumbhead, carve the neck first. It's easiest to see what you're doing if you carve the front view first, then the side view. See Figures 2 and 3. Leave the head until last. When the neck is nearly finished, turn the dumbhead upside down and chop the head to shape with a hatchet. It need not be fancy. The idea is simply to get as much of the wood out of the way of the user as possible, while maintaining

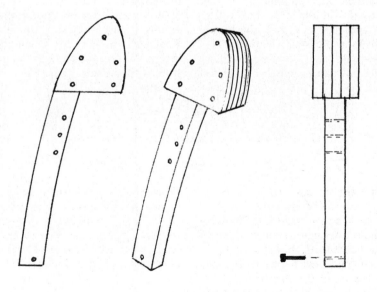

Figure 2. Dumbhead.

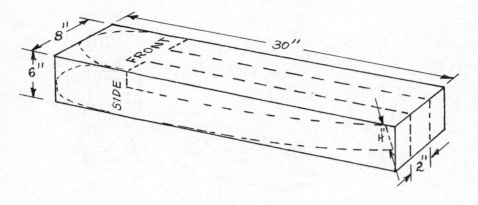

Figure 3. Laying out dumbhead on a 6 x 8 x 30 block.

the massive strength needed to sustain the constant pressure on the jaw.

Finish the neck smooth and square before making the treadle. The treadle must fit fairly tightly, yet be able to slide up and down the neck several inches. If you make the treadle first, **then** finish the dumbhead neck, the neck will be smaller than planned and may fit too loosely on the neck.

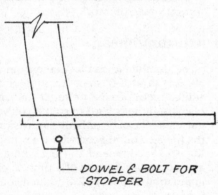

— DOWEL & BOLT FOR STOPPER

Figure 4. Treadle detail.

The treadle

The treadle is nothing more than a board with a rectangular hole near one end, fit loosely enough so it can slide up and down the neck about 6 to 8 inches. A scrap of 3/4" plywood works well. If you're working a particularly long piece of wood and have to sit right at the end of the shaving horse, you can slide the treadle up the neck to a comfortable position. To keep the treadle from sliding right off, pin the bottom of the neck with a bolt or a dowel. It

need not be terribly strong. The pressure on the treadle is taken up in friction on the neck, not on the pin at the bottom. See Figure 4.

Using the shaving horse

Adjust the jaw to the narrowest opening that will easily pass the work piece. Clamp the piece in the jaw with steady foot pressure on the treadle. You'll be amazed how little foot pressure is needed to securely clamp most objects. The best tool to use with a shaving horse is a draw knife or draw shave. These come in many styles, with straight or curved blades, handles at various angles, etc. For a beginner, a draw knife with a slightly curved blade and handles bent at almost a right angle to the blade is probably the easiest to use. Use it with the bevel **down** to take off long, slender shavings. Bevel **up** takes off more wood at a stroke, but can be much harder to control.

To get the feel of using a shaving bench, clamp a piece of scrap or firewood in the jaw and just practice taking off shavings. Work rhythmically and **watch the work piece**. Keeping your elbows in, toward your body will prevent you from endangering yourself with the razor-sharp blade. Stop every few seconds and release pressure on the treadle just enough to turn the work a bit, then resume. With only a few minutes practice, you can see the piece taking shape right before your eyes. Even a beginner looks impressive using a drawknife and shaving horse. Finish by scraping the wood smooth.

In the old days, most woodworkers had an assortment of spokeshaves and other smoothing tools for specialized jobs, but satisfactory results can be obtained by simply scraping the finished work with the edge of a piece of broken glass. When the edge gets dull or chipped, re-break the glass or find another piece. Of course, it's a good idea to wear leather gloves whenever handling broken glass.

Good company

Using a shaving bench is one of the most relaxing activities there is. There's something really down-to-earth about watching the shavings pile up while turning out stacks of beautiful tools, furniture parts, and other useful objects with effortless ease. President Jimmy Carter certainly thought so. That's why he kept **his** shaving horse in the White House basement the whole time he lived there. Δ

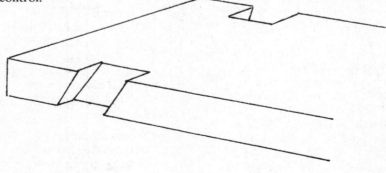

Figure 5. Bench top, morticed for 2 x 4 leg, splayed to the side and front.

Finding, growing, and eating Asian mustards

By Anne Westbrook Dominick

I love mustards and those called Chinese sometimes, Oriental others, are on the grow. They're growing literally (quick, early, and late season crops) and figuratively (more and more kinds in more and more seed catalogs).

About as pungent as any green can be, their foliage's nippy flavors range from the smooth clean bite of Green in Snow, to the multifaceted flavor of namfong, to the comparatively mild mizuna or Japanese Greens in China.

A brief history

Along with barley, wheat, and legumes it was among our first herbaceous foods. Native to Eurasia, mustards were embraced wherever sent. Enjoyed by the early Grecians and Romans, it took the Christian, Matthew, to record its importance. "The kingdom of heaven is like a mustard seed which a man took and sowed in his field; indeed it is the least of all seeds, but when it has grown, it is the greatest among herbs and becometh a tree, so that the birds of the air come and lodge in the branches thereof." (Mustard's height today ranges from one to six feet.) Made immortal in the bible, by the Middle Ages arrived mustard was a major foodstuff throughout most of the then-known world.

Both seeds and leaves were used. In India, where mustard was and is a dietary mainstay even among the extremely poor, both are crucial: seeds for flavor, foliage for nutrition. The leaves, which are fibrous without being stringy, are an excellent source of vitamins A, B1, B2, and C. The seeds, from early on, were used whole as a spice, crushed for their oil. To this day, the seeds attributes create the condiment used world-wide. Not

enough in olden days to be only a potherb and spice, mustard also had to heal and that it did: helping cure headaches, fevers, whooping cough, asthma, liver, stomach, and throat ailments.

Mustard is a crucifer, nowadays a Brassicaceae, along with broccolis, Brussel sprouts, cabbages, cauliflowers, kale, kohlrabi, rutabagas, and turnips.

3 ways to eat them

Alone mustards provide three distinct eatings:

- One, the condiment we call "mustard" and slop on hot dogs is the finished product of Brassica nigra or "black mustard." B. nigra is still grown commercially for those seeds. It grows 6 feet tall.

- Two, we use the seeds whole when pickling or in Indian (from India, not Native American) dishes. Powdered, these same seeds are the bright yellow, dry and very hot mustard we use on meat or fish for a bit of a bite. These are from B. hirta, formerly (as late as 1943) known as B. alba and still called "white mustard," which is still grown commercially for those seeds. It grows 4 feet tall.

- Three, we eat the leaves raw in salads or cooked as a potherb. Most mustards grown for their foliage are B. juncea, commonly called "brown mustard." Known these days as "Chinese mustard," it is a species of many names

and many forms. It is also the mustard I'm really writing about. The books say it grows 4 feet tall.

Now, the books aren't wrong, they just cover different varieties. In true American style, when we decided to develop a mustard to meet our needs, we took large B. juncea and made them larger.

Grown and enjoyed as a winter crop in the south, "Giant Southern Curled" or "Green Wave" or "Ostrich Plume" are of substantial size. Their leaves run about a foot and a half when harvested. Their seed stalks easily grow 4 to 6 feet high. But the B. juncea varieties sold specifically as Chinese mustards range from the "swollen stem mustard's" 8 inches to the "Green in Snow's" 20 inches.

Their seed stalks run 3 to 4 feet in height. Proportionately all mustards are long, broad leafed annuals that shoot seed stalks up when the weather turns hot. These are topped with four petaled, bright yellow flowers that become cylindrical seed pods which burst open when ripe.

Love cool weather

Oriental mustards grow in just about any soil, take 30 to 45 days from planting to harvesting, and produce two to three crops a year. Since they love cool weather, plant as early as possible in the spring and sow follow-ups every week or so until mid-May. For fall crops plant in August and September. As soon as young mustards are large enough to thin, thin them to six to eight inches apart and use in salads. With maturity they remain tasty in salads and become ideal ingredients in stir-fries or, in fact, just about any casserole.

Self-seeds well

Just as mustard grows quickly and easily for us, it self-seeds as well on its own. This has led many perfectionists to label mustard as: "weedy annual herbs," "nuisance," and even "very serious pests." This, I believe, is a stereotyping that took hold when mustard went wild on American farms. It did and does grow at will under certain conditions. I recall fall-plowed grain fields turning bright yellow from fence-line to fence-line before spring-planting. Unquestionably mustards are a hearty batch. A couple years ago a field in Chesterfield, New Hampshire, was plowed and by June it was one massive stretch of brilliant yellow. It was also abandoned. The next year it was put back into hay and the mustard never showed. It may be a rambunctious self-sewer but it doesn't take over. In fact, it is easily cropped out.

I always have a Chinese mustard self-seeding some place in the garden. The color is striking among the vegetables and, even mid-summer, there's a spicy green just waiting to be picked. If volunteers attempt a takeover, they are among the easiest pulled. Nor do they try to sprout new roots; once pulled, they're gone.

Interestingly mustard also stimulates soil micro-organisms, making it a decent green manure as long as the next crop isn't another crucifer. In fall as sections of the garden are cleaned up B. juncea can quickly germinate into a beneficial cover crop.

Some seed catalogs mention only one or two B. juncea, but a couple offer some very varied varieties including: namfong or "Chinese mustard cabbage" which is flavor at its ultimate, mizuna or "Japanese greens in China" which is a prime specimen for gourmet gardeners taking part in the mesclun fad (salad greens sown together for a one-spot mixed harvest), and "Swollen stem Chinese mustard" whose stem—technically its petiole—develops to be used like celery but with somewhat sweetened mustard flavor.

These and others should be tried for each is unique.

Two companies carrying a nice selection are:

- Stokes Seeds, Inc., Box 548, Buffalo, NY 14240
- Nichols Garden Nursery, 1190 North Pacific Highway, Albany, OR 97321.

Mustard greens as a stir-fry

1 pound mustard greens
1-2 tablespoons olive oil
1 clove garlic, minced
1 1/4 inch thick slice ginger root, minced
1/4 teaspoon sugar
1 teaspoon cornstarch
2 tablespoons water

Rinse and drain mustard greens and cut into bite sized chunks. Heat oil in skillet and fry garlic and ginger root for a few seconds. Add greens and stir to mix. Cover and cook, stirring occasionally, until barely tender—just a few minutes. Add a bit of water if mustard greens start to stick. Mix sugar, cornstarch, and water and add to mustard greens. Stir-fry until sauce thickens, another minute or so. Δ

Motes of dust,
My daughter saw
And asked,
"What kind of light
Is that
That sparkles?"
As a ray of sunshine
Fell upon the floor.
"Just dust?"
She asked,
At my reply,
"Just dust,"
I said,
She turned
And I
Watched her
As the wonder
Faded
From her eye.
Just dust.

John Earl Silveira
Ojai, CA

A BHM Writer's Profile

Richard Blunt writes a cooking column for *BHM* and is working with us to produce a cookbook that would, like his column, not just list a bunch of recipes but teach people how to cook.

A chef and dietary manager for 29 years, his first column appeared in *BHM's* Issue No. 19, which is not in this collection of issues. We mention him here because, if you are interested in cooking, his columns alone are worth your subscribing to *BHM*.

From chimney sweep to stone sculptor to worry wall, Ron Pruitt has decided his place is in the country

By Gary Williams
(Photos by Carl Carter)

Ron and Debbie Pruitt are used to doing things their way. From their beautiful self-built log home to Ron's current work in sandstone carving, the Summerfield, Ohio couple has pursued a completely self-sufficient lifestyle. And if recent successes are an indication, Ron and Debbie may be able to succeed in never punching a time clock again.

In using antique tools to fashion sandstone birdbaths and benches, Ron says he is reviving an old craft.

"This is stuff that everybody's great grandfather knew how to do and everybody had the tools. But mass production came along and nobody had any need for it anymore."

The Pruitts are throwbacks in other ways as well. For the past nine years, the couple has homesteaded on a 53 acre tract in Monroe County. They have designed and built their own home and subsisted with no job other than seasonal income from their business as S.O.S. Chimney Sweeps.

Ron and Debbie Pruitt built their log home themselves.

Ron Pruitt stands by his most recent sandstone creation — a beautifully symmetrical bird bath — in front of his Summerfield, Ohio home.

Ron and Debbie tried to live a more conventional lifestyle when they first got together. Ron worked as a steelworker in Cleveland but says, "I didn't like metal flake air and I didn't like living in the city." Taking advantage of property that Ron's father owned in Guernsey County, Ron and Debbie moved south and decided to become breadmakers instead of breadwinners.

A few years later they were able to buy land near Summerfield. The first summer on their land, they lived in an existing summer kitchen that now serves as a henhouse. Their goal that first year was to get a basement under roof before winter. With the help of neighbors who provided support, instruction, food and shelter, they were able to move in on Thanksgiving Day.

Help from neighbors played a big role in Ron and Debbie's learning of survival skills. Ron observes that the couple "learned to live on nothing, but the neighbors figured that if we were dumb enough to stay here, they'd better show us how to survive. If they think you're friendly and a hard

Ron and Debbie are proud of the unusual and efficient chimney which they designed and built for their rustic home.

One of Ron's first accomplishments was this sandstone birdbath.

Since then, he has completed five more birdbaths and a bench.

Ron gets much of his sandstone from abandoned barn foundations. When he suffers creative block or is otherwise unable to work, he stacks the stone on his "worry wall" at his outdoor studio. He hopes to be able to get grant money for an indoor studio in the near future.

Debbie Pruitt describes her husband's work as "trying to expand on what the tool can do." But it's obvious that the couple is expanding on what they can do as well. Δ

worker, they'll help. But if they think you're a bum, they won't."

Ron and Debbie soon became adept at gardening, canning, hunting and cutting firewood and this helped them get by without a steady source of income. Ron worked briefly in the CETA program, but he decided that

Ron at work on his "worry wall."

"if I couldn't do better than that on my own, then I'd starve."

For nine years, they swept chimneys, but most of that money went back into the house. A few years ago, they had enough money for indoor plumbing, but instead used the funds to purchase a Harley-Davidson motorcycle for Debbie to match the one Ron has. "You have to get your priorities straight," says Ron.

It was while building their fireplace that Ron discovered what he hopes will be his true calling. He was fascinated by stone work and with the aid of an antique stone scutcheon, or gangpick, that they purchased at the Muskingum Valley Trade Days in Reinersville, Ohio, he resolved to give stone sculpting a try.

Ron's first birdbath took over 200 hours of labor to complete but sold almost immediately. He entered his next birdbath in the Art on the Square show in Caldwell, Ohio, and took second place in the fine arts category.

July/August 1992
No. 16
$3.50 U.S.
$4.50 Canada

Backwoods
Home magazine

...a practical journal of self reliance!

FARM CRAYFISH
FOR A LIVING

DRIP IRRIGATION

SOLAR FOOD DRYER

DRIVING TO ALASKA

HOME VIDEO BUSINESS

TOM JEFFERSON/JOHN ADAMS

GROWING OLDER IN THE WOODS

Note from the publisher

A butt-burning and a raccoon dog

Since this is a "how to" magazine, I get a lot of people asking me how to do this or that. Since I'm no expert at anything, I just try and give them the best advice I can, but usually refer them to another "more expert" source.

But that wasn't the case when Maxine Montgomery, one of my nearest neighbors, asked me how I rigged up my temporary outdoor bathtub a couple of summers ago. "It's easy," I said. "Just put an old cast iron tub up on some rocks and light a fire under it. The more rocks around it the longer the water will stay warm because the rocks will retain heat for hours."

I forgot to tell her that I never sat in the tub because the bottom got too hot; I scooped water out and carried it into the tub inside the house. So she went home and put an old tub up on rocks, lit a fire under it, and when it got good and hot she sat down in the hot water and promptly burned her butt on the bottom of the tub. Her husband Doug laughed like hell. Max did too — after her bottom healed.

Now Maxine is wondering what to do about her 80-pound Rhodesian ridgeback dog named Squeaky. Twice in the past year she (the dog, not Maxine) has leaped through the living room window after spotting a raccoon outside. "Amazing dog," Doug said after replacing the window. "Didn't cut himself at all; didn't catch that damn raccoon either." I predicted Squeaky would jump through the window again before this issue went to print. If you have a suggestion to solve Squeaky's problem, drop us a line.

New BHM telephone: (503) 488-2053

We finally have an Oregon phone number. It is (503) 488-2053. The FAX is (503) 488-2063. Our former California number is now a recording.

Call Irwin for newsstand copies

If you can't find *Backwoods Home Magazine* on the newsstand, call our distributor, ADS, at 708-498-5014, and ask for Irwin Krimke. He's their national sales manager and will try to convince the magazine wholesaler who supplies stores in your area to carry *BHM*. This issue marks an increase in the number of magazines we are printing, from 39,500 last issue to 55,000 this issue. Surely your local store can use a few of those magazines.

Six-fingered thief on cover #15

Charles T. Lindberg of Deerfield Beach, Florida, sent me the following startling postcard: "On the cover of the May/June #15 issue of *BHM*, the 'kid' taking the pie has six fingers on his right hand . . . . WHY!!!??"

Why indeed! It was a complete surprise to me to find out we had produced a six-fingered pie-stealer on the cover of Issue No. 15. No one here noticed it until Mr. Lindberg's postcard arrived. Any of you other readers notice it? I called Don Childers, our artist, and asked him why he put six fingers on the pie-stealer, but all he could say was, "**WHAT!**"

Oh well. We were sure to count the toes on the coyote for this issue. Not that it will do any good. I don't even know how many toes a coyote is supposed to have.

Guerilla videos

We've decided to pay more attention to the guerilla videos that are being produced in people's homes around the country, so in this issue we have a feature about how to start a video business, a profile of Bill Myers and his video newsletter, and two pages of video reviews. We'll try to do a couple of pages of video reviews along with our couple of pages of book and magazine reviews from now on.

So if you're one of those gorillas who produce guerilla videos in your cellar or home workshop, send us a copy and we'll review it if we think it's of interest to our readers. No X-rated stuff please. We want reasonably well done "how to" videos that pertain to topics of interest to our readers. If you want them back send along the appropriate postage.

BHM Rental Boxes

An insistent reader has persuaded me to rent *BHM* "Rental Boxes" to our readership. The boxes are $10 per month, and the first one appears in this issue in the classifieds under the category "Business Opportunities." If you want more information, give us a call for the details.

Foreign countries and Tashkent

Don't ask me how they heard of us, but people in Finland, South Africa, Italy, Brazil, Australia, New Zealand, Mexico, England, Ireland, France, the Philippines, Latvia, and, of course, Canada, now subscribe to *BHM*.

Uzbekistan, one of the former Soviet republics, should be next. My friend Rich Hawkins, a Seattle actor, travels there in August to the city of Tashkent, where he will help set up an English Language Resource Center that would provide American instructors to teach English. The idea is to arm those budding capitalists with the international language of business and opportunity.

That worthwhile project is short of start-up funds, so if you'd like to help, contact the Seattle-Tashkent Sister City Committee, English Language Resource Center, 4112 NE 103rd Place, Seattle, WA 98125. Tel.: (206) 524-7729. As a bonus for *BHM*, Hawkins has promised to write some articles from Tashkent for future issues of *BHM*. Δ

Dave Duffy

My View

The black man's worst enemy is not racism

The recent riots in L.A. following the acquittal of four white L.A. police officers accused of beating black motorist Rodney King are yet another symptom of a serious disease in American society. No, the disease is not racism, although I'm sure the political opportunists will try and further their power bases by exploiting the racism issue. The disease is the same one we have editorialized against in the past — **Too much power in this country is now vested in our government, too little in the citizens!**

The acquittal of the four L.A. police officers astounded me. It looked like an open and shut case of police brutality, judging by what I saw on the videotape. But if the jury who acquitted them erred, it is one of many mistakes a justice system is bound to make. (Sometimes, to satisfy a mob's cry for punishment, they send the wrong people to jail.) We have to live with their decision under our laws, and it does not justify the resulting riots, looting, and especially the random attacks on innocent motorists who just happened to be in the neighborhood.

Nevertheless I sympathize with some of the rioters. Not the lawless bands of thugs and gang members who comprised the majority of the rioters, but with some of the ordinary blacks who, like you and me, can only be pushed so far before they push back, however so blindly.

Many blacks are locked into inner city poverty with little hope of ever getting out. There are a variety of reasons why this is so, including prejudice from the rest of us, but the main reason is that **government has destroyed the black family with a welfare check**.

"Do gooder" social engineers have created third and fourth generation welfare recipient families by offering black mothers more money than their jobless husbands can provide. The result is that 80% of L.A. black children grow up without a father figure in the home. Without a proper father figure, black children are at an extraordinary disadvantage. Many are forced to learn the ways of the world on the streets. And if their fathers do happen to come home, the cops and the D.A. are waiting to arrest them for failure to pay their child support payments.

The major foe of blacks in the inner cities of America is not racism or bad court decisions, but the friendly-faced "do gooder" bureaucrat with his easy welfare money. That bureaucrat doesn't say, "Here's some opportunity to help you get on your feet and into the mainstream of society." He says, "Here's some money; go enjoy yourself and leave everything to me." Then he goes back to his cushy job, secure in the knowledge that his job is safe because blacks don't have a prayer of getting out of poverty with such a dependency system. The problem with black families in L.A., and in most urban cities, is that welfare bureaucrats

Dave Duffy

have taken over their lives. They've hooked many on welfare, promising them ever-increasing benefits if only they'll vote for politicians that keep the bureaucrats in their jobs. Who wouldn't fall for such a trap? The wonder is that so many blacks **do** overcome this pernicious dependency system and make it on their own.

And when a gutsy black does make it on his own, what happens? A good look at the confirmation hearings of Supreme Court Justice Clarence Thomas will give you an idea. The politicians who depend on black impoverishment as part of their power base went after him like coyotes after a domestic dog who has strayed too far from home. They tried to rip out his guts. They accused him of being prejudiced against his own people because he had disdained the welfare system and all the other white bureaucratic "do gooder" traps. They couldn't stand an "uppity black" telling them to shove their welfare programs. The judge saw the "free money" programs for what they were — dead end roads designed by social engineers who don't understand that we live in a society in which the individual must learn to cope on his own.

The real tragedy of the riots in L.A. is that they will probably be used by misguided social engineers and opportunistic politicians to convince government to pour more money into the same welfare programs that have destroyed black families for generations.

People don't need welfare bureaucrats running their lives; they need jobs and their own small businesses so they can stand up by themselves. The way you create jobs is by giving small businesses a climate in which they can flourish. Rather than tax businesses to death to feed counterproductive government bureaucracies like the welfare system, encourage small businesses to open in the inner cities, or within traveling distance of the inner cities. Rather than offer bigger checks to welfare recipients and fatter retirement benefits to welfare administrators, offer incentives to black entrepreneurs. Rather than give the black mother a cash replacement for her husband, give the black man the opportunity to come home to his family. ∆

Farming crayfish for a living — the demand exceeds the supply

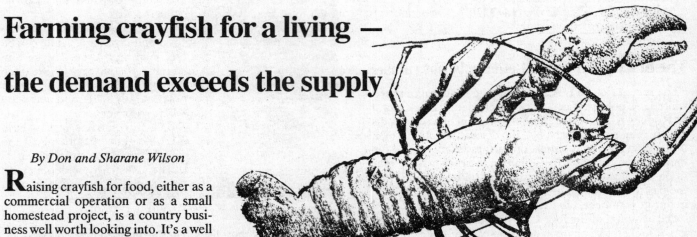

By Don and Sharane Wilson

Raising crayfish for food, either as a commercial operation or as a small homestead project, is a country business well worth looking into. It's a well established industry in much of the South. In Louisiana, commercial crayfish farmers raise and sell 85 million pounds yearly. Texas and Mississippi produce similar amounts.

Demand growing

There is a steadily growing demand for crayfish, also known as crawfish, on the East Coast. North Carolina, with 14 members in the state crayfish association, produces about 100,000 pounds yearly. The crayfish may be larger and tastier than the Louisiana crayfish even though most large operations raise the same variety—the Red Swamp Crayfish (P.clarkii).

Farming crayfish for profit is a newly established niche that has growers scrambling for production. The director of Aquaculture for the North Carolina Department of Agriculture (NCDA) says the North Carolina market for crayfish is "strong with definite growth potential," and that they "just need more people producing crayfish."

With over 400 varieties of crayfish in North America alone, there are bound to be dozens of varieties suitable for raising to a large food-size anywhere in the U.S.A.

In North Carolina, Georgia, and South Carolina the vast majority of crayfish are raised in the Coastal Plain. There are some crayfish farms in the panhandle of Florida. These states are all forming growers' associations to promote both the production and consumption of these tasty crustaceans. Annual crayfish festivals and give-aways happen during the harvest season.

Low investment

Raising crayfish for food and profit is a relatively low investment project, requiring only a moderate amount of labor for a short time period, and it has the potential for a good economic return. "Just about anybody can raise crayfish. The key is maintaining water quality," says NCDA's Tom Ellis. Aubrey Only, an Edenton crayfish farmer for three years, says "Crawfish can diversify an existing farm and add supplemental income."

Need at least one pond

To get started, you need at least one pond with a nearby freshwater source such as a creek, stream, or canal.

Low oxygen content is the main water quality problem. Although crayfish are exceptionally tolerant to low oxygen in their water, they can climb out and walk away from bad water.

Simply running fresh water to the habitat or aerating the water will correct this. If the water is aerated, then the water only needs to be pumped in to replace the ponds evaporation loss. This means the water source need not be very large to maintain the pond, and allowing the water to fall into the pond enough to make bubbles is all the aeration that is needed. A ram pump could be used in some cases to pump water without the need for electricity or gasoline.

The pond only needs to be 1-3 feet deep, and the water need not be crystal clear. Silted or turbid water may even be better, as crayfish don't like bright sunlight and predators would not be able to see them. Crawfish are normally placed in clear water after they are harvested to clear out their digestive system—sometimes called a "mud vein."

Food and growth

The natural food of the crayfish includes both living plant and animal sources—insect larvae, worms, other crustaceans, small fishes, snails, and tadpoles, as well as most dead animal matter.

The bulk of the crayfish diet comes from the high-protein bacteria, fungi, and other microorganisms which cover decomposing plant material. As the plants decompose, carbon changes to nitrogen and becomes more nutritious as well.

The crayfish detects food with its long antennae and the short antennules. It is believed that the sensing of meat juice or blood by the short antennules causes a reflex in the crayfish to turn and move toward the source. Crayfish do not drink; water is absorbed through the gill surfaces.

Crayfish mature in 3 to 12 months. The average life span is 24 months for most species. The Pacific and some American varieties can live 5-6 years. One Mississippi variety lives 6-7 years.

Crayfish possess the power of "Autonomy and Regeneration." That is, they can self-amputate, or drop a leg or have part of one taken by a predator, and grow a new one to replace it. The lost part is fully restored after several molts.

Environment needs

Although varieties of crayfish live within a wide range of environments, they all do best under similar conditions.

The ideal temperature range for rapid growth is 68 to 77 degrees F. Crayfish eggs will hatch in 2-3 weeks at these temperatures. At lower temperatures growth, activity and egg development slows—and stops completely below 50 degrees F. Above 81 degrees F most varieties seek shelter and become dormant.

The water must be fresh, with salinity less than 10ppt. Ocean water is about 35ppt.

There must be some calcium in the water (hard water) at between 50-200 ppm ideally. The acidity range is pH 5.8-8.2. Dissolved oxygen should be greater than 3 ppm. Total ammonia should be less than 1 ppm.

Crayfish can tolerate less dissolved oxygen and more ammonia levels, but they respond to these unfavorable conditions by slowing or stopping their molting rate.

When dissolved oxygen in the water falls below 2 ppm most crayfish will climb to the surface for air. They can survive this as long as the gills remain moist (100% humidity), but this is stressful. Crayfish can tolerate lower levels of dissolved oxygen, below 1 ppm, for up to 24 hours if they cannot get to the air.

All crayfishes are more susceptible to environmental extremes right around the time of molting.

Crayfish are very sensitive to synthetic chemicals, especially pesticides and weed killers. Creosote, turpentine, pine oil, nicotine, and pyrethins are toxic to crayfish in very small quantities.

Locating the pond

Choosing the location for raising crayfish is fairly important. The water source can be surface water or a well. A stream can be dammed to form a pond, or small pools can be dug out along the stream. A swampy area or marsh can be dug out or levied. Detailed advice on levee, dam, and pond construction may be obtained from the Soil Conservation Service, county agricultural agents, or local contractors.

In short, nearly any area that can collect and hold clean, fresh water is suitable for growing crayfish. The soil should have some clay to hold the water, and be thick enough that crayfish burrows will not drain the water.

The site should be limed if it is acid. The smaller the area used, the more efficiently it can be managed. Some provision should be made for draining the area, although some species of crayfish do not require an annual dewatering in their life cycle.

Pond construction

Crayfish ponds are generally constructed along the lines of catfish ponds—with a bulldozer—although the water need only be 1-2 feet deep and thus the levee or dam can be lower and less expensive.

The drain pipe should have anti-seep collars to prevent the burrowing of crayfish or rodents that would cause leaks. In order to promote better water circulation, the water input and the drain should be as far apart as possible. In large ponds, "baffle levees" and/or boat trapping lanes can be constructed so as to encourage water circulation. Water pumping, circulation and flushing is most impor-

tant in the fall, when vegetation in the pond decomposes and uses up the oxygen in the water.

In a boggy or swampy area that is too soft for a bulldozer, a dragline can be used to build up a levee. The bottom is left undisturbed except for the ditch created by the dragline. This type of pond is generally acidic and may need some lime treatment.

The walls (dikes, dams, levees) have to withstand the pressure of all the water in the pond, and must be watertight. The construction depends on the kind of soil in which the pond is being built.

A soil which is a mixture of clay and sand is best. If pure clay is used, it must be mixed with other soil, as pure clay will crack and leak. Do not use turf, humus, or peaty earth. All stones and pieces of wood or anything that will rot must be removed. These materials will weaken the walls if left there.

Start by placing layers of soil, about 8" thick, over the drainage pipes and tamping each layer down until it is compacted. Some people use a large rock or just jump up and down on the soil, but a tamping tool is best. The important thing is to pack the soil down tightly.

The finished height of the wall should be about a foot higher than the water level for small ponds, and about 20" for large ponds. The width of the wall at the top should be equal to its height. For a large pond, the wall is never less than 3 feet wide at the top. Most walls are built so two people can walk side by side along the top.

Grass should be planted on the walls to give added strength and prevent erosion. Do not plant trees.

Lime pond bottom

Most pond bottoms will have to be limed before filling. There are four kinds of lime that can be used for this, at the following rates:

- **Agricultural lime—2021 lbs. per acre**
- **Ground limestone—2508 lbs. per acre**
- **Quicklime—178 lbs. per acre**

● **Hydrated lime — 101 lbs. per acre**

The lime should remain on the pond bottom 2-3 weeks before filling the pond. This will counteract any acidity in the soil and pond water. Crayfish production can be more than doubled by liming acid soils. The best soil pH is 6.4.

Pond drain

The best type of drain is the double sleeve overflow system. This setup drains stale water from the pond bottom as water is added. The drain pipe goes through the wall or dam and turns up vertically at a "T" fitting inside the pond, to end at the desired water level of the pond. It is screened to prevent

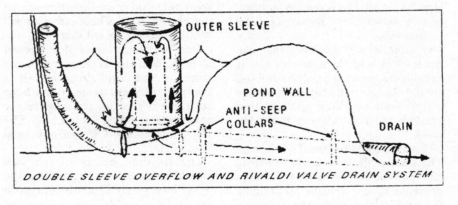

DOUBLE SLEEVE OVERFLOW AND RIVALDI VALVE DRAIN SYSTEM

escape of the crayfish. A larger diameter pipe is placed over this pipe, above the level of the water, and extending to near the bottom of the pond.

For the complete draining of the pond, the simple Rivaldi valve can be used along with this setup. It consists of a flexible pipe, screened, attached to the "T" fitting and kept staked above the water level until draining is desired: then it is allowed to fall to the bottom.

Water requirements

There needs to be some circulation in the water, although if some form of aeration/filtration is used, then only the evaporation loss need be replaced. The inlet and drain pipes should be screened (1/2" mesh), and be placed as far apart as practical to insure good circulation. Sometimes a screen on the inflow may not be necessary. It is needed mainly to keep out predatory fish. Smaller screen mesh can clog up, so a happy medium may have to be reached in some cases.

The inlet should be above the water level so that it splashes and mixes with air to add oxygen to the water. Both can be accomplished by allowing the input water to cascade over a series of mesh plates or screens on square frames mounted above each other.

Both stream and well water are typically low in dissolved oxygen, and this kind of aeration will overcome these problems. Be sure the water source is free of pesticides and pollution.

Silted or muddy water may have to be run through some kind of gravel-sand filter. This can be a tank or pool where the silt is allowed to settle out before it is drawn off the top into the habitat, or is filtered through gravel at the bottom.

Green, growing water plants add oxygen to the water (photosynthesis), and decaying plant and animal material use up the oxygen (oxidation). The living animals, in this case the crayfish, use up the oxygen to live (respiration). Respiration and oxidation go on day and night, while photosynthesis takes place only during daylight hours. Any stirring or splashing or even wind rippling of the water can add oxygen to the pond water.

The most important aspects of water quality to the crayfish farmer, beside temperature and dissolved oxygen, are alkalinity, pH, and hardness. These three factors are interrelated. The relationship can be summarized as:

low alkalinity = low pH = low hardness

In ponds, all three can be controlled by adding lime to the water.

Prefer shallow water

Crayfish prefer shallow water, between 6 inches and 1 foot deep. For optimum production, no more than 25% of the area should be over 3 feet deep. The bottom should be fairly level, with some small elevations, bumps or ridges. The slightly uneven bottom will give the crayfish more area to burrow. Of course they will thrive on most bottom contours, the main consideration being the form of harvesting planned upon. The smoother bottom allows for using nets or seines. When using baited traps, just about any bottom conditions will work.

Densely wooded areas will have to be cleared past the shoreline. If the brush is thick, it will make harvesting difficult, crowd out the useful plants, and shade the water, keeping it too cool for optimum production. The excess vegetation will also drop leaves and debris into the water, which decay and use up the oxygen.

The most common pest plants are cattails and water hyacinth. Remove these before they cover the pond, or crayfish production will be greatly reduced. Some good plants for crayfish food and cover are alligator grass and water primrose, as well as pondweed and duckweed. These are normally not discouraged unless they get too thick and hinder harvesting.

Beware of pesticides

Crayfish are extremely sensitive to synthetic chemicals, especially pesticides. Agricultural runoff is very dangerous to a crayfish farming operations. The crayfish can die, or they can accumulate some poisons in their flesh and be hazardous to human health when eaten. Locate as far from farm or pasture land as possible, or try to secure cooperation from the owners to avert contamination of the crayfish habitats.

Stocking

There are usually some naturally occurring local species of crayfish nearly anywhere one would plan on raising them. These are generally the best ones to stock the pond with, as they are already acclimated to the area climate and water. These wild stock can be trapped and placed into the pond as soon as possible. If enough are caught, one would be advised to select only the largest specimens to stock the pond. This will start the process of selective breeding right away—breeding for large size and fastest rate of growth.

One may also attempt to buy the stock from an established crayfish farmer who deals in such things. The stock crayfish should be freshly caught and kept cool and damp until put into the pond. In the south, the usual procedure is to stock ponds with adult crayfish (size—about 3/4 to 1 oz.) when prices are low, usually in March. Price may not be a big concern for the smaller operator. Crayfish below 1/2" are very vulnerable to predators. After the first year, the crayfish population becomes self-sustaining. Generally the southern specie do best where the pond is drained seasonally. Most northern varieties do not require this.

Jumbo sized

To grow really jumbo crayfish, avoid overcrowding. No more than 1 adult crayfish per square foot is recommended, with plenty of hiding places provided. Fighting and cannibalism of the newly molted and stunted adult size is the result of overpopulation in a crayfish habitat. More or better food will not correct this, as they are a solitary animal with a strong territorial instinct.

Crayfish growth and survival is best when they have plenty of both animal and vegetable products for food. A good portion of this can be grown or encouraged to grow naturally. Supplementing this with high-protein commercial fish feed or range pellets (cattle feed) produces truly huge crayfish. They cannot easily grow to this size in nature as wild crayfish.

In an aquarium

In my own experience there is some indication that raising crayfish in an aquarium from the very young and newly free-swimming size results in less fighting among them. Raised this way to an inch or so in size gives greater survival rate for stocking a habitat. About 18 juvenile crayfish per square foot of tank is a good recommended density. Trying to raise crayfish to adult size in an aquarium usually results in lots of fighting and competition. It is possible if they are kept separated with a screen or barrier of some kind.

I provide plenty of hiding places for these young, which are barely visible but fully armored minute replicas of adults. Young crayfish molt, or shed their shell, as they grow—sometimes once a month. For about a day the newly molted crayfish is soft and very vulnerable. The others will attack this soft crayfish unless it can hide. I have found that rocks or seashells piled along the rear long side of an aquarium with a gravel bottom makes for an efficient setup, providing plenty of cover with a clear area in front for feeding and observation.

An under-gravel filter or an outside flow-through filter keeps the water clear. Shrimp pellets seem to be the best feed, not fouling the water. Commercial crayfish feed is probably the best food for an outside pond or pool, supplemented with hay.

Raise them as pets too?

The arrangement of rocks allows you to view the crayfish, which are quite interesting creatures. They take an active part in their surroundings, making their own little shelters out of the gravel and rocks, almost like little bulldozers. I even use box turtle shells for the larger crayfish pets, which seem to be the right shape inside. Speaking of pets, pet stores are starting to carry crayfish now, sometimes calling them freshwater lobsters and blue lobsters. I picked up a pair of red ones hoping to get some eggs to hatch from them. Under a grow-lamp these creatures glow a bright fluorescent red in strange patterns. Someone was breeding these for pet stores, and also had blue ones available. Seems like a good market niche to me, raising red crayfish to sell for $2 or $3 bucks apiece.

How much can you make?

How much money can you make raising crayfish? It really boils down to how large you grow the crayfish and whether you want to sell them from the trap or process them yourself. You can even set up a soft-shell operation for some real profit (and intensive labor). Full grown crayfish average 1-2 ounces apiece, and sell for about $2 per pound live and $4 per pound cooked. Softshells and tail meat sell for $8 to $10 per pound.

And how much would you like to keep for your own eating, because these crayfish are excellent food, high-protein, low-fat, and as tasty as any lobster or shrimp? Try dipping the tail meat in melted garlic butter—you just might want to keep all you can grow. That's pretty much what I do, at least until I can get some more ponds in production.

(Don Wilson is author of the 47-page booklet, "Small Scale Crayfish Farming," available for $7.95 plus $1 shipping for a total of $8.95. The book can be purchased from him at Atlas Publications, Rt. 2, Box 190, Alto, GA 30510, or from Backwoods Home Magazine using the form on page 78.) Δ

Prelude to Fall

The damp, brown lane is
edged in gold
where leaves
come tumbling down.

An Elk-horn fire
flares by a log;
smoke hovers over town.

A group of sulky clouds
play tag
across the wan, blue skies.

Far above
the Cottonwood trees
a lone gull
lakeward flies.

June Knight
Caldwell, ID

A house that a tornado helped build

Almost 5,000 square feet, this house built from trees downed by a tornado cost $20,000. The logs provide such insulation that the entire house is heated even in the coldest weather by a wood stove in the basement and, when needed, a fireplace in the den. Some of the rooms are 36 feet long and 18 feet wide.

By Robert L. Williams

On May 5, 1989, tornadoes ripped through parts of three western North Carolina counties, including ours, and left piles of debris where houses, also including ours, once stood.

Our destroyed house was a restored 4,000 square foot pre-Civil War plantation house. And, like many other homeowners, we learned that the tornadoes were only the beginning of our problems.

Our insurance companies paid a grand total of $1,600 for the house, outbuildings, cars, and personal property. Federal, state, and local agencies' help was minimal at best, and we quickly learned that if we were to have a home, we'd have to build it ourselves.

As a freelance writer, I learned that I could not collect any unemployment benefits (because I could not fire myself, I was told) despite the facts that I had not time, place, or equip-ment for my work. Everything was literally gone with the wind.

We had $15,000 in ready cash, and, armed only with a chain saw, determination, and desperation, we went to work. The tornado that leveled our house had also uprooted a huge stand of mature trees, including poplar, oak, hickory, and maple. It was in the tangle of trees that we started to build our house.

We told ourselves that we had always dreamed of owning a log house, and now was the perfect time to build one. My wife, Elizabeth, 47 years old and a former newspaper editor, our son, 13 years old and a middle school student, and I, 57, retired public school and college teacher and freelance writer, tackled the formidable task of dealing with the monstrous trees.

We soon realized that the tornadoes, even though destroying our home, also did us a sort of back-handed favor. They had laid the trees down without wrecking or twisting them so badly that they could not be used. We did not have the worry and danger of cutting down trees: a degree of consolation.

Our first task was to select the types of trees we wanted to use. Availability dictated that we'd use poplars for the walls. The trees were tall, straight, and easy to reach. We'd use hickory for support posts, oak for door and window framing, and pine for wall covering, ceilings, and stairs.

Nearly everything we owned had been destroyed, so our tool supply was very limited. We spent a few precious dollars on a chalk line, measuring tape, gas can, oil, and chains.

The first step was designing our house, which we had done at night prior to starting work. It would be 52 feet long, 32 feet wide, and would have three levels: basement, with tornado-safe room, office space for me, summer den, recreation room, darkroom for my photo work, and a huge workshop — a total of 1666 square feet.

The first floor would have kitchen, laundry room, dinette, dining room, huge den, two bathrooms, and two large bedrooms: also 1666 square feet.

To cut squared logs without special chain saw attachments, first use a square and level to mark off on both ends of the log the dimensions you want, and then snap a chalk line from one corner of the layout to the corresponding corner on the other end of the log.

meaning visitors reminded us that we had no experience in building and that the logs were so heavy and the work would be so slow that we didn't have a ghost of a chance of succeeding even in our wildest dreams.

While they talked, we worked. We wanted no spliced or joined logs at any point in the house, so we made a list of lengths we'd need between doors and corners, between windows, and between windows and doors.

It took us a full week to saw one usable log, and we realized that at our current rate we'd devote two years to cutting the logs alone, and at least another year to assemble the logs and finish the house. There was also a highly discouraging amount of waste in the first tree trunk we cut.

Then we got wise. We cut a 60-foot log from the next tree and drew off a rectangle eight inches by ten inches on the small end. We made certain that

Cut a guide groove along the chalked line, and then cut along the layout line and, keeping the bar straight, through the entire length of the log.

The third level would consist of guest bedrooms, sitting room, and space for later use. The total square footage of the house would be almost 5,000 square feet.

For $15,000? Impossible, everyone told us. Friends, neighbors, and well-

Logs for smaller expanses can be loaded into the bed of the truck and weighted on one end to keep them from shifting in transit.

When the log is finished, pry up one end and rest it on chunks of unused logs. When the end is high enough, back the bed of a pickup truck under the end of the log, chain the log in place, and pull it to the building site. Take care that you do not overload the truck suspension system or engine.

the rectangle had perfectly vertical sides (by using our $4 level we had to buy) and we repeated the process at the other end. Then we chalked a line from one upper left corner to the corresponding corner at the other end.

I cut a one-inch deep groove along the chalk line, and then, using the groove as my guide, used the chain saw to cut down the vertical line until the tip of the saw was through the end of the log. From that point on it was simply a matter of keeping the saw bar straight up and down and following the guide cut.

A few minutes later we had a beautiful log with one square side. We chalked the other corners and when the cut was made, we had two square, or flat sides. Then we laid the log on its side and made the final two cuts.

We couldn't believe what we had produced: a perfectly straight log, square sided and ten inches high by eight inches thick. Now all we needed

The Third Year

To cut boards, square top and bottom of the log and then measure off the thickness of the desired board and cut as you did for the large logs. Finished results are very comparable to anything in the lumber yard. Use boards for flooring and wall covering.

was to go drag it to the building site and repeat the process about a hundred times more.

We had bought a come-along or power pull and log chains, and we hooked the log chains and one end of the come-along to our old pickup truck and the other end to the log. Then, with painfully slow six-foot progressions, we pulled the log to the makeshift road we had carved into the woods.

Loading the log into the truck was impossible, so we used poles as levers and chunks of logs as fulcrums and pried one end of the log high enough that I could back the truck bed under the log. We then chained the log in place as well as we could and I dragged the log to the house site.

Day after day we worked, squaring logs and dragging them to the site. We kept careful count, and when we had enough logs (four months later) we began to mix concrete. We had hired a man to dig our basement and footings, and we poured footings and basement floor, after which we laid concrete blocks for basement walls.

The cost of the masonry materials was demoralizing; we realized that a huge chunk of our budget had disappeared in the early stages of our work.

The bright part of the budget was that our chain saw did not wear out, we needed only half a dozen chains, and

we had no major repair bills. Our complete walls for the house cost us the grand total of $132.64. This was for tools, gas, oil, chains, and other related expenses, including gas for the truck.

We found that we could cut floor joists easily and quickly from pine logs. A large log would yield three or even four two-by-ten joists. I could cut one in about half an hour at a cost of less than half a dollar.

We bought plywood subflooring and then began to horse logs up to the floor area. We used the truck to pull the logs, on rollers, alongside the house, where we had earlier leaned smaller logs ripped down the center and placed, freshly-cut side up.

Using pry poles, we urged one end of a log up the leaning log nearest us until it was two feet off the ground. Then we nailed a wedge behind the log to keep it from sliding back down. We did the same at the other end, and afterwards we pried, shoved, or maneuvered the log, one end at a time, until it was on the sub-flooring.

Drill 1/4 inch holes every 2 feet all the way through the top log. Then use a 5/8 inch bit to drill a second hole 5 inches deep. Drive a fluted spike into the hole and into the log below. Use a punch to countersink the spike halfway through the log.

Cue sticks from our old pool table saved our backs and untold time and energy as we moved logs across the flooring. We used a crowbar to raise the ends of the log a couple of inches, and then we put a cue stick under and at right angles to the log on each end.

To our delight, the log could be pushed or pulled almost as easily as leading a puppy across the floor. When the logs were in place, we spiked them to the sills which had already been installed. We had used anchor bolts four feet long in the basement walls, and now we used countersunk fluted spikes spaced two feet apart the entire length of the log.

As the walls grew, we used short squared logs to hold the building logs as we levered them higher and higher and then pried them into position where they were spiked.

We did the interior finish work ourselves and also made a stab at wiring

Cut two-by-fours from smaller sections of logs and use these for railings. You can cut a superb two-by-four twelve feet long in about ten minutes at a cost of about twelve cents or less.

Cut support posts to reinforce girders. Use a level to get perfect positioning of the support post.

and plumbing. We read books at night and applied what we had learned the following day. Fireplaces and chimney were made of cement blocks and then covered with stones and jointed with black mortar.

We covered walls and cathedral ceilings with knotty pine boards and made staircases and railings from pine two-by-fours. By the time we had covered all the interior walls, including bathrooms, and all ceilings with knotty pine, we realized that our budget had been exhausted and we had not yet bought any lighting fixtures or installed a heating system. We had to spend money on roofing materials because of building code regulations.

Happily we learned that we could use the heat pump from the basement of our old house, and whatever money I earned through writing went into the light fixtures. By the time we moved in, our house and affordable furniture had cost us more than $20,000 rather than the $15,000 we started with.

Even at this point there is much left to do in terms of trim work and finishing touches, but the house is livable and we think that we came out with a spectacular bargain.

And a huge part of whatever success we realized came because of the questionable generosity of the tornadoes. We must admit that the task was at

times horribly demanding and discouraging, but at the same time we realize that the house we live in, while definitely not tornado-proof, is many times stronger and more comfortable than our pre-Civil War house.

What we learned was worth far more than the loss of a house. We learned that even out of the worst disasters, there is often a realizable good, and we learned, most importantly, that as human beings we are able to do—and do well—so much more than we ever dreamed possible. Δ

Alzheimer's: What Year?

*like the scarlet
flash of*

cardinal

*that flits
telephone line to
oak limb*

*the thought
paused in*

my brain

*but flew on
before it
reached*

my lips

Sheryl L. Nelms
Ft. Worth, TX

The Third Year

The genius of John Adams, Thomas Jefferson, and America's "Declaration of Independence"

By John Silveira

Backwoods Home Magazine has moved to Oregon—permanently. Though I'm still down here in California 700 miles away, my name is still carried on the masthead as senior editor. We'll see how long that lasts.

I regret I'm not going to see much of Dave and Ilene or Annie and little Jacob, who is now just eight months old. He's going to forget who Uncle John is.

However, I thought there was an upside to this. Now that they've moved, Dave can no longer look over my shoulder and discover I don't know what to write about.

Or so I thought. I forgot the telephone, and this morning its ringing woke me up. I stumbled out of bed half-asleep, crossed the house, stepping carefully in my grogginess, wary of my dog and three cats which have a way of blending in with the rug when I'm like this.

I picked my way to the living room like a soldier crossing a minefield and grabbed the receiver just as the ringing stopped. I said unpleasant things to the dial tone that must have had Alexander Graham Bell whirling in his grave like a dervish. I hung up and started back to my bedroom.

It rang again. I got to it on the third ring.

"Yeah?"

John Adams, left, and Thomas Jefferson.

"Did I wake you up?" It was Dave, my nemesis at deadline time.

"No, some idiot just called, then hung up just as I answered it."

"That was me," he said.

"Oh."

"I called to find out how your article's coming." he said.

"Fine," I lied.

"What's it about?"

"Ahh..." My mind was still in groggy gear.

"It's the July/August issue," he said.

"I know." I still couldn't think of what to tell him.

"Are you writing about anything we can tie to that time of the year?"

"Ahh..." I have a beautiful way with words.

"What happens in those two months?" he asked.

"Nothing," I said after some thought.

I could hear Ilene's voice in the background on his end. "There's the Fourth of July," she said.

"Hey, that's right," Dave said. He started sounding excited. "Can you tie your article to the Fourth of July?"

"Yeah," I said counting on the lie to get me off the phone and I even nodded, as if he would see how sincere I was.

"What's it about?" he asked.

"What's what about?"

"Your article."

With that question, all the lies were going to come home to roost like the buzzards returning to Hinckley, Ohio.

"There's someone at the door," I said hoping to buy time. "I'll call you right back." And then, like a wish come true, somebody actually did knock on my door. "Hey, there actually is someone at my door," I said in surprise.

"What do you mean 'actually?'" he asked.

"Let me call you right back," I said and hung up before he could object.

There was the knock again. I went to my front door, opened it, and there, looking bored and in need of coffee was Dave's poker playing friend, O.E. MacDougal. With Dave in Oregon, I really, really thought I'd never see him again.

"Hi," I said and, keeping in line with my gift for being expressive that morning, I couldn't think of anything else to say.

"Did I wake you up?" he asked. He sounded more concerned than Dave did when he had asked the same question.

"No, Dave did. He just called." Mac smiled.

"What's going on?" I asked.

"Nothing. I just put in some fishing this morning up in the Sespe. I thought I'd drop in before I went back to Ventura."

"Good," I said. "I didn't even know you knew where I lived."

"Dave told me."

"Come on in. Want some coffee?"

"Sure. What did Dave want?"

I stepped aside and let him pass. "Oh, he wanted to know what this month's article is about."

"What is it about?"

"I don't know, Mac. But now he wants it to tie in with the Fourth of July. What's there to write about the Fourth of July?"

Adams & Jefferson died the same day—on July 4, 1826

He shrugged and picked up my cat, Phideaux, before he sat down at the table. "Well, did you know three of the first five Presidents died on the Fourth of July?"

"They did?" I asked incredulously.

"Yeah, in fact, two of them, John Adams and Thomas Jefferson, died within hours of each other, on the same day, July 4, 1826. James Monroe, the fifth President, died on the Fourth just five years later, in 1831."

I turned on the flame beneath the kettle and put some coffee beans in the electric coffee grinder. I pressed the button on top of the grinder, and ground the beans to a powder. Phideaux gave me the look of disapproval he always gives me when I run the grinder, then he lay back in Mac's lap.

"Well, that's interesting, but I can't just write an article about three Presidents dying on the Fourth of July. It's got to be something interesting."

"Write about the men," he said. "Write about Adams and Jefferson. July 4th is about the Declaration of Independence and those two men

probably had more to do with it than any other two men."

"Really? Well, what can I write about them?"

"They're two of the most interesting men in American history. There's plenty to write."

"Would you mind if I took some notes?" I asked.

"Be my guest," he said and the phone rang again.

I got it on the second ring. "Yeah?" It was Dave.

"You hung up before you told me what you're writing about. What is it so I can get Don Childers working on the artwork?"

"It's about Adams and Jefferson and what they had to do with the Fourth of July."

I looked at Mac. He was nodding.

The kettle started to whistle. "Let me get going, okay?"

"Bye," Dave said.

I make coffee one cup at a time. I just haven't caught up with the rest of the twentieth century, yet. I put my little coffee cone on the first cup and started to pour.

Adams' son 'John Quincy'

"Adams's family was one of the most interesting and influential in American history," Mac said, "and almost as interesting and influential as Jefferson himself."

"What do you mean?"

"It is one of the great American families. Adams' eldest son, John Quincy, at the age of eight, watched the Battle of Bunker Hill from atop nearby Penn's Hill. When he was 14, he served the U.S. envoy to Russia as an interpreter of French—the language of the Russian Imperial Court at that time. Later, George Washington considered him the ablest officer in the foreign service of the United States. In fact, Washington, who saw many of the letters John Quincy wrote to his father, drew freely from them, and his Farewell Address, one of the great addresses of American history, is liberally sprinkled with phrases Washington lifted directly from those letters.

"You know, Washington's Farewell Address would make a timely article for one of your columns."

"Why?"

"Have you ever read it?"

I hate those questions. I feel like I haven't read anything. But Mac explained it as I made the second cup.

"He warned against permanent alliances with foreign powers, large public debt, a large military establishment, and the will and power of small and deceitful minorities who would try to control and change the government."

"When was that?" I asked.

"192 years ago."

"Okay," I said and made a note for a future article.

"John Quincy was also a major participant in drafting the peace treaty that concluded the War of 1812 and it was he, not James Monroe, who actually formulated the Monroe Doctrine that became the cornerstone of the United States's refusal to let European powers meddle in New World affairs.

"And, of course, he later became the sixth President of the United States and, after his Presidency, he went on to serve with distinction, for the rest of his life, in the House of Representatives. To the many, the thought of Adams going back to the House was demeaning to the office of the Presidency. But after leaving the Presidency, John Quincy said a man should be honored to still serve his country whether it's in the House of Representatives or as a town selectman. In 1848, he dropped to the floor of the House, the result of a cerebral hemorrhage, while arguing the case against slavery, and he died without leaving its doors.

"John Adams's wife, Abigail Adams, was a prolific writer. She was knowledgeable despite her limited education and was personally opposed to slavery and an advocate of women's rights, particularly championing educational opportunities for them.

"A second cousin, Samuel Adams, was another signer of the Declaration of Independence and later a governor of Massachusetts.

"During and after the Revolutionary War, John Adams, himself, served as a diplomat to the new American government and was, of course, the first Vice President and the second President of the United States. His thinking influenced the content of many of the state constitutions that now exist.

"What's all this got to do with the Declaration of Independence?" I asked.

"Before we get to that, I want you to understand that neither Adams nor Jefferson were the kind of political opportunists we seem to have in spades today.

"Adams was an original American thinker. He understood the American mind. He knew it differed from the European mind. The philosophical seeds of the American Revolution didn't happen overnight in 1776, and they were more deeply seated in the colonial psyche than they are in Americans today.

Adams opposed 'collective authority'

"The colonists were different from their English cousins, and when writing about his opposition to the Stamp Act of 1765 for the Boston Gazette, he argued that the colonists's opposition to the Act was a manifestation of the New World individualism opposing the Old World mentality of collective authority. It's the same collective mentality social programmers would have us go back to today."

"Are you editorializing?" I asked.

He shrugged.

"Why are some newspapers called gazettes?" I asked rhetorically, not really expecting an answer.

"The modern newspaper had its birth in Italy around the time of the Renaissance. Those documents were more like flyers and the price of one was one gazetta, a coin of the time. The name just stuck."

I stared at what I had just written. "How do you know...Never mind," I said. "Tell me more about Adams."

"Two years later the Stamp Act was repealed. But the same day it was repealed, parliament passed the Dec-

laratory Act which reaffirmed their power to rule the colonies. Adams saw this as them reaffirming their right to levy more taxes and, sure enough, they did exactly that before the year ended.

"In 1770, Adams, who would help lead the colonies on the road to independence, defended a group of British soldiers who participated in the Boston Massacre, even though colonial sentiment was heavily against them."

"Adams, a future president, defended them?"

"Yeah."

"How many were killed in the Boston massacre?" I asked, my pencil poised.

"Five."

"Five? That's a massacre? Doesn't seem like a lot to get shook about."

"Four were killed at Kent State and it moved the whole country to one side of the barricades or another; it's not the numbers killed but the act represented."

I nodded.

"Oddly, the first man killed was a black man named Cripis Attaks, and though the massacre was one of the acts that led to the War for American Independence, it would be a century before blacks would realize any of the benefits from the War for Independence."

"How'd the case against the soldiers go?"

"Adams got the commander and most of the soldiers acquitted, not on the grounds that the British were right, but that the soldiers had the right to defend themselves.

"Ironically, at the Second Continental Congress, five years later, it was Adams who nominated Washington to be commander-in-chief of the army that was destined to defeat the British Army and win the colonist's independence."

Phideaux rolled over in Mac's lap and Mac rubbed his belly.

"Adams also wrote a tract called *Thoughts on Government*, which was circulated throughout the colonies and formed the basis of the constitutions of many of the new states.

"Between 1776 and 1778 he served on committees that created the United States Navy, and in 1779 he helped draft one of the most famous of all Revolutionary state constitutions —

that of Massachusetts, in which he called for a government of laws and not of men."

"I may be remembering this wrong," I said, "But, in spite of what you're saying, it doesn't seem as though history has treated Adams very well."

"Adams made mistakes. He kept Washington's cabinet intact when he became President, not understanding that the members were divided by party loyalties. He also passed the Alien and Sedition Acts which, though he did not originate them, he signed into law. A popular sentiment rose up against them and his name will be entwined with them forever."

"What were the Alien and Sedition Acts?" I asked.

"They imposed restrictions on pro-French activities and attempted to curtail criticism of the Federal Government. They were really an attempt to keep anti-Federalist editors in line.

"To make matters worse, he lost the support of Alexander Hamilton because he had avoided war with France, though, in doing so, he was following in the footsteps of Washington who had done the same thing during his administration. Without Hamilton's support, he lost reelection in 1800 and Jefferson won the Presidency."

"Bummer," I said.

The most important election in history

"Actually, the election of 1800, between the Federalist Party of Adams and the Democratic-Republican Party of Jefferson may be the most important election in history."

"Why?"

"It was the first change of government, through the electoral process, in modern history. Electoral changes in government are so common in the industrial world today that we take them for granted. But until the election of 1800, it hadn't happened in over 1500 years, and suddenly, when it did, the two key players were Adams and Jefferson."

"By the way, that was the last election in which the candidate who finished second in the Presidential race be-

came the new Vice President, and Aaron Burr had finished second. So, four years later, while still Vice President, he killed Hamilton in a duel—the duel that would result in a Federal law against dueling, though later, Andrew Jackson killed a man in a duel and several other Presidents including Lincoln were challenged to duels."

"Did Lincoln fight in a duel?" I asked incredulously.

"No. On the way to the dueling site, he said so many funny things his opponent got to like him and the duel was called off." He smiled and shrugged. "Write something about Lincoln for the January-February issue," he said.

Phideaux purred loudly as he slept in Mac's lap. Mac stroked his fur and said, "You know, John, you should read more. There's a whole bunch of little tidbits you could throw into your writing to make it more interesting to your readers."

"Let's get back to the story. Did Adams's do anything good as President?"

"Sure, plenty of things. But his single most important act was to appoint John Marshall Chief Justice of the Supreme Court—perhaps the greatest justice ever to serve there. Marshall's someone else you should write about."

"What did he do?"

"One of the great landmarks in the formation of the American government is the policy of judicial review as established by Marshall in *Marbury v. Madison*. There, the court ruled certain government acts as unconstitutional.

"The irony is that Jefferson, the great democrat, opposed the right of the court—a bunch of nonelected officials who served for life—to do this on the grounds it was undemocratic, unrepublican, and unconstitutional. And he was right. Even today, the court has no constitutional authority to rule on the actions of the other two branches. But, no matter how you feel about the Supreme Court, the option for judicial review of the acts created by the other two branches is probably the last line of defense we have in the United States against tyranny. And if Jefferson had had his way, we wouldn't have it."

"Both men seemed to have had their faults," I said.

"Something about being human."

"What about Jefferson?" I asked.

An American original

"Jefferson is another one of those American originals. When he was 31, he wrote his first major essay on the rights of the American colonists. Like Adams, he saw rights and liberties as personal rather than collective things.

"In *A Summary View of the Rights of British America*, he put forth the view of individual rights as well as the view that the colonies, and other states in the Empire, were subject only to the king and not Parliament, and he further pressed the issue of independence."

"What did it matter, Parliament or king?"

"Parliament was the body taxing the colonists, and Jefferson presented the view that Parliament had no right to tax, rule, or impose military force in the colonies.

"He argued very persuasively, and by the time he was appointed to the committee of five who were to draft the Declaration of Independence, his literary skills were known, especially among the delegates to the Congress.

"Jefferson, a great believer in democracy, also advocated that public education be provided in the lower schools which, coupled with a free press, was necessary for the development of informed public opinion.

"He also felt a republican form of government would work only if property were available to all men—and, in the absence of property, acceptable work.

"He was also a profoundly religious man, but he was viscerally opposed to the entwinement of church and state, a stunningly un-European sentiment that we take in stride, today."

"Was he real popular in his day?"

"He had his enemies. It would be interesting, in today's electoral environment, to see if he could survive the mudslinging. He was a very sensitive man. At one point during the Revolutionary War, he served as governor of Virginia and, when a detachment of British soldiers attempted to capture him, he boogied. His critics used it as an excuse to slur his character, and Jefferson was so stung by the insinuation that he had deserted that after his term ended, he refused to serve as governor again, and thought he would never again serve in any public office.

Our smartest President

"Try to imagine how today's press would handle a man that sensitive. Many think he was the greatest President we've ever had but by today's standards he would be considered unfit to serve because he couldn't take personal slurs. So, we don't get men like Jefferson anymore. Look what we get instead.

"Which reminds me: Jefferson, if not the most intelligent President we've ever had, was certainly the most intellectual. He spoke Latin, Greek, French, Spanish, Italian, and Anglo-Saxon. He read Plato in the original and concluded he was overrated. He studied science and math, corresponded with some of the great European scientific minds of his day, and he excavated, collected, and classified fossils. During his European travels, he often sent back the latest European gadgets and inventions. He also conducted agricultural experiments on his farm at Monticello, and he may have been the first white man to systematically collect and classify Indian dialects."

"He did all that?"

"Yeah. He also influenced the direction of American architecture by his choices of Federal architecture during his administration.

"To put the man in perspective, try to imagine a George Bush, a Bill Clinton, a Jerry Brown, or a Ross Perot doing all this."

"What other posts did Jefferson serve in?"

"He served as minister to France from 1784-1789 and was there when the Articles of Confederation was replaced with the Constitution and, though he approved the Constitution, he criticized the omission of a Bill of Rights. He also criticized the lack of a provision to put a limit on the number of terms a President could serve, something we got 170 years later.

Advocated individual rights

"He also served as Washington's Secretary of State, a post he really didn't want but accepted reluctantly and soon found himself locking horns with Alexander Hamilton, the Secretary of the Treasury."

"Over what?"

"Hamilton believed that the individual was subordinate to the interests of the state. Jefferson believed just the opposite.

"He also disagreed with Hamilton's financial policies which he feared gave the central government too much power and were not in the interests of the majority. Jefferson feared a powerful centralized government, and he advocated state's rights. And there were foreign policy differences—Jefferson favored relations with the French and Hamilton sided with the British. The French and British were then, as they had been for centuries, at each other's throats. Large groups in the country took one side or the other and, though both men resigned their posts at the end of Washington's first term, each came to symbolize the two new emerging parties—Jefferson the Democratic-Republican and Hamilton the Federalist. The result was the foundation of the two party system.

"And though he would later use the party structure to defeat Adams, Jefferson actually hoped to do away with it."

"What kind of President was he?"

"You don't have enough room to cover everything he did, and the man has been practically canonized so let's hit a few things your readers may not know.

"As President, in an effort to mitigate Federalist policies and political appointees of the previous 12 years, he unwittingly introduced the spoils system.

"We all know he purchased the Louisiana Territory, a landmark event that would change world history by ensuring the United States was not merely a coastal nation, but on its way to becoming a continental nation. But even Jefferson knew he did not have the Constitutional authority to do so. He, in effect, out-Federalisted the Federalists with the purchase.

"His reasons were to remove the presence of one of the great European powers—France—from the North American Continent, as well as to ensure the availability of land which he was sure was essential to the success of the republican form of government.

"What's this republican form of government?" I asked.

"We're not a pure democracy," he said. "That was a Greek concept where every free man was allowed to vote on issues and all issues were decided by a general referendum. Nice in theory, but it's unwieldy, and unstable— public opinion being as mercurial as it is. The republican form of government provides for the democratic election of representatives to provide stability."

"Can we talk about how Adams and Jefferson figure into the Declaration of Independence?" I asked.

"Sure. Now's a good time.

"Jefferson was only 33 and a member of the Congress for less than a month when he, Adams, Benjamin Franklin of Pennsylvania, Roger Sherman of Connecticut, and Robert Livingston of New York were appointed to draw up a formal declaration of independence. Adams was actually the one who was supposed to write the draft but he, along with Franklin, another great colonial writer, insisted that young Jefferson write it because of the reputation he had already garnered as a writer. The style, the eloquence, and the force carried by the words in the Declaration of Independence belong to Jefferson alone, though Adams and Franklin made minor changes and the list of charges it contained against George III were inspired by the English Bill of Rights a century earlier, in 1689.

"But there was no jealousy between the two men, and when the document went to the floor of the Congress for debate, it was Adams who defended it.

"Though they were later to become political enemies, they were at this time great admirers of each other."

"What happened then?"

I watched Phideaux turn in his sleep and suddenly he was falling off Mac's lap. I didn't think Mac could move as fast as he did. He caught the little beast in midair and returned him to his lap. Phideaux hardly woke up.

"It was debated. On July 1st, John Dickinson, representing Pennsylvania, pleaded passionately against adoption of the declaration. However, in a vote, nine of the colonies voted for independence; only two—South Carolina and Pennsylvania—opposed it. The Delaware delegation was supposed to have three members, but only two showed up and they were split one-to-one. New York, adhering to instructions from home, abstained."

"Was Dickinson a traitor?"

"Far from it. He was later accused of being a Loyalist, but he served with distinction in the patriotic militia. In 1787, as a representative, then from Delaware, he was one of the signers of the Constitution."

"So what happened next?"

"On, July 2nd, South Carolina and Pennsylvania reversed their votes, and Caesar Rodney, the third member of the Delaware delegation, made a dramatic day-long 80-mile journey, and broke the deadlock in Delaware's delegation when he voted for independence.

The vote for independence

"Suddenly, the Congress was voting 12-0 for independence. New York still abstained. John Adams believed that that day, July 2nd, would live forever in celebration. It was the day of American Independence.

"Ironically, what we celebrate instead, is the adoption of the Declaration of Independence, which, of course, occurred on the Fourth.

"Why did it take two more days to adopt it?"

"There were several changes made. Some passages were amended, some were deleted. Most conspicuously, they removed a passage condemning the British people and their government. They also deleted a censure of the crown for disallowing colonial acts which would have banned the importation of slaves into the colony.

"Jefferson observed that the first of those two were attempts to please those who still hoped to retain British friends to the American cause, while the omission of the passages on slave importation were to mollify South Carolina which not only did not want the slave trade restrained but wanted it encouraged.

"On the Fourth, the final version was adopted.

"Five days later, July 9, New York ratified the declaration and made the vote for independence unanimous.

"But why don't we celebrate July 2nd?" I asked.

"I think because the document states, right at the beginning, 'In Congress, July 4, 1776.'"

"Oh," I said.

"Were Adams and Jefferson enemies the rest of their lives?"

"No. They were friends during the Revolution, bitter enemies during their Presidencies, then in later life they reconciled, became friends again and died within hours of each other on the same day, July 4th, 1826, the 50th anniversary of the adoption of one of the great documents of mankind.

"It's quite a coincidence for them to have died the same day."

"It may not have been all coincidence. In 1826, the semicentenial year of the Declaration of Independence, the two men so central to the drafting of the document were both dying—Adams in Massachusetts, and Jefferson in Virginia—but both wanted to live until the anniversary. They say the dying can do that and they both died that day, within hours of each other."

I looked at my notes. "Fishing?" I asked.

"Yeah, up in the Sespe."

Ah, yes. I think I'll see more of Mac, now. Δ

"You and I ought not to die before we have explained ourselves to each other."

Letter from John Adams
to Thomas Jefferson
July 15, 1813

The Third Year

prove this, let Facts be submitted to a candid World.

He has refused his assent to Laws, the most wholesome and necessary for the public Good.

He has forbidden his Governors to pass Laws of immediate and pressing Importance, unless suspended in their Operation till his Assent should be obtained; and when so suspended, he has utterly neglected to attend them.

He has refused to pass other Laws for the Accommodation of large Districts of People, unless those People would relinquish the Right of Representation in the Legislature, a Right inestimable to them, and formidable to Tyrants only.

He has called together Legislative Bodies at Places unusual, uncomfortable, and distant from the Depository of their Public Records, for the sole Purpose of Fatiguing them into Compliance with his Measures.

He has dissolved Representative Houses repeatedly, for opposing with manly firmness his Invasions on the Rights of the People.

He has refused for a long Time, after such Dissolutions, to cause others to be elected; whereby the Legislative Powers, incapable of Annihilation, have returned to the People at large for their exercise; the State remaining in the mean time exposed to all the Dangers of Invasion from without, and Convulsions within.

He has endeavoured to prevent the Population of these States; for that Purpose obstructing the Laws of Naturalization of Foreigners; refusing to pass others to encourage their migrations hither, and raising the Conditions of new Appropriations of Lands.

He has obstructed the Administration of Justice, by refusing his Assent to Laws for establishing Judiciary Powers.

He has made Judges dependent on his Will alone, for the Tenure of their Offices, and the Amount of payment of their Salaries.

He has erected a Multitude of new Offices, and sent hither Swarms of Officers to harass our People, and eat out our substance.

He has kept among us, in Times of Peace, Standing Armies, without the consent of our Legislatures.

He has affected to render the Military independent of, and superior to the Civil Power.

He has combined with others to subject us to a Jurisdiction foreign to our Constitution, and unacknowledged by our Laws; giving his Assent to their Acts of pretended Legislation:

For quartering large Bodies of Armed Troops among us:

For protecting them, by a mock Trial, from Punishment for any Murders which they should commit on the Inhabitants of these States:

For cutting off our Trade with all parts of the World:

For imposing taxes on us without our Consent:

For depriving us, in many Cases, of the Benefits of Trial by Jury:

For transporting us beyond Seas to be tried for pretended Offences:

For abolishing the free system of English Laws in a neighbouring Province, establishing therein an arbitrary Government, and enlarging its Boundaries, so as to render it at once an Example and fit Instrument for introducing the same absolute Rule into these Colonies:

For taking away our Charters, abolishing our most valuable Laws, and altering fundamentally the Forms of our Governments:

For suspending our own Legislatures, and declaring themselves invested with Power to legislate for us in all Cases whatsoever.

He has abdicated Government here, by declaring us out of his Protection and waging war against us.

He has plundered our Seas, ravaged our Coasts, burnt our towns, and destroyed the Lives of our People.

He is, at this Time, transporting large Armies of foreign Mercenaries to complete the works of Death, Desolation, and Tyranny, already begun with circumstances of Cruelty and Perfidy, scarcely paralleled in the most barbarous Ages, and totally unworthy the Head of a civilized Nation.

He has constrained our fellow Citizens taken Captive on the high Seas to bear Arms against their Country, to become the Executioners of their Friends and Brethren, or to fall themselves by their Hands.

He has excited domestic Insurrections amongst us, and has endeavoured to bring on the Inhabitants of our Frontiers, the merciless Indian Savages, whose

known Rule of Warfare, is an undistinguished Destruction, of all Ages, Sexes and Conditions.

In every stage of these Oppressions We have Petitioned for Redress in the most humble Terms: Our repeated Petitions have been answered only by repeated injury. A Prince, whose Character is thus marked by every act which may define a Tyrant, is unfit to be the Ruler of a free People.

Nor have we been wanting in Attention to our British Brethren. We have warned them from Time to Time of Attempts by their Legislature to extend an unwarrantable Jurisdiction over us. We have reminded them of the Circumstances of our Emigration and Settlement here. We have appealed to their native Justice and Magnanimity, and we have conjured them by the Ties of our common Kindred to disavow these Usurpations, which, would inevitably interrupt our Connections and Correspondence. They too have been deaf to the Voice of Justice and Consanguinity. We must, therefore, acquiesce in the Necessity, which denounces our Separation, and hold them, as we hold the rest of Mankind, Enemies in War, in Peace, Friends.

We, therefore, the Representatives of the UNITED STATES OF AMERICA, in General Congress, Assembled, appealing to the Supreme Judge of the World for the Rectitude of our Intentions, do, in the Name, and by Authority of the good People of these Colonies, solemnly Publish and Declare, That these United Colonies are, and of Right ought to be, Free and Independent States; that they are absolved from all Allegiance to the British Crown, and that all political Connection between them and the State of Great-Britain, is and ought to be totally dissolved; and that as Free and Independent States, they have full Power to levy War, conclude Peace, contract Alliances, establish Commerce, and to do all other Acts and Things which Independent States may of right do. And for the support of this declaration, with a firm Reliance on the Protection of divine Providence, we mutually pledge to each other our lives, our Fortunes, and our sacred Honor. Δ

Some thoughts on growing older in the backwoods

By Marjorie Burris

"Just how long are you going to be able to live in the backwoods like that?" my friend, Pat, asked. "You're not getting any younger, you know!"

I've known Pat for 30 years, and although she hasn't any tact to spare, she always makes me think. How long **can** we expect to live this special life-style which takes so much energy and endurance?

I remember when my grandparents, who lived on a farm, cut their own wood, grew their own food, and tended their own meat and milk cattle. When they became feeble in their eighties, they had to move to a little house in a small town. But they stayed on the farm as long as they were able, and to their dying day they never lost that independent but appreciative spirit honed by a life of living with the land and the elements.

Pat's question made me make an assessment of our life in the backwoods.

Why are we here?

We did not move to the backwoods to make a statement, join a movement, or drop out of society. In fact, in 1970 when we bought the "ranch" (a misnomer, but being westerners, we call it that) we had no inkling that there was an effort to make a "return to the land."

We had three reasons for wanting a place in the backwoods: the first, and at the time, the most important, was to have a place where we could teach our three boys how to do manual labor, how to solve problems, and how to rely on their own skills and judgment.

Knowing how to do things is empowerment. The feeling of being able, a sense of self worth, the satisfaction of seeing a job well done and knowing **you** have done it — these qualities are invaluable. And our sons **did** learn these things on our backwoods land.

I'd like to say here, though, that we did not immediately move onto the ranch when we first bought it. My husband and I kept our jobs in the city so we could pay for the land, make needed extensive repairs, and buy some equipment. We also accumulated a small savings which would let

us have at least some steady income when we finally made our move to the country.

For 10 years we came to the ranch and worked as a family on our days off and on our vacations. I took a leave of absence from my nursing job for a few summers and the boys and I stayed at the ranch. This was especially good because my sons learned responsibility by running the ranch and being guardians for momma.

On the very day our youngest son graduated from high school, my husband and I moved to the ranch. We felt we had waited long enough. Now, all three of our children bring **their** children to the ranch at every opportunity so they can pass on the legacy of backwoods values.

The second reason for wanting a place in the backwoods was to have a place of comparative security. I say comparative because no place on this earth is totally secure or even peaceful all the time. But if the economy fails, we do at least have a place where we can build shelter for the children and raise a great deal of our own food. In these unstable times our sons have the security of knowing if they lose their jobs they have a place to come to with plenty of room for all — and plenty to do!

The third reason we are here is because we like the solitude. It is impossible to go through life without jostling someone or being jostled, but at least out here in the wilderness there aren't so many elbows to scrape against.

Not that living in the backwoods gives us complete freedom. Here we are subject to the laws of the land and the weather. We don't plant a garden on a rock even if we do like that spot, but we plant where soil, sun, wind, and drainage do their thing.

We live by the weather and the seasons. We cut our firewood in July when the snow and mud doesn't hamper, even if we do have more time in the winter to cut wood.

But, all in all, it is much more satisfying to us to live in tune with nature than it is to live where our freedom ends because someone else's nose begins.

What are we doing here?

Well, for one thing, we **are** growing older. We've lived on the ranch since 1979. My husband is 65 and I'm 60. We've learned the joy of living simply within a small budget.

We've learned what is **really** necessary. And we've learned to be thankful for basic pleasures — the soothing of hot bath water, the taste of good fresh vegetables, the smell of fragrant apple blossoms, watching the grace of an eagle as it slowly spirals upward, upward out of sight.

Now, we are learning how to cope with the limitations brought on by one majestic sunrise followed by a glorious sunset, by yet another sunrise, sunset, sunrise, sunset to echo that haunting song in "Fiddler on the Roof".

In our sixties, we aren't really old, but as my friend said, we aren't any younger, either. We do notice that we can't work like we did even 10 years ago. Even though we are basically healthy, we don't have the strength we used to have. Realizing this, we are taking a few steps to enable us to stay on the ranch as long as possible. These include among other things:

1. We have cut back on the number and kinds of animals we have to care for. The Nearings were correct when they said you were slaves to your animals. Pigs and cattle are relatively easy for us to care for because the pigs are ham and bacon before winter sets in, and cattle fare well with just a little shelter during bad weather. We no longer raise milk cows, chickens, geese, ducks or goats. Caring for these use our energy, which we need to do essential jobs.

2. We set aside a couple of days a month to fix little things that annoy—like the screen door that hooks after us and locks us out when we go outside. Little things, but many little things become overwhelming and make you feel unable to cope.

3. I no longer feel obliged to serve a meal to everyone who wants to come and visit us. We live a long way out in the country and it is usually lunch time before our city friends make it to our house. I used to drop what I was doing and scurry around and "fix a bite to eat" for anyone who came.

Now, I tell everyone we have a lovely picnic area and they are free to use it. If people show up unexpectedly, I tell them they weren't expected and I'm not prepared. Our visitors are learning to bring their own picnic and I have cut down on a lot of stress. Because I am by nature a hospitable person, this has been hard for me to do.

4. When strength is limited, we find we are easily frustrated, and tasks seem harder. We try not to put unreal time limits on a job and we try to plan our essential jobs to be done well before a sudden turn in the weather puts pressure on us.

We have made a yearly calendar and written in each month the "must do" jobs for that month. For example: May—buy baby pigs and calves. Till and plant garden. Turn on water tank in forest. November—finish picking apples before freezing, make cider, prune orchard. Butcher and make soap. Till garden and sow with cover crop. Planning and **writing it down** helps us not to get sidetracked with things that are "nice" but not necessary.

5. We have become reconciled to the fact that our old homestead will never be a show place with everything freshly painted and all in good repair. We are only grateful that we are comfortable, the roof doesn't leak (for now), and the fire is warm on a cold winter day. A thankful heart makes the common things take on a golden patina.

6. We both studied diligently and both got a ham radio license. Then we spent some hard earned money for some adequate equipment so we can have communications with the outside world. Our sons in Phoenix insist that we contact them daily just to let them know we are all right.

In case of an emergency, we can dial 911 on the autopatch and get paramedic help almost as quickly as we could if we lived in a metropolitan area. This has given our family, and us, great peace of mind. We are isolated—yet we aren't. Now that you can get a ham radio license without knowing Morse code, it is easy to do. I would urge any backwoods person to look into ham radio.

Where are we going?

When Pat asked me that abrupt question, I looked her in the eye and asked, "How long are **you** going to be able to live in your big house in the city and take care of it?" She bit her lip and murmured, "I don't know." "That's my answer, too," I told her.

True, it is much easier to turn up a thermostat than it is to cut your firewood and keep a fire going, but I think your attitude has a lot to do about what you can do wherever you live. We plan to live on the ranch just as long as we possibly can. We will gradually cut back on our physical work, I'm sure, but perhaps our grandsons will be able to help us as we get older.

Eventually, though, this, too, shall pass away, and we may have to move to a small house in town. I hope if that time comes that I can learn to be in a receiving mode—just enough to make it easier for those whose lot it is to care for an old independent minded woman.

Life in the backwoods is a good life. We have savored the good times and have even learned to laugh about **almost** all the bad times. I think the poet William Cullen Bryant, when he wrote *Thanatopsis* almost 200 years ago, said it well when he concluded:

"So live, that when thy summons
      come to join
The innumerable caravan,
      which moves
To that mysterious realm, where
      each shall take
His chamber in the silent halls
      of death,
Thou go not, like the quarry-
      slave at night,
Scourged to his dungeon, but,
      sustained and soothed
By an unfaltering trust, ap-
      proach thy grave,
Like one who wraps the drapery
      of his couch
About him, and lies down to
      pleasant dreams." Δ

My season passes
So quickly and
Dreams,
Like fruit that never
ripened,
Hang withered
Among the branches.

John Earl Silveira
Ojai, CA

Photovoltaics in Arkansas' Meadowcreek community help make its self reliant ideas a model for the future

By Vern Modeland

It's the biggest photovoltaic installation in a six state area, they say. "They" are the folks who designed and who work with the 10,000-watt peak PV system that provides a significant portion of electrical power for Meadowcreek, a self reliant sustainable model community near Fox, Arkansas.

So far, no one has come forward to contest the claim to regional celebrity. But people in growing numbers are making their way to the Ozark Mountain valley about 120 miles north of Little Rock to see this exceptional grid-connected PV system and learn more about its place in a sustainable future.

Luke Elliott, director of the not-for-profit environmental education center, likes to point out that, when producing at its full design output level of 14,000 to 16,000 kilowatt hours of electrical power per year, Meadowcreek's PV system would more than meet the needs of two of today's average households.

"But the interesting thing is that if we look at households that really used electricity efficiently, we'd be producing enough power for probably 10 to 15 very efficient households. Sort of a micro-utility."

Hmmm. At 8 or 10 cents a kilowatt hour for utility-source electricity (or even as low as the 5 cent per KW base rate in Springfield, MO) and an average inefficient household's consumption of around 1,000 KWH a month, investing in a neighborhood-owned, PV-clean electrical system suddenly doesn't seem entirely out of reason.

That's the kind of train of thought that Luke Elliott likes to switch onto the track.

The energy-efficient education center at Meadowcreek nestles into a hillside. Solar hot water collectors are left-center. Fixed 5KW photovoltaic array is at right.

Meadowcreek's director, Luke Elliott, explains how a freon-powered tracking system works on the ground-mounted 5KW photovoltaic array. The gas in light-fixture-like tubes at front and at the rear of panel expands in the sun warmth to push at a piston in the container visible center-photo.

Utility-connected

The utility-interactive connection is real-time. There is no attempt to store PV-generated electrical energy in batteries. Rather, the system is connected to building wiring in parallel with incoming utility lines. The area's electrical utility became the supplementary supplier of power to Meadowcreek, Benson explains.

Meadowcreek doesn't attempt to sell back to the utility any surplus power it might generate.

"The economics of it were just not there for us. We'd be paid something like two cents a kilowatt hour for power we sold back. We would have to pay a monthly meter charge to do that. We figured the power we could sell back wouldn't pay the monthly meter charge.

And I think that is one of the misconceptions people have for alternative energy. People new to it come in and say, 'This stuff is great; I'm gonna put it on and sell power back to the utility!' The reality is that it makes better sense to produce only what you can use and not try for some scheme to sell it back," says Elliott.

All lighting and appliances in the building are standard 120 volt AC versions. No attempt was made to include direct current wiring or devices.

"People can see this is normal everyday stuff," Elliott explains.

Safety considerations for a grid-connected system

Hooking a PV system up to local power lines poses safety considerations as well as technical problems. According to Benson, the primary safety concern is to be sure any private system will quickly disconnect from the utility during any abnormal operations or outages for the safety of power company linemen who might be exposed to dangerous levels of power from a generation source of which they might not be aware.

The Omnion inverters were designed to disconnect within 25 frequency cycles. They've demonstrated an ability to go off-grid in two to five cycles after sensing an abnormality. A

"We want to give people an idea of the problems and an idea of the solutions also — practical solutions that are applicable in the real world," he says.

Meadowcreek's very remote location posed the power problem that sped the development of its showcase solution in alternative energy generation.

"The quality of electrical service at Meadowcreek was inconsistent due to its distance from the nearest voltage support and the rugged, heavily-forested terrain that the electric service had to pass through," recalls Chris M. Benson. Benson was project coordinator for the PV installation. He also is a senior policy analyst for the Energy Office, a division of the Arkansas Industrial Development Commission in Little Rock.

Electricity from the public power grid gets to Meadowcreek over a long single-phase distribution line. The nearest voltage regulation point is about seven miles away. The substation serving the area is nearly 20 miles distant.

Funding was obtained in 1990. The money came from federally mandated oil overcharge reimbursements earmarked for energy- related projects in Arkansas. The dollars came with a stipulation that an adequate PV system for Meadowcreek must also serve a role in energy education for visitors.

The installation was developed with support from the PV Systems Design Assistance Center at Sandia National Laboratories, Albuquerque, NM, the United States Dept. of Energy, and the Arkansas' Energy Office.

After everything was hooked up, plugged in and generating power, the bill added up to $118,635. Of that amount, $89,068 went directly for equipment and materials.

The Meadowcreek PV design includes two arrays operated in parallel. Output at peak power levels is five KW from a tracking mount array and five from a fixed array.

Each array is composed of three paralleled strings of 14 series-connected modules with a total of 84 Solarex photovoltaic cells in each. Each module operates at an average power level of approximately 55 watts and a nominal 230 volts DC. That is converted to 120 volts AC by inverters made by Omnion Power Engineering Corp.

Solar Engineering Services, Lacy, WA, was the vendor for the equipment and engineering services, Benson says.

manual disconnect switch also is readily accessible in case of emergency and for system and utility servicing and inspections.

Fixed and tracker arrays

Another unusual feature of the system is that half of the solar panel array is affixed to the building roof while the other is ground-mounted as a tracker. Up on the south-facing roof of the education center, one array is pitched at the local optimum angle for the latitude of 33 degrees.

The second array is behind the building, on a hill, on a rugged, north-south oriented pivoting steel frame. This design allows it to roll on its long axis. That's supposed to expose more of its face directly toward the sun. Energy to drive the pivoting movement is supplied by freon refrigerant in a device from Robbins Engineering, Lake Havasu City, AZ. The freon expands when heated and pushes a piston to rotate the array.

Collectively, the two arrays are producing 30 percent of the education center's annual electrical requirements. That's an average annual output of 15,000 KWH. Elliott and Meadowcreek's engineer-handyman, Reedis Allen, keep trying to push the percentage higher through a continuing program of uncovering and eliminating or reducing power-robbers—practicing the energy-conservation that is a part of the Meadowcreek commitment.

In summer, spring and fall, Meadowcreek echoes to youth leadership and educational retreats, Elderhostels, an internship program of global proportions, and workshops and conferences on topics related to energy, ecology, and agriculture that are as varied as PV water pumping and growing Shitake mushrooms for profit.

The education center building itself shows off environmentally innovative construction ideas that also are aesthetically pleasing. In its 18,000 square feet of floor space are an auditorium, environmental library, lounge, gift shop, kitchen and dining facilities, greenhouse, and offices. Eight-

hundred-square-feet of solar panels on the roof above the lounge heat water that is pumped to hot water heaters on demand or into the 5,000 gallon storage tank located in the mechanical room. The water storage tank was partially buried in the ground and bottom and sides insulated to R40-45. It keeps water at a temperature of 120-140 degrees Fahrenheit, according to Allen.

A wood-fired furnace and the big stone fireplace in the center's lounge are backup sources for warmth, if needed.

Solar energy also produces an average two gallons of water a day in a demonstration distillation unit located near the building's greenhouse. Seedlings grow there from late winter until early spring planting. Excess solar heat from the greenhouse vents

The workings of Meadowcreek's solar water heating system is outlined for visitors in a wall graphic that includes a real-time display of temperatures and status.

into the main part of the building as needed.

Low-E glazing in a couple of dozen skylights, and the abundance of windows that face a spectacular view of towering sandstone outcroppings and forested bluffs across the valley, keep the building sunny and serene most days.

Low-wattage compact fluorescent lighting is in evidence throughout the building. Replacing 75-watt incandescent bulbs with 7-watt compact fluorescents in overhead fixtures reduced their power consumption by

about 80 percent, Elliott figures. Thirty-two T-8 fluorescents with high frequency ballasts have been installed in other fixtures. Motion sensors in many rooms, including the restrooms, automatically turn lights on only when someone is present, and see that they are off otherwise.

A food service-size refrigerator and a walk-in cooler are the center's major offenders to energy efficiency, according to the director. The appliances are destined for replacement when funds allow, he says. So is the hot water booster heater necessary for sterilization during cleanup after meal service.

"It pulls 12 KW on just one shot. When we have a sunny day and we fire that thing up; it takes all the power we can produce."

The kitchen is staffed only as needed. Its two cooks see that menu selections lean to the healthy and also include a vegetarian choice. Produce from the center's terrace gardens and organic products, purchased locally, are used in cooking that stress natural ingredients and lots of "scratch." Food scraps go to compost that is returned to regenerate the Meadowcreek terrace vegetable gardens.

Recycling paper, newsprint, glass, aluminum, and plastic also are a way of life as Meadowcreek practices what it attempts to preach and, hopefully, spread as its gospel.

"We want to continue the demonstration aspect, but we want to build some good practical programs that have outreach and have something that we can take out into the world rather than have sitting down in this secluded valley," says Elliott of his plans for 1992.

He explains a concept that would target businesses:

"We would go into a business and look at what they're using energy-wise, look at what the environmental impact is, and provide a set of solutions that give a net dollar return, a good environmental return, and also offset CO_2 production by virtue of tree planting. My idea is to do it grassroots. I feel there are a lot of people that want to do something but so often organizations do a lot of talking and publicizing the problems with very little action. I think there is a grass roots audience—the wife of the plant manager, the son of the vice president—those connections. That's where we can implement change. I think."

Youth residency program

Meadowcreek offers a residency program each June for children entering 7th and 8th grades in Arkansas public schools. It's funded by the state department of education. Last year, 400 students applied for the 30 available openings.

"They come here for two weeks and learn about agriculture and organic gardening, renewable energy and energy efficiency. There's applied ecology and learning to appreciate what's in the natural world," says Elliott.

Another eight-week residential internship program for older folks integrates reading and lecture-based sessions with hands-on experience aimed at providing participants with knowledge and skills for making informed living choices.

"What we're trying to do is give people something they can take back to their own house, their own community, and apply. It's not a new idea but there are very few places where people can really learn about alternative energy and organic gardening and install a photovoltaic system or an active solar heater."

The Meadowcreek enterprise began in the 1970s as the commitment to action of two brothers who grew tired of only talking about the unsustainable direction in which they saw the world headed. David and Wilson Orr became of a mind to put their energy and money where their ideas were. They looked at locations in the Rockies, the Smoky Mountains, and elsewhere across the United States, then chose Meadow Creek Valley in the Ozarks.

Meadow Creek had the greatest combination of natural resources, David Orr observed. There were abandoned acres of farmland, stands of mixed hardwood forest, abundant water, a mild climate, and diverse wildlife.

The brothers bought 1500 acres.

Meadowcreek as David Orr envisioned it would be a model for viable communities and neighborhoods in an irrevocably interdependent world. But not a commune.

"Taking the best that 'soft technology' has to offer, we plan to set up not just a community, but an educational and research center that will encourage the exchange of information on successful responses to problems of sustainability," he wrote in describing his vision.

"I think we succeeded in many ways, including the construction of an extraordinary facility, the establishment of a variety of creative educational programs, some great conferences, and the initiation of off-site projects like the food studies we did at Hendrix, Oberlin, St. Olaf, and Carleton Colleges," he reflects today.

Wil Orr stayed with the project until 1989. David moved on in 1990 to teach in the environmental studies program at Oberlin. Luke Elliott arrived in 1990, taking over Wil Orr's role as energy specialist. Elliott then inherited David Orr's position as director, infusing a 32-year old's enthusiasm and energy.

His biggest task he says, has been to find funding that would keep Meadowcreek alive. One of his achievements in 1991 was a management and financial relationship with the Kerr Center for Sustainable Agriculture, Poteau, OK. The Kerr Center is a research and demonstration center providing education and technical assistance in agriculture.

"The ideas of self-reliance and sustainability are highly practical," David Orr observed more than a decade ago. "Applied widely enough, they would rejuvenate neighborhoods and communities, reduce environmental costs, lower energy demands, minimize burdens on government, cut inflation and unemployment, and preserve islands of diversity in an overly homogenized and vulnerable society."

Self-reliant thinking gave birth to Meadowcreek. Now, the largest photovoltaic installation in Arkansas attracts the people who can make such dreams come true. Δ

Semblances

You
Are trying
To be,
Like the person
In your poems;
Deep,
And intellectual,

While I
Am trying
Not
To be,
Like the
Dark
Brooding
Monster
In my own.

John Earl Silveira
Ojai, CA

More good reading:

The Coming American Dictatorship

By John Silveira

In Backwoods Home Cooking you'll find:

- **Breads**
- **Casseroles**
- **Cookies**
- **Desserts**
- **Jams & jellies**
- **Main dishes**
- **Pasta**
- **Salads**
- **Seafood**
- **Soups**
- **Vegetables**
- **Our favorites**

Searching for the right American health care plan —

Is the Medical Care Savings Account the answer?

By Martin P. Waterman

There have been many models put forward for a system that would provide all Americans with affordable health care. The Medical Care Savings Account is one of the newer plans being proposed and is, in part, modeled after a plan that is being used successfully in Singapore. It is sometimes called **The Singapore Plan**.

The biggest push for the Medical Care Savings Account has been put forward by an organization called the Citizens for Affordable Health Care, but more about them later.

In order to understand the Medical Care Savings Account, we need to look at the alternatives. There are basically three plans now before the Congress: private plans (such as the Medical Care Savings Plan), Mandated Employer plans, and the big topic this election year — a National Health Insurance Plan.

Mandated employer plans

The Mandated Employer Plans (also called "play or pay") are not a likely alternative for several important reasons. First of all, if they pass a bill like the one Senator George Mitchell proposes it will mean $6 billion in new taxes in the first year. And if they pass a bill like the one Representative Dan Rostenkowski proposes, the costs are $80 billion in the first year.

The new taxes would be raised by either a new payroll tax and/or a 9% surtax. History has taught us that once Congress has established a new tax they have relative ease in raising the rates. The reason that Mandated Employer Plans are unlikely to be

passed into law now is the opposition from businesses.

In a poll conducted by the National Federation of Independent Business, they found that 67.1% of small businesses objected to being mandated to provide health care, and 23% of them said they would let all the employees go if it is enacted into law. Still, another 21.5% said that they would just get out of business and this, of course, would be devastating to the economy.

National Health Insurance

That leaves us with the private and national health care plans. In Issue No. 15 of *BHM* I listed the benefits and drawbacks of a National Health Care Plan. In summation, the National Health Care Plan would cost around a quarter of a trillion dollars in its first year. This money would be raised (as proposed by some congressmen) by a new payroll tax in the 5% range, new excise taxes, and increased taxes on personal, corporate, and social security income.

In theory, although costly, the supporters of such a plan argue that it is a sound idea. However, the model from which an American national health care plan is likely to be drawn is the Canadian health care system, and that system, according to critics, has not lived up to its expectations. Former Presidential contender Paul Tsongas went as far as saying that if the Canadian System had been in place in the United States, he would never have received the treatment he needed to survive his bout with cancer.

Private plans

The final alternative is the private health care system and the Medical Savings Account. There are many private plans being talked about, but the one proposed by Citizens for Affordable Health Care may be the most acceptable, especially with the current discontent about the uncontrolled spending habits of Congress.

The Medical Care Savings Account

It is important to realize that one of the biggest beneficiaries of private plans is the insurance industry. They also have one of the most powerful and effective lobbies and were the major forces behind such legislation as mandatory seat belts and air bags for automobiles. Naturally, they want to protect their interests, and Medical Care Savings Accounts can keep them in the lucrative health care business.

Requires no new taxes

On the surface the Medical Care Savings Account seems too good to be true since it requires no new taxes.

This is how it is supposed to work: Your employer buys a policy to protect you and your family from the expenses of a major illness or serious injury so you have full coverage for catastrophic care. Your routine medical bills are also paid by your employer, but for these expenses he gives you the money in the form of a monthly benefit. The money the employer gives you goes into an account that you control. This account is your tax-free Medical Care Savings Account.

At this point, your employer is paying you 2/3 of the money he would normally be spending on health insurance.

Cost savings

The first cost savings are administrative. There are no forms for the insurance company or your employer to fill out and therefore you don't have to fight with an insurance company to receive a benefit. In addition, the medical decisions you make are between you and your Doctor.

There is no insurance company agent or government bureaucrat telling you what routine care you may or may not be entitled to. You choose the doctor and the medical service. Under the proposed plan, you will even be able to use the money for dental work and eye glasses.

You can keep the medical costs down by shopping around for the best medical service prices, which puts an incentive on the medical industry to help control costs since it is you and not some insurance company employee settling the bill. It is you who will have the incentive to find the best price and service available for you or your family.

A big incentive

Part of the incentive is that you get to keep any unused portion of the balance that is not spent in the Medical Care Savings Account. This does not punish those who take care of their health with higher taxes to pay for those who don't, as can happen under a National Health Care Plan. You keep the balance of the account just like an IRA, and the money would be tax-deductible. If you needed to withdraw excess funds, say for a backwoods home down payment or college education for your kids, you withdraw the balance and pay the taxes on it. Not a bad way to save money.

Employer benefits

But what about the employer? How does he benefit, that is, besides having an employee who feels his boss cares about his health and welfare? The employer benefits in many ways. First

of all, he is not taxed to death under a Mandated Employer Plan or National Health Care Plan.

One of the reasons that health care is so expensive is the high cost for the processing of small claims. It saves your employer money to purchase catastrophic health care for you and your family and then give you the other 2/3's of the money for your Medical Savings Account.

Your employer will also save money on buying the catastrophic policy since the insurance company will save money in not having to worry about endless reams of paperwork for the routine care. This saving will be passed on to the employer.

Most small businesses have flexibility concerning what they can pay their employees, thus they can convert part of the money they are paying in salary to a benefit. In doing so, the employer is not really paying out more money.

Under the proposed Medical Care Savings Account plan, the employer would pay you, on average, about $3000 a year, and any additional medical expenses would be covered by the policy which the employer has purchased for you.

It should be noted that the current national average cost (for medium-sized cities) of premiums per employee family is $4500. If you do not have any medical expenses in three years, you will have about $9000 dollars in your account. The plan rewards those who take care of themselves by providing a cash incentive.

When you take the excess money out of the account and pay taxes on it, you have converted your benefit back to a salary. Under the Medical Care Savings Account plan, you do not have to pay for medical care out of hard-earned (and taxed) dollars.

Of course, under the private plans, an employer does not have to offer the account. However, it places an incentive force in the job market place that the best employees will go to those businesses that offer the plans.

Citizens for Affordable Health Care argues that this is the best plan for America and that the reason there is a health care crisis is **not** that health care costs too much, but that we spend to much for it.

The key is incentive

Health care costs are rising at the rate of about 17% per year because there is little incentive for individual policy holders to keep the costs down. This is happening in the Canadian system where some doctors order a plethora of tests in order to boost their revenue, and patients often over-use the system because it seems almost free.

In America, if you are covered by a private policy that does not limit care, there is no incentive for you to save money or shop around, which also puts pressure on health costs to rise. Nor is there any incentive for doctors to avoid giving tests that are "useless but covered" under a particular plan.

Drawbacks

There are drawbacks to the Medical Care Saving Account plan. Some people may go without proper care so that they can keep the money in their accounts. However, this is better than having no plan and it does put the decision in your hands and not in the hands of an insurance company employee or a government bureaucrat.

The Medical Care Savings Account may not be perfect but it is worthy of consideration when one considers some of the alternatives. It protects the integrity of the free enterprise system by not taxing it to the breaking point.

Another point of contention is that the plan does not do much for the unemployed. This aspect could be addressed by government. If you do find yourself out of a job, you can use the proceeds in your Medical Care Savings Account to buy a policy until you are able to find work again.

For a growing number of people, the Medical Care Savings Account is the most logical plan to be proposed. If you are interested in learning more about this plan, you can contact the Citizens for Affordable Health Care at their offices at 220 North First Street, Albert City, Iowa, 50510. You can also call them toll free at 1-800-858-9621. Δ

Starting a home video business

By Doug Stevenson

One of the most difficult tasks facing anyone who leaves the city in search of a saner lifestyle is finding a way to earn a living. Let's face it. In rural areas jobs are scarce and those that are around pay very little. To survive one must discover unique talents and skills, and a way to tap into a cash flow that is either unrelated to or helps to bring a new service to the local economy.

Video production can be both of these. With a minimal starting capitol investment you can create a business that can tap into national markets or be one of the first in your community to offer video as a service.

About six years ago I faced a hard decision. Although I was already living in the country, the business I operated at that time kept me for the most part in the big city. I knew if my business was to succeed, I would need to move. Or find a new way to earn money from home.

I purchased a camcorder and a computer, and started asking a lot of questions. I've talked with people all over the country to find what they are doing to succeed. In the last five years the cost of professional level video gear has plummeted in price. Thousands are finding they can produce quality and impressive videotapes. By filling a need for information supplying the demand for documentation of local events, people are earning real money!

Starting locally

Just about no matter where you move, there will be some level of small town nearby where you buy groceries. These are your neighbors. Their kids are in dance recitals, playing sports, graduating, getting married, having reunions and on and on. People will

Doug Stevenson

pay to have these things taped and edited.

The key word is "edit". Editing is when you cut out the bad parts of a tape, and only save the good parts, putting them all together into something someone could stand watching. Only you don't cut anything, you simply record on to another tape, leaving out the places where the camera was pointed at your feet or out of focus.

What you need

Which means, yes, you do need more than just a camcorder. You have to be able to offer something different than what Uncle Bob can do. Editing is where you start. You need a second VCR. You have to put together a kit, a good mike, some lights, a tripod, a way to add titles.

You also need to spend a little extra and purchase video equipment that uses a professional format. Format means the type of tape you use. Regular VHS or the little 8mm tapes do not cut it. You need to buy what's known as Super VHS, Hi8mm, or even used 3/4". These types of tapes and their related equipment allow you to

produce tapes that will look acceptable.

In producing videos, first you shoot the tape, that is record the wedding or the commercial or whatever. This tape is the first generation. Then you edit that material to a second tape. That tape is the second generation. Now you are ready to make copies of the edited tape, and sell these to your client or customer. These copies are third generation. Every generation your picture loses some of its sharpness. You have to use equipment and a tape format that can withstand this loss and still look good.

Selling tapes nationally

The next type of video sales possible to tap into from the country is the sale of information. People have things to learn, need the facts, want to know how something is done. It can be basket making, fishing tips, build a log cabin, raising goats, cat lovers, you name it, and somebody's planning to make a video about it. It might as well be you. If you know something or know someone that has a skill or knowledge in an area that other people have an interest in, you have a potential market.

The trick is to find out what people want, and make a video about it. You've got to put it out where they can see how to buy it. This means mail-order, through display and classified ads in special interest magazines. There are hundreds of magazines, each catering to a specific group of people with a common interest.

Here again it helps to have quality equipment, but the key is the information. People are very forgiving if you are supplying them with information they really want.

More information

Interestingly enough, one of the best ways to learn about starting a video business, is on video. Several video entrepreneurs have put together sets of tapes that will help guide you through the maze of equipment, show you how to tap various markets, and basically help you get started by benefiting from their experience. If you are seriously considering this as a career move, then the price of this type of instant education is very minimal indeed.

There are also publications and newsletters dedicated to video and making money with video. Camcorder Magazine and Video-Maker are the two magazines found on the stand in almost any bookstore. The Video Marketing Newsletter by Bill Myers is considered by many to be the voice of the guru in starting a video business. He has gone in a few short years from starting out with no equipment at all, to a complex employing a number of people with an income into six figures, all from the backwoods of Arkansas!

Starting any new business is not easy. It takes hard work, but then what doesn't? The difference is you're working for yourself, at home, in the country, doing something downright fun!

Without a doubt the fastest growing segment of video production today is Wedding Videography. There is always an annual flow (2.5 million per year) of young and not so young couples getting hitched. Numbered in the millions nationwide. For years, photographers have had this market sewn up. But the trend now is video. While it will probably never replace the wedding photographer, video is becoming an essential part of the easiest ways to get started. The main thing you have to do is offer the bride (and her mother) something that Uncle Bob and his camcorder can't. Again it is editing, better sound, and some titles.

Fees for wedding video start out at around $150 for one person with a camcorder. More money comes with fancier productions, where you use two or three cameras, giving the finished piece a wider variety of shots, angles and in general a more professional look. One friend of mine is booked a year in advance. His services average $500 to $600 per wedding and his annual total is around $100,000 a year! Not bad for part time work on the weekends.

For more information:

- *The Bill Myers Video Marketing Newsletter*, 321 Ouachita Ave., Hot Springs, AR 71901, 1-501-321-1845

- *Wedding Videography Today Newsletter*, 1319 Carlsbad Drive, Gaithersburg, Maryland 20879, 301-869-6878

- *The Video Dave Desktop Video Production Newsletter*, P.O. Box 502, Antigo, WI 54409, 800-688-2001

- *Camcorder Magazine,* P.O. Box 6925, Ventura, CA 93006-9878

- *Videomaker*, P.O. Box 558, Mt. Morris, IL 61054

(Doug Stevenson is a staff writer for Camcorder Magazine and owner of Nashville Video Publications.) Δ

A Backwoods Home Anthology
The Sixteenth Year

* Build your own solar-powered water pumping station
* The art of chimney building
* Practical preparedness planning
* Catch your own bait
* Breaking ice on hard water fishing
* Build a trail
* The forever floor
* Removing mold
* Build a heated germination bed
* Some tips for aging gardeners
* Build a simple solar-powered outdoor light
* The art of living in small spaces
* Raising rabbits on the home place
* Paring down for off-grid living
* Solar window panels

* Rebuilding the homestead greenhouse
* Grid-tie solar-powered farm
* Starting over again without a man
* Lifestyle and cancer
* The care and feeding of solar batteries
* Making sausages
* Build a component water system
* The benefits of mulching
* 10 country do's and don'ts
* Preparing for home evacuation
* Make your own nut butters
* Frostbite — Don't flirt with this sneaky danger
* Gold panning for fun and profit
* Build a top-bar beehive
* Ice dams on roofs

Roughcut — a cut above?

By Kris Hartley

More and more people are discovering that roughsawn lumber provides an excellent alternative to the store-bought variety. Some folks choose the venerable standby over todays style of lumber because it's often less expensive.

Some use roughsawn lumber because of its rustic appearance. Others rely solely on roughcut for the wider selection of wood available, such as walnut, ash, oak, maple, etc. Another possible benefit to using roughsawn lumber is that you may already own the trees you need to make the lumber you want.

Having lumber cut from your own trees can be not only a money saving maneuver but also an environment saving one as well. By carefully selecting the trees to be harvested and replanting afterward, you can actually benefit the environment instead of detracting from it. In choosing between having lumber cut from your own trees or buying lumber from a sawmill, you'll need to consider what you intend to build and when you want to begin your project.

For most uses some amount of "drying" must take place before rough-sawn lumber can be used. This drying time is needed to either reduce or eliminate the shrinkage that will occur in the final project. The amount of time needed for the lumber to dry depends on many things, but one of the most important is how you want your project to look when it's finished.

If you're planning on using your lumber for something such as a board fence, you could use the boards after a short drying time. The shrinkage that would occur would add to the rustic appeal of the fence.

Of course if you want your lumber for woodworking instead of a construction venture you probably won't want any shrinkage in the final product. In

Squared log house built by the owners and their friends.

this case you can buy your lumber at the sawmill already cured.

If you want to use boards from your own trees for a project where you don't want any shrinkage, you'll either have to be patient while the wood dries naturally or have it kiln dried. A kiln is simply a controlled environment where lumber is placed to have it's moisture content reduced to a certain level to prevent any further shrinkage.

Drying your own lumber

You can dry your own lumber without using a kiln; it will just take longer. To dry your own lumber dry it where it's going go be used. Lumber

that is going to be used outside should be dried outside, preferably in the summer. Make sure the wood is off the ground and has 1" x 1" spacers across the width of the stack at about 2 1/2 foot intervals between the layers for air circulation. Keep all of the spacers in line with each other vertically. Always weight your drying stack down at the top to prevent warping and cover it if it's outside.

Lumber that's to be used indoors can be dried in a basement, heated garage, a spare room or under your bed if you can get away with it. Winter months are normally the best for drying wood indoors.

Drying times will vary with the type and thickness of the wood used, but if

Operator of a portable bandsaw type mill sawing boards from a log that has already been squared.

models of both circular and bandsaw types today and it is often easier to bring the mill to the logs instead of visa versa. (Several such mills have been advertised in *BHM*.)

The last item I'd like to mention about sawmills is the method of pricing. Although not all mills charge the same, most, whether selling you lumber from their stock or sawing your logs will charge by the board foot. A board foot is one inch thick, twelve inches wide and twelve inches long. A board that is one inch thick, twelve inches wide and ten feet long, would equal ten board feet. Three 2x4's that were five feet long would also equal ten board feet. The board foot method is a fair one, and once you learn the price per board foot you'll be able to determine the cost of any size of lumber easily. Δ

you use the methods described here, 3 to 4 months should be enough for most uses. Coating the ends of your boards with sealant will reduce cracks caused by the drying process. This can be done once you have your lumber stacked to dry.

If you're considering using rough-sawn lumber, the next thing you need to decide is what type of mill you want to use. When most people hear the word sawmill, they think of the contraption seen in the old movies or cartoons.

The descendants of this type of a sawmill, with it's large, round, steel blade is known as a circular mill. The other common type of sawmill in use today is known as a bandsaw mill. The bandsaw mill uses a thin metal blade that is in a continuous loop or band. Because of this thin blade, bandsaw mills normally produce more usable lumber per log. Wood sawn on a circular mill will usually have a rougher appearance. Whether this is an advantage, disadvantage, or unimportant will depend on your use of the wood and personal taste.

If you are planning to have lumber sawn from your own trees, there is another difference in sawmills that will concern you. You may be able to choose between a portable mill and a stationary one. There are portable

An outside drying stack of lumber that is to be used to build a workshop. This lumber is almost ready for use. Note the cover and weight on top of the stack.

A drip irrigation primer!

By Leon Springer

Drip irrigation is the process of applying the right amount of water slowly and evenly to the root zones of plants. This keeps the level of moisture in the soil within the optimum range for healthy growth and minimum stress. It's a sensible way to water your garden for several reasons:

Pinpoint water placement: Drip irrigation allows you to pinpoint water placement and adjust delivery rates to the changing needs of each plant. Fertilizers, using an inline injector, can be delivered in solution to the root zones of intended plants, increasing their response rate to feeding.

Saves time: A drip system will save you time wasted on hand watering or weeding. Timers can be installed to ensure that watering is done at the right time and in the desired amount. Enjoy your garden on your terms. Timers make gardening possible for many people who otherwise wouldn't have time for it. Or you can take a vacation knowing that your plants will be well cared for while you're away.

Saves money: You will use up to 70% less water with a drip system than with conventional watering. The payback period for lowered water bills, lowered food bills for vegetable gardens, and the value of your labor is usually one season or less.

Higher yields and quality: Drip irrigation is a total crop support system which will reward the gardener with higher yields, lower costs, and a quality garden. The slow, regular, uniform application of water and nutrients results in even growth and ripening with consistent quality. Drip irrigation, particularly when combined with mulching, helps break the cycle of too-wet-too-dry soils that stress plants and retard their growth.

Weed control: By pinpointing water to individual plants, water is unavailable for weeds. The most tedious part

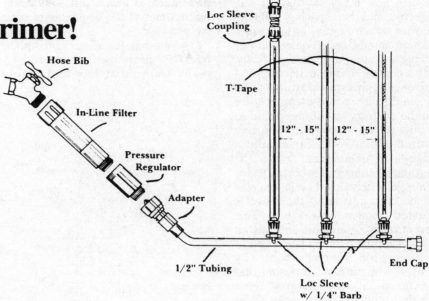

Example of a simple drip irrigation system.

of gardening—weeding—is minimized.

Designing a system

Designing a drip system is easy. Drip irrigation is flexible and forgiving. First, make a sketch or scale drawing of the area you want to irrigate. Note the location, size, and water requirements of each plant and tree.

Be aware that plants with very different watering needs will need their own watering circuits. For example, orchards that get watered weekly will need to have a different circuit than a garden that gets watered daily. Plants that are drought-tolerant will need to be watered differently than plants requiring a lot of water.

Note the distance between the water supply (hose bib, standpipe, etc.) and the plants to be watered. Long distances will require extra pipe.

Design considerations

Water supply: Most homes have sufficient water to meet the minimal water requirements of a drip system, but if your garden system needs more water than the supply will provide at one time, you can divide the drip sys-

tem into as many sections as necessary and schedule each section for a different time.

To check on how much water will be required, add up the output of your emitters and multiply by their gallons per hour rating. You can measure the output of your water supply with a one or five gallon bucket and a stopwatch. Time how long it takes to fill the bucket and use that number to calculate how much water is available per hour. Gallons/minute x 60 = Number of gallons per hour.

Elevation can cause a change in water pressure within the system. Elevation can add to the pressure or decrease it depending on whether water is moving uphill or down. Pressure-compensating emitters that provide a constant output regardless of line pressure were developed to alleviate this problem.

Friction will also affect pressure in the line. As water moves through half inch tubing, pressure is lost because of friction. In main line runs of more than 200 feet, there can be a significant drop in pressure that will lower the output of emitters at the end of the line.

Emitters are the most important parts of a drip system. They ensure that water is delivered in the desired amount at the intended rate. When deciding how many emitters to use, what type, and their spacing, **soil type and root structure** must be taken into account. Sandy soil requires closer spacing as water percolates vertically. With a clay soil water tends to spread horizontally, giving a wide distribution pattern. Shallow root systems require that the emitters be closely spaced so that the total surface of the soil gets watered. Deep roots can handle a wide spacing of emitters.

Automatic timers: It is best to water on a regular scheduled cycle. On clay soil or on a hill side, short cycles repeated frequently work best. This prevents run-off, erosion, and wasted water. Automatic timers help prevent the too-dry-too- wet cycles created by erratically timed hand watering that stresses plants and retards their growth. Automatic timers make a drip system work efficiently. They provide independence and worry-free gardening. For young plants, particularly those in a vegetable garden, a timer allows multiple small waterings during the day to keep the soil moist without saturating it.

Installation

Every drip system is unique. It's best to plan your system out on paper so you can visualize how the lines will be laid out, where the water source(s) is, and what parts you need. Steps 1-5 that follow can be done on site although it is convenient to use a workbench.

Note: All plastic fittings should be hand tightened only. All male plastic pipe threads, but not hose threads, should be wrapped with 2 to 3 turns of Teflon tape. Wrap in the same direction that the pipe is tightened into the fitting and leave a small bare spot at the top of the pipe thread to keep torn off pieces of Teflon from entering your drip system and clogging the emitters. Installation begins at the source of water, i.e. hose bib or water pipe and works outward. Much of the equipment is designed to work in only one direction. **Look for arrows pointing in the direction of flow.**

1. (optional) To control when and how much to water, install an **automatic timer** at the beginning of your system.

2. (optional) Install an anti-siphon **backflow preventer.** (Required by many water districts and highly

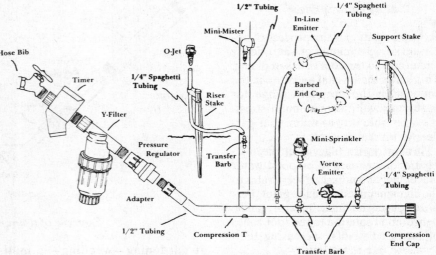
Example of a complex drip irrigation system.

recommended for automatic systems or where a fertilizer injector is used.)

3. (optional) **Install fertilizer injector.**

4. Install **pressure regulator** set at 20 PSI for all systems except those using T-Tape which should use a 10 PSI regulator.

5. Slip 1/2" **drip tubing** into **thread-to-tubing adapter.**

6. Attach **thread-to-tubing adapter** to pressure regulator.

7. **Uncoil tubing** and lay it on the ground near where its going in the garden. Let it warm up and become more pliable before forcing any bends. Hint: For a clean 90-degree turn below the valve, attach a **compression elbow** at ground level.

8. Set the main line in its permanent location. Stake down if desired.

9. After the main line is connected, laterals can be cut in at any point, connected with compression T's, and branched out to other areas.

10. To remove dirt and plastic fragments turn on water and flush the lines.

11. Install end caps or figure 8 closures at the end of all lines.

12. The emitters can now be attached. There are three ways to install emitters. In all three applications a punch is used for making holes in the main line.

● If the main line is close to the plants to be watered the emitter can be mounted on the main line.

● If the plants are away from the main line, as most plants are, **spaghetti tubing** is used to bring water to them. **Transfer barbs** are required to attach spaghetti tubing to the main line with emitters at the base of the plant.

● Many types of emitters can also be attached directly to the main line with spaghetti tubing connected to them and run to remote plants.

13. Inspect the system while running to ensure that all emitters are working. Check the soil for proper wetting after the first few waterings. Adjust the number or type of emitters if necessary. Set timers if used.

14. Inspect the system regularly. Filters need to be flushed out periodically, particularly with a home water supply. Check the filter after the first couple of waterings to gauge how often it must be flushed.

Drip hose can be left out all year but the filters and regulators should be removed if exposed to freezing. Hose mounted timers should also be taken in at the end of the season and the batteries removed.

- **Drip Tubing** is the 1/2" main tubing used throughout a drip system. It's inexpensive. If made of soft polyethylene, it comes without perforations but is designed to have emitters and spaghetti tubing punched into it and attached with barbed fittings. Drip tubing lasts about 10 years when exposed to sunlight, longer if mulched over or buried. Maximum flow rate is approximately 300 gallons per hour (GPH). Drip tubing is very easy to work with; it bends easily to conform to any layout.
- **Emitters** emit water to plants in a drip system. They attach to 1/2" drip tubing or to spaghetti tubing. Many emitters, including mini-sprinklers and misters, need to be mounted above ground to perform well. Supports, whether as stakes or as risers, are a fast and economical

way to do this. Stakes are also used for anchoring lines to keep them straight and to keep them from being inadvertently moved.
- **Spaghetti tubing** is small diameter tubing that carries water from drip tubing to emitters, or from emitters to individual plants. It is very soft and pliable; fittings and emitters are simply inserted into it. No clamps are needed to hold them in place.
- **Compression Fittings** are simple fittings that require neither glue nor clamps. Insert drip tubing into fittings while wiggling the fitting and pipe from side to side. Compression fittings work well up to 60 PSI.
- **Regulators** lower incoming water pressure to a pressure usable by the drip system so that components are not damaged. Regulators come either preset at a particular pressure or adjustable for individual requirements.
- **Soaker tubing** is designed to emit water throughout its length. Some of it has emitters spaced every few inches; some of it oozes water continuously. It's great for row crops. We don't recommend you bury soaker tubing because roots and dirt tend to clog it and its difficult to know whether its working properly until its too late. However, we highly recommend putting mulch over tubing; it helps conserve water, extends the life of the tubing, and keeps moisture more evenly dispersed in the soil.
- **Fertilizer injectors** require fertilizer that is water soluble (dissolves completely in water) and a backflow protection device.

(Drip Works, which prepared this article for BHM, sells a full range of drip irrigation products, including kits. Their address is 380 Maple St., Willits, CA 95490. Tel.: (800) 522-DRIP) Δ

A Backwoods Home Anthology
The Fourteenth Year

If you plan to drive the Alaska Highway for its 50th anniversary in 1992, here are some good travel tips

By Phil Wilcox

1992 is the 50th anniversary of the completion of the Alaska Highway. There will be celebrations all along the route and many Americans will be making the trip.

I drove from northern California to Alaska and back in 1991. There are many books available to advise you how to do this but I realize now that there are many little but important things they fail to tell you. So, I decided to write this article with some thoughts that will help you on your trip.

Most folks probably make this trip during July or August due to vacation time and better weather. That's fine and a good time to go. But I decided to leave August 15 and return October 1 for three reasons. I wanted to miss the crowds (I did); miss most of the mosquitoes (I did); and catch the beautiful September weather (I did partially).

Unfortunately, Alaska has a very cool and wet summer about every 10 years. They did in 1980 and again in 1991. Especially in the southeast area. As it turned out, it was just as bad in July and August! They really had no summer. Just rain and cool.

I experienced 16 consecutive days of rain from August 26 on Vancouver Island through Prince Rupert, Ketchikan, Sitka, and Juneau. The sun finally came through in beautiful Haines, Alaska.

So, realizing you can't do anything about the weather, pick the time that you can make the trip and go—hoping for the best. If doing it again I think I would go more in August than in September. Much of Alaska (and Canada) that deals with tourists (gas stations, resorts, etc.) closes down or severely restricts their hours after

The Alaska Highway

Labor Day weekend. Even the Alaska Marine Highway starts to reduce or drop ferry schedules in September.

Prepare your vehicle

With your time schedule set, think carefully about your vehicle and its condition. I drove a 1978 Chevy, 3/4 ton, four-wheel drive pickup with an 8' cabover camper attached. A good combination and perfect for one person—maybe a bit crowded for two. Suggested equipment would be two spare tires (most carry one underneath and one on a front bumper mount), heavy duty radials on the ground, two gas tanks, extra fan belts, fuses, and a good high-lift jack.

Gasoline in Alaska (except Fairbanks) and especially in Canada, is expensive!

Get your vehicle in good shape! Replace weak or suspected parts. I knew my brake master cylinder was a weak spot but didn't replace it at home. So I was forced to in Sitka, Alaska (by an honest, reasonably priced mechanic but, nevertheless, away from home in a strange place).

Purchase a bottle of "**Rain-X**". Follow directions and put it on your windshield. It's marvelous.

CB radio for emergencies

A **citizen's band radio** is a must for me. I don't use it often but it has been the reason for my rescue on more than one occasion. Generally in the "lower

Russian church in Sitka, Alaska

48" monitor Channel 17. Alaska and Canada seem to prefer 19.

I'm the sort of person who likes to know where I am. Both vertically and horizontally. So, my truck is equipped with both a **compass** and an **altimeter**. Also, if you have a camper, get (from your local RV dealer) two stick-on level gauges. Put one on the dashboard and one on the inside of the passenger door so as to be visible from the driver's seat. They really help you level your unit when parking at your campsite.

Food in Alaska is expensive

Food is cheapest at home (or in Oregon where there is no sales tax). Alaskan and Canadian prices are high! In Fairbanks a tunafish sandwich was $5.50. At Manley Hot Springs Resort a cheeseburger was $7.50.

I usually ate in my camper. Dinty Moore Beef Stew and Top Shelf dinners by Hormel were delicious. The latter you boil in its own pouch for 10 minutes, and no refrigeration is required. Great when you don't want the hassle of cooking a regular meal. I seldom ate out except to take advantage of local delicacies like fresh seafood!

Liquor prices are out of sight

In Alaska and Canada, the price of beer, wine and whiskey is sky-high! If you wish to drink these items while on your trip, stock up at home! I underestimated my consumption and paid high prices for my mistake.

Get mostly travelers checks from your own bank. I never had one refused—even in small places. Don't carry that much cash!

Bring some snack foods. They are not only great to munch on while driving down long highways, but they are a must in your daypack while on the ferry.

Daypack on the ferries

While on the ferry, you are not allowed to go to the car deck while underway to obtain items from your vehicle—so pack all you need (food, drink, reading, camera, towel and soap, etc.) in your day pack.

Most ferries have good hot showers so take advantage of them! If traveling overnight, bring a sleeping bag on deck. Some like sleeping topside on the covered solarium but I liked it better in the lounge chair area. Hint: usually the seat cushions are detach-able life cushions. Put three of them on the floor and you have a good bed.

Rain gear and cassette tapes

Take clothes designed mostly for cooler weather. And a good **rain suit is a must!**

In much of Alaska and Canada it is impossible to tune in any radio station. I mean hundreds of miles with no reception at all! Take plenty of cassette tapes if you enjoy music. My 10 tapes got old rapidly.

My cabover camper had no heater. I purchased an inexpensive stovetop heater at my local RV dealer and it worked beautifully to warm up and dry out my living space. Some type of **fire starter** helps in camping spots where the wood is damp and hard to start.

A friend loaned me his **bee-keepers hat**. It was great while fishing to foil the ever-present mosquitoes.

Unfold and place lots of newspapers under your cabover mattress. Keeps the cold from coming up underneath you!

Baggies are great for storing all sorts of things such as nuts and bolts, matches, left over food, playing cards, etc.

My camper had an ice box rather than a propane refrigerator. The ice

The Inside Passage to Alaska

The Third Year

Juneau, Alaska

box really does not keep items that cold and the price of ice is ridiculous. I paid as little as $.94 for a block in Eugene, Oregon and as much as $3.50 in Fairbanks. It is also not always readily available.

I purchased a bicycle rack that fit over my front-mounted spare tire. It worked well and I enjoyed being able to leave my truck and camper and use my 15-speed to explore the area.

GST tax refund

Canada has a new Goods and Services Tax (GST) which no one likes. It is levied on top of provincial taxes. U.S. citizens may claim a refund (save your receipts) when returning home except on items like gasoline.

The roads are in pretty good shape except certain areas where frost heaves bounce you up and down and wreak havoc by throwing things around in the back of the camper.

Abundant wildlife

Wildlife is abundant. I saw plenty of wild bald eagles, moose and caribou (reindeer), as well as roaming buffalo (bison). Although widely seen and feared, I never did see a bear. Heard one at a campsite one night though.

Of course, take a **camera**. Film is available everywhere and there is much to photograph.

Handy books

I strongly recommend you take and use the book *The Milepost*. It is a mile-by-mile log of all northern highways, including the Alaska Highway. I found it invaluable. I also took *The Alaska Wilderness Milepost*. It is a complete guide to 250 remote towns and villages. Both are available from Wild Rose Guidebooks, Box 240047, Anchorage, Alaska 99524. Write for their catalog of Alaska and Canada books, maps, and videos.

I will be glad to answer specific questions if you'll send an SASE to me at P.O. Box 1460, Lower Lake, CA 95457.

Have a good trip! The scenery and wildlife are spectacular but I was particularly impressed by the friendly people I met everywhere. Unlike the feeling often experienced by tourists—they make you feel at home. That's nice when you're a long way from familiar territory.

(Phil Wilcox, also known as "The Solar Man," sells and installs solar systems anywhere. He also travels a lot and loves to visit hot springs.) Δ

Night terrors
*I wake
In the middle of the night
And listen to the clock
Ticking
Like it was bulldozing
Eternity
Over a cliff
One
Second
At
A
Time.*

John Earl Silveira
Ojai, CA

A BHM Writer's Profile

Don Fallick lives in a primitive, wooded canyon in Washington State with his wife and nine of their ten children. He bought his first homestead in 1975 and says that since then he has raised "everything but his standard of living."

Don has learned woodworking, blacksmithing, building, and many other skills in his life, and shares them with our readers in almost every issue. Don has been writing for *Backwoods Home Magazine* since its first year, and is currently working on three books.

They may be old but they work—a solar food dryer

By Jj
(Photos by Eric Large)

Our rural canyon is home to several aging solar food dehydrators. Whether the original builders had plans, worked from their imaginations, or copied the first design of some original backwoods engineer I don't know.

I do know these rough-and-ready dehydrators, strange as they look, **do** dry food, without cost from June (and the first greens & berries) through the fall harvest.

It is possible to knock together a perfectly functional dehydrator from a photo of one, but for those less adventurous carpenters here are plans for a model similar to those dotting my landscape.

Author with dehydrator that came with her house.

Wood cut list for dehydrator:

From 3/4" stock—12-23" strips
   for tray supports
2-2x4's x 70" for back legs
2-2x4's x 68" for front legs
1-2x4 x 26 1/2" door support

From 3/4" (good one side) plywood:

Per illustration #1:
32" x 30" dehydrator top
24" x 30" dehydrator bottom
2-24" x 30"/32" dehydrator sides

Per illustration #2:
30" x 32" dehydrator door
30" x 30" dehydrator front

Wood cut list for collector:

1-1 x 6 x 30" ripped to 1 x 3 collector
   top end
   (save "scrap" 1 x 2 3/4 x 30)
1-1 x 8 x 30" collector bottom end

Per illustration #2:
2-6" x 67" collector sides
6" x 31 1/2" collector top from particle board or thinner plywood

58 1/2" x 31 1/2" collector bottom, painted flat black on top side
Glass: 60" x 31 1/2" (preferably double strength)

Wood cut list for trays

Using 3/4" stock: 12-23" lengths, and 12-23 1/2" lengths

Hardware

nails or screws
24 corner brackets
wood glue
30"x12" screening
2 hooks/eyes
2 hinges
staples
2 1/2 yards of nylon net

Dehydrator assembly

1. Nail & glue tray supports to inside (rough side) of dehydrator sides on indicated marks (illustration #1).

2. Nail or screw and glue legs to outside (good side) of dehydrator sides with 70" (back) legs on the 32" edge and 68" (front) legs on the 30" edge. Do not allow legs to extend above the top of the plywood.

3. Attach bottom, fitting around legs. Glue and screw or nail through bottom up into sides. Position door support between back legs, with support extending 3/4" to the back of the dehydrator). Nail or screw through legs into door support.

4. Attach front. Glue and screw or nail, positioning top of front flush with top of front legs.

5. Attach top. Nail or screw and glue, carefully, into top of sides & front, making sure top is centered and overlap is to the front.

6. Staple screen to inside front over holes.

7. Attach hinges to door, then to door support. Make sure screws are not too long for the door. You may need to get shorter screws for the door side of hinge and may want to use longer screws into the door support. Attach hooks to back legs and eyes to side of door.

Author removing dryer tray.

8. Place dehydrator in a permanent location in full sun if possible.

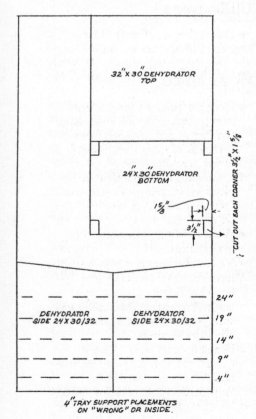

4" TRAY SUPPORT PLACEMENTS ON "WRONG" OR INSIDE.

Illustration #1

Collector assembly

1. Attach bottom and top ends between sides, **with bottom extending above** the sides and top flush with the sides. Attach collector top over top end. There will be a gap at the bottom of the top end; staple screen over holes in sides.

2. Attach bottom of collector top over top end. There will be a gap at the bottom of the top end.

3. Screw collector to dehydrator body, aligning gap at the top with screened holes. Make sure the collector fits snugly to the dehydrator.

4. Run a bead of silicone seal or other caulk along top of collector sides. Place glass in position; nail "scrap" to collector top extending down over glass. Silicone seal above & below "scrap"; at bottom where glass meets bottom stop and where collector and dehydrator meet.

Tray assembly

1. Glue and tack sides to front and back. Use a carpenter's square or **carefully** measure diagonals to ensure the trays are **square**! Screw in corner brackets, checking frequently to make sure trays remain square.

2. Staple on netting. Δ

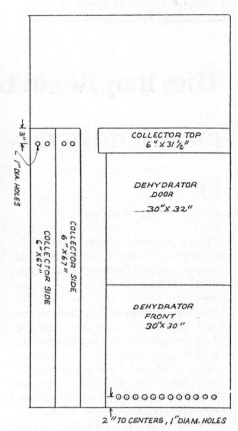

Illustration #2

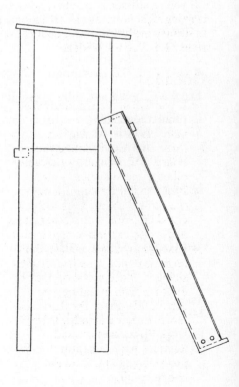

Illustration #3. Side view.

The Third Year

"Use it up, wear it out; make it do or do without!"

By Jo Mason

"Use it up, wear it out; make it do or do without." Over the years that old saying has deteriorated into a new phrase: "Throw it out and buy some more."

But if you live in the backwoods, you can't run to the store every time you need an item—or call a repairman to fix every little glitch. You have to be an expert in the art of making do.

And what, exactly, is that? It's conserving, it's recycling, it's practicing preventive maintenance. It's making an item yourself or finding a substitute. It's living within your means. In short, it's relying on your ingenuity to solve problems.

If you're still a city dweller, you can, starting right now, take one step closer to living your future, independent lifestyle. Here are a few ideas:

Outside

- If you live in the southern states, protect your water well from fire ants. Place wood shavings in a three-foot band around pump house. Then drizzle used motor oil over the shavings.
- Protect your air conditioner in the same fashion. Ants will crawl into relays and other parts and cause expensive repair bills.
- Emergency dog leash (or short term tie rope). Use your fishing stringer. Place metal tip (at one end) through metal ring (at other end). Place through once more, forming an adjustable loop. Place loop around animal's neck, and adjust to fit just snugly. (This is an anti-choke collar.)

- Need a quick garden trellis? Old coat hangers work fine.
- Instant garden hose weld. Heat the tip of a screwdriver and touch lightly against small hole in plastic garden hose. The plastic will melt together to form a patch.
- What's a good use for ashes from our woodstove or fireplace? Sift through a screen and mix with sawdust. Makes a great cleaner for greasy garage floors or driveways.

Bathroom

- Tired of running out of hot water in the shower? The Texas Water Development Board says installing a low-flow shower head is the single most effective step to save water that can be taken inside the home. These cost around $20 and can be installed easily.
- No toothpaste? Use salt and baking soda.
- Place a couple of bricks inside your toilet tank. They displace a gallon or so of water, and will save that amount with each flush.

Bedroom

- Don't buy fitted sheets. When time to change, remove only the bottom sheet, and move top sheet to bottom. Saves washing, water, and work.

Kitchen

- To remove tarnish from copper pots: Dip half a lemon in salt and rub pot with lemon. Allow to sit a few minutes, then wash and rinse.
- You can store bread in the freezer (great for those who only shop once or twice a month!) without it turning soggy. Wrap first in small paper bag, then in a plastic one.
- You don't need a dishwasher to sterilize glasses and utensils during flu season. Just add a few teaspoons of bleach in dishwater. Rinse well.
- Need to get a better grip on a stubborn jar lid? Put a large rubber band around the rim.
- All-purpose cleaner: Fill spray bottle with one part ammonia and 8 parts water.
- Out of coffee filters? Use a plain white paper towel. (Cut off corners to fit).

Utility room

- Out of fabric softener? Use a cupful of hair creme rinse.

Home office

- Here's a quick fix for postage stamps that won't stick: Moisten the flap of the envelope, then rub back of stamp over moistened area on envelope.
- Limit trips to the post office by purchasing stamps directly from your mailman. Ask him for details.
- Want to lower your phone bill? Write letters.
- Your ball-point pen may not have run dry. You may have been holding it at the wrong angle. To correct this, hold pen with point downward, and scribble a few seconds.
- Pen still won't write? Don't trash it yet. Place tip of pen into match flame for an instant. Repeat. Scribble until ink flows.
- No stickum? Remember that paste you made from flour and

water when you were in the first grade? It still works.

All around the house

- Don't panic if you lose that tiny screw from your glasses. Replace it with a stickpin. Bend once, then cut off excess.
- No cat litter? Use wood shavings sprinkled with borax.
- Magic Green Slime (for kids) Measure five tablespoons cornstarch and three tablespoons water into bowl. Add green food coloring and stir. Mixture should be thick, not runny.
- When buying appliances, be sure to check out the yellow EnergyGuide label. This rates the appliance as to efficiency and gives cost estimates to run the appliance for a year.
- When your new (or not-so-new) appliance acts up, don't forget to refer to the troubleshooting guide inside the instruction manual. (Sometimes this is printed directly on the appliance.)
- Parakeet food bought in those small boxes is expensive. Purchase five-pound bags of wild bird seed. The major ingredient in both kinds is millet. Sift through a colander and feed the large, inedible seeds to the wild birds.
- When adding shelves (or otherwise need to locate a stud in the wall) use a compass. The needle jumps when placed near a stud.
- Don't forget — free information (or almost free) is available on every subject from nutrition to house-building. Write to the Consumer Information Center, Pueblo, CO 81009, for their free index.
- Are you taking medication over a long-term period? Ask your doctor or pharmacist about generic prescriptions. You'll save a bundle. Δ

Backwoods Home Magazine's laboratory water test offer

Backwoods Home Magazine is working with Naturally Pure Alternatives (NPA) and National Testing Laboratories (NTL) to provide our readers with an outstanding value in water testing. This service is for our readers who are interested in knowing more about their water than what a cursory water test will show.

NTL is a nationally recognized leading laboratory with an extensive water test (see below) available for $129.00. If you are a subscriber, just tell NPA, and you will receive a $20.00 discount on your water test price. Call 1-800 TAKECARE (825-3227) to order with a VISA/MASTERCARD, or send check to Naturally Pure Alternatives, 575 Live Oak Ave., Ukiah, CA 95482.

We are not aware of a better bargain for testing your water for all of these parameters. Your water will be analyzed for 73 items, **plus** 20 pesticides. If you have any questions about your water's integrity, this is the test to give you peace of mind (or to help you give somebody a piece of your mind if the results confirm a suspicion you have). You will receive two pages of test results on the following parameters:

Metals:
Arsenic; Barium; Cadmium; Chromium; Copper; Iron; Lead; Manganese; Mercury; Nickel; Selenium; Silver; Sodium; Zinc.

Inorganics:
Total alkalinity (as CaCO); Chloride; Fluoride; Nitrate (as N); Nitrite; Sulfate; Hardness (as CaCO); pH (standard units); Total dissoved solids; Turbidity (NTU).

Volatile organics:
Bromoform; Bromodichloromethane; Chloroform; Dibromochloromethane; Total trihalomethanes; Benzene' Vinyl chloride; Carbon tetrachloride; 1,2-Dichloroethane; Trichloroethylene (TCE); 1,4-Dichlorobenzene; 1,1,1- trichloroethane; Acrolein; Acrylonitrile; Bromobenzene; Bromomethane; Chlorobenzene' Chloroethane; Chloromethane; O- Chlorotoluene; P-Chlorotuluene; Dibromochloropropane (DBCP); Dibromomethane; 1,2-Dichlorobenzene; 1,3-Dichlorobenzene; trans-1,2-Dichloroethylene; cis-1,2-Dichloroethylene; Dichloromethane; 1,1-Dichloroethane; trans-1,3- Dichloropropane; cis-1,3-Dichloropropane; 2,2- Dichloropropane; Ethylenedibromide (EDB); Ethyl-benzene; Styrene; 1,1,2-Trichloroethane; 1,1,1,2-Tetrachloroethane; Tetrachloroethylene (PCE); 1,2,3-Trichloropropane; Toluene; Xylene; Chloroethylvinyl ether; Dichlorodifluoromethane; cis-1,3-Dichloropropene; Trichlorofluoromethane; Trichlorobenzene(s).

Microbiological:
Coliform bacteria

Pesticides and herbicides:
Alachlor; Aldrin; Atrazine; Chlordane; Dichloran' Dieldren; Endrin; Heptachlor; Heptachlor Epoxide; Hexachlorobenzene; Hexachlorapentadiene; Lindane; Methoxychlor; PCBs; Pentachloronitrobenzene; Simazine; Toxaphene; Trifluralin; Silvex 2,4,5,,TP; 2,4-D.

After you have received your test results, feel free to call NPA to ask any questions about how to deal with your particular situation or problems. You will find them very helpful. Δ

Quick breads for summer

By Jennifer Stein Barker

It's summer, and who wants to spend all day hanging around the house waiting for bread to rise? Yet, you still want to eat wholesome bread that you bake yourself. You need something to snack on, something to make sandwiches out of, something to go with soup or soak up veggies and sauce.

If it sticks to your ribs till the next mealtime, all the better! The advantages of quick breads are: no kneading. No waiting for the bread to rise (and subsequent risk of failure if you wait to long). No spending hot sunny afternoons in the kitchen if the bread takes too long. With quick breads, you need only a few utensils, no experience, and you can be out of the kitchen in a little over an hour. The one disadvantage I have noticed is that quick breads are often too delicate and crumbly to make sandwiches. This is not a problem when your sandwiches get eaten as quickly as ours!

Quick breads depend on the chemical action of baking soda or baking powder to rise. These leaveners react with heat and moisture to produce little bubbles of carbon dioxide in the batter. A double-acting baking powder works first with the moisture as the liquid is combined with the leavener in the dry ingredients. Then it reacts to the heat as the bread begins to bake. For your health, please use a non-aluminum baking powder.

High-gluten flours such as whole wheat bread flour are not necessary and will indeed make quick breads tough. It is best to use whole wheat pastry flour, rye flour, or other low-gluten flour. Oat flour can be used instead of wheat, but will make the final product a little crumbly. If you cannot obtain whole wheat pastry flour, you can use fifty-fifty all-purpose whole wheat and white flour.

But why use whole grains anyway? The reason is more than just fiber versus lack of fiber. The refining process used to make white flour removes large amounts of vitamins from the grain, only a few of which are replaced by fortification afterwards. It is not enough to satisfy a need for carbohydrates, your body also needs vitamins, minerals, protein, fat, and fiber. In whole foods they are packaged in natural, usable proportions. Whole grains are no exception.

The big trick to mixing quick breads is to mix gently and thoroughly but **do not over mix**. The batter will begin puffing up as soon as the moisture hits the leaveners in the dry mixture. The more you mix, the more you deflate your bread. If the batter is mixed fairly uniformly, it's time to quit. Don't worry about the little lumps. Have your pans ready and your oven preheated so that you can scrape your batter into the pans and scoop them right into the oven.

To prepare your pans, oil or butter them. If, like me, you want the bread to slide right out without the least crumb sticking to the pan, you can line them with baking paper or wax paper. Fold it to fit in the pans **before** you oil them for a much cleaner job.

When the baking time is up, you can test for doneness by inserting a knife, fork, or toothpick into the center. It should come out cleanly. If it is gooey, bake for another 7-10 minutes. If the crust is already well-browned, a foil "hat" can be placed loosely over the loaf. When done, the top will feel springy and the sides will pull away from the pan just a little.

To cool, let the loaf sit a few minutes before removing from the pan to a cooling rack. Bread should be completely cool before it is put into a plastic bag or airtight container. Bread should be stored in a cool place. A refrigerator is too cold and will cause the loaf to dry out. If the location is too warm, the bread may mold after a few days (ours doesn't usually last that long).

Here are recipes for three very different breads. Starting with the basic proportions found in these recipes, you can create a huge variety of your own individualized breads. Have fun creating!

Date-nut bread

Moist and sweet with dates, a great snack bread.
Makes one 5" x 9" loaf:
1/2 cup whole wheat pastry flour
3 tablespoons buttermilk powder
1 teaspoon soda
1 teaspoon baking powder
1 cup water
3 tablespoons oil
2 tablespoons honey
2 tablespoons dark molasses
1 egg, beaten
1 cup chopped walnuts
1 cup chopped dates

Prepare a 5" x 9" loaf pan. Preheat the oven to 400 degrees. Sift together the flour, buttermilk powder, soda, and baking powder. In a medium bowl, whisk together the water, oil, honey, molasses, and egg. Add the dry mixture to the wet all at once, and stir just enough to thoroughly moisten all ingredients. Fold in the nuts and dates, and scrape the mixture into the prepared pan.

Bake at 400 degrees for 15 minutes, then turn oven to 375 degrees and continue baking for another 45 minutes, or until the loaf tests done.

Ricotta-herb-tomato bread

This crusty golden quick-bread has a heavenly aroma of herbs, and goes great with soups or stews. Makes one 5" x 9" loaf.

```
2 2/3 cups whole wheat pastry flour
1 teaspoon baking powder
1 teaspoon soda
2 teaspoons dried basil, crushed
1 teaspoon dried thyme, crushed
1/8 teaspoon freshly-ground black pepper
1 cup milk
3 tablespoons tomato paste
3 tablespoons oil
2 eggs
1 cup low-fat ricotta cheese
```

Prepare a 5" x 9" loaf pan. Preheat the oven to 350 degrees.

Sift together the pastry flour, baking powder, and soda into a medium bowl. Stir in the basil, thyme, and pepper until evenly distributed.

In a separate bowl, whisk together the milk, tomato paste, oil, eggs, and ricotta cheese until well-blended. Add all at once to the dry mixture and stir until all ingredients are moistened. Scrape the mixture into the prepared pan.

Bake for about an hour, or until the top of the loaf is crusty and golden, and the loaf tests done. Serve warm or at room temperature. Store in the refrigerator if it is not to be eaten the first day.

Quick sourdough rye bread

Nutty and delicious, this one will even stand up for sandwiches! Makes one 9" x 5" loaf.

```
1 1/3 cups whole wheat pastry flour
1 1/3 cups rye flour
1 teaspoon baking powder
1 1/2 teaspoons soda
2/3 cup sourdough starter
3 tablespoons oil
1 1/2 tablespoons honey
3 tablespoons molasses
1 egg
1 cup milk
1/3 cup sunflower seeds (optional)
```

Prepare a 5" x 9" loaf pan. Preheat the oven to 350 degrees.

In a medium bowl, sift together the flours, baking powder, and soda. In a large bowl, whisk together the starter, honey, molasses, egg, oil, and milk. Add the dry mixture to the wet, stirring until all ingredients are moistened. Stir in the sunflower seeds, if used. Scrape the mixture into the prepared pan.

Bake for 45-50 minutes, or until the cake tests done. Cool.

Δ

A BHM Writer's Profile

Jennifer Stein Barker has been writing for BHM since issue #2. She lives with her husband, Lance, on their 40 acre homestead in the Blue Mountains of eastern Oregon.

Lance built their solar electric home, which uses no back-up generator or propane appliances. Jennifer cooks and develops her recipes on a Pioneer Maid wood cookstove, which also serves as the heat source for the house. In her free time she skis, reads, chops wood, gardens, and works as a summer botanist for the Malheur National Forest. She is currently working on a cookbook of her recipes.

Embracing Mother Earth

The blaring of horns and grinding of gears,
The thunder of the freeway fell on deaf ears.

Under the overpass, weeding his backyard
Knelt an elderly gentleman showing little regard.

Knees stiff with arthritis, hands in the dirt,
He cultivated and planted his piece of earth.

Near a rocking chair, hollyhocks stood,
Tied to a fence made of scrap wood.

Seeding each row with played-out eyes,
Never complaining about the carbon monoxide.

He'd use his cane from time to time,
Untangling his feet from cucumber vine.

He turned his back to the Interstate and face to the sun.
Gardening was his life—his reward—his fun.

"When ya plant a garden, ya embrace mother earth."
The old man's philosophy—for what it's worth.

Hal Meili
Cheney, WA

Uncommon wines — another way to save the harvest

By Anita Evangelista

About July 15th, every year, I get exceedingly tired of canning tomatoes. The usual spring overplanting, carried on in a spirit of irresistible gardening enthusiasm and vigor, is actually just beginning its overkill yield by July— and we are engulfed in a growing avalanche of the red ovoids. Not to mention the large green baseball bats which were once zucchini, the unspeakable excesses of peas, and the yellow onions plumping out of the ground where I can't remember planting any.

There are only so many tomatoes a normal person can process in a given summer — and if friends start dodging you when they see you're carrying heavy, lumpy grocery sacks — it's time to try something else, particularly with those perishables which you just can't stand to dump on the compost heap while they're still in good shape.

Our farming ancestors were not blessed with such agricultural abundance — at least not enough to turn them into the wastrels we have become. They had a way to save each scrape of harvest, sometimes fed to chickens and pigs to be converted into usable protein, occasionally traded for some other commodity they desired, sometimes transformed into another valuable good: uncommon wines.

It's a frugal gardener who can take an excess bushel of carrots, or onions, or empty pea pods, and turn that into a pleasant beverage. The addition of only a few extra ingredients creates the miraculous transmutation of waste into true wines. These are not silly depersonalized, chemicalized drinks, found in any and every corner quickmart. These are as surprisingly flavorful, unique, and intricate as each season's harvest, as the person who troubles to make them.

But don't be misled by the strangeness of the main ingredient (Are you serious? Wine from pea pods? Tomatoes? Onions?). Tomato wine, for instance, is a lovely golden color, without even a hint of ordinary tomato taste. Pea pods make a white wine, with an earthy undercurrent. Onions develop into a strong, dry wine. Zucchini or other squash can become a remarkable Tokay-like beverage. And carrots, those humble garden regulars, become a delightful, rich sherry!

Our visiting friends have come to expect a bizarre guessing game — name the ingredients. Glasses are poured, toasts pronounced, and then the contest is on: "Tastes a little like a burgundy — is it beets?" "Beets and what else?" "What's that sharp, pungent undercurrent?" "It has the bite of turnips." "Could it be watercress?" "The pale golden color could be potatoes." "Or beets, turnips, or watercress." Whatever type of wine, it is the rare visitor who can name the primary ingredient, much less the secondary additions!

That homemade uncommon wines are also easy to prepare is seldom ob-

vious. The transformation of garden excess into a bright, sparkling, complex liquor is simpler (to my mind) than canning up a batch of anything. It calls for only basic, readily home-rigged equipment, the addition of commonly available sugar or honey, yeast (even the cooking variety will do in a pinch), and perhaps a couple lemons, oranges, or a pound of raisins. The only truly difficult thing about making these unusual drinks is waiting for them to mature to full flavor!

About the yeast and the air-locks

Grape wine connoisseurs shudder at the thought of using any yeast but one made specifically for wines — and there are a dazzling array available for home use. Unless you have specific wine variety preferences, a Montrachet yeast makes a good all-purpose beverage. Many health food stores now carry this kind of yeast. Nevertheless, a perfectly acceptable vegetable or fruit wine can be made with ordinary cooking (bread) yeast from the supermarket.

Air-locks can also be found at beer and wine-making shops, or you can construct an air-lock container fairly simply. The idea is to exclude outside air from the fermenting wine liquid, while allowing the beverage to expel excess carbon dioxide and other fermentation gasses. Some home-vintners have used a glass gallon juice jar, fitted a cork tightly in the top, and punched a narrow hole through the cork from top to bottom. Through the cork, a two-foot section of aquarium tubing is carefully slipped so that a couple inches extend from the cork bottom and the remaining fraction from the top, and the top edge of the cork is then sealed with wax around the tubing. After the jar is filled, the cork-and- tubing is fitted firmly in place, and the loose end of tubing is submerged in a jar filled with water. As the wine ferments, gasses will escape through the tubing, and bubble up through the water—but no air will be able to enter the jar.

I've had good results using plastic gallon vinegar jugs, punching a hole through the plastic screw-on cap with a leather punch, and inserting aquarium air-line tubing. It fits so snugly that wax isn't needed. As a plus, the cap is easy to attach and remove from the jug.

The process

Wine making from flowers, herbs, fruits and vegetables is not complicated. Like all fermentation-based foods—such as cheese or bread—it requires an adherence to strict cleanliness and attention to detail. In each of the recipes that follow, the steps are the same:

- 1. Wash the vegetable thoroughly. "Garden dirt" wine is not too appetizing. Chop or cook and mash as directed.
- 2. Add vegetable to water; put in dissolved sugar and other chopped ingredients, except yeast.
- 3. Cool or warm the water and added vegetable to room temperature, or a shade warmer. Add dissolved yeast, and mix thoroughly.
- 4. Set in room-temperature spot for about two days.
- 5. Strain off liquid into air-lock container. You can still consume the remaining vegetable "soup"; chickens and pigs can also get a share.
- 6. Let continue fermenting for one to two months—until all bubbling ceases.
- 7. Transfer to clean container by siphoning (use aquarium tubing, or special winemakers tubing). Leave sediments at bottom as much as possible. Taste the wine while siphoning—it will be quite strong, possibly terribly flavored or astringent. Don't despair! Once the wine has matured, the

flavor will be completely different.
- 8. Add clean eggshells (washed before cracking), with some white still clinging, to the liquid. This will draw all remaining sediments to the eggshells, so that the wine naturally clears. Cover tightly with cotton wool, or several layers of cheesecloth.
- 9. When wine has cleared, siphon into final storage bottles and cork, leaving behind shells and sediment. You'll notice that the flavor has already changed a little. It will continue to improve. You can use clean wine bottles or any type of sealable glass container. I've had good results with quart canning jars! Label with date of bottling, type of wine, and winemaker.
- 10. Store in a dark, cool closet; under kitchen counter; or back of refrigerator. Don't bother to try the tomato or pea pod wines for at least a year—they are remarkably nasty until they've aged. Begin sampling the other wines after two months until they reach a flavor you like. Enjoy with a good meal!

Recipes

Use the ingredients and follow the procedure previously outlined. Recipes are for a single gallon of wine—you can increase or decrease recipes to fit your container.

Carrot wine

(Sweet, potent, and a dark orange shade.)

1 gallon and 2 cups water
5-7 pounds fresh carrots, cooked and mashed
4 pounds white sugar or 1 quart honey
2 whole sliced oranges
1 lemon (yellow rind and juice only)
1/2 pound raisins, chopped
1 package yeast

Onion wine

(Delightful, pale golden and very intense—but no oniony taste).

1 gallon water
1/2 pound peeled, sliced onions
1 potato, washed and sliced thinly
2 pounds sugar
1 pound raisins, chopped
1 package yeast

Pea pod wine

(Can use empty pods, full pods, or just shelled peas alone! Makes a bright, white, earthy beverage.)

1 gallon water
3 pounds of pea pods, boiled until soft in some of the water
3 pounds of sugar or quart of honey
1-1/2 cups lemon juice
1 package yeast

Tomato wine

(Let the mashed tomatoes rest in the liquid during the entire period of fermentation, about 21 days. Stir every second day. Results in a blushing golden wine, with a complex, distinctive flavor—no hint of tomatoes!)

1 gallon water, poured boiling over tomatoes
10 pounds of chopped, mashed tomatoes
4 pounds of sugar
3 slices fresh gingerroot or 1/4 tsp. powdered ginger
1 tablespoon salt
1 package yeast

Zucchini or other squash wine

1 gallon water, poured boiling over the squash
3-4 pounds peeled, diced squash
1 cup lemon juice
3 pounds sugar or quart honey
1 package yeast

But don't stop with these vegetables—try any of your extra produce as a wine. If you come up with a new recipe that you really like, share it with a friend! Δ

The rise of guerilla videos

By Jojo Gunn

The Guerilla Video Network is not a reality yet, but if Bill Myers has his way, it may be sooner than you think. Myers, an Arkansas businessman, says people are fed up with American network TV. "It seems the networks try to create programming that appeals to the lowest elements of our society. Which means most of middle America has to stoop to their level of entertainment or do without."

His concept is "guerilla" video. Videos and TV programming produced by the people and for the people. Programming that could be created by anybody, and made available to those that wanted it via satellite or videocassettes. Programming produced in the home video studio.

Of course there was the problem of technology. Myers lives in the backwoods of Arkansas, a long way from the nearest TV studio. And Myers had no experience with TV productions, other than "30 years as a viewer", as he tells it. And a modern TV studio can be very expensive to put together, even if one knows what he is doing.

But Myers, who has a background in computers, felt sure that somehow a personal computer could be used to create the graphics and animation necessary for modern videos, and this could be combined with video footage shot and edited with camcorders and VCRs.

A desktop video solution

After six months of research, Myers discovered ways to mimic broadcast quality video productions in a studio that cost him less than $5,000 to set up. About half the cost was for the computer, the rest was for the camera, VCR, lights, and studio props. "The key to my success was that the technology I needed just happened to be

Bill Myers

available at the right time. The most important device, the genlock for the computer, just hit the market a few months ago."

With his **desktop video studio** up and running, Myers has found he can produce animation, graphics and special effects that rival those of the major networks at a fraction of the cost in time and equipment. Since putting together his studio, Myers has produced 11 different video documentaries and "how-to" tapes that are targeted for "the Americans that Hollywood forgot. Those who have above average intelligence and want to do more with their lives than just watch TV."

Myers said he feels that this new technology will open doors for people who have found they couldn't get their ideas aired on mainstream TV. "People are interested in this technology. They know how powerful TV can be, and people see desktop video as an opportunity to change the world, or at least let the world know how they feel. Anybody with their own desktop video system can put together a quality video production in a few hours with the cost limited to personal time and the blank tape."

Call them 'guerilla' videos

Myers says he isn't trying to compete with Hollywood. His videos, and others like them, are for people fed up with plastic images produced by Hollywood. "We don't use actors. We use real people and that's a major difference most people see right away. Viewers of guerilla video see people they can relate to, people like themselves, not "fancy pants" Hollywood actors."

While most guerilla video productions are not broadcast quality, most are well received by their audiences. Because the major studios have such tremendous overhead when undertaking any project, they can't touch the subjects that are available on guerilla videos. And this is the key to their success.

The TV revolution has finally reached the people

Many people are discovering that grass roots videos from real people have become a way to reach out and affect other people's lives with information not available in the mainstream media. Myers has found that his own guerilla videos on subjects such as pirate TV and desktop video technology have been very well accepted. "We've gotten hundreds of letters thanking us for making this information available."

One thing is certain. People are beginning to use some of the latest communications technology, including satellite transmission, to create alternate programming. Guerilla productions are showing up in the form of documentaries, news broadcasts and even satellite delivered home shopping shows, and maybe someday the Guerilla Video Network will be a reality.

(Bill Myers is the editor of The Video Marketing Letter and the founder of Group M Video, which markets several videos on how to set up your own desktop video system. Group M also offers a free desktop video hotline to help other people using this technology. For additional information, call 1-501-321-1845 or write Group M at 100 Bridge St. #27, Hot Springs, AR 71901.) Δ

Here's a few old books that are still great books!

By Mary Ann Hubbell

I've been searching through used bookstores, yard sales, thrift shops, and my shelves for old gardening and homesteading books. Here are some that I have found to share with the new generation of folk who desire a little more independence.

The Encyclopedia of Organic Gardening, by Steven Smyers and the staff of Organic Gardening Magazine, Rodale Press, 33 East Minor St., Emmaus, PA 18098, 1978, 1236 pgs, hardcover.

Written in dictionary format, this hefty volume has everything you want to know about organic gardening. Plants are listed by their common names rather than in Latin for those of us who neglected to get a degree in botany. Whether you are looking for information on insect control, companion planting, intensive gardening, or greenhouses, you will find what you need here and in everyday terms.

The Encyclopedia of Natural Insect and Disease Control, ed, Roger B. Yepson, Jr., Rodale Press, 33 E. Minor St. Emmaus, PA 18098, 1984, 490 pgs, hardcover; illustrations and color pictures.

Let's face it, not all of us had the inclination or the time to go to school and major in entomology. Rodale's encyclopedia not only teaches us insect and disease control but without the use of toxic chemicals—which is something you wouldn't have learned even with an "ag" degree from a Land-Grant college. You don't know the name of that critter bugging your garden? No problem; there are plenty of color pictures and illustrations to check. The next time you husk that corn only to find a fat worm looking at you, grab this book. If you can't figure

out a solution, you can at least use it to squash the worm!

Forest Farming, by J. Shoto Douglas and Robert A. de J. Hart, Rodale Press, 33 E. Minor St. Emmaus, PA 18098, 1978, 199 pgs, hardcover.

Not exactly for the layman, we came across *Forest Farming, Towards a Solution to Problems of World Hunger and Conservation* when we forgot to return the card instructing Rodale Book Club to "send nothing this month." I was going to send it back but before I could, my husband found it and became engrossed with the idea of farming with trees. Trees are not only important for our food needs, but for our basic survival. This book will tell you about tree products for food and raw materials, planting techniques, and suggestions on how to tree farm. If you love trees and yearn to have them surround you, let this be one of the books you read. Who knows, maybe it will inspire you too.

Getting the Most From Your Garden, Using Advanced Intensive Gardening Techniques, by Editors of *Organic Gardening Magazine*, Rodale Press, 33 E. Minor St. Emmaus, PA 18098, 1980, 482 pgs, hardcover.

Just when you think that you have got your intensive gardening techniques honed to perfection, you find this book and discover that there are "advanced techniques". *Getting the Most From Your Garden* claims that the key to getting the most from your garden is an individualized system that combines the best of several techniques: intensive gardening, interplanting, companion planting, successions, relays, and season-extending enclosed growing structures.

The most important part of intensive gardening is the growing bed. The bed is full of loose, airy soil which has been dug to at least a foot deep. This creates the perfect place to grow plants. This book shows you how to plan a compat-

ible garden for maximum results. Our family has used the intensive-gardening method since we discovered Mittleider (see next review). Going further than Mittleider, you will learn how to get a jump on the season by using seeds, transplants, and cold frames. A real "must" book, especially for those of us who live with limited suitable land and/or short growing seasons.

More Food From Your Garden, By Jacob R. Mittleider, UD, Woodbridge Press Publishing Company, P.O. Box 6189, Santa Barbara, CA 93111, 1982, 194 pgs. softcover.

This well illustrated, how-to book of intensive gardening shows in everyday terms how to grow abundant amounts of veggies in almost any condition. Some years ago, Loma Linda University in California sponsored Mittleider on a 24-nation survey of food production problems. The result was the Mittleider Method, which combines the best of both soil and hydroponic gardening. Jacob Mittleider showed that: ordinary people can do extraordinary gardening, simple hand labor can out-perform expensive equipment, abundant food can be produced on any kind of land—in the world.

Success is certain because nothing is left to chance. Some special features that you will find in this book are: "custom-made soil" recipes; grow box designs; plant nutrition formulas; systematic watering plans; step-by-step instructions for training, pruning, and pollinating plants; and plans for inexpensive greenhouse shelters, all explained in "user friendly" terms. So if you want to grow the maximum of vegetables with the least—think Mittleider!

Anything Grows, by Sheryl London, Rodale Press, 33 East Minor St., Emmaus, PA 18098, 1979, 405 pgs, hardcover.

Love gardening but short on growing space? I don't mean that you live on 1/4 acre and want to grow an acre of corn. I'm talking short of space—apartments, suburbs, and cities. *Anything Grows* shows you how to maximize whatever space you do have to grow things, whether it is your front yard, side yard, back yard, roof top, or parking lot. This book is split into 13 chapters guiding you through the world of container gardening. You'll learn how to garden—anywhere, how to wade your way through catalogs, how to find the equipment meant just for you. You'll find this book is not just another book about regional techniques or limited to city dwellers. It is a great book of ideas.

The Rodale Guide to Composting, Rodale Press, 33 East Minor St., Emmaus, PA 18098, 1979, 405 pgs, hardcover.

In our town, the city collects everyone's leaves and puts them into the community compost pile at the dump. When you need compost, you merely drive to the dump, load up, and take it home for your garden. *The Rodale Guide to Composting* teaches you the how and why, as well as the methods and practice of composting. And to think, we thought that we learned everything there is to know about composting in that magazine article we read.

Using Plants for Healing, by Nelson Coon, Rodale Press, 33 East Minor St., Emmaus, PA 18098, 1979, 272 pgs, hardcover.

In 1963, *Using Plants for Healing* was widely acclaimed as the best guide to medicinal plants in the United States. This book is a guide to over 250 medicinal plants, 160 of which are familiar plants with complete details on where to find them, how to identify them, how to prepare them for medicinal use, and what it is claimed that they cure. Anyone interested in alternative medicinal techniques is sure to find this book interesting.

Back to Eden, Jethro Kloss, Woodbridge Press Publishing Co. P.O. Box 6189, Santa Barbara, CA 93111, 1975, 684 pgs, softcover.

Back to Eden was one of the "musts" for the 70's back-to-the-lander. Originally published in 1939, you should be able to find a new copy at your nearest health food store or a well worn one almost anywhere. I can remember curling up with it at night, just to read it for fun and wishing that I knew more about herbal medicine. *Back to Eden* is still the bible of herbal medicine, filled with "old fashioned, time tested, good health advice." Tired of traditional medicine? Pick up a copy and see how our forefathers treated ailments and kept healthy.

Square Foot Gardening, Mel Bartholomew, Rodale Press, 33 East Minor St., Emmaus, PA 18098, 1981, 347 pgs, hardcover.

This book has been around for 10 years now, but I recently saw it in softcover at a bookstore. This has got to be the most logical way to garden that I have seen in a long time. Our family plans to combine the techniques in this book and intensive gardening for our own home garden this year. The basic idea is, you garden in squares—easy enough for the busiest person to manage. Each square is 12 inches by 12 inches and holds a different vegetable, herb, or flower. These 1-foot squares are grouped together in blocks of 4 feet by 4 feet. To avoid walking on the soil, garden paths are built out of lumber. This book is a step by step guide to growing by the square foot. One plus is that since you're constantly planting and replanting squares, you have your vegetables all maturing at different times! A **must** for the home library.

Growing for Market, by Roger B. Yepsen, Jr., Rodale Press, 33 East Minor St., Emmaus, PA 18098, 1978, 301 pgs, hardcover.

Keep your eyes peeled for this little gem if you have ever thought of producing and marketing fruit, honey, herbs, beef, cheese, mushrooms, wine, woolen goods, etc. because this book will tell you how to do it! Did you know that many profitable small-scale businesses started as hobbies? You don't need hundreds of acres—even a backyard will do.

The book is divided into five sections: Section One, "Direct Marketing," guides you through marketing techniques. Section Two, "Running the Business," tells you about costs and return, pricing, and government regulations. Section Three, "A Season in the Life of David Schonberg," follows one man's experience, his ups and downs. Section Four, "Specialties," gives you ideas concerning different small-scale specialties that can be developed. Section Five, "Profiles," shows you the experiences of successful small-scale businesses. If one of your goals is self-reliance, this book could help you attain it!

Five Acres and Independence, M.G. Kains, Dover Publications, Inc. 180 Varick St., New York, NY 10014, 1973, 397 PGS, softcover.

Five Acres and Independence — A Handbook for Small Farm Management, was written in 1935. The fact is that good advice is never too old and this book offers timely and factual advice for those of us who wish to rely more on the land for our needs. Easy to find, either new or used, it was very popular during the 70's. Need to know how to put in a septic tank? This book is for you! Full of all the useful information they neglected to teach us in school; this is an invaluable addition to your "Backwoods Home" library.

The Ruth Stout No-Work Garden Book, by Ruth Stout and Richard Clemence, Bantam Books, Inc., 666 Fifth Ave., New York, NY 10019, 1973, 161 pgs, softcover, Also Organic Gardening/Rodale Press Edition, 1971, hardcover.

I recently reread Ruth Stout's book after many years. In it she shares 40 years worth of organic gardening secrets. Did you ever wish that you could garden without any work? Ruth Stout tells you how. Her secret? **mulch!** For an in-depth look at mulching and meeting an interesting lady, find anything you can about Ruth Stout. She was a true gem.

Living on a Few Acres — The Yearbook of Agriculture, U.S. Dept. of Agriculture, Plume Book, New American Library, NY, 1979, 432 pgs, softcover.

The government puts out agricultural yearbooks every year. Some years they report progress in agriculture, other years they deal with a specific project. In 1979, the U.S. government saw a need and decided to give the people a "blueprint" to use as an aid to help with "going back to the land". The book deals with everything an amateur needs to know to find the right place and how to make that right place a success. If you find other agriculture yearbooks as you search, you might want to buy them, no matter what the year. They are full of interesting information and the older ones are also entertaining.

One Acre and Security, by Bradford Angier, Vintage Books Edition, Random House, Inc., NY, 1973, 319 pgs, softcover.

One of the "gurus" for the back to the land movement, Angier's books inspired many to pack their knapsacks and head to the wilderness. *One Acre and Security — How to Live Off the Earth Without Ruining It* was aimed towards homesteaders. His earlier books include *Free For the Eating, Skills for Taming the Wilds, How to Live in the Woods for Pennies a Day*, and *Survival With Style*. Angier got his experience by carving his own homestead out of the wilderness in Canada back when you could still do that.

Two Acre Eden, Gene Logsdon, Rodale Press, 33 E. Minor St., Emmaus, PA 18098, 1980, 237 pgs, hardcover, softcover.

Here's another one of those "acreage books." You remember them all don't you? Great titles like: "How to live on Five Acres and Have a Cow", or "Backyard Living with a BBQ". Only kidding about those titles but back during the 70's and early 80's you only had to close your eyes, reach into the bookshelf, and you would pull out a book designed for some amount of acreage. I think that most of the people who bought these books never actually became homesteaders; they were wish books to be drooled over — and I have them all! DROOL DROOL DROOL

This fun and informative book was written by Gene Logsdon, the Erma Bombeck for homesteaders. Sense of humor? Here are a few chapter titles: "Of Course I'm an Organic Gardener; I Just Keep That Sprayer Around for the Neighbors to Borrow," "The Most Unrottable Compost Heap I Ever Saw," and "If You Mean Rabbits, Praise Ecology but Pass the Ammunition." For a tongue in cheek approach to country living (and a good chuckle or two) read *Two Acre Eden*.

Harrowsmith Country Life Reader - The Best of North America's Award-Winning Journal of Country Living, intro by James M. Lawrence, Camden House Publishing Inc., Charlotte, VT 05445, 1990, 320 pgs, softcover.

For those of us who have watched the Canadian magazine, "Harrowsmith," start publishing a U.S. edition by the same name (which has evolved into the present Country Life), this book will be a rehash of their best articles since 1985. For neophytes, it's a good way to get a feel for the slick magazine. Beautifully illustrated and filled with great pictures, it is divided into six sections: Country Life (visits with homesteaders), Shelter, The Garden, Rural Arts, Husbandry, and the Pantry (yummy recipes). Not a real "must have" book but a nice addition to your library.

New Western Garden Book, Editors of Sunset Magazine, Lane Publishing Co., Menlo Park, CA, 1979, 512 pgs, softcover.

You'll find over 1200 plant identification drawings in this encyclopedia for all western climates. Our copy was used as a textbook for a college ag class back in '79. More recent copies can be found as close as your corner supermarket. If you want to save a few dollars, pick one up used; the information is eternal.

Rodale's Illustrated Encyclopedia of Gardening and Landscaping Techniques, Barbara W. Ellis, ed: writers Diane Bilderback...[et al.] Rodale Press, 33 E. Minor St., Emmaus, PA 18098, 1990, 426 pgs, hardcover.

Gardening and Landscaping Techniques is like having a library on all-organic gardening right at your fingertips. Between its covers, you'll find step-by-step directions and gardening techniques for not only food gardens but ornamental gardens as well. Divided into seven helpful sections, both the well-seasoned and the beginning gardeners will find page after page of hints and illustrations. Part one deals with the basics—how to know and work your soil, compost, start seeds, propagate plants and build cold frames and hot beds. Part two tells us about flowers—not only giving you types, but guiding you through garden design, harvesting, and use. Part three illustrates the successful food garden, including fruit trees and berries. The book is crammed full with charts so that you can see at a glance if a plant suits your area. Parts four and five cover lawns, ground covers, trees, and shrubs. Part six helps you with growing houseplants and container gardens. Part seven covers the tools you will need to do it all.

The book also lists addresses of sources and gives recommended reading lists throughout. Whether you are in the market for a first gardening book, your only gardening book, or you can never have enough gardening books, **this is that book!**

Living on Less from the Editors of the Mother Earth News, Mother Earth News Inc., Hendersonville, NC 28791, 1984, 256 pgs, softcover.

Divided into 12 sections of old fashioned, Mother-type info on: Affordable Housing, Buying Land and Homesteading, Gardening, Canning and Preserving, Foraging, Livestock, Cutting Energy Costs, Clothing and Housewares, Health and Beauty, Recreation, and Barter, Bargaining and Auctions. *Living on Less* is a great book to keep an eye out for at yard sales or your favorite used book store.

Rabbits

If you have entertained the idea of raising rabbits for show, pets or meat, any of the following books will help:

How to Start a Commercial Rabbitry, by Paul Mannell, Bass Equipment Co., Box 352, Monet, MO 65708, 1985, 120 pgs softcover.

Raising Rabbits the Modern Way, Bob Bennett, Garden Way Publishing,

Charlotte, VT 05445, 1975, 158 pgs, softcover.

Raising Rabbits, Ann Kanabe, Rodale Press, 33 E. Minor St., Emmaus, PA 18098, 1977, 191 pgs, softcover.

Rabbit Production, Cheeke, Patton, Lukefahr, McNitt, The Interstate Printers and Publishers, Inc., Danville, IL, 1987 472 pgs, hardcover.

Backyard Rabbit Farming, Ann Williams, Prism Press, Stable Court, Chalmington, Dorcester, Dorset, DT2 0HB, 1978, 123 pgs, softcover.

How to Raise Rabbits for Fun and Profit, Milton I. Faivre, Nelson-Hall, Chicago, 1973, 212 pgs, hardcover.

The above books basically give the same information about rabbits—only in different depth. If you are seriously into rabbits, choose the Oregon State University book—*Rabbit Production*.

Goats

Goat's milk. You either hate it or you love it. If you yearn for the taste of fresh goat's milk, the following books will help you learn how to get it—and not something that smells and tastes like a buck!

Raising Milk Goats the Modern Way, Jerry Belanger, Garden Way Publishing, Pownal, VT 05261, 1975, 152 pgs, softcover.

Written by Jerry Belanger of *Countryside* magazine fame, this is considered the best goat specialty book for the novice. Contrary to popular belief, goats are not smelly, disgusting creatures that eat everything in sight. They are friendly, docile, and picky eaters. With the right care and handling, they will give you and your family years of milk-drinking and good companionship.

Starting Right with Milk Goats, Helen Walsh, Garden Way Publishing, Charlotte, VT 05445, (1947) 1975, 138 pgs, softcover.

Part of the old "Have More" Plan Reference Library (for more information, this plan was reprinted in TMEN #2), this book about goats might be found at a used book store or on the dusty rack of a country market. Chock full of illustrations containing not only

goats, but also good directions for building a goat barn and a milk stand. It was replaced by Belanger's book, but is still a good read.

Herbal Handbook for Farm and Stable, Juliette de Bairacli Levy, Rodale Press, 33 E. Minor St., Emmaus, PA 18098, 1976, 320 pgs, hardcover.

If you own animals, it is wise to have on hand a book for their medical care. We have three at home that we use. Two cover basic vet care and this one fits in where the others leave off. Even if you are not familiar with herbal medicine, you will have at your fingertips the name of the herb and directions for its use. She also takes you from animal to animal, discussing different ailments that you might find and the treatments you can use, complete with suggested dosage. Whether you believe in herbal medicine or not, a good book.

A Veterinary Guide for Animal Owners, C.E. Spaulding D.V.M., Rodale Press, 33 E. Minor St., Emmaus, PA 18098, 1976, 420 pgs, hardcover.

One of the most used books in our family. I've thrown it down to catch baby goats as they fell from their mother at birth, read the directions as I dehorned or castrated a baby goat, *A Veterinary Guide for Animal Owners* has paid for itself many times over. If animals are in your future, make sure that this book is too. It covers all farm-type animals and also a few pet-types for those of you who may never own a cow.

Starting Right with Poultry, G. T. Klein, Garden Way Publishing, Charlotte, VT 05445, (1947), 1973, 177 pgs, softcover.

Part of the old "Have More" Plan Reference Library. For more information on the "Have More" plan, locate the 2nd issue of the old *Mother Earth News*. That whole issue was devoted to it. *Starting Right With Poultry* contains everything that you wanted to know about poultry from egg to table. Another good used-book find.

Raising Animals for Fun & Profit, by the editors of *Countryside* magazine,

Tab Books Inc., Blue Ridge Summit, PA 17214, 1984, 298 pgs, hardcover.

This book, as well as a subscription to *Countryside* magazine (not the slick one), is a must for those of you who yearn to live "beyond the sidewalks." If you can't afford to buy individual books on each animal, buy this one to use as an informational guide for cattle, horses, swine, sheep, goats, poultry, rabbits, and bees. It provides plenty of hints and good advice for animal husbandry.

Worms

Let's talk worms. Yes, worms—the fishing kind, the kind that will make your garden the talk of the town. With a little help from the following books and pamphlets, you could be a successful worm rancher with over a million head in those beds.

There's a Fortune in Worms, Hank Haynes, Brook House, Los Angeles, CA, 1976, 57 pgs, softcover.

On his way to the bank, Hank Haynes stopped to write this little book sharing with us a picture of his ranch! Nothing is overlooked here, from red wigglers to African night crawlers. We learn how to make a worm bed, who to look for as worm enemies, the secrets of worm reproduction, and how to sell worms once they do reproduce.

Jimmy Carter may have been president of the United States, but that barely holds a candle to the achievement of his cousin Hugh, president of the Carter Worm Farm in Plains, GA. For a price, Hugh A. Carter will share with you the *18 Secrets of Worm Raising, What to Feed and How to Feed the Hybrid Red Wiggler, How to Raise the African Red Worm, Over 300 Questions and Answers on Worm Raising*, and *Raising the Gray Cricket*. Once you are successful with raising the little buggers, he shares *How and Where to Sell Fishworms and Crickets*. Yes sir, there's big money in worm farming. Don't take my word for it; Hugh suggests you read about his success story in *Life Magazine* in the Dec. 28, 1959 issue, page 73. If you are serious about worms you might want to drop Hugh a line at the Carter Worm Farm, Plains, GA 31780. Δ

Just for kids — life in a rotten log

By Lucy Shober

This is the perfect time of year to pull out your magnifying glass, pack up a picnic and go on an expedition. Bring along several old plastic bags, some writing paper and a crayon. If you are lucky, you won't have to travel far before you come to a woodlot. This is where your explorations will begin. As you walk, try to find a healthy acorn or hardwood nut to put into your pocket. Now choose a rotted and moss covered log and set up shop!

What a treasure chest of life you will discover when you gently pull the rotted wood apart. First scrape together a handful of the soil around your log. It's hard to believe that the

A pill bug, left, and a Betsy beetle.

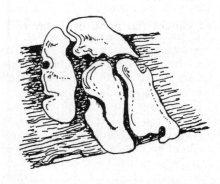

Honey fungus is also called a fox fire because of its eerie nightime glow.

clump of dirt was once a majestic tree maybe 200 feet high. Take a deep breath and smell it's pleasant earthy odor. What you are holding is the product of many workers who have devoted their entire lives to changing this tree into soil.

Layer by layer you can meet the workers in your rotten log, just remember to treat them gently.

First you will notice on the bark of decaying wood several different kinds of fungus. Brown, green and blue,

these lacy looking decorations send long root like threads called hypha deep into the wood. Hypha digest the inside of the tree, and open the door for an army of little demolition experts. If you carefully pull the outer layer of bark away from the log, you might find some of these busy fellows. Study the inside of the bark and try to find signs of an engraver beetle. Tiny tunnels will course through the wood. Some of them will

be in the shape of beautiful flowers, and others might look like scary

Puff Ball fungus. Millions of tiny dust like spores are released when these fungi are disturbed.

Engraver Beetle markings are tiny tunnels of excavated wood.

monsters. The engraver beetle chews through the wood laying her eggs as she goes. She plants little patches of fungus for her children to feed on, then even fertilizes them. These patches will produce more hypha for the babies to eat.

Other important members of the demolition team belong to the pill bug family. You might have heard them called roly-poly bugs or wood lice. They travel along and gobble up any wood pulp that the engravers might have left behind. Though they are closely related to lobsters and crabs, these shy creatures don't have the strong claws of their larger cousins and have to depend on leftovers for most of their meals.

Those huge black shiny black beetles scurrying about the inside wood of your stump are probably Betsy beetles. They are the parents of those large white grub worms that you probably also see. Betsy beetles are good mothers, they chew up and digest the hard inner wood, then feed it to those

fat little babies who are helpless at this point.

Of course with all of this activity, you are bound to notice that there are several predators lurking about ready for lunch. Wasps, salamanders and spiders might all be found waiting their turns in this moist dark food line. Slowly, over a period of years, these little demolition experts change the fallen tree into a decaying log, and finally into the rich humous all around you. That's when things start happening all over again!

Take the nut that you found, and gently but firmly lodge it into the rotted wood at the base of the fallen tree—maybe when you visit your rotten log next year, there will be a different story to tell!

Some log exploration projects

Make a spore print: If you see mushrooms growing on your log, pick one and carefully put it into your plastic bag. At home place the mushroom onto a piece of paper and cover it with a glass jar. After several days, lift the cap and see the print on your paper. This is left by spores from the inside of the mushroom cap. Spores aid in the reproduction of fungi.

Make an engraver beetle print: Take your writing paper and lay it on top of a pretty engraver beetle tunnel. With the side of the crayon, rub the paper until the print shows through. This will be a permanent record of your log exploration.∆

This Spotted Salamander stalks a wood-eating termite.

Why I like living in the country

*An essay by
"Beezer" Matthews (age 6)
Centralia, Missouri*

I like to go walking in the woods and hunting. There is a tree in our woods that lies down across a creek. We can climb the tree and play on it. I like it when Mom and Dad take us fishing. I like to play around the water and throw rocks in it. I like school too.

We used to have pigs and horses and dogs and cats and chickens and goats and sheep and rabbits and geese and ducks and guineas. We used to have a miniature horse named Gussy that I could ride. We sold most of our animals when we decided to move to Canada. I hope we get more animals when we get there.

When it snows we can go sledding. I like to skate on our pond too. Mom or Dad checks the pond everyday to make sure the ice is thick enough. We build snowmen and snow forts in the winter. We also have snowball fights. Sometimes we go over to our neighbor's farm and play in his hayloft. His name is B.L. Sims. He raises cows. He has lots of real cute calves. My little brothers think that all the cows in the world belong to B.L. Whenever they see cows anywhere they yell, "B.L. cows!" Sometimes we cut firewood in B.L.'s pasture. Dad cuts the wood and splits it and Mom and Scotty and I load it on the trailer. Dad lets Scotty and me use the hatchet to cut little limbs. He tells us to be really careful.

Mom and Dad give us allowance if we do our chores. We gather the eggs and check the chickens' feed and water. We clean our room and help with the babies.

I like to play in the tree in our front yard.

When I grow up I want to be a writer like Dad. I want to live in the country forever. ∆

Accessories can make shooting safer, more productive

By Christopher Maxwell

One of the most important accessories for any firearm is the owners manual which comes with every gun. If you buy a used gun you probably won't receive one, but you should be able to get one from the manufacturer for little or no cost. If you have a military surplus rifle, the proper manual can be found at a gun show or from one of the distributors of surplus or reprint manuals.

Your owners manual will tell you the proper method to disassemble your firearm if that should become necessary, and other important information for operation and maintenance.

Complete disassembly may be needed if you get caught in the rain, or drop your firearm overboard. Unnecessary disassembly should be avoided, as it may cause wear and loss of small parts. You may want to try it once just to make sure you understand the directions and have all the tools needed.

Cleaning equipment

Your firearms will last longer and work better if you keep them properly cleaned and lubricated.

Modern ammunition and materials take some of the urgency out of cleaning. You can take a bath yourself before cleaning your gun when you come in from shooting these days.

I like Government Issue bore solvent and LSA weapons lube. Many commercial products are fine, but nothing but the best is good enough for Uncle Sam. Surplus products are cheaper too, if you forget that you already paid for it.

If you use surplus military ammunition of dubious foreign origin, you have to assume it may be corrosive. This means commercial solvent will not dissolve the mercury salts from the primers. You need to use military solvent or commercial solvent made for black powder guns.

Whenever possible cleaning rods should be inserted from the breech end to avoid damage to the rifling at the muzzle. If you can't clean from the breech, don't worry too much. Just use a cleaning rod made from aluminum or brass and try to keep it centered in the bore. Rifle barrels are made from some pretty hard steel.

The G.I. cleaning rod for the M-16 is very useful. It comes apart into sections 7.5" long and is thin enough to fit a .22 but strong enough for larger calibers. You will need an adapter to use civilian cleaning tips and brushes, but these are available. The handle folds into the rod, allowing the entire disassembled cleaning rod to be carried in a 1" diameter tube.

Safety

Eye and hearing protection are very important and should be used any time firearms are used.

If you wear glasses make sure they have safety lenses. If you don't wear glasses you will need safety glasses. I don't like them either, but I wear them whenever possible.

Repeated exposure to high decibel sound (like gunfire) will cause permanent hearing loss. You lose the high frequencies first. This may be the reason some people don't notice the damage until it's too late.

Shooting without ear protection may also prevent you from ever learning to shoot well, as you may develop a flinch which jerks your shot off target whenever you shoot.

The most convenient effective hearing protectors are the foam earplugs. While these are not as effective as the "head phone" type hearing protectors, they are adequate and they don't get in the way of your glasses. Most safety glasses prevent the headphone type hearing protectors from fitting tightly against your head. Wadded cotton is not effective hearing protection.

It may not be possible to run for your glasses and earplugs while the coyotes are dragging your calf away, but you should use them whenever possible.

Carrying cases

If you have a telescopic sight on a firearm, that firearm must be transported in a hard case to protect the telescope. Any long-time hunter can tell you stories about a broken scope or mount which ruined a long anticipated hunting trip.

Iron sights can be much more rugged, but may not be rugged enough to stand being dropped on a parking lot. I know YOU would never do anything so clumsy, I just mention this for those others who might. A hard sided case is a good idea for any firearm.

In addition to protecting your firearm from damage, there is also a legal problem in many places. You may only be permitted to transport firearms in a locked hard case.

Information on exactly what the law is in your area may not be easy to come by. Most Police Departments and other government agencies are forbidden to tell you what the law is under the idea that this would constitute giving you "legal advice".

The local NRA affiliate should be able to provide you with a copy of your local firearms laws.

For reasons of security and privacy, I prefer gun cases which are not shaped like guns. My favorite pistol case is a plain old briefcase, and my favorite shotgun and rifle case is a covered golf bag. Most of my busybody neighbors think I'm a real fanatic for golf.

Transport cases are not good storage cases for your fire arms. Keeping your gun in a gun case locks the moisture in with it. In addition, leather is often treated with chemicals which can be corrosive if left in contact with your guns, so don't store your guns in leather holsters or cases.

Locks, cabinets, books

Many of the simplest things you can do to protect your guns are also the most effective.

A padlock through the frame of a revolver will prevent the cylinder from closing. A bicycle lock through the magazine well of a rifle will prevent the bolt from closing. The lever can be padlocked to the stock on most lever action rifles.

Display cases or racks for firearms are usually a bad idea. They display your guns to anyone who enters your home or looks in your window. To secure your guns you either need to attach them to something practically immovable with a bicycle lock or cable, or keep them in a safe-type cabinet. A converted closet can also work well.

Regarding books, a good general primer on firearms for practical use is Mel Tappan's *"Survival Guns"*. While some of his specific brand recommendations are dated now, and the conditions he postulates for use of his guns may not seem realistic, he did a fine job of explaining general firearms to novices in very practical terms.

"The NRA Guide to Firearms Assembly" is a great book for anyone who buys, sells or trades in used guns. Despite the title, it has excellent disassembly instructions for almost any gun you may run into.

While not a complete replacement for an owner's manual, this book is the best thing available for many old guns.

Sources

The best source of information about firearms, firearms law, instruction and where to find things is the National Rifle Association. They also have a book sales and publishing division with many useful titles.

Gun Parts Corp. has one of the largest supplies of parts for old guns in the world. They frequently buy the remaining parts from manufacturers who go out of business or discontinue a model, so they are sometimes the only source for parts.

Brownells is an excellent source of tools and accessories. They are set up to supply gunsmiths, but will sell to the public.

There are other sources for all these needs which may be as good or better. These are sources which I have found to be reliable, and are provided as a convenience. Don't bother mentioning my name; I don't get any commissions from them.

National Rifle Association
1600 Rhode Island Ave. N.W.
Washington, DC 20036

Gun Parts Corp.
W. Hurley, NY 12491

Brownells, Inc.
107 S. Mill
Montezuma, IA 50171 Δ

A Backwoods Home Anthology
The Ninth Year

* Build your own solar hot tub
* Five building tricks for super-strong framing
* Make mead the easy way
* Plant fruit trees, pick big bucks
* Make "split pulley" bookends
* Grow unusual plants on your windowsill
* Save big $$$ by installing your own septic system
* Compost the quickie way
* Forget the dog, the chicken is man's best friend
* Remembering the good life
* Perk up the cash flow by selling farm produce
* Build a fish pond, just for fun
* Build your own portable forge
* Try growing the popular potato
* Kerosene lamps — a brilliant idea
* Convert dead space to closet space
* Try this gravel road waterbreak
* Cash in on those windfalls
* Whole-grain sourdough recipes
* Build a simple through-the-wall woodbox
* Victory gardens
* Canning your meats and vegetables at home
* Long term food storage
* Dreaming of a Civil War Christmas dinner
* Use common herbs to treat the common cold

Women, self defense, and the 20-gauge shotgun

By Michelle Richards

Self defense, speaking as a woman, means many things to me. Protection of my physical self, protection of my homestead in the wilderness of northern Minnesota, my livestock, pets, and my food supplies—be it garden, crops, or storage facilities, and, of course, my loved ones.

It's a hard decision for some women to come to the conclusion that they need protection from two-legged varmints and four-legged ones. Our politicians and media have somehow persuaded us a knight in shining armor will come to our defense or that somehow nothing will ever happen to us.

Your own defender

The truth is, violent crimes against women are epidemic in our society, and if you are living the self-reliant country lifestyle or contemplating it, that self-reliant philosophy naturally extends to self defense. I myself live without electricity and telephone. I cannot call 911. So anything that arises here I must handle myself.

Now I know there's a few of you reading this that are saying, "But I'm only 5'1" tall and weigh 98 pounds; how can I do this?" Read on. I write from a somewhat unique perspective. I am a woman over the hill in age, physically challenged, of medium frame, and I'm also a licensed gun dealer.

I see and handle many firearms and help women in my area into firearms that are appropriate for their circumstances. I also find a great feeling of satisfaction in helping physically challenged people get an appropriate firearm for their defense. There is a firearm suitable for you, if you choose to use one.

When I first decided to be responsible for my own defense, I sat down and said, "Mick 'ol girl, there are predators out there who see me as prey; some are furry and have four legs, others only two." I do not want to hurt people or animals, but I deserve to live and do not deserve to be hurt or killed. If it becomes necessary, I will shoot a predator, and if it dies I will be sad, but alive.

Know the law

If you've followed my logic to this point and you are saying to yourself, "OK, fine; I have made a rational decision to protect myself and all I hold dear, but where do I start? What firearm is appropriate for me?" Your first step is to know your local and state laws concerning firearms ownership.

In my state, to purchase a rifle or shotgun one must be of legal age, possess identification that she is a resident, and fill out a form at purchase time. For a handgun purchase, Minnesota residents must go to the Sheriff's Office and fill out a form for a background check, which is done in approximately two weeks time. A card will be mailed to the applicant, who then shows it to the licensed dealer. Your laws will vary from state to state.

Join the NRA

I believe your next step should be to join the National Rifle Association (NRA). Their number is 1-800-538-4NRA). Contact their Office of Women's Issues and Information. The NRA is a valuable tool for you as they fight anti-gun legislation, and by joining at $25 per year you receive a monthly magazine, some very good insurance coverages, and other benefits. In 1992 the NRA's Office of Women's Issues and Information launched the Gun Safety and Personal Protection Seminar program, a series of free, four-hour seminars for new or potential gun owners. There will be 10 or more of these seminars around the country. Ask them if one will be held in your area.

Why the 20-gauge?

Next step is deciding what type firearm is suitable for you. Rifle? Shotgun? Revolver? Autoloading Pistol? I put my opinions on firearms on the line daily and I'll do it here. If I had to pick one firearm for a homesteader that would fit the average and smaller-sized woman, be easy for her to learn and control, and that would take care of two-and four-legged varmints, I'd suggest a 20-gauge shotgun in **youth** and **ladies** configuration.

Here's why: First, the stock is designed to fit smaller-framed people. The trigger is set back for easier reach for smaller hands and the gun is lighter. This does not mean it's somehow a lesser firearm. It is a formidable, useful, and strong firearm—just scaled down to fit your smaller frame.

I also suggest 20-gauge because the recoil is less than a 12-gauge, which can be substantial.

Also, a 20-gauge shotgun has more muzzle energy than a 357 magnum. It will handle any two-legged predator with ease. The gal operating this tool of defense knows she doesn't have to be a sharpshooter or pistolero. Just bring the shotgun to your shoulder, point, and shoot.

Won't go through walls

Another very important fact, in this day and age of flimsy wall construction, a 20-gauge shotgun's pellet energy, once in a wall, is significantly reduced vs. a bullet that can travel through 2, 3, or 4 walls and across the street to your neighbor's house, or out across your field and into your livestock barn. This to me is important and might very well be important to you and yours also.

As for the four-legged predator, the 20-gauge is good for 30 to 40 yards. With good shot placement and the proper shells, it should handle predators up to the size of coyotes.

If you hunt, this shotgun can fill many requirements: quail, grouse, pheasant, and rabbits of the small huntables, and with slugs you can take small to medium-sized deer. All in all it is a very versatile tool for self defense, and one that can also provide food for the table. Please check your local hunting laws for legal firearm calibers to hunt within your locality.

Buying your gun

OK, now it's time to go see that firearms dealer. Don't be intimidated because you don't know the lingo. Remember, dealers don't always stock all brands in all calibers, so you may be limited to some brands in your area. Check around. Go to a couple of dealers.

As to handling the firearm: Look it over, pick it up, and ask how it works. Does it feel good to you? Is it too heavy? Don't hurry this. Walk around with it in your hands, and work the action. Is it smooth? Is it short enough for you to reach? Is the trigger com-

fortable? I suggest you start with our well known American manufacturers because of any future servicing that may need to be done or replacement parts that you may need. Also, gunsmiths are more knowledgeable of American manufacturers' goods.

20-gauge brands

Here are some good 20-gauge American-made firearms in small stock configuration:

- Remington 1100 Autoloading in youth configuration
- Remington 870 Express Pump in youth configuration
- Mossberg 500 Bantam Pump
- Winchester Model 1300 Ranger youth pump
- Winchester Model 1300 ladies — youth

These 12-gauge shotguns vary in stock material — some are birch, some walnut — so some cost more than others. Retail prices in your area should range from $250-$275 for the birch-stocked pump guns to about $500 for the Remington autoloader. All are serviceable and will do the job at either end of the price scale.

When you buy your gun, remember to buy ear and eye protection and a cleaning kit.

Practice, practice, practice

OK, you've now come home with your shotgun and you need to practice. Don't skimp on this. It is important. Get out the manual and read it front

to back. Understand it front to back. Then and only then go to your firing range and practice, practice, practice. Then rest or do your chores.

Do this daily until you are sure you know how to operate the firearm safely. **Do not over practice until you exhaust yourself; you will become careless.**

When you first start to practice, shoot at close range. Don't go back 50 yards and try to hit a tin can. Get up close. Try 10 yards and see what happens. Practice and correct your mistakes at this distance. Then back up a couple of yards and practice and correct.

Continue this to the maximum range of your firearm. This way you will know what limits you and your firearm may have. Later, "brush up" often enough to remain competent.

I hope this article has helped some women out there who have questions, or who are confused about firearms. In the next issue of *Backwoods Home*, I'll talk more about self defense and guns for women — from the woman's, not the man's, pespective.

(Michelle Richards is a licensed gun dealer and a homesteader in the wilderness of northern Minnesota.) Δ

> *I think that we should be men first, and subjects afterward. It is not desirable to cultivate a respect for the law, so much as for the right.*
>
> Henry David Thoreau
> 1817-1862

In Backwoods Home Cooking you'll find:

- *Breads*
- *Casseroles*
- *Cookies*
- *Desserts*
- *Jams & jellies*
- *Main dishes*
- *Pasta*
- *Salads*
- *Seafood*
- *Soups*
- *Vegetables*
- *Our favorites*

The Third Year

Low overhead, sense of humor, and personal touch are key ingredients to running a good small business

By Linda Rainey

My husband, Richard, and I are currently in the process of setting up a small business (a second hand store). This will be our third store in the last ten years. We would like to show you how it can be done without major investments.

A second-hand store

We started our original business in 1982. We were greenhorns, from the word go. We bought an old motel and restaurant in rural Arizona. We converted the restaurant into a second hand store and we later made apartments from the motel.

The building had been vacant for years and was in a total state of disrepair. Richard, with the help of a handy man, spent a week scrubbing and repairing the old restaurant. It was so bad that I thought the floors were bare concrete. After the years of dust were removed, we discovered a nice vinyl tile floor.

The next project was to install the store fixtures. Richard built the shelves from scrap 1 x 12's then painted them. Our counter and cash register came from the flea market, where we had lived for a few months. As we made money, he continued remodeling until the day we sold the store.

We opened our store with the merchandise we had at the flea market and sixty cents in our pockets. Luckily the first few customers did not ask for change.

Note: Think low overhead! Rent an inexpensive building and fix it yourself. You can obtain materials for fixtures from junk yards, flea markets and second hand stores. You can be on a budget and still make a store attractive. More businesses fail the first year because of the expense of opening the business.

Be wary of shoddy goods

The merchandise at our first store consisted of new and used items purchased at yard sales and flea markets. After months of trial and error I assembled a list of wholesalers. I then obtained a catalog and obtained samples of merchandise, in our price range, that I thought would interest our customers. One wholesaler offered costume jewelry at a ridiculously low price. I was so excited by this good deal that I persuaded Richard to let me order instead of getting samples first. To my horror, the merchandise was not even good enough for a Cracker Jack box.

Guard your catalog sources

Note: This may sound selfish, but guard your catalog sources well. I made the mistake of giving a jewelry wholesale catalog to a close friend. He, in turn, gave the catalog to several flea market dealers. Within a month, everyone was underselling me on earrings.

Buying at auctions

The next source of merchandise is auctions. This is the most fun way of buying. The thrill of underbidding someone for a desired item, can't be compared.

There are certain steps you need to follow when going to an auction. First you need your resale tax number. This enables you to purchase items and defer sales tax, until you resell the item.

When you arrive at the auction you register and receive a bidding card and a catalog of items for auction. Using the catalog, you locate the merchandise that you are interested in bidding on. Make notations next to the item as to the high and low you're willing to give.

When the bidding starts, position yourself to the back of the room. This enables you to observe the actions of all bidders. Caution! Do not bid against yourself. A good auctioneer, to stimulate more bidding, will sometimes indicate he has a bid, when he doesn't.

When you are first getting started in business, a way to fill your shelves is to buy small boxes of merchandise offered at most auctions. Auctioneers, wanting to move these items, will usually accept $.50 to $1.00 a box.

Pricing merchandise

Pricing merchandise is the hardest part of doing business. This involves research of competitors prices, supply and demand of the item and also, taking into account the purchase price of the item.

Richard always tries to double his money. This rough rule of thumb usually gives you a small profit margin.

Gather it ... eat it

- *Clover*
- *Greens*
- *Asparagus*
- *Flower buds*
- *Raspberries*
- *Blueberries*
- *Wild garlic*
- *Acorns*
- *Wilderness wine*

Harvesting the Wild
gathering & using food from nature

A self-reliance guide from
Backwoods Home Magazine

Finding that rare find and selling it for millions is the fantasy of every second hand store owner.

My rare find wasn't worth millions but it was profitable. Richard and I were at a church rummage sale. As I was examining a coat, I felt a hard object. I discovered a pocket watch. Very casually, I paid the $.25 for the coat. Richard knew the item was worth more than $.25 but thought it was broken, since he could not find a way to reset it. A friend, who was a watchmaker came in several months later. Richard asked him about the watch. Our friend casually took the front off the watch and reset it. He then offered Richard $100.00 for it. Our $.25 coat was the home for an old railroad watch.

Rearrange your display

An attractive display of merchandise increases your profits. People always complimented Richard on his clean, attractive merchandise. If you clean, repair and put effort into your displays you will attract more customers. Rearranging merchandise frequently will give the impression that you have new merchandise.

Recordkeeping

My best advice is to read some of the excellent books on the market, such as *Small Time Operator* by Bernard Kamaroff CPA, or you can get free information packets for setting up small businesses from the IRS.

Employees?

Richard and I work better without employees. The headaches and increase in overhead is not worth it for a small starting business.

Advertise!

The most important aspect of any business is to attract customers. The key word is **advertise!!** A small well worded ad in a newspaper, magazine, or a shopper is worth it's weight in gold.

Richard is famous for his gimmicks, ads and craziness, which are all factors in running a successful business. Our first store was:

"Crazy Richard's Trading Post #3"

and our motto was:

"Worse crap than a second hand store"

Richard would run a catchy three-four line ad in the local shopper that gained readership all over the country. Our most famous was:

"We cater to the poor and tolerate the rich."

Richard grew a beard to his waist, had long hair, wore a gun, and acted crazy in our first store. This brought people in the store and they usually bought something before they left. We have customers that remember him from Alaska to Mexico and from Florida to California.

To summarize:

- 1. You have to like what you're doing.
- 2. Be prepared to work long hours.
- 3. Keep the overhead low.
- 4. Spend the first few years putting the profit back into the business.
- 5. Stay small.
- 6. Have a sense of humor.
- 7. Be attentive to your customers. People like the personal touch. That's what a small business has over the chain stores.
- 8. Give the people bargains. High volume works better than high prices. Δ

Fan

*The only other soul
on the mountain with us
was a big mafia man
from Chicago.
In his bedroom
he had a swimming pool
and usually around 6 P.M.
he swam from his bed
out onto his patio
and dried off with
a big blue towel.
His big thing was
putting the record player
out on a cane chair
each evening
and playing
Strangers in the Night
and drinking
hot Coca-Cola
sometimes past dawn.
Frank Sinatra had a house
on top of the mountain
a long flat pink house
with many windows.
Not once did Frank
come to the window.
The mafia man sat way out
at the edge of the patio
and looked back up there.
He smoked black cigars
in the steamy moonlight
and never gave up.*

Kyle Jarrard
Suresnes, France

Waterpower for personal use

By Rudy Behrens

(This introductory overview to waterwheels is the first of a three-part series. The second installment (Issue No.17) will be about undershot and no-head wheels, and the third installment (Issue No. 18) will deal with overshot wheels. — Editor)

The creak of an old, wooden moss-covered wheel lazily driving a gristmill in a long lost past is how most people think of a small scale water power. Of course water power is old. Historical records put it at around 4000 years old. While that makes it an ancient technology, that doesn't make it an antique technology. If you have ever considered windmills, think of a water wheel as a windmill that uses a fluid 824 times as dense. In other words, 824 times as powerful. On the negative side, you need access to a good stream, while the wind is everywhere. I am making this comparison to show that water power isn't any more complicated than wind power to understand.

How they work

Waterwheels run because "gravity" causes a "mass" of water to fall some distance (HEAD). This energy is absorbed by the wheel to do work. There is more than one way to absorb the energy, so wheels have evolved into two classes:

● **reaction**

● **impulse**

Reaction, uses the moving water to create a pressure differential like an airplane wing. These are correctly called "turbine's." A propeller is the most common example of the type.

They have many advantages, but most of the advantages benefit professional or large-scale users. While very efficient and compact they require more "tending" than a non-professional may be able to provide. While they can be automated sufficiently to allow unattended operation, these controls are very costly and really can't be justified for a non-professional power plant.

For this reason I recommend **impulse** type water wheels. These function by transferring the momentum of the moving water to the machine.

The energy transfer is similar to one billiard ball transferring its energy to another. Because of this, impulse wheels have a very high efficiency, and more importantly, have a constant efficiency over varying stream conditions.

On a small, variable stream (a typical home/farm stream) an impulse wheel can produce more than twice the kilowatt hours of a reaction wheel. Impulse wheels are available in several types, each designed for a specific type of stream.

No-head water motor

No-head- If you have a stream with an average velocity of 4 feet per second or higher (preferably higher), you can use a no-head water motor. These are a relatively new innovation. While they are somewhat inefficient compared to more traditional designs, they have the advantage that they **do not** need a dam of any sort. The time, expense and just plain hassles associated with building a dam make these designs very desirable. There are three choices:

● 1. a simple paddle wheel (Be sure to use a large diameter).

● 2. a Scheider Lift Translator. This is a patented design. The company is located in the area of Sacramento, CA.

An all-welded steel undershot Poncelot waterwheel ready for installation.

● 3. A FITZ C-Rotor and the Scheider Lift Translator are autonomous generators, containing the wheel, generator, and regulator in a single unit. You just place one in a stream and connect the power cable to a load. Both designs are quite cost-effective as a personal power source.

Undershot wheel

Undershot wheels range from simple paddle wheels placed in a stream to Poncelot Wheels. They were developed in France during the 18th century. They are good for small to medium flows and heads from 1 foot to 12 feet. If properly designed, a Poncelot can be 85% efficient or more. Even an amateur-built wheel can be over 75% efficient.

Overshot wheel

Overshot wheels are the kind people associate with Currier & Ives engravings. While many were made of wood, after 1840 most were made of metal. For small streams and heads up to 25 feet, these are still the best choice for a home/farm user. The old FITZ I-X-L designed in 1862 was tested at the University of Wisconsin in 1913. It proved to be 93% efficient.

Crossflow turbines

Crossflow turbines are incorrectly called a turbine since they work on the impulse principal. They can best be described as undershot wheels in a can. They are useful for small to large flows and heads from 10 feet to 100 feet. They are close tolerance devices so we wouldn't recommend this design to an amateur builder unless you have some machining experience. A Pelton wheel is a high head variant of the crossflow, best used with heads of 50 feet or higher.

Site selection

Basically, the problem you have to solve with site selection is this: How can I make the most kilowatt hours per

The undershot wheel from the previous page, plus attached generator, installed.

year with the least expenditure of time and money.

Surprisingly, wheel horsepower and efficiency are not the most important factors. This is because stream flows vary over the year.

The best choice is the wheel that delivers 50% or more of the theoretical power of the stream. In other words, the total annual production should be at least HALF of the production you would get if the wheel ran at full power all year long.

For example, there are 8760 hours in a year. If you had a 100 kilowatt wheel, it should produce 438,000 kilowatt-hours annually. (100 KW * 8760 * 50%). If it doesn't, you should use a smaller wheel. This isn't as difficult to calculate as it sounds. Power available can be calculated as flow (in cubic feet per second) times head (in feet) divided by 11.8. This will give you power in kilowatts. Divide this answer by 0.746 to get horsepower.

Also remember a stream varies over the year. The most important thing to know for any waterwheel installation is **how much water is available,** and **how much can you use.** An oversized wheel is both inefficient and a waste of money. Plot the flows if you can, or get stream flow data from the U.S.

Geological Survey. Usually a flow that is **met or exceeded** 25% of the time is a good flow to size your generator. While you may miss some power during spring floods, remember that they don't occur often enough to justify the expense of a larger waterwheel.

Generator type?

When selecting a generator type, decide if you want AC or DC power. Will you co-generate with the electric company or go it alone? If your power plant is 25 kilowatts or larger, a self regulated AC system is the best. If it is smaller, or you want to supplement with wind power or photovoltaics, DC is the simplest to use. If you are co-generating, a simple AC induction system will work for any size power plant. This is the absolute least cost arrangement. Here is where the self-regulating characteristics of impulse wheels really pay off.

Wheel selection

Head is the real factor when selecting your wheel. Review the descriptions above and make your choice.

Speed increaser

Impulse wheels turn slowly. This was one reason reaction turbines were invented. Today gearing is very reliable so it is no longer necessary to direct drive a generator. This also allows use of more efficient 4-pole (1800 rpm) generators. Any industrial enclosed drive will work. Do not use auto transmissions. They were never intended for continuous duty. The bearings and casing are too light unless you are making 10 kilowatts or less.

This is an overview of how waterwheels can be used for personal power plants. As in anything, attention to detail is what separates success from failure. Measure your stream carefully, and don't over-estimate your power needs or building skills. Waterwheels are **heavy** industrial machines.

On the other hand, don't under-estimate what one person looking to change their piece of the world can do. Before I bought the FITZ Waterwheel company, I had been through some hard times. Now 6 years later, I operate 1250 kilowatts of generators commercially, providing clean, environmentally safe power to over 1000 homes. I hope you have as much fun and satisfaction with your waterwheel, whatever the size.

(Rudy Behrens owns the FITZ Waterwheel Company. 118 Sycamore Ct., Collegeville, PA 19426, Phone: (215)489-6256.) Δ

Summer Rain

The angry ones behind the hill
just shook those dusty clouds until
the thunder roared,
the lightning came
to bring through
          the summer rain.

June Knight
Caldwell, ID

Coyote

Ow-ow a-ooooo, she howled
Drowning out the hooting of the last spotted owl.
If you'd listen sharply, you'd hear shrill cries
As her pups poked their noses into the skies.

The temperature plummeted when the moon rose
Capturing their silhouettes as shadows transpose.
Their coats were priming for the winter ahead.
The pups knew not of blizzards or being underfed.

You say their existence appears somewhat bleak
Serving no purpose — reaching no peak?
Why, nature itself set-forth their goals
To chase prairie dogs, to unearth moles.

I can't imagine sleeping out in a tent
Rolling over at night without ear half-bent,
Listening for the song they alone can sing,
The song of our wilderness...vanishing.

Ow-ow a-ooooooooo.

Hal Meili
Cheney, WA

September/October 1992
No. 17
$3.50 U.S.
$4.50 Canada

Backwoods
Home magazine

...a practical journal of self reliance!

THE SENSIBLE WAY TO STORE AND USE FOOD

BLACKSMITHING

HEATING AND WINDOW SYSTEMS

THE "OTHER" TEXAS FRENCHMAN

WATERWHEELS

HOME CANNING

HERBAL FIRST AID

Note from the publisher

Backwoods Home Magazine will no longer accept credit cards

Backwoods Home Magazine can no longer accept credit card orders for either the magazine or any of the handful of products, such as books and a T-shirt we sell. We had been processing credit card orders through TGE, a company owned by my computer friend, Tim Green, who is president of Tim Green Enterprises (TGE).

His bank has informed us they will no longer allow *BHM* to process credit card orders through TGE, and that we have to apply for our own processing number.

We have, but it'll take three months—if they give it to us. It seems the credit card company wants us to have a store-front and do at least 20 per cent of our business as walk-in business. We have no store-front and process no orders as walk-in business. Everything is done over the phone or by mail.

Even if they give us a processing number, I'm doubtful we'll resume accepting credit cards. Credit cards are a trap sprung on the American people by big banks. It gets the banks rich but puts the average American in debt over his and her head. Since it's a free country, I have no quarrel with people who want to use their credit cards (I have none), but I'm sick of paying the big banks the three per cent fee on all orders. I dislike big banks about as much as I dislike big government.

So if you have a credit card and would like a country magazine, don't use it to order one from us. There are lots of country magazines that will take a credit card. They're no good, and they will soon go out of business, but they'd appreciate your money. But if you have a check, money order, or cold hard cash and would like to read a good country magazine, send it to us. We'll send you a magazine that's worth reading, and you'll have the pleasure of knowing you have neither increased your debt nor enriched the big banks.

Down with PR releases

While I'm on a roll, let me tell you about all the public relations (PR) releases that clog up the *BHM* mail box. They come from all over, from companies too cheap to take out an ad and too stupid to write a news release that would be acceptable to your average newspaper. The PR releases are labeled "news releases" by the dunces that write them, but they are really self-serving advertisements for products that generally stink. I throw them in the post office trash can.

About twice a week I get a call from one of the companies asking if I got their "news release." I say "Yeah and I threw it in the stinking trash can; don't send me any more." Then I slam down the phone and laugh like hell.

Dave Duffy

So if you're working for a PR firm, cross me off your list and save yourself a stamp.

Preparedness and Eco Expos

There are two interesting shows coming up in the West in September. One is the Preparedness Expo at the Spokane Center in Spokane, Washington, the other the Eco Expo in San Francisco, California. We have booths at both shows, but unfortunately they take place on the same weekend (Sept. 18-20) so we'll have to solve a a logistics problem to be at both.

I hate to miss either show. Not only do they have a lot of useful products to offer the person who is self sufficient, but for me they are educational. The shows are basically political and stem out of very different political beliefs. Eco Expo people, for example, are crusaders for the environment, and many of them wouldn't be caught dead at a Preparedness Show, which features people whose main concern is that America's government stop its march toward socialism and adhere to the U.S. Constitution.

My main interest in the shows is that I get to talk with political activists of both the left and right. It gives me a close-up feel for what people actually think. The political views are so different from show to show, you wonder what would happen if the two shows ever met face-to-face, such as in adjacent auditoriums. I think there'd be a riot.

Andre Marrou interview

With all the talk about Ross Perot running for President, and all the dissatisfaction with Bush and Clinton and everyone else in Government, we decided to interview another third-party Presidential candidate for this issue. He is Andre Marrou, candidate for the Libertarian Party, which is the nation's third largest political party.

We told Christopher Maxwell to go toe-to-toe with Marrou and ask him all the tough questions. Marrou, unlike the other three Presidential candidates, met the questions head-on. I think you'll find his direct answers refreshing. Δ

My View

Media juveniles and Big Government

I have been told by a number of readers that I should drop the politics from *Backwoods Home Magazine* and concentrate on the "how to" information. I find that to be an impossible request for a couple of reasons.

First, you cannot get away from politics by moving to the woods. Government has a long arm, ranging from its oppressive system of taxation of our property no matter where it is, to its outright confiscation of it for a variety of "it's-good-for-society" reasons.

Second, if you ignore politics, you condemn yourself to living by the rules of those who control politics. Right now those in the mass media tend to drive politics in whatever direction they want, and our two major political parties—the Democrats and the Republicans—are more interested in securing their hold on political power than they are in solving the nation's problems.

Those who do not know history . . .

Many Americans suffer from a political short-sightedness that is based on historical forgetfulness. They think we are **safe** from our Government because we live in the "land of the free." Our forefathers may have lived in the land of the free, but we do not; we live in the land of Big Government. Just as former communist countries have moved in the direction of more freedom, we have moved in the direction of less freedom. It's almost as if we have met the communists half way.

Our forefathers protected their freedoms by constant vigilance of Government; they fought Government attempts to ignore parts of the U.S. Constitution, fought state Government's attempts to usurp the powers of local Government, and fought the federal Government's attempts to usurp the powers of the state Governments.

But for decades now we have largely ignored Government at all levels, letting it take care of itself. It took care of itself alright, by growing like the predator it is: it gobbled up many of our freedoms all the way down the food chain of politics. We now have little local Government and an enormous federal Government that everyone is dissatisfied with but nobody knows what to do about.

One reason Government has grown like a rotten tumor is because the mass media is probably more short-sighted and more historically forgetful than any other segment in society. They are the first to cry about freedom of the press, but they are the most guilty when it comes to forgetting about the freedoms the rest of us would like to have.

The bulk of the mass media in this country is on an unwitting socialist binge. Unwitting because most members of it probably think they are doing the right thing. Their handicap is that they are too young to understand what is really going on. The average age of a news reporter is somewhere in his or her mid-20s, and every year enough college journalism majors graduate to replace every working journalist in the country.

That glut of would-be writers depresses journalists' salaries to the point it guarantees that the age of your typical journalist will remain young. Visit any newspaper and look around at who is writing the stories; you'll think you're in a college classroom. Only a couple of reporters and some of the editors will be over 40.

What we end up with in the mass media is a handful of veterans and an army of youthful idealists who think you can solve the world's complicated problems by wishing them away with clever phrases and other people's money. They jump on evey idealist bandwagon that comes along, quote the phrases of the politicians whose ideas more closely reflect their own young idealism, and cling to an old and stupid theory: if Big Government (or Big Money) has been unsuccessful at solving a problem, then Bigger Government (or Bigger Money) will probably solve the problem.

We have a bunch of juveniles in possession of the enormously powerful tool of modern mass communications. The wily politicians of the entrenched Establishment understand this, so most have little difficulty dealing with the mass media—just play their tune and you have a loud and eager election ally.

Unfortunately the positions the media juveniles advocate do not bode well for the future of American freedom. Here are two examples:

Gun control is necessary to control crime. This tragically erroneous view is not shared by the majority of Americans, but our dull-headed politicians in power hear it so often that they routinely propose and often pass legislation that restricts our Constitutional guarantee to bear arms—not just as hunting weapons but as a last resort of rebellion against a Government that no longer responds to the will of the people.

Government should provide a mass social welfare net for all citizens. This absurd notion is socialism, the same socialism that it took the former Soviet Union and Eastern Europe 70 years to realize doesn't work. But the juveniles in the mass media have little recollection of history, even history that occurred only yesterday. They still believe that if money were transferred from society's producers (the media calls them businesses and the rich) to society's non-producers (the media calls them the poor) that everything would work out just fine.

They have been very successful at convincing Government to do this in big cities like New York, which is now virtually bankrupt, and in state's like California, where one fourth of businesses in the state are considering plans to move out of state. Ten years from now, when California's business exodus causes the unemployment rate to go through the roof, the media will still be writing editorials about transferring more money to the poor to solve the problem. They just don't get it.

So what's the solution? Us! Vote, get involved, support laws that solve problems, and ignore the juvenile rambling of the mass media. Δ *Dave Duffy*

The sensible way to store and use food

By Russ Davis

Acquiring and maintaining adequate food reserves is a prudent concept which country folks have always practiced. Crops harvested in the fall had to last until the next crop came in. Period. A well-stocked pantry and/or fruit cellar shielded them from the frailties of bad times. As a boy growing up, I spent long hours every fall helping to fill hundreds of sterilized Mason jars with the bounty of the garden. The work was hard and not a lot of fun, but it filled our tummies with good food all

winter long and into the next summer. It's only been the last few decades that people, especially in the cities, have developed a "we can always run to the super market" mentality which has relegated the well-stocked larder concept to a place alongside buggies and kerosene lanterns.

In the light of today's uncertainties, with the potential for natural disaster, extended unemployment, or war — all of which could close the supermarkets we have become so dependent on — a survival-conscious person needs to revive the old concept of the full larder. For most people, the question is not whether this is a sound concept, but

rather how to do it within the constraints of today's budgets.

Of course, for the person with a pocketful of spare cash, the answer is simple: just look up any of the dozens of reputable producers and distributors of storable food supplies and buy yourself a year or two of reserves. The options range from Spartan basics to super deluxe combinations of freeze-dried goodies, with prices resembling telephone numbers to match.

Thus, for the rest of us, the question is how to get started on an already strained budget. The most reasonable answer is not to wait until you've won the lottery, but rather to try to squeeze a few extra bucks each week and to convert them into pantry-stuffers. Or to try to overbuy your actual needs by a few cans or containers of this or that each time you visit the market. (This would be in addition to any home canning and preserving you might be doing from your own garden, etc.) It might not sound like much, but you'd be amazed what an extra five dollars a week could do. For example, in just three months, that extra five dollars could buy you, say, 50 pounds of assorted dried beans, 50 pounds of rice, and still leave a buck or two over for some other incidentals. To be sure, far short of a balanced and complete food supply, but a lot of eating.

The central idea, then, is to accumulate, as quickly as your budget allows, a reserve supply of basic food which can be stored for long periods, and which provide maximum nutrition at minimum prices.

Six guidelines

To succeed at this, here are six prudent guidelines to follow.

1. Be determined to be regular in your accumulation of food and supplies.

Buy as much as you can, as quickly as you can, but then continue to accumulate stuff every week. Just like making car payments or any other obligation. Don't allow yourself to say "Gee, I really want to do it, but I need the money for something else, so I'll just double up next week." Next week might turn into week after next or next month and before you know it, your plan is weeks or months behind schedule.

2. Be inventive in creating new sources of funds.

Hold a garage sale, collect returnable bottles, try to get in a little overtime—whatever you can do to accumulate a little extra money. Then use it to buy items for your emergency food supply.

3. Keep your pantry shelves stocked.

Establishing an emergency food supply should never be done at the cost of your daily needs. Besides, a well-stocked pantry for every day use can be a valuable addition to your emergency reserves. Conversely, do not rob your emergency supplies to meet your daily needs. The idea is to build up your reserves to the level you feel is appropriate for your needs (a month, six months, a year, or whatever) and then to keep it as fresh as possible by using the oldest stock for your daily cooking while replacing it with new stock. Establish a permanent system of rotation and replacement.

4. Buy those items for long term storage which lend themselves to it, and which are things your family can and does eat on a more or less regular basis.

This is important: Don't fill your emergency larder with foods you don't normally eat. For example, rice is an excellent basic staple which can be stored for many years, but if your family doesn't like rice, it would be foolhardy to store it. There have been cases in which children actually starved to death, refusing to eat food which was alien to them.

It is absolutely false to assume that hungry people are willing to eat anything. They might, but then again, they might not. Dry dog food is edible, but would you want to make 300 pounds of it your sole reserve food?

A reasonable approach would be to gradually and systematically introduce your family to some of the easily stored items on the list contained later in this article. In that way, they will be getting used to a variety of wholesome foods which can enrich their daily lives and minimize any "shock" to their systems when switching over to emergency supplies. For example, lentils are loaded with nutrition and are relatively easy to prepare, but the common variety is ugly. They're mottled brown and cook up looking like a bowl of mud. But, properly prepared, they taste delicious. Don't forget that old Bible story about Esau selling his inheritance to Jacob for a bowl of pottage—that's Bible-talk for lentil stew. Taste them once and you'll know why Jacob knew what he was doing.

Another popular fallacy, even among those who should know better, is that your system can instantly and easily convert over from what you normally eat to whatever is available. This myth belongs in the same category as the one about goats eating tin cans. They don't and you can't.

For example, much "to do" is made about reliance on a basic supply of whole wheat berries to be consumed pretty much in a cooked but otherwise unaltered state. Make no mistake about it: If you are on the typical soft white bread and low fiber don't-give-me-anything-I-have-to-chew-on-all-American- McDiet, converting immediately to a high fiber whole wheat diet will rip your intestines out and hand them to you on toilet paper. After a couple of days, you'll begin to think someone skated through your boudins with razor blades.

Don't fill your emergency larder with foods you don't normally eat.

Don't get me wrong. Wheat gruel, whole wheat breads, etc., are very nutritious. Our ancestors probably ate them as a basic diet. The Roman army consumed them daily and marched over half the known world, but their digestive systems were used to it. Yours is not, but it could be by gradually introducing such foods into your diet and consuming them on an ongoing basis. Do it gradually, ok? To make an immediate total conversion is an open invitation to flatulence, "runny-gits", and perhaps even intestinal bleeding.

On the other hand, if your family is used to eating whole grain breads, cooked whole cereals, etc., then the changeover is a piece of cake—actually a piece of bread. By extension of this principle, trying "survival" recipes on your family during normal times helps to determine likes and dislikes, and it practices sound nutrition in your daily life.

Do not be bashful about trying some of the more "exotic" foods which lend themselves to home manufacture. Many oriental products such as tofu, a type of soy bean curd which is easily produced, is an excellent source of high quality protein. Others include miso and tempeh. Reference books on their manufacture and use are found at the end of this article.

5. Always practice good economics by comparison shopping, buying in the most economical quantities, and using cooperative purchasing and other plans to save money.

Use your calculator to determine the best buy. Prices for identical items can vary tremendously. I save 50% on some staples such as dried beans, rice, and pasta by stocking up at a warehouse type of grocery outlet. Bigger is not necessarily cheaper. I have found that the per pound price for many items such as rice and navy beans may be actually cheaper in one or two-pound bags than in 25-pound sacks. The only way you'll know for sure is to run it through your pocket calculator. Sometimes you might also be able to buy in bulk directly from local farmers or grain mills.

6. Inform yourself. Establish a library of books on the subject.

Several good ones are listed at the end of this article. Read them and use them. You need to have an intimate knowledge of nutrition and how to make the most of what you have. Being caught in a roaring blaze is a poor time to read the instructions on how to operate your fire extinguisher!

What you need

Having elected to prepare your own survival larder, you now need to know what should go into your emergency food reserve supply. The master list (Table 1) contains two columns. In the left one, you will find the absolute basic essentials in each category. In the right are supplemental items which will add to the variety, effectiveness, and palatability of the basic supplies. In essence, take all of column one and as much of column two as you have time, money, and interest.

All amounts are for one average person for one year. Those doing heavy labor will require somewhat more, those doing less hard work, somewhat less. Split the proportions up according to your individual tastes. One well-known authority, Ann Elliott, has

Table 1. Master List

	Must have	Nice to have
Grains — total 350 lbs.:		
wheat	200-250	millet
corn	50	buckwheat groats (kasha)
rice	50-100	barley, popcorn, rolled oats
Beans/legumes — total 100 lbs:		
soy beans	30	kidney beans
navy beans	35	pinto beans
split peas	15	lima beans
lentils	20	
mung beans	20-40 (to sprout)	alfalfa seeds - 20 (to sprout)
		whole dried peas-yellow or green
canned peanuts		
Epsom salts or calcium sulfate (to convert soybeans into tofu)		
Miscellaneous:		
assorted pastas (spaghetti, etc.)	25-50 lbs.	assorted pasta dinners (Kraft dinners, etc.)
		assorted instant noodles (Ramen)
honey	50 lbs.	white and/or brown sugar molasses
non-instant dried milk	50 lbs.	an assortment of spices
peanut butter	5-10 lbs.	canned tuna and/or sardines soda crackers (saltines)
apple cider vinegar	1-2 gallons	powdered eggs
oil (peanut, corn, etc.)	6-7 gal.	instant coffee/tea (a coffee sub. can be made from roast grains such as wheat)
onion and tomato flakes		other dried veg. flakes such as parsley, cabbage, carrot, celery, etc.
salt - non-iodized	50 lbs.	salt petre for preserving meat
black pepper	1-2 lbs.	red pepper
dried garlic powder		baking soda
liquid bleach (Chlorox)	2 gal.	protein powder
all purpose soap	10-20 lbs.	spirulina powder (high protein)
dried yeast	1-2 lbs.	fruit cakes
assorted dried fruits	10-15 lbs.	baby formula mix (good for adults, too!)
baking powder	1-2 lbs.	
assorted bouillon cubes		dried soup mixes/bases
vitamins and supplements		Texture Vegetable Protein in assorted meat flavors
an "emergency garden" kit consisting of a variety of garden seeds — do not buy hybrids or you will not be able to collect seeds from your first crop. Seal this packet tightly and renew each year. (Use last year's to plant this year's home garden.)		freeze-dried starter for yogurt, and tempeh soy sauce, miso as "last splurge" items, all the dehydrated and freeze-dried commercially packed foods your budget will allow. Concentrate on meats, fruits, cheese mixes, desserts, etc. - only after your column one has been filled.

made the recommendations in Table 2, below, as bare-bone minimums.

Our master list uses a somewhat different breakdown and provides for a more variety and a higher caloric intake.

If you do not make regular use of a hand-operated grain mill, you may wish to buy one for emergency use. Steel-burred models are the cheapest, but stone-burred ones are the nicest.

Table 2. Minimums

	per person per day	per person per year
grains	12 oz.	300 lbs.
beans/ legumes	4 oz.	100 lbs.
honey	1.5 oz.	35 lbs.
salt	1/4 oz.	6 lbs.
dry milk	1.6 oz.	36 lbs.

Some interpretations

First, bear in mind that the recommended amounts of each item are based on average tastes and consumption. If you have a good reason to vary yours, do it. For my personal tastes, I would reduce the amount of wheat by 100 pounds and bump the rice up an additional 180 pounds, plus 20 pounds of millet. I would also just about double the pasta and beans. Why? Because my family eats more rice, beans, and pasta, and a lot less wheat.

Grains

A reasonable guideline is to figure approximately one pound of **grain** per person per day. This, when supplemented with beans, legumes, and a few other items, constitutes a reasonable daily ration.

Wheat

Wheat is the standard for most Americans. Fine milled, it can be used to make breads and pastas. Cracked (meaning run through a very coarse setting on your grinder), it can be turned into a cooked breakfast cereal. When cooked for a short period of time in enough water to cover it, then dried in a very slow oven, it becomes **bulgur**, an Eastern European delight which can be used to extend meats and stews. Bulgur keeps for a very long time; a healthy supply is part of my personal larder.

Rice

I can scarcely say too much good about **rice**. It is **the** basic food for most of the world's population. It cooks up rather easily, provides a lot of nutrition (especially in combination with beans), and can be prepared about three zillion different ways. It also keeps well.

Recently, I found a couple of five-pound plastic sacks in one of our storage tubs (one of those snap lid five-gallon plastic buckets that once held salad dressing for a restaurant) which had been placed there eleven years earlier. We opened them, inspected them, and then ate the rice. It tasted every bit as good as the "fresh" rice in our regular bin.

Barley is great for soups. **Buckwheat groats** is another one of those Eastern European foods which is both easy to use and high in nutrient value. **Millet** is an easy to cook, easy to digest grain which is used all too seldom by Americans except for bird seed. It is, however, a main crop in many African countries. **Grain sorghum** is not mentioned above. It, too, is an extremely nutritious grain. It was originally grown to feed slaves, but has never found much acceptance. Too bad.

Regular **corn** yields cracked corn, corn meal, and corn flour, depending on how finely it's milled. With it you can make a wide variety of tasty items including corn bread, mush, polenta, even tortillas.

Popcorn has been added to the list. In addition to its popular form with salt and perhaps some butter or other fat, you may be surprised to know that popped dry and without salt, all you need is a little milk and sugar to turn it into a tasty breakfast cereal! Honest. Ask anyone who grew up in the depression when it was called "depression delight."

Rolled oats are super. They kept the Scots bounding around the highlands, no doubt because they are full of energy—and cheap.

Beans and legumes

Beans and legumes are the heavy artillery of nutrition. They are loaded with energy and are an excellent source of protein. Beans and other legumes of all descriptions should be in abundance in your reserve larder. They store very well, though older beans do take longer to cook tender.

Most Americans, if they know what **tofu** is, think of it as something they buy in the fresh vegetable section at the super market and use as an ingredient in oriental cooking. It can be made easily and fairly quickly from soy beans. Protein-starved orientals call it the meat without a bone. It is, truly, one of the wonder foods. It is very bland in flavor and takes on the taste of whatever it's cooked with. It is easily digested and a powerhouse of protein. The book on tofu listed in this article is a "must" reading. **Soybeans** also provide bean sprouts as do **mung beans**, which are a tad easier to sprout. Sprouting is simple, virtually idiot-proof, and each pound of dry beans yields as much as six pounds of vitamin and energy packed sprouts in only four or five days. **Alfalfa seeds** also spring into a mountain of green munchies with no more encouragement than a little water, darkness, and time. If you have some starter, you can also convert cooked soybeans into tempeh, a solid white mass which has the texture and, according to many, also the mild taste of chicken. It can be sliced and fried.

Lentils are, as was previously mentioned, plain looking. Kind of ugly dull brown disks. Oriental shops also carry some of the Mideast and Indian varieties—bright oranges and yellows. Same great taste and super nutrition in fancy colors. Lentils require less preparation and cooking time than beans.

Honey

Honey is the recommended sweetener because it is chemically different from regular white sugar and will keep for a long, long time. In fact, honey was used as a preservative back in ancient Egypt. According to some scholars, merchants during the middle ages were known to have created a shortage of mummies by buying up those preserved in honey, throwing out the body, and selling the honey to unsuspecting buyers. It's ok to keep some of your sweetener supply in sugar, but try to keep as much of it in honey as you can.

Powdered milk

Buy the non-instant, variety of **powdered milk**. Dairies and bakeries are often good sources of this in bulk. It can be easily reconstituted by adding water and beating with a wire whip. Back in my boy scout days we used an over-sized cocktail shaker with a loose piece of fine chain in it. When shook, the chain flayed the water and the milk powder into a frothy liquid in about a half a minute. With a little effort, you can also turn reconstituted milk into yogurt or cheese — real taste treats and nutritional bonuses. Dairies and bakeries are also good sources to check about **powdered whole eggs**. Some of those fellers who were G.I.'s back in W.W. II would still shudder at the mention of powdered eggs, but they're a lot better these days.

Vinegar is something which is generally ignored by others when making suggestions about what to include in your reserve food supply. That's an oversight which should be corrected. It is just the thing to preserve and pickle, or to liven up the taste of stuff like bean soup. **Pure apple** cider is medicinal in a number of ways. Vinegar can also be used to make tofu and to make more vinegar, sort of like using a little of the old sour dough or yogurt as a starter for a fresh batch.

Textured vegetable protein (TVP) is listed in the right column. I'd give it very serious thought. TVP or TSP is a soybean product and comes unflavored as well as in beef, ham, or chicken. It might be a little harder to find this than most of the other items on the list. In this country it is found most commonly in granule form. In Europe, it's available in chunks which,

when soaked briefly in water, swell up to look like cubes of veal.

Oil is important in cooking and fats are very important in your diet. Buy it by the gallon in plastic jugs. **Dried vegetable flakes** are available in little bitty containers in the spice rack and in big cans from supply houses. Buy the sizes you want, but buy plenty. They add taste and variety to your meals. The same is true of **bouillon** cubes or powder. I recommend buying the big jars of beef, ham, and chicken- flavored soup base.

The amount of **salt** may seem high, but remember it can also be used as an antiseptic for wounds and sore throats, as a preservative in canning, and a lot of other things. Make sure you get the non-iodized kind if you intend to use it for canning.

Watch the expiration dates on items which have them. This is especially true of stuff like baking powder and dry yeast. Speaking of yeast, you can preserve its baking qualities virtually forever if you convert it into sour dough starter and use it on a regular basis.

Spirulina may require an explanation. It is a type of green fresh water algae which can be had in powdered or tablet form. It is a highly concentrated protein which can be taken by itself or added to just about anything else. Buy it in bulk to save money.

The listing of **fruit cakes** may have caused your eyebrows to raise, but high quality fruit cakes last about forever, if stored properly and rubbed down once in a while with an ample amount of rum. They taste great and they are highly concentrated "food bombs" loaded with both calories and nutrients. The best time to shop for them (unless you want to make your own, which is a lot of fun and not very difficult) is right after Christmas when merchants close them out for 50% or more off regular price.

Don't forget to include a supply of **vitamins and supplements**. The "one-per-day" multi-vitamins with minerals are ok for starters. Supplement them with extra B-complex in the 50 mg. dosage. Include extra C in the 500 or 1000 mg strength.

Vegetable seeds

Another must is to invest 10 or 15 dollars in **vegetable seeds**. Kept tightly sealed and fairly cool, most garden vegetable seeds have at least a year or two germination life. Many are viable for much longer periods of time. Make sure that you buy the non-hybrid varieties. They may not bear so prolific as the fancy hybrids, but their seeds are true, so that you can collect them to act as a starter for the next year's garden.

Include tomatoes, turnips, lettuces, radishes, onions, carrots, cukes, melons, collard, corn, beans of all sorts, peas, cabbage, and anything which turns you on. Seed stores have fantastic varieties to choose from, but most are of the hybrid kind. Luckily, most discount stores run a garden shop in the spring and usually have big display bins of vegetable seeds at very low prices — often for 12 or 15 cents per package. It has been my practice to buy five or six dollars worth of these and to pop them into a seal-a-meal bag. These go into storage for next year. Meanwhile, I take out last year's bag and plant those seeds this year. Thus, I always have next year's seeds on hand.

The last items, in terms of priorities, are those you buy with the money you have left over after you have filled your reserve food list. Any surplus dollars can and should be splurged on the kinds of things which the professional suppliers sell: dried cheddar cheese powder, dehydrated butter, dessert mixes, freeze-dried meats, etc. Anything which strikes your fancy. The variety is infinite.

Even overruns of government field rations — called **M.R.E.'s** by Uncle Sam and "Lurps" by the grunts — are readily available, though at about 3-4 dollars per meal packet, pretty expensive.

Another item which fits into this category is a supply of salami or summer sausage which has a long expiration date. At least two national chains sell such sausages. Aldi food stores (among others) carry a brand of Danish salami or summer sausage weighing a couple of pounds. It's on the salty side but unopened, it probably has a shelf life of a couple of years at average room temperatures, and no doubt even longer at lower temps. Lasting just as long and tasting much, much better are the Hungarian salamis sold by K-Mart. They come in two varieties and two sizes: six ounces and a larger one about one pound. All of the items in this category share two characteristics in common: good taste and high costs, so despite their "toothsomeness," take care of your other needs first.

Storage considerations

Except as noted, nothing on the master list has a nutrient shelf life of less than three to five years when stored properly. Watch the temperature in storage areas very carefully. Anything above 50 degrees F. will start to significantly shorten shelf life of foods like peanut butter and dried milk, among others. Grains and beans should be good for 10 years or even longer. As mentioned above, honey lasts for decades, though it has a tendency to crystallize. That's not a problem and if you prefer it in its more common liquid form, all you have to do is to heat it gently by setting the jar (with the top off) in some boiling water and stirring occasionally until it turns back into the familiar golden ooze.

If you are following the basic principles put forth in this article, long term storage is not a problem, because you will be practicing "R and R" — rotation and replacement. Since your reserve food supply will contain many of the kinds of foods you normally use, all you have to do is to take the oldest item from the reserve stocks (rotation) and replace it with a new one. For example, your regular food supply of cooking oil runs out. You simply take the oldest gallon of oil from your reserve supplies and replace it with a gallon of fresh oil. In this manner, you are using up the oldest while it is still relatively fresh and tasty, and replacing it with fresh stock. The only discipline required is to always take the oldest and **never, never** take anything from the reserve supplies without replacing it immediately.

The type of storage you choose depends on your requirements and life style. If you are fairly mobile, your reserve food supply is best kept in smaller, easily moved containers. Unless you have the strength of an Irish longshoreman, avoid large barrels and big boxes. (They're fine for more permanent locations.)

Most people do not realize that there are plenty of free and low cost containers to be had which are perfect for this kind of storage. Restaurants normally obtain salad dressings and such things in screw top glass or plastic jars and big five-gallon plastic buckets with snap-on lids. Bakeries are another source of these. Sometimes you can get them for the asking, other times you might have to pay a little. In those areas of the country where I've lived, the most I ever had to pay for even one of the five-gallon buckets was 75 cents, though a buck or two is not an uncommon asking price. Another neat container can be obtained from those bakeries which get their bread mixes in 40 or 50 gallon fiber barrels. These have metal tops and bottoms. The tops are removable and are held in place with a shaped metal snap-on rim. These beauties will hold perhaps a couple of hundred pounds of wheat berries. I've also got somewhat smaller fiber barrels from a sausage maker who bought his spices in them.

Bug free containers

To make your sealed containers bug free, place a 2"x2"x1" piece of dry ice in the bottom under a disposable aluminum pie tin in which you've poked several holes. Then fill, leaving the lid somewhat ajar. The dry ice will evaporate, giving off carbon dioxide which will push all the oxygen out of the container. Once this has subsided, you can then seal it tightly, leaving a hostile oxygen-free atmosphere behind for any bugs which might hatch. To seal before the carbon dioxide has done its thing is an invitation to a bulged or burst container. If your storage area is subject to any moisture problems, you may want to take a little extra time and give the outside of your fiber barrels a waterproofing. Shellac is ok for this

job. So are some paints. When in doubt, check the labels or ask the sales clerk.

Helpful books

There are all kinds of books on the subject. Some are a lot better than others. The following are included in my library and are recommended for your consideration. If you are limited in funds, the four best ones for the beginner are probably Dickey, Ewald, Lappe, and Longacre. Each of the books on this list is special in some way. Quite naturally, each author has a somewhat different idea on what should go into a reserve food supply, how to store and prepare it, etc. For example, the *Natural Foods Storage Bible* by Dienstbier and Hendricks is written with the vegetarian in mind and outlines a reserve food supply selected especially for the lacto-vegetarian. The recipe section is a treasure trove.

Esther Dickey's original book, *Passport to Survival*, is a tribute to Mormon ingenuity. She has taken four basic foods — wheat, honey, salt, and dried milk — and created a rainbow of recipes, the variety of which is nothing short of amazing. If there is anything I've learned about Mormons, other than that they are hard-working, honest, and decent folks, it's that they take survival very seriously.

The majority of books that I am familiar with on establishing and using reserve supply systems are printed by Utah-based publishers like Bookcraft Publishers in Salt Lake City and Horizon Publishers in Bountiful who cater to Mormon (and non-Mormon) needs. You might want to write for their catalogs to see what other neat books they have in print. Other good sources are the shelves of your local library, natural food coops, and the catalogs of those companies specializing in so-called survival supplies.

Davenport, Rita. *Sourdough Cookery* (NYC: Bantam Books, 1977).

Densley, Barbara. *New Concepts In Dehydrated Food Cookery* (Bountiful, UT: Horizon Publishers, 1982).

Dickey, Esther. *Passport To Survival* (Salt Lake City: Bookcraft, Inc. 1969, rev. 1975).

_____ *Skills For Survival* (Bountiful, UT: Horizon Publishers, 1981).

Dienstbier, Sharon B. and Hendricks, Sybil D. *Natural Foods Storage Bible* (Bountiful, UT: Horizon Publishers, 1976).

Erwald, Ellen Buckman. *Recipes For a Small Planet* (NYC: Ballantine Books, 1973).

Keys, Margaret and Ancel. *The Benevolent Bean* (NYC: Noonday Press, 1967, rev. 1972).

Jones, Dorothea Van Gundy. *The Soybean Cookbook* (NYC: Arco Publishing, 1963).

Lappe, Frances Moore. *Diet For a Small Planet* (NYC: Ballantine Books, 1971).

Larimore, Bertha B. *Sprouting For All Occasions* (Bountiful, UT: Horizon Publishers, 1975).

Longacre, Doris Janzen. *More-With-Less Cookbook* (NYC: Bantam Books, 1981).

Nelson, Louise E. *Project: Readiness* (Bountiful, UT: Horizon Publishers, 1974).

Salsbury, Barbara G. *Just In Case* (Salt Lake City: Publishers Press, 1975).

Shurtleff, William and Aoygi, Akiko. *The Book of Miso* (NYC: Ballantine Books, 1979). *Book of Tempeh* (NYC: Harper and Row, 1979). *The Book of Tofu* (NYC: Ballantine Books, 1979).

Stevens, James Talmage. *Making The Best of Basics,* 6th Ed. (Salt Lake City: Peton Corp., 1980).

Zabriskie, Bob R. *Family Storage Plan* (Salt Lake City: Publishers Press, 1966). Δ

It is thrifty to prepare today for the wants of tomorrow.

Aesop, The Ant and Grasshopper

*Go to the ant, thou sluggard; consider her ways, and be wise:
Which having no guide, overseer, or ruler,
Provideth her meat in the summer, and gathereth her food in the harvest.*

Psalms 6:6-8

The Best of the First Two Years
Our first big anthology!
In these 12 issues you'll find:

❋ A little knowledge and sweat can build a home for under $10,000

❋ Tepee to cabin to dream house

❋ From the foundation up, house-building is forgiving

❋ A first time horse buyer's guide

❋ A greenhouse offers advantages for the organic gardener

❋ Canning meat

❋ Backwoods Home recipes

❋ In pursuit of independence

❋ Canning blueberries

❋ How we keep humming along on the homestead

❋ Pioneer women on the trail west

❋ Some tips on first aid readiness for remote areas

❋ Whip grafting—the key to producing fruit variety

❋ The basics of backyard beekeeping

❋ Co-planting in the vegetable garden

❋ How to make soap—from fat to finish

❋ The instant greenhouse

❋ The old time spring house

❋ Getting started in a firewood business

❋ For battling ants or growing earthworms, try coffee grounds

❋ Sawmills: a firm foundation to homesteading

The Third Year

Give a country kid a camera

By Robert L. Williams

One of the first things adults do when they move to the backwoods country and get settled is to grab a camera and head for the fields, hills, and streams to photograph the natural wonders there.

One thing they do not do is provide their children with a similar camera and film and urge them to learn to see the world, not simply with the eye but through the lens of the camera.

And while the instruction sessions are going on, the adults would do well to watch what the kid sees and photographs and maybe learn a lesson or two.

When our son was two years and ten months old (he is now 15), we were taking photos one day and he asked for the camera. Somewhat reluctantly we gave it to him, along with very brief and simple explanations as to the operation of it.

That was it. He went off, shooting wildly, we thought, at everything that moved or remained still. Because we do our own darkroom work, we were not particularly worried about the cost of the film. If you buy a basic bulk loader and a few canisters, you can roll your own film at a remarkably low price.

Better still, you can put whatever number of shots you need on the roll, anywhere from a half-dozen up to forty or more. And if you rig up a makeshift — or permanent — darkroom, you can develop and print the photos in a short time and with little expertise.

We decided to let Robert III have his own way, and we finally bought him his own camera, a Vivitar .35mm manual instrument that he could handle and operate easily.

When we printed the first roll of film he shot, we were shocked at the quality

Robert L. Williams III, age 5, with his camera.

of the photos. And if he was not shocked as well, at least he was delighted, so much so that he decided when he was three years old that he wanted to learn to develop and print his own photo work.

We taught him and let him try his hand. He made mistakes, as all kids — and adults — will, but he learned, and he became so very enthusiastic that soon he wanted to submit his photos along with my own to editors of newspapers, magazines, and books.

We submitted the photos, without bothering to inform editors who had taken the shots, and to everyone's delight they began to buy the kid's, along with mine.

And, if the truth is a must, at times they bought his **instead** of mine.

What we learned is not that we had a son who can take photos but that nearly all children, at incredibly early ages, can take fine photos after only a brief period of instruction.

So if your finances and blood pressure will allow it, let your young son and daughter borrow your camera on the next hike through the woods or while you lounge under the shade trees in your back yard.

Buy the kids a simple but effective camera if they show real enthusiasm and interest. Give them only as much instruction as they need, and don't try to see for them. They probably see much better than you do. Let them

Cat kiss of Dad was the result of a shot taken when photographer was four-years-old.

Mill pond was taken when photographer was four years old.

experiment. Use black and white film at first, so they can really see what can be done with light and, later, with filter.

When they shoot out-of-focus shots, print them and show them to them the next time they go out with the camera. Let them see that they can correct the problem by simply turning the lens until the fuzziness disappears and the image is sharp and clear.

The best type of camera is one with shutter speeds down to one second and up to one-thousandth of a second, minimum. At least one lens should be capable of close-up work, with range down to a foot or so and up to infinity. Largest shutter apertures should be no less than 2.8, larger if economically feasible. Smallest openings should be 22 or at least 16.

Don't engage in flash usage at first. Let the kid learn to use available light. Show him how to open the lens wider and wider if there is poor light, and tell him how to shut down the lens if the light is too great.

Show him that by wide lens openings he can achieve sharp close-up focus and blur background for dramatic effect. Show him or her, too, that he can shut down the lens as far as possible and get sharp focus up close and at great distances, at the same time.

Above all, don't fuss and complain and insist that your way is right. It may very well be right, but the child needs the chance to learn from his mistakes.

Soon the child will be seeing details with perfect recollection and be able to describe with astonishing accuracy what he has seen. He will begin im-

proving his memory, a feat which will serve him well in later years.

Two of the leading characteristics of nearly all superb readers are visual acuity and visual memory. The camera can help a child to improve his acuity, or his ability to focus his eyes quickly, and his visual memory is likely to grow with leaps and bounds.

But more than anything else he will begin to see the world of nature and to understand the relationships between himself and his surroundings. He will soon grasp the fact that a rusting soft drink can or styrofoam cup clash with the beauty of the natural world. He will comprehend in his own way that a plucked wild flower is not quite as satisfactory as one left growing.

He will start to see and relate to the subtle changes that occur hourly and

The Third Year

Bridge and reflection make ideal shot for Robert when he was five years old.

seasonally. He will learn that a cloud passing between him and the sun will create changes in light diffusion or refraction or simple availability that will require him to change his own perspective—and that of his camera—as he attempts to record the shot for his permanent records.

Encourage him to take several shots from a variety of angles of a particular scene or detail. Let him learn, as he will surely have to learn later, that nearly everything we encounter looks very different as we change our viewpoints, whether of a photo challenge or social and political positions.

As he grows older, let him go "hunting" with a camera rather than a gun, not because guns are bad but because at his young age a gun is dangerous. But he can learn to stalk game, to sneak up on deer, birds, snakes, and any other "game" that he discovers lurking in the fields and trees.

Few items in our possession teach us as much courtesy as does a camera. Let the child learn to be thoughtful of others and to ask them if it is permissible to take a photo. And by all means let adults learn not to walk between a child—or adult—with a camera and his subject.

Photography is a splendid way for children to meet and relate to other children and older people. The activity is one that inspires curiosity and reaction, as well as admiration and respect for the person using the instrument capably.

Buy your child a scrapbook for his photos, and either mount these in the book or on mounting paper or other materials so that he can see them whenever he wishes. Let him develop the ability to distinguish superb photos from mediocre ones.

Explain to him the importance of anchor points or the rule of thirds. These terms mean, in the most applicable sense to a child, that there should be something in the foreground to provide genuine drama or setting for the photo composition, and that "good" photos are naturally divided into thirds from left to right or from top to bottom.

Let the child learn about natural and darkroom contrast. Let him discover the magic of seeing light fall on a special paper which is then immersed into a developing chemical and, as his eyes grow wider and wider, he sees the

The Third Year

Girl in tree was shot when photographer was four years old. He composed the shot alone.

image start to appear as if by magic on the paper.

It **is** magic, in its own way. But it's magic that he can learn to comprehend and appreciate.

There's much more for the child to learn, but he will learn much of it without your assistance. You will, of course, be highly nervous when he takes the relatively expensive camera out to "work" with it. But you can stress to him that it is not a toy and that if he is careless with it, he will be deprived of its use for a period of time. If he handles it with adult care, he will be rewarded.

Contented cat and empty bird cage seem ominous, but three-year-old Robert moved the empty cage beside the sleeping cat, then added the cat food bag for emphasis.

(And later on, these same observations will apply to trips to the homes of friends, where delicate objects on coffee tables are not to be handled carelessly and even later when he begins to learn to drive the family car or use his own gun or other equipment. Anything he can learn well and positively as a child will serve him doubly well as he grows into adulthood.)

One rule will eventually apply to the camera and to all other applicable items: You may use but not abuse.

Children can learn these concepts and apply them to Nature and to their possessions and items for which they are to be held responsible.

Now, if we could only get adults to learn and understand them! Δ

His first deer: he was able to get close enough to catch not only the deer but the flies on his back. Taken when he was five.

> Dost thou love life? then do not squander time; for that's the stuff life is made of.
>
> Benjamin Franklin, June 1746

Selecting the right heating system

By Martin S. Harris

If you look at a map of the U.S. showing zones for plant hardiness, you'll see a climatic range all the way from zone 3 (Northern New England and the upper Plains states) to zones 10 and 11 in Southern California and Florida). Zones 10 and 11 are the only places where buildings might be constructed without heating systems, and so readers in that area need not worry about the subject of this discussion. For all the rest of us, the question is not whether to install a heating system, but rather what type to choose.

A couple of centuries back, there would have been one choice, a fireplace. By the 1830's, cast-iron stoves were becoming available. By the 1880's, people were installing gravity hot-air furnaces; and before the turn of the century, steam and hot-water boilers as well. Electric heat came into the residential market in the 1910's and '20's, about the same time that some Californians and Floridians began experimenting with solar-based systems. Since then, we've improved combustion efficiencies and distribution systems, but we've developed no new basic designs.

The same basic pattern holds for heating fuels: wood and then coal, gas and oil by the turn of the 20th century, electricity and solar after that. A few hydroponic greenhouses are using radio-activity waste heat from generating stations, but all the rest of us are either still in the carbon-fuel stage or tentatively experimenting with solar.

Today's problem is that there's such a wide range of fuels, combustion systems, and system efficiencies that making a design choice seems like a daunting task. Actually, it isn't.

In terms of pure cost-effectiveness (the largest amount of heat delivered inside the living space per dollar of fuel cost) there's only one choice: a state-of-the-art ultra- high-efficiency gas-burning furnace or boiler. If you want to go outside the dollar economy, there's also only one choice: wood (except for you West Virginians who own your own coal seams), for which you don't count your time as a harvesting cost.

Nevertheless, the most popular system remains the domestic oil burner, consuming (usually) No. 2 fuel oil to heat water for a hydronic system, to make steam for a steam system, or to heat air for—what else—a hot-air system.

Steam probably hit its peak of popularity back in the '50s, and since then the residential market has been about split between baseboard hot-water and ducted hot-air. The latter is usually viewed as lower in cost and quality, but when built right that isn't true.

Wood came back into favor briefly in the 70's when oil prices went up, but has since declined because it's neither cheap nor clean nor automatic.

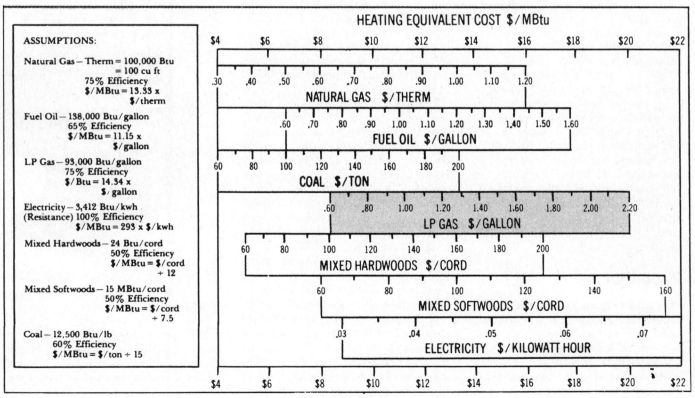

Fuel cost comparison

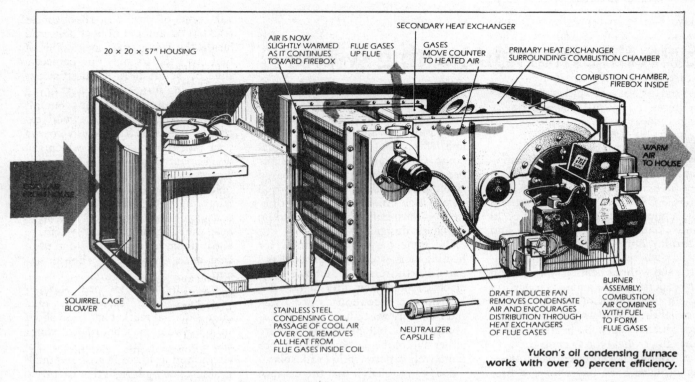

This cut-away drawing of an ultra-high-efficiency unit shows how those 90 + % numbers are achieved. Note that no chimney is needed — a boon to cash-strapped first-time builders or owners of an old place with a substandard masonry stack.

Solar, on the other hand, hasn't made much market penetration because oil is still artificially cheap and can under-price the hardware costs for all except simple passive solar systems.

Coal is a "fringe" fuel, popular in limited areas just like wood pellets or chips, various kinds of bio-mass, geo-thermal, land-fill methane, and so on. Another "fringe" fuel is waste oil: remarkable strides in the technology of this one have been made in just the last few years, and I would count it as the only real innovation in the space-heating field. Probably the best way to analyze this range of choices is to look at each in terms of strengths and weaknesses, as follows:

Wood/coal

Let's start with wood or coal. Unless you require automatic stoker systems, wood or coal stoves are the least expensive and least complex way to heat a house, hardware-wise.

Whether they're the cheapest fuel-wise depends on how you cost out your fuel-acquisition method. They're the least efficient, combustion-wise (the quantity of heat delivered vs. the theoretical heat content of fuel burned), about as bad as space-heating electricity from a nuclear plant; well below 50%.

That's for relatively modern units; old stoves can easily be down around 20%, fireplaces half that number. On the other hand, stoves don't require ducts or piping, registers or baseboard convectors, thermostats or fuel pumps. They don't require professional maintenance, and they don't even require a masonry chimney, now that insulated metal stove-pipe systems are available.

On the other hand, they're not cheap to operate if you have to buy all your fuel at top-dollar retail prices. They're dirtier and more labor-intensive to operate than gas or oil systems. Not all stoves will even hold a fire overnight or while you're off at work during the day. And finally, most mortgage-writing banks today won't accept stove-type heating systems.

Fulton pulse combustion steam boiler

Oil

Oil, specifically No. 2 fuel oil, the same viscosity as diesel fuel, is the basis for more extensive steam, hot-water, or hot-air systems. In fact, some of the older ones are oil-burners which have been converted from coal or wood, back in the '40's and '50's when the going price was 6 cents per gallon, as compared to almost a dollar today.

Heavier and cheaper oil, up to No.6, is used in industrial applications, but it requires special pre-heat and pumping equipment.

No.1 — kerosene viscosity — is used in cookstoves and space heaters, some of which have such high combustion efficiencies that they require no venting.

Oil for single-pipe steam was popular back before WWII: it requires a fairly bulky radiator at each window and a fairly bulky combustion unit, usually in the house basement. Most of these old-timers are insulated, pipes and all, in asbestos: be real careful with the legalities in renovating or removing such systems.

Oil for dual-pipe hot-water was more expensive but a quieter-operating system, and therefore considered to be higher-quality; it used either radiators even larger than steam units or else long base-board convector units.

Oil for hot-air can be a high-quality system, if the ducts are large enough to keep air velocities low, the operating systems quiet and draft-free, and a cold-air-return system provided so room doors can be kept closed.

Unfortunately, it's been easy for installers to save pennies by undersizing ducts and even skipping the cold-air returns, so hot-air systems have developed a reputation for poor quality. Lots of all this stuff — ducts, pipes, registers, radiators, and so on — is available on the salvage market today at very modest prices. Most older oil-fired units are lucky to achieve a combustion efficiency of 67%, while the newer ones are usually up around 85%.

There are one or two ultra-high-efficiency oil-fired units — Yukon is one trade name — with a combustion efficiency in the low 90's.

Gas

To get a wider choice of combustion units in the 90% range, one must turn to gas. Gas-fired systems have been around about as long as oil, in the underground piped natural-gas ser-

This gas-fired boiler manufactured by a well-known member of the industry is typical of modern combustion systems which run in the mid-80% range of combustion efficiency. That's a substantial advance over units of the '60's and '70's which rarely got their combustion efficiencies above the mid-60% range. Payback to shift over usually occurs in the 4-5 year range, although, ironically, the better the insulation level, the slower the payback on combustion efficiency.

vice areas. Since WW II, bottled gas, usually liquified propane, has enabled consumers to use the product out into suburbia and the countryside beyond the gas mains. Most appliances are built for easy conversion to either fuel. No matter which gas is burned — piped-in or bottled, natural or LP — the rest of the distribution system is the same as for oil: supply and return pipes for hot water and baseboard convectors, supply and return ducts for hot-air registers and grilles. The combustion efficiency difference for the ultra-high units is based on a process called condensing, where heat is drawn not only from the flame of combustion but also from the vapors of the combustion process. Ultra-highs do such a good job of this that they need no conventional chimney, only a 3/8 inch drain for water condensate and a 1 and 1/2 inch plastic pipe for CO_2 and H_2O exhaust. They're tiny, too; unlike earlier coal or oil burners, these units are no bigger than 3 or 4 cubic feet in size for the average size house.

Electric

Electric-heat advocates sometimes argue that their system is 100% efficient, that every watt or electricity consumed is converted into building heat. That's technically true within the building, but such accounting conveniently forgets the combustion inefficiency back at the generating station, the line loss in moving electricity to the consumer, and the fact that even the supposedly inefficient oil burner warms a basement which in turn warms the upper floors. Electric heat is cheap to install, no doubt about that. With no pipes or ducts, it costs far less than, say, hot-water or hot-air to put in wiring and baseboard resistance heating units which look much like baseboard hot-water convectors. It's also, in most parts of the countryside where electricity costs 8 to 10 cents or more per kilowatt hour — sometimes even more under a winter-rate schedule — far more expensive to operate. If there's a strength to electric heat (beyond the low installation cost, that is) it's that it can be used to beef up weak areas in a conventional system; extra heat in a bathroom, for example, or in a study which is infrequently used.

Solar

By the same selective accounting, solar advocates sometimes argue that their system uses zero-cost fuel. That's true. And it's a fact that the simplest kinds of passive solar — greenhouse glazing, for example, are highly cost-effective. Solar's problem lies in the cost of its plumbing, in the hardware needed to store heat until it's needed and to move it to places where the sun doesn't shine. It's the cost of collectors and piping, pumps and automated controls, of storage banks and re-distribution systems, which makes it tough for supposedly free-fuel solar to compete with, say, dollar-a-gallon oil. That's not to say that people can't control costs by home-building collectors, storage banks, and plumbing systems: many have done just that.

Solar's biggest problem, I suspect, lies not in the technology or the plumbing hardware cost but rather in

The Third Year

the sales pitches of the equipment industry itself, which tries to discourage passive solar and even do-it-yourself applications so it can sell more hardware.

The solar argument, like the electric-heat argument, is further confused by the insulation argument, wherein advocates try to compare highly insulated solar or electric buildings with low-insulation traditional-fuel buildings to show some sort of cost advantage.

It's my own view that passive solar, including earth-sheltering, simple glazing, night-curtains, and generous insulation levels, is the most cost-effective way to go. In fact, I've done studies in which simply raising the insulation level of an older electric-heat building reduced heat loss so much that there was no longer a rapid payback to replace the electric heat.

Waste oil

Which brings us to another free-fuel system: waste oil. Of course, people have been burning waste oil for years, but in highly inefficient and environmentally destructive ways; now the industry has developed a system for waste-oil combustion which meets all environmental standards. These units are not cheap — about $3,000 each, minimum — and they can't be home-

Waste-oil burners such as this model are not yet available in heat capacities small enough for the average house, but they may be a good value anyway.
An over-size unit simply works less hard to perform its heating task. They come with the full range of necessary industry and government approvals.

A girl and her horse

made like a sheet-steel wood-stove. Nor are they yet available in the relatively low BTU outputs needed for the typical dwelling: 50,000 BTU or so. But they are available in the 100,000 BTU size; the fuel is free (technically, one is supposed to burn only the waste oil one generates on-premises) and they're as safe as any other appliance bearing the UL label. They can be adapted for hot-water systems, although the vast majority of applications is hot-air. A couple of trade names — Black Gold and Clean-Burn. Here in northern New England most home-owners expect to spend about $4 per square foot to have a contractor put in a more-or-less conventional heating system, and about $.60 per square foot to operate it through the heating season. Some of us spend a lot less than that by investing sweat-equity in both system and fuel; some spend a lot more because they weren't willing to spend for insulation or because they like to wear sheer blouses in December. We used to have a lot more choice in system design, before the banking

industry in some areas began telling us how to live; and those who can't escape that sort of control will probably have even less choice in years to come. The nice thing about this country is that most of us can escape; if not with our purchasing patterns or ballots, then with our feet.

(Martin Harris is a Vermont architect, cofounder of "The New England Builder," and author of numerous articles on home building.) Δ

We must all hang together, or assuredly we shall all hang separately.

   Benjamin Franklin, July, 4, 1776

"To disarm the people is the best and most effectual way to enslave them."

   George Mason

Ingredients for an herbal first aid kit and how you can use them effectively

By David W. Christopher M.H.

Many of you have discovered the deep satisfaction and savings that comes from making your own clothing, growing and processing your own food, repairing and maintaining automobiles, and in some cases defending yourselves in legal matters. The expertise in these areas is commendable, but nothing compares to the exhilarating feeling of being free from the current health care system, of becoming self-sufficient in your health care needs. In this regard, you will find natural health care to be extremely simple and greatly rewarding.

If you have stored food and supplies sufficient to tide you over during a natural or man-made crisis, keep in mind that you will not be able to use these supplies if you are sick or injured, with no access to outside help.

Take a lesson from the riots

Let us take a cue from the past unrest experienced in Los Angeles and other parts of the country. In particular is the case of the young father who ventured out during the riots to buy milk for his baby and ended up being shot. We should all store at least 72 hours worth of provisions so we do not repeat history. A medicine kit should be in every home, car, and place of business.

You could go to a well equipped pharmacy and purchase a kit supplying the basics but they will also contain the same old unnatural, poisonous, and sometimes habit forming materials that give temporary relief but do not go to the cause and correct the underlying problem. So let's put together our own, and make it as natural and effective as possible.

An herbal medicine kit

A medicine kit first of all should contain the basics which include, but are not limited to, first aid tape, sterile gauze, and assorted bandages including butterfly and knuckle. Other items would include good scissors, tweezers, a thermometer, and an instruction manual on CPR and other lifesaving techniques.

As you prepare your medicine kit you will want to include something to counter infections. This is where herbs should be used, mainly because they are safer and more effective. The simple herb, **cayenne pepper** stops bleeding and helps to heal wounds. The herb **golden seal root** will counter any infection and also aid in healing. **Comfrey** is another healing herb that I have seen work miracles. **Oak bark, bayberry bark**, or any other astringent herb will help pull tissue together, further assisting in the healing process.

Cayenne to the rescue

I remember the last time I cut myself seriously enough that the blood was spurting, I found that my biggest danger wasn't in bleeding to death, but losing it all through going into shock!

So the first thing that I put in my personal first aid kit was **cayenne extract** which prevents shock. All it takes as a dosage is one dropperful. This same cayenne extract can be used to stop a heart attack.

My father who was a practicing herbal doctor, never lost a client due to heart attack when cayenne was administered. His method was to mix a heaping teaspoon of cayenne in a glass of warm water and have the patient drink the whole amount.

This same procedure was used in cases of gunshot wounds, where the blood stopped spurting within 10 seconds of drinking the **cayenne tea**. I personally suffered from bleeding stomach ulcers, which were arrested with one day's therapy using this same cayenne tea.

Cayenne works equally as well externally. Many people have reported excellent results of immediate secession of bleeding, wound healing, and no scarring by immediately placing cayenne on the wound when the occasion arises.

Cayenne should also be used in cases

cayenne

of hypothermia. After getting the person dry, warm and calm, administer the dropperful of cayenne extract or a heaping teaspoon of cayenne, which has been mixed into a cup of warm water. Warm the torso first and then the extremities—with your own body if necessary. Since the person is most likely exhausted, nourish him or her with warm liquids, soups, warm vegetable juices, honey in warm water, etc. **(Honey should never be given to babies. —Editor)**

One more situation in which you can use cayenne is in cases of frostbite. Use one tablespoon in a gallon of warm water, not hot, and soak the extremities. We could go on for days about the uses of cayenne.

For bites and stings

The next item that I would want for my medicine kit would be used for venomous bites or stings. The herb of choice is **echinacea** in extract form.

I would take a dropperful every hour and also use an **echinacea** compress on the bite or sting. A compress is made by soaking gauze with the extract and taping the gauze over the bite, or the dry herb is mixed with water or saliva to make a paste that is placed on the bite. It is important to keep the person still and calm, while restricting lymph flow with slight even pressure between the injection and the heart, around the circumference of the affected limb. All toxins are eventually eliminated through the bowels, so it is imperative that this channel is kept operating. Enemas and herbal laxatives would be in order to accomplish this goal. The best herbal laxative, Naturalax #2, can be purchased in any good health food store.

Gastro-intestinal disorders

The most common health complaint is that of gastro-intestinal disorders. There is absolutely nothing in drug stores that can approximate the effectiveness of herbs for these disorders.

For example in double blind studies, conducted at Brigham Young University, **ginger root** was found effective in alleviating nausea experienced by volunteers who were spun in circles.

While in the same experiments, Dramamine, one of the most popular drugs, barely beat out the placebo. I would definitely have ginger root in my medicine kit. Cayenne can also be effective in digestive disorders by stimulating hydrochloric acid production which effectively breaks down the food in preparation for the intestines.

Sometimes when it seems like we have too much stomach acid, we might reach for an antacid. Don't do it! In reality we are actually deficient in stomach acids. By eating too many acid-forming foods, we trick the body and it doesn't provide the hydrochloric acid necessary to break down the food.

The body, in an attempt to correct the problem, will allow a backwash of alkaline juices from the intestines into the stomach, which then triggers more hydrochloric acid production. It is this sensation that we wrongly identify as excessive stomach acids, and by reaching for the antacids, we upset the delicate balances of the body.

So the worst treatment for bloating, gas, heartburn, etc., is that of using antacids, which allows foods to pass

comfrey

into the intestines without the benefit of being acted on by stomach acids. This procedure interferes with the enzymatic action in the intestines, thus allowing undigested food to pass into the bowels, where no enzymatic activity takes place. In the bowel, remaining substances are broken down by bacterial action, and the by-product of bacterial action is gas.

When the gastro-intestinal tract is abused and becomes stagnant, many disorders are manifest. Constipation is the first sign of stagnation and is easily resolved by using the **Naturlax #2 combination.** Greater stagnation is evident with nausea. At a time like this, a quick cleansing of the upper digestive tract is in order and calls for a wonderful herb named **lobelia.** This herb acts as an effective emetic (to induce regurgitation). After emptying the stomach and upper intestines we can then go to work on the lower intestines, with the herbal laxative.

If nothing is done to eliminate stagnation, the body is then more likely to be subject to infestation of parasites, be it pin worms, E. coli, giardia, or whatever.

This leads to a **vermifuge** as my next candidate for inclusion in this medicine kit. **Wormwood** is my favorite, especially mixed with molasses. A good substitute is my own VF Syrup. After three days usage, a strong herbal laxative is used. This procedure should be used every week for three weeks.

If gastro-intestinal problems are not quickly resolved they may become chronic and result in ulcers or colitis.

I mentioned before the use of cayenne to eliminate stomach ulcers, which is a rough but effective treatment. Colitis (ulcers of the intestines and bowels) is not treated effectively with cayenne, but instead we use an herb named **slippery elm bark**. This herb is very soothing and gentle and over a longer period of time (several weeks to several months) will eradicate any aforementioned conditions. I also find combining **licorice root** with the slippery elm root will effectively stop diarrhea, and helps counter inflamed hemorrhoids. Slippery elm gets my vote for being in a natural medicine kit.

Slippery elm is a very soothing herb that can be used on any irritated surface such as bed sores, diaper rash, bruises, scrapes, etc. It is just sprinkled on dry. When combined with small amounts of water it makes an excellent band aid. It sticks to the skin by itself! A small amount of **golden seal** could be added to this natural bandage to counter infection, and maybe some **comfrey** could be added to speed up the healing process. Of course, cayenne could be combined with the slippery elm to stop bleeding.

Burns

These herbs minus cayenne would be excellent for burns. A very excellent herbal combination to use for burns

plantain

and healing is my BF&C Ointment. It is a combination of what I consider the most effective herbs for skin problems in a natural base of olive and wheat germ oils. This would be an excellent inclusion in any medicine kit but

should be refrigerated for long-term storage.

Poison oak

For those of us who encounter some poison oak, poison ivy, or just some harmless but irritating stinging nettle, good drawing herbs would be essential. My favorite is **plantain** and it definitely is in my personal kit. I have it combined with **pine tar** and it never needs refrigeration. **Clay** can also be used and is prepared and applied in the same manner as slippery elm bark.

When I finally find time to slip away into the mountains, I tend to overwork my muscles so I have included in my first aid kit an analgesic. I

have combined essential herb oils like **cassia, eucalyptus,** and **mint** in olive oil and use it effectively for any muscular pain including temple headaches and toothaches.

(If you are interested in learning more about the medicinal use of herbs, contact David Christopher by writing to The School of Natural Healing, P.O. Box 412, Springville, Utah 84663. The herbs listed in this article can be purchased at any good health food store or by calling The Herb Shop at 1-800-453-1406.) Δ

Gather it ... eat it

Harvesting the Wild
gathering & using food from nature

A self-reliance guide from
Backwoods Home Magazine

- *Clover*
- *Greens*
- *Asparagus*
- *Flower buds*
- *Raspberries*
- *Blueberries*
- *Wild garlic*
- *Acorns*
- *Wilderness wine*

A Backwoods Home Anthology
The Seventh Year

❋ It took a lot of weed-eating fish & work to make our lake usable

❋ Our homestead motto: Make-do

❋ Beans — they may be a poor man's meat, but they are also the gourmet's delight

❋ The amazing aloe

❋ Try these smaller breeds of multi-purpose cattle

❋ Soil pH is the secret of a good garden

❋ Protect those young trees from frost and vermin

❋ Don't have a cow! (Get a steer instead)

❋ Blueberries are an affordable luxury

❋ A brick walk with little work and less money

❋ For some surprises in your garden, grow potatoes from seed

❋ Make your own lumber with a chainsaw lumber mill

❋ Felting is an ancient art that's still useful today

❋ Those leftover fall tomatoes are a delicious bounty

❋ Sheet composting saves work

❋ Make grape juice the easy way

❋ These chocolate treats make great gifts and delicious holiday desserts

❋ Save time and money, and get that custom look with hinges you make yourself

❋ Grow winter salad greens on your windowsill

The magic of home canning —
great food at the best possible price

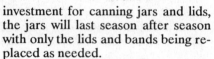

By Darlene Campbell

Nothing compares to the feeling of personal satisfaction gained when looking at row upon row of gleaming glass jars filled with home canned food—enough food to last a family for one entire year, or until the garden is producing again. Each jar bears the bright color of its contents: red beets and tomatoes, green beans and pickles, yellow corn, orange carrots. There are chutneys, sauces, relishes and sauerkraut to add zing, and hearty soups made from the last harvest before frost to warm you on a cold day in January. There are fruits for pies and cobblers or to be served with honey for breakfast. Jars of jams and jellies sparkle like jewels and every ingredient is pure and natural.

Canning was done by our grandmothers out of necessity, but with the arrival of the supermarket few of our mothers learned this task to pass on to their daughters. But despite changing times, learning to can is not difficult and the rewards are so abundant that you will find yourself looking for recipes to can long after the garden is covered with a blanket of snow. Such as your own homemade spaghetti sauce! Since gifts from the kitchen is an American tradition, what could be more pleasing than giving or receiving home-prepared jams, jellies, and pickles.

Free food

Although the main reason we can is to preserve food, it is also a great money saver. Aside from the sugar and pectin in jellies, and the vinegar, salt, and spices in pickles, all that food is free. Once you have made the initial investment for canning jars and lids, the jars will last season after season with only the lids and bands being replaced as needed.

Begin early to prepare for the canning season. The season varies across the country just as the growing season does. Don't fool yourself into believing that canning is done only at the end of summer. Canning begins as soon as the garden starts producing. After all, you want only the freshest, best produce to put up, not tough end-of-season products which are beginning to go to seed.

How much to can?

As soon as the garden is in, begin preparing by making sure you have the proper equipment. How much to can? That depends on the number of persons you are going to feed. With four in our household, I always plan to put up at least 300 quarts of vegetables. Relishes can also be counted with this number as they can be served in place of a salad during the winter. But don't include jams or fruit juices in this. Figure how many meals are needed per day, and multiply that by the number of days until your garden produces again in the spring. Naturally, for those persons with short growing seasons, the number of days that they will need to live from the pantry will be greater than for someone who lives as I do in a warm climate with short winters and long growing seasons. But with 365 days in a year, 300 quarts is a pretty good figure.

Equipment

By far the most important equipment is the **canner**. I purchased my first canner 13 years ago at a garage sale. We were planning to make our move to the country and I discovered this old canner with clamps around the lid and a pressure gauge. I took it to our extension service to have the gauge checked and it checked out fine. I have used this large, ugly canner for years because it is so big, and it cans up to seven quarts in one load. So don't think a canner must be new or expensive to do the job.

Later I added a deluxe model **pressure cooker** with a rubber gasket so I could have two canners going at one time. I found this new one ideal to do smaller jobs as well as pressure cooking meals for the family.

You may want to add a **water bath canner**, which is simply a deep pot with a rack and lid. It is recommended for sealing jellies, jams and preserves, fruits, and acid vegetables such as rhubarb, sauerkraut, and tomatoes.

Water bath canners must be deep enough to cover the tops of the jars with boiling water to a depth of one to two inches. I bought one years ago but never used it for canning. Instead it ended up being used for a dish pan. For water bath canning I simply use the old and ugly garage sale canner without clamping the lid to prevent the build up of pressure.

A **large mouth funnel** is a must for filling the jars, especially if you use the hot pack method. A good choice is "Busy Liz" which comes with several screw-on attachments for straining and separating. Another good choice holds up to five cups. These are aluminum funnels with a width of six inches and are available through mail order houses.

A **metal jar lift** is also essential. It works by closing around the jar and tightening itself as you lift the jar. It is impossible to drop hot jars as you handle them using this practical device.

A **canning book with recipes** is indispensable. You must have correct processing times for every item you plan to can to protect against botulism.

Protect against botulism

Botulism is a toxin that can grow in a tightly sealed jar of any low-acid food if not properly processed. Only correctly processed food which has been processed in a steam-pressure canner will destroy the spores that produce botulism.

The temperature inside the canner is equal to 240 degrees at 10 pounds of pressure, and at 15 pounds it is equal to 250 degrees. Scientists have developed the correct length of time corresponding with these temperatures to make food processing safe without destroying the natural flavor, color, or texture of the foods you can.

Do not take chances; follow recipes for canning to the last letter to protect your family. Books on canning are available through the agriculture extension service in your area, manufacturers of canning jars such as Ball and Kerr, the library, and through mail order houses such as Rodale Press. They are also included with pressure canners.

A **timer** is handy, but so is the kitchen clock which means it is not absolutely necessary.

I have satisfactorily used mayonnaise jars for canning, but they are not recommended by the experts. The only fault against them is the fact that they are made of thinner glass than regular canning jars and you are taking a chance that one will break in the canner. I have never had one break, but if I did, I would simply clean the canner and proceed with another jar.

It is recommended that **jars be made of glass tempered especially for home canning**. They come in a variety of sizes from half-pint to half-gallon capacity. There are wide mouth and regular mouth. Although I prefer the wide mouth jar for ease of filling and cleaning (I can easily get my hand into a wide mouth jar for thorough washing), the lids which must be replaced each time the jar is used are more expensive. So invest in a good jar brush for cleaning, and purchase the less expensive regular jars and lids except for special large items such as meat cuts.

The **most common lids in use today are two-piece**. They consist of a flat metal disc containing a sealing compound around the edge and a separate metal screw band. Although the screw bands are reusable for many canning seasons, discard them if they become rusted, bent, or otherwise damaged. A misshapen band can prevent a good seal resulting in food spoilage.

Sealing and spoilage

Always check the jars before storing them away to make sure a good seal is made. If a jar is not sealed and it is caught immediately, you have two choices: either reprocess the jar using a new lid, or store the jar with its contents in the refrigerator until ready to use, up to 10 days.

Test the seal with a spoon and check the safety button

Check the seal by striking the jar lid with a spoon. There should be a clear ringing sound. If the sound is dull or thuds instead of ringing, it is not sealed. Also, the lid has a safety button in the center, this button is flat if a good seal is made, but if it is popped up, or pops up later, the seal is inadequate.

What causes a good seal to release or the safety button to pop? The spoilage of food within a jar causes pressure inside which breaks the seal. Never use food from a jar with a broken seal. Tiny microorganisms such as molds, yeasts, and bacteria are always present in food. They also inhabit the air, water, and soil. These microorganisms are destroyed during the canning process, but in the event a seal is broken, air invades the jar and the organisms begin to grow.

If you discover discolored food, mold, spurting liquid, or an off odor when you open a jar, discard the contents. I have canned for many years and have never had a jar go bad on the shelf. Occasionally a jar will not seal and I reprocess it or use it immediately.

Processing

Before starting to can, wash all jars and lids in hot soapy water. I like to wash them the evening before and let them air dry on a towel. Then first thing in the morning, I harvest the vegetables from the garden, wash them, and sort them for quality. Over-ripe vegetables are placed in the refrigerator to be used fresh.

Harvest and can for peak nutritional value

The harvesting is done on a daily basis, so canning is a daily event all through the summer months at our house. I may can only 4 or 6 quarts one day, and 12 or 20 quarts the next.

This assures that the food is processed at its peak of nutritional value, not saved over until more jars can be filled the next day. As the beans are ending, the tomatoes are beginning to produce. So it goes right up until fall.

Usually our cool weather crops are harvested first, that is, carrots, spinach (which I prefer to freeze), turnips, and cabbage. Then the beans, cucumbers for pickles, tomatoes, corn, and okra.

Don't allow veggies to soak

To wash the vegetables, handle them as little as possible. Rinse under running water or through several changes of water in a basin. Do not allow them to soak or remain in water for any period of time as the water soluble vitamins will leach into the water and be lost. Prepare the vegetables as directed in the recipe you have chosen, or cut them to the size you normally serve at the table.

Scald the jars and fill

Scald the clean jars by filling with boiling water and pouring it out. Now fill the jars with the prepared vegetables; add the correct amount of salt or spice according to your recipe; and fill the jar with boiling water, syrup, or brine to within 1/2 inch of the top. Take a table knife and insert it into the jar along the sides in several places to release any trapped air. Using a clean paper towel or damp cloth wipe the rim of the jar clean.

Place scalded lids on the jars, screw the bands in place, and tighten. As each jar is filled, set it on a rack in the canner.

When all the jars have been filled, add water to cover them one or two inches if using the boiling water bath, or follow the manufacturer's recommended amount of water if using a pressure canner.

After the proper processing time has elapsed, use a jar lift to remove the jars from the canner. Place them on several thicknesses of towel away from drafts. Do not disturb the seals. If liquid has boiled out, that's okay. Allow to cool undisturbed for 12 hours or overnight.

Check seals before storing

The next morning, check the seals as described earlier. Wipe each jar with a damp rag to clean its surface and to make it sparkle. Store in the pantry for future use. If you don't have strong shelves (do not underestimate the weight of canned goods), the filled jars may be stored in their original cartons and stacked several cartons high.

Mark each carton as to the contents so you can locate needed vegetables at a glance. Most foods are identifiable, but you may want to label each jar individually, especially if you plan to give any as gifts. An important note to place on the label is the date the food was processed. This way you can use the earliest processed foods first.

Once you've put up your first year's harvest, you'll look with pride at the bounty you've preserved. Δ

> "And what country can preserve its liberties, if its rulers are not warned from time to time, that this people preserve the right of resistance? Let them take arms..."
>
> Thomas Jefferson

A Backwoods Home Anthology
The Sixth Year

* Here's a simple device to improve rough roads
* Backwoods firearms
* Make your own tool handles
* Home brew your own beer
* Make a heated seed germination flat
* Elderberries—the undiscovered fruit
* Wild turkey, goose, and venison for the holidays
* Tractor maintenance saves you more than money
* How to buy your first sheep
* Try a cement block garden
* Greens—delicious, nutritious, and easy to grow
* Raising goats can be profitable
* Making teas from wild plants and herbs
* Need a privy? Here's the right way to build one
* Enjoy zucchini all year
* Start a home-based herb business
* Try these fresh ideas in your dairy
* Install rafters alone—the easy way
* This is one way to make applejack
* Build a homestead forge and fabricate your own hardware
* Soups for winter
* If you'd like to get started with chickens, here are the basics

EXCLUSIVE INTERVIEW

The other Texas Frenchman —
An interview with Andre Marrou,
Libertarian candidate for President

(Despite the considerable media coverage of Ross Perot, he is not the only "third party" Presidential candidate. Others like Bo Gritz, Howard Phillips, and Andre Marrou are also running for President, but they have been largely ignored by the mass media. In our continuing effort to give readers "alternatives," here is an alternative of a different sort—an interview with Andre Marrou, one of the other third party candidates. Like Perot, he is a Frenchman from Texas; unlike Perot he represents a viable political party—the Libertarian Party—which is the third largest political party in America (next to the Republicans and Democrats). In the 1990 Congressional election, The Libertarian Party received two million votes, a sizable sum for a party begun in 1971 by disaffected former Republicans and Democrats.

Andre Marrou was born in Texas and earned a degree in Chemical Engineering from the Massachusetts Institute of Technology (MIT). He was elected to the Alaska state legislature in 1984 as a Libertarian, and subsequently voted against every new tax and every tax increase, and was part of the successful effort to repeal Alaska's income tax. Divorced and the father of three children, Marrou, 53, now lives in Las Vegas where he is a commercial real estate broker.

This is an exclusive interview given to Backwoods Home Magazine.— Editor)

By Christopher Maxwell

QUESTION: Mr. Marrou, your press kit doesn't say what happened in the years between MIT and the Alaska state legislature? What led you to become a Libertarian Party activist?

ANSWER:
After I graduated from MIT I worked in the Boston area for ten years as an engineer and an engineering manager. I got married, raised a family; two of my three sons were born there. I was in Boston a total of seventeen years, the same length of time I was in Texas,

where I lived until I graduated High School.

In 1973 I moved to Alaska. For three years I had a wholesale distributorship in restaurant and bar supplies. I worked on the pipeline and in radio. I moved out into the woods for two years with the woman who later became my wife. Then in 1980 I made a conscious decision to move back to town and fight the government.

I originally intended to only start a local Libertarian Party. In 1981, when I was trying to get somebody to run for the legislature, somebody said "Why don't YOU run for the legislature?".

I was taken aback at first, but people said "Why not? You're well educated, articulate...". They had a lot

Nancy Lord, running mate

Andre Marrou, Presidential candidate

of nice words and maybe I listened to the nice words too much, but about three months later I decided to run for the legislature.

I finished second out of three; I beat the Democrat but not the Republican. I came back in 1984 and defeated the Republican on the same day that Ronald Reagan was re-elected by a landslide.

QUESTION: What did you do for that two years you were "in the woods"?

ANSWER:
The first year we lived on an island, Perl Island off the southern tip of the Kenai Peninsula. It's about three by three miles. The second year we lived at the head of Kachemak Bay.

On the island we were taking care of a homestead and some cattle. When we got there they had some cattle, a couple of geese, some ducks and two cats. It was our responsibility to take care of the buildings — one of the two buildings was the log cabin we lived in — and the animals.

The second year we were in a better location; there were more buildings. The building we lived in was sort of between a cabin and a house. It had separate rooms but no doors. There we had no animals to take care of except our own. I had a dozen laying hens.

We did have neighbors there, as opposed to the Island. There were no people on the island except us. In both places we would go into town once a month. The homesteader would hire an air taxi to come out and get us and take us into town one day a month.

QUESTION: Were you trying to be self-sufficient?

ANSWER:

Yes, I was deeply interested in self-sufficiency. During the first year on the island we easily became self-sufficient in food, and during the second year we were overly self-sufficient in food and traded with our neighbors. We had probably enough food to support two or three couples. I was really getting into that.

The next step would have been to become self-sufficient in energy, which was natural for me being an engineer. I did a lot of study in that area.

I even proposed to the two universities in Alaska the establishment of a course of study leading to a doctorate in homesteading. I thought they would laugh at it, but they took it seriously. I don't know if they did anything about it but they were considering it.

I was doing some healing, since we had no doctor. I studied herbal remedies and various natural and home remedies and was able to help some people out.

I think everybody would be wise to learn some ability in self-sufficiency. You never know when it may come in handy.

QUESTION: Why did you get involved in politics?

ANSWER:

I had moved to Alaska to get away from government, at least to get away from too much government. Then I moved out into the woods to try to get away from government.

I used to cut wood a lot. We used wood for fuel so every day I would chop wood anywhere from two to

six hours a day. I not only got into pretty good shape, I had time for a lot of thinking. I finally came to the conclusion that you cannot get away from this government. They will come get you—no matter where you are—if you don't do what they tell you, if you don't pay your taxes, especially property taxes.

I finally figured out how to get away from almost every kind of government except property taxes. No matter where you are you have to have land and you have to pay property taxes in cash.

Up until the 1930's or '40's you could pay your taxes in kind, in chickens or corn or whatever you had. Now you have to pay in cash; you have to have an income, so then you have to pay income tax and Social Security tax, everything I was trying to get away from.

I finally came to the conclusion that you cannot get away from this government. They will come get you—no matter where you are—if you don't do what they tell you, if you don't pay your taxes, especially property taxes.

I finally concluded after a lot of thinking that you just can't get away and the better thing to do instead of trying to get away from them is to fight them.

So we moved into town in mid 1980 with the express intent of fighting the government. I didn't know quite how I was going to go about it; as I said I only intended to start a local chapter of the Libertarian Party, which I did. One thing led to another and eventually I got elected to the legislature in 1984.

QUESTION: I'd like to move on to some specific issues that the readers of this magazine may be interested in. What would a Libertarian government do about the environment? Some people seem to think that Libertarians would abolish the EPA and

turn big business loose to rape and plunder the environment.

ANSWER:

Well, it's actually not big business by itself who is raping and plundering the environment; it's big government. The government is either doing it consciously, or they are letting others do it on government land. The federal government owns a lot of land, which it is not supposed to; it's unconstitutional. There is nothing in the constitution which says the federal government is supposed to own land, yet it owns 84% of Nevada and even larger percentages of other states.

The clear cutting of old growth forest that is being done is almost never done except on government land. Overgrazing of cattle is also done almost entirely on government land. What we need to do is transfer that land by various means to private ownership. Not only selling some to ranchers and timber companies, but also allowing people to homestead that land. We can sell some of the more environmentally-sensitive land to private conservation organizations like the Sierra Club and so forth. And of course, some will need to be sold to mining companies; we need some minerals unless we want to go back to the stone age.

The EPA is doing a rotten job. Everyone knows this, but it seems like no one knows what to do about it. What we say is: first of all restore the right to sue companies or individuals in federal court for pollution. This right was removed when the EPA was established 23 years ago. Secondly, the right to sue the government for polluting should be established. If a bureaucrat or a group of bureaucrats allows pollution to go on, they should not be immune to being sued. Also, we would extend the time of a temporary restraining order to stop pollution from the three to ten days now granted to six months or maybe even a year.

Mainly what we need is to get the government to stop polluting. Not only is the government the largest polluter, they also have the worst pollutants like highly toxic radioactive waste. They produce most of it.

The second tier of polluters are the government-licensed and protected utilities. It's not industry who is doing the worst of the polluting; it's the federal government and the utilities they control.

QUESTION: What happens to the poor under a Libertarian government?

ANSWER:

First of all, we need to be mature enough to understand that utopia is not one of our options. There will always be some poor; some people will not be successful no matter what society does. We cannot eliminate poverty, but we can reduce it.

The first thing we can do is to leave as much money in their hands as possible. Not give them somebody else's money, just let them keep their own earnings. Don't take any money from them in taxes. If they earn $100, let them keep the $100; don't tax them down to $75, with Federal taxes or down to $53 with all the state and local taxes. Reducing taxes is going to make it much easier on the poor.

Other things we can do: stop price supports on the things the poor need to buy. The price of milk in this country is about twice the price of the rest of the world. Why? Because the federal government subsidizes it to help the farmers, ignoring the poor who have to buy this milk and other milk products such as cheese and butter.

We also need to remove some of the restrictions on people, most of which are not federal. Most of these are state and local, about what people can do with their time, their bodies, and their money. When I was 12 I was working for 25 cents an hour. Today that would be equal to about $2.50 an hour, and it would be illegal. It is also illegal to hire a 12-year-old now. That job probably doesn't exist anymore, and some 12-year-old is hanging around looking for some kind of trouble to get into.

Minimum wage is $4.25 an hour; that means after the employer adds his part to the Social Security tax, plus unemployment tax, and state unemployment insurance it costs an employer over $5.00 an hour to hire somebody at minimum wage. Some jobs just aren't worth that much; they aren't that important. There are millions of potential jobs out there that it would be nice to have done, things like having the sidewalks swept or having somebody watch the parking lot, that just aren't important enough that a small business can pay $10,000 a year to have them done. These jobs would benefit society also. Not just in their immediate effects but by keeping kids and unemployed adults busy they would reduce street crime and teach good work habits. Employers would still have to pay competitive wages to attract good workers to the more important jobs.

The other restrictions, such as zoning restrictions, prevent the poor from operating businesses from their homes. Licensing laws prevent people who can't work full time or can't read the forms from making a living in self-employment. This is wrong. There should not be restrictions to prevent these people from working.

But mainly, the answer for the poor is the same as the answer for the rich—get the government off their backs and out of their pockets. Quit taxing the poor; let them do what they want to do as long as they don't hurt or defraud anybody and I guarantee we'll have more prosperity and more happiness in this country.

Repeal income tax

QUESTION: Part of your platform is repeal of the Federal Income Tax. Are you serious? How would the government operate?

ANSWER:

Yes, I am serious. First, we repeal the income tax; second, we abolish the IRS; third, we release all the tax protesters from prison; fourth, we sell the IRS buildings; fifth, we burn all tax records; and sixth, we declare April 15th a national holiday.

The IRS is the most powerful, and the most hated and feared agency in the government. This isn't Eastern Europe or the Soviet Union. This is America, the land of the free and the home of the brave. We shouldn't have to hate and fear our government.

The personal income tax brings in only 37 percent of federal revenues, leaving 63 percent to operate the government. How far back in history do we have to go to find a federal government that is 37 percent smaller than in 1992? To 1917? 1941? 1960? We have to go back only five years to 1987.

If we just get rid of the excessive government that the Republicans and Democrats have given us over the last five years, we could set ourselves free from the income tax.

Were people saying that the government was too small in 1987? Do you remember hearing people say "Gee, what we need is 37 percent more government by 1992." No, they weren't. The government was already much too big in 1987.

The IRS is the most powerful, and the most hated and feared agency in the government. This isn't Eastern Europe or the Soviet Union. This is America, the land of the free and the home of the brave. We shouldn't have to <u>hate and fear our government.</u>

The government could also raise a lot of money to finance the government and retire a large part of the National Debt by selling off some of the valuable properties it now owns. Some examples are the Presidio in San Francisco, and Camp Pendleton. This real estate is worth billions of dollars and the military doesn't do anything there they couldn't do on less valuable property, like the 84% of Nevada the government owns. And this is only two of the thousands of federal installations in the U.S.

The government also does many things that are not needed, and has many programs which are in conflict with each other. For example, the federal government spends money subsidizing tobacco farmers, then spends more money campaigning against smoking. The results of these programs cancel each other out. We could drop both programs and get the same net effect.

Federal government employees have an attrition rate of 7 percent to 10 percent per year. We could reduce the federal bureaucracy by 28 percent to 40 percent in four years without any layoffs or firings. When the taxes that support this army of bureaucrats are repealed, and the oppressive regulations they have written are rescinded, the expanding economy will be able to absorb these people with no trouble.

Military spending, and foreign aid to prop up repressive and socialist governments all over the world are other areas where huge savings could be made. The Cold War is over, but the Pentagon sees the world as its oyster and thinks its mission is to preserve the status quo. The Bush administration has made simple-minded stability-preservation the basis of U.S. security policy.

A Marrou administration, based on Libertarian principles, would define American vital interests precisely as our physical security from attack, our independence as a nation, and our constitutional liberties. Preventing and defending against any direct threat to these vital interests is what the Pentagon's job should be.

The Pentagon's latest plans are self-serving justifications for the future budgets and careers of civilian policy analysts and bureaucrats in uniform. Communism is dead. But the military-industrial complex is imagining new enemies and dreaming of more places to go to war.

QUESTION: Since the government is now the largest employer and such a huge part of the economy of the U.S., how do you think you can reduce the size of the government without massive layoffs that would create a ripple effect through all the businesses and services that government and its employees use and could cause massive unemployment?

ANSWER:
All we have to do is stop replacing federal bureaucrats. Federal government employees have an attrition rate of 7 percent to 10 percent per year. We could reduce the federal bureaucracy by 28 percent to 40 percent in four years without any layoffs or firings. When the taxes that support this army of bureaucrats are repealed, and the oppressive regulations they have written are rescinded, the expanding economy will be able to absorb these people with no trouble.

QUESTION: What is your position on the War on Drugs?

ANSWER:
The war on drugs is a failure. Drugs should be re-legalized. Drugs were all legal before 1914, and there was no drug problem. The problems — crime and violence — are caused by the high price of drugs. The high price of drugs is caused by the drugs being illegal.

We tell people not to take drugs, then we make the taxpayers pay for welfare for drug addicts and ambulances and emergency rooms when drug users overdose. We have to let people make their own decisions and bear the consequences of their decisions.

Most Libertarians don't use drugs and don't approve of drug addiction, but the war on drugs is not preventing these problems. Drugs are more easily available now than before they were outlawed, especially to children. Nobody is giving out free samples of whiskey at schoolyards; there isn't enough profit in it to risk the loss of your license.

The War on Drugs is an excuse to do away with the remainder of the Constitution and violate the Bill of Rights. It is one of the greatest threats to our freedom today.

The War on Drugs is an excuse to do away with the remainder of the Constitution and violate the Bill of Rights. It is one of the greatest threats to our freedom today.

QUESTION: Many people will vote for one of the major party candidates, not because they like him but because they hate the other one and they are afraid if they don't vote for the one they don't like, the one they hate will win. Do you understand this? What difference do you see between the major party candidates?

ANSWER:
I do not see any difference between the major party candidates. One of the problems we have in American politics is that Americans tend to vote against a candidate they don't like instead of voting for a candidate they do like.

If they voted for the person or for the philosophy they liked, more Libertarians would be elected because Libertarianism is the basic American philosophy. Leave us alone, let us do what we want to do, you get what you pay for and you pay for what you get; these are basic American statements and basic American Libertarian philosophy.

So, if people voted for the person or philosophy they liked, they would elect Libertarians. For example, ten years ago we ran a guy for Governor of Alaska. Two weeks before the election he did a poll and there were two questions on the poll. There were three candidates — Democrat, Republican and Libertarian. The first question was "Who are you going to vote for governor?" That very precisely predicted the actual results. The poll predicted 16% for the Libertarian, he got 15.7%. The other question was, "If you thought all three candidates had an equal opportunity of winning, who would you vote for?" That question was won by the Libertarian.

Not by much, but he did win. He got about 35%, which was enough to win. If people voted for what they really believed in, we would have had the first Libertarian Governor ten years ago.

If we can get Americans to vote **for** *a candidate or philosophy instead of voting* **against,** *then we would get many more Libertarians elected.*

We will eventually elect a Libertarian President and Congress; I just don't know who or when. I may not get elected this year; that doesn't really concern me because I'm building the next major party. We will elect Libertarians because we have to elect Libertarians. If the government continues to grow at the pace of the last thirty years for the next thirty years, there won't be anything left. The government will own and run everything. And judging by their past and present performance, they will run everything irresponsibly, inefficiently, and ineptly.

If the government continues to grow at the pace of the last thirty years for the next thirty years, there won't be anything left. The government will own and run everything. And judging by their past and present performance, they will run everything irresponsibly, inefficiently, and ineptly.

QUESTION: If you don't win, aren't the people who vote for you wasting their votes?

ANSWER:

Absolutely not. Every election we get more votes than the previous election, we prove we are still growing and will be back even stronger for the next election. Every vote for every Libertarian candidate brings us closer to the goal of getting government's hand out of our pockets and nose out of our business.

We have received enough votes in the past to have automatic ballot status in some states. That means we don't have to petition to get on the ballot, and voters can register as Libertarians. We need almost one million signatures to get on the ballot in all fifty states now.

Every time we get enough votes to make automatic ballot status in another state, that means we don't have to spend all our money and burn out all our volunteers just to get on the ballot, we can devote more money and work to campaigning on the issues. Fifty-state ballot status is our immediate goal. Fifty-state automatic ballot status is our next goal. Every vote for every Libertarian candidate will help us achieve automatic ballot status in '94 and '96. We must have this to mount a serious challenge to the status quo.

(Andre Marrou's running mate is Nancy Lord. She holds doctorate degrees and licenses to practice both medicine and law. Her legal practice specialized in medical issues and constitutional liberties, but she has given up her practice for this year to campaign with Marrou. A quote from one of her speeches: "National Health Care will combine the efficiency of the Postal Service, the compassion of the Internal Revenue Service, and the cost controls of the Pentagon." —Editor)Δ

A BHM Writer's Profile

John Silveira is the senior editor for *BHM*. His articles have generated numerous reprint requests from other magazines and many requests from teachers to use them as part of course curricula.

He is a mathematician by training, but a fiction writer and poet by avocation. His ability to marry fiction writing style to nonfiction articles for *BHM* has resulted in major articles that are not only well researched but engaging to read. Silveira often writes his articles in tandem with O.E. MacDougal, who does not work for *BHM* but who is well known to long-time readers.

Silveira grew up on a farm in New Hampshire where he says he spent much of his time playing hooky from school. As a boy, he says his father used to give him one bullet per day for his .22 rifle to teach him how to shoot straight. It took him hours of stalking before he pulled the trigger, but he developed considerable skill as a marksman. Once, using an unscoped rifle, he outshot *BHM* publisher Dave Duffy, who used a scoped rifle, at 100 yards.

He says he worships amoebae, which is how he justifies drinking beer instead of water.

Waterwheels . . . Part 2 . . .

Design calculations for no-head, low-head waterwheels

(This is the second of our three-part series on waterwheels. The third installation (Issue No. 18) will deal with overshot wheels. — Editor.)

By Rudy Behrens

For those of you who are still awake after reading my first installment, I will now continue. This part will deal with the design factors you will need to know to build a low-head waterwheel. It's somewhat technical, but it is essential to know if you are to build a successful no-head or low-head waterwheel.

Head, spouting velocity

The most important thing to determine is **head**, or how far the water falls. If you have a small dam or waterfall, the answer is the difference in height between the free water surface on the **upstream** side, and the free water surface on the **downstream** side, in inches or feet. If you have a swift moving stream, the answer is only a bit harder to figure out.

The answer is in the equation for spouting velocity, which is the equation that describes the speed of any falling mass: **velocity squared divided by two times a gravitational constant**, which is expressed mathematically as $V^2/2G$. The gravitational constant (G) is 32.2.

You can measure the velocity of a stream by running two strings across it, some measured distance apart. You then throw in corks, or pingpong balls and time their travel between the strings, in feet-per-second. Do this several times at several points along the stream and calculate an average velocity. Once this is done, you take this figure and multiply it times itself, then divide that number by 64.4, which is two times the gravitational constant. This will convert your velocity into a **head.**

Diameter of wheel

When designing an undershot wheel, you must know the **head** since the optimum diameter of the wheel is three to six times the head. Let's say you measure your stream and get an average velocity of 10 feet-per-second. That number times itself is 100. Divided by 64.4, we get an answer of 1.55 feet. In other words, the water is moving as fast as it would if it had fallen 1.55 feet. Your wheel should then be at least 4.65 feet to 9.3 feet in diameter (E.g.: 3 x 1.55 = 4.65 or 6 x 1.55 = 9.3).

Whenever possible, make the wheel as large as you can. However, there would be no improvement in performance if it were larger than 9.3 feet.

The next step is to compute the working diameter. This is the overall diameter minus the head. Now, multiple this number times **PI** (which is the mathematical constant equal to approximately 22/7 or 3.14) to get the working circumference. The answer will also be in feet.

Blade spacing

When you install the wheel, you will **submerge the blades a distance equal to the head.** Therefore, the spacing between the blades should be some convenient number times **PI** to get the working circumference. The answer will also be in feet.

In our example I have decided to work with the 9.3 foot diameter from the figurs above, so the working circumference is 24.35 feet (9.3 minus a head of 1.55 = 7.75 feet. 7.75 x PI = 24.35 feet.)

The space between the blades should be less than 1.55 feet, which in our example is te head. Let's use 1.5 feet, so the number of blades is 16.23 (24.35/1.5 = 16.23) or rounded to 16. So, we will build a wheel 9.3 feet in diameter with 16 blades.

Making it efficient

But how fast will it turn? The most efficient energy transfer occurs when the wheel speed is between 67% and 90% of the water speed. For undershot wheels, I usually go for the lower figure to allow for slow days. Sixty seven percent of 10 feet per second is 6.7 feet per second, which is the same as 402 (6.7 x 60 = 402) feet per minute. You divide this by the working circumference of 24.35 feet per revolution. This gives you an answer of 16.5 (402/24.35 = 16.5) revolutions per minute. That is your best rotative speed.

As you can see, it is rather slow. That is why you will need a speed increasing system, as we said in the last issue.

Actual power of wheel

The power you will get depends on the width. For our example, I have chosen three feet. The working cross section will then be width times submergence. In this case 1.55 feet times 3 feet, or 4.65 square feet. Multiply this times our velocity of 10 feet per second and we get a design flow of 46.5 cubic feet per second. Power is equal to **flow** times **head** divided by 11.8. Therefore, we have a **flow** of 46.5 cfs **times** a **head** of 1.55' divided by 11.8. 46.5 x 1.55 = 72.075. 72.075/11.8 = 6.1 kilowatts or kw/.746 = horsepower. 8.2 horsepower. We should assume an efficiency of 70%. So, our hypothetical wheel will produce 5.7 horsepower or 4.3 kilowatts.

These calculations apply to **any** low-head waterwheel. The only thing that changes among the various designs is the speed or efficiency. If we were to make our example as a **poncelot** wheel, all the design parameters would be the same. The blades would not be straight. Instead, they would be offset from the radius of the wheel by

a negative 30 degrees and the lower portion would be curved to 60 degrees of arc in a radius equal to the **head**. This change will raise efficiency to the 80 + % range.

Wheel should be steel

Materials should always be a good grade of steel. A steel grade of A36 or B36 works very well. Twenty gauge or thicker is good. We always use 1/8" at FITX Waterwheel Company, and ours have withstood direct hits by ice flows of more than a ton. If you use **corten**, a weathering steel, it will not need painting and it will acquire a reddish color that resembles wood. Statically balance the wheel before installation.

No matter how tempting, never use wood. It rots and holds water unevenly. This unbalances the wheel and makes it unsuitable for any use except

grinding grain. Be very accurate in all you measurements, especially those concerning **flow** and **head**. If they are wrong, everything is wrong.

Use wood bearings

I recommend oil-impregnated wood bearings. They can be obtained from the POBCO Bearing Company of Worcester, MA. Waterwheels turn too slowly for ball or sleeve bearings; they cannot maintain a uniform lubricant field. This tends to ruin the bearing quickly. The wood bearings have a "wick" action that maintains uniform lubricant.

Next issue, we will adapt these equations to overshot wheels and get into the economics of going into the co-generation business.

(Rudy Behrens owns the Fitz Waterwheel Company, 118 Sycamore Ct., Collegeville, PA 19426. Phone: (215) 489-6256.) Δ

A FITZ Waterwheel Company all-welded steel undershot wheel..

How to get started in blacksmithing

By Don Fallick

Just six things are needed to forge iron: a hunk of metal, a way to heat it, a tool to hold it with, a hammer of some kind, and something to hit it **against**. Also, a tub of water to quench the hot metal in. We're talking real low tech here.

Iron

Strictly speaking, there is no such thing as wrought iron any more. The last country to smelt pure wrought iron was the Soviet Union, and that was decades ago. What we're left with is called "mild steel", though it's actually **not** steel, but another alloy of iron. For simple blacksmithing, mild steel will work just fine. I get most of my iron from the local farm implement dealer. Old farm implements have **lots** of long, thin rods, square shanks, and flat bars of iron and steel that are just perfect for blacksmithing. Most dealers will be happy to sell you such junk for next to nothing. The price of scrap iron varies, but seldom costs more that $.50 per pound. You may already have just the piece you need in your **own** junk pile if you look!

It is certainly possible to forge other metals besides mild steel, but stay away from **cast** metals. They'll break, no matter what you do to them. Spring steel, such as you find in old saw blades, is also easy to forge, after you heat it. It makes excellent knives. Some mild steel is so soft you can forge it without heating it. This works okay for gentle bends, but sharp bends may break the metal if it's not heated first. Cold-forged steel will never be as strong as hot forged, anyway, because the heat and hammering actually packs the molecules closer together, making a very dense, strong metal. Mild steel doesn't pack.

Heat

I'm not going to tell you how to make a forge out of an old truck brake drum. You can do it, and it's not hard, but it takes time, and a certain investment of money. You may not know whether you **want** to be a blacksmith, and it's not necessary to own a forge to find out. **Any** source of heat will do. I've done lots of forging just using the firebox of my hundred-year-old, wood-fired cookstove. Even a good, hot campfire will do in a pinch.

Blowing on the fire makes it hotter. Traditionally, blacksmiths used a bellows (and an appretice) to do this, but a blow-dryer will also work. Ideally, you want the air to blow up through the center of the fire, so you need a pipe of some kind to direct the air to the right spot. This pipe is called a **tuyere**, pronounced "tweer". A place to build a fire, with provision for a tuyere of some kind is called a forge. You can make it out of a brake drum, or out of fire brick stacked together, with the cracks filled up with sand. It's **not** a good idea to use rocks, as some rocks explode when heated. You can even use sheet metal, or even **wood**, lined with lots of damp sand. Many modern, professional smiths use a welding torch to heat metal. It's safe, effective, and quick. Who cares if it's "authentic"? The idea is to heat the metal up until it glows. That's all. Everything else is icing on the cake.

Color

Iron and iron alloys change color at specific temperatures. If you knew the exact composition of the metal, you could tell the exact temperature by the color. Fortunately, you don't need to know the **exact** temperature to do excellent blacksmithing. What you need to know is, "Is the metal hot enough (or cool enough) to do what I want it to do?" The color of the metal tells you this. There are books on blacksmithing with excellent color photographs, so you can see just what color the author means by "cherry red" or "straw color". For most work this is totally unnecessary. Iron progresses from black, through red, orange, yellow to white as it heats up. White heat is used only in welding, and this is **advanced** stuff. As a beginner, you'll be working mostly red, orange and yellow metal.

If you hit anything less than brick red, you risk pieces breaking off and putting your eye out. An old blacksmith's joke says that there are only two sins

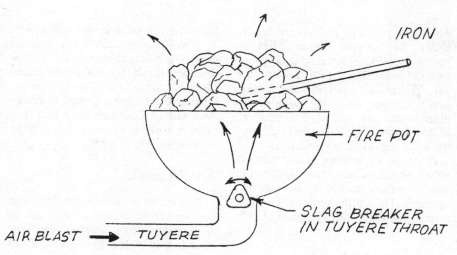

IRON

FIRE POT

SLAG BREAKER
IN TUYERE THROAT

AIR BLAST → TUYERE

that can send a blacksmith to Hell: hitting black iron and charging too little! If you feel you **must** know what temperature your iron is, put a piece in the kitchen oven and heat it up! Heat is heat, and the color will show it. In general, cherry red to orange is a good color range for forging most stuff. The iron will cool off as you work it, anyway, so you'll always be working within a **range** of colors.

If the iron isn't soft enough to do what you want it to, heat it up a little hotter and try again. If it's too soft, let it cool a bit, or quench it and reheat. This can take a bit of extra time and use up extra fuel. It's what comes of "having too many irons in the fire".

Fuel

The absolutely best fuel for a forge is hardwood charcoal, but it's expensive. Anthracite or "hard coal", also called "blacksmith's coal", is used by most smiths when they can get it, because of its purity and long-burning ember. Soft coal contains a percentage of sulfur, which will contaminate the hot iron, altering its physical properties. But soft coal **will** work for forging, as will hardwood, softwood, or anything that'll leave a hot-burning ember. My first "mentor" used Douglas Fir bark, which he picked up in the woods for free. It sparked a lot, but it worked.

The fire

The trick in forging is to burn your fire from the center out, so the iron is never in contact with the raw fuel anyway, but only with the "coke" or charcoal. (Coke is to coal what charcoal is to wood.) Build a **deep** fire and keep feeding the fuel in a circle, so the coke or charcoal is always next to the iron. You don't want to allow air next to the iron, to prevent oxidation from weakening the metal. Pack the coke around the metal with a fire shovel. It helps to wet the coke first. Coal packs better than any other fuel.

Actually, for the sort of projects a beginner is likely to attempt, most of these problems are not important. But there's no sense deliberately weakening your project when it's so easy to prevent it.

Tongs

If your rod is long enough, you'll be able to hold it in your bare hand, but if not, you'll want something to grab the metal with. An old pair of locking pliers works fairly well, but don't use a new pair. The heat of the metal will eventually take all the hardness out of them, making them useless. A pair of cheap, cast pliers with the handles stuck in foot-long lengths of 1/2" iron pipe works OK too. Often, beginners try to use leather gloves to protect their hands. This is one of those wonderful ideas that just doesn't work. The leather will heat up from the outside in. By the time the heat reaches your hand, it'll be **really** hot! You'll likely drop the iron in your hurry to get the glove off, possibly burning yourself worse in the process. The safest way is to work a rod long enough to hold bare-handed, or else use some kind of metal tongs.

While we're talking safety, wooden floors **don't** go with forging. Most old-time smithies had hard-packed dirt floors. Bare concrete works well too. If you do use some sort of a forge to heat your iron, make some kind of arrangements to contain the sparks.

Hammers

Virtually any kind of hammer can be used for forging iron. Remember that anything that hits hot iron is going to leave an impression in it. If you hit a piece of iron with a knurled framing hammer, it's going to show the imprint of the knurls in the finished product. This may not bother you. If you are trying to flatten a fairly thick piece of

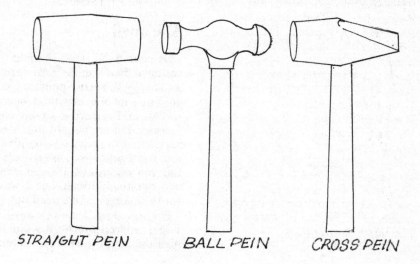

STRAIGHT PEIN   BALL PEIN   CROSS PEIN

metal, you'll want a heavier hammer than a carpenter would use. If you want to spread the metal in all directions, a ball pein hammer will do it. A straight pein hammer, which looks like a small, short-handled splitting maul with a very blunt blade, will spread the metal in only one direction. A flat-faced hammer will flatten the metal. Heavy hammers work faster and easier than light ones, but also leave a deeper impression. That's one reason blacksmiths have such a large collection of hammers—heavier and lighter ones of each shape for rough and fine work. I use a 3 1/2 lb. maul for rough work, and a 2 lb. ball-pein hammer for most shaping. I also have a couple of 1 lb. hammers of various shapes, and even an 8 oz. hammer for very delicate work.

Another reason that blacksmiths have such large collections of hammers is that most of what non-blacksmiths take for hammers are actually "sets"—tools placed against the hot metal and then struck with the hammer, to leave a specific size and shape dent in a particular place. One way to tell a "set" from a hammer is to look at the handle. The handle of a set tool is just used to hold it still, keeping the hand out of the way of the hammer and the hot metal. It doesn't have to be very sturdy. The handle of a hammer, used for striking, must be quite strong.

Tools

You will probably want to make your own set tools, eventually. Bolting or

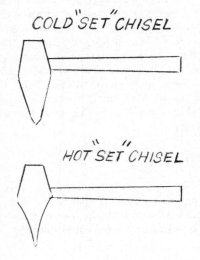

COLD "SET" CHISEL

HOT "SET" CHISEL

welding a piece of rod onto a "cold chisel", for example, makes it into a passable hot chisel, for cutting off your finished piece. Since it can be difficult to hold a set tool, a pair of forge tongs, and a hammer all at the same time, blacksmiths have invented a number of "third hand" types of tools. Probably the most important is the hardie.

A hardie is nothing more than a chisel, punch, or other tool made to fit into a square socket in the anvil, point upwards. The smith then can hold the iron in one hand over the point of the

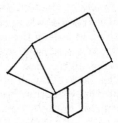

HARDIE

hardie, and hammer the iron down onto the hardie with the hammer. If you are going to do this, remember that the hardie and the hammer can damage each other, so make the last few strokes just "off" the hardie.

Other smithy tools are basically either concave or convex forms, used to shape iron to a particular, exact shape. Make your own, harden them, and if you keep them cool, and the iron is yellow or orange hot, you can forge the same shape repeatedly.

The anvil

Of course the basic shaping tool is the anvil. Blacksmiths' anvils are large and heavy, to absorb pounding, and to soak up a lot of heat without becoming too warm. Both are desirable characteristics, but are not absolutely necessary. What you need is something hard and flat. I sometimes use a piece of an old iron woodstove. It's cast iron, and will eventually break, but it was free for the taking and it's **dead flat**.

For rounding, a smith's anvil has a large, tapered "horn". It's tapered to give the smith a choice of diameters

for his bends, but this isn't vital either. A piece of pipe clamped in a large, heavy vise works almost as well. I know folks who do all their forging on an old piece of railroad rail. This may be too light unless securely bolted to something immovable, such as a stump, but there is nothing wrong with the shape or composition of a rail.

An old anvil

Used anvils are not cheap, if you can find one at all. If you do find an old anvil at less than $2.00/lb. you may want to buy it. But first, check it out carefully. Is the square hardie hole broken out? A functional hardie hole can be real important. Is the top flat? If it's badly dished, you won't ever be able to make anything flat. Has it been broken and repaired? Check for welds. They won't hold up under constant pounding and differential heating. The only way I know to adequately repair an anvil is to bolt it together.

Finally, hit it with a hammer. Does it ring? Most folks these days have never heard the rhythmic **"bang! di-di-di-ding...bang!di-di-di-ding!** of a working blacksmith. If they have, they may assume that the deliberate ringing of the hammer on the anvil in between

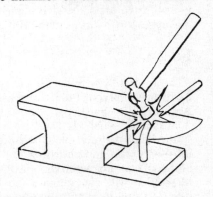

BENDING ROD OVER ANVIL HORN

blows on the metal has something to do with timing of the blows, or was done for some other technical reason. Actually, it's done to save the smith's hand. An anvil that won't ring will hurt your hand, just like hitting a brick wall with a wrench. All the vibration that would normally cause the anvil to sound will instead travel up your arm, causing fatigue, pain, and eventually tendon problems if you keep it up long enough.

Basic techniques

The most common operation in smithing goes like this: heat a hunk of metal, beat it to shape, reheating as necessary, quench in stagnant water or brine, then reheat again and temper, quenching when the metal reaches the proper temperature.

It seems silly to say it, but it is only necessary or desirable to heat the part of the metal that you want to work. If you heat a ten-inch length rod to cherry red and bend it, the whole ten-inch length will bend. If you want a shorter bend, heat a shorter length of rod. Then when you place the rod under bending stress, by banging it over the edge of an anvil, or by clamping one end in a vise and bending the rod by hand, the "cool" part of the rod stays stiff and only the hot part bends. Remember, though, that iron is a good conductor of heat, so if you take very long to accomplish the bend, the heat will travel up and down the rod. This can be prevented by wrapping the cold part of the iron in wet rags, to slow down the travel of heat. Keep an eye on the color of the iron, and when it gets down to a dull, brick red, **re-heat it**. You **can** bend such (relatively) cool iron if you beat it hard enough long enough, but you risk seriously weakening the iron there.

Shaping iron

The basic techniques for shaping iron are hammering, drawing-out or **fullering** (thinning), **upsetting** (thickening), twisting, cutting, punching and **swaging**.

Hammering is used in most general shaping. With practice, you can use a hammer to make round rod square, square rod round, bend rod over the horn of the anvil or some other form, thin the edges of bars, draw out their length or width, and flatten lumps. You will probably want to use at least one very heavy and one fairly light hammer. Ball pein hammers of various sizes are readily available in used tool stores, pawn shops, and garage sales.

In making something such as a hook, out of a "rod" (perhaps an old bolt?), remember that the end of the rod may be inaccessible after the middle of the rod is bent, so form the end first, then make the bend.

Quenching

As soon as the end is formed, quench it in the slack (or slake) tub of water or brine. Stagnant water works best for quenching most work. Fresh water contains dissolved oxygen, which combines with the hot iron, chemically oxidizing it, and reducing its strength. Plunging the hot iron into the cold water hardens the iron, but only where the iron actually gets cold. If you just stick it in the water and remove it right

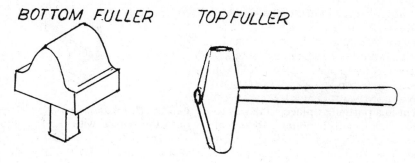

BOTTOM FULLER   TOP FULLER

away, the center of the iron will still be hot, and so shortly, will the surface. So it's necessary to leave the iron in the water for a few minutes.

Don't just leave the iron resting in the tub, though. If you do, there will be a sharp line (at the water line) where the strength of the iron changes suddenly, making it very weak there. When you first quench the iron, move it up and down in the water, to make the change from hard to soft take place over several inches. When the water no longer boils, it's safe to leave the iron in it without moving it. Cutlers (smiths who specialize in blades) like to use oil for quenching the spring steel they normally work, but water works fine for most practical smithing. Don't take the iron out of the water too soon. It'll take several minutes for the cold to reach the center of the piece. You want it to have time to cool off before you heat it up again for the next bend.

Fullering

It's strange that the technique for making iron thinner should be called "fullering" but that's the way it is. You can draw out a bar of iron with a flat hammer, but if you try to do this to the center of the bar without first thinning the edge you won't get far. To fuller the center of a bar, lay it flat on the anvil, with a rounded piece of cold iron on top, then hammer the two pieces together, pinching the hot iron between the "fuller" and the anvil. Blacksmiths who do a lot of this make special tools, consisting of two hunks of iron held apart by a bow of springy steel. They can place this 2-piece fuller around the hot iron and strike with the hammer. The spring bow holds the

two pieces in perfect alignment. It's a very handy, but not vital tool.

Remember that whenever you fuller a piece, the iron has to go somewhere. If you heat up a flat bar and hit it in the center with a hammer, the bar will grow wider and longer. If you use a cross-pein hammer, you can extend just the length or just the width of the piece. If you thin one edge of a piece, such as a knife blade, for example, **that edge** will grow longer. **The other edge won't.** The result: your knife blade will curve away from the thinned edge. To allow for this, bend the knife in the other direction before you thin the edge.

Upsetting

The opposite of fullering is **upsetting**, or thickening the metal. This is most often done by heating the part to be upset to yellow heat and holding it vertically, repeatedly **slamming** it down onto the anvil. Hammering on the piece will upset it, too, but is more difficult to control, since the hammer only moves the part of the iron it actually contacts. If you heat a rod and try to hammer the end of it, either the rod will bend, or one or both ends will mushroom, or maybe all three. In slamming the rod down onto the anvil, every molecule of the rod acquires the same inertia, and when the anvil stops that motion, and all the molecules try to pack together, some of them get pushed to the side, thickening and shortening the whole rod. Remember, the iron to upset your part has to come from somewhere, so if you are going to have to upset any part of your piece, allow extra length.

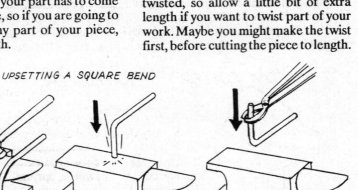

UPSETTING A SQUARE BEND

Upsetting a piece does more than just thicken it. It also changes the shape. To keep the same shape, immediately after upsetting, turn the rod so it's flat on the anvil and restore the shape with the hammer. Then, if necessary, reheat and upset again. It's easier to see what you're doing if you maintain the shape while upsetting, than to do all your upsetting at once and then try to restore the desired shape.

Square corners

Upsetting is used for more than just thickening one part of the piece you may be making. Sometimes you'll want to make a square corner in a piece. If you try to **bend** a corner square, it'll be weak and may even break as you work it. To make a square corner, you upset the end of a rod, then extend the upset portion in the direction you want, by

drawing it down with the hammer. Or, you can make a gentle bend over the horn or edge of the anvil, then upset it square.

Twisting, cutting & punching

Twisted iron looks neat, and is easy to make, but it's not necessary for the function of anything I've ever made. Basically, you twist iron by heating up a length of stock, clamping one end in a vise, and twisting the other end by hand or with pliers. Remember, twisted iron will be shorter than untwisted, so allow a little bit of extra length if you want to twist part of your work. Maybe you might make the twist first, before cutting the piece to length.

The hard way to cut a bar of iron is to use a hack saw. It's much easier to heat the bar up orange or yellow hot and cut it with a hot chisel. Technically, a hot chisel (used to cut hot iron) should have a much sharper angle on the blade than a cold chisel has, but a store-bought cold chisel will work. You can sharpen it sharper later, if you decide to get serious about blacksmithing. Now you know why a cold chisel is called a **cold** chisel.

In cutting iron, remember that the point of the chisel and the top of the anvil can damage each other. **Never** cut into the anvil with a chisel. Cut nearly all the way through the bar, then break it over the edge of the anvil, or use a piece of soft scrap iron to "pad" the anvil top for the final cut.

Another real common tool is the punch. The easy way to make a hole in iron is to punch it. To prevent the iron from just tearing out, hit it with the punch over the flat face of the anvil

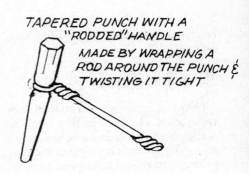

TAPERED PUNCH WITH A "RODDED" HANDLE MADE BY WRAPPING A ROD AROUND THE PUNCH & TWISTING IT TIGHT

until it's 3/4 of the way through, then turn the iron over and punch the piece out through the round "pritchel" hole.

Swaging

A swage is a concave form, used to shape iron to a predetermined shape. The iron is heated yellow hot, then hammered into the swage. Most commercial forging done today is actually swaging. It's faster and more standardized than hand-forging, but it

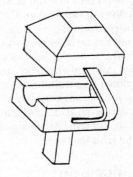

2-PIECE SWAGE

doesn't allow for the use of different techniques on different parts of the same piece of iron. Old-time smiths used swages to make round, square, and ornamental-shaped rods, as well as specialized swages for making nail

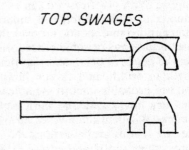

TOP SWAGES

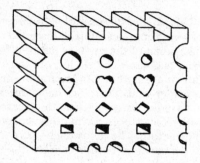

SWAGE BLOCK - FORMS
BOTTOM HALF OF SHAPE

and bolt heads. This is somewhat advanced for a beginner.

Hardening

Mild steel won't harden, but real steel will, if heated to the proper temperature and immediately quenched. Steel heated too hot will be brittle, too cool and it may not harden at all. Unless you are a metallurgist with a complete lab and reference library, or you know the exact alloy you're working, you'll have to test the steel to find out how hot to heat it.

You test it by heating a thin sliver of the same metal you're working, from one end, so it shows all the colors from white hot to dull red. Mark the sliver with a cold chisel where the colors change, and quench the whole piece. Test for hardness by breaking off pieces of the sliver over the edge of the anvil. Look for a fine, even grain. That's the proper hardening color. Where strength is not a factor, or speedy fabrication **is**, choose the proper alloy from Table 2 and harden to cherry red. But it's much better to test and **know** what you're doing.

Tempering

Most people think tempering means hardening. Actually, it means softening metal that has been hardened, so it won't be brittle. You'll use a different set of colors to judge its temper. Heat the test sliver to its hardening temperature and quench thoroughly. Polish off all scale from the test sliver until it shines, with a whetstone or a piece of emery paper glued to a stick. Then

heat one end until it turns gray again and re-quench. The heated end will appear gray, the coolest end will still be shiny, and in between will be a rainbow of "tempering colors", showing how hot the steel got before being quenched. The hotter it got, the more of its hardness was "drawn" from it by the fire. See Table 1.

Test for desired hardness by lightly running an old, worn file over each color. Only you will know exactly how hard you wish the finished product to be, so there is no hard and fast rule about how much temper to draw. It depends on the intended use of the piece and on the specific hardness of the particular alloy. There are hundreds of recognized alloys of steel, but for practical purposes, most smiths classify them as carbon steel, spring steel, and tool steel, in increasing order of hardness. Tool steel, even tempered to blue, may be harder (and more brittle) than carbon steel even at its hardest. Only by experience can the smith tell exactly which alloy to use, at what temper, for a given application. Fortunately, if a tool turns out to be too hard or too soft for its intended use, it can easily be re-hardened and tempered. For a rough idea of that

---

Table 1*

Temper color	Approximate temperature	Uses
pale straw yellow	430 degrees	files, metal-cutting tools
yellow	440 degrees	razors
darker straw	470 degrees	very sharp knives
dark straw yellow	490 degrees	cold chisels, wood-working tools
brown-yellow	500 degrees	axes, plane irons, most knives
yellowish purple	520 degrees	chisels, saws
light purple	530 degrees	swords, springs
dark purple	550 degrees	stone-cutting tools
dark blue	570 degrees	small saws
pale blue	600 degrees	large saws
very pale blue-green	630 degrees	too soft to use

*Adapted from Spon's Mechanics Own Book (out of print).

Table 2. Characteristics

Type of steel	Characteristic	Uses
tool steel	extremely hard & brittle, grind to sharpen, can't be filed when heated to cherry red & quenched	files, drills, taps & dies
spring steel	quite hard, springy when tempered, grind to sharpen, can't be filed when heated to cherry red & quenched	coil & leaf springs, garden tools, wood tools, screwdrivers, pry bars
carbon steel	tough, holds edge, file to sharpen, shock-resistant, can be filed when heated to cherry red & quenched	saws, shafts, axles, steering rods, king-pins, hardened bolts
general steel	easily cut & shaped cold, won't hold an edge, easily filed when heated to cherry red & quenched	angle iron, rods & plates, ordinary bolts & chain, structural & auto parts

---

kind of steel to use for a given application, and where to find it, see Table 2.

Unfortunately, there is a trade-off between strength and hardness. Really hard steel is brittle; really strong steel is soft. Many tools require a bit of both. Really hard parts, like the point of a cold chisel, should be tempered just a little. Parts that have to be strong, like the striking end of a chisel, may be heated further before being quenched. A problem occurs when very thin metal, such as the point of a chisel or the blade of a knife have to be hardened. The thin metal heats up rapidly, and will burn before the rest of the tool gets even cherry red. The solution is to heat the **other end** of the chisel until the point is straw colored, while the butt or striking end of the chisel is still blue, then quench. With a very thin edge, such as on a knife blade, even this technique may not be safe. Cutlers keep thick bars of iron around for just such occasions. They heat a bar up and lay a polished blade flat on top of it. As the knife blade soaks up the heat of the bar, the edge will turn colors faster than the rest of the blade. Bands of color can be seen flowing down the polished blade toward the edge. When the edge reaches the exact, right temperature, the cutler quenches it, edge first, to prevent warping. Thus the blade can be strong while still holding an edge.

The black metal

Working iron can be a satisfying hobby, or even a profitable business. After a little practice, you'll discover a seemingly endless list of things you can make that can't be bought ready-made anywhere. Things like lantern hooks, and specialized tools for log builders. Using the four classical elements of earth, air, fire, and water to produce beautiful, durable goods can be very satisfying.

Blacksmithing is lots of fun, but it is not particularly clean. Iron has long been known as "the black metal". You will get dirty playing with iron, but liquid hand cleaner, such as auto mechanics use, will get the black off your skin. Nothing will get it out of your clothes, though, so wear old ones you don't care about. Remember, goldsmiths, silversmiths, even tinsmiths are known by the names of the metal they "smite". Only blacksmiths are known by its color.

Good reading

This article is a **simplified** treatment of a very complex subject, intended to take some of the mystery out of it for rank beginners. I have left out lots of information that other smiths may consider vital. There are many different traditions of blacksmithing, each with its own tools, techniques, and nomenclature. The following books contain a much more thorough treatment of the "black art": *The Art of Blacksmithing*, by Alex W. Bealer. Harper & Rowe. A classic. Exhaustive treatment of all facets of blacksmithing. Profusely illustrated. Many tables.

The Woodwright's Shop, by Roy Underhill. The University Of North Carolina Press. Mostly about woodworking, but the section on blacksmithing is cogent and well-written, with truly excellent photographs. Strongly oriented toward historical authenticity.

Cumberland General Store *Wish & Want Book*. Everything a blacksmith needs but the fire. Not cheap junk, but durable, high quality tools. Write for catalog: Rt. 3, Crossville, TN 38553. Δ

A Backwoods Home Anthology
The Seventh Year

Headwaters homestead: backwoods living in the Boston Mountains of Arkansas

By Vern Modeland

Ten years into homesteading on a stony shoulder of the Boston Mountains in Arkansas, Howard and Kate Kuff can't think of a reason to trade places with anyone.

They have an attractive, comfortable, pay-as-you-go owner-built homestead. They have two healthy children, Lenni, 8, and Heron, 4. There's income from Howard's computer-based businesses, and Kate finds time to craft custom leather footwear when she's not busy at the local alternative community school.

Life beyond the beaten path is good, Howard and Kate Kuff will tell you.

There are annoyances. Chain saws and bulldozers slice up the quiet some days. One of their neighbors, the U.S. Forest Service, has begun clear cutting vintage stands of hardwoods very close to their common property line. And winter can produce an ice storm or two that makes travel off the mountain more than exciting. But, for the most part, the homesteading life is everything Howard, Kate, Lenni, and Heron Kuff want it to be.

Heron has her cats, King Tut and Pawpaw, to keep her company. Lenni has young friends who live close enough to drop by for a computer game or to watch a VCR movie.

PV power

With the TV playing, and Howard's business computers whirring, it's hard to remember that all the electricity used at the Kuff homestead comes out of eight Kyocera solar panels that are

Howard Kuff cooks lunch in kitchen built as a one-room cabin in 1982.

700 feet up a hill in the middle of the garden plot. The PV system has been on-line for three years, feeding three computers and a printer, two stereo systems, a 19-inch color TV, the VCR, a vacuum cleaner, wringer washing machine, refrigerator, and a 3/4 horsepower industrial sewing machine. It supplies a mixture of 110-volt alternating current and 12-volt direct current power for compact fluorescent, quartz halogen, and incandescent lights. If wintertime's cloudy days string out longer than ten in a row, a 1,600 watt generator is used to re-charge the 2,700 amp-hour lead-acid battery bank.

Howard said the total cost for the PV panels, generator, batteries, charge regulator, inverter, control panel, wiring and miscellaneous was less than $6,000. With the nearest utility lines about a mile away, the installation of PV-generated electricity costs about equal to what grid-connect charges would have come to.

"And this is clean energy, almost maintenance free, with no monthly energy bills," Howard also likes to add.

A 12-cubic-foot Sun Frost refrigerator-freezer has replaced their aged propane refrigerator, and Howard

Howard Kuff works from home as an information management consultant.

talks about pumping water from their spring up to the house. A 12-volt pump could do away with every-other-day walks 100 yards down to the stone cistern to get a couple of five-gallon pails of the clear, cool ground water captured there.

Overflow from the cistern gurgles off down the hollow and abruptly tumbles

The Kuff's seven-room backwoods home in the Arkansas' Ozarks.

several hundred feet off a bluff to join other rivulets that become the Buffalo National Scenic River.

Wish list

The addition of the Sun Frost refrigerator and water pump will mean adding four more 63-watt panels to the Kuff's PV system.

Several other improvements also are planned for the family's multi-level, seven-room house. The post and beam cabin that started it all, built in 1982 for $1,200, is due for replacement. Howard wants to more than double the space of the original cabin in a clerestory window design. The added space will provide for laundry and more room for cooking and visiting around the Kuff's kitchen table — recycled from a treadle sewing machine.

Howard explains: "That (building project) will hold us for a while. But the kids are sharing a room. When Lenni gets to be a teenager, he's going to need his own room, so I've got another expansion planned. And I want to build a stone and cedar bath house down below in the spring. Once I get those things done, I'll start to feel I'm done working on my 10- year plan."

An air-tight, high-efficiency wood stove has a place on the wish list. That

will mean retirement for the $35 steel barrel conversion stove that has heated the expanding home for years from a spot where the kitchen opens into later room additions.

Choosing the site

The Kuff's house sits below the top of a ridge, in a hollow that opens eastward.

"We chose the spot so that the trees would keep us cool and protect from the late afternoon sun," Howard said.

Ash, walnut, hickory, and tall oaks, with an understory of pawpaw, dogwood, and cherry provide seasonal shade.

"We found this place on a camping vacation," Howard recalls.

"It originally was a 150-acre farm. We bought part of it with some other folks. We're trying to keep development so that people will always have their privacy."

He credits *The Owner Built Home* by Ken Kern as a guide in original planning and designing.

"And I've learned to utilize people's skills. There are a lot of folks with building skills among our neighbors and friends."

The nearest house is about a quarter-mile away.

Kate and Howard Kuff work by a spring that is one source of the Buffalo National Scenic River. At rear is a stone cistern that is used to collect water.

"We're good neighbors, but not really close friends. We hold 60 acres in common and share organic vegetable and fruit gardens there. We bring water from the community pond down to a cistern to use for wash water."

The Kuffs get a fair amount of their food from the garden, especially in spring and fall, canning some which then goes into a root cellar under their living room. Bountiful years allow selling some of the garden's harvest. They supplement their home-grown food with once-a-month trips 60 miles to the Ozark Cooperative Warehouse at Fayetteville, Arkansas, a regional supplier of natural foods for 16 years.

Working from home

"For the first four years, living here was like a long camping vacation," Howard now recalls.

"But money got tighter and tighter. We inherited a little money and that helped us for a while. We both were teaching at Headwaters School (a one-room parent-teacher-student co-operative at Pettigrew, Arkansas). We were getting paid, but it wasn't enough to live on.

"I realized it was just a matter of time before our money was going to run out completely. So, rather than wait until there was none, then go out and do something, I started thinking about what I could do here, so I wouldn't

have to drive away to a job to be able to make enough money to support us.

"I started thinking about computers and the way telecommunications was growing. I applied to NASA. I applied at a lot of different places before I found a job with Energetics at Columbia, Maryland. It's an energy and environmental engineering company that employed fewer than 20 people in 1985. They accepted me because of my mathematics training. We rented our cabin to some friends, and Kate, Lenni, and I moved east.

"I had used personal computers a little, but I wanted to really get into it and this company was high-tech. They hired me at a decent rate and I was going to get involved in computer uses. I really ate it up. I started working 60, 70, 80 hours a week.

"I got in at the right time. There was a real niche there in 1985. They had three computers, and everybody was using them peripherally. My job was data analysis and research—digging up data for specific things.

"In a few months, I became the expert on their computers. They had me setting up systems to manage various accounts on Lotus spreadsheets and databases. They started adding more computers and I got to be the person in charge of specifications. I became the computer systems manager. And then we added data processing and I helped them move from dedicated word processing systems and work station PCs onto a local area network.

"By the time I left, three years later, we had graphics capability, desktop publishing, word processing, and databased management and information systems. And we did programming. I had nine people who worked for me. I managed 45 computers, and the information and database management systems for clients, including the U.S. Department of Energy."

Lenni Kuff and a friend challenge a computer game.

Howard, Heron, Kate, and Lenni Kuff in their Buffalo River headwaters homestead.

Making it pay

What Howard learned and taught himself, and some of the contacts he made, evolved into Headwaters Micro Systems, a homestead-based information management consulting business and supplier of customized computer software and hardware.

The Energy Related Inventors Project at the Department of Energy sought him out to implement a program to monitor and manage the financial and technical support of energy related inventions. Another client's business involves computer-programmed and managed parking meters.

The computer's capability for communications over phone lines, and a program called PC Anywhere, allow Howard to link up in seconds with far-flung software clients and help keep Kuff-devised computer programs running trouble-free.

Love to learn

Howard and Kate met while both were students at Northland College, Ashland, Wisconsin. They shared interests in backpacking, hitchhiking, and camping. Together, they explored Wisconsin's woods, the shores of Lake Superior, and the mountains of the western United States before discovering the Ozarks.

A native of Baltimore, Maryland, Howard has degrees in philosophy and mathematics and an advanced degree in mathematics and statistics.

Kate, who is from Kansas City, has a degree in child psychology and early childhood development. She also has an affection for early education. She teaches two days a week at the 16-year old Headwaters School and serves on the board of directors for the 350-member National Coalition of Alternative Community Schools (58 Schoolhouse Road, Summertown, Tennessee 38433).

Kate talks of getting three dozen kids at Headwaters, who range in age from 3-16, "to love to learn."

"We have just two rules at our school. We follow the Golden Rule and then we have the 'Stop Rule.' If somebody says 'stop,' you need to stop.

Headwaters School is a magnet for homesteading families in rugged northwest Arkansas.

"We've met people who have moved here from all over the country," Howard observes.

"They seem to want to be away from the mainstream of American culture. They've found just too many things about it that are bothersome or distracting. They like the beautiful natural area—so much open space, so much opportunity here. There's not much restriction. No building codes. Basically, if you buy a piece of land and you go out and live there, the state will leave you alone to build your house and live the life you want, as long as you aren't breaking any major laws. There's not many places where that's still possible these days."

"The people who've moved out here—most had to drop their standard of living. We went from living in a fairly nice apartment in the city to living in the woods. But over the years, our standard of living has risen again to where now I think it is very comfortable—for us. It's not exactly what most American families would have, but I'm not up to here in debt, either." Δ

Do-it-yourself "take-out" food

By Jo Mason

You may be a dedicated, dyed-in-the-wool backwoodsman, but do you ever go a little wacky and get a craving for "junk food?" Do you feel a nostalgic ache for the Dairy Queen—or the corner deli? Do words like **greasy and fattening** begin to creep into your conversation?

You have three choices: Ignore the urge until it goes away; drive into town, wait in line, and plunk down your money; or in true pioneer spirit—make it yourself.

Some "convenience" items have been used in these recipes. Canned beans are used in the three-bean salad, and already-skinned and boned chicken breasts are used in the fajitas. Still, all of these are about half the price of what you'd pay at a deli or fast food place. You can save more money by doing more of the work yourself. For instance, if you're good at baking, by all means whip up a batch of hoagie buns instead of buying them. Or make your own fruit filling for the turnovers.

Crispy onion rings

> 4 or 5 medium sized yellow onions
> 1 1/2 cups flat beer
> 1 1/4 cups flour
> 1/4 cup corn meal
> shortening for frying
> salt, to taste

Combine flour, cornmeal, and beer. Cover bowl and let sit at room temperature for about three hours. Cut onions into 1/4-inch slices. Separate into rings. Heat shortening in deep fryer or large, heavy skillet. Using fork, dip onion rings into batter. Place in hot fat (375 degrees). Fry until golden, turning if needed. Drain on absorbent paper. Salt to taste and serve immediately.

Corn chips

> 1 package corn tortillas
> shortening for frying
> salt, to taste

Using sharp knife, cut each tortilla into about six "pie" sections—but do not slice all the way to the center. (This makes it easier to fry six chips at once.) Place shortening in heavy skillet (enough to cover tortillas). Dip each sliced tortilla into hot grease. Fry until golden, turning if needed.

Drain and salt to taste. Press center of each tortilla to break apart into chips.

The following sauce is often served along with corn chips in Mexican restaurants.

Hot chili sauce

> 3 Tablespoons bacon drippings
> 3 cloves minced garlic
> 3 Tablespoons flour
> 6 Tablespoons chili powder
> 3 1/2 cups water
> 1 beef bouillon cube

In large saucepan, melt bacon drippings over **low** heat. Add garlic, flour, and chili powder. (Be careful at this point. Chili burns easily.) Stir in water and bouillon cube. Simmer 10 minutes.

3-bean salad

> 1 can red kidney beans
> 1 can green beans
> 1 can yellow wax beans
> 1/4 cup minced bell pepper
> 1/2 cup minced onion
> 1/2 cup salad oil
> 1/2 cup cider vinegar
> 3/4 cup sugar

Drain beans (using colander). Put in glass container. Add onion and peppers. Combine remaining ingredients and pour over beans. Refrigerate several hours before serving.

Super submarines

> 4 Hoagie buns, split
> Italian dressing
> Swiss cheese slices
> Thinly sliced meat (ham, pressed chicken, salami, etc.)
> 1 large tomato, sliced
> shredded lettuce
> sliced ripe olives
> thinly sliced bell pepper
> thinly sliced onion

Drizzle Italian dressing on each side of buns. Layer on meats, cheese, and vegetables. When sandwich is made, cut in half. Makes four servings.

Chicken fajitas

> 3-4 skinned, boned chicken breasts
> 1/4 cup salad oil
> 1/4 cup vinegar
> juice from 1 lime
> 1 teaspoon sugar
> 1/4 teaspoon ground cumin
> 2 cloves minced garlic
> flour tortillas
> 1/2 cup shredded cheese
> 2 bell peppers, sliced and sauteed
> 1 onion, sliced and sauteed
> salsa
> guacamole

Cut chicken breasts into long thin strips. Combine the next six ingredients (the marinade), and marinate chicken in it (in glass bowl, in refrigerator) for a few hours. Cook on foil-lined grill over hot coals for about 15 minutes, turning once. (Chicken is done when no pink shows after piercing with fork). Heat tortillas until soft. Place everything on the table and allow each person to fill his tortilla.

The following recipe is the result of about ten years experimentation to match the flavor of the cole slaw at Kentucky Fried Chicken.

Jo's Kentucky fried cole slaw

> 1/2 medium-size head cabbage
> 1 small carrot
> 1/2 bell pepper
> 1/2 cup mayonnaise
> 1/4 vinegar
> 1/4 cup sugar
> 1/2 teaspoon dry mustard
> dash of salt
> dash of black pepper

Shred cabbage finely. Grate carrot and pepper finely. Place vegetables in large bowl. Put mayonnaise in small bowl. Stir in sugar, then gradually add vinegar while stirring. Add remaining ingredients to small bowl. Mix well. Stir dressing into vegetables. Cover and chill several hours before serving.

Fruit "turnovers"

> 10 small-size flour tortillas
> 1 can Comstock pie filling (apple, etc.)
> vegetable oil for frying

Warm each tortilla until soft (in heavy skillet on high heat). While tortilla is still soft, immediately place 1-2 heaping tablespoons of pie filling in the center. Fold over sides like an envelope. When all are filled, place one inch hot oil in skillet. Carefully place each pie, seam side down, in hot oil. Fry until golden brown, turning once. Remove with slotted spoon. Drain on paper towels.

Glazed doughnuts

> 1 loaf frozen bread dough
> vegetable oil for frying
> 1/4 cup powdered sugar
> 1 teaspoon water

Grease frozen loaf and two large cookie sheets. Allow to thaw. Roll out dough to about 1/4 inch thickness. Cut with doughnut cutter. Place on cookie sheets and allow to rise until tripled in size. Using spatula, carefully place doughnuts in hot oil (in heavy skillet or preferably a deep fryer). Fry until golden. Remove with slotted spoon. While still warm, brush with glaze made from a mixture of the powdered sugar and water.

Sweet and sour pork

> 1/2 pound lean pork, cut in 1" cubes
> 1/2 cup flour
> 1/4 cup cornstarch
> 1/2 teaspoon baking powder
> dash salt
> 1 egg, beaten
> 1/4 cup water
> vegetable oil
> sweet and sour sauce (see recipe below)*

Combine flour, cornstarch, baking powder, salt, egg, and water to form smooth batter. Heat oil to about 375 degrees. Dip pork in batter and add one at a time to hot oil. Fry until golden brown.

*Sweet and sour sauce

> 3/4 cup sugar
> 3/4 cup water
> 2 to 4 tablespoons soy sauce (to taste)
> 1/2 cup catsup
> 1/2 cup cider vinegar
> 1/2 bell pepper, chopped
> 1 small can chunk pineapple, drained
> cornstarch/water mixture

Combine sugar, water, soy sauce, and catsup in a saucepan and bring to boil. Add vinegar and peppers. Stir cornstarch mixture into sauce a little at a time and cook and stir until thickened. Add pineapple. Δ

Packable salads

By Jennifer Stein Barker

Fall is coming, but the weather's still warm. Labor Day picnics are still to be packed, and soon after that, school begins and there are lunchboxes to be fixed. Hearty, packable salads make a nice addition to a picnic or sack lunch while the weather is still warm (and something crunchy and fresh sounds better than another PB & J sandwich). These salads can all be prepared the night before an event, refrigerated overnight, then transferred to a serving bowl or individual-sized container and carried along with you.

Don't feel obliged to use only the vegetables listed in the recipes, either. Let your creativity take you to the garden or the grocery store, and use whatever's in season. Suggested variations on the themes are listed after the recipes. When the recipe calls for blanching the vegetables, slice them as desired, then place them in a steamer basket over boiling water until **just barely** tender. Remove from the heat, pour the vegetables in a thin layer into a container, then cover and cool in the refrigerator. Dunking them in cold water, as is often recommended, preserves the fresh look and stops the cooking process more quickly, but washes off valuable vitamins. It's your choice.

Oriental pasta salad

This is a hearty, full-flavored salad. For a main dish, chunks of fresh or fried tofu can be marinated in the dressing for two hours before adding the rest of the ingredients. Serves 6 as a main dish, or 10 as a side dish:

> 1 lb. sesame-rice spirals
> 2 small yellow zucchinis, quartered and
>   sliced 1/4" thick
> 2 red bell peppers, diced 1/2"
> 1/2 cup chopped fresh cilantro leaves
> 2 cups oriental pea pods
> 4 Tbsp. raw sesame seeds
> 1 lb. firm tofu (opt.)
>
> sauce:
> 1/2 cup dark sesame oil
> 2 cloves garlic, finely chopped
> 1/2 cup tamari
> 4 Tbsp. balsamic vinegar
> 4 tsp. fresh ginger root, peeled and minced
> 2 tsp. honey
> 2 tsp. hot oil

Mix the sauce ingredients in a small bowl. Whisk well until the honey is thoroughly incorporated. If you are using the tofu, add the chunks now, and chill in the refrigerator for two hours.

Blanch the zucchini and the pea pods until just barely tender. Cool. Place the sesame seeds in a small dry pan over medium-high heat and toast, shaking frequently until golden. Set aside.

Bring eight quarts of water to a boil, then add the pasta spirals. Stir briefly with a fork, return the pot to the boil, and boil, uncovered, for 9 minutes (until the pasta is cooked but still a little chewy). Drain the pasta thoroughly in a colander. To assemble the salad, add the warm pasta to the sauce and toss briefly. Then add the vegetables and fresh cilantro, and toss again. Sprinkle the toasted sesame seeds over the top, and chill for two hours or overnight before serving.

Name some other vegetables that would be good in this: cabbages, bok choi, thin-sliced turnips, asparagus, bean sprouts.

Italian pasta salad

A picnic standby, this pleases folks of all ages. Kids love the tomatoes, and the shape of the pasta. Serves 6 as a main dish, or 10 as a side dish:

> 1 lb. vegetable rotini (whole wheat preferred)
> 4 oz. button mushrooms
> 1 head broccoli
> 2 carrots, sliced thin
> 1 pint cherry tomatoes
> 1 oz. mozzarella cheese, julienned
>
> Sauce:
> 1/2 cup olive oil
> 1 dash Tabasco (1/8 tsp.)
> 2 Tbsp. tamari soy sauce
> 1 Tbsp. fresh herbs (choose at least two from
>   basil, thyme, marjoram, and oregano) or
>   1 tsp. dry
> 3 Tbsp. red wine vinegar
> 1 clove garlic, minced
> black pepper

Blanch the carrot slices until just barely tender. Cut the broccoli into individual florets. Peel the broccoli stems, and cut them into 1/2" chunks. Blanch the broccoli chunks and florets just until they turn bright green. Cut the mushrooms in half and saute gently in olive oil in a small skillet, just until tender. Cut the cherry tomatoes in half. Chill all the vegetables.

Boil the pasta as directed in the recipe for oriental pasta salad. While the pasta is boiling, mix all the sauce ingredients except the herbs. If you are using dried herbs, crush them between your fingers as you add them. If you are using fresh herbs, pick the leaves from the stems and chop them coarsely before adding to the sauce.

When the pasta is drained, pour the sauce over the warm pasta and toss. Add all the vegetables and toss again. Chill in the refrigerator for two hours or overnight. Slice and add the cheese just before serving.

What else can you use for vegetables? Red onions, olives, zucchini, celery, green beans...

More-than-tabbouleh

This traditional Middle Eastern salad can be turned into a main-dish salad with a few simple additions. Serves 4 as a main dish:

> 1/4 cup dry lentils
> 1 small cucumber, peeled, quartered, and sliced
> 1 1/2 cups bulghur
> 2 medium-sized tomatoes, diced
> 1 medium carrot, sliced thin
> 3 Tbsp. minced fresh parsley
> 3 Tbsp. lemon juice
> 3 green onions, thinly sliced
> 1/2 cup olive oil
> 1 tsp. minced fresh mint
> salt and pepper to taste

Boil the lentils in a small pan with 2 cups of water until they are tender, but still whole. Place the bulghur in a large bowl, and drain the cooking water from the lentils over it. Put the lentils in the refrigerator to cool. Add enough more boiling water to the bulghur to cover it, and let soak until all the water is absorbed. Taste the bulghur, and if it is not tender, add a little more boiling water as necessary and soak until tender. If you add too much water, the bulghur will have to be drained and squeezed in a cheesecloth to remove the excess moisture.

When the bulghur is tender, add the lentils and all the other ingredients. Toss to mix thoroughly, then cover and chill for two hours or overnight.

What else can you put in this salad? Zucchini, bell peppers, peas, cauliflower, olives, shell beans.

Don't stop with just changing the vegetables. Change the type of grain, the flavor of the oils and vinegars, and the herbs and spices in the dressings to create an unlimited variety of hearty, whole-grain salads!

Need a recipe for a special vegetarian dish? If I don't have one, I'll create one! Requests may be forwarded to Jennifer Stein Barker through this magazine. Δ

A BHM Writer's Profile

Lucy Shober was born and grew up on Lookout Mountain in Tennessee along with eleven brothers and sisters. Her motley assortment of pets included monkeys, goats, pigeons, and racoons. She has worked in wildlife rehabilitation and environmental education and writes children's columns for several local newspapers.

She and her husband, John, have three children and run "The Flying Turtle Farm" in Cloudland, Georgia. They raise and sell organic vegetables, flowers, minor breeds of poultry, and Irish Dexter cattle.

Hand loading your ammo is far cheaper than buying it

By Christopher Maxwell

The only way to become truly proficient with firearms is practice, practice, practice. You can learn a lot with a .22, but if you are going to use more powerful firearms you will have to practice with the guns you plan to use. This can get very expensive.

Assembling your own ammunition can substantially reduce your ammunition cost. You can also make special purpose ammunition that is not available from any factory.

Easier than you think

Making your own ammunition can be much simpler than you may think, and the equipment is not too expensive. Often you can buy used equipment for a fraction of new prices from former fanatics who don't shoot enough any more to justify the trouble.

All there is to reloading is removing the used primer from the fired case, resizing the case to its proper size, inserting a new primer, charging the case with powder, and seating a new bullet in the case.

Save 30-60% of ammo cost

You can save 30% to 60% of your ammunition cost by making your own. How much you will save will depend on how much and what equipment you buy, and how much you shoot.

You can increase your savings by reloading instead of buying expensive premium ammunition rather than reloading instead of buying low priced ammunition. (OK, I'm sorry. I just couldn't stop myself. My friend keeps telling me he saved $5000 buying a Samurai instead of a Jeep. I'm going to save $30,000 by buying a Samurai instead of a Range Rover. I'll be rich!)

If you will only use five rounds per year to check your zero and shoot your deer, you don't need to worry about ammunition cost. Reloading won't be worth the bother for you.

But if you use your guns for pest and predator control and practice once a month or more you will probably be money ahead the first year. I say probably because you may find yourself shooting more often when you start making your own ammunition. You may end up spending your savings on more practice and find yourself shooting much better instead of saving money.

Equipment considerations

The equipment you will need to start will vary depending on what and how much you shoot.

You can buy something simple like the Lee Loader for under $20, but it is slow and should only be used to make moderate power loads for a single firearm. If you have more than one gun or may want to shoot more than 20 rounds per month, I don't think you will be well served with this.

If you shoot rifles or handguns you will need a press, a scale, a powder measure, some type of case measure and trimming device, and a separate set of dies for each caliber you intend to reload. If you find your volume increasing, there are other devices such as case polishers, auto priming tools, and even multi-stage presses which work like table top assembly lines and can turn out hundreds of rounds per hour doing a different operation to several cases at once.

You can buy a complete outfit for under $100, which will turn out factory quality ammunition in enough quantity for most people, or you can spend most of $1000.

You can buy a simple, single-stage press to reload all metallic cartridges for anywhere from $20 to $75. The low priced presses take more effort to use, and do not offer the option of adding more features later. If you don't shoot anything longer than .30-06 and won't want to make more than about 50 rounds at a time, they are a good value. You can load larger cartridges on them, and larger lots, but you would be better off with a larger press.

I like my Lyman AccuPress because it can be used as either a bench mounted press or a hand press. I can do the relatively mindless operations like decapping and resizing while watching a movie, then use my larger bench-mounted press to do the more critical operations. I also use the AccuPress as a light duty bench mounted press.

The larger presses offer better leverage for easier operation, more durability, and the option to add such features as auto primer feed and multi stage operation.

A multi-stage or progressive loader can cost $300 to $700 and can turn out an amazing quantity of ammunition. Some are only meant for pistol and revolver ammunition but many will also load rifle cartridges.

A scale will cost anywhere from $20 up to as much as you've got. Even though you will measure powder for most of your reloading, you will still need a scale to check the accuracy of your measure. The closer you are to the maximum load for your cartridge, the more important it is for your charges to be precise.

You can get by without a powder measuring device but if you will be making large runs of ammunition you will find it very time consuming to scoop or weigh every charge.

Dies will cost $15 to $35 depending on brand and caliber. I have used RCBS, Lyman, and Lee and find very little difference to comment on. I prefer to spend the extra few dollars on carbide dies in pistol calibers, and carbide expanders for my rifle dies.

These reduce or eliminate the need to lubricate the cartridge cases when resizing. Lubricating and then cleaning the lubricant off are some of the most time consuming jobs in the entire reloading process.

Improved versatility

Many firearms only offer one level of power. My favorite rifle is a WW2 Mauser converted to .308 which is capable of shooting better than I do. When I'm just plinking, or using this rifle for pest control, I don't need full power loads.

A load about 30% less powerful than standard is easier on my shoulder, my rifle, and my neighbors' nerves. It's almost like having two different rifles, but more convenient because all I have to do is change ammunition and turn the sight four clicks. No factory makes this load.

Instead of buying several different rifles for different size game you can just buy the largest size you may need and load down for lighter uses. The same idea works for handguns. You can load a .44 Magnum with a lighter bullet and less powder to make a comfortable small game or pest elimination load, or load it up to handle deer

or large predators. Just be sure to follow the loading instructions for whatever powder you use. Some powders may detonate rather than burn if not used at the recommended density.

I have a break open .30-30 which I like quite a bit, but the factories only make .30-30 ammunition with flat nosed bullets. This limits the effective range to just over 100 yards. My loads with pointed bullets are effective to 200 yards. No factory would ever make .30-30 ammunition with pointed bullets because the tubular magazines of the lever action rifles in .30-30 place the nose of one cartridge against the primer of the one in front.

These are just a few examples of the things you can make which the factories don't make.

Reloading is not a substitute for a bigger gun

While making less powerful ammunition rather than buying a smaller gun is practical, the reverse is not true. If you find you need more power than the maximum loads listed, get a bigger gun. Overloading your gun will wear it out faster and reduce your case life even if it doesn't blow up.

Powder, primers, and safety

Propellant powder and primers are extremely flammable. They wouldn't be much use otherwise. Store your materials and do your loading away from heat, flame, and sources of electrical sparks.

Safety glasses should be worn, especially when handling primers. While the chance of a primer being accidentally crushed or otherwise activated may be small, it only takes a tiny metal fragment to do serious eye damage.

Substituting powders is not safe, even similar powders. Two companies, Hogdon and IMR, make some very similar powders which have the same stock numbers. H-4895 is NOT the same as IMR 4895.

They are not interchangeable. Make sure you are using the correct data for your powder.

My system for avoiding accidental substitution of powder is to use as few

different powders as possible. I use 748 in my rifles and Unique in my handguns and shotguns. These two powders look different, meter differently, and bulk differently enough that accidental substitution would be almost impossible.

Dispose of any unidentified powder. Don't try to guess what it might be; powder doesn't cost enough to risk damaging your gun and injuring yourself.

Buy factory ammunition when you need maximum loads. The most accurate loads in most guns will be found about 5 to 10% below the maximum loads listed. Hitting with a moderate load gets better results than missing with a maximum load. The small increase in performance is not worth the extra trouble and risk.

When starting out, try the easiest cartridges first. Large revolvers are the least picky about their ammunition. Almost anything you make which fits into the cylinder will fire. If you followed the directions, it will probably shoot well. Automatic pistols are more demanding. The size and shape and power of the cartridge must be within tighter limits. Bottleneck rifle cartridges are more difficult, and bottleneck cartridges for autoloading rifles have to be perfect.

Most of the large bullet manufacturing companies and many of the manufacturers of propellant powders publish loading manuals. Naturally, such a manual will promote the use of products made by the manufacturer who published it. They still contain a great deal of useful general information. I like the reloading manuals produced by Speer and Hornady. That doesn't mean there is anything wrong with the others; it just means I like these two.

Reloading shotgun shells?

Reloading shotgun shells requires different equipment and is not usually cost effective for anybody but fanatical trap or skeet shooters. You can spend $100 to $500 on equipment to load shotgun shells, then you need primers, powder, shot, and wads. Most of the equipment and materials used will not be useful for anything else. Shotgun shells can usually be picked up cheap as loss leaders at Walmart or K-Mart stores and you will find that you have to shoot hundreds of rounds per month before reloading becomes a significant saving unless you don't value your time highly.

In addition, reloaded shotgun shells rarely perform as well as factory ammunition. I have tried ammunition reloaded by people who knew what they were about and I just wasn't very impressed.

Metallic cartridges can be reloaded to equal or exceed the performance and accuracy of factory ammunition with very little practice and experimenting. Shotgun shells have more variables which affect their performance such as shot hardness, wad shape and flexibility, case thickness, crimping, and others. The factories can afford the research to find the right combination, and the shooters

who fire hundreds of rounds per month can; I can't.

This article can't even begin to cover the options available in making your own ammunition. Entire books have been written just on such subjects as bullet casting. True fanatic handloaders can spend hours polishing and trimming cases and months or years experimenting with different combinations of components in their pursuit of the perfect load. I must admit I have never found it that interesting. For me, loading my own was always a way to shoot more on a limited budget, or make something I couldn't buy.

This may help you decide whether this is a subject you might be interested in researching further. If you do, read the manuals and be careful. I don't know of a single accident with firearms or ammunition which could not have been prevented.

This article concludes my series of basic articles about firearms. These

articles were not intended to be a complete education on the subject of firearms for country living. They were intended as an introduction to the subject for those who may have had no information, or only had misinformation. The basic knowledge in these articles will enable you to learn more from other, more widely available sources.

While Dave and I agree there is no need for another gun magazine on the market, we both thought there was a need for this type of article. If there are other subjects you would like to see covered in

BHM, drop Dave a line and let him know.

BHM #11—Shotguns
BHM #12—.22 rimfire
BHM #13—Learning to shoot
BHM #14—High Power Rifles
BHM #15—Ammunition
BHM #16—Accessories Δ

A Backwoods Home Anthology
The Eighth Year

* Considering life in rural Arkansas
* Where I live: Nine-patch, baby, and log cabin quilts
* Here's the best way to split gnarly firewood
* Here's an easier (and cheaper) way to make wooden beams
* Rid your garden of snails and slugs — organically
* Try these 13 metal cleaning tips to keep your house shining
* I remember the day the lynx attacked
* Raise your own feed crops for your livestock
* Lay vinyl flooring the foolproof way
* These double-steep half stairs save space
* Think of it this way...Science and truth — are they related?
* Commonsense preparedness just makes sense
* Grandma will love this personal "Helping Hands" wall hanging
* Try these pasta desserts for unusual holiday fare
* Protect your small buildings from wind damage
* Winterize your animals without going broke
* Enjoy snap beans — fresh from the garden
* Set 100 steel fence posts a day with a home-made driver
* Plant your Irish potatoes this fall or winter
* From apple crisp to French tarts, tasty apple treats are just right for fall
* Here are four sure catfish baits
* Save time and energy with the fenced chicken coop/garden
* Rough day? You need to sip some yeller wine

Social conditioning, women, and self-defense

By Michelle Richards

For years I've read articles written by men telling women what is appropriate for them in a handgun for self-defense purposes. These so called experts give what appear to be rational, well thought out reasons for what they perceive women should have to defend themselves. But it's technical balderdash as far as I can see. Men see it as a particular weapon and power source, but I approach the subject differently. I approach it psychologically, and as a woman who knows firearms.

Gun makers and women

Until recently women have been ignored by the firearms industry. Guns are produced to fit the average male, i.e., longer arms, hand length, and width. When we women have purchased guns we've had to work around these restrictions, to our disadvantage. Grips on handguns were too fat to hold comfortably which made it hard for us just to hold on while firing.

Triggers were set too far out for us to reach, thus our accuracy was severely reduced. **If a gun does not fit you well, and you are uncomfortable firing it, you will not shoot well. Period.**

I now see things changing. Being a cynic at heart I know it is not because anyone in the firearms industry heard us demanding guns that fit us, but because advertising executives have decided 51% of the population is too big a market to ignore any longer.

We now have Smith and Wesson advertising their slicked up Lady Smith series, and Mossberg, a shotgun manufacturer, pushing their .410 shotgun as a woman's home defense weapon, just to name two.

Unfortunately the advertising is directed at men and continues the myth that women cannot make choices for themselves. For example, an ad has been running lately in gun magazines by Mossberg for their .410 shotgun. The picture in the ad shows a woman with a handgun pointed straight out in front of her and her head turned sideways with her eyes closed and her face all contorted. The text of the ad has a man going through options in what's available in the marketplace for women for self-defense. Through trial and error **he** determines the Mossberg product is just what **she** needs and suggests other men get this product for their women.

I don't fall for it. Not because the product is poor, not because it wouldn't do the job (it would), but because I am tired of being called a simpleton to my face. Needless to say I wrote Mossberg and told them I was insulted and if they wanted me to buy their product they'd have to appeal to my intelligence, not some long-standing myth directed at men that women can't understand firearms and their uses without a male's help.

Through the years manufacturers and gun dealers have told women the .25 ACP was just the ticket for them. These little guns are cheaply made, all dolled up with "pretty" grips, and marketed as "women's guns." Knowing what I know of guns and ballistics, a .25 would be just about dead last on my list of a firearm for self-defense. Because I deal with firearms on a daily basis I'd only be comfortable carrying two brands out of the many on the market, and they are very expensive when compared to the usual assortment in gun stores.

From the history above, it is very easy for me to understand why women have not been quick to see the merits of gun ownership and the necessity of self-defense. First, we are told guns are a "man's pervue" because they aren't made to fit us, then we are told we are ignorant and that a man has to tell us what to buy, and then when a gun is marketed for us it is a wimpy, poorly-made "prettied-up" piece that is suppose to appeal to us aesthetically. It's not really a firearm capable of hurting an attacker, but a pretty piece of metal with roses on the handle.

We are being told that the thought of shooting and maiming or even maybe killing someone in the defense of our lives is something we can't psychologically handle. We will obviously have a nervous breakdown and regret the rest of our days the fact we defended ourselves. We have been societally conditioned to believe it is wrong and even unladylike to meet violence with violence. As sad as this state of affairs is, I believe we women can turn that around to our advantage. This social conditioning truly gives us the upper hand **if** we can recognize it as such.

We're so shell-shocked by violence on the nightly news, movies, and newspapers, we curl up into our own little world and figure it'll never happen to us; it's so much easier to get through the day that way. We've got so much else to consider in our hectic lives, the thought of having a nightmare happening just seems so remote we get on with what's pressing and let anything that's not slide away.

Besides, you have rape counseling now, and a good insurance policy to cover your injuries, right? **Well gals, I call that shutting the barn door after the horse gets out.** I also call that **victim thinking.** You come by it honestly. Our society tells you it's expected and proper.

Going on the offense

Never having been proper, nor done what's expected, I've decided to go into an **offensive** stance. Notice I did not say **defensive.** I said offensive and I meant it. Remember earlier I said women can turn our societal conditioning around to our advantage? Here's how we can:

We as women have been taught to think like victims, behave like victims, and therefore be victims. Men believe this too. Do you really believe a man would attack you if he believed you could defend yourself and maim or kill him? Do you really believe men aren't afraid of a gun in their face?

It is my contention that I will win in an encounter based on a man's perceptions and expectations of what will happen in the encounter. He will attempt to use his physical size to intimidate me and threaten me. If that does not work he will use his greater strength to overcome me.

He knows he can, and that I have been conditioned, and he will believe I will accept it. But here's the monkey

wrench. I won't. I will use his perceptions to overcome him. If the situation is such that it's to my advantage I will growl menacingly, raise by voice, and race toward him with my gun drawn and ready to use. I will act "crazed."

If the perpetrator is too close I may use another technique—scream in a high voice. He expects this, and he will concentrate on my face while my hand moves for my gun, thus allowing me that split second I need in close quarters.

Whatever I choose to do in the situation at hand I will not stand still, I will not do as I'm told. I will not do what he wants because that's what he expects. For what may be just a split second or a second or two things will be unfamiliar to him. He won't understand. It's not working right. I'm supposed to be whimpering on the sidewalk or in a corner and he knows what to do then. But by taking the offensive I confuse him and my chances to survive go up dramatically. He's not ready and he cannot react. I have done the unthinkable.

Whatever I choose to do, in the situation at hand I will **not** stand still, I will not **do as I'm told.** I will not do what he wants because that's what he expects. For what may be just a split second or a second or two things will be unfamiliar to him. He won't understand. It's not working right. I'm supposed to be whimpering on the sidewalk or in a corner and he knows what to do then. But by taking the offensive I confuse him and my chances to survive go up dramatically. He's not

ready and he cannot react. I have done the unthinkable.

This type of thinking does not come easily, nor does the skill necessary to carry this out. It is a mind-set backed up by years of mental scenarios played out in my head. What would I do if . .

Seeing myself defend myself and win, backed up by practice using guns. Building my confidence by practice. Rolling around my back 40 acting out scenarios of self-defense. Setting an alarm at 2 a.m. to see how quickly I can find my handgun and get it into firing position while groggy. It may seem silly as you picture it while reading this, but it makes me so familiar with my firearm I don't **think**; I react. I don't fumble, wonder, and think. I know. This takes dedication and commitment. Are you willing to do this?

Are you willing to take the time to have your gun be an extension of your hand? So familiar with it, it's like second nature? If not, don't use a firearm. If so, welcome to the sorority. I believe you have made a very rational, intelligent choice, saying you are valuable and deserve to live with dignity. You have empowered yourself. The first step to live a full and meaningful life without fear.

If you wish more information geared especially for women there's a magazine published called Women & Guns, P.O. Box 488, Station C, Buffalo, N.Y. 14209.

In my next article I want to discuss the get down, get gritty subject of particular guns and calibers that I believe are especially appropriate for women and their defense. For you fellas who have read this far, there even may be some surprises for you. Δ

Grounding and lightning protection for solar-electric power systems

By Windy Dankoff

Lightning and related static discharge is the number one cause of sudden, unexpected failures in PV systems. Lightning does not have to strike directly to cause damage to sensitive electronic equipment, such as inverters, controls, radios, and entertainment equipment. It can be miles away and invisible, and still induce high voltage surges in wiring, especially in long lines.

Fortunately, almost all cases of lightning damage can be prevented by proper system grounding. Owners of independent power systems do not have grounding supplied by the utility company, and often overlook it until it is too late.

My own customers have reported damage to inverters, charge controllers, DC refrigerators, fluorescent light ballasts, TVs, pumps, and (rarely) photovoltaic panels. These damages cost many thousands of dollars, and all reports were from owner-installed systems that were **not grounded**.

Grounding

Grounding means connecting part of your system structure and/or wiring electrically to the earth. During light-ning storms, the clouds build up a static electric charge. This causes accumulation of the opposite charge in objects to the ground. Objects that are **insulated** from the earth tend to accumulate the charge more strongly than the surrounding earth. If the potential difference (voltage) between sky and the objects is great enough, lightning will jump the gap.

Grounding your system does four things:

- It drains off accumulated charges so that lightning is **not highly attracted** to your system.
- If lightning does strike, or if a high charge does build up, your ground connection provides a

safe path for discharge directly to the earth rather than through your wiring.
- It reduces shock hazard from the higher voltage (AC) parts of your system.
- It reduces electrical hum and radio caused by inverters, motors, fluorescent lights, and other devices.

Also, it is required by the National Electric Code. Photovoltaic systems are included in Article 690 of the Code. Low voltage systems are **not** exempt from grounding requirements or from the NEC.

To achieve effective grounding, follow these guidelines:

Install a proper grounding system

Minimal grounding is provided by a copper-plated ground rod, usually 8 ft. long, driven into the earth. This is a minimum procedure in an area where the ground is moist (electrically conductive).

Where the ground may be dry, especially sandy, or where lightning may be particularly severe, more rods should be installed, at least 10 feet apart. Connect or "bond" all ground rods together via bare copper wire (#6 or larger, see the NEC) and bury the wire. Use only approved clamps to connect wire to rods. If your photovoltaic array is some distance from the house, drive ground rod(s) near it, and bury bare wire in the trench with the power lines.

Metal water pipes that are buried in the ground are also good to ground to. Purchase connectors approved for the purpose, and connect **only** to cold water pipes, **never** to hot water or gas pipes. Beware of plastic fittings—bypass them with copper wire.

Iron well casings are super ground rods. Drill and tap a hole in the casing to get a good bolted connection. If you connect to more than one grounded object (the more the better) it is **essential to electrically bond (wire) them to each other.** Connections made in or near the ground are prone to corrosion, so use proper bronze or copper connectors. Your ground system is only as good as its weakest electrical connections.

If you have rocky soil

If your site is rocky and you cannot drive ground rods deeply, bury (as much as feasible) at least 150 feet of bare copper wire. Several pieces radiating outward is best. Try to bury them in areas that tend to be moist. If you are in a lightning-prone area, bury several hundred feet if you can. The idea is to make as much electrical contact with the earth as you can, over the broadest area feasible, preferably contacting moist soil.

You can save money by purchasing used copper wire (not aluminum) from a scrap metal dealer, and stripping off the insulation (use copper "split bolts" or crimped splices to tie odd pieces together.) If you need to run any power wiring over a distance of 30 feet or more, and are in a high-lightning, dry, or rocky area, run the wires in metal conduit and bond the conduit to your grounding system.

What to connect to your ground system

Ground the metallic framework of your PV array. (If your framework is wood, metallically bond the module frames together, and wire to ground.) Be sure to bolt your ground wires solidly to the metal so it will not come loose, and inspect it periodically. Also ground antenna masts and wind generator towers.

Ground the negative side of your power system, but **first** make the following test for leakage to ground: Obtain a common "multi-tester." Set it on the highest "milliamp" scale. Place the negative probe on battery neg. and the positive probe on your ground system. No reading? Good. Now switch it down to the lowest milli- or microamp scale and try again. If you get only a few microamps, or zero, **then ground your battery negative.** If you **did** read leakage to ground, check your system for something on the positive side that may be contacting earth somehow. (If you read a few microamps to ground, it is probably your meter detecting radio station signals.)

Connect your DC negative to ground **only in one place**, at a negative battery connection or other main negative junction nearby (at a disconnect switch or inverter, for instance.) Do **not** ground negative at the array or at any other points.

Ground your AC generator and inverter frames, and AC neutral wires and conduits in the manner conventional for all AC systems. This protects from shock hazard as well as lightning damage.

PV array wiring should be done with minimum lengths of wire, tucked into the metal framework, then run through metal conduit. Positive and negative wires should be run together wherever possible, rather than being some distance apart. This will minimize induction of lightning surges. Bury long outdoor wire runs instead of running them overhead. Place them in grounded metal conduit if you feel you need maximum protection.

Surge protection devices bypass the high voltages induced by lightning. They are recommended for additional protection in lightning-prone areas or where good grounding is not feasible (such as on dry rocky mountain top), especially if long lines are being run to an array, pump, antenna, or between buildings. Surge protectors must be special for low voltage systems, so contact your PV dealer.

Safety first! If you are uncertain of your ability to wire your system properly, hire an electrician!

(Windy Dankoff if the founder of Flowlight Solar Power, a leading manufacturer of solar water pumping systems. He says the company grew up and is no fun to play with anymore, so he's back to working at home, supplying solar-electric power systems to folks who live beyond the power lines.His phone: (505) 351-2100) Δ

A well-regulated militia, being necessary to the security of a free State, the right of the people to keep and bear arms, shall not be infringed.

The second amendment to the Constitution of the United States

Rabbit diseases and how to cope with them

By Darlene Campbell

Even if you keep your rabbits healthy through sanitation and good management, eventually even the best managed herd will develop some health problem. Most of us recognize simple ailments such as diarrhea or abscesses, and can treat them with remedies we use on other animals on the farm. There are some diseases however, that are peculiar to rabbits alone, such as sore hocks which can prove troublesome unless you know what the symptoms and remedies are.

I've discovered the best remedy for disease is prevention, and often prevention means isolation. This is not to imply that rabbits are to be kept in isolated quarters, but that visitors should be kept to a minimum. Persons can carry disease from one rabbitry to another, so it is best to avoid showing your stock to strangers who may have spent the day visiting various herds, or who may have sick rabbits at home.

Stray dogs, cats, and wild animals such as mice, rats, and wild rabbits also are carriers of disease and contaminants. Store feed so as to prevent the invasion of mice, and never introduce a new rabbit to the herd without knowing about the health of the herd it comes from.

Just like in humans and other animals the infectious agents that cause disease in rabbits are bacteria, viruses, parasites, and fungi. Although direct contact is necessary in some instances, it is not always necessary as viruses and fungi are carried in the air. This explains how an outbreak of a virus can spread rapidly through the herd.

Learn to give antibiotic shots yourelf; you will save a lot of veterinary expense in the long run. I have tried to list the most common rabbit ailments along with their usual symptoms and treatments to make rabbit raising what it should be — uncomplicated.

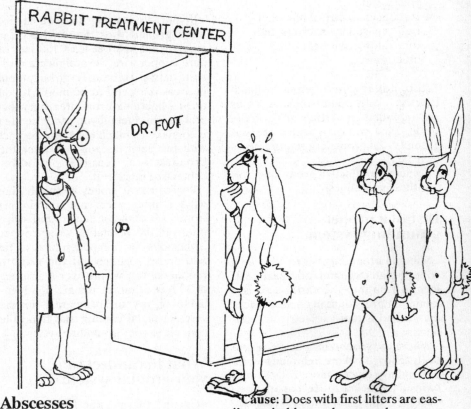

Abscesses

Symptoms: Lumps under the skin in the back, neck, cheek, or dewlap areas.

Cause: Abscesses are a collection of pus caused by the invasion of a bacteria, streptococcus.

Treatment: Clip the fur from around the lump. Using rubbing alcohol or iodine, sterilize the area. Make an incision in the lower portion of the lump and squeeze out the infective material. Clean the incision with peroxide, and apply an antibiotic ointment. Antibiotic ointment should be applied twice daily or a topical spray or powder such as Furazolidone can be applied once or twice daily.

Cannibalism

Symptoms: Scattered bits of flesh, or missing young from the nest box within two weeks after kindling.

Cause: Does with first litters are easily excitable, and are under stress. They may eat their young if disturbed suddenly such as by a strange dog. However, it has been the author's experience that cannibalism will present itself when no disturbance has occurred. There seems to be two factors involved. The first is diet and the second is heredity. It may also be a method in which the doe reduces the number of young to what she can satisfactorily nurse.

Treatment: First decide the cause. If the doe was frightened and she became cannibalistic, prevent any further disturbance. Also, be careful to avoid unusual happenings or move her cage to a secluded spot before the arrival of future litters.

If diet is the cause, a protein supplement added to the diet a few days before kindling will give a protein boost, and aid in the production of milk.

Where the litter is too large, moving some of the young to a doe having a small litter may save them. This is discussed in a later chapter.

Never save does for future breeding stock from the litter of a doe who shows signs of cannibalism as the tendency may be passed to the young.

Caked udder

Symptoms: Does that are heavy milk producers are the most commonly affected, particularly when nursing only a few young. The teats become sore, and the udder inflamed. It is hard and hot to the touch. The doe may refuse to nurse the litter.

Cause: The most frequent cause is too few young to relieve the flow of milk. A doe will easily bruise herself when leaping in or out of the litter box if the sides of the box are too high. Improper weaning.

Treatment: For mild cases, such as improper weaning where the young were removed suddenly before milk production slowed, cut back on feed and return one or two of the litter for a day or two. Where too few young are being nursed, add one or more young from a doe with a large litter.

Where the teats are injured, sore or cracked, apply an antibiotic ointment which will not only aid in healing, but will soften the skin to prevent further cracking. This is frequently seen in does with their first litters.

Do not fail to treat a caked udder as soon as detected. If untreated it can lead to the destruction of the udder leaving it non-functional.

Sore hocks

Symptoms: Sitting in a hunched position. Inactivity and off feed. The presence of scabs or sores on front or hind leg hocks. Infection may cause swelling and inflammation.

Cause: This is a painful condition that is caused mainly from unsanitary conditions in the cage, sharp wire flooring, or cage bottoms that are not solid enough to support the rabbit's weight without sagging. Some rabbits inherit thin fur covering on the feet and are more susceptible.

Treatment: Wash the sores with mild soap and water. Apply an antibiotic ointment until condition clears, or administer 1/4 ml of combiotic daily by injection. Placing a board on the cage floor will give relief until healing is complete.

Fungus infections

Symptoms: Patches where hair is missing with a flaky, dry crust. The lesions appear on the nose, feet, around the mouth, on the eyelids, and on the backs of the ears.

Cause: A fungus invasion of the hair follicles. Fungus is transmitted by persons handling the stock, or spread from one rabbit to another on contact. This condition is also transmissible to man so caution should be used when handling affected animals.

Treatment: Rub a fungus powder or ointment into affected area daily until new hair growth appears. Replace bedding in nest boxes and apply fungus powder to the fresh bedding to prevent transmission to the young.

Mucoid enteritis

Symptoms: Diarrhea as evidenced by feces on the hind feet or not forming into the usual round pill shape, hunched back, rough coat, grinding the teeth, or sitting hunched over the water dish with front feet in the water. The stomach may be bloated and the eyes appear to be squinting.

Cause: Fifty percent of all rabbit deaths from birth to 8 weeks of age are caused by Mucoid Enteritis. The exact cause is not known, but it is suspected to be caused by one or more of the following: coccidiosis, intestinal parasites, fungi, virus, unsanitary conditions, and/or improper feeding.

Treatment: A water soluble antibiotic, terramycin, aureomycin, or neoterramycin can be added to the drinking water at the rate of 1 teaspoon per 2 1/2 gallons of water. Continue treatment for one week. As a preventive measure, the entire herd may be treated with a low level mixture at the rate of 1 teaspoon per 5 gallons of water.

Sulfaquinoxoline or sulfa solutions such as Sulmet which are primarily used by poultry breeders prove to be highly beneficial when coccidiosis is the cause. The amount recommended for poultry is printed on the label of the bottle and is satisfactory for rabbits. Mix this solution with the drinking water and offer as the only water available to sick animals, or use it periodically to treat the entire herd as a preventive measure.

Since the death rate is high with mucoid enteritis, it is recommended that all animals that die be disposed by burning or burying. Do not administer two drugs at the same time.

Coccidiosis

Symptoms: A listless appearance, pot belly, loss of appetite, thinness, and diarrhea. Upon examination, the liver will be spotted white and the intestines inflamed. A heavy mucous will be found in the intestines.

Cause: Coccidia is a microscopic parasite which grow in the intestines. It is transmitted by drinking contaminated water or by the normal eating of the offal.

Treatment: The use of sulfa solutions such as Sulmet on a regular monthly basis is a control measure. For acute cases use the solution for 3 days, then off for 3 days, then give for a final 3 days. Follow instructions printed on the label as given for poultry.

Pneumonia

Symptoms: Rapid breathing, a temperature above 103 degrees, nasal discharge, and a bluish tint to the eye color of albinos.

Cause: Drafty, cold, or damp quarters. Stress, and a general run down condition which weaken the rabbit's ability to fight off bacterial infections. The infection invades the lungs and nasal passage. It is a major killer of adult rabbits, and can infect and kill a rabbit within 24 hours. Suspect pneumonia when a member of the herd is discovered dead without any previous sign of illness.

Treatment: Speed in diagnosing and treating this disease is upmost important. Inject antibiotic deep into the hind leg muscle following the dosage recommended for rabbits by the manufacturer. Either penicillin or combiotic is effective. Combiotic is a good all around antibiotic which can be kept on hand by the rabbit breeder to fight a variety of illnesses and infections. Continue the dosage recommended for 2 days past the last sign of symptoms.

Conjunctivitis

Symptoms: This is an inflammation of the eye, and shows itself with tearing or a discharge of pus. In severe cases the eye may be stuck closed.

Cause: Bacteria which has infected the eye, or irritants such as dust, pollen, or foreign objects.

Treatment: Cleanse the eye with a mild solution of boric acid, or sterile water. Apply an antibiotic eye ointment once or twice a day until the condition clears.

Ear canker

Symptoms: Shaking of the head and scratching at the ear. The formation of crust deep within the ear.

Cause: Ear mites which embed into the soft parts of the ear.

Treatment: The mites which cause ear canker will spread quickly within the herd. Isolate affected animals. Apply a drop or two of baby oil to suffocate the offending mites, and repeat the treatment in 10 to 14 days. Effective remedies are available which contain insecticides and fungistats.

Mastitis

Symptoms: Tender, sore, or swollen milk glands with bluish coloring. Severe cases may be abscessed.

Cause: An injury to the milk glands. The doe may have bruised herself when jumping into the nest box, or damaged herself on sharp objects such as nails, wires, rough edges of the nest box. This is also caused by a bacterial infection entering the system, and young from an infected doe should not be placed in the nest box of an unaffected doe.

Treatment: Sanitize the nest box and hutch after each litter. Remove any sharp object within the hutch, and ensure that each litter box has one side considerably lower than the other three. Treat with combiotic or other antibiotic by injection continuing for 2 days after symptoms have disappeared.

Snuffles

Symptoms: Snuffles is called by many breeders the common cold in rabbits because of the nasal discharge. There may be sneezing prior to the runny nose, and the affected rabbit try's to wipe away the discharge with his front paws.

Cause: An infection entering the mucous membranes of the nasal passages due to stress and lowered resistance.

Treatment: Treat the entire herd by administering a water soluble antibiotic such as Aureomycin in the drinking water. Follow the manufacturer's directions on the package, usually 1 teaspoon to every 5 gallons of water. Do not use metal water containers while using this medication.

An antibiotic such as Penicillin or Combiotic may be given by injection. Do not use two medications at the same time.

Stress

Symptoms: All growing and breeding animals are under stress. Also, stress is seen in animals which are hauled to and from shows or otherwise moved from their normal quarters. Extremes of temperature, poor diet, parasites, illness, and strange visitors are other causes of stress. There may be diarrhea, unthriftiness, loss of weight, and in the case of pregnant does, aborted litters.

Causes: Any situation which puts a strain on the emotional or physical condition of the animal.

Treatment: Use a vitamin mixed with the water and feed a highly nutritional diet. Avoid drafty quarters or overheated quarters which may cause bucks to go sterile. Treat disease and parasites as quickly as they become recognized.

Slobbers

Symptoms: The rabbit will be wet about the face or throat, and the face may be swollen.

Cause: The feeding of fresh greens in excessive amounts when the digestive system is not accustomed to them. A sudden change in diet from pellets to greens is harsh on the animal's system and any change should be made gradually.

An abscessed molar tooth may also be the cause.

Treatment: Discontinue the green feed until the conditions clears itself. Do not give more greens than a rabbit will eat in 30 minutes time. Where a tooth is involved, it can be removed.

Tapeworm larvae

Symptoms: There are no symptoms of tapeworm larvae in the live rabbit. Examination of the liver tissue will disclose white streaks, or there may be small, white cysts attached to the membranes on the stomach or intestines.

Treatment: No treatment is available. Prevention is the method of control. As it is brought into the rabbitry by dogs and cats with the parasite. These animals should not have access to the feed, water, or nest material.

Ketosis

Symptoms: The rabbit refuses to eat, usually after kindling and following a normal pregnancy.

Cause: This is a metabolic disorder which releases ketone bodies into the blood stream. The presence of ketones prevents hunger and produces the normal action of the body to absorb body fat. This in turn causes weight loss and eventual death.

Treatment: A change of diet is effective. Changing from pellets to alfalfa hay and grain will stimulate an interest in food. Also, adding sugar or molasses to the drinking water will get sugar into the blood stream rapidly and stop the manufacture of ketones. Does that are heavy producers of mild are more generally affected by ketosis.

Vent disease

Symptoms: The appearance of blisters or scabs on the genitals. Swollen genitals.

Cause: Vent disease is highly contagious and is frequently referred to among rabbit raisers as rabbit syphilis. If left untreated the rabbit will become a dormant carrier of the disease without any outward symptoms. It can then be transmitted to unborn young. The disease is caused by a bacteria.

It is possible to confuse vent disease with fungal or urine infection caused by unsanitary bedding. For proper diagnoses, consult your veterinarian and have laboratory tests run.

Treatment: Wash the genital area with warm water and a mild soap. Apply an antibiotic ointment daily until the condition improves. Where solid floors are used, the straw or other litter material should be changed daily.

An injection of Penicillin or Combiotic may be given deep into the rear leg muscle. Consult the package insert for dosage and continue injections for 2 days after the disappearance of the symptoms.

Orchitis

Symptoms: Inflammation of the testicles.

Cause: Bacteria which is transmitted from one rabbit to another during mating. Unclean cages and hutch floors.

Treatment: It is best to cull the affected buck from the herd rather to attempt treatment with antibiotics.

Metritis

Symptoms: A white, thick putrid discharge 7 to 10 days after breeding has taken place. This infection can invade the uteri and cause sterility in the doe.

Treatment: The infection is difficult to reach and it is recommended that affected does be culled from the herd as they may cause bucks to develop orchitis.

Malocclusion or buck teeth

Symptoms: Loss of weight. Possible drooling and wetness about the mouth. Lower teeth that curve upward into the mouth, and upper teeth that curve inward into the mouth.

Cause: This is a hereditary condition where the upper or lower jaw is too long or too short. Rabbits must be able to gnaw on objects to keep the teeth worn down. Where the teeth do not meet properly, the proper gnawing action is lacking to wear them down, and the teeth continue to grow. Death will result unless treatment is available.

Treatment: Using a pair of sharp wire nippers, temporary relief can be given by clipping the incisors. This will give relief and the rabbit can eat. However, since the condition is hereditary, the animal should not be used for breeding. With proper selection of breeding stock this condition is easily eliminated in future generations.

Spray leg

Symptoms: Young rabbits with difficulty in standing. The legs spread away from the body and the animal sprawls on its belly. The very young rabbit will eat satisfactorily, but as it grows and gains weight moving about becomes more difficult. Once weaning occurs so that the doe does not enter the nest box to nurse the litter, spray leg causes the growing youngster to find difficulty in reaching the feed. Soon it gives up and dies.

Cause: This is another hereditary condition which can be eliminated through careful selection of breeding stock. The bones and muscles of the young never develop strength and there may even be some malformation of the hip joint.

Treatment: Dispose of young rabbits that show signs of having spray leg.

Heat prostration

Symptoms: Rapid breathing, prostration, and blood-tinged fluid emerging from the nostrils and mouth in severe cases.

Cause: Does that are due to kindle and overweight, older rabbits are most susceptible to extreme outside temperatures. Rabbits are heat sensitive animals.

Treatment: Reduce the temperature of surrounding air by spraying with water. Place wet blankets or frozen jugs of water inside the cages for the rabbits to lie on or near to reduce body temperature.

Myxomatosis

Symptoms: Inflammation and swelling of the eyes, ears, nose and genitals accompanied with a high fever. The death rate among mature animals is high.

Cause: This is a virus infection affecting rabbits only along the west coast of the United States, Mexico, and South America. It is spread by biting insects such as mosquitoes.

Treatment: The best control is prevention since there is no cure. Spray or drain mosquito breeding places. There is a vaccine proven to be effective in the prevention of Myxomatosis.

Warbles

Symptoms: Irritated, raised areas under the skin usually on the back, neck, or flanks. Movement can be felt under the skin. A visible hole.

Cause: This is the larval stage of a bot fly which has entered under the skin and feeds upon tissue. It obtains oxygen from the hole in the skin and must frequently surface to breath.

Treatment: A drop of chloroform or ether on the larvae will quiet it for easy removal with a pair of tweezers or forceps. The larvae may be as much as 1 1/2 inches in length. After removal, apply a skin antiseptic to the wound.

Skin mange

Symptoms: Intense itching, red, scaly skin, loss of hair. A crust of yellow, dried blood serum may be present.

Cause: A microscopic mite that burrows under the skin.

Treatment: Dust with a powder especially for external parasites such as fleas. Use two dustings, one week apart. Δ

Just for kids — feather your vest

By Lucy Shober

A magic jacket

Pretend that you have found a jacket covered in thousands of magic zippers. As you try it on, you realize that it will carry you to anywhere in the world your heart desires.

If you decide to spend the week on an ice flow in Alaska, your magic jacket keeps you snug and warm. If a balmy Carolina beach is the next choice, you whisk yourself south and bask in the noon-time sun. The magic zipper jacket will protect you from heat and rain. You can even use it as a float while you relax in the warm ocean tides.

A bird's jacket

The next time you spot a stray feather in the yard, pick it up and examine it to see why every bird has it's own magic zipper jacket.

If you use a magnifying glass you can see that each **vane** of the feather is covered with hundreds of tiny **barbs**.

As a bird preens, (passes its beak over it's feathers) it locks these barbs together to form an air and water tight raincoat. Water birds have a small button above their tail feathers which is full of oil. As they preen, the oil is passed over the zippers, making them act like miniature life preservers.

That's why ducks float

That's why ducks float! When a bird is cold on a drizzly winter day, it's feathers are fluffed up to make pockets which trap body heat. On hot days, the feathers are flattened close to the body so that heat is free to escape.

We humans have found plenty of our own uses for bird feathers. We've borrowed them for everything from down filled pillows and sleeping bags to plumage covered hats and jewelry.

The next time you find a sizable feather, save it, examine it, then use it as Thomas Jefferson would have — as a quill pen! Have an adult help you to follow the directions below. While you wait for the perfect magic zipper to drop out of the sky, see if you know the answers to these feathery questions:

Three feathery questions

● 1. Why are flamingo feathers pink?

Answer: They absorb color from shrimp that they eat. If flamingos had another type of diet, their plumage would be white.

● 2. Why is a vulture bald-headed?

Answer: If vultures had head feathers, they would become matted and filthy. Being a baldy lets the vulture thrust it's head deep into the bodies of dead animals that it feasts upon.

● 3. What bird has soft combs extending from the edges of it's flight feathers?

Answer: The owl. These little combs break up the air so that unlike most birds, the owl glides through the night noiselessly (watch out mice!).

Make a quill pen

Find a large feather with a sturdy quill. Have an adult use an Exacto knife or single edged razor blade to shave the tip of the quill so that it is flat on one side. Now insert a tooth pick or match tip into the center of the quill to remove the crusty interior. Lay the feather on a flat surface with the shaved side up, then carefully use the

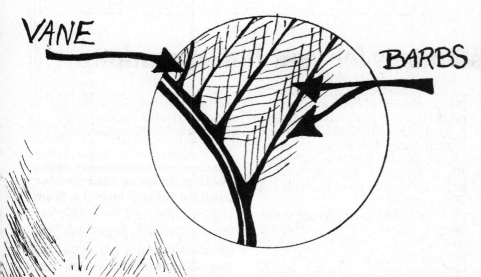

VANE

BARBS

tip of your blade to slice a **vertical** cut into the center of the quill. If the tip of the feather seems to be uneven, slice it so that both ends are flat and of the same length. If you want to make a fancier pen, you can strip some of the "vanes" from the base so that it's easier to hold. To create a set of different colored pens, you can wash the feathers in soap and water, then tint them with food coloring. Dip your finished product into ink or water based paint or food coloring, then practice your writing technique!Δ

FRONT & SIDE VIEW OF QUILL PEN

I Like This Place

You know, I like this place,
I really do.
It's rough, run down,
The buildings beyond paint
But in its half wild rustic state—
Somehow it speaks to me—
Telling of people not afraid
To let a tree grow wild,
And secure enough to let each
Flower or weed grow free.
Someday these people will be gone.
Then the grove will be pruned
And mowed, the land subdued.
Birds will wing on past,
Deer won't flit through the woods.
Even squirrels and rabbits won't linger
And I won't like this place any more.
I really won't.

Janet K. Collins
Conrad, IA

Why I like living in the country

An essay by
Scotty Matthews (age 7)
Centralia, Missouri

I like the country because I can make stuff. I make clubhouses and I like to dig in the dirt. I like to make little tiny houses. I like the country because you can fish and hunt.

When Dad takes me hunting with him sometimes I bring my BB gun. Sometimes I shoot it. I get to see wild animals. I have seen squirrels and deer and rabbits and wild turkeys and cardinals and blue jays sometimes. I don't shoot anything because Dad says I am not old enough yet.

I eat healthy food that we grow in our garden. One time I planted tomatoes and my plants had more tomatoes than Mom's plants.

We are going to move up to Canada and live in the mountains. Up there you have to be 10 years old to hunt. There are rivers with rocks in them. There are bears and moose and it gets really cold in the winter. The land where we will live has a big beaver lake where we can go fishing in the summer and skating in the winter. If you look on the pond up there where my mom and dad are going to live with me and if you look up there in Canada you'll see that you might like it in the summer a lot. Now, do you like it?

Today is Tuesday and my dad's name is Scott and my brother's name is "Beezer". My mom's name is Ann and my twin brothers' names are Bobby and T.J. My last brother is Andy.

What I want to say last is when it's fall you can swim in the leaves and your mom and dad will like it too.

I wish everybody could be as happy as me and live in the country. It's not really nice in the towns but it's really nice in the country. It's nice in the towns sometimes too. Δ

Don't spend a lot of money for your house windows

By Martin Harris

Don't spend a lot for a muffler. Don't spend a lot for house windows either. For, truth be told, the huge variation in retail window price conceals the fact that all major window manufacturers build products which are almost identical in terms of thermal performance.

Manufacturers which are considered the Tiffany of the industry (and price their product accordingly) don't actually create and sell a product much different, energy-wise, from those sold by more modest firms. Conversely, you'll get just about the same thermal quality from a less promotion-oriented manufacturer who doesn't have so much overhead tied up in color TV advertising.

Advertising is, indeed, the place to start this analysis. That's because of two facts.

Black holes of energy loss

One: Compared to any other part of the building envelope—walls, floors, or roof-ceiling assemblies—windows are black holes of energy loss. That's true of even the best products on the market.

Consider these R-value numbers, which reflect energy efficiency of building components: most housing today is built with overhead insulation to the R-38 level, walls to R-19, foundations to R-10 (that's 12 inches of fiberglass, for example, in the overhead; 6 inches in the walls; and a couple of inches of closed-cell bead board around the foundation). Even the very best of super-high-tech windows don't get up to R-5.

Two: Compared to the overall building envelope, windows are only a tiny percentage of the total square footage exposed to the weather. In most housing, for example, windows are less than 15 percent of floor area, and the rule of thumb is that usable floor area is about a fifth of total exterior surface. A 1200 square-foot house, for example, would have less than 180 square feet of surface in windows, while it would have about 6000 square feet of walls and roof.

So, in a typical house, glazing makes up only 3% of total heat-losing (or -gaining) surface. Even if you swap out all your windows and double their thermal efficiency, you aren't going to make much of a dent in your total heating (or cooling) costs.

You may make a very noticeable difference in occupant comfort by going to a better window: that's because both kinds of window energy loss—radiation and drafts—are very noticeable to people who sit or work near inefficient glazing. If the glazing is really inefficient and drafty, improvements may even show up in your energy bills.

Going from a 19th century window which fits its frame reasonably well to a 21st century unit with high-tech double-glazing and poly coatings, therefore, won't gain you more than 3 points on the scale of R-values. That's not much, considering the typical cost differential between units of these two types.

Typical Glazing Characteristics				
Glazing type	R-value	Shading coeff.	Vis. trans.	Perf. index
Single-glazed clear	0.90	1.00	90%	0.90
SG gray-tinted	0.90	0.69	43%	0.62
SG bronze-tinted	0.90	0.71	52%	0.73
SG green-tinted	0.90	0.71	75%	1.09
SG reflective	0.90	0.51	27%	0.53
SG low-E clear	1.40	0.74	84%	1.14
SG low-E gray	1.40	0.50	41%	0.82
SG low-E bronze	1.40	0.52	49%	0.94
SG low-E green	1.40	0.56	71%	1.27
Double-glazed clear	2.00	0.84	80%	0.95
DG gray-tinted	2.00	0.56	39%	0.69
DG bronze-tinted	2.00	0.59	47%	0.80
DG green-tinted	2.00	0.60	68%	1.13
DG reflective	2.00	0.42	26%	0.62
DG low-E clear	3.12	0.67	76%	1.13
DG low-E gray	3.12	0.42	37%	0.88
DG low-E bronze	3.12	0.44	44%	1.00
DG low-E green	3.12	0.47	64%	1.36
DG poly film clear	4.50	0.42	53%	1.26
DG poly film gray	4.50	0.27	26%	0.96
DG poly film bronze	4.50	0.29	32%	1.10
DG poly film green	4.50	0.29	45%	1.55

Source: Lawrence Berkeley Laboratory's Window 3.0 program

Table 1. This tabulation, courtesy of Consulting & Specifying Engineer (C&SE), shows the narrow range of R-values between the simplest, single glazing at .90, to the most advanced, double glazed with poly film at 4.5. Even a low-cost window-quilt drape will give you an R of 7 or so.

But, most likely, you won't. That's because even the most traditional of windows—single-pane glazing and a storm window—has an R-value of R-2, while the best on the market is under R-5. Going from a 19th century window which fits its frame reasonably well to a 21st century unit with high-tech double-glazing and poly coatings, therefore, won't gain you more than 3 points on the scale of R-values. That's not much, considering the typical cost differential between units of these two types.

Next, get the manufacturer's catalog. Practically all will tell you, on a reference page, the exact performance of each window style and size compared to one of those standards. There's only one difference: sometimes they'll give the total infiltration for a given size window, sometimes the infiltration per lineal foot.

Here are some manufacturers and their performance results for double-hung windows, taken from recent catalogs:

- Andersen double-hung — .17 CFM per LF
- Marvin double-hung — .14 CFM per LF
- Pella double-hung — .13 CFM per LF
- Weathershield double-hung — .12 CFM per LF

Although these manufacturers vary considerably in retail pricing, they all out-perform the industry infiltration standard by a wide margin and by more or less the same amount.

If manufacturers don't vary much in their ability to produce draft-free windows, they vary even less in their ability to raise the R-value of glazing. Very simply, each separate pane of ordinary glass has an R-value of about 1, so that a double-glazed (sometimes called insulated glass) window will have an R-value of about 2—the same as an old-fashioned single-glazed unit with storm window.

As Table 1 shows, the addition of various tints or films will affect the R-value somewhat, but it will affect the window price even more. Table 2 shows how the price range, in dollars per square foot of glazing, goes up as

more sophistication is employed in manufacture.

My conclusions are simple:

- select your windows on the basis of price, performance, and design/appearance
- go for the lower cost products and put your savings into real energy savers, like high-R-value window quilts for drapes
- keep window square footage low unless you're specifically designing for solar heat gain.

Let's take a closer look at design/appearance. We have only a few choices for operational design:

- the side-hinged or casement unit
- the top-hinged or awning unit
- the bottom-hinged or hopper unit
- the horizontal slider
- the vertical slider or double-hung unit.

In general, the casements have the best infiltration numbers and the sliders have the poorest, while the double-hungs are somewhere in between; but the variations aren't enough to base a style choice on. Style choice is usually based on looks, the double-hung being considered the most traditional, even though casements and horizontal sliders go back many centuries earlier in Europe.

Awnings and hoppers are a little out of fashion currently, for two reasons; they became associated with institutional design; and they haven't overcome the poor infiltration reputation they acquired decades ago, even though it's no longer accurate.

Very simply, each separate pane of ordinary glass has an R-value of about 1, so that a double-glazed (sometimes called insulated glass) window will have an R-value of about 2—the same as an old-fashioned single-glazed unit with storm window.

Comparative Costs of Glazings in 1991	
Glass type	**Dollars/ sq. ft.**
Single-glazed	$3.00
SG tinted	3.75
SG reflective	5.50
Double-glazed	8.00
DG tinted	8.75
DG reflective	10.00
DG low-E	10.50
DG low-E poly film	11.00

Source: Southern California Edison's "Design for Excellence" brochure

Table 2. This tabulation, also courtesy of C&SE, illustrates how rapidly glazing prices climb as the product becomes more technically complex. For a typical 12-square-foot window, the price range is even greater: from less than $50 at a discount millwork outlet to more than $300 through franchise or industry

It's not so here in New England, but for the country as a whole, the casement is currently the most popular among home-owners and builders.

Usually, they're purchased as double-glazed units, needing no storm sash. An interior screen usually comes with the unit, which therefore has to be crank-operated. Some units come with lever-type closure handles to insure a tight seal when the unit is closed.

In New England, and elsewhere in the country where owners want a traditional appearance, the double-hung is still popular. In fact, it's become so popular that manufacturers are now again offering long-obsolete styles, with one sash larger than the other, with small panes, with historically accurate muntin bars (the dividers between panes) inside and out.

Even major manufacturers which for years refused to offer anything beyond plastic snap-in grills have now bowed to market pressure and are now offering double-hungs which look fully authentic. Double-hungs are available with insulated glass and similar expensive niceties, just like all other styles,

Figure 1. This illustration, courtesy Andersen Corporation, shows a traditional double-hung unit. Such authentic-appearing units with excellent energy-efficiency qualities are now available from all major manufacturers.

but most buyers seeking a traditional appearance buy them as single-glazed units with a separate storm/screen combination.

Hoppers and awnings are simply casements turned on their sides; not as popular as they used to be, but still available from most manufacturers. The screen problem requires awnings to be crank-operated, while hoppers can be set by hand, usually with hinge friction or counterweights to hold them at the selected tilt.

Horizontal sliders in smaller sizes are even less popular; in the largest sizes we see them as patio doors.

Fixed-glazed windows

And, of course, there's always fixed glazing, windows which are built into a surrounding frame and are non-operable. These are becoming increasingly popular for three reasons:

- You can have any geometrical shape or size you like. Most manufacturers will build to order, using single, double, or even triple glazing. Many do-it-yourselfers find it easy to buy the glazing in stock sizes and build it into the wall themselves.
- You can save a bundle on the window costs in your construc-

tion budget by going to fixed glazing.
- Recent advances in low-cost mechanical ventilation units make it possible to reduce the amount of operable glazing that used to be needed for natural ventilation.

Roof-windows, skylights

There's also roof-top glazing; those units called skylights or roof-windows. The basic design principle goes back to Victorian times, with glass set into steel frames, but it lost popularity because of problems with leakage and condensation, with poor energy-efficiency, even with access for cleaning.

Within the last score of years, skylighting has made a comeback: new roof-windows are now typically glazed in a slight bubble-shape, in residential sizes from 2 feet square on up. Energy, leakage and condensation problems have been solved, but at a price: typically, these units are not cheap. It's been my experience that a homeowner can put a dormer with standard window on his upstairs bedroom for less cost than he can install an equal size roof-window.

Finally, I'll mention the non-standard window market. It falls into two categories: local enterprises which

focus on recycling old sash and millwork from altered or demolished buildings, and other enterprises, also local, which focus on custom-manufacture of sash and millwork.

Windows are available, in all sorts of styles and sizes, from salvage operations which range from real junkyards to up-scale architectural-detail outlets. Costs vary widely, but even the most expensive offer second-hand products at a fraction of their modern reproduction price. Sometimes only sash units are available, but frames can be custom-built to their dimensions; conversely, for the purchaser who buys some handsome old intricate frames, most manufacturers now offer custom sash sized to fit.

Windows are also available from small custom manufacturers who can make up about anything you'd want. The infiltration performance of units manufactured at the small industry level isn't likely to be quite as high as for those manufactured by industry giants, but that doesn't matter to customers who prefer to control the design they want or to deal with local artisans. Such producers can't compete in price with the stock products of the industry giants, but their overhead is low and they can usually produce at prices competitive with the custom items of the big names in the industry.

It's been my experience that a homeowner can put a dormer with standard window on his upstairs bedroom for less cost than he can install an equal size roof-window.

In short, windows are about like any other product in the American economy. Yes, there's misleading advertising; there's also amazing quality. There's a broad range of products at a broad range of prices. And yes, the industry does respond, although not overnight, to new trends in consumer demand. The uninformed buyer won't do well in this marketplace; but the informed buyer will. And that is what the free market is all about. Δ

A saddle shop created self sufficiency for Idaho family

*Story and photos
By Rosemary LeVernier*

Cliff Stansell had had enough. He was tired of traveling, tired of being away from his home and family, and tired of the daily rat race associated with working for someone else. So, he turned his lifelong interest in horses into a thriving homebased business.

Cliff, 40, is a tall, dark-haired custom saddle maker who is as much at home in his shop as he is the woods, working with horses, or playing the fiddle. His soft-spoken, easygoing manners put those around him at ease.

The "lack of people" drew him to northern Idaho from his native Gold Beach, Oregon in 1974. After moving to the small logging town of Priest River, Idaho, he worked at his trained profession of surveyor for many years. But surveying jobs took him all over the northwest, and away from home and his wife and two children for extended periods of time.

"I didn't want to do that anymore," he said. "I needed something that would keep me home and give me a livelihood — and something I wanted to do."

A saddle business seemed a natural choice for Cliff, who had worked with horses most of his life.

Saddle-making school

The nearest saddle making course was in Spokane, Washington, a 90-minute drive in good weather. Five days a week for two years, Cliff made the 150-mile round trip commute from his home to Spokane Falls Community College, and spent six hours a day in class.

"You get out of it what you put into it," he said, "I figured this was going to be my livelihood, so I would go to school, then sometimes I'd go to a saddle shop after school to learn firsthand from other saddle makers. Then I'd

Cliff Stansell in his saddle shop north of Priest River, Idaho, sewing leather.

come home and work until 10 or 11 o'clock every night."

He opened Stansell Saddlery at a rented shop in downtown Priest River in 1984. Five years later, Cliff was ready to move the shop to his cabin 12 miles north of town in the woods, something he had planned from the start. "I figured I had to put in my time in town until I got established," he explained.

"Now, I don't get the walk-through traffic I got in town, which is good and bad," Cliff said. "It's bad because I don't sell little retail items or do repair jobs that I normally got in town. But it's good because I get my work done. In town, I was there 8 or 10 hours everyday, and half of it was talking to people." With a chuckle, he added, "I like talking to people, but you have to get your work done too."

Photovoltaic power

The move home presented a problem — no electricity. For years, Cliff

The Stansell family (left to right: Cliff, Ben, Betsy, Katie enjoy a musical evening at home.

and his family used kerosene lamps, wood heat, and a propane stove and refrigerator in the log cabin they built. But some of Cliff's saddlery tools required power, so he turned to the sun for a solution.

Now his 1,000-square foot cabin and 300-foot shop are powered with electricity produced from photovoltaic panels mounted on the cabin's roof. They turn sunlight into electricity, which is stored in 12-volt nickel cadmium batteries and run through an inverter to provide AC power.

"I wanted to stay off the (power) grid," Cliff said. "I wanted to be more self-sufficient and eliminate another monthly bill."

The solar system cost was far less than the $10,000 the utility company wanted to run in electricity from the nearest power line half a mile away.

Winter's lack of sunshine doesn't worry Cliff. He simply plugs his batteries into his truck's alternator and lets it idle for a few hours each week to charge them.

"I didn't expect to have power, so it was a luxury when we got it," said Cliff's wife Betsy. "I couldn't do without it now," she laughed.

For daughter Katie, 12, electricity means listening to her favorite tapes, watching television and videos, and playing her electric keyboard. Son Ben, 6, is more interested in helping Pop than thinking about electricity.

The leather business

Out in the shop, where the stitchers, grinder, and lights hum along happily on sunpower, Cliff shared a bit about his trade.

"There's quite a price difference between good quality and poor quality leather, hardware, and saddle tools," said Cliff. "There's also a tremendous quality difference. To me, if you skimp on quality in the materials, then you're going to skimp on other things too."

He uses leather tanned with bark instead of chemical-tanned leather which breaks down more quickly. "If you take good care of a saddle and the leather is good quality, then it'll last for 100 years easy," he said.

Cliff Stansell and horse Rusty head for home.

"I've got about 60 hours into a plain saddle," he said. "I'm a little bit slower than a lot of saddle makers, but if I went faster I'd probably be cutting corners. I'm more of a perfectionist."

Cliff's base price for a saddle is $1200. "I've seen factory made saddles for $250. I've got about $600 just into materials."

"I do the best job I can and I'm fair with the price," he said. "I think it's important to be a service to the community. When people lose that, they start ripping people off."

To a limited degree, Cliff has displayed and sold his handiwork at various horse shows. Now, his plan is to start selling more of his items at the working cowboy shows. He feels the shows will be a good source of potential clients. "The people who appreciate the quality of the work are the ones who use the stuff the hardest," he said.

He also plans to branch off into mail orders, and is currently putting together a catalog of his products. In addition to making saddles and doing repair work on saddles and leather items, Cliff's handiwork includes briefcases, chaps, gun scabbards, bridles, belts, knife sheaths, hatchet satchels, and family album covers.

Betsy helps her husband in the shop. "I do mostly finish work, like slicking

and oiling saddles," she said. She also cleans saddles, does small repairs, braids leather, makes small items such as leather straps, and does the paperwork.

When not in his shop, Cliff can often be found working with his Percheron-class horses. He uses them for logging, haying, plowing snow, and riding. He enjoys working with the horses because it gets him out in the woods and moving around.

He's always willing to work out trades for his work. He once made a saddle in exchange for a truck, and has accepted building materials and labor in exchange for horse logging.

"To me, this is the ideal setup" he said, gazing out over the hayfields and forest visible from his shop. "A day where it's raining I can be inside doing leather work, and on nice days I can be outside working with the horses."

(If you think you might have some saddle-making for Cliff to do, his address is P.O. Box 959, Priest River, ID 83856. Tel.: (208) 448-2711.) Δ

November/December 1992
No. 18
$3.50 U.S.
$4.50 Canada

Backwoods
Home magazine

... a practical journal of self reliance!

REMEMBERING
MOTHER'S KITCHEN

A CELLAR THAT WORKS

ONE WOMAN'S FARM

AUSTRALIAN SHEPHERDS

ROPE AS A TOOL

PREDICTING WEATHER

HEALTHY HOLIDAY BAKING

Don Childers

Note from the publisher

Three cheers for Willits' energy show

The Solar Energy Expo and Rally (SEER) in Willits, California, was a great experience for us. Friendly people, eye-opening exhibits into our energy future, and a beautiful tree-shaded spot for our booth. Not only was it a well organized show with as much attention paid to the comfort of the exhibitors as was paid to the comfort of the attendees, but we took more subscriptions there than at any previous show.

We also met a number of subscribers. One, who had previously bought Don Wilson's *Crayfish Farming* book from us, said he had put crayfish in his catfish pond in an attempt to breed them. "They (the catfish) thought they were delicious," he told me with a big laugh. Another guy made a similar mistake by placing the crayfish in his bass pond. "Those bass never ate so good," he said. So that's a lesson for all you crayfish entrepreneurs: be careful where you plant the tasty critters.

Halfway through the first day of the show a customer took a calling card from the plastic holder on my exhibit table, read it, and asked me, "Your name Ilene?" I looked at the card and discovered I had been giving out my wife's cards as my own. Details have always been my weak point.

This is one of two major alternative energy shows in the country. The other, the Midwest Renewable Energy Fair at Amherst, Wisconsin, is as good as SEER I am told. We had to cancel out of that show earlier in the year because of a scheduling conflict. Next year we'll exhibit at both shows and give you plenty of advance information about them.

Preparedness show in Salt Lake City

Best show coming up for the remainder of this year is the Preparedness Show November 5, 6, and 7 at the Salt Palace Center in Salt Lake City, Utah. Mormons play a major role in this show, and for good reason. As a group they are experts when it comes to "being prepared." I had met only a few Mormons before I visited Salt Lake City for my first Preparedness Show there last year, but I have come to know many since then.

Mormons are practical survivalists, much like the way I view survivalism and preparedness. They are not screwballs who see doom around every corner, but pragmatists who believe in prudent planning so that they are ready for any emergency. Chances are good that any Mormons caught up in the recent hurricanes, fires, and floods in this country were not taken totally off guard. They are always prepared for such emergencies.

And if you want to see a big city that not only works, but is beautiful and one in which you feel safe while taking a walk at night, visit Salt Lake City. You'll probably ask yourself the question: "Why can't other cities do this?"

Lifemates found in "PERSONALS"

I am happy to report that two readers have informed me that they have found mates through ads in our "PERSONALS" in the classified ads at the end of the magazine. Congratulations! We give a half price discount to individuals using the "PERSONALS" category, so it's nice to see the ads paying off for some people.

How this issue's cover came to be

As a study for the cover for this issue, Don Childers used a photograph taken by Robert L. Williams III, of Lawndale, North Carolina. Robert was four years old when he took the photo, and we printed it on page 17 of Issue No. 17. Don turned the photo's summer scene into a winter scene. He also changed a few other details as you'll see by comparing this cover to last issue's photo.

We now pay writers in advance

As many of our contributing writers are painfully aware, we often take a long time to get back to a writer who has submitted an article to us. This has changed. Thanks to the help of Don Fallick, who was in Utah preparing to take his wife-to-be home to Washington to get married, but interrupted his plans for a week and flew to *BHM's* offices in Oregon to help us out from under the pile of manuscripts here, we've caught up.

And we've also changed our policy on paying the many excellent writers who contribute to *BHM*. We now pay writers of articles in advance of publication. It will be better for the writers and better for us because we'll make quicker "accept" or "reject" decisions on articles and won't fall so far behind again.

The Breadboard

As I write this I'm sitting in The Breadboard restaurant in Ashland, Oregon having breakfast with Lenie and Jacob. We come here about once a week and usually use the occasion to plan articles for the next issue.

This restaurant is small but great. The owner—Tim Richardi—is also the cook, giving the food that good personal touch only an owner-operated business can have.

One-year-old Jacob always sits in his highchair at the end of our table, sloshing around in his bananas and cheerios and eating the occasional scraps of toast, egg, and broccoli we give him. He has been a great help to me in my attempt to lose about 15 pounds of excess weight I have accumulated since starting *BHM* nearly four years ago.

Midway through breakfast Jakey inevitably gives me a mouth-full-of-food smile. As the food oozes past his two bottom teeth and down his chin, I give him a half-hearted smile, stop eating, and delve into the pile of magazine work I bring to the breakfast table. Thanks to Jakey, I seldom finish the delicious food at The Breadboard, get a lot of work done, and have lost a few pounds. Δ

My View

Rewriting the Bill of Rights

Russian Communists and German Nazis were the most efficient rewriters of history. Both were ruthless in the beginning, killing anyone who disagreed with the new histories that supported their peculiarly warped ideologies.

The Nazis, fortunately, were defeated in war, but the Russians (the Soviets) continued to rewrite history with ideological fervor, discovering in the process that it was easier to teach the historical lies to the nation's youths than it was to kill millions of unbelieving adults, although they did still manage to kill or forcibly reeducate millions of unbelievers.

Now that the Russian system has collapsed under the weight of its own lies, that discredited socialist ideology seems to have found a new home—here in the United States—and the rewriters of history are at work again.

Here's one example: Eric Grig of Boone, North Carolina, went into a North Carolina bookstore and asked the clerk if he had a book on the Constitution of the United States. The clerk gave him a book titled, <u>The Constitution of the United States</u> by Floyd G. Cullop. Mr. Grig sent the book to me.

Cullop, who has taught history for 17 years to junior and senior high school students in Tennessee, has a simple premise for his book: "The United States Constitution is often difficult to read and understand." So he sets out to explain it, not just with his personal opinions but with his rewriting of what the Constitution actually says.

Here is the most glaring example: Part III of the book is titled, "The Bill of Rights." The Second Amendment, according to Cullop, is written as follows:

Amendment 2. Right to Bear Arms

For their protection and for purposes of having a well trained militia the people of the states may keep and bear (own) arms (weapons), but the federal government or the state governments may pass laws against owning certain weapons and the way others may be used.

Now, anyone casually familiar with the U.S. Constitution knows that that is not how the Second Amendment reads. It reads as follows:

A well-regulated militia, being necessary to the security of a free State, the right of the people to keep and bear arms, shall not be infringed.

However you may interpret those words, those are the words. There's nothing in it about government being able to "pass laws against owning certain weapons and the way others may be used," as Mr. Cullop asserts.

Like so many ideological zealots before him, Cullop's attempt to rewrite history—in this case the most important historical document this nation has—cannot stand up to

Dave Duffy

the scrutiny of an informed adult like Mr. Grig of North Carolina, but it could easily get by a younger person, such as the junior and senior highschoolers Cullop has been teaching for 17 years. And I think that's exactly the intention of Mr. Cullop—to hoodwink younger readers so they will grow up to believe what is simply an ideological lie.

Mr. Cullop is not unlike many in the mass media who routinely distort current events and history to promote their own ideology. In this particular case Mr. Cullop obviously believes guns should be controlled somehow, and he knows that the only way guns can be controlled is if the Constitution is somehow distorted to read that the Government can change the Second Amendment simply by passing a law. Cullop, like the Russians, is in it for the long haul—he's hoping to pollute those young minds for the future.

To be fair, Mr. Cullop does give the real Constitution at the end of the book, long after the damage has been done.

Fifteen reasons to vote in November

While we're on the subject of writers distorting the truth, have you noticed that the mass media has lined up staunchly against "term limits?" Nine out of 10 editorials in the press warn of the dangers of term limits. One editorialist at one of my local papers, the *Medford Mail Tribune*, suggested that term limits was a remedy that would be worse than the disease of having an inept entrenched political establishment. That's like saying a promising experimental cancer treatment should not be tried because it may kill the terminally-ill patient.

Term limits to limit federal officeholders has already been enacted in Colorado, and 15 more states will vote on similar initiatives this November. The states are: California, Florida, Michigan, Ohio, Washington, Oregon, Nevada, Arizona, Wyoming, Nebraska, Missouri, Arkansas, North Dakota, South Dakota, and Montana.

In my opinion these term limit initiatives will not only not kill the patient, but will be the first step in wrestling the country back from the professional quacks who have been misgoverning the nation. Ignore the mass media editorialists; they're in bed with the quacks. Δ

How to build an inexpensive cellar that works

By R. Lee Rose

The trouble with gardens is that the short life of our surplus produce forces us to either jam everything into our freezers, dry it, or can everything immediately—or (more often) give our excess away to friends.

The cellar is an old invention that takes some of the pressure off the preservation activities, and even keeps some foods all winter in quite good condition without significant processing. Probably some Neanderthal family discovered that food wilted less rapidly in summer, and kept from frost damage better when stored in the family cave instead of being left out in the dooryard.

Okay, so a cellar is a glorified hole-in-the-ground. Some improvements have been discovered that are worth considering. I know. I built one cellar incorrectly, and came to realize its shortcomings. I did some research, and built a second one that serves us very well.

We live in a cold climate, (British Columbia, Canada) and find a cellar a virtual necessity to keep our fruit jars and root crops from freezing. However, I believe it would be a boon to a gardener in a warm climate, too, since produce deteriorates just as rapidly when stored in an environment that is too warm.

Excellent results

We find our cellar stores certain things better than others. Carrots, potatoes, yams, turnips, rutabagas, parsnips, and beets keep very well. Our last year's carrots and potatoes were still crisp and firm until May. We have even used the cellar as a convenient place to store latex paint, which is ruined by freezing. We store our carrots parsnips, and beets in buckets (or wooden boxes) of sawdust, but we simply place other root crops, and potatoes in the bins, or in cardboard boxes in the bins.

Good results

We successfully store cabbage, Brussels sprouts, onions, tree fruits and squash for a few weeks to several months, sometimes wrapping delicate items in little squares of newsprint, and placing them in shallow layers to prevent crushing. We usually tie our onions in bunches and dry them before storing, and hang our cabbages by their roots.

We have had very poor success with very soft bodied items, like tomatoes, eggplant, cucumbers, cauliflower, green vegetables, dried foods (except in jars) etc. In my opinion they would be better stored in the freezer, or dried and stored in dry containers.

Choosing the best location

First, you really need a small hill into which you can make an excavation. Otherwise, you will have to haul in a lot of fill. A cellar is not just an insulated shed, like the old fashioned ice house. In addition to insulating your

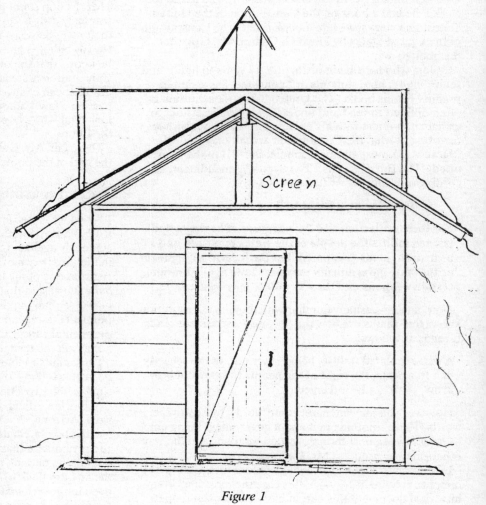

Figure 1

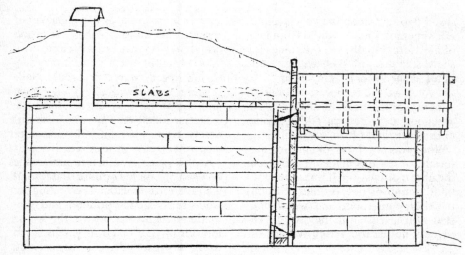

Figure 2

food from the cold outside, it really needs to absorb heat from the earth—which is, in fact, a large heat sink. So it must be surrounded, as much as possible, by earth.

Avoid choosing a spot at the base of a large ridge where a great deal of runoff comes spilling down after a heavy rain, or during spring thaws. We want the cellar to be moist inside, so foods won't dry out, but excessive water is a nuisance. If you absolutely must use such a location, you will have to dig a slanted ditch above the spot, and put in drainage tile, or washed gravel (or both) to divert the excess water.

Also avoid places where you have observed heavy drifting during winter snows. It is a pain to find your entrance blocked by a big drift. Sometimes, a new structure encourages—or may even prevent—drifting. You are going to have to make a judgment here.

Avoid locations where you see evidence of underground boulders. Heavy clay makes a firm foundation, but huge boulders, or massive rock can only be excavated by blasting. Similarly avoid places near large trees, because they may have numerous roots you will have to dig through, and they may send new roots in through your cellar wall, and cause damage to your walls or roof. Large aspen trees have a nasty habit of breaking off and falling on things we don't really want crushed, too.

Design features

Having an anteroom on your cellar offers some valuable benefits. We find it a great place to store empty canning jars, extra buckets, hose, garden tools (behind the doors), and even the wheelbarrow.

Equally important is the shelter it provides for the entrance of the inner room. It keeps wind-driven rain and snow from accumulating in the space between the thick beveled door and its casing, which would freeze and swell the door making it impossible to open. It also keeps moving soil from the walls from building up near the lower corners, and it prevents snowdrifts from piling against the door. I advise you to include one in your cellar plans.

Both rooms should be sloped downward for drainage. There will be seepage into your cellar, and it must have drainage. Dig your walls in so they will be level, and if you do not find heavy clay, or hardpan, you will need footings. These walls must support several

tons of earth. I did not build footings, and have had no movement, but your location may require it. I laid a plank down the center of my inner room, and filled around it with washed gravel to prevent having to step in mud. The plank is for the wheelbarrow, to keep its wheel from sinking in the soft clay. Notice the location of the ventilator shaft (Fig. 2). It's needed to carry excess atmospheric moisture out. It draws air in through the small cracks in the door casing. I keep it sealed in winter (by stuffing an old fertilizer bag in the bottom of the shaft), and in spring, when the weather begins to warm up, I open the inner door for more circulation.

You will see from Fig. 3 that the bins are wider than the shelves. This is to gain freer access to the bins, and prevent lumps on your head when you stand up from one of the bins. Speaking of headaches, you should adjust the height of the ceiling to match your own (or your friends') height. Avoid making it taller than you need, since a tall ceiling encourages circulation: cold air to the floor, and warm air to the ceiling. You might freeze your spuds that way.

Building materials

Expensive is not always the best. I have seen beautiful workmanship and some very successful cellars done in cement and stone masonry. I didn't have the time or money—or the masonry skills to use those materials, but they do have some advantages, and frankly, some disadvantages.

Cement and masonry is rot proof, and has greater strength—if it is reinforced with steel. It can be, but will not always be water tight. It is cleaner

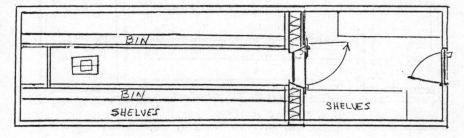

Figure 3

looking than wood, and can be swept out, or even scrubbed easier than one like mine. It is less likely to be invaded by insects and rodents.

The disadvantages I have seen are: the greater expense, the more difficult skills needed to work with stone or concrete, and the longer building time and labor to be expended on the project. Cracks in the structure may develop, and seepage may be a problem. Good drainage may be more difficult to achieve.

I had an acquaintance who built a beautiful stonework cellar (in a level place—below ground) in which water stood two feet deep the year around. His vegetables never wilted from lack of moisture. Finally, the fastenings for shelves, doors, and such are more difficult to anchor in a stone cellar.

If you have the resources to build in concrete or masonry, by all means do, and good luck. You can still use some of the basic ideas from my design.

Wood was my choice of building materials for reasons made obvious from the above discussion. It was quicker to build, requiring only ordinary carpentry skills and tools, and wood construction is easier to modify, or replace if necessary, and fastenings for shelves is as simple as driving a nail or screw. The disadvantages for wood construction are significant, too. Wood eventually rots, and it may sag, shrink, swell, warp, or break. Nails (except galvanized ones) may rust, and the wood may attract termites, insects, rodents, and fungus. Unfortunately, wood may not be as inexpensive for you as it was for me.

At this point I want to mention the danger of using pressure treated wood. The phenols used in treating the wood are systemic poisons, and aromatic enough to permeate the whole interior of your cellar. If you insist on using a preservative, I suggest you paint the outside of your wall and roof planks with a copper sulfate solution. It is poisonous, too, but not nearly so dangerous, because its vapors are not very volatile. Be warned that copper sulfate will hasten the corrosion of your spikes and nails.

Construction notes

Hire a backhoe to dig the excavation into the hillside; you would do better to live the rest of your life without a cellar than to endure it with an injured back. Dig into the hillside for a distance of at least 25 feet to make the natural slope of the hill taper out in the middle of your anteroom wall. (See Figure 2.) The coldest part of your cellar will be the upper front corners of the inner room. These corners are difficult to cover. The slope of the sides is steep here, and soil does not easily remain where you place it. But the corners must be covered in cold climates.

Make the trench at least nine feet wide, to give you some room to work around the outside of the wall after it's built. You need to line the outside with 6-mil plastic, before filling around the wall with earth. Remember to slope the floor at least a quarter-inch to the foot for drainage.

If you use different dimensions than I have indicated, do remember to leave a wide enough access for your wheelbarrow.

I made my alley 30 inches wide. Remember, you need a little swinging room for your knuckles when you

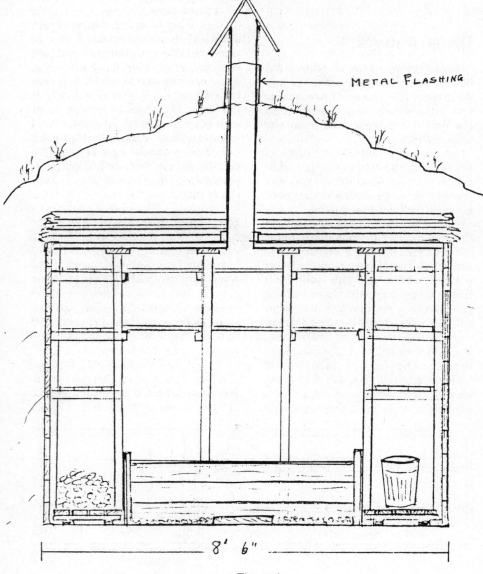

METAL FLASHING

8' 6"

Figure 4

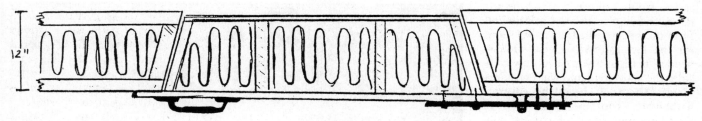

Figure 5

make course corrections with the barrow. I also designed my bins thirty inches wide — you may want yours narrower, to make them easier to clean. Whatever size you settle on, I suggest you remember to make the shelves above them narrower, as I have mentioned above, and to leave out the lowest shelf to give you freer access to the bins.

I chose to leave out the shelves behind the doors in the anteroom, to allow them room to swing fully open. Of course, you may change that arrangement if you really need the storage.

The inner door is filled with fiberglass insulation, and is about 10 inches thick in spite of its appearance in Fig 5. It is faced on both inside and outside with half-inch plywood. Its sides are beveled at an angle of about 10-15 degrees, and you may want to bevel the top and bottom, too. I didn't, and mine works well. The bevel is to allow such a thick door to swing shut without its inside corner binding on the casing. Put a stout handle on the door, in case some moisture does freeze in the casing. You might have to pull really hard to get it open sometime. The direction of swing is really important for both doors — especially in snow country where drifts may form. The outer door can be very simple. It has no insulating duties to perform. Beware of latches that can lock you in, if a gust of wind blows it shut while you're inside. (Experience talking, here.)

Wall construction

I used heavy (full 2-inch) planks and stacked them like logs. I think you could use ordinary framing techniques, but you must remember that the inward pressure of the surrounding earth as it settles is tremendous.

Build strong! I even used a special notch in the inner corners in my planks (Fig. 6). I cut these out with a skill saw. Notice that they are placed so as to resist the inward pressure from either the back or the side. Galvanized spikes are a must here. If you use the heavy planks like mine, remember to stagger them so you don't have two splices near each other (Fig. 2).

Place cross planks every four feet across the bottom on the floor to brace the lower wall planks. This is where the inward pressure will be the greatest. You will fill around these with washed gravel later. Install vertical shelf supports (two-by-fours) around the walls about every three feet. Nail them with 3.5-inch twist nails. In addition to holding up your shelves, they also keep your wall planks in line and prevent their warping inward.

Over your washed gravel, lay a sill under each door, to allow drainage under the door, and to position the door up off the floor, so it will never drag when you open it. You may want to build little ramps on either side, so your wheel barrow will ride over these sills more easily.

Main roof construction

Use heavy lumber for the roof — the heavier the better. If you only have 2-inch lumber, then use full width lengths, laying it crosswise, and covering it with a layer or two of 6-mil plastic. Then lay good strong slabs from a lumber mill, or sound poles, or old bridge timbers, or railroad ties, or whatever you can find that will add strength. Place everything crosswise, from wall to wall. Use no short pieces here, since they will only add weight, not strength. Then cover this layer with another piece of plastic, and cover the whole roof with at least two feet of earth. Don't forget to install the ventilator shaft before you cover its place! When the earth is in place, wrap the ventilator shaft with sheet metal to keep animals from climbing in. Plant a good variety of lawn grass on the surface, to keep the soil from washing down and leaving the roof exposed.

Anteroom roof construction

Choose a roof slope that will allow a two-foot overhang on the sides as well

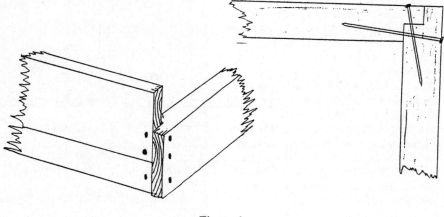

Figure 6

as the front. I chose a 1:2 slope for mine, and had to dig out a little soil from the back corners to make room for the last rafter. No insulation is needed here, and you need only consider the snow load and wind requirements. The roof should be covered with waterproof material, such as rolled roofing, or other roofing surfaces.

If you construct your anteroom well, it makes a good place to cool a small carcass after slaughtering, if you install strong timbers overhead. I left the gable end of the anteroom open, and covered it with screen to keep birds away from my meat. It is also a good place to hang cheesecloth bags of beans or peas for drying.

Evaluation

We built our cellar in 1983, and so far have seen no sign of weakness, shifting, or sagging of walls or roof. We do have a bracket fungus growing in one plank, but can't see that it has damaged the plank, yet. I also had to trim the inside door during the first winter—I fitted it too tight. We have a continuing battle with our free-run chickens, who like to take dust baths on the cellar top. They ruin the grass, and kick the soil down the slope.

Although, I can't see where they get in, we have had mice chew our potatoes twice. One winter, we even had a weasel come in to feast on the mice. (Couldn't find his means of access, either.) We had to set traps for the mice the second time, when the weasel didn't report for duty.

We also stored our paint cans over the potato bin once and had one of the cans spring a leak. It didn't ruin many potatoes, but it taught me a lesson.

We learned that some tree fruits, especially apples, exude a compound that stimulates sprouting in potatoes and other root produce, shortening their shelf life. Fruits should be stored in wrappings, or not in the cellar at all.

One unexpected benefit of our cellar, has been the fun the children have, starting their toboggan run from the top of the cellar. It really gives them a fast send-off. Δ

A Backwoods Home Anthology
The Fifth Year

* Odd-jobbin' can be a country goldmine
* How to keep those excess eggs
* Make better pizza at home than you can buy
* How we bought our country home
* Cooking with dried fruit
* Garden huckleberries
* Short season gardening
* The 10 most useful herbs
* Simplified concrete and masonry work
* Raising sheep
* Free supplies for your homestead
* Learning in the pickle patch
* Good-bye old friend
* Three great bread recipes
* Firewood: how and what to buy
* A bit about ducks
* Choosing superior bedding plants
* How to build the fence you need
* Improving poor garden soil
* Learn the basics of wall framing
* Build a fieldstone chimney
* Sun oven cookery
* Determined woman builds distinctive vertical log studio
* Turkeys — fun and profitable and not as dumb as you think
* Raising fish in the farm pond
* You have to learn to shovel crap before you learn to be the boss
* How to build a low-cost log lifter
* Choosing and using a wood cookstove

Remembering the magic of mother's kitchen

By Jean M. Long

During the Great Depression, I grew up on a farm in Arkansas 25 miles from Little Rock. Before the arrival of Rural Electric of Arkansas and butane gas, our lights were generated by Delco battery and we cooked the fruits of our own garden on a wood burning Home Range.

The center of our world was Mother's kitchen. We each had our favorite dish and she used it to comfort, inspire, reassure, and celebrate the milestones in our life. Some of her greatest culinary triumphs have been added to an "endangered" list by the health obsession. Others have been rendered obsolete by the required preparation time. Her kitchen has become historically significant to a new generation.

In the summer of the early 1940's our house sat in the middle of a cotton field with the noon sun beating down upon its shingled roof. All that separated it from the rows of blooming stalks was a neat lawn and two silver maple trees.

"Expected" visitors

In the distance came a four door sedan Ford ploughing its way down a dusty road across the flat fields with a trailing brown cloud to mark its progress toward the house and farm headquarters. The driver was a salesman from J.R. Watkins & Company and the back seat of his car was filled with the redolent smells of cloves, nutmeg, cinnamon, and pure vanilla extract. That is why he was coming to see my mother. She was always good for the giant economy size bottle of his vanilla. Like every other salesman in the area, he timed his annual visit to coincide with lunch.

Around the big oak table in the dining room, my mother happily shared with the insurance representative, the World Book encyclopedia man, the Luzier cosmetic lady, the crop dusting pilot who had to make an emergency landing in the alfalfa field, and the Methodist preacher who came most Sundays after church. There was always plenty no matter who happened to be there at meal time.

My mother smiled with pride as her guests complimented the excellence of her culinary talents. She had an instinctive natural ability coupled with years of experience. At age nine she began preparing the family meals when her mother died.

On summer mornings, I was awakened by the aromas drifting from our kitchen. Mother and any help she could find on the farm were busy shelling peas, canning tomatoes, simmering strawberry jam on the stove, or making crisp sweet pickles from the prolific cucumbers in her garden.

It was a joy to watch her quick efficient motions and hear her singing as she stirred a batch of corn bread and poured it into the sizzling black skillet to form a golden crust. I loved to listen to the steady rhythm of her hand whisk popping against the glass bowl as she beat egg whites into the fluffy makings of a towering angel food cake.

The ice house and ice cream

Summer Sundays meant homemade ice cream and a four mile-trip to the ice house before church.

On our back porch, my father crushed the ten pound frozen block inside a burlap bag with a sledge hammer while my mother poured a mixture of fresh peaches and cream into the metal container that revolved inside the hand-cranked freezer. We each took our shift turning the handle, hearing the grinding crunch of ice and salt as the cream hardened and the process became more difficult.

When the mixture expanded and began to spill over the sides, we knew it was time to cover our frozen creation with towels for insulation and let it "ripen" before lunch.

A veggie feast

Summertime was also a feast of vegetables. My father rose at 4 a.m. and was ready for a large noon day meal. The turnip greens were young and tender, just out of the garden. Yellow squash was cooked with onion, corn was cut from the cob and sauteed in a skillet, green tomatoes were fried in corn meal, okra and fresh tomatoes

joined together in a delightful medley, green beans were boiled with new potatoes, and tiny fresh butter beans were cooked in butter and their own sweetness. There was often a cobbler made with berries picked from the thick bushes beside the road or a watermelon iced in the cold water of the irrigation ditch that ran through the cotton fields behind our house.

Chickens from the yard

Long before the neat packages of segregated chicken parts in the supermarket, our mother went right out into the back yard, cornered a chicken, grabbed it by the neck and slung it in a circular motion until the body flew across the yard dancing frantically as its life ceased. Holding the bird by its legs, she bore it in the kitchen where she doused its white feathers with boiling water from a teakettle and plucked it with precision. To rid the skin of any residual fuzz, she lit a crumpled sheet of newspaper and singed it thoroughly.

She then cut the chicken into parts, including the wishbone, a prize the butchers no longer can find. Dipping the fresh meat into milk, she dusted it with flour and dropped the pieces one by one into the boiling grease.

Never taking her eyes from the frying pan, she held a big fork in readiness for the proper moment to turn each morsel. When they were just the right shade of brown on both sides, she piled them high on my grandmother's blue china platter.

Sprinkling flour over the crispy parts remaining in the skillet, she waited for the mixture to turn bronze and then added milk, stirring constantly as it thickened to become the best part of all, "milk gravy."

Biscuits and banana fritters

Then came the biscuits. Mother cut up shortening and flour into tiny pea sized morsels and poured in the buttermilk. After spreading the dough with hard sure strokes of her rolling pin she cut round circles with the shell of a small Pet Milk can.

Mother's Boston Cream Pie consisted of several layers of light yellow cake, separated by creamy custard with chocolate icing on the top. Sometimes when we had "spend the night" company, she fried banana fritters for lunch and served them to us hot, right out of the skillet.

There were dinner parties when we ate early in the kitchen and went to bed, straining to hear the adult conversation lulling us to sleep. Sometimes ladies' luncheons inspired Bing cherry salads, tomato aspic, and home made mayonnaise, but no occasion was so grand to us children as the wiener roast in our front yard.

The wiener roast

Our friends from the small town nearby arrived for these gatherings with their entire family. There was no generation segregation. We built a big fire on the hill and set up long tables made of planks and sawhorses covered with table cloths.

The buns came from the store, but the pickle relish, chili and cold slaw came from mother's kitchen. The guests, young and old, were responsible for their own hot dog on the end of a tree branch or a wire spear fashioned from an elongated coat hanger. We held the spicy meat over the hot fire until it was charred on the outside and pink and warm on the inside.

For dessert there was always a large chocolate cake. The icing was made with cocoa, powdered sugar, and a swig of morning coffee with the double purpose of melting the butter and adding a hint of mocha to the flavor. Sometimes marshmallows, and chopped nuts covered the cake which might have a touch of the fresh banana hidden in the batter.

When guests were coming, Mother hurried to make her table a festive one. The natural spontaneous beauty of her flower arrangements was achieved at the last minute using unusual material and on occasion, dangerous ones. Admiring the white edges of its leaves, she once gathered milkweed along the side of the road. A sudden allergic reaction prompted a trip to the doctor and made her late for her own dinner party.

For more traditional "fillers," she robbed the privet hedge of its summer blossoms or cascaded sprays of "bridle wreath" amidst the flowers. She took great pride in the proliferate clumps of daisies which she displayed on the grand piano in a green punch bowl. She anticipated the appearance of her "surprise" lilies that popped from no-where every July. She planted a whole garden of pink Zinnias every summer. After arranging them in her favorite crystal bowl, she stood back smiling to enjoy the results of her seemingly careless but effective efforts.

First frost meant "hog killing" time

The first frost heralded "hog killing" time. Early in the morning when our breath formed a mist in the cold air, the prime hogs were slaughtered. This meant fresh bacon, side meat for cooking greens and black eyed peas, hog cheese, chitterlings, smoked ham and sausage spiced with pepper and sage.

Winter night brought pork roasts with thick brown gravy and sweet po-tatoes baked in their skins. On cold Saturday mornings when we came into the kitchen for breakfast, there would be a big pot of spaghetti sauce already simmering on the stove in preparation for our day at home from school. On Sunday a standing rib roast with pota-toes oven-browned in the meat juices would be waiting when we returned from church.

Christmas turkey

On Christmas morning, when we rushed into the living room to gather around the tree, the delicious scent of a roasting turkey filled the house. Mother always rose at 4 a.m. on this holiday to assure the bird's readiness before the relatives arrived.

The quality of her dressing was very important to her. The process began the day before when she allowed "light bread" (the store bought variety) to dry until it was crisp. She made fresh corn bread, sauteed onion and celery,

and mixed them all together with plenty of sage, turkey broth, a bit of "sweet" milk (as opposed to butter-milk), and eggs. The mixture had to be rather liquid, not too thick, and baked in the oven until brown on top but never dry. She never literally "stuffed" the turkey but baked the dressing as a casserole and side dish.

On this holiday morning, she also made the eggnog. This delicacy was limited to adult consumption because it was heavily endowed with our father's secret supply of bourbon. We never missed the exclusion because our mother's boiled custard with whipped cream was much more to our taste. Sometimes, it was ambrosia and cake made from fresh coconut. To achieve this, she banged the ugly brown coconut shell with a hammer to reach the white meat inside. Taking the broken pieces, she carefully cut away the hairy surface and grated the remains into mounds of moist snow to cover her white cake or stir into fresh oranges which were then a seasonal fruit, only obtainable at Christmas time.

Jam cakes and cream puffs

Winter was also the time for fruit cakes and jam cakes with caramel icing. Mother claimed that caramel icing was one of her most difficult feats. She had to be very careful to let the white sugar brown just enough without burning it before adding the cream to the skillet.

The meringue on her chocolate or lemon cream pies stood tall and firm and she knew exactly how to pour the thickened white sauce into beaten eggs for a perfect dessert filling. Her cream puffs popped up larger than base balls. Biting down on that crusty bubble would send whiffs of powdered sugar to cover our noses and clothes like a magical dust.

There was magic in my mother's kitchen. I have often thought that she had been granted some secret power at age nine to make up for her great loss. Instinctively, she knew just how "long," how much was "just enough" to come forth with something that was "just right".

She was a tall slender woman with large hands and great strength. She greeted her guests at the door, holding the bottom edge of her apron and fan-ning it like a little girl tugging on the skirt of her best dress. Her hair curled around the classic beauty of her face as she came from the hot kitchen, breathless with excitement. All of the preparations had been made. She re-moved her apron. She was on stage now and her finest presentation was about to begin.

I saved all of her scraps of clippings, handwritten recipes on napkins, note cards and her stacks of recipe books, but I can never come close to her pro-ficiency. I search my memory for bits of culinary wisdom that she shared with me as she worked but they are all mixed up with her mother/daughter advice. We had great soul searching talks in her kitchen.

Years later, I gathered my own chil-dren in our kitchen where we made fudge, homemade ice cream and broke a coconut together once, just so they would know. I felt it was an im-portant part of their education. Some-how these joint adventures always brought us closer together. Maybe that was the magic of my mother's kitchen after all. Δ

For three years running
I washed my clothes in a laundromat
On Christmas Eve,
And while the machines agitated
And the dryers tumbled,
I stood in the doorway
Watching the street,
Empty,
But for an occasional traveller bound,
I imagined,
For the warmth of
A not too distant home.
My third Christmas in that doorway
I surprised myself
When I started to cry.
I wiped my face,
Afraid someone would come
And embarrass me.
But there was nothing to worry about.
No one goes to a laundromat
On Christmas Eve.

John Earl Silveira
Ojai, CA

Life of the "prairie tenor"

By Vernon Hopkins

The coyote is midway in size between a fox and a wolf. An average male is about 44 to 52 inches long, including its 14-inch tail, and weighs an average of 25 to 40 pounds. Eastern coyotes are larger, with many weighing 50 pounds or more. Females are generally one-fifth smaller in size and weight.

As there are a number of varieties of timber wolves, so it is with coyotes. In the southwest, there are several distinct varieties, showing considerable differences in size and color. Altitude of habitat seems a factor in coloration, with those at higher elevation being of a lighter color. Most will have black tips on their tails but occasionally there is a white one.

Originally, it was an animal of the open plains. "Prairie Wolf" was, at that time, an accurate name as its habitat was mostly prairie country. As settlers moved west, cutting away the forests, farming the land, and eliminating the timber wolves to protect their livestock, coyotes migrated into areas formerly dominated by wolves.

Coyotes do not mate for life, although some pairs may remain together for a number of years. The mating season for most areas is from January through March. Gestation is 60 to 63 days, with the average litter being 4 to 7 pups. However, as many as 19 pups have been found in one den. Occasionally, two females use the same den. The second female is likely a daughter unable to find a suitable den of her own. Some females breed at less than one year of age.

A female may clean out or dig several dens before pups are born. If one den is disturbed, pups are moved to another by the mother, carrying one pup at a time. Pup's eyes are sealed for about 10 days. The female stays close to the den for the first few days after having pups, then spends more time outside, resting some distance from the den and down wind from it — always alert for any danger.

Male coyotes carry food to his mate and pups when they are very young and continue helping provide food until pups are large enough to leave their den. Pups gain strength quickly on their unstable legs and are soon play-fighting, wrestling, and stalking bugs and insects near the den.

When strong enough to travel, pups are moved to an area near water and some open space where they are taught to catch grasshoppers and insects. They soon graduate to hunting mice, young squirrels, and rabbits. By fall, they are nearly full grown and are on their own. If half the litter survives to be one year old, the coyote population is doing well. Predators that capture and kill pups are bear, wolves, eagles, and cougars.

"An opportunist" is a phrase that best sums up the coyote's eating habits, if not his lifestyle. Both a scavenger and predator, its diet consists of small animals, birds, livestock, deer, carrion, reptiles, amphibians, insects, and many plants and fruits. You name it, he eats it. This is the reason it has been able to live in such a variety of habitat.

They will consume an average of 10 percent of their body weight per day. It may survive on about three hares every two days, but since deer provide much more energy per pound, they are the preferred food. A heavy toll is taken on fawns during the first few weeks of their lives. Under certain conditions, a lone coyote is capable of killing adult deer.

Coyotes often bury food they cannot consume at a single meal and return later to dig it up for another meal.

The coyote seems to have an excessive number of parasites and diseases. This may be caused by the great variety in its diet, much of which comes from its skill as a scavenger. In general, it is a host to every parasite borne by domestic dogs — tape worms, mange mites, ticks, lice, and fleas — and it is subject to distemper, relapsing fever, and salmonella poisoning. They all take their toll on the coyote population, along with tularemia and rabies, which must also be considered a real danger to mankind.

Social system

Being very social and territorial they use a complex vocalization to communicate and establish dominance. Their social system is built upon a strict hierarchy in which each member of the society holds a dominant or submissive position. Dominant males guard their territories with a passion and intruders are severely dealt with. I once saw a large male ruffed up by two smaller coyotes and escorted out of the field. He knew that he was trespassing and made no effort to defend himself. They have a dialect with which to signal others of danger, tell of opportunities, ask for information, or call for assistance. The coyote is constantly saving himself from danger or securing his food by co-operating with others.

Having heard the "where are you" call—consisting of two short barks and a short, lonesome howl—many times, I stopped and listened early one morning when a male coyote sounded off. Within seconds, his mate and their pups answered. Beyond them, two adults and their pups answered. Still farther to the west two more adults and their pups answered; beyond them two adults, then three adults to the east answered, and then all was quiet. Within less than a minute, the first coyote knew the whereabouts of all the resident coyotes within the area.

Each year, one or two litters of pups are raised in or around our irrigated pasture, located in the Siskiyou Mountains of southern Oregon. Over the years, I have witnessed several interesting episodes. When Happy, a labrador-collie cross, was a big awkward pup he found a lonesome coyote pup one day who, not knowing having a dog for a playmate was a no-no, joined Happy in a game of "catch me if you can." Later, when Happy was older, he chased a coyote pup out of the field only to be cut off at the pass by the pup's parents, who followed him back telling him in no uncertain terms they would not stand for such nonsense.

Many times, a coyote has come to the edge of our field and challenged our dogs, who gave chase but soon returned, only to have the coyote return and challenge them again. Once, while cleaning a ditch, I heard a lonesome howl, then another. Looking a short distance away, there was a big-eared pup no larger than an average-sized house cat. Its second howl was answered by the mother and the rest of the litter at the other side of the field. The pup went wobbling off in their direction.

Another time I had just put out a block of salt for the heifers. They were standing around it when a two-year old doe came toward us licking out her tongue in anticipation of the salt. The heifers chased her away but she tried from another direction only to be chased away again. She went a short distance away and started feeding when suddenly she looked up the hill as a coyote chased a squirrel into a small brush pile. The coyote rushed up to the doe from one side, then dashed around it and caught the escaping squirrel.

Coyote population is self-limiting in that they limit their numbers before running out of food. Their population density is directly related to the food supply.

In areas where coyote population is high and livestock depredation common, predator control agents operate the year around to reduce coyote numbers, but it is not surprising that their control operations have had only limited success because of the coyote's ability to control its own numbers.

The coyote actually responds to empty territory by increasing it's birth rate. When they have reached the carrying capacity of their environment, their average litter size remains fairly stable at about 4. However, when they are heavily hunted, litter sizes increase to 7 to 9 and the age of sexual maturity in females declines.

During late fall, family groups increase their home range and begin to break up, with juveniles seeking out and establishing their own territories. Knowledge of their migratory movements have been gained through ear tagging programs by the Fish and Wildlife Service. Some tagged animals have migrated more than 100 miles within a few months; others were recaptured years later within a few miles of where they were tagged. This is one reason that it is impossible to eliminate coyotes from a given area.

Coyotes readily mate with domestic dogs. The hybrid known as a "coy-dog" may be confiding and playful with the person who raises it, but suspicious and timid around strangers. Both sexes of this hybrid are fertile, and while they have successfully been bred through several generations, the benefits of such a cross is of doubtful value.

Although attacks on humans are not common, they have been documented. There have been 14 recorded attacks in Yellowstone National Park and Alberta National Park. Several years ago, coyotes attacked and killed a three-year old girl in Los Angeles. Coyotes are masters at finding and fitting into new habitat niches, and some of their heaviest concentrations occur in urban areas.

An estimated 2,000 to 3,000 live within Los Angeles city limits. They drink the chlorinated water from expensive swimming pools, prey on small dogs and house cats, and eat bowls of dog food left at back doors for family pets. At one time, they were called the "Prairie Tenor," but now it is often "The Song Dog of the Suburbs."

Sheep and poultry ranchers traditionally despise the coyote for the raids on their flocks. Cattlemen appreciate a reasonable number on their land, as they recycle the rabbits and mice that compete with the cows for available forage. Most wildlife biologists believe the coyote has a vital role when its numbers are in balance with their environment. It is then a beneficial predator and scavenger.

While all segments of society may never agree on how, when, or if control measures should apply to coyotes, we must agree that an animal as intelligent, cunning, versatile, and interesting as the coyote deserves our admiration—even as he steals our Christmas goose.

(Vernon Hopkins, 80, is a naturalist and retired trapper. He was the subject of our profile in Issue No. 2.) Δ

The Third Year

Moving houses — good bargains for backwoods living

By Robert L. Williams

When the typical urban dweller decides to have a go at backwoods living, one of the first questions to be settled is that of housing. Often there is the problem of affordability, of having to build or buy a country house while making payments on the city dwelling. For those with such questions, there is an answer you may not have thought of — one that is affordable by nearly everyone, and one that can actually result not only in money saved but in money earned.

This solution involves moving the entire house to your land. As hard as it is to believe, you can have a fantastic house, or a simple rural structure, for as little as $10,000 and often much less.

Our first "moved" house

When we moved our first house several years ago, we found the perfect place for us, located the owner, and asked him what he wanted for the house.

"I'll take $50,000," he said, and when he noted our doubts about paying such a price, he quickly added, "Get rid of that old barn of a house on it and it's a perfect place for a mini-mall or supermarket or specialty shop."

"We don't want the land," we said. "All we want is the house."

He answered, "Hell, you can have it. In fact, I'll pay you to tear it down and clear the land for me."

We made a deal. He deeded us the house for the token sum of one dollar and then we agreed to leave the land perfectly clear of debris in exchange for remuneration for our demolition services.

As you expected, we did no demolition work. Instead, we hired a house mover in need of business, agreed to pay him $2,500 to move the house to our property in the South Mountains

Huge houses, brick or frame, can be moved for very long distances and across very congested highways. Regarding the brick on this house, the owner has two options: he can move the house, brick and all, at a higher cost, or he can have the brick removed and re-laid later.

range of western North Carolina, a distance of more than 20 miles, the last leg of it over rugged terrain where there had never been a road.

The mover brought in his equipment, jacked up the house, attached the wheels to the towing frame, and pulled the house from its foundation and started up the road with it. At our property he had already bulldozed a roadway over fields and up hills and through small growths of pine and poplar and wild cherry.

At the site, he set the house down on the foundation we had started, and he left. And for $2501 we had bought and had delivered a house with a huge kitchen, large den, immense living room, dining room, two baths, two bedrooms, and a library. On the back of the house and connected to it were a laundry room and servants' quarters. On the front was a wide front porch supported by huge columns, and on the side was a screened-in porch that could serve as sleeping quarters in warm months.

And we had our road into our property cut for us, as part of the bargain.

As part of the "services rendered" deal we agrred upon in exchange for our labors, we received enough money for digging a well and septic tank, re-plumbing and re-wiring the house, and building two large chimneys. Each of the upstairs bedrooms had its own fireplace, as did the den and the living room downstairs.

Not bad for $2501!

Prices better today

But that was years ago! Things, prices among them, have changed. There is no way to get a deal like ours in the modern economic structure.

True. You can actually get a better deal.

All over this country there are houses like ours or much better than ours that can be had for a song, even one sung out of tune. And the cost of moving a house, while considerably higher in some areas, has actually dropped in many areas of the country.

Here's how to get a bargain-basement house, delivered to your property, just like the morning paper. In fact, it is much easier to have a house delivered in some parts of America than it is to get the paper carrier to your place.

Locating a house

There are several ways to find the house of your dreams—or the edifice of your fantasies. The most casual way is to take a drive through your part of the nation and look for the tell-tale signs of a house ready to be moved. You might see a sign in front of a stately house, a sign that proclaims: "Future site of McDoogle's Supermarket."

Once a house is moved, the mover leaves it on the steel while the owner arranges to have a foundation built under it. When the foundation is completed, the house is lowered to the top of the wall and the steel is removed.

That sign also says the stately house has got to go, so approach the owner and make him a deal. Agree to clear the property in exchange for everything moveable on the lot. Then locate a house mover, strike a deal with him, and agree to pay him to move the house—if he consents to clear the property as part of the deal. So he does your work and you get the house.

A second way to locate a house is to read the newspaper legal sections

daily. Also read for donations to colleges, universities, urban renewal projects, libraries, hospitals or churches. Look for notices of wills and bequests. You will often see brief statements that inform readers that a local man or woman died and left five acres or so to the school or library.

Again, common judgment dictates that the college can't hold classes in the house and the hospital can't treat patients there. The major value of the land, to them, is for a parking lot or as the site of a new building. And, to them, the land is far more valuable once the old house is dealt with.

When urban renewal projects are started, often many houses will be in the way. The same is true when a new stadium, parking lot, or shopping center is started. You can often buy a house for as little as the legal one-dollar fee and sometimes they, too, will agree to pay you to get the house off their land.

When a church builds a new parsonage, the old house is often available to anyone willing to move it.

Read notices of building permits. If a man secures a permit to build a house on a lot where an existing house stands, he will in all probability need to deal with the old house first. You

can deal handily with these people, as well.

The best possibilities

But the best possibilities by far is in locations where the state highway department is either widening an existing road or building a new highway, or where the local airport is lengthening and improving runways, etc.

In such building projects, there are often as many as several hundred houses, ranging from small bungalows to mansions. You have a superior choice of house sizes, styles, and designs.

Buying the house

Rule Number One: Don't approach the owner and offer him money. Let money be a final consideration, and if he asks for a couple of thousand dollars, walk away, leaving him to hire a demolition crew and lose money and time. Generally speaking, unless the house is in great demand and is in splendid condition, there won't be any racy bidding on the house.

Rule Number Two: When you visit a housing development where a road, airport, or school is to be built, you will need to submit a sealed bid on the house of your choice. If you are the high bidder, you will usually have 60 to 90 days in which to move the house or lose your purchase price.

So submit a bid of $10 on every reasonable house in the entire development! Chances are great that a half dozen of the more eye-catching houses will receive nearly all of the bids. You may find that your ten-buck bid was tops on a dozen or so houses.

If so, after first determining that it is legally correct to do so in your area, select the house you want, then put the other houses up for sale by you as the new owner. You may be able to sell the houses for a couple thousand dollars or more to people who want to move them.

If nobody is interested in the houses, you still have two choices: **1)** Hire the mover (you can get a special rate on volume business) to move <u>all</u> of the houses. **2)** Borrow money and buy building lots and have the houses set up on them; then put them on the real-estate market.

It is not at all unusual to buy a house for $10, pay $4000 or even more to have it moved, and then sell it for $125,000. A man in South Carolina did exactly what is prescribed here, and he moved his first house, sold his $10 investment for $40,000, while it was still on the wheels, and delivered it to the new owner's property. He eventually sold $600,000 worth of houses within a period of a few weeks, and he started his own housing development. With his profits he bought some moving equipment and went into the house-moving business.

And, in a worst-case scenario, if you can't find a soul who will buy your houses, you can leave them where they are and forfeit your investment. So you lose $120 or so, but you saved thousands on the house you bought and moved.

Setting up the house

Once the house is on your property, you dig your basement, if you want one, and build your foundation walls **after** the house is in place and still sitting on the steel. This is also an excellent time to do any electrical or plumbing work that is needed.

You can move brick houses as easily as frame houses, and you can move houses of several stories. Recently a 12-story building was moved in North Carolina. If your house is brick, you can buy matching brick so the new foundation wall will match the old bricks.

If there are problems with termite or decay damage, replace the defective timbers while the house is on the steel. When the house is on the foundation walls, you can build chimneys, if needed, or you can actually move a house with the chimney intact.

Final considerations

Several questions always arise, such as how far a house can be moved, what happens if the house is damaged, and how much the house is weakened by moving.

First, there is often a limit to moving distance, usually 20 miles. However, the mover can haul the house 20 miles, then pull into a parking area and wait unil the next day and move it 20 more miles. He could, theoretically, cross

This house, all 4,000 square feet of it, was bought for less than one dollar. The owner wanted to use the land for commercial development and needed the lot cleared. It cost $2,500 to move the house and another $5,000 to restore the house to its original condition.

the country if so desired, in 20-mile segments of the trip.

Second, while en route, the mover's insurance will cover any damage. Once the house is in place again, regular home- owners insurance will take over.

Third, a house is not weakened by moving it. The opposite is often true. Uneven houses will be leveled again; shifting corners will be squared and braced. One mover reports that he moved a huge house more than 20 miles while a pot of beans sat on the kitchen range — and he didn't spill the beans.

Finally, you can get a bank loan on a moved house — once it has been moved. Such loans do not differ essentially in most states from loans on permanent houses.

Caution: do not get over-anxious and jump at the first chance you have. Shop around; keep options open. But don't delay beyond a reasonable time. Remember that other people want bargains, too, and a good buy will not sit there long waiting for you.

You will have headaches, naturally, with the move. You must work hard to get the deal you need. Movers, like the rest of us, want the highest possible prices for their services, and costs vary greatly from section to section. Even at the best, there will still be some headaches; you have them when you buy a stationary house. Find people who have moved their houses and ask their advice. Then make your own move. Δ

MAKING A BACKWOODS LIVING

Medical transcription —
a recession proof career?

By Barbara Elig

Is it possible that there truly is a recession- proof career? If there is, medical transcription comes mighty close, and the best part is you can do it right at home! I have successfully operated a medical transcription service from my home for more than seven years, and with the right skills, knowledge, and mind set, I believe you can too.

What is involved?

Here's what medical transcription involves:

Physicians dictate reams of information about their patients. This is being done in private practice, hospitals, nursing homes, clinics, sports medicine facilities, etc. They usually use a hand-held dictating machine utilizing a small micro-cassette.

This is in turn handed over to the medical transcriptionist who uses a transcriber that will accommodate the cassette. The transcriptionist then listens to the physician and types what she/he hears, ending up with a medical record. The physician should normally review the typed document and sign it, and it is then placed in the patient's file where it becomes part of a permanent record.

This record is very important as it will stand as a legal document in case of lawsuit. It is not hard to see how a well-qualified medical transcriptionist could be kept pretty busy with the volume of information needed not only to satisfy the physician but also the many government regulations pertaining to such programs as Medicare and Medicaid, plus the private insurance carriers.

What training is needed?

If you can type 60 wpm, spell, have good grammar, and have an "ear" for words, I believe you can learn medical transcription.

The American Association for Medical Transcription, located in Modesto, California, offers a training program at a very good price for anyone wishing to learn.

It goes without saying that medical transcription requires long hours at a typewriter or computer so you must be able to withstand long hours sitting. However, I have found with well-planned breaks this is not a problem. Besides what better place to be than home if you are typing all day. You can take breaks and accomplish some of the many chores you'd have to do anyway around the house.

Many community colleges also offer courses in medical transcription and medical terminology at very reasonable prices. That is the way I learned.

How much can you make?

You can make quite a lot of money. If you are an average transcriptionist you can earn between $8.00 and $25.00 per hour depending on your area and your level of skill.

Of course you must be able to hear and understand and then translate what you are typing. But as you progress and learn more and more you will find it becomes easier. A background as a nurse, lab tech, or any health field related experience would be very helpful in understanding the medical lingo on the tapes.

I have often heard from other transcriptionists that at some point everything "just clicks" and you are off and running with medical transcription. I know that's what happened to me. It is a lot like learning a foreign language; you just develop the "ear."

How to find customers

I saw a recent newspaper article about a medical transcription company who had 415 medical transcriptionist's positions to fill and were only able to hire 50 because of lack of basic skills in grammar, typing (ability to type 60 wpm), and spelling. The company was willing to train their employees in medical terminology and transcription, but it could not get the basic skills to begin with.

Even if you live in the backwoods, you will find physicians who will need your skills as a medical transcriptionist. A well-presented flyer listing your qualifications—either hand-carried or mailed to the area physicians—will soon net you your first customer. You can then build your base from there.

The best part is that if you do a good job you will not need to prospect for new customers. They will be so happy to have you they will never let you go.

What kind of equipment, supplies do I need?

Although it is possible to do medical transcription on a typewriter, I think getting a personal computer makes more sense. You may need the storage capabilities of a computer and certainly you will almost always have to make some corrections to the dictation as you go.

My first set-up cost somewhere in the range of $5,000 for a personal computer and printer, but computer prices and printers are now much cheaper. For $1,500 you could be up and running.

Your transcribing machine can be rented or purchased. I have bought only one and had it repaired once and it has served me well.

Transcriptionists who work in small towns or rural areas are able to work for hospitals or large transcription services via modems connected to their computers and telephone lines. The hospital or transcription service will usually set you up with all the equipment and then you send your finished product over the phone lines.

You can also offer your customers pick-up and delivery if you are not too far off the beaten path.

Conclusion

There may not be a truly recession-proof career these days, but I do believe the well-qualified medical transcriptions will not be out of work long.

This is a very specialized field but one in which bright capable people can enter. You don't need years of education or even a college degree.

You of course must learn the basics but after that you will have a skill that can be done in any part of the world, in any setting—rural or big city—and best of all it can be done at home. You will find you have more time to spend with your family and friends, more time to garden or just enjoy the beauty of nature, but most of all you will be a skilled, highly sought after person who can write your ticket in the field of medical transcription. Δ

> *Give an Irishman lager for a month, and he's a dead man. An Irishman is lined with copper, and the beer corrodes it. But whiskey polishes the copper and is the saving of him.*
>
> Mark Twain
> 1835-1910

Grow your food Can your food

- *Gardening basics*
- *Canning supplies*
- *Growing fruit*
- *Growing and canning tomatoes*
- *Pickles, relishes, and sauces*
- *Raising and canning meats*
- *Meals-in-a-jar*
- *Canning dairy products*
- *Great recipes*
- *Food storage ideas*

Moonlight and newspapers

By Natalie Lund

Journal entry: December 30, 1989

It is 1:25 a.m. on Sunday morning. Soon I'll be leaving for a 2:00 a.m. rendezvous with Shirley, the woman whose Sunday morning newspaper route I'll be taking over at the beginning of the month.

It's bitterly cold outside, and my house has frozen water pipes. So I've brushed my teeth with water from a Tupperware pitcher, and I'll stop to buy a cup of coffee on the way to the newspaper shack—if I can find a coffee shop open at this hour.

I'm still wearing jeans and a sweatshirt from yesterday. But I've added tights to make sure I'll be as warm as possible. My supplies are assembled—flashlight, billing envelopes, knife for cutting newspaper bundles. I'm ready to head out and start stuffing Courier-Journals into rural mailboxes.

Is this insanity? Is the extra cash worth the effort and loss of sleep? Or the risk of being out on slick winter roads in the middle of the night?

For now, my plan is to do the carrier route for a month or two and then re-assess. I'm told there's enormous turnover in newspaper delivery; maybe those who drop out early have special insight. I suspect I'll know soon enough.

Update: Mid 1992

I am now a veteran newspaper carrier with over 14,000 miles of road trek. The Saturday night work routine has become an integral part of my life. I do the 96 miles on my route entirely by rote; I know where to make each stop and what time I need to arrive at each new road in order to stay on schedule—even though a schedule is not really required.

It turns out I really like this job. It provides a peaceful change of pace from the more chaotic work I do on Monday through Friday. I like driving down country roads and seeing rabbits and cows—and being paid as I do it.

My friends' initial response to the paper route wasn't entirely positive.

"I can't believe you're doing this," said one of my friends. "Only roosters are up before sunrise on Sunday mornings."

"You'll never be able to leave town on weekends," said another friend. "I don't think this will last very long."

"You don't seem like the newspaper delivery type," added a third critic. "I figured you'd design brochures or teach a class if you needed something else to do."

These are people who fail to see the romance of having a middle of the night mission. They simply don't understand that an unlikely activity can add a little spice to an otherwise rather predictable life.

Of course, a paper route is not an entirely mysterious undertaking. In a nutshell, the job consists of assembling sections into complete newspapers, loading the assembled papers into cars, and delivering them to designated mailboxes and vending locations. Except for minimal bookkeeping, that's really all there is to it—a job perfect in its usefulness and simplicity.

But even uncomplicated work holds occasional surprises. I had always assumed, for example, that virtually all households subscribed to a Sunday newspaper. So the fact that I pass by far more mailboxes than I fill each week came as a bit of a jolt to me. Evidently reading the Sunday newspaper is not as necessary to American normalcy as I had believed.

I also never would have guessed that grocery store promotions could influence newspaper sales. But it's definitely true. Here in Barren County, Kentucky, subscriptions increased significantly when local grocery stores began redeeming coupons at double their face value. Theft from newspaper vending racks also increased at about the same time. The allure of Sunday newspaper coupons is not to be underestimated.

My reasons for taking on a newspaper route were pretty typical. I needed car repair money, and I simply didn't want to cut back on the good things in life to keep resuscitating an aging Stanza. An additional job might be the answer, I thought. It wouldn't stop the hemorrhaging of funds, but at least there would be a better way to keep up with the outpour.

It was my friend Shirley who convinced me that newspaper delivery was a sensible choice. "It's not much work," she said, "and if you're willing to adjust your Saturday evening sleep schedule a bit, you'll never even notice that you've been up most of the night."

So when Shirley and her husband started making plans to move to a different part of the state, I signed on as their replacement. I assumed responsibility for route #9G930921U.

I bought a map showing the backroads in Barren County. I paid a bonding fee and ordered supplies necessary for route maintenance. And most important of all, I outfitted my cassette recorder with new batteries, enabling me to listen to a training tape — road directions and landmark notations deemed important by the previous carrier.

"Just follow the play-by-play, and there's no way you can get lost or miss any of the stops," said my circulation manager. "You'll love the tape."

"...OK, you come on out Highway 63 until you pass Siloam Road," intones the Southern voice on the cassette. "Pretty soon you'll see a little bridge. Just beyond the bridge you'll turn left onto Redbud Lane..."

It takes about six weeks to learn the geography and pacing of a hundred mile route, I discovered. And then one's mechanical tutor can be retired. Visual cues replace verbal ones, and the process becomes automated and comfortable. Now there is time for thinking or listening to music or playing tapes of full-length books read by men and women with mellifluous voices.

Entertainment in place? Now add coffee, cranberry streusel muffins, and moonlight. These are the appointments of a perfect evening.

Of course, not all evenings are perfect. Sometimes there's fog. Or car trouble. Or exhaustion. Or mailboxes that have been knocked over or mislabeled or don't exist.

"Prospective builders," says my circulation manager.

"Right," I agree.

Along my route I encounter roosters, cows, horses, peacocks, tobacco fields, pastures, and bullfrog-filled ponds. There are also landmark buildings—old schools, deserted farmhouses, churches. Plus lots of cats, dogs, possums, and rabbits—typically out in greater numbers on slightly rainy nights.

"This is like being on vacation from the rest of my life," I've explained to friends who wonder at my commitment to newspaper delivery. Over time I'm absorbing the details of rural Kentucky; I'm being imprinted with the best of what my state has to offer. Essentially, this is a job so enjoyable the extra income is almost incidental—but nice, nevertheless.

So I continue to turn down out-of-town weekend excursions and continue to keep the car repair fund alive with money received from my subscribers. My goal, of course, is to expand the number of newspapers I deliver each week. So, if you'd like to sign up for Sunday delivery, give me a call. You have my promise that the paper will be in your mailbox by 7:00 a.m. Even if the weather is bad and my water pipes are frozen. Δ

A Backwoods Home Anthology
The Eighth Year

* Considering life in rural Arkansas
* Where I live: Nine-patch, baby, and log cabin quilts
* Here's the best way to split gnarly firewood
* Here's an easier (and cheaper) way to make wooden beams
* Rid your garden of snails and slugs — organically
* Try these 13 metal cleaning tips to keep your house shining
* I remember the day the lynx attacked
* Raise your own feed crops for your livestock
* Lay vinyl flooring the foolproof way
* These double-steep half stairs save space
* Think of it this way...Science and truth — are they related?
* Grandma will love this personal "Helping Hands" wall hanging
* Try these pasta desserts for unusual holiday fare
* Protect your small buildings from wind damage
* Winterize your animals without going broke
* Commonsense preparedness just makes sense

Selling chickens to an ethnic market

By Dynah Geissal

If you live near an immigrant population, you may have a ready market for products that you already produce on your farm. While most Americans seem to prefer "sanitized," wrapped in plastic super-market fare, people from less developed countries often have values similar to ours as low impact farmers. If you appreciate different cultures, the rewards of dealing with other groups of people may be greater than merely monetary.

Missoula, Montana has been lucky to be a resettlement area for many nationalities including Hmong (Laotian), Tibetan, and Russian. There is also a university that attracts people from many African and Asian nations.

Many of these people prefer to see animals on the hoof when they buy their food. They like to choose a living animal and slaughter it in their traditional way. That works well for me since the law forbids the sale of home-butchered meat. Pigs, cattle, geese, ducks, chickens, and goats are all candidates for the ethnic market.

I have concentrated my efforts on the sale of chickens, although I occasionally sell other animals also. The Hmong population is my primary customer. That community is large enough that they have been able to maintain many traditions.

The Hmong people are smart, honest, hardworking, and despite the hardships they have been through almost always seem upbeat and optimistic. I have really enjoyed getting to know them, although there are some difficulties that you should be aware of if you are considering a similar venture.

An obvious problem is the language barrier, but with patience on both sides this can be overcome. It gets easier as you both learn what to expect too. The young people learn our language quickly and they can often be counted on to help with the transactions.

A second problem involves the tradition of bargaining that is prevalent in other cultures. In my early dealings with the Hmong I had to face this every time. While I understand that this is a normal part of life for them I made the decision not to participate. For one thing, they're better at it than I am; but also I'm the only one that knows how much it cost me to raise the animal to the point of sale. I can't bargain for feed or for chickens. My figures are clear and I know what profit margin I need to make the enterprise worthwhile. These are not variables, so for me there is no room for haggling.

A third problem is a combination of the above two—language and the desire to bargain. When the language is new many sentences come out as a command. It is intimidating at first. An example:

"Old Uncle buys ten red chickens today. He pays $2."

"I only have black chickens today and they are $2.50."

"Old Uncle buys those red chickens."

"Those are for eggs. I don't sell those."

"Old Uncle needs red chickens today."

This can go on and on. Denying Old Uncle's needs was very hard for me at first. I learned though that this is their way of bargaining exaggerated by a quirk of learning a new language that causes it to be a command instead of a request. Some people are angered or annoyed by this way of talking. Others are talked into selling something that they don't want to sell. To be successful a person must be firm but cheerful about what they have for sale and what it will cost. I don't have the problem

anymore except with an occasional newcomer. One man even teases me by offering a very low price when he comes to buy. Then we both laugh and appreciate the rapport that we have established that even allows for joking.

A fourth problem is that the young people are sensitive about what Americans think of them. Because of that they hesitate to talk about their native celebrations. If a person needs black chickens today, is it for a personal reason such as honoring the birth of a child or is it a community wide holiday? If they need red today and black next month, what does that mean? How will I know? Even most of the people that I regularly deal with are very difficult to communicate with on this matter. They have had too many bad experiences. Many Americans have laughed at their traditional rites and called them pagan. In fact most Hmong are Christian and want to be accepted as Americans. It has become somewhat easier as trust has developed between us. Still it's a constant struggle to pick up hints about what will be needed three or four months in the future. Hardly ever is it spoken right out.

I enjoy my marketing arrangement with these warm wonderful people. If you think you might enjoy a similar setup read on and I will tell you what I've learned over the years.

I had never raised large numbers of chickens before. I have 100 layers and in addition I raised 50 butcher chickens every year. Now I raise for sale 100-200 every eight weeks. It's a very different proposition. Starting 50 chicks in your kitchen every spring is one thing. Having chicks in your kitchen all year is not something you would enjoy. Keeping expenses down is primary as is conservation of labor. These are things you don't worry too much about when you raise chickens for the freezer but if it's to be a business you will want everything streamlined.

Unless you live in a very warm climate you will need a brooder house. It should be erected near the house because you will need to check your chicks at least four times a day. A 10' X 10' building will house 100 chicks and 200 if the weather is warm enough

for them to run outside. My brooder house is double-walled with insulation in between. It is good at -20 degrees Fahrenheit unless the wind is blowing from the east which is where the door is. In those circumstances I have to use a small electric heater if the chicks are very young. Your brooder house should have at least one adjustable vent near the ceiling on a wall not facing the prevailing winds. A window in the south wall will add warmth, light and ventilation when necessary. It will also serve as an exit for the chicks when they are old enough to go outside.

You will need a hover about 4' X 3' with sockets for two heat lamps. With the two lamps the chicks don't tend to pile up and it also serves as a safety feature in case one lamp burns out. A thermostat is cheap and is a good investment. If you have to be gone early in the morning it is good to know that the lamps will stay on until the house warms up but will go off before your birds are overheated. It is also helpful if the hover can be raised and lowered. Install a light with a switch near the door. You will need it for checking on the chicks and at times you may want to leave it on.

If you can afford it, get commercial feeders and especially waterers. When you're only raising birds for yourself you can improvise but when you're raising them continuously you will want the convenience of having the right equipment. Buying a five gallon waterer was one of the best things I've done for myself. A feeder you can fill just once a day is wonderful too. Then your time can be spent checking on their health and well being instead of on menial tasks repeated several times a day.

You will probably want to try several hatcheries before you find one that's just right for you. Price is important, of course. Most hatcheries have specials that may meet your needs. Note: Many cultures need certain colors for certain purposes or, more importantly, cannot use certain colors. All the hatcheries I've used seemed to be reputable but some seem to have chicks with greater liveability. That may be genetic but more likely it's how fast the chicks get to you after hatching.

Keep records! Write down every expense beginning with the material for your brooder house. When you have broken even you can celebrate! It's very important to see where your expenses are and how much you make on each chick. Keep a diary. How long did you feed chick starter? When did the birds reach market size? What weight had they attained? To make a decent amount of money on this you have to be really good at it. You won't remember everything; so write it down.

If you encounter disease write down symptoms and what you did about it. Did it work? Almost any disease involving butcher chickens can be prevented. The major causes of disease are not enough warmth, overcrowding, insufficient diet, lack of ventilation and lack of cleanliness. All are easily correctible.

Setting your price list will be hard at first — another reason records are absolutely necessary. I found that charging 25 cents a week until ten weeks of age and then 25 cents every two weeks works well for me. An eight week old chicken would cost $2.00. At first I sold eight week old chickens for $1.50. That didn't work because the cost of raising the birds to that age is much greater than when they're old enough to eat whole grain. At $2.00 I can make a reasonable profit even if they are all purchased at that age. After the chickens are on whole grain my profit margin increases considerably and the purchaser also gets a better deal with the heavier bird.

My price is much higher than supermarket prices but comparable to those in health food stores. I am as fair in price as I can be and still have it worthwhile for me.

The Hmong people are just one group who appreciate the fruits of a small farmer's labors. There are many other groups that are happy to buy animals that are alive and raised more naturally. If you enjoy people from other places you may find this market a very special one just as I do.

Note: Possible sources for markets are refugee centers, cultural centers, ethnic stores. My experience has been that once you get your first customers, word of mouth will take over. Δ

Riving shingles for your roof the old-fashioned way

*By Johnny M. Ernst
and Theresa Neville*

Dan Pulley (Ozark Dan to his friends) is a Bunceton, Missouri artisan who may have been born a hundred years after his time. His passion is to breathe new life into the old, nearly forgotten skills that were once part of America's cultural past.

The art of shingle riving is one such old skill he has mastered through research and long hours of hands-on experience. He does it the way it was done more than a century ago, and this article will show you how it used to be, and still can be, done.

Splitting with the grain

First, let's define riving. Riving, pronounced with a long "i," means to split with the natural grain, thus giving the finished shingle the ability to shed water. If you place a log section on end you would see the lines making their

Red oak shingles on display as they would appear on a roof.

Walter Bonecutter debarks a quarter section of a stick of red oak using a Black Hawk.

way toward the bark from the center. To "rive" is to split the wood with these natural lines.

The procedure of turning hardwood logs into shingles begins with the selection of the right kind of tree. Dan uses red oak because its grain generally runs straight, more so than other hardwoods in the area. Black oak also will work as will virgin white oak. Be careful to avoid second growth white oak because its grain is likely to be twisted. The tree must be at least 20 inches in diameter, preferably found on the south side of a hill. There, the wind has had little opportunity to whip the grain into a gnarled nightmare. Once the tree is down, strip off the limbs and branches. Cut the log into sections, each 20 inches in length. Referred to as "sticks," these sections are the raw material for the shingles. It is best to begin riving your shingles soon after you have cut your logs. Dan has learned that seasoned red oak is reluctant to cooperate with your efforts.

Stand the "stick" on end. Now, using a long handled steel maul and a steel wedge find a natural split in the center of the stick and split it into two pieces. Now, take each half and split these in similar fashion. You now have four sections. Next, using the same maul and wedge, remove the "heartwood" from each section. The heartwood is the very center of the stick. Since you split the stick into four parts, each a pie-shaped section of the stick, the heartwood is the narrow pointed part of the section. Next, use a hand ax or a "black hawk" (both tools resemble a hatchet) to chip the bark away from each pie-shaped section. Underneath the bark you will find a soft, sponge-like, grainless part of the wood called the "sap edge." It will decay in time so it is not necessary to remove it. The sections of wood that remain, denuded of bark and heartwood, are called "bolts."

Tools of shingle riving, from left, are large froe, hand-hewn red oak maul, hand ax, hand-hewn maul, Black Hawk, small froe with hand-hewn hickory handle, hand-hewn maul, and medium froe.

The shingle brake

The bolts are ready to be rived into shingles. This step takes place in the "shingle brake." Dan made his shingle brake from a natural fork from a hedge tree that resembles the letter "Y." This "Y" crotch should be cut to about six feet in length. Place the single end on

Walter Bonecutter uses a maul to split away the heartwood from a stick of Red Oak.

a 20-inch log section. At the double end crisscross two mulberry poles and apply downward force on them to secure them in place.

Nails or other bracing are not necessary because the poles work against each other. The mulberry poles are about four inches in diameter and are about six feet long. Make certain that the top surface of the brake is level. Now, place a block of wood under the brake for the "bolts" to rest on while riving. Dan uses a seasoned walnut stump for this job, but any such short block of wood will do.

The bolts that you have previously made from your logs are ready to be placed in the crotch of the shingle brake. If the bolt is too large for the brake, stand it on end on the ground. Then use a large froe and wooden hand maul to split the bolt in half. A "froe" is a tool designed to split wooden boards (shingles) from logs. It is a spring steel blade with a cone shaped eye for the handle to slip through. The edge of the froe does not need to be sharp, in fact a froe's edge should be dull. This dullness is what causes the wood to split. An old expression says it best—"as dull as a froe."

Place a bolt between the two arms of the shingle brake with the bottom of the bolt resting on the block under the brake. Place the froe on the top of the bolt in the center aligning the blade with natural lines as much as possible. Strike the froe blade with the wooden hand maul sharply a couple of times, driving the froe into the bolt. Then using the shingle brake as lever and brace, pry the shingle off the blot. Sometimes there is a tendency for the crack to run out to the edge before it reaches the end of the bolt. When this occurs, place the thin side of the bolt on top. With a free hand apply pressure on the end of the bolt. By pushing down on the handle of the froe you can use it as leverage to straighten the crack. This will give a straight shingle.

Continue to rive each quarter "pie" section down until you get the desired thickness for each shingle, usually one half inch. Remember the less seasoned the wood the easier this part of the process will be. Throw the rived shingle off the side of the brake. Dan estimates that it takes about 500 shingles to make a square. A square is ten feet by ten feet.

If the shingles have an uneven look or are very rough they can be dressed

With a bolt of red oak placed firmly in the Shingle Brake, "Ozark Dan" Pulley trims off the excess before splitting the bolt with his hickory-handle Froe. The Shingle Brake is a "Y" branch of a hedge tree.

"Ozark Dan' Pulley is using a hand-carved red oak Maul to strike the Froe in order to split the red oak bolt into two shingles. This is called "shingle riving."

up a bit by placing them on the shaving horse. Clamp the shingle into place on the shaving horse and use a drawing knife to shape the shingle. The "drawing knife" is a spring steel tool with two handles and a beveled blade sharp only on one edge. The user draws the blade toward himself. The "shaving horse" is more or less a jig or vise and is vital to the proper use of the drawing knife. The shaving horse incorporates the use of the human body as a vital part. It has a bench, three or four legs, and an angled bridge. It also has a swing arm through the center, and a foot pedal to help firmly hold the shingle in place on the bridge.

Dan built his shaving horse out of an old bridge plank and nailed it together with reproduction blacksmith nails. These nails are hand forged with a square taper on the end.

When you have finished riving the shingles, begin to stack them by crisscrossing each layer. On top of this stack place a large stone or some form of heavy weight. The force of the weight will strengthen any bow in the shingles over a period of time. Let the shingles season about six months, as they will become darker in color. Use the shaving horse and drawing knife

again, which will put a taper on the upper edge of the shingle. This causes them to lay as flat as possible on the roof.

When it is time to put the shingles on the roof, it is best to let the shingles soak over night in water. This reduces the chance that they'll split now that they have seasoned. Properly installed shingles should last thirty to forty years. "Some old-timers have told me that they've seen this type of shingle on houses that they knew were in place for at least sixty years. And you could stand in the attic, see shafts of light coming through and the roof would not leak when it rained," says Dan.

Nail the shingles to the furring strips that run across the rafters. Each row has two courses of shingles. Repeat this step all the way up to the ridge. How much you overlap will depend on the pitch of the roof. At the top of the roof continue to overlap until you can see that the possibility of leakage is prevented. If you find this or any other part of the installation tricky, Dan won't mind if you call or write. He will

be glad to help you through any difficult situations you may encounter.

Some tools that Dan uses must be made by hand. For instance the froe can be found with a little diligent effort in flea markets or antique shops, but the handle is usually missing. Dan fashioned his froe handle from a piece of seasoned hickory. He used a drawing knife to shape it on the shaving horse. He then smoothed it down with a broken piece of glass just like the old-timers used to do it (of course sand paper will work just fine). He then worked in linseed oil as a finishing touch. You should never use a steel maul to drive a froe into a bolt of wood. Although you will find some froes in shops have been damaged by a steel hammer, they are still usable. The purpose of the wooden maul is to drive the froe into a bolt. It is made from oak heartwood and should be hewn with a hand ax or black hawk.

(If you have particular questions about riving shingles, Dan will be glad to help you with your questions. Just write or call: Ozark Dan (Pulley), Box 177, Bunceton, MO 65237. Tel. (816) 427-5316.) Δ

A BHM Staff Profile

Jennifer Brown handles the telephone, the mail, and some of the typing and art layout at *BHM*. She is also our "woman on the move" because we send her around the country to represent *BHM* at the dozen or so Preparedness, Ecology, and Alternative Energy Expositions where we have booths.

Jennifer grew up in the Siskiyou Mountains of southern Oregon where the deer are "as thick as cattle." She went to live in Los Angeles for a few months to see how she'd like it and summed up the experience with her now famous words: "What a dump!"

Want the kids to learn shooting? Try Whittington!

By Robert L. Williams

I confess I never really liked shooting; primarily, I suppose, because I was never much good at it. But when the national director of the Whittington Adventure Camp just outside Raton, New Mexico, came to our house and offered me, my wife, and our son jobs for the summer as writers/photographers, it was too good to turn down.

We'll always be glad we went.

What we learned would fill several books, and virtually all of it was miles higher than anything we expected, in both the literal and figurative senses of the word.

The National Rifle Association's (NRA) Whittington Center is open

Pistol competition is fierce and instruction high-level.

A student becomes familiar with a shotgun.

year round, but during the middle of the summer the 53,000 acre range and accommodations are geared toward the Adventure Camp in which two sessions of kids, ages 14-17, learn to shoot everything from high-powered rifles and shotguns to black powder rifles and pistols.

But they learn a heck of a lot more than just shooting. They learn outdoor living, social skills, photography, and, especially, self-respect, respect for their fellow man, and respect for Nature. Above all, they learn safety.

They have safety drilled into their heads and hearts from the time they wake in the morning until they fall asleep, happy but exhausted, at night.

"There has never been a shooting death in the history of the Whittington Center," said Mike Ballew, who heads the center. "There has never been even a shooting accident in any form," he continued, "and there damn well better not be one. Such a thing is not only unthinkable but inexcusable."

Ballew points out that no matter where you stand on one of the shooting ranges, you cannot fire any weapon permitted on the range and have the projectile land outside the range. Shooting is done against a backdrop of Rocky Mountain peaks, and the splendor of the scenery is almost matched

by the beauty of the ranges and the manner in which the kids are taught.

The campers sleep in log cabins, and they eat breakfast in the center's mess hall. The first day they were treated to a speech by the national director who said, "You young men and women are here for one reason, you think: to shoot, shoot, shoot. You are wrong, wrong, wrong. You are here for several reasons: to learn gun safety, hunting safety, etiquette, consideration for others, cleanliness of mind and body, and concern for the world you live in. You are here to grow toward becoming part of the body of men and women and young people who know that a gun, properly used, is one of the finest inventions ever; improperly used, it is without doubt one of the worst devices ever unleashed upon the public."

He added, "While you are here, you will see hundreds of big game animals walking around you. If you even think of shooting at one of them, you're on the next plane home. If you want another quick ticket out of here, let me hear profanity, abusive language in any form, disrespect for anyone else's faith and way of life or ancestry, or let me learn of any conduct that is not in keeping with the highest standards of our society."

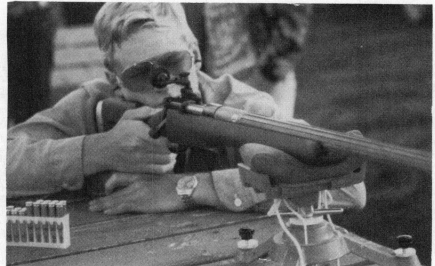

A barrel rest helps stabilize this single-shot rifle.

The kids spent hours learning the proper ways to handle a weapon and its ammunition; they shot until their shoulders ached and their arms felt like lead. And within minutes kids who had never held a gun in their hands were suddenly blasting clay pigeons out of the sky or blasting out the black in targets.

During the final week of camp, the kids packed their gear and moved to Coal Canyon, where they were responsible for setting up their own camps, cooking their meals, and keeping their houses clean and orderly.

One particularly challenging task was that of making their way across a mountain crest where targets of all sorts awaited them. If they spotted the big buck and shot it properly, they scored points. If they shot at the buck but failed to see the silhouette of the hunter beyond the buck, they were penalized severely. If they shot the silhouette of the "buck" which turned out to be a doe, they lost points. If they lost their way, they lost even more points.

They completed their week with their first real "hunt." Armed with cameras, they stalked the deer, bear, elk, and other big game that infests the NRA Whittington Center. And part of their camp fee paid for the processing and printing of the photos they snapped.

When it was over, minor miracles had occurred. One kid who was taking 14 different prescribed drugs when he arrived had, by the fourth day, stopped all medication and was feeling the best

he had felt in ages. He didn't take any more during the entire camp and left for home a totally new person.

Youngsters who were depressed and frustrated by the end of the second day were calling home on the third day with a wide range of messages for their parents. Hanging around the pay phones, I heard such messages as, "Dad, everything's fine here. I just thought you might be wondering who won the shotgun competition, especially since I had never used a shotgun before I got here," Or, "Mom, are you

too busy to hear what your son just won?" Or, "Hey, Mom. Get Dad on the other line while I tell you something that just might make you proud of your tomboy daughter."

The teaching staff of the camp, which is held during June and July every year, includes a bizarre range of talents. Included on the staff of the camp we attended were one newspaper editor, one flight surgeon, a psychiatrist, several college professors in fields ranging from farm management to literature to ROTC classroom work, one carpenter, a Border Patrol guard, an airline executive, several high school teachers, housewives, and an array of other professionals and amateurs all having one common denominator: they were all amazingly proficient in shooting, gun safety, outdoor living, and teaching techniques.

They came from a dozen states, from the East to the South to the Far West and points in between. And they used their vacation time to help kids learn to live better and longer.

When at the pistol range a metal target was hit but not knocked to the ground, the instructor was reluctant to stop the entire firing line. So he simply used his own pistol and blasted away

The campers are expected to set up and strike their tents while in the canyon phase of the Adventure Camp.

The Third Year

at the edge of the target and knocked it off with his first shot.

Classes met all day and well into the night, with nocturnal instruction centering around survival skills, creating comfortable camp sites, field dressing game shot and killed (a pig, later barbecued and served as supper, served also as the big game), and legalities and etiquette of hunting.

And what of the writer/photographer staff members who had never fired a shotgun or rifle except rarely during their entire lives? A college professor, a Ph. D. from the University of New Mexico, took us to the shotgun range for our first shots at the clay pigeons. I missed my first five, then Chris, the tutor, called a halt and gave me a couple of tips, and I proceeded to hit 27 of 30 clays, including some doubles coming toward me and from behind me at international skeet speeds.

My wife hit a respectable number of them and then our son, who was actually very frightened of guns before the trip, took over and blasted everything out of sight that sailed past him.

We moved to the black powder range where within five minutes we were loading our own weapons and hitting

If dinner isn't good, the campers have no one but themselves to blame.
They do their own menu planning and cooking.

the small silhouettes at considerable distances. We did the same with .357 magnum targets and with .22 pistols and .22 rifles.

Like the kids, we didn't realize what our capabilities were until we tried and after we received expert instruction from the best in the country.

But even kids who already shoot well or even those who do not benefit greatly from the instruction can and, in all probability, will find the Whittington experience to be memorable. What could be better for a young man or woman than to wake in the morning to the glorious sunrise over the Rocky Mountain peaks? Or to hear the howling of coyotes during the night, the foraging of the black bears that enter campgrounds and latch onto anything edible that isn't stored properly, or the excitement of seeing a herd of hundreds of elk after they find their way down from the higher elevations to the lush grasslands near the ranges?

Or the campfires at night, with the singing and story-telling and legends of the Old West being resurrected? Or the wild thunderstorms with jagged lightning illuminating the peaks and creating unforgettable visions of heavenly powers? Or the sight of a dozen mule deer or antelope grazing contentedly within ten feet of your cabin?

When we returned to North Carolina, richer and rewarded in dozens of ways beyond our wildest expectations, I dreamed every night of the Raton area and the Whittington Adventure. And for months afterward I'd dream of the incredible beauty, majesty, and wonder of one of the most magnificent parts of America.

Want to know something else? I still do. Δ

A group portrait. Kids come from all over the country to experience the adventure.

The Third Year

Self sufficiency & non-hybrid seeds

By Reynolds Griffith

There are two basic forms of seeds—hybrid and non-hybrid or open pollinated. Hybrid seeds are created by crossing carefully selected varieties of plants. The plants which grow from hybrid seeds have desirable characteristics from both parents and so are superior to either. Open pollinated seeds are produced by a plant which is pollinated by itself or a plant of the same variety.

Why use non-hybrid seed?

If hybrid seeds produce plants that are "superior", why would we use non-hybrid seeds? First, the term "superior" may be from the viewpoint of the commercial grower, which may not be best for the backyard or homestead gardener. For example, the hybrid crop may ripen all at once or be tough enough to ship across the country. We would prefer it tender and giving us an extended harvest.

Also, we cannot save the seeds from a hybrid plant and plant them the next year. (Actually, we could plant them, but there's no telling what would grow—almost certainly not anything as good as the parent plant.)

Seeds from a nonhybrid plant generally grow into plants almost identical to the plant which produced the seed. By saving seed from our gardens to plant the next year, we reduce our reliance on commercial sources. By careful selection of the plants from which to save seed we also end up with varieties which do well in our particular location.

Sources of non-hybrid seed

Most commercial seed dealers have non-hybrid as well as hybrid seeds. Hybrids must be indicated in the name or description in the catalog so it is easy to avoid them. However, there are suppliers who specialize in open pollinated varieties. These often are seeking to preserve and develop varieties that are no longer being carried in the major catalogs. By ordering from them instead of the big commercial dealers, we encourage the preservation of a wide range of varieties that are particularly suited for home gardeners. Here are some of the specialized sources:

Bountiful Gardens, c/o Ecology Action, 5798 Ridgewood Road, Willits, CA 95490. Their stock includes herbs and cover crops as well as vegetables. The catalog has very good descriptions. They also carry books and other materials on the biointensive gardening method. The catalog is free.

Garden City Seeds, 625 Phillips, Missoula, MT 59802. It carries vegetable seeds for northern climates.

Native Seeds/SEARCH, 2509 N. Campbell Ave., #325 Tucson, AZ 85719. They specialize in rediscovering, propagating, and distributing seeds of plants native to the Southwest. The catalog cost is $1.00.

Redwood City Seed Company, P.O. Box 361, Redwood City, CA 94064. They offer a variety of unusual vegetables, fruits, nuts, and herbs with interesting background on them. The catalog costs $1.00.

Seed Savers Exchange, R.R. 3, Box 239, Decorah, IA 52101. Not a seed company, but puts gardeners who save heirloom vegetable seeds in touch with each other. Send a long stamped addressed envelope for information.

Seeds Blum, Idaho City Stage, Boise, Idaho 83706. Their catalog has many heirlooms and unusual vegetables with good descriptions, suggestions for planting, gardening tips, and information on seed saving. It is arranged by a botanical family to help seed savers avoid unintended crossing of varieties. Catalog costs $3.

Southern Exposure Seed Exchange, P.O. Box 158, North Garden, VA 22959. Another good one—their catalog has very detailed descriptions, planting instructions, etc. Mostly open pollinated heirloom varieties. Many varieties are especially for the climates of the Mid-Atlantic region, but some are more widely adapted. It also carries some books. Catalog costs $3.

Territorial Seed Co. P.O. Box 157, Cottage Grove, OR 97424. They carry seeds primarily for the Pacific Northwest and similar climates. The catalog is free.

Saving seeds

To save seed, we select a couple of plants that seem to be doing especially well and let them "go to seed." For some (e.g. lettuce) this means not harvesting them so that they mature and produce seed (some will take until the next year to do so). For others (e.g. okra or squash) it means leaving a fruit or two on plants to fully ripen (or dry out in cases like beans or okra).

You should save at least twice as much seed as you expect to want to plant the next year. That way, if your crop should fail next time, you will still have seed to plant the year after (and perhaps some to share with others). Seeds of most plants will last at least two or three years if properly stored.

Be sure the seeds are completely dry before you store them (allow at least a week). Put them in airtight containers (e.g. vitamin bottles). Label each bottle with the variety and year.

Store them in a cool location where varmints can't get to them. Also save any catalog description or planting instructions that you have for each variety.

Conclusion

Using non-hybrid seeds makes sense for the homesteader or home gardener. It can be fun to try out several more of the many available varieties each year and develop your own seed stock of your favorites.

Sources for additional information: Bubel, Nancy, *The Seed-Starters Handbook*, (Emmaus, PA: Rodale Press), 1978. Δ

Waterwheels . . . Part 3 . . .

Design calculations for overshot waterwheels

(For good background information for this article, the reader should read "Waterpower for personal use" in Issue No. 16 and "Design calculations for no-head, low-head waterwheels" in Issue No. 17. — Editor)

By Rudy Behrens

This installment deals with the classic overshot waterwheel. This is the type most familiar to people where the water is introduced to the top of the wheel by a chute, known as a flume. In spite of the public impression that these machines are low technology, they were actually quite extensively studied by academicians. The first to study them was a Roman named Vetruvius, who wrote what is considered to be the earliest known engineering treatise. The work on waterwheels by Lazare Carnot´ in the early 1700s not only advanced fluid dynamics, but his study was the groundwork for the study of thermodynamics.

As we discussed in previous articles (Issues No. 16 and 17), the most important thing to determine when utilizing a waterwheel is **head**, or how far the water falls. This is important because it has a lot to do with the diameter of the wheel. Ideally, the wheel diameter should be 90% of the **head**. For convenience we choose some even number, in feet, that is nearly 90%. Unless the wheel is unusually large, we choose a diameter equal to the **head** minus two feet. This two-foot difference will be the depth of our flume.

Spouting velocity

We will now return to the concept of "spouting velocity." The water in the flume will flow to the end where it will fall two feet. We must determine how fast it is moving horizontally **and** vertically. You see, once it reaches the end of the flume, it begins to fall again, and gravity causes its downward speed to increase.

The answer is in the equation for spouting velocity, which is the equation that describes the speed of any falling mass: **velocity squared divided by two times a gravitational constant**, which is expressed mathematically as $V^2/2G$. The gravitational constant (G) is 32.2. We used this last time to convert a velocity into a head. Now we will use it to convert a head into a velocity.

Instead of the $V^2/2G = \text{Head}$, we will use the form: $\sqrt{\text{Head} \times 2G} = \text{velocity}$. It is the same equation; we re-arranged the terms to solve for a different variable.

If our water falls 2 feet, the equation tells us the velocity will be 11.35 feet per second. At the same time, gravity is pulling the water down as it is moving horizontally.

Bucket curvature

If we plot several points on a graph (see Figure 1) showing how the water travels horizontally as it leaves the flume, then vertically as gravity pulls on the water, we will get an arcing line. This line is very important. It will be the curvature of our buckets. By curving the buckets this way, the water enters smoothly and without splashing. It is then possible to make use of the velocity energy. Figure 1 is a graph of points for water leaving a two-foot flume.

Working diameter

The next step is to compute the working diameter. This is equal to the **total head** minus the depth of the flume. We will use a hypothetical head of 12 feet. This means our diameter will be 12' minus 2' = 10'. Now, multiply this number times **PI** (which is the mathematical constant equal to approximately 22/7 or 3.14) to get the working circumference. The answer will also be in feet—31.4 feet.

The number of buckets is relatively easy to determine. They should be approximately one foot apart, more or less, depending on the diameter. I recommend that it be an even number to simplify construction. Therefore, for our example we use 32 buckets. It is an even number and they will be almost one foot apart. The buckets should be around one foot deep.

Rotative speed

But how fast will it turn? The most efficient energy transfer occurs when the wheel speed is at 93% of the water

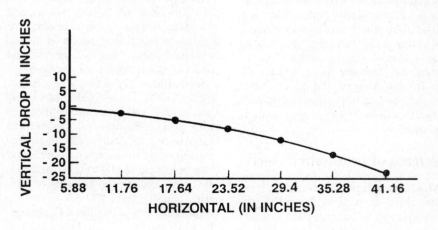

Figure 1. Bucket curvature graph

speed. For our example, the spouting velocity is 11.35 feet per second. So 93% of that is around 10 feet per second, which is the same as 600 feet-per-minute. You divide this by the working circumference per revolution. This gives you an answer of 19 revolutions per minute. That is your best rotative speed.

As you can see, it is rather slow. That is why you will need a speed increasing system, as we said last issue.

Power considerations

The power you will get depends on the width. For our example, let's assume you have a design flow of 50 cfs (cubic feet per second). When you divide this by the design speed of 10 feet per second, you see you need a bucket area of 5 square feet. If our buckets are 1 foot deep, the wheel should be 5 feet wide, **plus** one foot extra on each side to ventilate the buckets. As the water comes in, the air **must** get out.

One important detail: Put a one-inch diameter hole near the bottom of each bucket. This is to prevent them from sucking air when they are submerged. That can use up half of your power, while only a negligible amount of water leaks out. As I said last issue, power is equal to **flow** times **head** divided by 11.8. Therefore, we have a **flow** of 50 cfs **times a head** of 12' divided by 11.8. 50 X 12 = 600. 600/11.8 = 50.8 kilowatts. To state it another way, 50.8 kilowatts/.746 gives you 68 horsepower. We should assume an efficiency of 90%, so our hypothetical wheel will produce 61 horsepower or 45 kilowatts.

These calculations apply to **any** overshot waterwheel. The only thing that changes among the various designs is the speed or dimensions.

Materials should always be a good grade of steel. A36 or B36 works very well. 20 gauge or thicker is good. We always use 1/8" and ours have withstood direct hits by ice flows of more than a ton. If you use corten, a weathering steel, it will not need painting and will acquire a reddish color that resembles wood.

Never use wood

Staticly balance the wheel before installation. No matter how tempting, never use wood. It rots and holds water unevenly. This unbalances the wheel and makes it unsuitable for any use except grinding grain. Be very accurate in all your measurements, especially those concerning **flow** and **head**. If they are wrong, everything is wrong.

I recommend oil-impregnated wood bearing. They can be obtained from the POBCO Bearing Company of Worcester, MA.

Waterwheels turn too slowly for ball or sleeve bearings. They cannot maintain a uniform lubricant field. This tends to ruin the bearing quickly. The wood bearings have a "wick" action that maintains uniform lubricant.

(Rudy Behrens owns the Fitz Waterwheel Company, 118 Sycamore Ct., Collegeville, PA 19426. Phone: (215) 489- 6256.) Δ

Gather it ... eat it

- *Clover*
- *Greens*
- *Asparagus*
- *Flower buds*
- *Raspberries*
- *Blueberries*
- *Wild garlic*
- *Acorns*
- *Wilderness wine*

A Backwoods Home Anthology
The Eleventh Year

※ Wild greens: when weeds become vegetables
※ A portable bench for your better half
※ Keeping poison ivy under control
※ Cooking for a crowd
※ Rural building: Construction q's and a's
※ Radiant floor heating
※ Jackie's tips for hardcore homesteading
※ Solar building design
※ Make a sure-fire live trap
※ Good homemade jerky
※ A passive solar-heated tower house

※ Preparation for successful painting
※ An easy-to-make pot rack
※ Make your own insulated waterer
※ Home canning safety tips
※ Masonry stoves — what's old is new
※ Lye soap making in the modern home
※ Integrated PV/roofing
※ Basic livestock vetting
※ Tale of a country family
※ Dealing with ticks
※ Electricity from the wind: Assessing wind energy potential

The Third Year

Rope as a tool—as versatile as ever

By Jim Sullivan
(Drawings by Linda Parker)

Rope is one of our oldest and most useful tools and for those of us living in the backwoods, it is a relatively inexpensive tool, capable of making dozens of tasks easier and safer.

Types of rope material

Natural fiber ropes tend to be heavier, more subject to rot, and in the long run, less cost effective than synthetics. They also can't be stored wet.

But there are some occasions when natural fiber cordage and ropes are preferred. For example, when rope or cord must be abandoned in the field—only natural fibers will biodegrade.

Today most rope and cord is made of four synthetic materials:

1. **Nylon**, which is strong, stretchy, and expensive.
2. **Dacron**, which is also strong and expensive, but doesn't stretch.
3. **Polypropylene**—frequently used as a utility rope. Although a lot stronger than any natural fiber, it is not as strong, elastic, or as pleasant to handle as nylon, but it is less expensive and it floats.
4. **Polyethelyne**, which is similar to polypropylene, but cheaper in every way—and harder to knot.

Rope performance, for both natural and synthetic materials, is also determined by the method of construction. Figure 1 illustrates three methods that I'll discuss: Traditional **three-strand twisted (or "laid" rope** is reasonably strong, spliceable, and inexpensive. It doesn't flatten under a load, so it's suitable for pulleys or winches. But it can rotate under a load.

Solid braid rope is not as strong as twisted rope, but wears better and has greater abrasion resistance. It handles well, doesn't flatten under a load and doesn't twist. But it isn't spliceable, and it is expensive.

Double braid rope is two ropes in one: usually a strong, abrasion-resistant jacket braided over a braided core. It doesn't flatten or rotate. It is flexible, spliceable (with a fid), attractive, strong, and very expensive.

Other construction methods are used for various specialty ropes. If you love that "natural feel," rope-makers can—for a price—combine the "feel" and knot-holding capacity of natural fibers with the durability and strength of synthetics. There are specially designed ropes for nearly every task you might imagine, from tree pruning to clothes drying.

The **Recommended Working Load (RWL)** is recorded on the package or spool label or in the manufacturer's catalog. You will note that the RWL is usually only 8 to 14 percent of the breaking strength for new twisted ropes and 15 to 20 percent for new braided ropes. The RWL may seem overly conservative to inexperienced workers, but several factors can combine to drastically weaken rope under a heavy load: To begin with, most traditional knots weaken rope by 60 to 90 percent (unlike splices, which are much stronger). Dynamic loading, or sudden or extreme stress, can additionally—and unexpectedly—reduce strength, as can age, abrasion, and other sometimes undetectable damage. Whenever safety is a factor you should know the RWL of the ropes you are using.

Not so hard to tie

Some people are intimidated by knots, but there is no reason to be. If you can tie your shoe laces, you can tie just about any knot you'll ever need. In fact, the shoe lace knot is relatively complicated and difficult. Technically it is a double-slipped square knot, which most of us can tie in the dark using a genuinely sophisticated technique, even if we can't tie a normal square knot.

3 STRAND TWISTED

SOLID BRAID

DOUBLE BRAID

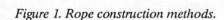

Figure 1. Rope construction methods.

The real problem with knots is not lack of dexterity or the temporary difficulty of figuring out how to tie a knot from the diagrams in a book, but that we don't use knots in our daily routine so we forget what we already know about them. It's like forgetting the words to a song.

The way most of us solve this problem is to stick to a dozen or so tried-and-true standbys out of the 4,000 plus known knots. These will cover 90% of the jobs you ever need to do. Nearly everyone knows at least half of these already, which means that with 5 or 6 more knots most of us would be fairly competent rope users. When you need a special knot, look it up. A good knot book should be part of your reference library.

Whipping the ends

Before starting to use a rope you need to whip the ends to keep them from unraveling. An easy and effective way is to tape them with electric or duct tape or one of the special tapes or plastics now available. Synthetic ropes can be flame sealed but the fumes are toxic, and on larger ropes sharp, finger-cutting edges can form.

The best way to whip the ends is with one of the traditional palm and needle whippings using a special waxed or tarred thread, although few of us have time for such labors on any but our best ropes. The worst—but sometimes necessary—way is to tie off the end

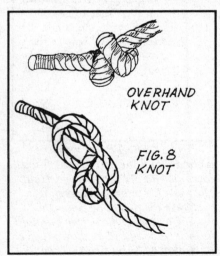

Figure 2. Stopper Knots.

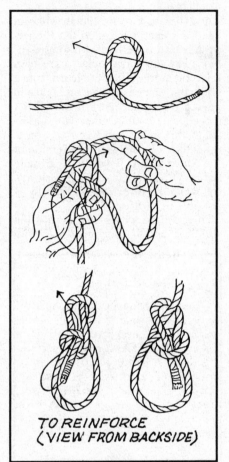

Figure 3. Instructional Bowline. Form the hitch part of the knot by passing the working end up through the loop from below. Continue to form the interlocking loop by passing the working end around to the left behind the standing part and back down through the original loop (which is now the center of the 3 loops you have made—the loop on the right will be the final open loop of the knot). To provide additional security, you can turn the knot over and trap the working end under the hitch as shown.

with a **Stopper Knot**, usually an overhand or figure eight as in Figure 2.

A knot for the job

Try to think about knots in terms of the jobs you want them to do. I don't mean the specific task such as tying up your dog or making a lanyard for your flashlight or hoisting a chain saw up to your partner in a tree. Rather "job" in

the sense of what the knot does to the rope.

Loop knots make a loop in the end of the rope, which common job knots are asked to do. A loop in the end of a rope enables you to attach the rope to an object and do a task with it. There are quite a few good loop knots, but the undisputed king is the **Bowline**. You can't get your black belt in knot-tying without learning it. But don't worry—it's easy. Figure 3 shows what is sometimes called an Instructional Bowline.

For most people what is hard about the Bowline is not so much learning it, but actually trying to tie it in the field when your physical orientation to the knot may be different, or the rope (and you) may be wet, cold, stiff, frayed, or under tension. Or you may have to tie it around an object instead of tying it in hand and slipping it around the object later on.

Five or six different methods of tying it have evolved to cover these kinds of situations. If you take the trouble to learn at least three of these, you will not only be able to get your Bowline tied, but you'll develop a feeling for how to deal with most other knots under similarly difficult field conditions.

When you tie a Bowline directly around an object, use the Bowline Hitch, as shown in Figure 4.

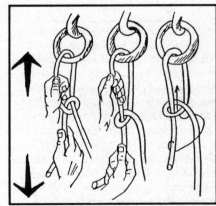

Figure 4. Bowline Hitch. Pass the working end around the object, then bring it back around and make a hitch on itself. Release the rope with both hands and regrasp the working end on both sides of the hitch and jerk the hitch apart—the hitch will transfer to the other side.

The Third Year

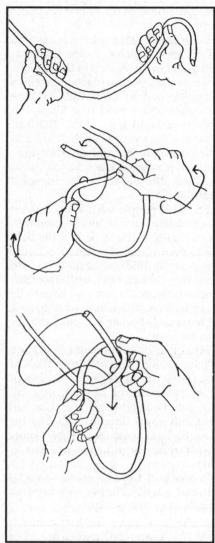

A stylish way to tie the Bowline in hand is sometimes called the **Fingertip Bowline**, a method with some flair, more like the way shoelaces are tied. It is a bit more difficult to learn from a book, but very easy to use and teach in person once you figure it out. Don't forget, style counts. Once you understand this move you will find something like it in the weaver's version of the **Sheet Bend**. If you have trouble figuring this one out, try it very slowly, following the directions as literally as possible in Figure 5.

This method works well even if the standing end is hanging down with

Figure 7. Reinforced Sheet Bend, above, and Becket Bend, below.

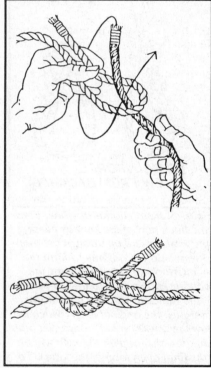

Figure 5. Fingertip Bowline. A) Start with palms up, working end to the right. B) Bring hands together while rotating both wrists so the palms are more or less down. Lay the working end across the standing part, pinching these two parts between the thumb and forefinger of the right hand. C) Rotate both wrists back outward. While you are doing this, lower your right hand a bit and raise your left hand, moving it simultaneously in an arc directly away from your body, down, then back under, wrapping a hitch around the working end as shown. Now reach under the standing part with your left hand to grasp the working end and bring it around to insert back down through the hitch as shown by the arrow.

Figure 6. Instructional Sheet Bend. In your left hand form the loop (in the thicker rope if you are using different sized ropes). Position the short working end on the right side and allow the long standing part to hang over the back of your hand with gravity. Form the hitch by threading the other rope up through this loop, passing it all the way around to the right, behind the loop, then pinning it under itself as shown. Both short ends must wind up on the same side. Completed Sheet Bend must be drawn up carefully before use.

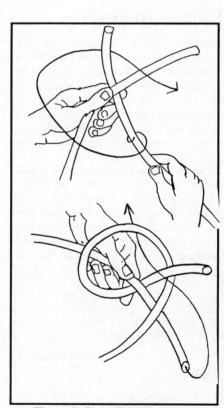

Figure 8. Sheet Bend, weaver's method. Place the end of the left rope over the end of the right rope. Hold between left thumb and forefinger. Grasp the right rope below the crossing and wrap it clockwise around its own working end as shown (twice for reinforced Sheet Bend). Then fold the other end back through the hitch.

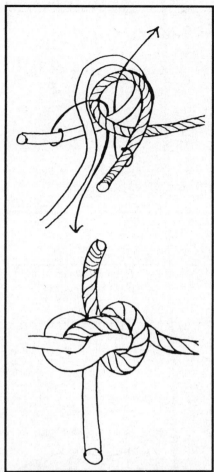

Figure 9. Zeppelin Bend. Form the two loops as shown and lay the right loop on top of the left loop. Thread the ends through the center from opposite directions as shown by the arrows.

gravity but, to reduce the confusion while learning, you may want to tie the standing end off to another object so that it leads to your hands as shown in the drawings. Try this exercise: tie off to a table leg or drawer handle or other object with a Bowline Hitch, then tie a Fingertip Bowline in the other end.

When there is a possibility of the Bowline slipping, you can tie the working end off to the standing part with any of a number of hitches — Two Half Hitches being about as good as any — or directly reinforce it in any of several different ways, one of which is shown in Figure 3, at the bottom.

A **Bend** is a knot that attaches the end of one rope to the end of another (or itself). The classic bend is the

Sheet bend. Although it is not a particularly secure knot, especially in synthetic rope, it can easily be reinforced. It is the standard utility bend, especially when joining different sized ropes.

If you take a look at the Sheet Bend you will see that it is virtually identical in form to the Bowline, consisting of one hitch interlocking with one loop. Turn it over and note how each stops the other from slipping out — a very elegant formation.

The instructional way to tie the Sheet Bend (Figue 6) involves forming the loop first, then threading the hitch up from under the loop, around behind, and pinning it back under itself. Consider also Figure 7, the **Becket Bend**, which uses a similar principle to attach a rope to a loop. To make either of these more secure, take an extra turn as shown in Figure 7, top. You have to take extra care to work the Sheet Bend up carefully, or else it may capsize.

A stylish weaver's method for the Sheet Bend is shown in Figure 8. If you can tie the Fingertip Bowline and the **Weaver's Sheet Bend** you are going to walk around feeling good about yourself.

Since knot tying is as old as our earlier ancestors, you'd think that by now, with all that practice, it would be hard to come up with anything new. But the introduction of synthetics 40 or 50 years ago stimulated the invention of several brand new secure knots for slippery rope as well as new applications for some old knots. **The Riggers Bends**, for example, both old and new, have come into their own as outstandingly secure, easy to untie bends for general use. The handsome **Zeppelin Bend** (Figure 9) was used to tether dirigibles. It has a better lead than the Sheet Bend, is stronger, and more secure.

Hitches attach a rope to an object or another rope. Snug hitches are tied directly around the object. Loose hitches involve passing the rope around the object and tying it back on itself.

There are more hitches than anyone could hope to learn. They are indispensable and a lot of fun to tie. You should study the **Half Hitch**, the knot called **Two Half Hitches** (Figure 10,

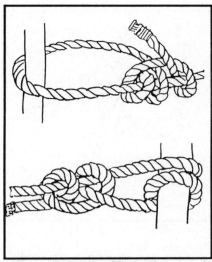

Figure 10. Rolling Hitch, above, and Round Turn and Two Half Hitches.

bottom), maybe the Clove Hitch (Figure 11), and a few others.

The versatile Rolling Hitch

But if you had to pick only one hitch, you couldn't do much better than the **Rolling Hitch** (Figure 10, top). Just knowing that it also goes by at least five other names (**Tent Peg Hitch, Tautline Hitch, Midshipman's Hitch, Magner's Hitch, Magnus Hitch**) lets you know that craftsmen both ashore and at sea have treasured it. It is adaptable to many different tasks, easy to tie, easy to untie, strong, secure, and — rare for knots — adjustable. It can be tied as a loose hitch or snug hitch. It is an important rescue knot. And it is easy to remember.

The rolling hitch is probably most often tied as a loose hitch, that is, the rope is first led around the object and then tied back on itself with what is known as a Round Turn and then secured by a Single Half Hitch (Figure 10). It's hard to believe such a simple knot could be so reliable. Although it is adjustable, it won't slip under tension. Put the round turn on the side you don't want the knot to slip toward. You can make the hitch in either the same direction as the round turn, or opposite it. If slipping is a problem, the second half of the round turn can be slipped over the first for added friction. When this hitch is tied directly to

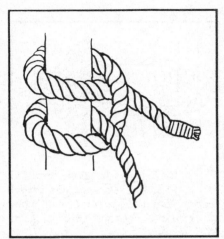

Figure 11. Clove Hitch

an object as a snug hitch it is considered the most reliable single knot under lengthwise pull.

These fundamental loops, bends, and hitches will enable you to put your rope to use. Don't neglect to work them carefully into their final forms. Incorrectly tied knots can be dangerous. You can expand naturally on this core as you learn the other knots you need to get your work done. It helps to carry a practice cord around in your pocket. You'll be surprised how often you find yourself experimenting with it. Moreover, a lot of good knot tiers are positively compulsive about demonstrating their currently favorite knot to any one who will listen.

(Jim Sullivan is a retired landscape contractor working on a book tentatively titled "Learn to Tie Knots," due out soon. This article is extracted from the chapter on Materials. For more information write Knots, P.O. Box 92, Bodega, CA 94922. Phone: (707) 874-2174.) Δ

The Australian Shepherd is a good dog choice for the self sufficient person who values brains and loyalty

By Susan P. Weiss

Ask a self-sufficient country person about the ideal dog and words like intelligence, loyalty, and diligence would probably come up. It is not surprising, then, that the Australian Shepherd is an increasingly popular country dog, since the breed has all of these qualities and more.

This dog, named Blue, has the typical markings of an Australian Shepherd.

Although they arrived in California with Australian sheepherders and cattledrovers in the early 1900s, there is some debate concerning the exact origin of these dogs. Similar to a breed that arrived with Spanish sheepherders, "Aussies" have been traced to the Basque region in the Pyrenees Mountains between Spain and France. Although they are thought to be a cross between the Kelpie and the Scottish Border Collie, another theory has it that in New South Wales in the middle of the nineteenth century, a squatter searching for the perfect working dog crossed a Smithfield Cattle Dog with a German Collie. The crossbreeds were brought to America, where their working instincts were soon put to the test.

Although the Australian Shepherd earns top ranking in obedience and sheepdog trials, it was not until September of 1991 that the American Kennel Club opened registration to Aussies. Prior to this, the breed was registered with the United Kennel Club, the National Stock Dog Registry, and the Australian Shepherd Club of America. (ASCA) The ASCA, founded in 1957 in Tucson, Arizona, is one of the largest independent breed club registries in the U.S. Because the Aussie is primarily a herding dog, fanciers of the breed didn't press for AKC recognition, as they were concerned that the breed's appearance would become more important than its keen work instincts.

When Ed Buterbaugh and Christl Moran began raising Peruvian Pasos horses several years ago, they were looking for a good work dog.

"We wanted a herding dog that would keep up with us when we're out riding, and Aussies do keep up. Not only do they bring the horses in from pasture, but they are very good companions," comments Moran. Buterbaugh and Moran live on a horse farm outside Indiana, Pennsylvania. The former dairy farm has been in the Buterbaugh family since 1884. A skilled carpenter, Buterbaugh recently completed a brand new barn on the historic property. Although they grow corn for feed, the couple's ultimate farming goal is self-sufficiency. Moran artfully converts the milk of their Nubian goats into goat milk cheese. Having adopted an Australian Shepherd, Buterbaugh and Moran were so taken with the breed that they are now breeders themselves.

Aussies are generally reserved with strangers, and should be allowed to take their time in getting acquainted. They are extremely alert without being too intense. Their innate split-second timing is both awe-inspiring and necessary at the heels of powerful beasts of the field. In addition to their herding ability, Aussies are warm companions. Their heavy, water-repellant coat makes them a natural outdoor dog. Although excellent guard dogs, they are rarely vicious. Moran credits them with keeping pests out of the garden. Rather quiet, they generally bark only with good reason. According to Moran, Australian Shepherds "like to be where the action is." They are quick learners who are very good with children.

In Australia, the breed is called simply "The Shepherd dog." Sensitive and easily trained, these dogs are loyal protectors, both of herd and master. There have been several accounts of Australian Shepherds who saved their rural owners from danger. Some Aussies, in their owners' absence, have brought in herds just prior to a treacherous storm. One dog even attacked a rattlesnake which was wrapped around a child's leg, saving the child's life and taking the majority of bites himself (luckily, in a bony area of his head, so the poison didn't spread). Australian Shepherds also make excellent tracking dogs. Roy Rogers included several of his own Australian Shepherds in his television episodes.

On a typical day, Moran, mindful of the breed's versatility, might take her dogs riding in the morning and to her son's Little League game in the evening. Moran and Buterbaugh took their first group of Aussies to a herding clinic, where the puppies were trained with a flock of sheep. If a sheep strayed, the dogs were taught to retrieve it. Some authorities advise owners to begin training their puppies with comparatively non-aggressive animals such as ducks. Although they are natural herders, Australian Shepherds intended to be working animals should receive early command training.

"Like other breeds, Aussie puppies are frisky and playful, but as they mature, they learn to listen," advises Moran. For this reason, they should not work cattle until they are about a year old. Litters average five to eight puppies. A puppy from Moran's most recent litter was receptive to obedience training at only four months of age. All of Moran's customers have been pleased with their puppies. Some have returned from hundreds of miles away, just to visit and talk about the breed.

The color of these intelligent dogs varies, and includes blue merle, red (liver) merle, solid black and solid red (liver). All of these colors may occur with or without white markings and or tan (copper) points, and there is no order of preference. Moran and Buterbaugh consider the dog easy to

breed, but caution that breeding merle to merle can result in excessive white. This can result in a deaf or blind litter. Although salt and pepper coat splashes are desirable, a dog with more than one third of whiteness would be disqualified from the breed standard. Technically, eyes and ears of the Australian Shepherd should be entirely surrounded with color other than white. The American Kennel Club recommends choosing a puppy at least six weeks old. Look for an alert and curious puppy with a shiny coat.

Shep, also Australian Shepherd, is more solid-colored

Moran and Buterbaugh found their first Australian Shepherd through a classified ad in a horse trade magazine. "We were not particularly interested in show dogs, so the magazine was a good source for us. We have been perfectly happy with our choice." Moran says that a buyer will pay more for an Australian Shepherd of show quality. Dog shows provide a chance to observe many breeds and to speak with breeders. One might also find Aussie breeders at horse shows. Veterinarians are another source for finding local Australian Shepherds. The American Kennel Club can provide guidance in finding a nearby breeder.

With their expressive eyes and gentle nature, Australian Shepherds are natural companions. Moran is not the first owner to claim that when happy, members of the breed actually smile!

For more information about the Australian Shepherd, contact:

The American Kennel Club Customer Service, 580 Centerview Drive,

Raleigh, North Carolina 27606, (919) 233-9767.

The Australian Shepherd Association, Attention: Maria Pino, P.O. Box 964, Dallas, Texas 75221.

The Australian Shepherd Club of America (ASCA), 1706 East 29th Street, Suite E, Dept. 16, Bryan, TX 77802-1425, (800) 892-ASCA, (409) 823-3491. Δ

God forbid we should ever be 20 years without such a rebellion...What country can preserve its liberties if its rulers are not warned from time to time that this people preserve the spirit of resistance? Let them take arms. The remedy is to set them right as to facts, pardon & pacify them. What signify a few lives lost in a century or two? The tree of liberty must be refreshed from time to time with the blood of patriots & tyrants. It is its natural manure.

Thomas Jefferson
1743-1826

My best winter meals

By Darlene Campbell

If your backwoods home is like mine, there are drafty cracks around the windows and under the doors, no insulation and winters are harsh. This makes cooking one of the most pleasant winter chores as opposed to breaking ice on the pond to water animals or stacking firewood on the porch for easy reach when temperature and wind chill take a dive. Cooking in winter not only warms the house and fills it with aromas to tempt the appetite, it satisfies that urge to create.

Although I cook on a gas burning stove, in the living room is a wood burning space heater for heat. It is our only heat source and that means the coals are never allowed to go completely out. This is where I keep a kettle of water hot for herb tea or cocoa while it adds humidity to the air.

This is the stove I place a stool behind to let bread dough rise to perfection while children's wet boots and mittens are drying, while on its top I set a pot of stew or soup to stay hot for serving. I even use the wood stove to warm cold plates or bowls pulled from a cold cupboard before setting them on the table.

But the main source of cooking is done in the kitchen. No fancy kitchen here, but the meals that come from it are nutritious and economical to prepare. The secret to stocking a kitchen is maintaining a selection of herbs and spices along with basics like flour, cornmeal, baking soda, baking powder, yeast, sugar and salt. Add to this such staples as dairy products, rice, pastas, potatoes, cereals (hot and cold), a selection of canned, frozen, dried or fresh vegetables and fruits, eggs and (unless you're vegetarian) meat. With this list you are on the road to complete nutrition. You may or may not choose to cook with oil or shortening but it is necessary for baking. And since bread, rolls, pies and cakes are part of winter cooking, shortening is on my list of necessities. Once you learn how much of each staple you use each month, you will find that shopping can be done monthly and becomes the major project for family survival.

Picking up items on sale are profitable, but only if you intend to use them and can rely on the quality. For example, tomato sauce is frequently used in my kitchen so I stock up when it's on sale. But be wary of off brands of items such as coffee or flour. You may end up drinking coffee for a month that would be better used for opening drains, or bread and biscuits that are heavy and hard to digest.

Storing a month's supply of food does not have to be difficult. Most rural kitchens are equipped with plenty of cupboards, and some even offer the luxury of a pantry—a small room or large closet lined with shelves for storing canned goods. But if your kitchen is not designed with lots of storage, you can use a back bedroom closet or any place that is dry and does not freeze to store surplus items. Even covering them and placing them under the baby's crib is satisfactory. Place them in cardboard boxes and tuck the flaps over the top to protect them. Be cautious of mice that may find the store and chew through. Keep your home rodent and insect free.

The following recipes are some of winter's best eating.

Hamburger soup

1 pound ground beef
4 carrots, cut in 2-inch chunks
3 potatoes, quartered
1 onion, chopped
1/2 bell pepper, sliced
1 16-oz. can tomatoes
1 6-oz. can tomato sauce
1 cup water or stock
1 teaspoon thyme
1/4 teaspoon each black pepper and garlic powder
1 bouillon cube

In a large soup pot, cook the ground beef over medium heat until brown and crumbly. Drain off excess fat. Add remaining ingredients and simmer, stirring occasionally, until vegetables are fork tender. I do not use salt in this recipe, but if you omit the bouillon cube, you may add salt to taste.

For variety, substitute stewed tomatoes for regular canned ones, or add celery or corn. Serve with hot biscuits.

In the country a cook soon learns to improvise. By substituting what is on hand for ingredients called for in recipes, new tastes are developed as well as minimizing trips to town when you run short. For example, few people know that mayonnaise can be substituted for either shortening or eggs in recipes. Just be careful not to overdue the mayonnaise or the flavor comes through. In the following recipe, mayonnaise takes the place of shortening.

Mayonnaise biscuits

2 cups self rising flour
1 cup milk
3 tablespoons mayonnaise

Place flour in medium size bowl. Stir in mayonnaise and milk. Knead dough lightly adding additional flour if necessary. Roll out on a floured board and cut with a medium size biscuit cutter. Bake at 450 degrees until lightly brown.

Angel biscuits

> 1 cup buttermilk
> 4 cups all-purpose flour
> 2 teaspoons baking powder
> 1 teaspoon salt
> 1 package dry yeast
> 1/2 cup warm water (105 to 115 degrees)
> 5 tablespoons shortening
> 2 tablespoons sugar
> 2 tablespoons butter or margarine, melted

Heat buttermilk in a small pan until bubbles form around edge, careful not to overheat as buttermilk will curdle. Cool to lukewarm. While milk is cooling, sprinkle yeast over warm water in a small bowl. Add sugar to yeast mixture. Stir in lukewarm buttermilk. Into a large bowl sift flour with baking powder and salt. Cut shortening into flour mixture with a pastry blender until mixture resembles coarse cornmeal.

Make a well in the center of the flour mixture and pour buttermilk and yeast mixture into it all at once. Stir with a wooden spoon to mix well. Dough will be stiff. Knead as you would for bread until smooth. Roll out with a rolling pin to 1/2-inch thickness. Cut with a floured 2-inch cutter. Place one inch apart on greased cookie sheet, cover with a kitchen towel and let rise in a warm place free from drafts until double in bulk. Brush tops with melted butter and bake at 400 degrees 10 to 12 minutes.

There is usually plenty of plump young fryers or broiler chickens in the freezer, so chicken recipes are treasured. Here are two that can be served at home or taken to a church supper.

Mexican chicken

> 1 large package tortilla chips, crushed
> 2 chickens, de-boned
> 1 can cream of mushroom soup
> 1 can cream of chicken soup
> 1 cup chicken broth
> 1 can Ro*Tel tomatoes
> 1 pound Cheddar cheese, thinly sliced
> 1 onion, chopped

Boil and de-bone the chicken. Combine soups, Ro*Tel tomatoes and broth. Place chopped onion in a pan and follow with layers of chicken, 1/2 the cheese, 2/3 package tortilla chips, soup mixture, remaining cheese; top with tortilla chips. Bake in 300 degree oven for 25 minutes.

Schoolhouse chicken pie

> 2 tablespoons margarine
> 1 cup sliced mushrooms
> 1 clove garlic, minced
> 2 tablespoons cornstarch
> 1 1/2 cups milk
> 2 1/2 cups cooked chicken, cut in bite-size pieces
> 2 cups peas, canned or frozen
> 1 whole pimiento, chopped
> 1/2 teaspoon dried thyme leaves
> 1 teaspoon salt
> 1/4 teaspoon pepper
> 1 recipe for double crust pastry

Melt margarine in a skillet. Add mushrooms and garlic. Saute over medium heat until lightly browned. In a saucepan stir together cornstarch and milk until smooth. Mix in mushrooms, garlic and pan drippings. Bring to a boil over medium heat, stirring constantly; boil 1 minute. Stir in next 6 ingredients. Pour into pastry-lined 9-inch pie pan. Cover pie with pastry; seal and flute edge.

Cut slits in top and bake in 375-degree oven for 35 minutes or until crust is golden brown.

Winter and the kids can empty the cookie jar almost faster then you can fill it. Here's a recipe that makes enough cookies to fill that jar two or three times. These keep well and can also be frozen.

Dishpan cookies

> 4 cups all-purpose flour
> 2 teaspoons soda
> 1 teaspoon salt
> 2 cups brown sugar
> 2 cups granulated sugar
> 2 cups oil
> 4 eggs
> 2 teaspoons vanilla
> 1 1/2 cups quick-cooking oats
> 4 cups cornflakes

In a very large bowl or pan combine sugars, oil, eggs and vanilla. Mix well. Blend and sift flour, soda and salt. Add flour mixture to sugar mixture, mixing thoroughly. Blend in the oats and cornflakes. Drop by spoonful onto greased cookie sheets. Bake 8 to 10 minutes at 325 degrees. Makes 9 to 12 dozen cookies.

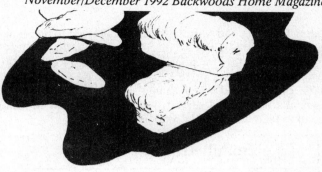

If you are not feeding a tribe, the following cookie recipe is ideal for between meal snacking. It contains lots of wholesome ingredients like oats, coconut and pecans.

Earth's greatest cookies

> 2 sticks margarine
> 1 cup sugar
> 1 cup brown sugar
> 1 egg
> 1 cup vegetable oil
> 1 cup rolled oats
> 1 cup crushed cornflakes
> 1 cup shredded coconut
> 1 cup pecans
> 3 1/2 cups all-purpose flour
> 1 teaspoon soda
> 1 teaspoon vanilla

Preheat oven to 350 degrees. Cream margarine and sugar until light and fluffy. Add egg; mixing well after each addition add oats, cornflakes, coconut, and nuts. Blend well. Form into balls the size of a walnut and place on ungreased cookie sheet. Flatten with the bottom of a glass dipped in sugar, and bake until lightly browned.

No collection of winter recipes would be complete without a hearty bread. Since most cookbooks contain recipes for wheat or white bread, I like to find unusual bread recipes and bake them to chase the chill from the house. Here are two breads that can be baked in coffee cans for fun. They should slide out of the cans for easy slicing, but if they stick, remove the bottoms of the cans with a can opener and push the bread through from the bottom.

Boston brown bread

> 1 1/2 cups yellow cornmeal
> 2 cups all-purpose flour
> 2 teaspoons baking soda
> 1 teaspoon salt
> 1 1/3 cups milk
> 1 1/3 cups buttermilk
> 3/4 cup molasses
> 1 cup raisins

Sift cornmeal, flour, baking soda and salt into a large bowl. In a small bowl, combine the molasses, milk and buttermilk. Slowly add the molasses milk mixture to the flour mixture. Mix with a spoon. Stir in raisins. Spoon dough into well greased coffee cans, filling two thirds full. Cover the cans with foil and place on a rack in deep kettle.

Add boiling water to the kettle to come halfway up sides of cans. Cover the kettle and steam 2 1/2 to 3 hours adding more water as needed. Remove loaves from cans and cool on a rack.

English muffin bread

> 2 packages dry yeast
> 2 tablespoons sugar
> 1 cup warm water
> Small amount cornmeal
> 1 teaspoon salt
> 5 cups flour (approximate)
> 1 1/2 cups warm milk
> 1/2 teaspoon baking soda dissolved in 1 tablespoon water.

Combine yeast and sugar with warm water (about 110 degrees) in a large bowl and let stand for several minutes until puffy. Using an electric mixer, slowly beat while adding alternately into the yeast mixture the salt, 3 cups of the flour, and 1 cup warm milk. Beat well after each addition. Add soda-water mixture and beat well to blend.

With a wooden spoon, beat in the remaining 1/2 cup milk and enough remaining flour to make a stiff dough. Dough should be too sticky to knead with the hands. Spoon the dough into coffee cans that have been greased and sprinkled with cornmeal on the inside. Top with their lids. Place in a warm spot to rise until the lids pop off, about 45 to 60 minutes. Carefully remove lids.

Bake the cans upright on a rack in the oven at 375 degrees for 25 to 30 minutes or until loaves are well browned on top and the sides and bottoms are golden. Slide loaves out of cans and stand upright on wire racks to cool. Slice in rounds and toast to serve.

The above bread will keep well if stored in an airtight container at room temperature. It also freezes well for longer storage. If setting the dough behind the wood stove to rise, be sure to turn the cans occasionally to allow all sides to rise evenly. Do not set directly on the wood stove or it will over heat killing the action of the yeast.

A good standby is spaghetti sauce. Started early in the morning it takes over two hours to simmer and the rest of the day sitting on the back of the stove to enhance its flavor. It doesn't have to take that long if you are not tied to ethnic traditions, but I like to think of the longer cooking time as adding humidity and warmth to the kitchen, not to mention the aroma. This sauce is wonderful, and I found it will can beautifully adding to my stock of homemade fast food. It can be served over pasta or rice, used as a base for lasagne, pizza, or chili, and when canned it can be heated at a moment's notice and served over sliced English Muffin Bread to feed hungry after schoolers.

Spaghetti meat sauce

> 1 pound ground beef
> 1 medium onion, chopped or grated fine
> 3 6-ounce cans tomato sauce
> 3 6-ounce cans water
> 1 can tomato paste
> 1/2 teaspoon garlic powder
> 1 tablespoon salt
> 1 tablespoon dried oregano leaves
> 1 tablespoon dried basil leaves

In a 5-quart Dutch oven, saute ground beef over medium heat breaking it up into chunks with a wooden spoon. Add onion and continue cooking until beef is crumbly and no longer pink, and onion is transparent. Drain off excess fat. Add tomato sauce, water and tomato paste. Stir well to blend. Add remaining ingredients and blend. Bring sauce to a boil and reduce heat to very low. Place the lid off-set on the Dutch oven to allow steam to escape. Continue cooking at a slow simmer for 2 1/2 hours, stirring occasionally. Sauce will thicken as it cooks.

To can this sauce, pour, hot, into sterilized jars. Leave 1inch of head space and adjust caps and bands. Process pints 1 hour, and quarts 1 hour and 15 minutes at 10 pounds of pressure.

Not all the meals prepared are eaten indoors in winter. Many don't even require long hours of cooking. When I go to the woods to help John I take along two thermos bottles of coffee, one with sugar and one without; some cheese; graham crackers and apples. And while John cuts trees and brush with a chainsaw, I stack firewood and drag brush and branches. When we tire we find a spot to sit down and enjoy our take-out meal. Δ

A BHM Writer's Profile

Marjorie Burris and her husband have lived in an old hand- hewn log house on their forty-acre homestead in central Arizona for over 10 years. Their next-door neighbor lives five miles away.

They have a quarter-acre organic garden and an organic apple orchard from which they make cider on an 80-year-old cider press. They have raised chickens, ducks, geese, and rabbits in the past, but now only raise pigs and beef cattle, which they process themselves. Marjorie cooks and cans on a wood stove, and shoots rattlesnakes with her Smith & Wesson .38.

Her husband recently installed a solar electric system in their home. Before moving to the mountains, she was an operating room nurse at the V.A. hospital in Phoenix, Arizona.

She is delighted to have her four grandchildren come to the homestead and learn backwoods skills and values. She recommends the backwoods life for "them that can take it."

I believe there are more instances of the abridgment of the freedom of the people by gradual and silent encroachments of those in power than by violent and sudden usurpations.

James Madison
1751-1836

Healthy holiday baking

By Jennifer Stein Barker

Does baking for the holidays make you dream of buttery, sugary confections chock-full of candied fruits and sprinkled with sparkly colored sugar? Or do you dream of presenting healthier goodies to your friends and family that taste every bit as wonderful? Many people gain weight over the holidays, but even worse is that listless, drained feeling that follows too many weeks of indulging in empty calories. Every time you eat a goodie full of fat, sugar, and refined carbohydrates, you are losing the chance to acquire fiber, vitamins, minerals, and complex carbohydrates along with your calories.

At our house, we indulge a little over the holidays. We order extra honey, dried fruit, and nuts. We make sure the spice shelf is well-stocked. But we don't sacrifice the nutritional quality of our food. Make sure you use whole wheat **pastry** flour for these goodies, and honey with a light, sweet flavor, and they will be every bit as tender as the baked goods you are used to. The flavor of the wholesome ingredients can't be beat. Can you feel righteous and self-indulgent at the same time? You bet!

Whole wheat apricot bars

Use unsulphured, organic dried apricots for a fresh taste. Makes one 8" X 8" pan:

> **Filling:**
> 1/2 cup honey
> 3/4 cup water
> 1 1/2 Tbsp. cornstarch
> 2 1/4 cups dried apricots, sliced thin
>
> **Pastry:**
> 1 cup whole wheat pastry flour
> 1 1/2 cups rolled oats
> 1 Tbsp. lemon peel
> 1/3 cup honey
> 1/4 cup oil
> 1 egg yolk

Prepare the filling: combine ingredients in a small saucepan stirring frequently, until filling is cool slightly while you prepare the pastry.

For pastry: Sift the flour, and stir in the rolled oats and lemon peel. In a separate bowl, combine the honey, oil, and egg yolk, beating vigorously. Add all at once to the dry mixture, stirring until well blended.

Oil an 8"X8" square pan and line it with wax paper or parchment. Spread one half the pastry mixture in the bottom of the pan (it will be thick—I use a rubber spatula). Spread the filling over the pastry in the pan, and then **very carefully** spread the other half of the pastry mixture over the filling. I have found the best way to do this without mixing them together is to drop the pastry mixture over the filling in little dabs and then to spread the little dabs together.

Preheat the oven to 350 degrees and bake 40 minutes, or until the top of the pastry is golden brown. Cool. Cut in square or oblong bars. These keep wonderfully for a week or even two, if kept in an airtight cookie tin.

Fruit cake

Rich, moist, and dark with fruits and nuts. Makes one 5" X 9" loaf.

> 1 2/3 cups whole wheat pastry flour
> 4 Tbsp. buttermilk powder
> 1 tsp. soda
> 1 tsp. baking powder
> 1/2 tsp. allspice
> 1 cup water (use apricot water for part or all)
> 3 Tbsp. oil
> 3 Tbsp. honey
> 1 Tbsp. dark molasses
> 1 Tbsp. brandy
> 1 egg
> 1 tsp. grated orange peel
> 2/3 cup dried apricots
> 2/3 cup date pieces
> 2/3 cup dried pineapple, cut into bits
> 2/3 cup almonds, chopped
> 2/3 cup pecans, broken

Prepare a 5" X 9" loaf pan by oiling it and lining with baking paper. Preheat the oven to 375 degrees.

Place apricots in a small bowl, and pour over enough boiling water to cover. Let soak 5 minutes. Save the water, and slice the apricots thin.

Sift together into a bowl the flour, buttermilk powder, soda, baking powder, and allspice. Add the sliced apricots, date pieces, pineapple bits, almonds and pecans. Toss to coat the fruit.

In a medium bowl, whisk together the water (use the apricot soaking water, and add enough to bring the measure to 1 cup), oil, honey, molasses, brandy, egg and orange peel.

Add the liquid mixture all at once to the dry mixture, and stir together just until all ingredients are thoroughly moistened. Scrape the mixture into the prepared pan and smooth over the top.

Bake for 1 hour or more, until the top is golden and springy and a knife inserted into the center of the loaf comes out clean. Cool on a wire rack before serving.

Applesauce raisin spice cake

I made this one for my wedding cake!
Makes one 8" round cake:

```
1 1/2 cups whole wheat pastry flour
1/2 tsp. baking powder
1/2 tsp. soda
1 tsp. ground allspice
1 tsp. ground cinnamon
1/4 tsp. ground cloves
1/4 tsp. ground ginger
2 Tbsp. buttermilk powder
2 eggs, separated
1/4 cup oil
1/2 cup honey
2/3 cup applesauce
1 1/2 Tbsp. dark rum
1 1/2 Tbsp. brandy
1/2 cup chopped walnuts
1/2 cup raisins
```

Prepare the raisins: chop them finely, then place them in a small pan with 1/2 Tbsp. each of the dark rum and brandy, and 2 Tbsp. boiling water. Place the pan over low heat and stir the raisins frequently until the liquid is absorbed. Set aside to cool.

Prepare the pan: oil and line an 8" round springform pan with baker's paper. Preheat the oven to 350 degrees.

Combine the pastry flour, baking powder, soda, allspice, cinnamon, cloves, ginger, and buttermilk powder. Sift together three times into a medium bowl and then set aside. In a small bowl, beat the egg whites until stiff peaks form. Set aside.

In a large bowl, combine the egg yolks, oil, honey, applesauce, and remaining rum and brandy. Beat well with an electric mixer, then add the dry mixture in four installments, beating each time until smooth. Fold in the beaten egg whites, then fold in the raisins and nuts.

Bake 45-50 minutes, until the cake tests done. Cool in a wire rack, then frost with cream cheese frosting and decorate with flowers.

Cream cheese frosting:

Use light or natural creamcheese:

```
5 ounces creamcheese, softened
3-4 Tbsp. honey (to taste)
1 Tbsp. dark rum or 1/2 tsp. vanilla
```

Beat the creamcheese and honey until they are well blended and creamy. Beat in the rum or vanilla. If the frosting is too soft to put on the cake, refrigerating for 15 minutes or so will firm it up. Swirl on with a spatula. Δ

> *What country before ever existed a century and a half without a rebellion? . . . The tree of liberty must be refreshed from time to time with the blood of patriots and tyrants. It is its natural manure.*
>
> Thomas Jefferson
> 1743-1826

A BHM Writer's Profile

Dave Duffy is the founder, publisher, and editor of *BHM*. He built his own home in the Siskiyou Mountains of Southern Oregon while launching the magazine, and that home has now become the magazine's office.

Duffy spent his first 29 years in Boston, Massachusetts, and the next 20 years in the West, mainly in Ventura, California. He was a newspaper reporter for 10 years and a technical writer for the defense industry for another 10. He patterned *BHM* after his own successful effort to "leave the rat race, the crime, and the congestion behind and be my own man by building a house and becoming self sufficient in every way".

Just for Kids — a short possum tail (tale?)

By Lucy Shober

" When I look into your eyes...I see the wonder of the world in your eyes." Doctor Doolittle, the famous veterinarian who could talk with the animals, sang this sweet lullaby to a seal friend of his before he tossed her gently into the sea.

Though there is no mention of her in his books, I can bet that the good doctor would have fallen as deeply in love with a friend of **mine**, had he known her.

Virginia O'possum was a Virginia Opossum. She had every bit as much understanding of the world as Dr. Doolittle's famous seal, plus an added charm that endeared her to anyone who met her. Her warm gray and white frosted fur kept a sweet scent of possum/cedar. Her crinkled papery ears flapped in the breeze as she held tightly to whoever carried her. Virginia was an orphan who had fallen off of her mother's back during a late winter storm. After being brought to the animal hospital she was mauled by an upset chipmunk when she wandered into his cage. These two experiences left her a tad daffy and were the beginnings of her life as a house possum.

"Ginnie" didn't worry about her condition at all. In fact, with a brain that is very small when compared to the size of their bodies, possums don't worry too much about anything! Like all possums, Ginnie loved to eat...and eat...and **eat**. Berries and bugs are the favorite treat for these little marsupials, (cousins of the Kangaroo) and the sight of a fat rolly beetle or crunchy katydid bug would send that possum into a mouth watering frenzy.

When a bowl of grapes was set before her, she would use her dainty hands to place each berry into her mouth, then tilt her head back so that the sweet juice could roll down her throat, then **snap**! the dry leathery peeling would flip out like unwanted garbage. She could sit by the hour, almost in a trance as she filled the floor with little wads of discarded grape skins.

Virginia lived four years, which is about two years longer than is usual for her wild cousins. During that time she taught her human friends a lot

Possums use their tails as an aid in gathering leaves for a warm bed and to help in keeping balanced while picking berries, but they never hang by them.

The Third Year

about possum lore. Read about some of the things she showed me, and see if you don't develop a weak spot in **your** heart for these timid little animals.

Opossums are **nocturnal** marsupials, they have pouches on their tummies for carrying young babies. Ginnie would let me slip my finger into hers, and I could feel the tiny bumps which would have become large and full of milk if she had ever had children.

Baby possums are born after only 12 1/2 days of gestation. (Gestation is the time a child spends inside its mother's womb.)

When she feels that it is time for the children to be born, a mother possum licks a pathway of moistened fur from the birth doorway to her pouch. The blind and naked children climb until they reach the safety of this warm little purse. There they find a tiny bosom and swallow it! This will ensure that they aren't thrown away from their breakfast if Mrs. Possum has to dodge an angry chicken farmer or out run a pickup truck.

After two months, the babies have grown a good coat of fur and developed all 50 of their teeth (more teeth than any other North American mammal). Then you might see them peeping out of the pouch or hitching a ride on mama's back.

Possums date back to pre-Ice Age times, and have changed hardly at all since those times!

Sometimes if a possum is terribly frightened, it's whole body just freezes up, and with that sickly smile plastered onto its lips, the terrified creature will become so stiff as to seem dead. This along with the fact that many predators (meat eating animals) dislike the taste of possum meat has worked to save quite a few of these little varmints from being killed.

If you would like to learn more about these interesting critters, you can create a **possum pantry** in your back yard or even at your bedroom window. Remember though, don't try to catch or make a pet of a wild possum. Adults rarely learn to like humans, and if you scare them enough, they might be forced to put some of those 50 sharp teeth to work!!

A possum pantry

To invite wildlife into your back yard, you must provide three things, **food, shelter and water.** Go to some nearby woods, and collect an assortment of branches, underbrush and twigs. Make a mound of these about as high as your head, and four or five feet long. This will provide shelter. Water must be provided in a flat dish unless you live close to a pond or creek. Be sure to keep the water supply constant and fresh. You wouldn't like it if you moved into a new home, then found green sludgy water coming from the faucet!

The food department is the fun one. First create a platform high enough that dogs cannot reach it. Securely place a log pole or sturdy ladder next to the feeding platform so that your possum (and raccoon?) friends can climb it to reach the food.

who would become so entranced while eating corn bread that you could knock loudly on the window beside his platform, and he wouldn't even notice the commotion.)

Keep your possum pantry clean! That will ensure that flies and other pests don't become a problem. Have fun learning more about these walking history books, and be sure to ask an adult to help you in your discoveries!

Find and circle the following words from Virginia O'possum's story in this **word find** game:

**POND
DISCOVERIES
DAFFY
GESTATION
OPOSSUM
ICE AGE
MARSUPIAL
POUCH △**

AEJDIOMARSUPIALWEUNXOLIERPADW
LEMTERODESNOCTURNALJOTCPEMBTA
DLHIREOPOSSUMRKDSPOCZWEQRITGH
AALWNERIASHCDAOHMQGESTATIONOP
FARNTLXTYPEHWEMTOLPWQEGALTEVM
FELRTMNYIRWYRLPONDSLRIENTERES
YDISCOVERIESWINLRTUXUYZMONTEL

WORD FIND.

Now become a scavenger. After dinner, raid the leftovers and uneaten food portions. At first, take only breads and fruits...things that won't be too horrible when they become rotted or rained on. Later after you are sure that your feeding station is being visited, you can add just about anything that you want. Discover the favorite menu of your neighborhood varmints! (We once had a wild possum visitor

The Electoral College — how we elect the President

By John Silveira

I've been getting a lot of telephone calls from Oregon lately. My article is late—again—and Dave Duffy, the fellow who publishes this magazine, keeps calling to ask me when I'm sending it up.

I don't mind him asking when. I just mind when he asks what this month's article is going to be about, because I haven't got the slightest idea. That's usually why I'm late.

O.E. MacDougal, Duffy's poker playing friend, still lives and plays down here in California, and he's been by a few times. Anyone who reads my articles knows he's usually very helpful when I'm trying to write them, but this time it was apparent I was on my own.

In fact, he dropped by this morning and was sitting across the room from me, reading a magazine while I slouched at the computer waiting to be inspired.

I couldn't think of anything, so I tried to bait him. "Who do you like for the World Series?"

He looked up and shrugged. "I'm not following baseball this season." He went back to reading.

That killed a baseball article.

"How do you feel about November's presidential election?"

"It'll be either Tweedledum or Tweedledee," he said without elaborating.

"What do you think about the Soviet Union?"

He didn't even look up. "It's gone, John."

"Oh, yeah."

I went to my coffee pot. It was empty. Mac drinks more coffee than anyone I've ever known. I started another pot.

"Bobby Fischer's going to play chess again," I said.

He nodded.

The phone rang. I hoped it was a bill collector and not Duffy asking about his article. But it was Dave's voice on the other end. It's the curse of good credit.

He wanted to talk about the election.

"I know," I said when he asked if I realized he was supporting the Libertarian candidate.

"That's right," I said when he said that from one election to the next nothing really changes.

"I am too," I responded when he said he was disappointed with the entire political process.

I agreed that the electorate had to do something about it. "Not enough people vote," I said.

Out of the corner of my eye I saw Mac look over his magazine at me and then he went back to reading.

"We should encourage more people to vote," I added. "Yeah, whip your readers into a frenzy and get them out to vote."

"Goodbye," I said and hung up without either of us mentioning the article. I sighed the sigh of a reprieved man, then stared at the monitor and realized no article was coming out of me. This was going to be the second issue in a row without anything by me.

"Why?" Mac asked.

"Why what?"

"Why should more people vote?"

"Because it's the way democracy works best," I said.

He shrugged and started reading again.

"Don't you think so?" I asked.

"I don't know," he replied. "It bothers me that most people don't know what they're voting for and now we want more of them to vote."

I stared in his direction. He was reading again but he said, "Most people have no grasp of what the issues are," he said.

I didn't say anything.

"Very few people even know the names of either their Representative in Congress or the names of the United States Senators from their state."

He looked at me in anticipation. I realized I didn't know who they are.

"Gallegly is your Representative and Cranston is your Senator. Seymore is the other Senator."

I smiled and made a note of it on the computer.

"It's symptomatic of the problems in our society that most people know the name of the judge on *The Peoples Court*..." He hesitated.

"Judge Wopner," I said showing him I wasn't completely ignorant.

"...but, not one in ten knows who the Chief Justice of the Supreme Court is." He hesitated again.

I didn't say anything.

"I'm not sure we'll benefit by having even more people voting. It would be different if they were voting and they were informed."

He went back to his magazine.

"Um, who is the Chief Justice on the Supreme Court?" I asked.

"Justice William Rehnquist," he replied but kept reading.

I made another note.

"Well, what would you do to change the electoral process for the better?" I asked.

He looked at me again. "First, I'd either make Election Day on April 15th or make taxes due on the first Tuesday following the first Monday in November."

"That's Election Day, right?"

He nodded. "Second, I'd make all the ballots blank—if you don't know who or what you're voting for, you can't vote."

"Be serious," I said.

"I am. I think people should have to know something before they cast a ballot. I'm not saying they have to have college degrees, or be rich, or have any particular beliefs. I'm just saying that when they start marking a ballot, they should have done some homework and find out who's who and what's what. They're voting for people who spend hundreds of billions of our dollars, start wars that cost us our lives, and in general are influencing the course of history. They should have to know something before they mark their ballot."

"Well, it must be comforting to you that in the last twenty years, the percentage of eligible voters who actually vote has fallen," I said.

"It's an illusion."

"It's cold, hard math," I said. "The percentages have fallen."

"No, twenty years ago we lowered the voting age by three years and enfranchised a bunch of people who don't vote. People twenty-one and over still vote in roughly the numbers they always have, but those in the 18-20 year range are notorious for not voting and

when they're averaged in with the older people it makes it look like there's been an across the board drop."

"Oh," was all I could muster.

"Is there anything else you'd change?"

"Yes. Several states, like Nevada, have the option of 'none of the above' on their ballots. Of course, the way it works now, if 'none of the above' wins, like it did in some district in Georgia in a primary this year, second place is the winner. But I think if 'none of the above' wins, a new election should be mandated—I don't care if we're talking the presidency or dog catcher."

"What would we gain by that?"

"The electorate would have the choice of voting for other than Tweedledum and Tweedledee and if the major parties see enough of this 'none of the above', one or the other will have to listen up and become more responsive to our needs."

I made a few more notes.

"Most people don't even realize, when they vote in a presidential election, that they're not actually voting for a president or vice president."

"We're not?"

He looked at me just a little surprised himself. "No. You're voting for a slate of electors who will vote for the President. You're not voting for the President at all."

"Are you kidding?"

"No. What do you think the electoral vote being tracked on television during the election means?"

He didn't wait for my answer.

"Each state's electoral vote represents a group of electors you are voting for who will vote for the President in December. It's the vote of these electors in December that makes the presidential election official.

I stared at him for several seconds. I'd always known about the electoral vote, but I'd never really given thought to what it meant. "We don't vote for the President?"

"No."

"How many electors are there? And who are they?"

"The number of electors a state has is equal to that state's total representation in Congress. The least populous states have at least one Representative

and two Senators, so, states like Wyoming, North Dakota, and Vermont have three electoral votes. California, with 52 Representatives and two Senators, has 54 electors."

"Big difference," I said.

"It is, and if a candidate carries a plurality in a state his slate of electors wins the state contest. If Bush wins California, his slate of electors will cast their 54 ballots for him and he'll carry all of California's electoral vote.

"Forty-nine states have the winner takes all approach. Maine splits its electoral vote in proportion to the popular vote, but in reality, an elector, once elected, can vote for whomever he pleases as long as that person is 35 or older, is a natural born American citizen, and has been a resident in the U.S. for at least 14 years."

"Anyone?"

"Electors are not bound by any Constitutional Articles or Amendments to vote for the candidate who won. That's why, in the election of 1820, though James Monroe won every state and should have won every electoral vote, he didn't. An elector from New Hampshire cast his vote for John Quincy Adams, Monroe's opponent."

"Why?"

"He said only one President, George Washington, should ever be accorded the honor of 100% of the electoral vote. So, he voted for Adams. Today, Washington is still the only President to win unanimously—and he did it twice."

"Wasn't John Quincy Adams President at some time?"

"Yes. Ironically, he won the following election, in 1824, in an electoral contest where no one could win a majority in the electoral college and the decision was thrown into the House of Representatives for the second time in the nation's history, and Adams won the presidency there in a contest racked with scandal.

"What happened?"

"When the electoral votes were tallied, there were four men who had significant electoral votes: Andrew Jackson, John Quincy Adams, Henry Clay, and a man named William Crawford. But none had a majority. The Constitution, states that if no Presidential contender has a clear majority of electoral votes the names of not more than the three top finishers are to be submitted to the House, and Jackson's, Adams', and Clay's names were submitted. Jackson had garnered more popular votes than Adams and Clay combined and many thought he was going to win. But, when the election is tossed to the House, each state casts one vote and Henry Clay threw his support to Adams and Adams won. Then, when Adams formed his cabinet, he named Clay Secretary of State. Jackson's supporters cried scandal and made it an issue for the next four years. In the election of 1828, Adams won one less electoral vote than he had in 1824 but Jackson won virtually all the rest and along with it a landslide ride into the presidency.

"If that weren't enough, four years later, Jackson won again, this time beating Clay."

"You said that was the second time it went to the House. Who won the first time it happened?"

"That was the election of 1800. Thomas Jefferson and Aaron Burr each won 73 votes. After something like three dozen ballots, they chose Jefferson."

I looked at my notes. "What happens if the House is deadlocked and can't choose a winner?"

"The Constitution provides that the names of the two to have garnered the greatest vote should then be presented to the Senate and the Senators choose by casting individual ballots."

"What do you think would have happened if Ross Perot had stayed in the race and tied up the electoral vote so no one got a majority. Could he have wielded any power?"

"Probably not. It's not likely he could have influenced his electors, and if the election were thrown to the House, he had no power to broker there as Henry Clay did in 1824. If the race had gone to the House, there were no state delegations he could swing. There are no Representatives who owe him allegiance."

"So, who would win?"

"Figure it out. Each of the state's delegations would get one vote. About 30 of the states have more Democratic Representatives than Republican Representatives. Another 10 have more Republicans. The remaining 10 are split."

"Clinton wins."

He nodded.

"But you say the electors can vote for someone else if they want."

"Yeah. It's even happened several times in this century. As recently as 1988, an elector from West Virginia cast his ballot for Lloyd Bentsen, though Michael Dukakis had carried the state."

"Why do we elect the President with an electoral college?"

"It's actually a very clever way of ensuring the likelihood of a President being elected, particularly if there are more than two strong candidates. In 1860, Lincoln was elected out of a field of four contenders with less than 40% of the popular vote because he still carried enough states to win a majority of the electoral vote. In 1968, Nixon

won less than 44% of the vote against Humphrey and Wallace but still won the electoral vote. It just increases the chance of a winner if there are a lot of candidates."

"So how many electoral votes are there altogether?"

"There are 538 electors, total. This is because there are 435 Representatives and 100 Senators in Congress—that makes for 535 electoral votes—and since 1964, Washington, D.C. has been allowed to elect a slate of three electors, rounding the electoral college out to 538. It takes a majority, or 270 votes, to elect a President-Vice President and that will elect them regardless of the popular vote."

"The popular vote doesn't matter?"

"No. In fact, twice, in the case of Rutherford B. Hayes, the 19th President, and Benjamin Harrison, the 23rd, the winners received fewer popular votes than the Democrats who lost but Hayes and Harrison won because they carried the right combination of states to give them an electoral majority."

"Then you don't even have to be the big winner of the popular vote. You can win by just carrying the right states."

"Right."

"What's the smallest number of states a candidate can win and still be elected President?"

He looked around the room and, when he saw it, he grabbed my World Almanac from a shelf and leafed through the pages. "Figuring it takes 270 electoral votes to win..." he said as he leafed through the pages until he found what he was looking for and I guess he was doing some mental calculations, "...winning just 12 states—California, New York, Texas, Florida, Pennsylvania, Illinois, Ohio, Michigan, New Jersey, North Carolina, Georgia, and Virginia, a candidate would garner 270 electoral votes and guarantee a win regardless of how the other 38 states voted or what the popular vote was."

"How does someone become an elector?"

"Electors for each candidate are generally nominated by the political parties at their state conventions. There are certain restrictions on the electors.

For instance, they can't be members of Congress or hold any Federal office of — as the Constitution says — trust or profit."

"Trust or profit? That's what it says?"

He nodded. "If you were to vote for Clinton in this election, you would actually be voting for that slate of electors, from your state, chosen by the Democratic Party at their state convention, and you're not likely to know who any of those people are."

"And they don't have to vote for Clinton if he wins?" I asked.

"No, though more than 99% of the time, the electors vote for the candidate they represent. But each elector can vote for whomever he or she pleases, as long as that person is Constitutionally qualified for the job and as long as, of the two persons he casts his votes for, President and Vice President, are not both residents of the same states as he is."

"So, neither Bush's nor Clinton's electors have to vote for them?"

"No."

"I never knew that."

"Some states have tried to pass laws forcing its electors to vote for the candidate to whom they are pledged, but I don't think the state could prosecute an elector who voted otherwise. And though electors from Maine must, by law, split their vote in proportion to the popular vote from that state, if the state tried to prosecute an elector who violated the law, and the state won in its own courts, I'm sure the law would be overturned if the case were appealed to a federal court."

"Why don't we just do away with the Electoral College? It doesn't seem democratic."

"It's not. But we're not really a democracy. We're not like in ancient Athens where all the enfranchised voters met in the town square and voted on every issue. We're a democratic republic. We vote for many of our public officials democratically, but after the election those officials can go off and do their job unbound by the will of the people."

"You're saying a person elected to carry out the will of the people can do whatever he wants?"

"Sure. I know that most people believe elected officials are supposed to

go off and carry out the popular will and when they don't they're doing something illegal or immoral. But elected officials who act contrary to the popular will are neither illegal or immoral and there's no provision in the Constitution for the elected officials to survey the Gallup or Roper polls and act accordingly. In fact, the Founding Fathers didn't know a public opinion poll from a telephone pole because neither existed then. The modern public opinion poll didn't exist until after World War II."

"So, what is an elected official required to do?"

"To do the job to the best of his or her ability. If that means making unpopular decisions, so be it. Of course, ever since the founding of the Republic, elected officials have almost unanimously felt that the right thing to do is whatever will get them reelected and going against the public will is rarely the way to do that, even if the public is wrong."

"But what if we don't like what the guy is doing?"

"If we don't like what he does, we can throw him out in the next election and in extreme cases, there are provisions for impeachment proceedings and recall."

I thought about what he'd said. "I guess that makes sense. But why was the electoral college system selected over any other?"

Mac stared off for a moment and I knew he was organizing his thoughts.

He began, "We think of the political system of the United States as being a two party system. It's not. Otherwise, the Ross Perot phenomenon could not have happened nor could the numerous small parties like the Libertarians exist. Most people, including most media people, lose sight of this and the term 'two party system' rolls off their tongues as if it was the law.

"George Washington didn't belong to any party. Neither did the second President, John Adams. Ironically, the party system in this country was created by a person who didn't believe in parties — Thomas Jefferson. He used it to defeat John Adams in the election of 1800, and he regretted it later."

"Why?"

"He sincerely believed political parties would corrupt the democratic process and in many ways it has."

"But why do we have the Electoral College?"

"It wasn't critical that the President represent an absolute majority. What was important was that a President be elected in a decisive and orderly fashion and without the hangups that could lead to discord. In the election of 1860, it may have been impossible to have elected a President without the electoral system, but because of the system we got Lincoln elected. Also, the electoral college system makes it possible for there to be a wide range of candidates, and although we seem content to operate as with a de facto two party system, the Founding Fathers did not want to institutionalize such a two party system."

"We always hear about how our democracy evolved from Greek democratic traditions," I said. "Do you know if our form of democracy is the same as the form of democracy the Greeks enjoyed?"

"Not even close. Not all the Greek city states were democracies. Sparta, for instance, had a king. But some of the democratic states, like Athens, went through a phase where they used a method called sortition to select officials."

"How did that work?"

"They chose public officials by lottery."

"Are you kidding? Did they pull names out of a hat or something?"

"Yeah, and except for a few notable exceptions like military leaders and financial officials who were elected, all government offices were filled by lot."

"Why did they do that?"

"It eliminated political races, ensured a regular turnover of officeholders, but most importantly, it guaranteed universal participation in the political process — at least among free Greek citizens. But you've got to remember that women, slaves, and people of foreign birth, no matter what contributions they made to society, could not participate in the Greek political process. That left only about 10% of the citizens in Athens enfranchised."

"Not much of a democracy."

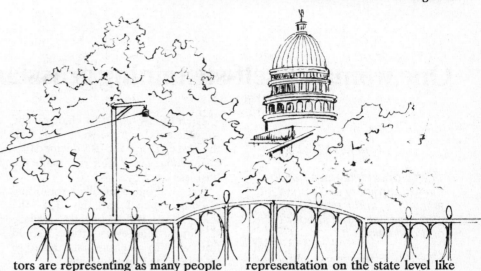

"No, it wasn't."

"But you're saying you could open your mail one day and find out you're governor whether you liked it or not?"

"No, if you were chosen by the lottery it was because you had volunteered to be in it. If you hadn't volunteered, your name wasn't in the hat, or barrel, or whatever it was they used."

I glanced at the page of notes that was growing.

"You know," I started, "I never really thought about this before, but how come the states have different numbers of Representatives in the House but they all have two Senators?"

"The House was meant to reflect the popular will so the number of Representatives a state has is based on the size of its population and is reviewed every 10 years, right after the Census. California had 45 Representatives after the 1980 Census but after the 1990 Census, they picked up seven more. The more people in your state, the more Representatives you have.

"The Senate exists because, in the early days of the Republic, the smaller states were afraid of being completely dominated by the more populous states. Equal representation in the Senate meant that, no matter how few Representatives a small state has in the House, it has a voice as big as anyone else's in the Senate.

"As an example, Wyoming has only one representative to California's 52. Citizens in Wyoming are not going to swing many decisions in the House. However, in the Senate, Wyoming has two votes — just like California — and it has just as much influence there."

"So, in the Senate, the voices of the smaller states will always be heard," I said.

"Yes, but the result is that there is disproportionate representation for citizens of small states in Congress. California has more than twice as many people as the six New England states combined and accordingly has more than twice as much representation in the House as all those states combined. But those six states have a combined representation that is six times that of California in the Senate, though they have less than half as many people. Another way to look at it is that those 12 New England Sena-

tors are representing as many people as just one Senator from California."

"Sounds like a good deal for the smaller states. Will the Supreme Court ever overrule it?"

He shook his head. "The only way that will change is by constitutional amendment."

"But it sounds like the small states can really ride roughshod over the big states if they wanted to."

"Not really. Another thing most people don't know is that all bills not only have to clear both the House and the Senate to become law, but bills that involve spending always have to originate in the House."

"So it's not easy for the smaller states to take advantage of their position," I said.

"No."

I looked at my notes again. I was seeing my article develop. "Are the legislatures of any of the states set up like the House and Senate?"

"Not since the 1960's. Back then, in a lot of states, the rural areas were disproportionately represented in the state legislatures although most of the people in those states lived in urban areas. Huge cities had one or two state representatives or state senators and so did Podunk towns. But, in the early '60's, the Court, under Earl Warren, ruled that the guarantee of equal protection meant the state legislature in Tennessee had to reapportion itself to reflect the population distribution and a couple of years later the Court said that all states with bicameral legislatures had to balance both houses according to population. There couldn't be different forms of

representation on the state level like the House of Representatives and the U.S. Senate have."

"What's a bicameral legislature?"

"Bicameral means a state has two legislative bodies — usually called a house and senate. Forty-nine of the states are bicameral. Nebraska is unicameral. It has a single legislative body."

I reread my notes. "This is a lot of material," I said and suddenly realized Mac was writing my article — again.

"Do you want a byline on this story?" I asked.

He smiled and shook his head, no.

"Can I ask you one more question?"

"Sure."

"Have you given much thought to who's going to win the Presidency in November?"

"Uh-huh."

"You look pretty sure."

He smiled.

"Who?"

"I'll tell you, under one condition."

"What's that?"

"You can't include it in your article."

"What?"

He stared at me.

"You have a bet placed on this, don't you?"

He smiled, again.

"Oh...Well...I'm not sure..." I fumbled for words. "Let me think about it."

He started reading his magazine again.

My curiosity got the best of me.

"Okay," I said.

Then he told me. Δ

One woman's self-sustaining grassland livestock farm

By Vern Modeland

"It was grass that gave rise to the extraordinary and abundant animal life, and it was the complex grassland that supported and maintained it."

Jean M. Auel
The Plains of Passage

Luane Schroeder likes to quote Auel when describing her different way of thinking about farming.

Lean and short-shorn, aglow with energy that comes from working out-of-doors every day, Luane Schroeder, at age 50, is proprietor and only full-time hand for 144 valley and mountainside acres appropriately named LedgeRock Farm. She's also become a missionary for the use of intensive, controlled grazing in livestock management and of maximizing Nature's ability to produce rich forage.

Fifteen years ago, Luane, her husband and their two young children fled a financially comfortable life in Houston, Texas. Crime and fear had become so prevalent that Luane didn't feel it was safe in the city to allow her young son to go alone into public bathrooms, she recalls.

The Schroeders settled in North Arkansas' Boston Mountains, and the kids grew up there. Luane became single again—in need of finding a way to support herself.

"I decided I'd make purebred cattle production profitable," she says as though that was nothing remarkable.

"I started out typical of a lot of seedstock producers in that cost of production didn't influence most of my management decisions. I had supplemental income. If I wanted to use a lot of feed to maintain my cows and grow my young stock, I could get it by the truck-load. If I wanted to change a field from one type of forage to another, I could plow, poison, and fertilize to my heart's content.

"Then things began to change. The supplemental income went first, then the nest egg, then the IRS decided that losing money year after year made the business a hobby.

"I read about controlled rotational grazing. Once I had the idea—the teaser, if you will—I began to explore the limits, read every article I could find, went to meetings, and talked to people using that approach.

She was influenced by several sources, including novelist Elmer Kelton, editor Allan Nation of *Stockman Grass Farmer*, *Stockman Grass*

Luane Schroeder looks for vigor and variety in new forage growth at her LedgeRock Farm in the Ozarks.

Productivity author Andre Voison, and *Holistic Resource Manageent* author Alan Savory. But she said she developed her own working model.

Sustainable concept

What she has built is a tightly managed livestock operation that is true to a principle of changing grazing locations daily and closely monitoring the health of both the animals and the pasture.

This year, Luane is feeding 23 Beefmaster cows, including 15 calves and three working bulls. She also has introduced 26 Barbados sheep and 76 Spanish goats to the operation as a test of diversification and to further fine tune her pasture management.

"Beef production is my business," she says, "but the basic raw material is forage grasses. Forage production is steady, and here (at LedgeRock Farm), it is harvested as it is ready, not after it has passed the peak of nutritional quality and is being wasted.

"It's kind of like thinking about too much food being prepared for dinner and becoming leftovers. Leftovers usually wind up going bad in the fridge and being thrown out. Forage is my raw material and my harvester is cattle."

Hard choices

Hard choices are part of her business. "I can't afford to keep a cow that doesn't bring a calf to the weaning pen," she says, "and I can't afford to raise cattle if it costs more to produce the calf than I can sell it for."

It took time and a lot of thought to develop and understand this land management system, Luane admits, and it has taken detailed records to show her what works and what doesn't.

In 1982, she added up expenses of $8632 for feed, $741 for medicines and veterinarian visits, and $2562 spent on fertilizing forage—a total of nearly $12,000. It figured out to $362 in expenses for each of 33 calves born that year.

Costs didn't much change over the next four years, other than by eliminating the fertilizer bill and buying some different strains of forage seeds. But her 1986 accounting showed the cost of calves (there were 36 that year) was down to $294 each.

Then, in 1987, the hay supply ran out in mid-February, and the money ran out a little later. So Luane turned her cattle out to live off the land through to December, feeling guilty that she might be "short changing" the cows. At year's end, she again figured costs. The bill came to $8,345 for another 36 calves produced, down to $232 each.

The one-woman farm relies on high-power electric fencing for stock control.

Nineteen eighty-eight was what she calls her "pivotal year." Just reducing production costs would be to no avail if production fell off. But it didn't, reflecting, she decided, that what she had seen in 1987 was not a carryover from earlier nutritional practices. Her "cow factory's" product was holding its own on quality, and that would pay back at sale time.

Managing the overhead with electric fencing

With sustainable quality apparent, Luane set about to better manage her farm's overhead. That included retiring debts for machinery and mortgage and attacking the biggest overhead factor on most farms—labor.

"When I describe how I run the farm, many people are immediately turned off by what they think is too much work," she says.

"The work was in setting it up. Execution is simple. Five to 25 minutes a day, depending on where the livestock are. That beats three hours or more hauling and unloading feed once or twice a week, then another three to five hours feeding.

"I remember spending all day one time, looking for a calving cow when she had 50 to 70 acres to hide in."

No more. LedgeRock farm is separated into cells which in turn are divided into paddocks of 1 1/2 to 3 acres in size. The paddocks are defined, and quickly re-definable, by electric fencing.

"All I do is open and shut gates. The most time-consuming part is monitoring forage growth in order to plan the moves. My cattle are so used to being moved that it's just one more thing that happens.

"The cows eat the plant, extract what they need for themselves and their calves, then return most of what they eat to the soil where the plants retrieve the usable portion and makes more plants for the cows to eat, and so on."

Monitoring is important

"The contribution I make to this cycle is to monitor the recovery period for the plants and match the cow cycle to the plant cycle. I supply logic. It's illogical to try to grow plants that require a lot of soil preparation on land that is mostly rock, especially when there are plants that will grow without all that preparation.

"Anything, plant or animal, that requires heroic measures to maintain isn't suited to my low-input system and will eliminate itself. What I'm left with is very hardy, tenacious things—animal and plant—which will produce very well when conditions are good, and well enough when conditions aren't so good."

Like during a drought. One came in 1988. It rained some, but plant growth in April was slow. Days were warm to hot and nights were cooler than normal. Cool season forages, Luane observed, were sprouting seeds with less-than-expected leaf production. Warm season forages hadn't even begun to grow.

In May, 1988, lack of moisture was beginning to be noticeable, but it happened during breeding season and Luane could only hope the dry spell would be temporary. She took note that cool season grasses were growing well. What she hadn't noticed, she recalled later, was that seed head production was far ahead of earlier years.

The drought-induced reduction in forage production began to impact the cattle operation in June.

"On June 29, 1988, I had to abandon close attention to my two breeding herds in favor of grass management. I just hoped that everything that would breed was bred."

Luane sold some cows. Reducing the number of cattle she had to feed would buy time for adequate recovery periods for the forage paddocks.

Charting grass growth

By measuring and charting the grass growth, it seemed to her that it might be possible to predict what would happen. Crabgrass and other forage plants native to Arkansas' Boston Mountains at times in their growth cycle become so palatable that cattle can go through them in a matter of weeks, Luane discovered. Short grazing periods and regular rotation allow for recovery growth time. And recovery was consistent even in times of relatively dry weather.

Her painstaking measurement showed her that the grasses grew about an eighth of an inch a day even with no significant amounts of rainfall.

"While most people might not notice the growth, cattle can find that eighth inch. If the pastures were uneven when a dry period started, and if the cattle were allowed to pick and choose, they'd first go back to the new growth, however slight. In order to have any grass at all, it's essential to provide at least 30 days rest between grazings, to allow the root systems to recover. When there is adequate moisture, roots aren't called upon to provide growth nearly as much as they are in dry conditions. But, stressed for growth too quickly after grazing, the grass roots get weaker and weaker until even an eighth-inch a day growth is impossible."

"After you get the hang of it, you can almost tell by looking what you have and how long it will last," says Luane after that first drought experience.

"The main thing to remember is that it's not a static program. Growth rates don't stay the same, whether you're discussing stock or forage."

Unconventional thinking

Conventional wisdom among cattle people is that controlled grazing will lower animal performance. Luane Schroeder is a person who automatically questions conventional wisdom.

"One of the things that has given controlled grazing a reputation for lowering animal performance is the practice of forcing cattle to eat poorer quality forage before moving them to a new paddock. Once you get the paddocks to where everything is green and vegetative all the way to the ground, I think individual performance is as good or better than any other grazing system. The trick is to keep quality high with regular harvesting."

The next step

Sitting before the big open fireplace in the 2200-square-foot post and beam addition that she designed and helped build onto the original LedgeRock homestead, Luane Schroeder closes her fingers around her coffee cup and dreams of taking the skill and knowledge she's gained in sustainable agriculture on the road.

She'd like to find a bus—cheap or free. The bus would be converted into a mobile classroom, with its own audio/visual and computer equipment. Luane wants to get out and network on a regular basis, to establish and maintain contact and put on some "how-to" workshops.

(For more information on least-cost, sustainable forage marketing programs, you can write Luane Schroeder at P.O. Box 125, Dogpatch, AR, 72648.) △

LedgeRock's electric fences

A major livestock management tool in Luane Schroeder's one-person sustainable grassland livestock operation at LedgeRock Farm is "New Zealand-type" electric fencing.

"I can do the land managing I have wanted to without having to build (or battle) miles of barbed wire. I can use the best water source on the farm anytime I want to. I can keep cattle out of ponds at will. I can move cattle anywhere I need to as quickly as I can walk the temporary line of paddock fencing (bright orange-colored electrically conductive plastic tape strung betwen fiberglass rods).

"I can separate animals from the herd quickly. I make lanes 8 to 12-feet wide and they get in line and go wherever the lane takes them. This psychological approach to animal control works so well that it was hard to convince the cattle to cross any line where the tape has been.

"So far I've not had anything completely shut the system down. I've had snow and ice on the wires and insulators, I've had grass growing in the wires, I've had trees down on it, and I had wires down at one point. The worst the energizer did was about 1,900 volts when there was an eighth of a mile of wire on the ground, some of it touching other grounded wires."

High power electric fencing requires more attention to construction than other electric fences, Luane points out. LedgeRock's fences incorporate a grounded wire strung between two other 12 1/2 gauge, high-tensile "hot" wires.

"You wouldn't depend on one strand of barbed wire as permanent stock control. Electric fence is no different. The object is to make a fence that is a good, strong fence even if the power is off."

Where steel "T" posts are incorporated, the ground wire in the system is tied to each one all along the fence line. There is never more than a maximum of one-half mile between earth ground reinforcement points.

"My permanent fence is my transmission line to get power where I need it. I build the best quality I can so that I won't have to be chasing trouble spots."

A hand held volt/ohm meter can quickly isolate fence problems.

"I can turn on a section of fence a mile from the energizer, read the voltage at the switch, and know if there is a problem in that section."

Lightning strike protection and shielding from other forms of possible power surges also has been important in designing and building dependable electric fences on LedgeRock Farm. △

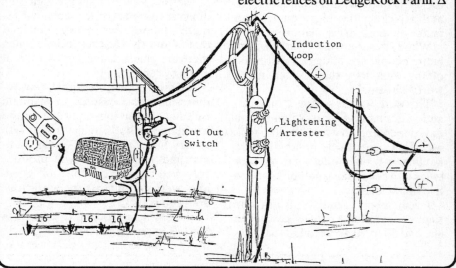

Here's a handy chart to help predict your local weather

By Michael Simmons

Here's a handy weather prediction chart for do-it-yourself weather forecasters, especially for those who might be located many miles from a radio station and need to know what their local weather is going to be like.

To use it one only needs an aneroid barometer (the type you usually see in one's home) and some way of determining wind direction as by simple observation of wind effects or a windvane.

The chart is good year-round for 24 to 48 hour forecasts and will offer plenty of fun sharpening your weather predicting skills! I keep my chart right underneath the barometer along with a calendar-type log that I printed with my computer to keep a daily record of weather events. Such a log lets me know how well my predictions come out as well as aid in future weather prediction. The more record-keeping one does, the more information one can draw upon to make a forecast.

To use the barometer, you should first calibrate it using the barometric reports from the nearest radio or TV station. There should be a small screw on the back which can be carefully turned with a screwdriver to the reported barometric pressure. Refer to the unit's instructions for any other considerations. Tap it once or twice to make sure it stays on the intended reading.

Once calibrated, it's ready for use. There should be a pointer that can be turned by a knob on the front. This is set to your first reading as reference. A second reading may then be taken two to three hours later and compared to the original quite easily. Make sure you always gently tap the barometer before reading it. This will "settle" the needle (and tell you if the barometer is rising or falling in case you have forgotten to take a prior reading for quite a while!). Record your second reading and the difference between the two.

Note: If you need to buy a barometer, please don't purchase one of the cheap types commonly seen in large discount stores. These can be woefully inaccurate. Go ahead and spend the extra dollars for a good unit which will last a lifetime to hand down to your children.

A slow rise or fall in barometric pressure is 3 millibars or about 0.09 in. per 3 hours while a moderate rate is considered 3 to 6 millibars or about .09 to 0.18 inch per 3 hours. A rapid rise or fall would be anything above 6 millibars or 0.18 inch per 3 hours.

Although such do-it-yourself weather predicting can't replace the government (NOAA) VHF weather stations, it's certainly more fun and educational. Besides, even the pros miss it once in awhile, so your personal forecasting just might prove more accurate occasionally! Δ

Weather chart

Wind direction	Barometric pressure	Expected weather
SW to NW	30.10 to 30.20, steady	—fair, with little temperature change for one or two days
SW to NW	30.10 to 30.20 rising fast	—fair, followed by rain within two days
SW to NW	30.20 or above, steady	—continued fair, with little temperature change
E to NE	30.10 or above, falling fast	—rain probable in summer within 24 hours; in winter, rain or snow and windy
SE to NE	30.00 or below, falling slowly	—steady rain for one or two days
SE to NE	30.00 or below, falling fast	—rain and high wind, clearing within 36 hours
S to SW	30.00 or below, rising slowly	—clearing within a few hours, fair for several days
S to E	29.80 or below, falling fast	—severe storm soon, clearing within 24 hours; colder in winter
Going to W	29.33 or below, rising fast	—clearing and colder
E to N	29.80 or below, falling fast	—severe northeast gale, heavy rain; in winter, heavy snow and cold wave

The case against modular housing

By Martin S. Harris

It's a source of constant amazement to me that the general public doesn't shop for housing with the same skill that it uses when purchasing anything from potatoes to auto parts.

No one would cheerfully hand over $25 a hundredweight for spuds or $150 for a Chevy starter. Why, then, do people sign on the dotted line (and mortgage themselves for the next 30 years) for pretty ordinary wood-frame housing in the form of pre-packaged, pre-fabricated, or "modular" housing at prices equal to $80-90 a square foot?

Although most modular housing being offered on the market today is more expensive than a custom-construction home and have severe design limitations when compared to the custom-built home, the modular houses still sell well. Why?

In my search for an answer, I've seized on the possibility that perhaps people think there's the same sort of competition in the housing industry as exists in agriculture or mechanics, and that 1ist prices therefore represent the same sort of reasonable profit over production costs that prevail in other sectors of the economy. Not so.

There is, of course, a kind of competition in residential construction; but it's rather limited in scope, and therefore it produces some interesting results when examined from an economic point of view.

Urban vs. rural costs

To prove my point I'm going to use construction numbers from New England, my home base; but numbers from elsewhere in the country are basically similar. Even a casual glance at any of the construction-cost estimation manuals published every year shows that there's far more difference in costs between urban and rural locations than there is, say, between the costs in the rural Northeast and the rural Northwest. That's because of two factors:

(1) a taxpayer-subsidized Interstate Highway system which enables commodities like lumber to move anywhere in the country at costs to producers and consumers well below the real costs of transporting tonnage.

(2) the fact that urban construction (for reasons ranging from Code requirements to union wage rates) is more expensive than rural.

Modular (pre-packaged) housing, left, is convenient and can be made livable in a few days, but it is almost always much more expensive and has severe design limitations than custom-built housing, right.

Wood frame construction, even if it were Code-approved in urban areas (mostly, it isn't) would cost more than the same work executed out in the countryside, even though the cost of the lumber is just about the same everywhere.

Here in Vermont, it costs a builder in the $30-to-$40-persquare-foot (SF) range to build a wood-frame house or condo, with the level of quality in finishes and appliances that most buyers expect to see.

Land costs vary widely, from an average of about $30,000 per lot in suburban locations with all utilities down to a few hundred an acre in truly rural locations where bringing in utilities will cost, on average, another $10,000. Professional builders can sub-divide raw land, build streets, and bring in utilities for an average of $20,000 per house; since most houses average 1200 SF in size, the land and services add less than $10/SF to the builder's cost. Let's assume that all his other costs, from permits at the beginning to advertising at the end, add another $5000 per unit to costs; even so, the builder's investment, for a product which will sell for maybe $150,000 is about half that number, or $75,000.

One could fairly conclude, then, that a builder who offers to set up a prefabricated house (the owner has already paid for the house lot and all utilities and landscaping) is going to incur a cost of about $30-$40 per SF; and at, say, 10-15% mark-up (which is what the construction identifies as its usual margin for overhead and profit), should be selling for $33-$60 per SF.

Note the choices the buyer doesn't get. Yes, he gets to select cabinetry, flooring, and finishes (within certain cost limits, that is), he doesn't get to change the floor plan, the window arrangement or the roof pitch, or any of a host of options open to one who contracts for custom construction.

If the best price the package-housing market will offer is about $60/SF, and if, by intelligent shopping a buyer can readily achieve a target price of $40/SF in the custom-built, stick-built market, why do so many buyers opt for the package? The answer comes in three parts.

Part 1: The package building industry does an excellent job of marketing. Buyers don't seem to realize that most of the housing inventory in America is carrying a price higher than its equivalent replacement cost, and when they see a price like $65,900 they think they're seeing a huge bargain.

Part 2: Most buyers have no idea of actual construction costs, or actual builders' margins for profit and overhead. Further confusing the pricing issue is the fact that "address counts," i.e. Americans have historically bid up the price of housing in neighborhoods regarded as prestigious. It's all too common for the same house, in two adjacent (and differently-evaluated) school districts to show a price differential in the tens of thousands.

Part 3: Many buyers are afraid of builders. They've heard enough war stories about fighting between owner and builder on custom housing that they're ready to opt for a package design which, they believe, will be argument-free.

Reasonably independent and self-sufficient people should be doing better than this. People with enough initiative to prefer *Backwoods Home Magazine* over, say, *Suburban Existence*, should be capable of evaluating the industry's marketing gambits, of getting a basic grounding in construction costs, of dealing with house-builders as they would with stockbrokers or auto mechanics: as informed equals.

For those willing to make the effort to become informed participants in the housing market, the rewards are substantial: both monetary and esthetic. Monetary isn't more important than esthetic, but it comes first simply because the informed consumer is in a better position to get what he wants in housing, without some outrageous fiscal penalty, whether it's a customized floor plan or a favorite color scheme.

And that's why almost all the forms of modular housing being offered to the public shouldn't look terribly attractive to the informed buyer: they combine no-bargain pricing with severe design limitations.

Target pricing

The alternative is something I've come to call "target pricing."

Target pricing can be used by anyone; in fact, general contractors use it (without that label, of course) when they solicit bids from sub-contractors for specialized parts of a construction project. They know what such work should cost, and so they shop around until they find a skilled sub-contractor ready to do it at that price.

Architects and owners can use target pricing too. We do it by being able to estimate, with a high degree of accuracy, what each sector of a project should cost (including a comfortable contractor profit, of course) and seeking a builder for the whole thing or for its component parts, at that figure.

Learning prices isn't as tough as it may sound; in fact, it's far easier than the supermarket pricing every food-shopper learns, simply because there's so much less to learn. I suppose one could enter the marketplace simply knowing that ordinary wood-frame construction housing costs $30-$40/SF, thereby shrinking the learning curve to one item; but most owners will want to know more. Table 1, below, gives a few examples. For each item, the first price shows the material cost,

Table 1.

Item	Material	In-place
Concrete	$55/cubic yard, delivered	$125-150 formed, poured, and stripped
Framing lumber	40-50 cents/board foot	$1.20-1.50
Sheetrock	$.20/face foot	$.60 hung, taped, and cemented
Wood siding	$.50/face foot	$1.50
Asphalt shingle roofing	$.30/face foot	$.75-$1.00

The Third Year

and the second the in-place cost which includes the value of installation labor.

One can approach component systems the same way. For example, the fixtures for a 3-piece bathroom — one-piece tub/shower enclosure, water closet, fiberglass lav in vanity — will run around $600; installed with supply, waste, and vent piping they'll run 3 times that number.

Actually, sharp eyes will notice that the "3 times" factor is a widespread one in the construction industry. Many products will show a 3x spread between the materials cost and the in-place cost; so that do-it-yourselfers should be able to build a $40/SF 1200 SF house for under $20,000.

Non-do-it-yourselfers can pocket some of that amount by administering their project, as opposed to turning the entirety of the work over to a single general contractor. GC's typically mark up a sub's work 10-15% — sometimes more — in putting together a total project price; and so, on the typical $50,000 project, the savings might amount to $5000. These earnings are not free, however: sub-contractors must be selected and supervised, their work coordinated among the various trades, even if the coordination is so simple that it consists of nothing more than keeping the carpenters off the job until the concrete work is done. Owners who want to accept the responsibility can do this sort of administration without difficulty, it seems to me.

Even if owners don't want to accept the responsibility, they can buy the same result by hiring a clerk of the works, an ancient term still in use in the industry to describe an employee of the owner who visits the job periodically to see that everything is going properly, and report back to the owner. A clerk might be a retired builder, for example with enough experience to be able to appraise work quality and to advise the owner accordingly. Since he's not on-site full-time, his wages are a modest addition to project cost.

All of the above isn't to say that package — or modular, or kit, or pre-fabricated, or whatever — housing is for no one. There is a niche market, particularly if units are available at substantially less than usual list prices. A kit can be on-site overnight and habitable in a few days; no stick-builder can match that. A kit will come with local code compliance permits and approvals, and sometimes that's worth a lot. A kit reduces the hassle factor to a minimum (usually); and sometimes that's worth a lot, too.

I do believe, however, that barring the conditions just listed, there isn't much of an argument for modular as opposed to stick-built, and my reasons sugar down to the two basics of price and design. I will admit that stick-built can be purchased out of consumer ignorance, and that in such cases a kit may, comparatively, look pretty good. But when you start with the informed buyer I think you'll end up with stick-built just about every time.

(Martin Harris is a Vermont architect, cofounder of The New England Builder, and author of numerous home building articles.)∆

Starting Over

If you want to read a motivating story, this book is for you. Jackie has inspired thousands of readers with her articles in *Backwoods Home Magazine* with her perseverance, homesteading knowledge, and wisdom. Come step into Jackie Clay's world and watch this modern day pioneer carve a home in the wilderness.

Backwoods Home Cooking

- *Breads • Casseroles*
- *Cookies • Desserts*
- *Jams & jellies*
- *Main dishes • Pasta*
- *Salads • Seafood*
- *Soups • Vegetables*

Making a great rug from the rag bag

By Lois A. Adams

Recycling makes a lot of sense in these days of dwindling landfill space and non-renewable resources. But I can remember practicing recycling in my home when I was a kid, too, only we didn't know back then that that's what it was called. We flattened tin cans and bundled newspapers. Every Saturday we had soup made from the week's leftovers. Nothing ever went to waste.

My parents had just survived the Depression, and they knew how to stretch a buck. My mother never threw anything away if another use could be found for it. When a towel wore out, or a sock was widowed, it became a scrub rag. Holey undershirts made good dust rags, and thin old bed linens could be torn and used for a lot of things—paint rags or tie-ups for tomato plants, or even kite tails.

My favorite recycling memory involves the rag bag. The summer after kindergarten, when I outgrew my best grey and yellow plaid dress, my mom and I tore it into strips for making rugs. First, we took out the hem and some of the seams, and pulled out the gathers at the waist. We removed the buttons, of course, and saved them in the button box. Mom made little snips as starters, about two inches apart, along the edge of the fabric. And then we tore.

When we finished, we put the strips of fabric into a big brown paper bag, jumbled together with blue flowered apron strips, brown and white striped shirt strips, pink blouse strips, and red flannel nightgown strips. There were even some mysterious pieces of cloth that I'd never seen before, colors that I'd never personally experienced, in the pile of clothes we tore up that day.

Other bags of rug rags were stored in the attic. We opened the door at the foot of the attic stairs and battled our way through the cobwebs with rolled newspaper swords as we creaked up the wooden steps. The attic was as hot as melted butter, like it always was in summer. The sun slanted through the dirty window, dancing with dust motes.

After shaking and blowing layers of dust off the bags, mom unrolled the tops and dug her hands in, sifting her fingers through the cloth strips, dragging them out in bunches, judging quantities and colors. I can still remember the smell of cotton and dye, soap and sunshine and mothballs.

After they passed her test we brought them all downstairs, and that's when the magic began.

She sewed the strips end to end, choosing each next piece by whimsy or by art. Sometimes the colors shaded from dark to light, sometimes they changed abruptly from yellow to black to green to red. Long exotic snakes of fabric coiled onto the floor behind the sewing machine.

Years later, our old black and gold treadle Singer was converted into an

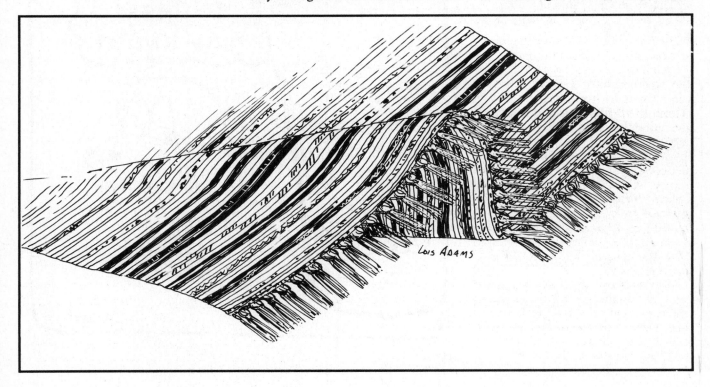

Lois Adams

electric portable. But I can't picture my mother sewing any way except with her right foot flat on the treadle, and the left cocked so that only the toes touched. She'd hit the flywheel with her right hand to start the needle driving up and down, then set the rhythm with her feet, start and stop, start and stop, adding in new scraps of color.

The next step was to roll the cloth strips into balls. Both my father and I got to help with this part. Pieces of my dress showed up in each of the balls.

Mom packed them into May Company bags with handles and carried them to Mrs. Rodecker, who had a loom. She was a widow supporting herself by doing needlework for neighbors and weaving rag rugs.

The next time I saw my grey and yellow plaid kindergarten dress, it was part of three different rugs, along with other scraps of our lives, woven closely with stout white threads and fringed at the ends. Each rug was a kaleidoscope of memories, and lasted for years.

You can buy rugs sort of like these now, for a buck or two, at the discount drugstore. They look the same, almost. But if you look closely, the cloth strips they make them with are cheap spongy synthetics, and the threads they are woven with are thin and far apart, making them flimsy landfill fodder.

And there's never a memory in a whole pile of them. Δ

A Backwoods Home Anthology
The Fifteenth Year

* Canning basics
* Benefits of mulching
* Water and winter tree injury
* Birch tree syrup
* Selecting a breed of chicken
* Grow your own dishrags
* Solar & propane powered super home
* How to shoot a handgun accurately
* Make a poor man's safe
* Hogs belong on the homestead
* Fighting tomato blight
* Water is the key to gardening
* Herb boxes from fence boards
* Controlling aphids
* Dairy goats are for you!
* The poor man's ceramic knife sharpener
* Protect your house from lightning
* Double wall adobe construction
* Living with kerosene
* Save money when you buy your next vehicle
* Tree planting tips
* Sweet big fat squash that keep all winter
* Removing pine sap
* Split shake siding the modern way
* Beekeeping basics

Thoughts While Doing Laundry

*If I had it to do
All over,
   I'd start writing
   Younger,
   I'd kiss
   More women,
   I'd buy
   All the same colored socks.*

      John Earl Silveira
      Ojai, CA

Other books available from
Backwoods Home Magazine

❋ The Best of the First Two Years
❋ A Backwoods Home Anthology—The Third Year
❋ A Backwoods Home Anthology—The Fourth Year
❋ A Backwoods Home Anthology—The Fifth Year
❋ A Backwoods Home Anthology—The Sixth Year
❋ A Backwoods Home Anthology—The Seventh Year
❋ A Backwoods Home Anthology—The Eighth Year
❋ A Backwoods Home Anthology—The Ninth Year
❋ A Backwoods Home Anthology—The Tenth Year
❋ A Backwoods Home Anthology—The Eleventh Year
❋ A Backwoods Home Anthology—The Twelfth Year
❋ A Backwoods Home Anthology—The Thirteenth Year
❋ A Backwoods Home Anthology—The Fourteenth Year
❋ A Backwoods Home Anthology—The Fifteenth Year
❋ A Backwoods Home Anthology—The Sixteenth Year
❋ A Backwoods Home Anthology—The Seventeenth Year
❋ A Backwoods Home Anthology—The Eighteenth Year
❋ A Backwoods Home Anthology—The Nineteenth Year
❋ Emergency Preparedness and Survival Guide
❋ Backwoods Home Cooking
❋ Can America Be Saved From Stupid People
❋ The Coming American Dictatorship, Parts I-XI
❋ Chickens: a beginner's handbook
❋ Starting Over: Chronicles of a Self-Reliant Woman
❋ Dairy goats: a beginner's handbook
❋ Self-Reliance: Recession-proof your pantry
❋ Making a Living: creating your own job
❋ Harvesting the Wild: gathering & using food from nature
❋ Hardyville Tales
❋ Growing and Canning Your Own Food
❋ Jackie Clay's Pantry Cookbook